Vatican II

Vatican II

Renewal within Tradition

EDITED BY
MATTHEW L. LAMB
AND MATTHEW LEVERING

OXFORD
UNIVERSITY PRESS

2008

OXFORD
UNIVERSITY PRESS

Oxford University Press, Inc., publishes works that further
Oxford University's objective of excellence
in research, scholarship, and education.

Oxford   New York
Auckland   Cape Town   Dar es Salaam   Hong Kong   Karachi
Kuala Lumpur   Madrid   Melbourne   Mexico City   Nairobi
New Delhi   Shanghai   Taipei   Toronto

With offices in
Argentina   Austria   Brazil   Chile   Czech Republic   France   Greece
Guatemala   Hungary   Italy   Japan   Poland   Portugal   Singapore
South Korea   Switzerland   Thailand   Turkey   Ukraine   Vietnam

Published by Oxford University Press, Inc.
198 Madison Avenue, New York, New York 10016

www.oup.com

Oxford is a registered trademark of Oxford University Press

Library of Congress Cataloging-in-Publication Data
Vatican II : renewal within tradition / edited by Matthew L. Lamb & Matthew Levering.
    p. cm.
Includes bibliographical references and index.
ISBN 978-0-19-533268-1; 978-0-19-533267-4 (pbk.)
1. Vatican Council (2nd : 1962–1965)   2. Catholic Church—Doctrines.
I. Title: Vatican 2.   II. Lamb, Matthew L.   III. Levering, Matthew, 1971–
BX8301962 .V3725 2008
262'.52—dc22   2007029552

Printed in the United States of America
on acid-free paper

Contents

A Proper Hermeneutic for the Second Vatican Council

Pope Benedict XVI

The last event of this year on which I wish to reflect here is the celebration of the conclusion of the Second Vatican Council forty years ago.
This memory prompts the question: What has been the result of the
council? Was it well received? What, in the acceptance of the council,
was good and what was inadequate or mistaken? What still remains to
be done? No one can deny that in vast areas of the Church the implementation of the council has been somewhat difficult, even without
wishing to apply to what occurred in these years the description that
Saint Basil, the great Doctor of the Church, made of the Church's
situation after the Council of Nicea. He compares her situation to a
naval battle in the darkness of the storm, saying among other things:

> The raucous shouting of those who through disagreement
> rise up against one another, the incomprehensible chatter,
> the confused din of uninterrupted clamoring, has now filled
> almost the whole of the Church, falsifying through excess or
> failure the right doctrine of the faith. (Saint Basil, *De Spiritu
> Sancto*, XXX, 77; PG 32, 213 A; SCh 17ff., p. 524)

We do not want to apply precisely this dramatic description to the
situation of the postconciliar period, yet something from all that occurred is nevertheless reflected in it. The question arises: Why has the
implementation of the council, in large parts of the Church, thus far
been so difficult?

From an address of Pope Benedict XVI to the Roman Curia, December 22, 2005, "Ad Romanam
Curiam ob omnia natalicia," *Acta Apostolicae Sedis* Vol. XCVIII (6 Januarii 2006): 40–53 (© Libreria
Editrice Vaticana, 2006). These remarks are excerpted from pages 45–52.

Well, it all depends on the correct interpretation of the council or—as we would say today—on its proper hermeneutics, the correct key to its interpretation and application. The problems in its implementation arose from the fact that two contrary hermeneutics came face-to-face and quarreled with each other. One caused confusion, the other, silently but more and more visibly, bore and is bearing fruit.

On the one hand, there is an interpretation that I would call "a hermeneutic of discontinuity and rupture"; it has frequently availed itself of the sympathies of the mass media, and also one trend of modern theology. On the other, there is the "hermeneutic of reform," of renewal in the continuity of the one subject-Church that the Lord has given to us. She is a subject that increases in time and develops; yet always remaining the same, the one subject of the journeying People of God.

The hermeneutic of discontinuity risks ending in a split between the preconciliar Church and the postconciliar Church. It asserts that the texts of the council as such do not yet express the true spirit of the council. It claims that they are the result of compromises in which, to reach unanimity, it was found necessary to keep and reconfirm many old things that are now pointless. However, the true spirit of the council is not to be found in these compromises but instead in the impulses toward the new that are contained in the texts.

These innovations alone were supposed to represent the true spirit of the council, and starting from and in conformity with them, it would be possible to move ahead. Precisely because the texts would only imperfectly reflect the true spirit of the council and its newness, it would be necessary to go courageously beyond the texts and make room for the newness in which the council's deepest intention would be expressed, even if it were still vague.

In a word: it would be necessary not to follow the texts of the council but its spirit. In this way, obviously, a vast margin was left open for the question on how this spirit should subsequently be defined and room was consequently made for every whim.

The nature of a council as such is therefore basically misunderstood. In this way, it is considered as a sort of constituent assembly that eliminates an old constitution and creates a new one. However, the Constituent Assembly needs a mandator and then confirmation by the mandator, in other words, the people the constitution must serve. The Fathers had no such mandate and no one had ever given them one; nor could anyone have given them one because the essential constitution of the Church comes from the Lord and was given to us so that we might attain eternal life and, starting from this perspective, be able to illuminate life in time and time itself.

Through the Sacrament they have received, bishops are stewards of the Lord's gift. They are "stewards of the mysteries of God" (1 Cor 4:1); as such, they must be found to be "faithful" and "wise" (cf. Lk 12:41–48). This requires them to administer the Lord's gift in the right way, so that it is not left concealed in some hiding place but bears fruit, and the Lord may end by saying to the administrator: "Since you were dependable in a small matter I will put you in charge of larger affairs" (cf. Mt 25:14–30; Lk 19:11–27).

These Gospel parables express the dynamic of fidelity required in the Lord's service; and through them it becomes clear that, as in a council, the dynamic and fidelity must converge.

The hermeneutic of discontinuity is countered by the hermeneutic of reform, as it was presented first by Pope John XXIII in his Speech inaugurating the council on October 11, 1962, and later by Pope Paul VI in his discourse for the council's conclusion on December 7, 1965.

Here I shall cite only John XXIII's well-known words, which unequivocally express this hermeneutic when he says that the council wishes "to transmit the doctrine, pure and integral, without any attenuation or distortion." And he continues:

> Our duty is not only to guard this precious treasure, as if we were concerned only with antiquity, but to dedicate ourselves with an earnest will and without fear to that work which our era demands of us. . . . It is necessary that this certain and unchanging teaching, which is to be faithfully respected, be deeply studied and presented in a way that corresponds to the needs of our time. The substance of the ancient doctrine of the deposit of faith is one thing, and the way in which it is presented is another, retaining nonetheless the same meaning and message. (S. Oec. Conc. Vat. II, *Constitutiones Decreta Declarationes* [1974], 863–865)

It is clear that this commitment to expressing a specific truth in a new way demands new reflection on this truth and a new vital relationship with it; it is also clear that new words can only develop if they come from an informed understanding of the truth expressed, and on the other hand, that a reflection on faith also requires that this faith be lived. In this regard, the program that Pope John XXIII proposed was extremely demanding, indeed, just as the synthesis of fidelity and dynamic is demanding.

However, wherever this interpretation guided the implementation of the council, new life developed and new fruit ripened. Forty years after the council, we can show that the positive is far greater and livelier than it appeared to be in the turbulent years around 1968. Today we see that, although the good seed developed slowly, it is nonetheless growing; and our deep gratitude for the work done by the council is likewise growing.

In his discourse closing the council, Paul VI pointed out a further specific reason why a hermeneutic of discontinuity can seem convincing. In the great dispute about man that marks the modern epoch, the council had to focus in particular on the theme of anthropology. It had to question the relationship between the Church and her faith on the one hand, and man and the contemporary world on the other (Paul VI, *Discourse Closing the Council*; cf. ibid. 1974, pp. 1066ff). The question becomes even clearer if, instead of the generic term "contemporary world," we opt for another that is more precise: the council had to determine in a new way the relationship between the Church and the modern era.

This relationship had a somewhat stormy beginning with the Galileo case. It was then totally interrupted when Kant described "religion within pure reason" and when, in the radical phase of the French Revolution, an image of the State and the human being that practically no longer wanted to allow the Church any room was disseminated.

In the 19th century under Pius IX, the clash between the Church's faith and a radical liberalism and the natural sciences, which also claimed to embrace with their knowledge the whole of reality to its limit, stubbornly proposing to make the "hypothesis of God" superfluous, had elicited from the Church a bitter and radical condemnation of this spirit of the modern age. Thus, it seemed that there was no longer any milieu open to a positive and fruitful understanding, and the rejection by those who felt they were the representatives of the modern era was also drastic.

In the meantime, however, the modern age had also experienced developments. People came to realize that the American Revolution was offering a model of a modern state that differed from the theoretical model with radical tendencies that had emerged during the second phase of the French Revolution.

The natural sciences were beginning to reflect more and more clearly their own limitations imposed by their own method, which, despite achieving great things, was nevertheless unable to grasp the global nature of reality.

So it was that both parties were gradually beginning to open up to each other. In the period between the two world wars and especially after the Second World War, Catholic statesmen demonstrated that a modern secular State could exist that was not neutral regarding values but alive, drawing from the great ethical sources opened by Christianity.

Catholic social doctrine, as it gradually developed, became an important model between radical liberalism and the Marxist theory of the State. The natural sciences, which without reservation professed a method of their own to which God was barred access, realized ever more clearly that this method did not include the whole of reality. Hence, they once again opened their doors to God, knowing that reality is greater than the naturalistic method and all that it can encompass.

It might be said that three circles of questions had formed which then, at the time of the Second Vatican Council, were expecting an answer. First of all, the relationship between faith and modern science had to be redefined. Furthermore, this did not only concern the natural sciences but also historical science for, in a certain school, the historical-critical method claimed to have the last word on the interpretation of the Bible and, demanding total exclusivity for its interpretation of Sacred Scripture, was opposed to important points in the interpretation elaborated by the faith of the Church.

Secondly, it was necessary to give a new definition to the relationship between the Church and the modern State that would make room impartially for citizens of various religions and ideologies, merely assuming responsibility for an orderly and tolerant coexistence among them and for the freedom to practice their own religion.

Thirdly, linked more generally to this was the problem of religious tolerance—a question that required a new definition of the relationship between the Christian faith and the world religions. In particular, before the recent crimes of the Nazi regime and, in general, with a retrospective look at a long and difficult history, it was necessary to evaluate and define in a new way the relationship between the Church and the faith of Israel.

These are all subjects of great importance—they were the great themes of the second part of the council—on which it is impossible to reflect more broadly in this context. It is clear that in all these sectors, which all together form a single problem, some kind of discontinuity might emerge. Indeed, a discontinuity had been revealed but in which, after the various distinctions between concrete historical situations and their requirements had been made, the continuity of principles proved not to have been abandoned. It is easy to miss this fact at a first glance.

It is precisely in this combination of continuity and discontinuity at different levels that the very nature of true reform consists. In this process of innovation in continuity we must learn to understand more practically than before that the Church's decisions on contingent matters—for example, certain practical forms of liberalism or a free interpretation of the Bible—should necessarily be contingent themselves, precisely because they refer to a specific reality that is changeable in itself. It was necessary to learn to recognize that in these decisions it is only the principles that express the permanent aspect, since they remain as an undercurrent, motivating decisions from within. On the other hand, not so permanent are the practical forms that depend on the historical situation and are therefore subject to change.

Basic decisions, therefore, continue to be well grounded, whereas the way they are applied to new contexts can change. Thus, for example, if religious freedom were to be considered an expression of the human inability to discover the truth and thus become a canonization of relativism, then this social and historical necessity is raised inappropriately to the metaphysical level and thus stripped of its true meaning. Consequently, it cannot be accepted by those who believe that the human person is capable of knowing the truth about God and, on the basis of the inner dignity of the truth, is bound to this knowledge.

It is quite different, on the other hand, to perceive religious freedom as a need that derives from human coexistence, or indeed, as an intrinsic consequence of the truth that cannot be externally imposed but that the person must adopt only through the process of conviction.

The Second Vatican Council, recognizing and making its own an essential principle of the modern state with the Decree on Religious Freedom *Dignitatis humanae* has recovered the deepest patrimony of the Church. By so doing she can be conscious of being in full harmony with the teaching of Jesus himself (cf. Mt 22:21), as well as with the Church of the martyrs of all time. The ancient Church naturally prayed for the emperors and political leaders out of duty (cf. 1

Tm 2:2); but while she prayed for the emperors, she refused to worship them and thereby clearly rejected the religion of the state.

The martyrs of the early Church died for their faith in that God who was revealed in Jesus Christ, and for this very reason they also died for freedom of conscience and the freedom to profess one's own faith—a profession that no state can impose but which, instead, can only be claimed with God's grace in freedom of conscience. A missionary Church known for proclaiming her message to all peoples must necessarily work for the freedom of the faith. She desires to transmit the gift of the truth that exists for one and all.

At the same time, she assures peoples and their governments that she does not wish to destroy their identity and culture by doing so, but to give them, on the contrary, a response which, in their innermost depths, they are waiting for—a response with which the multiplicity of cultures is not lost but instead unity between men increases and thus also peace between peoples.

The Second Vatican Council, with its new definition of the relationship between the faith of the Church and certain essential elements of modern thought, has reviewed or even corrected certain historical decisions, but in this apparent discontinuity it has actually preserved and deepened her inmost nature and true identity.

The Church, both before and after the council, was and is the same Church, one, holy, catholic and apostolic, journeying on through time; she continues "her pilgrimage amid the persecutions of the world and the consolations of God," proclaiming the death of the Lord until he comes (cf. LG 8).

Those who expected that with this fundamental "yes" to the modern era all tensions would be dispelled and that the "openness towards the world" accordingly achieved would transform everything into pure harmony, had underestimated the inner tensions as well as the contradictions inherent in the modern epoch.

They had underestimated the perilous frailty of human nature which has been a threat to human progress in all the periods of history and in every historical constellation. These dangers, with the new possibilities and new power of man over matter and over himself, did not disappear but instead acquired new dimensions: a look at the history of the present day shows this clearly.

In our time too, the Church remains a "sign that will be opposed" (Lk 2:34)—not without reason did Pope John Paul II, then still a cardinal, give this title to the theme for the Spiritual Exercises he preached in 1976 to Pope Paul VI and the Roman Curia. The council could not have intended to abolish the Gospel's opposition to human dangers and errors.

On the contrary, it was certainly the council's intention to overcome erroneous or superfluous contradictions in order to present to our world the requirement of the Gospel in its full greatness and purity.

The steps the council took towards the modern era which had rather vaguely been presented as "openness to the world," belong in short to the perennial problem of the relationship between faith and reason that is re-emerging in ever new forms. The situation that the council had to face can certainly be compared to events of previous epochs. In his First Letter, Saint Peter urged Christians always to be ready to give an answer (apo-logia) to anyone who asked them for the logos, the reason for their faith (cf. 3:15).

This meant that biblical faith had to be discussed and come into contact with Greek culture and learn to recognize through interpretation the separating line but also the convergence and the affinity between them in the one God-given reason.

When, in the thirteenth century through the Jewish and Arab philosophers, Aristotelian thought came into contact with medieval Christianity formed in the Platonic tradition, faith and reason risked entering an irreconcilable contradiction. It was above all Saint Thomas Aquinas who mediated the new encounter between faith and Aristotelian philosophy, thereby setting faith in a positive relationship with the form of reason prevalent in his time. There is no doubt that the wearing dispute between modern reason and the Christian faith, which had begun negatively with the Galileo case, went through many phases, but with the Second Vatican Council the time came when broad new thinking was required.

Its content was certainly only roughly traced in the conciliar texts, but this determined its essential direction, so that the dialogue between reason and faith, particularly important today, found its bearings on the basis of the Second Vatican Council.

This dialogue must now be developed with great open-mindedness but also with that clear discernment that the world rightly expects of us in this very moment. Thus, today we can look with gratitude at the Second Vatican Council: if we interpret and implement it guided by a right hermeneutic, it can be and can become increasingly powerful for the ever necessary renewal of the Church.

Acknowledgments

We owe a debt of gratitude to many. Clearly the credit for this volume belongs to the contributors. Each one of them made this project a priority, and their contributions constitute a rich theological conversation about the council's documents from the perspective of a hermeneutic of reform within continuity called for so eloquently by Pope Benedict XVI. We have been encouraged and sustained in this work by many at Ave Maria University. For their untiring support, we wish to thank Mercedes Cox and the entire faculty. Moreover, for the preparation of this volume we also owe a special debt to Dianne Boffetti for her editorial assistance, along with Louise Mitchell, who helped both editorially and theologically with her knowledge of Vatican II. Bishop Basil Meeking and Shannon Gaffney also assisted with their expertise. We are most grateful for the expert guidance provided by Theo Calderara, Keith Faivre, Daniel Gonzalez, and their associates at Oxford University Press as well.

In addition, we have been encouraged in this work by many faculty and students at Ave Maria University, and although we cannot name everyone, we wish to mention Fr. Joseph Fessio, S.J., and Michael Dauphinais, Dean of Faculty at Ave Maria University. Their friendship and support have been a great blessing. Moreover, we acknowledge the decisive importance of Thomas Monaghan in founding Ave Maria University and supporting, together with President Nicholas Healy, Jr., the undergraduate and graduate programs in theology, whose aim is to foster the ongoing *ressourcement* that the Church requires for "renewal within tradition."

In particular, two of the contributors to this work have placed the appropriation of the Second Vatican Council at the heart of their theological and pastoral ministry: Avery Cardinal Dulles, S.J., and

Francis Cardinal George, O.M.I. The Catholic Church in the United States owes enormous gratitude to these two great thinkers and leaders, and in evident ways their work inspired this book. We are privileged to count them as friends. To them and to all of the supporters and contributors to this volume, we offer our gratitude. May God continue to bless their labors in his vineyard.

Contributors

Anthony A. Akinwale, O.P., is president of the Dominican Institute in Ibadan, Nigeria, and author of several important studies on the church and religious life in Nigeria.

M. Prudence Allen, R.S.M., has authored *The Concept of Woman: The Aristotelian Revolution, 750 BC to AD 1250* and *The Concept of Woman: The Early Humanist Reformation, 1250–1500.* She teaches at St. John Vianney Theological Seminary in Denver, Colorado.

Khaled Anatolios is the author of *Athanasius: The Coherence of His Thought.* He teaches at Weston Jesuit School of Theology in Cambridge, Massachusetts.

J. Brian Benestad has most recently edited the three volumes of *Ernest L. Fortin: Collected Essays.* He teaches at the University of Scranton.

Don J. Briel is the founder of the Catholic Studies Department at the University of St. Thomas, Minnesota, and of the journal *Logos.*

Romanus Cessario, O.P., is the author of numerous books, among them *A Short History of Thomism* and *An Introduction to Moral Theology.* He teaches at St. John's Seminary in Brighton, Massachusetts.

Avery Cardinal Dulles, S.J., is the author of numerous books, among them *The Assurance of Things Hoped For* and *Newman.* He holds the Laurence J. McGinley chair at Fordham University.

Denis Farkasfalvy, O.Cist., is coauthor of *Formation of the New Testament Canon: An Ecumenical Approach.* He serves on the Pontifical Biblical Commission and teaches at the University of Dallas.

Brian Ferme is dean of the School of Canon Law at the Catholic University of America and the author of *Canon Law in Medieval England: A Study of William Lyndwood's Provinciale with Particular Reference to Testamentary Law.*

Francis Cardinal George, O.M.I., is archbishop of Chicago and author of numerous scholarly studies, including *Inculturation and Ecclesial Communion: Culture and Church in the Teaching of Pope John Paul II.*

F. Russell Hittinger is Warren Professor of Catholic Studies at the University of Tulsa. He has authored *The First Grace: Rediscovering the Natural Law in the Post-Christian World* and *A Critique of the New Natural Law Theory.*

Pamela E. J. Jackson teaches at the University of Notre Dame and has authored *Journeybread for the Shadowlands: The Readings for the Rites of the Catechumenate, RCIA,* and most recently *An Abundance of Graces: Reflections on Sacrosanctum Concilium;* she has also written scholarly articles on the history and present practice of the liturgy.

Arthur Kennedy teaches at the University of St. Thomas in St. Paul, Minnesota, and is an expert on ecumenical relations. He has published articles on Flannery O'Connor, Christopher Dawson, and Bernard Lonergan.

Benoît-Dominique de La Soujeole, O.P., teaches at the University of Fribourg, Switzerland, and has authored *Le sacrement de la communion: Essai d'ecclésiologie fondamentale.*

Matthew L. Lamb has been professor of theology at Boston College and is the author of numerous articles and books, including *History, Method, and Theology; Solidarity with Victims: Toward a Theology of Social Transformation; and Eternity, Time, and the Life of Wisdom.* He teaches at Ave Maria University.

Matthew Levering is the author of *Christ's Fulfillment of Torah and Temple; Scripture and Metaphysics;* and *Sacrifice and Community.* He teaches at Ave Maria University.

Guy Mansini, O.S.B., is the author of *What Is Dogma?* and *Promising and the Good;* he is the coeditor of *Ethics and Theological Disclosures: The Thought of Robert Sokolowski.* He teaches at St. Meinrad's Seminary in Indiana.

Francis Martin holds chairs at the John Paul II Cultural Center in Washington, D.C., and Sacred Heart Major Seminary in Detroit, Michigan. He is the author of numerous books, including *The Feminist Question* and *Sacred Scripture: The Disclosure of the Word.*

Charles Morerod, O.P., is dean of philosophy at the Angelicum in Rome. He has most recently authored *Oecuménisme et philosophie.*

Richard John Neuhaus is founder and editor of *First Things* and author of numerous Books, including *Death on a Friday Afternoon* and *The Naked Public Square.*

M. Judith O'Brien, R.S.M., is professor of pastoral and canon law, St. John Vianney Theological Seminary in Denver, Colorado.

Robert W. Oliver, B.H., is professor of systematic theology, St. John's Seminary, Boston, and author of a major study on the Decree on the Laity of Vatican II.

Geoffrey Wainwright is Robert Earl Cushman Professor of Systematic Theology at Duke University Divinity School in Durham, North Carolina. He is the author and editor of numerous books, including *Doxology* and *The Oxford History of Christian Worship*.

Lawrence J. Welch has authored *Christology and Eucharist in the Early Thought of Cyril of Alexandria*, in addition to numerous articles. He teaches at Kenrick School of Theology in St. Louis, Missouri.

Chronology of Vatican II

October 28, 1958	Angelo Giuseppe Roncalli is elected pope and takes the name John XXIII
January 25, 1959	Pope John XXIII announces that he plans to call a council
December 25, 1961	*Humanae salutis*, the formal summoning of the council
October 11, 1962	Opening of the council
October 11–December 8, 1962	First session
June 3, 1963	Pope John XXIII dies
June 21, 1963	Giovanni Battista Montini is elected pope and takes the name Paul VI
September 29–December 4, 1963	Second session
December 4, 1963	*Inter mirifica*
	Sacrosanctum concilium
September 14–November 21, 1964	Third session
November 21, 1964	*Lumen gentium*
	Orientalium Ecclesiarum
	Unitatis redintegratio
September 14–December 8, 1965	Fourth session
October 28, 1965	*Christus Dominus*
	Gravissimum educationis
	Nostra aetate
	Optatam totius
	Perfectae caritatis
November 18, 1965	*Apostolicam actuositatem*
	Dei verbum

December 7, 1965   *Ad gentes*
                                    Dignitatis humanae
                                    Gaudium et spes
                                    Presbyterorum ordinis
December 8, 1965   Closing of the council

Abbreviations

Vatican II

Introduction

Matthew L. Lamb and Matthew Levering

The Second Vatican Council stands out as one of the most important religious and ecclesial events in the twentieth century. It was certainly the most extensively covered by the mass media. Pope Benedict XVI calls attention to the theological difficulties in implementing the reforms of Vatican II. He sees that commentators have distorted the teachings of the Second Vatican Council by means of a "hermeneutics of discontinuity and rupture." The "spirit" or "style" of the council was often severed from, or set in opposition to, the texts promulgated by the council. The pope mentions that, for some, the texts were wrongly interpreted as "compromises" that contain "many old and ultimately useless things that had to be dragged along" in order to "make room for the new." This way of interpreting the council, the pope asserts, found "favor among the mass media" and in some sectors of contemporary theology.

Never before was an ecumenical council of the Roman Catholic Church so extensively covered and reported by the modern news media as Vatican II (1962–1965). The impact of this coverage was pervasive and profound in its portrayal of the council in the ideological categories of "liberal versus conservative." The council was dramatically reported as a liberal or progressive accommodation to modernity that aimed to overcome Catholicism's traditional, conservative resistance to modernity.

For foreign correspondents from 1962 to 1965, two news sectors required ongoing coverage: One was Vietnam, the other the council in Rome. Journalists of the print and electronic media flocked to Rome. Few had any expertise in Catholic theology and so were dependent upon the popularized accounts of the council's deliberations and debates offered by *periti* and theologians with journalistic skills.[1] An

American Redemptorist, Fr. Francis Xavier Murphy, contributed much to the
propagation of an ideological reporting on the council debates with his widely
read "Letters from the Vatican" under the pen name of Xavier Rynne in the
New Yorker.[2]

It is important to understand what is meant by ideological distortions. At
the time, certainly the young German theologian Joseph Ratzinger was well
aware of the lively debates at the very beginning of and throughout the council.[3]
Any coverage of the council, however, that fails to penetrate to the theological
aspects of these debates will inevitably distort them. Reporting on the council
for the French publication *La Croix,* Fr. Antoine Wenger warned against
"explaining everything categorically" in terms of "conservatives and progressives," while Pope Benedict XVI clearly indicates the consequence of such
distortions: The council's new initiatives are set in opposition to the old—to
tradition—with the result that the texts are misread as only compromising documents that fail to fully embody the spirit of the new initiatives. These politically ideological categories in covering the council then distorted the event of
the council by interpreting it as a political and an ideological happening. In the
pope's words, the discontinuity of the new situation the council addressed
obliterates the deeper continuity of the Church's magisterial tradition, the principles of which were used to evaluate the new situation.

The daily celebrations of the Holy Sacrifice of the Mass at the council, the
countless prayers and invocations of the saints, whose holiness in Christ Jesus
are a mark of the Church—all of this rich theological context was ignored. The
genuine event of the council was truncated to a struggle between liberals and
conservatives, and the documents of the council were misread within what
Benedict XVI accurately terms a hermeneutics of rupture and discontinuity.
Whenever a document referred to traditional Catholic teachings and practices,
these were misread as if they were simply compromises made to get the conservatives to vote for the liberal and progressive agenda. Such conciliations were
to be ignored by those imbued with the spirit of the council. As Pope Benedict
indicates, it was more the spirit of the age (Zeitgeist) than the Holy Spirit.

In fact, Vatican II can be adequately understood only in the Catholic context of reform and renewal within the continuity of the Church's two-millen-
nial tradition. Pope Leo XIII expressed this tersely in the phrase "vetera novis
augere et perficere"—to strengthen and complete the old by the new.[4] The
wisdom tradition within Catholicism is very much opposed to the Enlightenment opposition of the new to the old. Yet this opposition tends to dominate
post-Enlightenment cultures, and it is not surprising that theologians who
became journalists or communicators fell into this hermeneutics of rupture
between the old and the new.

The place of the council within the tradition was clearly articulated by Pope
Benedict XVI in his very first statement as pope:

> Pope John Paul II indicated the [Second Vatican] Council precisely as
> a "compass" with which to orient oneself in the vast ocean of the third
> millennium (cf. apostolic letter *Novo millennio ineunte,* nos. 57–58). In

his spiritual testament he noted: "I am convinced that the new generations will still be able to draw for a long time from the riches that this council of the twentieth century has lavished on us" (March 17, 2000). Therefore, in preparing myself also for the service that is proper to the Successor of Peter, I wish to affirm strongly my determination to continue the commitment to implement the Second Vatican Council, in the footsteps of my Predecessors and in faithful continuity with the two millennial tradition of the Church.[5]

What does it mean to implement Vatican II "in faithful continuity with the two millennial tradition of the Church" and thereby for it to serve as a "compass" to guide us at the dawn of the third millennium? This broad panorama of the millennia involves the Church in a vast *ressourcement* or recovery of two thousand years of traditions if it is to renew and orient an *aggiornamento*—a bringing in of the new—to the tasks of our times.

The first millennium of Catholicism could be characterized as a patristic-monastic era in which the fidelity to the truth of revelation set up the dioceses, cathedral schools, monasteries, and convents, which emphasized the importance of a dedication to wisdom and holiness. The ecumenical councils defended the truth of the Word of God as revealed in the sacred scriptures against heretical distortions. Theological problems were often traceable to philosophical ones. In the evangelization of the Greek and Roman cultures the Church fathers demonstrated how the true Word of God revealed the redemptive wisdom of the Word incarnate in his life, suffering, death, and resurrection. The greatest philosophers of Greece and Rome had taught the need for intellectual and moral excellence and for living a virtuous life according to right reason. They could not, however, account for the pervasive evil and injustice that eventually led, as the Apologists and Augustine showed, the intellectually excellent to surrender to skepticism and the morally excellent to either retreat into Stoic indifference or degenerate into Epicurean distraction.

As the great Roman culture was collapsing from its own vices, Augustine wryly remarked that it would have been better had they built temples in honor of Socrates or Plato rather than the gods and goddesses that were projections of their own disordered and irrational desires. Thus throughout Europe, the Church's first millennium developed intellectual and ecclesial apostolates in parishes, convents, cathedrals, and monastic communities dedicated to the quests for wisdom and holiness. Benedict XVI has emphasized the "decisive importance" for world history in the "rapprochement between Biblical faith and Greek philosophical inquiry."[6] What derailed the philosophical life of reason, as the Church fathers and monastic founders like Saint Benedict indicated, was the root sin of pride with its accompanying "acedia" as the flight from God as friend who creates, sustains, and redeems the universe and human history.

While the first millennium was a patristic, cathedral, and monastic period, the second millennium witnessed the emergence of a new form of the intellectual apostolate as universities emerged in Catholic Europe. Theology was pursued in communities committed to the quest for science and scholarship. Because of pride, the differentiation of science and scholarship from the pursuit of wisdom and holiness was always in danger, as Bernard warned Abelard, of becoming a separation and an opposition. Indeed, despite the efforts of the mendicant theologians such as Aquinas, Bonaventure, and Cajetan, the spread of nominalism and voluntarism eroded the notion of wisdom as a serious contemplative-theoretical attunement to the whole. With the loss of wisdom traditions, modern enlightenment cultures cultivated empirical sciences of the particular. There is no heuristic attention to the intelligibility and pattern of the whole; instead there is attention only to the individual elements, and any efforts to pattern or order them are considered conventional and arbitrary. The intellectualism of an Augustine or an Aquinas, as Pope Benedict XVI reminds us, was replaced by a nominalist voluntarism.[7]

A major fault in the post-Enlightenment cultures' rejection of wisdom is the lowering of expectations and standards. These are not only privatized but also identified as resulting from force and fraud. In the face of these cultural challenges, it is important to emphasize that the holiness of the Church has its cause in the infinite holiness and goodness of Jesus Christ as truly God and truly man. The hierarchical successors of the apostles are sent by Christ, as he was sent by the Father. They are one with the mystery of Christ's redemptive mission from the Father in the Holy Spirit. Charles Taylor has analyzed how the post-Enlightenment evaluations of everyday life developed from a rejection of the Roman Catholic notion of an ecclesial and a hierarchical mediation of the sacred.[8] In these cultures there is no notion of the church in the full Catholic sense of sacramentally carrying forward the missions of the Son and Spirit. All Christians are alone before God and are individually responsible for their personal commitment to Christ. There is no ship in the Catholic sense, no bark of Peter, no common movement carrying humans to salvation. All believers row their own boat. Indeed, the bark of Peter was rather roundly denounced by Spinoza, who was later followed by Hobbes and others, as little more than a clerically dominative "Leviathan" that seduced the credulous and superstitious by fraudulent force.[9]

Without wisdom and holiness to attune the minds and hearts of theologians and scholars to the revealed realities, the sense of development of doctrine is lost. It is misunderstood as arbitrary decisions on propositions whose truth is not recognized as the revelation of the infinite wisdom and love of the Triune God. Sacred doctrine loses its very soul. Spinoza set forth the presuppositions of this denigration of revealed truth in his *Theologico-political Treatise*. Like nature, the Bible can no longer be treated as a whole; it must be broken up into fragmented parts. These isolated texts must then be interpreted only by other texts. Because the wise attunement to the whole was lost, Spinoza remarks that one must never raise the truth question, only the meaning question to be answered solely with reference to other fragmented texts. The development of doctrine within the Bible from Old to New Testament and within the ongoing mission of the Church is rendered impossible. Wisdom is replaced with arbitrary power.[10]

Not a few commentators and Catholic theological experts at the council picked up this ideological framework. These texts were approached as products of power struggles between the liberals and the conservatives, with one side winning this passage and the other side winning that. What began at the council continued and spread in subsequent decades. Illustrations of the distorting impact of the hermeneutics of discontinuity and rupture abound, for example, in Archbishop Agostino Marchetto's excellent studies of scholarship on Vatican II.[11] He provides a careful analysis of many writings on the council and often criticizes distortions and biases in their presentations.[12] Marchetto sees a general flaw in many of these works insofar as they are attentive to the event of the council interpreted as a new and progressive opening to the modern world, while failing to understand the profound theological continuity with tradition in the conciliar texts. Instead some texts are read as compromises and are considered to be of less importance than the liberal event of the new against the old.[13] Given Pope Benedict's clear and compelling criticisms of such distortions, it is not surprising that some historians of the council complain that the present pope is far from the spirit of Vatican II.[14]

The specifically theological import of the conciliar documents and their continuity with the two millennial traditions of the Church were also neglected because of the woeful lack of adequate theological formation as fewer and fewer graduate theological programs educated their graduates in the linguistic skills, philosophical and theological habits of mind, and scholarly judgment they needed to appropriate the primary patristic, monastic, scholastic, and counterreformation sources.[15]

In contrast to this "liberal or conservative" reading of Vatican II as a power struggle, then, the present volume seeks to make a modest contribution to what Pope Benedict XVI calls a hermeneutics of reform in continuity with the two millennial traditions of Catholic thought and wisdom. The contributors are theologians dedicated to the renewal of Catholic theology in the light of Vatican II.

The Constitutions

Avery Cardinal Dulles, S.J., opens the volume with a discussion of *Lumen gentium*. Dulles is well aware of interpretations of *Lumen gentium* that find in the dogmatic constitution an opening for reconceiving the Catholic Church along more democratic, pluralist, and postmodern lines. In such interpretations Dulles sees at work not only mistaken characterizations of the document's teaching on the Church but also an erroneous hermeneutic of the entire council. If the council is interpreted as a rupture from past teachings rather than as an authentic development of tradition, then the very nature of conciliar teaching is profoundly undermined: If one council can decisively break from the teachings of past councils, one could no longer affirm that conciliar teaching is other than an exercise of arbitrary power that constructs "doctrine" in a fluid manner for particular epochs. After critiquing this erroneous hermeneutic, Dulles evaluates the central ecclesiological concepts set forth in *Lumen gentium*: the Church as "sacrament," the membership of the Church, the Mystical Body, the Kingdom of God, missionary activity, the people of God, the hierarchical structure of the Church, the episcopate, collegiality, the magisterium, and the "sense of the faithful." Dulles identifies the ways in which the council presents these realities and makes clear that while the council's presentation often allows for a development, such developments constitute a deepening of, rather than a break with, the tradition of the Church's self-understanding. For Dulles the key to this deepening is the council's envisioning of ecclesiological realities through the lens of sacrament.

Father Benoît-Dominique de La Soujeole explores the second half of *Lumen gentium* and devotes particular attention to chapters 5, 7, and 8. In chapter 5 he examines the holiness of the Church (the "universal call to holiness") in light of the members' sinfulness: The Church offers to her members the holiness of the divine life that Christ bestowed upon her through the Holy Spirit, while the members, in their gradual conversion, are configured over time to the divine life. The holiness of the members is charity, or love. Chapter 7 engages another seeming tension in the mystery of the Church: The Church is one and yet exists both on earth and in heaven. How can these two modes of existence, so different, constitute a unity? De La Soujeole notes that *Lumen gentium* draws the two together by means of the supernatural virtues, especially hope, by which the members of the Church reach out to heaven, and by means of the intercession of the saints in heaven on behalf of the Church on earth. Lastly, chapter 8 offers a Mariological reflection upon the Church. Here de La Soujeole exhibits *Lumen gentium*'s ability to set forth the fullness of the tradition without thereby including all of the aspects of theological and pastoral expression that are specific to various time periods but are not essential to the reality expressed. The council raised two issues in particular: the range of Marian titles to include and the question of whether to place the theology of Mary in a separate document or within *Lumen gentium*. De La Soujeole details the opposed positions on these matters with sympathy toward both sides, and in this way he makes manifest the way in which the council's approach integrates the concerns of those who sought, on the grounds of tradition, a different treatment.

Father Francis Martin examines the first half of *Dei verbum*. The great challenge for the council, he states, was how to integrate modern historical work with the teaching of tradition as it relates to scripture and revelation. Such work was already under way in papal encyclicals published before the council. Martin pays particular attention to the preamble of *Dei verbum*, which places the entire document in the light of 1 John 1:2–3: "We announce to you the eternal life which was with the Father and has appeared to us: that which we have seen and heard we announce to you that you might have fellowship with us and our fellowship may be with the Father and with his Son Jesus Christ." The purpose of *Dei verbum*, then, is to take its place within the ecclesial continuity (the "fellowship") of this announcement of the Gospel. For this reason, too, the preamble remarks directly upon *Dei verbum*'s continuity with the councils of Trent and Vatican I.

Martin then treats *Dei verbum*'s account of revelation, which provides a theology of history that emphasizes God's intimate presence as creator and redeemer. For *Dei verbum*, the biblical covenants trace the stages by which God prepared mankind for the coming of his incarnate Son. Other themes include the apostolic transmission and appropriation of revelation, the relationship of scripture and tradition, the role of the magisterium, and the inspiration and truth of the scriptures. Having exhibited these themes with attention to prior Catholic teaching, Martin addresses in some detail the question of the interpretation of scripture, including topics such as authorial intention, the canon, the analogy of faith, and God's condescension in conveying divine truth through human writing. Throughout Martin shows how *Dei verbum*'s treatment opens up to contemporary hermeneutical and metaphysical insights into the communication of truth.

Abbot Denis Farkasfalvy focuses upon the second half of *Dei verbum* and takes his cue from the issues raised in chapter 3. His insights complement Martin's. Placing *Dei verbum* in the context of the 1943 encyclical *Divino afflante*, as well as standard textbooks on scripture from that period, he observes that *Dei verbum* harvests some of the fruits of the encyclical's awareness of the role of literary genres in scripture. In turn, this appreciation for literary genre, when united with the insights into history provided by the ressourcement theology that flourished before the council, made possible a deeper reflection upon the key questions of the theology of scripture. For *Dei verbum*, revelation includes propositional truth but cannot be *reduced* to the conceptual level. With regard to the chapters on the Old and New testaments, he demonstrates that this point enables the council to approach inspiration and inerrancy from the perspective of the historical economy of salvation, in a manner similar to that of the fathers and the medievals. Similarly, the canonicity of books of scripture makes more sense from a perspective that begins, as *Dei verbum* does, from the apostolic Church and its teaching. For Farkasfalvy, in short, *Dei verbum* is engaged in a retrieval of the Church's ancient understanding of revelation and scripture, one that accords with the tradition of the Church but also offers a more nuanced and textured historical framework so as to avoid certain pitfalls of modern rationalism. In this regard he believes that *Dei verbum* could have gone still further, especially with regard to the issue of divine and human authorship. He also raises concerns about the reception of the second half of *Dei verbum*, especially the chapter on the Old Testament, and argues that its patristic Christological emphasis has not been taken up by the Pontifical Biblical Commission.

In the following chapter Dr. Pamela Jackson addresses *Sacrosanctum concilium*'s theology of the liturgy. She first summarizes the basic principles laid down by *Sacrosanctum concilium* in its opening paragraphs, where the liturgy is placed within the Trinitarian context of the history of salvation and human beings' incorporation into Christ's saving work. In this regard she notes *Sacrosanctum concilium*'s well-known description of the liturgy as the "summit" and the "source" of the Church's activity, as well as its integration of Christ's presence and action in the liturgy with the Church's action in the liturgy. Turning to the document's later chapters, she provides a general overview of themes such as the Holy Eucharist, the Liturgy of the Hours, and the liturgical year. In Jackson's view, which she illustrates in some detail as regards each section of the document, *Sacrosanctum concilium*'s approach corresponds closely with that of the fathers and draws heavily as well on the 1947 encyclical *Mediator Dei* (influenced, Jackson notes, by the liturgical movement of the early twentieth century) and contemporaneous Church documents. She finds similar background to the liturgical reforms proposed by *Sacrosanctum concilium*. While the Council of Trent does not play a leading role, its teachings are upheld and deepened, Jackson affirms, by means of the council's careful attention to the fathers' liturgical theology and to the magisterial documents that appeared in the decades before *Sacrosanctum concilium*.

Father Romanus Cessario also takes up *Sacrosanctum concilium* and focuses upon its teaching on the sacraments. As he observes, *Sacrosanctum concilium* does not intend to offer a new teaching on the sacraments but instead presumes that of the Council of Trent. Its aim is to reform sacramental practice, not to enunciate new sacramental doctrine. Cessario identifies the twentieth-century liturgical movement as the key source for *Sacrosanctum concilium*'s understanding of the liturgy. Although many of the liturgical movement's historical claims and perspectives no longer obtain, its emphasis on active participation and its influence on Pius XII's encyclicals *Mediator Dei, Mystici Corporis Christi,* and *Divino afflante Spiritu* exhibit its significance in overcoming what Cessario calls a "juridicism associated with the administration of the sacraments, especially of Penance" in the early twentieth century. As he shows, *Sacrosanctum concilium* introduces a development in Catholic theology by contributing to a new emphasis on liturgy within the Church's catechetical presentation of the sacraments. Yet this is not to say that *Sacrosanctum concilium* warrants an anthropocentric view of the sacraments. Cessario observes in this regard that the council "Fathers were set upon making the causal efficacy of the sacraments more attractive and comprehensible to the Catholic people, not reducing the sacraments to empty symbols of a creature-centered religious ritualism." He suggests in conclusion that today sacramental theology, as shown by *Redemptionis sacramentum* and other recent Church documents, requires renewed attention. The result would be to complement the work of *Sacrosanctum concilium* by expositing the sacramental causality by which we are enabled to share in the justice of Christ.

In the following chapter Dr. J. Brian Benestad engages the first part of *Gaudium et spes*, which, he maintains, should be read in light of *Lumen gentium.* Benestad observes that one can agree with some of the criticism of *Gaudium et spes*'s foreword without thereby sanctioning its misreading by other scholars who understand the world in an undifferentiated fashion not justified by *Gaudium et spes.* In a clear manner, *Gaudium et spes* points out the existence of an interior moral disorder of individuals that corresponds to moral and political disorder in modern societies. Above all, *Gaudium et spes* does not simply affirm human dignity; rather it seeks to assist in perfecting it in the light of Christ. In this vein *Gaudium et spes* challenges the presumptions that modern societies make about what constitutes the dignity of the human person: Human dignity is not lessened by dependence upon others. Instead, it rests upon and is *perfected* by a threefold human relationship with God: creation, redemption, and the call to Trinitarian communion. Ultimately the dignity to which God calls human beings can be understood only Christologically (*Gaudium et spes* 22). Benestad shows that the same understanding of the need for the perfecting of human dignity characterizes the tradition of Catholic teaching on the human person. Discussing the topics raised in chapters 2 through 4, he finds that these chapters appeal to principles of Catholic social teaching that long predate *Gaudium et spes*, although Benestad suggests that *Gaudium et spes*'s teaching on the duties of the clergy and laity seems somewhat unprepared for the movement of dissent that followed upon the council.

Next, Dr. Matthew Levering discusses part two of *Gaudium et spes*. The Church is a privileged instrument of human development because she knows the end to which the Father, through Christ and in the Holy Spirit, seeks to draw human beings. Only such knowledge of the goal allows for a true measure of what constitutes progress. In part two of *Gaudium et spes* five central areas of human development receive attention: marriage and the family, culture, economics, politics, and the use of coercive military force. In outlining *Gaudium et spes*'s treatment of these issues, Levering asks whether *Gaudium et spes*'s sometimes innovative presentations constitute a moment of disjunction from previous Church teaching on the topics. With regard to marriage and the family, he observes that *Gaudium et spes* rearranges the discussion in terms of the covenantal mutual gift of husband and wife. Yet this does not alter the Church's traditional teaching on the procreative and unitive ends: The mutual gift of husband and wife is ordained to the supreme gift, children. Similarly in this framework of mutual gift the imaging of Christ and the Church, as well as the indissolubility of marriage, receive clear expression. Regarding culture, *Gaudium et spes* both celebrates the birth of a new humanism and warns that, without knowledge of the human ordering to fulfillment in Christ, such a humanism will result in a cultural and technological deformation of the human being. Similarly, with respect to economic development, *Gaudium et spes* reaffirms the principles of *Rerum novarum* and, with respect to political development, emphasizes the common good as prior to individual choice, thereby insisting that rights are not markers of individual autonomy. On the issue of Church and state, *Gaudium et spes* argues primarily that the Church cannot be seen as a mere political community alongside other political communities since the Church embodies the transcendent common good of the human race. Finally, with respect to war, *Gaudium et spes* retains the traditional teaching on "just war" while nonetheless decrying both war and the ominous emergence of nuclear weapons.

The Decrees

Msgr. Brian Ferme delves into *Christus Dominus* and demonstrates how the council, which drew upon the long tradition of bishops as successors of the apostles, was able to complete and complement the work of Vatican I on the roles of the pope as successor of Peter. As the chapters on *Lumen gentium* indicate, the hierarchical character of the Church is intrinsic to her mission of sanctifying, teaching, and governing. The universality of the Church is concretely instantiated in the many local churches whose bishops are in communion with the pope as bishop of Rome. Indeed, the council itself witnessed to the participation of all the bishops in hierarchical communion caring for the universal Church. Ferme treats the juridical teachings of *Christus Dominus* with regard to the bishops' relationships with the Petrine ministry, as well as their responsibilities in their own dioceses and their cooperation in attending to the common good of many churches through synods and episcopal conferences. These juridical responsibilities flow from the theology of the bishop in the Church brought out in *Lumen gentium*.

Father Guy Mansini and Dr. Lawrence J. Welch treat *Presbyterorum ordinis*. Focusing on paragraph two as the hermeneutical key to the document's Christological account of the ministerial priesthood, they explore the document's genesis, its relationship to the Church's tradition of reflection on holy orders, and its reception since the council. A key task of *Presbyterorum ordinis*, they suggest, was to bring together the three *munera* (functions) of the priest, namely, sanctifying, preaching, and ruling. Put another way, the priest should be understood as consecrated to God in order to offer the Eucharistic sacrifice and as prolonging the apostolic mission of preaching and ruling. At stake in the interpretation of *Presbyterorum ordinis* since its promulgation, Mansini and Welch suggest, has been the question of whether the munera of preaching and ruling absorb or eclipse, in *Presbyterorum ordinis,* the *munus* of sanctifying (especially through the Eucharistic sacrifice). In other words, has the cultic understanding of the Catholic priest, affirmed by the Council of Trent and elsewhere, been dislodged or undermined by *Presbyterorum ordinis?* Mansini and Welch, appealing in particular to paragraph five, argue that the answer is no. They also show that in both *Presbyterorum ordinis* and *Lumen gentium* the ministerial priest is presented as representing Christ not only when acting *in persona Christi* in the Eucharistic sacrifice but also in preaching and ruling. This is a development of doctrine that goes beyond both Trent and the encyclical *Mediator Dei* but that, as a true development, does so without distorting the traditional teaching.

Father Anthony A. Akinwale examines *Optatam totius*. He begins with a brief exposition of John Henry Newman and Yves Congar on the development of doctrine, so as to rule out from the outset the idea that the council succumbed to an undifferentiated acceptance of modern culture. Akinwale then focuses upon the *munus triplex Christi* that the priest undertakes in representing Christ in and for the service of the Church's communion. It seems, he notes, that *Optatam totius*'s insistence upon engagement with the world in priestly formation marks a sharp disjunction from the Council of Trent's more strictly ecclesial formation of priests. Akinwale argues, however, that the two approaches to priestly formation are united by the role of the three munera, whose foundations are of course scriptural. The emphasis on the three munera is found not only in *Presbyterorum ordinis* and *Optatam totius* but also, according to Akinwale, in Trent and the encyclical tradition, as well as in the fathers and scholastics. For both Trent and Vatican II, says Akinwale, the goal of priestly formation was to shape priests who, in exercising the munus triplex, are "of the world" but not "in the world," that is to say, who embody Jesus Christ in the world today. Given this goal, *Optatam totius*, like earlier documents on priestly formation, insists on the necessity of seminaries set apart for priestly formation. Seminarians should be given the tools needed for exercising the munus triplex, including preaching the revealed word of God, celebrating the sacraments, and governing through service. As Akinwale puts it, this means an integrated formation in holiness, intelligence, and competence, such as the writings of the fathers display. He then reviews *Optatam totius*'s specific teachings on formation in cruciform holiness (Christological and Mariological), which requires intellectual formation guided by not only the method but also the basic content of St. Thomas Aquinas's theology so as to model the intelligence of faith needed for inculturation.

Next, Sr. Prudence Allen and Sr. Mary Judith O'Brien explore *Perfectae caritatis*. Drawing upon a study of ten essential elements of religious life, Allen and O'Brien focus upon *Perfectae caritatis*'s presentation of three such elements: relation to the Church; consecration by public vows of chastity, poverty, and obedience; and communion in community. For each of these themes, they review in some detail representative texts from the tradition of the Church's teaching on religious life, especially since the medieval period. They observe that religious orders were traditionally conceived as "cooperators" with the Church and as set apart for the sanctification of their members. However, St. Thomas Aquinas, as well as Pius XII in his 1947 apostolic constitution *Provida Mater Ecclesia*, recognized that the religious state affects all persons in the Church. In this vein, *Perfectae caritatis*, like *Lumen gentium*, affirms that the complete gift of self made by consecrated persons assists the Church's missionary creativity and provides a measure of the Church's depth of faith. With respect to consecration by public vows, *Perfectae caritatis* did not challenge its necessity or place, despite the experimentation that occurred after the council. Rather, both *Perfectae caritatis* and *Lumen gentium* affirmed the value of the vowed life of chastity, poverty, and obedience, although they did so in less juridical language than did some earlier ecclesial texts (in this they were preceded by documents issued by Pius XII). Finally, with respect to communion in community or "common life," they show that *Perfectae caritatis*'s statements both affirm the value of common life in deepening the self-giving service that is charity and accord with earlier ecclesial texts.

Father Robert W. Oliver discusses *Apostolicam actuositatem*, whose stated goal is to stimulate service of Christ and the Church on the part of the laity. As Oliver points out, *Apostolicam actuositatem*, like *Lumen gentium*, places such service not in a "horizontal" but in a "vertical" context, as a sharing in the Trinitarian work of salvation. The document grounds its teaching on baptismal incorporation into the common priesthood of Christ. Rather than viewing the laity as fundamentally passive in their membership in the Church, *Apostolicam actuositatem* depicts the laity as active members of the Body of Christ. For this reason and in light of early-twentieth-century debates about the work of Catholic Action, *Apostolicam actuositatem* presents a broader meaning of "apostolate" than found in previous Church teaching: "Apostolate" (individual or organized) now includes not only the direct evangelization and sanctification of the world but also the penetration of the Gospel into every aspect of the world. Oliver traces this meaning through the chapters of the document and sees in its range a development away from earlier juridical understandings of "apostolate" as requiring canonical authorization. *Apostolicam actuositatem* does not envisage individual believers asserting their authority over against ecclesial authority, but it does distinguish between apostolates whose ecclesial ends require direct Church governance and those whose ends preclude it. In this regard, Oliver remarks, *Apostolicam actuositatem* clarifies a controversy regarding a pontifical congregation's 1920 ruling that the canons of the 1917 *Code of Canon Law* did not apply to lay associations. Similarly, *Apostolicam actuositatem* offers a new conception of the variety of relationships between lay initiatives and episcopal oversight. Yet, in making these various canonical distinctions, *Apostolicam actuositatem* does not conflate the role of the laity with that of ecclesial authority.

Francis Cardinal George examines *Ad gentes*. After noting the Church's missionary activity throughout history, George summarizes the insights of *Ad gentes* in five areas: the Church's mission; Jesus Christ, the origin and source of mission; the nature of mission; proclamation and dialogue; and conversion. With respect to the Church's mission, George states that *Ad gentes*, like *Lumen gentium*, thinks of the entirety of the Church as the embodiment of the Son and Spirit's historical mission from the Father, a charge whose purpose is to draw all people into the communion of the Trinity. Mission is thus linked with communion, enacted visibly and historically in and through the apostolic structures of the hierarchical Church. Second, George turns to Jesus Christ as the origin of mission. *Ad gentes* teaches that, although God may unite human beings to Christ through implicit faith and outside the Church's visible bounds, all salvation nonetheless comes about through Christ and incorporation into his Body, the Church. *Ad gentes* likewise affirms that mission, in its most proper sense (which includes evangelization), is spreading the Gospel and planting the Church in non-Christian countries. The content of such missionary work cannot be reduced, according to *Ad gentes*, to the witness of a charitable life or social services but must include preaching the Gospel, which should take place within a context of respectful dialogue. In this regard George sees *Ad gentes* as developing a more positive understanding of the value of other religions, without thereby renouncing the particularity of Christian salvation. *Ad gentes* rules out proselytism, understood as inducements or pressure, but clearly states that the goal of missionary activity is conversion to Christ. In conclusion he briefly traces the reception of *Ad gentes* since the council.

Father Charles Morerod surveys *Unitatis redintegratio* in the context of the history of Catholic ecumenism. He notes that consciousness of permanent division did not fully emerge until the end of the sixteenth century, after which it was sometimes interpreted positively as an indication of the defeat of one side or the other. Vatican I noted that the Reformation divisions led to significant loss of faith. Contemporary ecumenism began only in the late nineteenth century, and not until John XXIII's 1959 encyclical *Ad Petri cathedram* were ecumenical gatherings looked upon in a more clearly positive fashion. Morerod suggests that the central theological notion of *Unitatis redintegratio* is "fullness." Fullness is present in the Catholic Church, which possesses the whole of the means of salvation; yet the existing fullness, impaired by the separation of Christian brethren, can increase. *Unitatis redintegratio* also teaches that a "hierarchy of truths" exists: While everyone must be held in faith, some are nonetheless closer to the heart of Christianity than others, and this hierarchy allows for the appreciation of degrees of participation. Christians not united to the visible Church can be imperfectly united by degrees of participation through faith, baptism, and other shared elements. As Morerod shows, *Unitatis redintegratio* thus engages the Orthodox churches and the Protestant communions by applying the Church's traditional understanding of degrees of participation to the situation of Christian division.

Next, Dr. Khaled Anatolios comments on *Orientalium Ecclesiarum*. This document, which pertains to the Eastern churches in communion with Rome, gives insight, in Anatolios's view, to the council's commitment to theological ressourcement. Anatolios first summarizes the document with particular attention to the changes it makes to canon law—for example, allowing patriarchs to appoint bishops within their patriarchal territories—out of respect for the Eastern churches' need to remain in organic continuity with their tradition. He notes, too, *Orientalium Ecclesiarum*'s respect for Eastern liturgical rites as equals to the Latin rite, which constitutes a change from the perspective taken in Benedict XIV's 1755 encyclical *Allatae sunt* but accords more closely with Pius XII's 1944 encyclical *Orientalis Ecclesiae*. Anatolios also points to the conciliatory tone adopted with regard to the Eastern Orthodox by Leo XIII in his 1894 encyclical *Praeclara gratulationis*. In the same year Leo XIII published the encyclical *Orientalium dignitas*. Anatolios devotes a significant portion of his treatment to comparing the opening paragraphs of Leo's *Orientalium dignitas* to those of Vatican II's *Orientalium Ecclesiarum*. He finds that both documents praise the Eastern churches, but the latter does so more specifically for their conservation (as bearers of tradition) of the Church's doctrinal heritage. In this way, there is both significant continuity and significant development in the Church's understanding of the Eastern churches.

Father Richard John Neuhaus takes up *Inter mirifica*. He points out that *Inter mirifica*, although about social communication (the media), was generally ignored by the news media. To the extent that any paid it attention, it often received bad press. The responses to the document, as Neuhaus shows, found *Inter mirifica* to be overly cautious with regard to the media and too concerned to lay down rules for communicating the faith. Neuhaus grants that the tone of *Inter mirifica* is at times too negative, although he also observes that the present state of the media justifies much of this negative concern. By emphasizing the risk of abuses and the need to advocate for the Church, however, *Inter mirifica* seems to Neuhaus to lack some of the boldness of other documents that, indebted to the program of ressourcement, display the fathers' missionary zeal to convert the world rather than to retreat fearfully from it.

Yet, this tone does not, Neuhaus makes clear, distort the substance of the document's teaching, which conveys the Church's traditional understanding, unchanged today, of the communication of the faith. The key point of *Inter mirifica* is that evangelization, as an ongoing task of all Christians, will be carried forth by Christians who are proficient in the instruments of communication precisely through those instruments. Just as Catholics must actively evangelize through the media, so also, according to *Inter mirifica*, must the media exemplify truth, charity, and justice in order not to become the obverse of true communication. *Inter mirifica* therefore defends the freedom of the media but does so within the due limits of justice in accord with the state's concern for the common good. As Neuhaus concludes, *Inter mirifica*'s content is neither new nor outdated but constitutes simply a modest effort to encourage the full communication of the Gospel and to uphold the standards of truth and justice as they concern the communications industry.

The Declarations

In this section Dr. Russell Hittinger engages *Dignitatis humanae*, which he reads as meaning what it says in its first paragraph with respect to leaving "intact the traditional Catholic teaching on the moral duty of individuals and societies toward the true religion and the one Church of Christ." Hittinger asserts that *Dignitatis humanae* is best read as a very limited statement on the duty of states to protect the freedom of religious worship. He notes that historically one finds three models of the Church's situation vis-à-vis temporal authorities: (1) a single body, in which the king participates in Christ "pedes in terra [feet on earth]" and the episcopal authority participates in Christ's "caput in caelo [head in heaven]"; (2) a separation in which the Church enjoys liberty under certain rubrics; and (3) a conflation in which the government takes over the Church. In Hittinger's view, faced with the twentieth-century rise of fascist and communist regimes, *Dignitatis humanae* strongly rejects the third model and offers only tangential comment upon the first. Instead, in accord with the second model, *Dignitatis humanae* aims at articulating the particular kind of religious liberty that the Church, along with individuals and other communities, requires. This does not mean that *Dignitatis humanae* supposes that governments can be neutral toward truth. Rather, absent recognition of the existence of divine truth, human religious liberty would not be sufficient to ground its claim to inviolability. Hittinger points out that *Dignitatis humanae* teaches that liberty comes not from the state but from Christ, who has purchased the Church's liberty by his cross and requires her to speak the truth to all cultures. Human beings possess religious liberty precisely in order to find and affirm such truth. Governments should not control religious activity but rather should facilitate people's ability to engage in religious activity. In making this limited claim, Hittinger observes, *Dignitatis humanae* both fully accords with the tradition of Church teaching and avoids the thorny issues that would mark a broader discussion of the temporal authority's responsibilities in relation to the Church.

Next, Dr. Don J. Briel discusses *Gravissimum educationis*. He grounds his discussion in a thorough acquaintance with earlier papal teaching on education, above all Pius XI's 1929 encyclical *Divini illius magistri*, as well as remarks in documents such as Pius XI's 1937 *Mit brennender Sorge* (regarding the Nazi restriction on Catholic schooling) and Pius IX's 1849 *Nostis et nobiscum* (regarding the detachment of education from the Church's authority and pastoral oversight). Briel also reflects upon postconciliar magisterial documents and commentary on *Gravissimum educationis* by theologians, in particular Joseph Ratzinger, who criticized the document as weak. As Briel points out, *Gravissimum educationis* is far more optimistic in terms of its anthropology and its assessment of modern technological development than is Pius XI's *Divini illius magistri*. In addition, *Gravissimum educationis*, while privileging Catholic schools, does not restrict its scope to them; it also treats the needs of Catholic students in non-Catholic schools. In Briel's view, where *Gravissium educationis* could have gained most from an increased incorporation of *Divini illius magistri* is in the area of distinguishing between parents' competencies and responsibilities, the Church, and society with regard to the education of children. Yet, as Briel shows, *Gravissimum educationis* is attuned to the distinct roles of parents, Church, and society and aware too of the threat posed to the common good by a purely secular education that excludes God.

Finally, Fr. Arthur Kennedy interprets *Nostra aetate* as an exercise in appropriating and transposing traditional teaching on the Church in light of developments in historical knowledge and cultural appreciation of other religious communities. At the heart of *Nostra aetate*, Kennedy observes, is Saint Augustine's dictum that "our hearts are restless until they rest in Thee." It is in this light that *Nostra aetate* envisions the aims of non-Christian religions. Thus *Nostra aetate* seeks to value all that is good in these religions while proclaiming that Christ alone gives the salvation that fulfills human beings. Kennedy describes in some detail the theological presuppositions of *Nostra aetate*'s teaching on Judaism. Without smoothing over the discontinuity and historical tensions, *Nostra aetate* takes up Saint Paul's affirmation in the Epistle to the Romans that God has not rejected his people or revoked his covenants and also continues and develops the catechism of the Council of Trent's teaching that our sins, not the entire Jewish people, are responsible for Christ's death. Here again Kennedy points to Augustine as a significant source for *Nostra aetate*'s perspective, and he notes as well the emergence of Jewish-Catholic dialogue, particularly in the early twentieth century. Augustine and Saint Thomas Aquinas also contribute, in Kennedy's view, to the document's understanding of other non-Christian religions in relation to the capacities of natural reason, strongly affirmed by Vatican I, and to the virtue of justice. Kennedy concludes by remarking upon the reception of the document through the wide variety of efforts to foster dialogue and understanding between Catholics and non-Christian religions.

Lastly, from a Methodist perspective, Geoffrey Wainwright comments on *Unitatis redintegratio* and *Sacrosanctum concilium* in light of the twentieth century's ecumenical and liturgical movements. Emphasizing the patristic roots of both documents, Wainwright employs three liturgical terms to guide his reflection: *anamnesis* (remembrance), *epiclesis* (invocation), and *prolepsis* (anticipation). With regard to *Sacrosanctum concilium*, he states that the renewed "service of the word" directs attention to the Paschal mystery and points to the ecumenical significance of the new anaphoras. He also finds in the 1972 Rite for the Christian Initiation of Adults a renewal of patristic practice. Placing *Unitatis redintegratio* in the context of the ecumenical movement of the first half of the twentieth century, he observes that the recurrent question in ecumenism is ecclesiological: Where is the one Church to be found? Important in this regard, he shows, was the patristic theology of baptism, especially Augustine's affirmation that the baptism administered by the Donatists did not need to be repeated. Building upon this foundation, the ecumenical movement and *Unitatis redintegratio* set forth an understanding of "degrees of communion" and of the Church as a "sacrament." Wainwright argues that these approaches make possible further ecumenical convergences among Christians regarding the marks of the Church. He then turns specifically to exploring the concept of "renewal within tradition." Renewal, he notes, has its Christian meaning in an "eschatological newness" that requires the pilgrim Church, guided by the Holy Spirit, always to deepen the union with Christ that the Paschal mystery has accomplished. He shows that in fact this is precisely the meaning of "renewal" at work in the revisions and reforms proposed by the council's documents. Included within this "renewal within tradition" was a new mode of doctrinal dialogue between the Catholic Church and various Protestant communions, as Wainwright demonstrates by means of particular attention to recent dialogues between Catholics, Methodists, Lutherans, and Anglicans.

How do the chapters of this book, taken as a whole, contribute to our understanding of the Second Vatican Council? First, the variety of the documents that constitute Vatican II become clear. The point that the conciliar documents do not mark a break with prior teaching obviously does not mean that they all integrate earlier teaching in the same way or to the same degree. Likewise, continuity with tradition does not mean a static or stale repetition. Rather it is precisely the continuity, or complementarity, that allows for true renewal. Renewal does not mean deconstruction or rupture but instead entails the enriching and deepening of what has gone before.

Second, as befits a truly "Catholic" approach, the council's documents exposit realities of faith and recommend courses of pastoral practice, with the aim of moving ever closer to the Word incarnate, Christ Jesus, who offers each person, by the Holy Spirit, true freedom through faith, hope, and self-giving love. The council's task is to lead believers more deeply into the contents and requirements of faith, hope, and love. In this task the council is sustained by the awareness that Christ Jesus has never left the Church bereft of his truth and sanctifying power. The tradition upon which the council draws is itself the work of the Spirit, which draws believers closer to Christ. Far from rejecting this tradition, which would bring about an unintelligible rupture at the heart of the Spirit's work in the Church, the council aims to enter ever more deeply, in a doctrinal and pastoral fashion, into the realities that are handed down within this tradition.

Some recent remarks by philosopher Robert Sokolowski recall the importance of appreciating the council's work in this Catholic, rather than liberal or conservative, fashion. Sokolowski offers a metaphor, taken from American football, that explains the "rupture" model of interpreting the council: "The impression was given that the tradition of the Church was not a continuous handing on, through the centuries, of something received; it was more like a long pass from the apostolic age to the Second Vatican Council, with only distortions in between, whether Byzantine, medieval, or baroque."[16] In this view, the progressive teachings of Jesus have been distorted by centuries of conservative overlay—the work of what Hobbes might call "priestcraft"—that Vatican II then bravely seeks to overcome. Vatican II here becomes the great force against ideology. The problem with this perspective is that Vatican II would thereby seem to deny the continuity of the Spirit's work in the Church and ipso facto would turn itself into an ideology (thus the attraction of the liberal-conservative schema). As Sokolowski points out, however, from a fully Catholic perspective rooted in the historical missions of the Son and the Spirit, "the Second Vatican Council is only one council among many, and all the others—including the First Vatican Council and the Council of Trent—as well as the tradition of the Church retain their force and importance."[17]

Sokolowski goes on to call for Catholic scholars to place the council within a properly Catholic theology of history. The Church is no mere ideology but is instead the locus of Christ's sanctifying truth by the power of his Spirit. The Church draws us into a personal encounter with the Redeemer, who invites us to share in the very life of the Trinity. This is good news indeed, and it cannot coexist with an ideological reading of the Church's tradition. Sokolowski observes, "Without episcopal teaching in continuity with the apostles and with Christ, there is no sanctification and government, and there can be no Catholic Church."[18] Other kinds of churches and theologies of history might be possible without such continuity, but not a Catholic one. As he says, therefore, "One of the greatest challenges to the Church is to reestablish the continuity between the present Church and the Church throughout the centuries, to revalidate the tradition of the Church."[19] This task requires a theological hermeneutic of the council.

This book, we hope, contributes in an initial way to the needed task. If these chapters inspire other theologians to take up this charge with a Catholic hermeneutic appropriate to the council, then the book will have achieved its aims. Much more work remains to be done. The renewal sought by the Second Vatican Council requires all Roman Catholics to deepen their lives of faith and learning, their sacramental participation in divine worship, as well as their many spiritual and corporeal works of mercy. In opening the council John XXIII prayed that the "sacred deposit of Christian doctrine should be guarded and taught more efficaciously" in order to respond with an intelligent and loving faith in Christ Jesus and his Church to the challenges facing both the Church and humanity at the end of the second millennium of Christianity and the dawn of the third.[20] Will those hopes and prayers be fulfilled? As one perceptive historian has written, "No one knows whether, in the twenty-fifth century, Vatican II will be remembered as another Lateran V—a reforming council that failed—or another Trent—a reforming council that was so successful that it set the course of Catholic life for more than four hundred years."[21]

NOTES

1. One theologian who was obliged by his superior to give daily reports for *La Croix*, Fr. Antoine Wenger, A.A., called attention to the danger of ideological distortions in the mass media coverage: "The journalist is in danger of writing merely ideological information, explaining everything categorically in terms of conservatives and progressives, integralists and modernists, doctrinal and pastoral, curia and pastors, Italians and non-Italians, etc." *Vatican Council II: The First Session*, trans. Robert J. Olsen (Westminster, Md.: Newman Press, 1966); his complete coverage (in French) appears in *Vatican II* (Paris: Centurion, 1963–1965), 3 vols. See also Yves Congar, *Le concile au jour le jour* (Paris: Editions du Cerf, 1963–1966), 4 vols.

2. These are collected in Xavier Rynne, *Vatican Council II: With a New Introduction by the Author* (1968; New York: Orbis, 1999).

3. Joseph Ratzinger, *Theological Highlights of Vatican II*, trans. Henry Traub, Gerard Thormann, and Werner Barzel (New York: Paulist Press, 1966).

4. Leo XIII, *Aeterni Patris*, an encyclical on the restoration of Christian philosophy (Aug. 4, 1879), no. 24.

5. First statement of Pope Benedict XVI after the Mass with the cardinals (Apr. 20, 2005), no. 3: "Iustissima quidem de causa Pontifex Ioannes Paulus Secundus Ecclesiae in Concilio illo demonstravit indicem seu ut dicitur quasi 'nauticam pyxidem,' qua in vasto mari tertii millennii dirigeretur (cf. Litt. Ap. *Novo millennio ineunte*, 57–58). In suo spirituali quoque Testamento scripsit: 'Persuasum mihi habeo advenientes homines diutius etiam quaedam sumpturos ex divitiis illis quas hoc Concilium saeculi vicesimi nobis est elargitum' (Mar. 17, 2000). Nos quoque propterea munus ingredientes quod est proprium successoris Petri, firmam certamque voluntatem declarare volumus Concilii Vaticani Secundi continuandi exsecutionem, Praegredientibus Decessoribus Nostris, atque in fideli perpetuitate duorum milium annorum Ecclesiae traditionis."

6. Benedict XVI, "Faith, Reason, and the University: Memories and Reflections," lecture at the University of Regensburg, Sept. 12, 2006, in James Schall, S.J., *The Regensburg Lecture* (South Bend, Ind.: St. Augustine Press, 2007), 233–47.

7. Ibid. On the consequences of voluntarism on academic cultures see Alasdair MacIntyre's *Three Rival Traditions of Moral Inquiry* (Notre Dame, Ind.: University of Notre Dame Press, 1990), in which he charts how contemporary universities and cultures take their bearings from two Enlightenment traditions: the encyclopedists and the genealogists. The encyclopedists attend carefully to the endless particularities open to human study but lack any internal intelligent ordering of the whole. The alphabet provides the scholars, as it also does the administrative bureaucrats, with their impoverished substitute for order: the filing system. God is filed under "G," along with "gold" and "gorillas." The genealogists then come along to claim that any language is only a dialect with an army and a navy, so that all orders are only conventions imposed by dominative power. All order and pattern are merely conventional, so whatever pattern is operative is due to those in power deciding it is so. Truth becomes just another name for arbitrary dominative power.

8. Charles Taylor, *The Sources of the Self: The Making of Modern Identity* (Cambridge, Mass.: Harvard University Press, 1989), 215ff.

9. See Jonathan Israel, *Radical Enlightenment: Philosophy and the Making of Modernity, 1650–1750* (New York: Oxford University Press, 2001), 218–29, esp. 227–29.

10. Ibid., 157–274, 445–76; and Spinoza, *A Theologico-political Treatise* (New York: Dover, 2004), 98–119, esp. 101.

11. Agostino Marchetto, *Il Concilio Ecumenico Vaticano II: Contrappunto per la sua storia* (Vatican City: Liberia Editrice Vaticana, 2005), 84ff., 358ff. An English translation is in preparation.

12. The Italian five-volume *Storia del Concilio Vaticano II*, under the general editorship of Giuseppe Alberigo, has been published in several languages. The English version is *History of Vatican II*, ed. Joseph Komonchak; trans. Matthew J. O'Connell (Maryknoll, N.Y.: Orbis, 1995–2006).

13. Marchetto, *Il Concilio Ecumenico Vaticano II*, 223–43; also 93–165. See also Camillo Cardinal Ruini, *Nuovi segni dei tempi: Le sorti della fede nell'età dei mutamenti* (Milan: Mondadori, 2005); and Sandro Magister, "Vaticano II: la vera storia che nessuno ha ancora raccontato," *L'espresso* (June 22, 2005): 7.

14. "Alberigo: Ratzinger lontano dallo spirito conciliare," *Corriere della sera* (Mar. 15, 2007); also "Pope subverts Vatican II, historian charges," *Catholic World News* (Mar. 16, 2007): 2. Alberigo accuses Pope Benedict of being fearful of modernity: "A noted Italian Church historian has denounced the opposition of the Catholic Church to the legal recognition of civil unions, and blasted Pope Benedict XVI, saying that the current Pontiff is 'worse than Pius XII. . . . It is a restoration that cancels a century of Church history,' he said. Alberigo argued that 'it is difficult to find cohesion between magisterial documents and the spirit of the Second Vatican Council.' "

15. See Matthew Lamb, "Will There Be Catholic Theology in the United States?" in *America* 162 (May 26, 1990): 523–34. Also, "The Catholic Theological Society of America: Theologians Unbound," *Crisis: Politics, Culture, and the Church* (Dec. 1997): 36–37; "The Catholic Theological Society of America: A Preliminary Profile," *Fellowship of Catholic Scholars Quarterly* 21 (1998): 8–10; also, the responses in *Crisis: Politics, Culture, and the Church* 16 (1998): 3, 14; and in *Fellowship of Catholic Scholars Quarterly* 21 (1998): 2–5. From 1968 to 1997, 75 percent of doctoral dissertations in theology written by members of the Catholic Theological Society of America were on twentieth-century thinkers; 10 percent discussed nineteenth-century thinkers. Of the remaining 15 percent, most were in biblical studies. Research on specifically Catholic theological traditions—patristic, monastic, scholastic, counterreformation—was woefully meager. See Walter Principe's plaintive presidential address and the responses in *The Proceedings*

of the Catholic Theological Society of America (Atlanta: Catholic Theological Society, 1991), 75–107.

16. Robert Sokolowski, *Christian Faith and Human Understanding: Studies on the Eucharist, Trinity, and the Human Person* (Washington, D.C.: Catholic University of America Press, 2006), 129.

17. Ibid.

18. Ibid., 130.

19. Ibid., 129.

20. Opening speech to the council by Pope John XXIII (Oct. 11, 1962).

21. George Weigel, *The Courage to Be Catholic: Crisis, Reform, and the Future of the Church* (New York: Basic Books, 2002), 4–5.

The Constitutions

I

Nature, Mission, and Structure of the Church

Avery Cardinal Dulles, S.J.

Conciliar Hermeneutics

There exists a general impression that Vatican II accomplished a major revolution in ecclesiology. John O'Malley credits it for achieving a reform by transformation or revolution rather than by adjustment or development;[1] Gregory Baum holds that its documents reflect a "Blondelian shift" from extrinsicism toward experience and immanence.[2] Richard P. McBrien speaks of "Copernican" and "Einsteinian" revolutions that overcame the unhealthy ecclesiocentrism of the past.[3] George Lindbeck finds in the council documents a mixture of classical and progressive elements but holds that the old is to be understood in terms of the new rather than vice versa.[4]

These authors, together with many others who might be named, popularized a rather radical interpretation of the council's impact on ecclesiology. Before the council, it is held, the Church was regarded as an institution founded by Christ with definite and immutable structures. After the council the Church was seen as a pilgrim community constantly restructuring itself to suit the times. Before the council the Church was regarded as necessary for salvation; after it, as one of many places in which people could live a life of grace. Before Vatican II, the Catholic Church saw herself as the sole legitimate Church; after it, as one of many realizations of the Church of Christ, all imperfect. Until the council, the Church was seen as a divinely instituted monarchy in which all authority descended from the pope; after it, as a People of God that governed itself through consensus.

All of these generalizations, I maintain, are false. They overlook the nuances both in the preconciliar period and in Vatican II. The council did effect a number of important developments in ecclesiology, but they were not revolutionary in character. Any aggiornamento that it accomplished was intrinsically connected with the principle of *ressourcement*. "Every renewal of the Church," for the council, "essentially consists in an increase of fidelity to her own calling" (*UR* 6).

The principles of interpretation are of vital importance. Concerned by misinterpretations, Pope John Paul II convened an extraordinary assembly of the Synod of Bishops in 1985. That synod in its final report taught that the council's teaching should be interpreted "in continuity with the great tradition of the Church," including the teaching of earlier councils and popes.[5] At a special audience on February 17, 2002, Pope John Paul II warned against partial and prejudiced interpretations. He went on to declare that "The Church has always known the rules for a correct hermeneutic of the contents of dogma. They are rules inscribed within the texture of faith and not outside it. To read the council supposing that it involves a rupture with the past—whereas in reality it situates itself in the line of the abiding faith—is decisively misleading. That which has been believed 'by all, always, and in every place' is the authentic newness that permits every epoch to feel itself enlightened by the word of God's revelation in Jesus Christ."[6] In light of this "authentic newness," in this chapter I explore the teaching of the Dogmatic Constitution on the Church, *Lumen gentium*, on the nature, mission, and hierarchical structures of the Church (chapters 1–3).

The Church as Sacrament

The first chapter of *Lumen gentium*, which deals with the mystery of the Church, begins by describing the Church as being, in Christ, a sacrament of unity: that is to say, a sign and an instrument of the unity of the whole human race in Christ the Lord. This vision of unity recalls the opening words of Vatican I's *Pastor aeternus*: "The eternal Shepherd and Guardian of our souls (cf. 1 Pet 2:25), in order to continue for all time the saving work of redemption, determined to build his holy Church so that in it, as in the house of the living God, all who believe might be united together in the bond of one faith and one love. For this reason, before he was glorified, he prayed to the Father not for the apostles only but for those also who would believe in him on their testimony, that all might be one as he, the Son, and the Father are one (cf. Jn 17:20ff)" (DS 3050). Vatican I did not apply the term "sacrament" to the Church, but it did speak of the Church as a "standard lifted up among the nations" and as inviting all, by her Catholic unity and other wonderful properties, to believe in her divine testimony and to enter her fold (DS 3013–14).

For Vatican II, the idea of the Church as sacrament is of foundational importance. Four times in *Lumen gentium* (*LG* 1, 9, 48, 59) and six times in other documents (*SC* 5 and 26; *GS* 42 and 45, *AG* 1 and 5) it so designates the Church. A sacrament is a symbolic expression of the great mystery of grace and salvation centered in Jesus Christ. For the New Testament and the fathers, Christ is the great sacrament or mystery of salvation, but Christ is not complete without the Church, which is his visible and effective presence on earth. Thus the Church may be seen, in Christ, as the encompassing sacrament.

The history of the concept of the Church as sacrament cannot be reviewed here, but others have traced it.[7] Anticipated by Augustine and his mediaeval followers,[8] sacramental ecclesiology came into special favor in the nineteenth century, with outstanding representatives such as Johannes Kuhn, Heinrich Klee, Johann Adam Möhler, and Matthias Scheeben. Pius XII in his encyclical on the mystical Body, without calling the Church a sacrament, portrayed it as a visible, grace-filled institution through which Christ carries on his saving work. In 1949 the Holy Office spoke of the Church as a *generale auxilium salutis* (DS 3870), which is practically equivalent to "general sacrament."

In the decades that preceded Vatican II many theologians, such as Henri de Lubac, Otto Semmelroth, and Karl Rahner, spoke of the Church as a great or fundamental sacrament in which the grace of Christ was mysteriously at work. The German bishops were primarily responsible for getting the sacramental concept written into the Constitution on the Church.[9] A few theologians at Vatican II opposed the application of the term "sacrament" to the Church. They feared that it might be misused to imply that the sacraments were not constitutive of the Church and that the Church could institute or suppress individual sacraments at her discretion. American theologian Joseph Clifford Fenton attributed this view to Modernist George Tyrrell and expressed the apprehension that the same view would resurface after the council.[10] His concerns were not unfounded even though the idea of the Church as general sacrament did not imply the her temporal priority over the individual sacraments. If it is true that the Church makes the sacraments, it is no less true that the sacraments make the Church. She does not have creative power over them.[11]

Membership

In the light of its sacramental ecclesiology, *Lumen gentium* revisited the question raised by Pius XII in *Mystici corporis* regarding membership. For Pius XII, the mystical Body had two aspects, the visible and the invisible, which were not two bodies or two churches but two aspects of a single complex reality analogous to the union of the two natures in Christ (MC 63).[12] Approaching the question of membership in terms of the Church as a visible and an organic body, the pope held that only Roman Catholics could be members in the full sense of the word (*reapse*, MC 22). Non-Catholics could be spiritually united to the Church by desire and intention but could not qualify as members (MC 103).

Vatican II, relying on a sacramental ecclesiology, handled the question of membership somewhat differently. Avoiding the term "member," which had become bogged down in controversy, it spoke of perfect and imperfect realizations of the sacrament. The sacrament of the Church is fully realized only in the Catholic Church, the visible and grace-filled society in which the bonds of professed faith, ecclesiastical government, and sacramental communion remain fully intact (*LG* 14). These bonds belong together insofar as the true Church indefectibly possesses them all. But the bonds are separable in the sense that some may survive in the absence of others. Non–Roman Catholic communities may possess some authentic ecclesial elements and be able to make fruitful use of them as channels of grace (*LG* 15; cf. *UR* 3).

Individuals in different ecclesial situations may enjoy various degrees of communion with, or incorporation in, the one Church of Christ. To be fully incorporated and fully in communion, one must possess the Spirit of Christ and accept the full system of Catholic Christianity, including all of the means of salvation given to it (*LG* 14). Catechumens can be joined to the Church by explicit desire (*voto*, *LG* 14). Baptized non-Catholics can be in partial or imperfect communion, thanks to their faith, their devotion, and the means of salvation available to them in their respective communities (*LG* 15). Non-Christians are not in communion with the Church but are ordered toward it in various ways (*diversis rationibus ordinantur*, *LG* 16).

The Church of Christ and the Catholic Church

Mystici Corporis, relying on the analogy of the body, stated that the Church of Christ is identical with the Roman Catholic Church. The early drafts of Vatican II's Constitution on the Church took a similar position, but once the sacramental idea was introduced, a change was in order. Responding to complaints that the language seemed to rule out ecclesial elements in other churches, a subcommission eliminated "is" (*est*) and inserted in its place "is present in" (*adest in*). However, the council fathers were not content to assert that the Church of Christ is present in Roman Catholicism, which had always claimed to possess in itself the fullness of the Church. Thus the Theological Commission on November 25, 1963, dropped the term "adest" and replaced it with "subsistit." The new term was proposed by Sebastian Tromp, S.J., who had previously favored "est" and was a stout defender of the positions of *Mystici Corporis*.[13]

It is regrettable that the commentaries generally give the impression that *subsistit in* was a replacement for *est* and was introduced to provide for the ecclesial reality of other Christian communities.[14] In point of fact, it was introduced as a replacement for "adest in" in order to safeguard the full presence of the Church of Christ in the Catholic communion.

Since the council it has become common to say that *Lumen gentium* contradicted and corrected *Mystici Corporis*, which had taught that the Catholic Church is the same as the mystical Body. In reality, the council agreed with *Mystici Corporis* that the mystical Body had full or substantive existence in the Catholic Church and nowhere else. According to Cardinal Ratzinger, speaking at Menlo Park, California, in 1999, the council, far from contradicting Pius XII, simply explicated his formula. He went on to say:

> The word *subsistit* derives from ancient philosophy, as it was later
> developed among the Scholastics. It corresponds to the Greek word

hypostasis, which of course plays a key role in Christology in describing the union of divine and human natures in the one person of Christ. *Subsistere* is a special case of *esse.* It refers to existence in the form of an individual subject.... With the word *subsistit,* the council wanted to express the singularity and non-multipliability of the Church of Christ, the Catholic Church: the Church exists as a single subject in the reality of history. But the difference between *subsistit* and *est* also embraces the drama of ecclesial division: for while the Church is only one and really exists, there is being which is from the Church's *being*—there is ecclesial reality—outside the Church.[15]

Necessity and Mission of the Church

Many commentators have used the sacramental ecclesiology of Vatican II as grounds for belittling the importance of the Church for salvation. They speak as though the Church were a mere sign (*sacramentum*) that points to the reality of salvation, which is found in the Kingdom of God (*res sacramenti*), as something external to herself. In an early book, Richard McBrien took the position that while all are called to the Kingdom, only some are called to the Church. The Church, in his view, was one of a number of agents for bringing the values of the Kingdom (freedom, justice, peace, charity, compassion, and reconciliation) into human society. The Church, consequently, should abandon the illusion that she is the ordinary means of salvation and that all people are invited to belong to her.[16]

This understanding of the sacramentality of the Church, although it became popular in some circles after the council, departs substantively from *Lumen gentium.* According to the council, the Church and the Kingdom, without being in all respects identical, are intimately conjoined. The Church is "the Kingdom of Christ now present in mystery" (*LG* 3). In proclaiming and extending the Kingdom, the Church "becomes on earth the initial budding forth of that Kingdom" (*LG* 5). The Church is not a bare sign or a mere instrument; as a sacrament, it precontains in germ the reality that it effects: The Kingdom of God is already present in Christ and the Church; it grows in and through the Church.

In his encyclical on missionary activity, *Redemptoris missio,* Pope John Paul II criticized authors who speak of the Kingdom in purely secular terms and limit the Church's mission to the promotion of "values of the Kingdom" such as peace, justice, freedom, and brotherhood. He insisted that the Kingdom cannot be detached either from Christ or from the Church. Even the temporal dimension of the Kingdom, he said, remains incomplete unless it is connected with Christ present in the Church.[17]

The necessity of the Church is powerfully affirmed in several passages of *Lumen gentium.* For example, article 9 states that Christ uses the Church as "an instrument for the redemption of all," while article 14 declares that Christ, "made present in his Body, which is the Church," is "the one Mediator and the unique Way of salvation." In affirming the necessity of faith and baptism (Mk 16:16 and Jn 3:5), Christ implied the necessity of the Church, to which faith and baptism give admission. Anyone who knows "that the Church was made necessary by God through Jesus Christ" is obliged to enter the Church and remain in her under pain of forfeiting eternal salvation (*LG* 14).

In addition, article 17 presents a very strong rationale for the Church's missionary activity. Through the Apostles she has received the solemn mandate to evangelize the whole world, a task she is impelled to embrace because of the inner compulsion of the Holy Spirit: "In this way the Church simultaneously prays and labors that the entire world may become the People of God, the Body of the Lord, and the Temple of the Holy Spirit, and that in Christ the Head of all, there may be rendered to the Creator and Father of the Universe all honor and glory." These statements of *Lumen gentium* on the importance of spreading the faith are reinforced by Vatican II's Decree on the Church's Missionary Activity, *Ad gentes*.

In accord with previous papal teaching, especially since Pius IX, the council acknowledged that persons who were inculpably ignorant of the Gospel could attain salvation. Those who "through no fault of their own do not know the gospel of Christ or his Church, yet sincerely seek God and, moved by his grace, strive by their deeds to do his will as it is known to them through the dictates of conscience" can attain to everlasting salvation (*LG* 16). But rather often, according to the council, those who have not been privileged to hear the gospel "have become caught up in futile reasoning and have exchanged the truth of God for a lie, serving the creature rather than the Creator (cf. Rom 1:21, 25)" (*LG* 16). To believe the gospel is consequently not just a duty but also a signal benefit.

The People of God

One of the distinctive features of *Lumen gentium* is its use of the image of the people of God as a description of the Church. This image was introduced partly to offset the limitations of the image of the Body of Christ, which did not do justice to the personal freedom and responsibility of each member. Protestant exegetes such as Ernst Käsemann and Nils Dahl had popularized the idea of the Church as the pilgrim People of God still en route to its eschatological destiny; Catholic exegetes such as Ceslas Spicq, Lucien Cerfaux, and Rudolf Schnackenburg found merit in this image.

The image of the People of God helped to overcome what some council fathers characterized as triumphalism. Shifting the emphasis from the divine Head to the human members, this image called for a humble Church, open to purification and reform. It favored sociological studies of the Church and the process of inculturation.

Along with its assets, the image of People of God had its limitations. Cardinal Ratzinger, in various studies, found that it had only a meager basis in scripture and in the fathers. Even in the New Testament, he discovered, the term generally referred not to the Church but to the Old Israel. The members of the Church can become the People of God only through union with Christ, thanks to faith and the sacraments. Christians are the People of God because they partake of the Body of Christ.[18]

Ratzinger concludes that the term "People of God" must be combined with "sacrament" to be serviceable in ecclesiology: "One only remains faithful to the council if one always takes and reflects on these two core terms of its ecclesiology together, sacrament and people of God. Here it becomes clear how far the council is still ahead of us: the idea of the Church as sacrament has hardly entered people's awareness."[19]

Yves Congar gives a critique not unlike that of Ratzinger. Under the new dispensation, he remarks, the People of God receive a spiritual status that can be expressed only in the categories and theology of the Body of Christ. According to Congar, "St. Paul never contented himself with adding the attribute the Body of Christ to the concept of the People of God, just as he had received it from Judaism. He introduced the idea of the Body of Christ as the essential concept in treating of the Church. This idea was needed to explain what the People of God had become since the incarnation, Easter and Pentecost. The People of God *was* truly the Body of Christ. Only thus does it secure its adequate Christological reference."[20]

In its overview of the images of the Church, Vatican II by no means dismissed Body of Christ, or "mystical Body," the central theme of articles 7 and 8. The council used the categories of People of God and Body of Christ as mutually complementary. It would be a mistake to imagine that with Vatican II the concept of the Church as People of God simply replaced that of Body of Christ. Both images were used to give concreteness to the more abstract and technical concept of sacrament.

Hierarchical Structure

In July 1963 it was decided to remove from the chapter on the laity the passages that deal with the people of God as a whole and to place those sections near the beginning of the document, immediately after chapter 1, on the mystery of the Church, thus constituting what became the new chapter 2.[21] From this fact proponents of democratization have drawn sweeping inferences. Because the vast majority of the People of God are laypersons, some contend, the new ordering of the chapters gives priority to the laity and leaves the hierarchy in a secondary role as servants.[22] Some imagined that all of the baptized bear within them the power conferred by ordination and that the hierarchical ordering of the Church is merely a matter of good order.

In fact, the reordering was prompted not by a desire to place the laity ahead of the hierarchy but rather to treat the Church in general before taking up any of her components. The chapter on the laity did not become the new chapter 2; it became chapter IV, which follows the chapter on the hierarchy. The new chapter 2 does not say or even suggest that the Church was originally a community of equals without hierarchical leadership. On the contrary, it states that the People of God were from the beginning made up of people of various ranks who had different ministries (*LG* 13).

In chapter 2 *Lumen gentium* draws a sharp distinction between the common priesthood of the faithful and the ministerial priesthood of the ordained. To its great credit, the council here gives new prominence to the biblical and patristic notion of the baptismal priesthood. After undergoing at least a partial eclipse, the notion reemerged in the early twentieth century. Fruitfully used by Pius XII in his Encyclical on the Liturgy, *Mediator Dei* (1947),[23] the theme was extensively studied in theology during the next decade.[24] Vatican II, unlike some of its commentators, did not confuse the two priesthoods or play off the one against the other. It taught that the common priesthood and the hierarchical priesthood differ in essence and not only in degree (*LG* 10). The ministerial priest, by the sacred power he enjoys, "molds and rules the priestly people.... Acting in the person of Christ, he brings about the Eucharistic sacrifice and offers it to God in the name of the people," thereby enabling the faithful to join in the offering by virtue of their royal priesthood (*LG* 10; cf. 17).

To insist on the indispensable role of the hierarchy is in no way to minimize its obligation to serve the whole People of God. This has been almost self-evident to Christians because of the strong exhortations to selfless service in the New Testament and throughout Christian tradition. Gregory the Great made a classic statement when he called himself "servus servorum Dei." But the servant who holds pastoral office is sometimes called to exercise authority firmly on behalf of Christ the Lord.

The Episcopate

Chapter 3, which deals with the hierarchy, contains the most important doctrinal pronouncements of the entire council. On two occasions *Lumen gentium* uses the solemn words "This sacred Synod teaches . . ." The first instance is in article 20, which affirms that bishops have by divine institution succeeded to the place of the apostles. The second instance is in article 21, which states that episcopal ordination confers the fullness of the sacrament of orders. The council here exercises its doctrinal authority to settle a question previously disputed among theologians in the West. It builds on patristic sources and in particular on the writings of Cyprian and the ordination rituals of Hippolytus of Rome and Leo I. Although *Lumen gentium* does not here deliver a dogmatic definition in the strict sense, its judgment seems to be definitive. By an act of the extraordinary magisterium, it confirms the common teaching of the ordinary and universal magisterium. Such, at least, is the conclusion of Yves Congar, who takes into consideration the views of many qualified experts.[25]

Although the clarification of the episcopal status is a clear advance over previous doctrinal pronouncements, it is not a reversal of anything previously taught. It stands in perfect continuity with the Council of Trent, which taught under anathema that bishops are superior to presbyters in the hierarchy (DS 1777). The advance follows the normal lines of dogmatic development.

Collegiality

Much the same may be said about the treatment of collegiality in the following article. Just as the Apostles with and under Peter constituted a college, so do the bishops as successors of the Apostles. "Together with its head, the Roman pontiff, and never without its head, the episcopal order is the subject of supreme and full power over the universal Church" (LG 22).

The doctrine of collegiality is new in Vatican II, in the sense that it is not taught in the same language by previous popes and councils. The doctrine, however, has deep roots in patristic theology, notably in the work of Cyprian, Celestine I, Leo I, and Gregory I.[26] Somewhat obscured in the Middle Ages, it reemerged in the eighteenth century.[27]

Pope Gregory XVI, in a work published in 1832, the year before he became pope, declared that by virtue of ordination "each bishop enters into membership in the episcopal body, and consequently enters into the right to govern and teach the entire Church, when he is in union with all the others and forms a body with them."[28] In his encyclical of the missions, Fidei donum (1957), Pope Pius XII taught that "even though each bishop is the pastor of that portion only of the Lord's flock entrusted to him, nevertheless as lawful successor of the Apostles by God's institution and commandment he is also responsible, together with all the other bishops, for the Apostolic task of the Church."[29]

The doctrine of collegiality does not appear in Vatican I's Constitution on the Church, Pastor aeternus. But in his official relatio on the first three chapters, Bishop Federigo Maria Zinelli expressed his conviction that the bishops collectively participate in the government of the universal Church and assured the fathers that this aspect of episcopal ministry would be taken up in the projected second Constitution on the Church.[30] In his draft for that second constitution Joseph Kleutgen, S.J., affirmed that the supreme power of the Church was to be found in two subjects: the pope alone and the body of bishops united with the pope. Since the two subjects were inadequately distinct, there was no possibility of conflict between the two. The bishops could not act as a body if they were in disagreement with their head, the pope.[31]

Theologians looking for discontinuity in doctrinal development often write as though Vatican II's teaching on collegiality, correctly understood, had overturned the "papal absolutism" imposed by Vatican I. At Vatican II a conservative bloc opposed collegiality on this very ground, but before the final vote its fears were allayed. Partly because of the clarifications given in the Nota explicativa praevia, only ten votes were cast against the constitution on November 19, 1965, and at the solemn final vote of November 21, the number fell to five.

The section of Lumen gentium that deals with collegiality was carefully composed so as to make it unmistakably clear that the pope's powers of teaching and jurisdiction, as defined by Vatican I, were in no way curtailed (LG

22–24). The college of bishops can never act without his consent. The pope, however, is never obliged to act collegially. Enjoying supreme power over the whole Church, "he can always exercise this power freely" (*LG* 22). In teaching this, Vatican II enacted almost exactly what Kleutgen had proposed at Vatican I. One looks in vain, therefore, for a contradiction between the teaching of the two councils on Church governance.

Magisterium

Since the authority to teach rests in the same persons as those who govern, all that we have said about ecclesiastical governance applies to the magisterium. Vatican I had recognized two subjects of the supreme magisterium, both equipped to enunciate binding and irreversible doctrines concerning faith and morals. The first subject, treated in *Dei Filius*, is the bishops as a body. They, in turn, can teach in either of two ways: through their ordinary and universal magisterium or through solemn judgments (DS 3011), which normally emanate from ecumenical councils. The second subject, treated in *Pastor aeternus*, is the pope, who can on occasion make ex cathedra pronouncements on matters of faith and morals by virtue of his authority as successor of Peter. His pronouncements are binding on the assent of all the faithful and are irreversible (DS 3074). Regarding the object and exercise of infallibility, Bishop Vincenz Gasser, speaking for the Deputation on Faith, gave helpful explanations and answered many questions too involved to be treated in the conciliar texts.

Vatican II in *Lumen gentium*, article 25, did little more than repeat the essential teaching of Vatican I on magisterial infallibility and incorporate a few helpful points from Bishop Gasser's *relatio*. The main difference between the two councils on magisterium is that Vatican II speaks also of official teachings in which the magisterium does not engage its full authority, demanding definitive assent. On this question *Lumen gentium*, article 25, incorporates materials from Pius XII, who taught in *Humani generis* (1950) that when the pope teaches authoritatively, even without appealing to his supreme authority as successor of Peter, he is to be reverently heard as speaking in the name of Christ (DS 3995). Vatican II teaches that in such cases the faithful should proffer "a religious submission of will and mind" (*LG* 25). Although the term "obsequium religiosum" is new, it aptly summarizes, as much as a single term can, traditional teaching regarding the response due to nondefinitive magisterial teaching.

Lumen gentium did not mention dissent, nor did it intentionally open the way to dissent. It did speak of the sense of the faithful but not as an alternative that could be used against the magisterium. Because the same Spirit is operative in the magisterium and in the body of the faithful, it stated, the assent of the faithful to definitive teaching will never be wanting (*LG* 25).[32] The sense of the faith that the Spirit of truth arouses in the People of God, inclines them to cling to the faith once delivered to the saints and to defer loyally to the sacred Magisterium (*LG* 12). The teaching of Vatican II on the nature, mission, and structures of the Church should by rights have brought about a peaceful consensus within the Church and launched a new era of confident evangelization. In point of fact the council was followed by several decades of contestation, polarization, and confusion. Often enough, dissenters tried to justify their stance by appealing to Vatican II, as though it had broken sharply with the past and ushered in a new era of critical thinking and innovation. Such appeals to the council were hollow and unwarranted. With a sounder hermeneutic, it may still be possible to retrieve the council's actual teaching. If so, the Church may appear more radiantly as the sacrament of Christ, who remains forever the light of the nations.

NOTES

1. John W. O'Malley, *Tradition and Transition: Historical Perspectives on Vatican II* (Wilmington, Del.: Michael Glazier, 1989), 73. He has continued this theme in many articles, most recently in "Vatican II: Did Anything Happen?" *Theological Studies* 67 (Mar. 2006): 3–33.

2. Gregory Baum, *Man Becoming: God in Secular Experience* (New York: Herder and Herder, 1970).

3. Richard P. McBrien, *Do We Need the Church?* (New York: Harper and Row, 1969).

4. George A. Lindbeck, *The Future of Roman Catholic Theology: Vatican II—Catalyst for Change* (Philadelphia: Fortress, 1970).

5. Synod of Bishops of 1985, "Final Report," *Origins* 15 (1985): 445–46.

6. John Paul II, "Udienza al convegno internazionale di studio," in *Il Concilio Vaticano II: Recezione e attualità*, ed. Rino Fisichella (Rome: San Paolo, 2000), 739.

7. Leonardo Boff, *Die Kirche als Sakrament im Horizont der Welterfahrung* (Paderborn, Germany: Bonifacius, 1972), esp. ch. 4.

8. Ibid., 98–99; M. J. Le Guillou, *Christ and Church: A Theology of the Mystery* (New York: Desclee, 1966), 138–55; Erwin Iserloh, "Sacramentum et exemplum: Ein augustinisches Thema lutherischer Theologie," in *Reformata reformanda: Festgabe für Hebert Jedin*, vol. 1 (Münster: Aschendorff, 1965), 247–64.

9. Günther Wassilowsky, *Universales Heilssakrament Kirche* (Innsbruck: Tyrolia, 2001).

10. Wassilowsky gives a detailed account of the written controversy between J. C. Fenton and O. Semmelroth. He shows that Cardinal Ernesto Ruffini's speech of Oct. 1, 1963, bears the imprint of Fenton's influence; ibid., 390–97.

11. Giuseppe Colombo accepts the idea of the Church as sacrament but rejects Semmelroth's term *Ursakrament* on the ground that it inverts the objective relationship between the Church and the sacraments. See Colombo, *Teologia sacramentaria* (Milan: Glossa, 1997), 57.

12. The letters MC in parentheses refer to Pius XII, encyclical *Mystici Corporis Christi*, in *The Papal Encyclicals 1939–1958*, ed. Claudia Carlen (Wilmington, N.C.: McGrath, 1981), 37–63.

13. Alexandra von Teuffenbach, *Die Bedeutung des subsistit in (LG 8): Zum Selbstverständnis der katholischen Kirche* (Munich: Herbert Utz, 2002), esp. 363–92.

14. For one such commentary see Heribert Mühlen, *Una mystica persona* (Munich: Schöningh, 1969), 399–405. The official *relatio* is partly responsible for the confusion. In a previous draft the explanation given was the following: "It is stated '*adest in*' so that

the expression may better agree with the affirmation of the ecclesial elements that are present (*adsunt*) elsewhere." When the further change was made (introducing the term *subsistit in*), the explanation was left unchanged. In fact, however, the word "subsistit" was chosen to emphasize the full and unique presence of the Church of Christ in the Catholic Church—almost the opposite of the reason for choosing "*adest in.*" See Teuffenbach, *Die Bedeutung*, 389.

15. Joseph Cardinal Ratzinger, "*Deus locutus est nobis in Filio:* Some Reflections on Subjectivity, Christology, and the Church," in *Proclaiming the Truth of Jesus Christ: Papers from the Vallombrosa Meeting* (Washington, D.C.: United States Catholic Conference, 2000), 27–28. Ratzinger presents a similar interpretation of *subsistit* in his paper "The Ecclesiology of the Constitution '*Lumen gentium,*'" in his *Pilgrim Fellowship of Faith: The Church as Communion* (San Francisco: Ignatius, 2005), 148.

16. McBrien, *Do We Need the Church?* 229.

17. John Paul II, encyclical *Redemptoris missio* (1990), ch. 2, esp. 17–20.

18. Joseph Cardinal Ratzinger, *Church, Ecumenism, and Politics* (New York: Crossroad, 1988), 14–20.

19. Ibid., 19.

20. Yves Congar, "The Church: The People of God," in *The Church and Mankind* (Glen Rock, N.J.: Paulist, 1965), 36–37.

21. For the history see Giuseppe Alberigo, ed., *History of Vatican II*, vol. 2 (Maryknoll, N.Y.: Orbis, 1997), 411.

22. See, for example, the discussion in Richard P. McBrien, *Catholicism*, rev. ed. (San Francisco: HarperSanFrancisco, 1994), 670.

23. Pius XII, encyclical *Mediator Dei*, no. 88, in Carlen, *Papal Encyclicals*, 134.

24. For a sense of the richness of the Catholic literature on the royal priesthood of the faithful, see the footnotes in Yves Congar, *Lay People in the Church* (Westminster, Md.: Newman, 1957), 112–221.

25. Yves Congar, "En guise de conclusion," in *L'Église de Vatican II*, ed. G. Baraúna (Paris: Cerf, 1966), 1366–67.

26. Jean Colson, *L'épiscopat catholique: Collégialité et primauté dans les trois premiers siècles de l'Église* (Paris: Cerf, 1963). See also Joseph Lécuyer, *Études sur la collégialité épiscopale* (Paris: Xavier Mappus, 1964), and the historical articles in *La collégialité épiscopale*, ed. Yves Congar (Paris: Cerf, 1965).

27. Giuseppe Alberigo, "La collégialité épiscopale selon quelques théologiens de la papauté," in *La collégialité épiscopale*, 183–221. He discusses most of all the work of Vincenzo Bolgeni, S.J. (1733–1811).

28. Mauro Cappellari, *Il trionfo della Santa Sede e della Chiesa* (Venice: Giuseppe Ballaggia, 1832), 119; quoted in J. Robert Dionne, *The Papacy and the Church* (New York: Philosophical Library, 1987), 388–89.

29. Pius XII, encyclical *Fidei Donum*, no. 42; in Carlen, *Papal Encyclicals*, 326; cf. Dionne, *Papacy and the Church*, 64–65, 389–90.

30. On Zinelli's *relatio* see Jean-Pierre Torrell, *La théologie de l'épiscopat au premier concile du Vatican* (Paris: Cerf, 1961), 149–59.

31. Kleutgen's schema is lucidly treated in ibid., 247–79.

32. Here, as in other cases, Vatican II acknowledges in a footnote that it is paraphrasing Gasser's *relatio* at Vatican I. For the statement on the "assent of the Church" see Iohannes Dominicus Mansi, *Sacrorum Conciliorum nova collectio*, Florence 1759ff; Paris and Leipzig 1901–1927, vol. 53, col. 1214A; English translation in James T. O'Connor, *The Gift of Infallibility: The Official Relatio of Bishop Vincent Gasser at Vatican Council I* (Boston: St. Paul Editions, 1986), 44.

2

The Universal Call to Holiness

Benoît-Dominique de La Soujeole, O.P.

The Constitution on the Church, *Lumen gentium*, aims at teaching at length the mystery of the Church. It seeks to provide an ecclesiological synthesis. In spite of a difficult beginning, the final document constitutes an undeniable success. The text is very unified, with its many parts forming a harmonious whole. The framework that organizes the entire subject matter is the first teaching of the constitution, which comprises two major parts. The first (chapters 1–4) presents the Church as a single, Catholic, and apostolic body. The second (chapters 5–8) concerns various aspects of the Church's holiness. The document can be outlined as shown in the following sections.

Part I: The Church Is a Living Organism

1. The mystery of the Church ⇒ one and unique (permanent identity)
2. The people of God ⇒ Catholic (the mystery in history)

⇒ *Nature* of the Church

3. The hierarchical structure of the Church ⇒ Apostolic (the mediation between Christ and the faithful)
4. The laity (the receivers of Apostolic mediation)

⇒ *Edification* of the Church

5. The universal call to holiness
   in the Church   ⇒ *Vocation* of the Church

6. Religious

7. Eschatological nature of the
   pilgrim Church and its union   Holy
   with the Church in heaven

8. The Blessed Virgin Mary,
   Mother of God, in the mystery
   of Christ and the Church   ⇒ *Realization* of the Church

Part II: The Life of the Church

Cardinal Dulles has discussed the first part of *Lumen gentium*, which deals with
the nature of the Church as a mystery that carries forward the one, Catholic,
and apostolic mission entrusted by Jesus Christ to his apostles and their successors. He has shown how this Church is indeed the mystical body of Christ.
Now we turn to the life of the Church as called to holiness.

The Apostolic Hierarchy as Mediating Sanctification of the Faithful

The final two chapters of part I of *Lumen gentium* show how the community
receives Christ's divine life in order to live from it and to communicate it. This
is truly the daily edification of the ecclesial mystery that is presented here by
the distinction between pastors (chapter 3) and the lay faithful (chapter 4) in
the heart of the community. The apostolic character of the Church says this:
Christ configured to himself, in a particular fashion, certain disciples—the
Apostles—so that they and their successors may ensure, for the time of
the Church here on earth, the permanence of the preaching of the true faith,
the constancy of the celebration of authentic sacraments, and the conduct
of the community. These men are not the successors of Christ, as he lives
forever with us (Mt 28:20), but are his *vicars* (literally: representatives).

One finds here an application of what I stated about the ecclesial mystery-
sacrament. The presence of pastors in the community is first and foremost a
human need: All communities need leaders to ensure their unity. However, in
the mystery of the Church, this human given is taken as a sign and an instrument of a divine reality; it is the authority of God, who, in Christ, conducts
his Church. Only those who express their faith through charity and pastoral
service can know the presence of Christ, who teaches, gives his grace, and
directs. The council develops this hierarchical aspect of the community at
length because it is not without very strict conditions that the ministers have
the function of representing Christ, who edifies his Church. The most important principle that governs them is that the pastoral hierarchy transmits the
gifts that come from Christ. In this sense, the ministers precede the faithful, as

cause precedes effect, and this is the reason this point (chapter 3) is taught before the chapter consecrated to the laity (chapter 4).[1]

Cardinal Dulles has called attention to those who misrepresented the council as if the people of God were opposed to apostolic hierarchy. As he indicated, this is a false opposition, rooted in what Pope Benedict XVI terms a hermeneutics of rupture. The Church is the work of God, and this work is realized in Christ and by the Holy Spirit, who act through "intermediaries" or *mediators* (the hierarchy), who are the true causes of grace ("efficient ministerial cause"). Thus a cause always precedes its effect. It is in this sense that the hierarchy precedes the laypeople. If one reverses this order and supports the primacy of the baptized over their ministers, one runs the risk of conceiving of the hierarchy as the fruit, the effect, of the charity of the faithful. According to this line of thinking, the constituted community would "produce" in its bosom the pastoral service entrusted to some of its members. Then, however, the question arises as to *how* this community was constituted. If one responds that the constitution comes "directly from Christ," one does not consider the ministers as *mediators* in the line of efficient causality instituted by Christ but as a solely human disposition that comes from the community and is variable according to its needs. Such reasoning echoes a typically Protestant perception that denies any mediation between Christ and the faithful.

This explains why, during the age of "classical" theology of the Counter-Reformation, one insisted on the efficient causality exercised by the ministers. The response is accurate, but it is true (if one only honors this aspect) that one runs the risk of concentrating all ecclesiology in the study of the ministers. This was the case with many manuals at the end of the nineteenth century and the beginning of the twentieth. The reaction against the Reformation need not be excessively the inverse. For this, it is necessary to add other considerations to the line of efficiency. Two principles must be considered. The first is that charity, once it is received by the faithful through the ministers, "circulates" throughout the entire organism with the grace that is the Church. Charity comes from Christ through his ministers; this is first in the order of efficiency. However, once received in the ecclesial Body, charity reacts on the ministers in such a way that all of the acts for which the ministers are secondary causes (preaching and governing) will be more or less successful as a function of the concrete state of the charity in the entire organism.[2]

In chapter 2 the priority of the consideration of the faithful, before making any distinction, is therefore not intended to negate the ministers' causal role. Furthermore, the development of the Body of Christ (ch. 1, nos. 7–8) clearly mentions this. In sum, the order clergy-laity differs according to one's point of view. As for efficiency, the clergy engenders the laypeople both personally and as a community. As for finality, the clergy serves them again both personally and as a community. It is this second point of view—finality—that is the key in determining the order of the chapters of *Lumen gentium*.

Part II carries forward this context: The mystery of the Church, simultaneously sign-instrument and reality of salvation, is engaged in history by the way in which it progressively embraces everyone's life. The relationship between ministers and laypeople is the very expression of Christian life and comes through Christ by the ones he sends to bear his fruit. What is this fruit? In a word, it is holiness, a holiness that is not limited by the life of this world but allows participation in the glorious and eternal life of the family of God already in heaven, the family of which the Virgin Mary is the most eminent member and perfectly illustrates the vocation of all.

The Universal Call to Holiness in the Church

Chapter 5 contains four sections (*LG* 39–42), including a preamble and three paragraphs, and is the shortest chapter of the constitution. This does not indicate that it is not important; on the contrary, it has a central place because it recalls the principal teachings.

The preamble begins by restating that the Church is a *mystery* and that consequently only faith can grasp its profound identity. The particular issue to *believe* here is the holiness of the Church, which comes from its union with the only Holy One, Christ Jesus. This holiness is not, however, given and definitive; rather, it calls for the holiness of each member of the community, which is their sole purpose.

PREAMBLE AND UNIVERSAL CALL TO HOLINESS (*LG* 40). This preamble therefore affirms that which is a determining teaching—the apparent paradox of the Christian condition. The Christian condition is first of all a gift received at baptism, but at the same time it is a vocation, a personal work for which no one can substitute for anyone else. Then the council teaches that this holiness, to which all people are called because Christ has redeemed them all, is both a gift and the great concern of life: "They are justified in the Lord Jesus, because in the Baptism of faith they truly become sons of God and sharers in the divine nature. In this way, they are really made holy. Then too by God's gift, they must hold onto and complete in their lives this holiness they have received" (*LG* 40). Because we are weak and sinful, we are constantly dependant on God's mercy if we are to be able to fulfill our vocation.

This may seem obvious. In fact, the Church has never taught that holiness was a privilege reserved for an elite group in the Church (the religious, for example). The age-old practice of canonizations, which honor the faithful in various states of life, illustrates this. However, Christians have been more or less aware of this point throughout the ages. One does not have to look too far back in history to find an era when one thought, confusedly, that the fullness of Christian life could be found only in consecrated life and that the rest of God's people would be content with a necessary minimum. However, nothing could be further from the truth. The *commandment* of charity is not mere *advice* suggested for some; it is, instead, the most demanding and the greatest commandment of the Christian life, and it is addressed to all without distinction: "Thus it is evident to everyone that all the faithful of Christ, of whatever rank or status, are called to the fullness of the Christian life and to the perfection of charity" (*LG* 40).

The council is not simply engaging in a contradiction here. The Church is holy, but she is composed of sinners. How can the community itself be authentically holy when its members are sinners? The council never intended to imply that the Church was sinful (*LG* 8, §3), following the teaching of Saint Paul: "Husbands, love your wives, as Christ loved the church and gave himself up for her, that he might sanctify her, having cleansed her by the washing of water with the word" (Eph 5:25–26). To attempt to understand what seems to be a contradiction to us (the community is holy, but its members are sinners), one must consider the most intimate mystery of the union of Christ with the Church, which is his Body and his Spouse. It is necessary to distinguish the *sancta* (i.e., the Church's holy and sanctifying realities: the truth of the Gospel and the authentic sacraments) and the *sancti* (i.e., the people who receive the sanctifying realities).

The community of the faithful—pastors and laypeople, both according to their vocation—enjoys the assistance of the Holy Spirit to keep the sanctifying gifts of Christ intact throughout history (*LG* 12). In this way the Church is called Holy because she continually offers the source of divine life in all its purity for the spiritual life of her members (Gospel and sacraments). However, this fecund source only progressively nourishes the lives of the faithful, which are, thanks to these gifts, in the constant process of conversion. If the Church is unfailingly holy (the offer of the sancta), she must also tend toward holiness in her members (the life of the sancti). Thus in remaining faithfully connected to the sources of grace—the Gospel and the authentic sacraments—holiness, as *a gift of God,* begets holiness when accepted, as the human vocation, which is progressively realized.

THE DIVERSE FORMS OF HOLINESS (*LG* 41). After having presented holiness in general, the council briefly develops the many forms this holiness takes in the life of the people of God and recalls that it is always about the same fundamental holiness (charity), even if it is lived with many differences, depending on the place, the culture, and one's personal state in life.

Vatican II begins by evoking the holiness of the Church ministers. It is the occasion of a very profound teaching on the holiness of the priest: This holiness is not merely an accompaniment to his sacerdotal functions (to preach, sanctify, and govern) as if it were necessary to separate the individual from the function, but is a central component of the ministry: "The shepherds of Christ's flock must holily and eagerly, humbly and courageously carry out their ministry, in imitation of the eternal high priest, the shepherd and guardian of our souls. They ought to fulfill this duty in such a way that it will be the principal means also of their own sanctification" (*LG* 41). This means that charity is the soul of the ecclesial ministry, without which this service is disfigured and the personal holiness of the priest is absent. Certainly, a sacrament celebrated either by a holy priest or by a mediocre one is the same sacrament because the value of the sacrament comes from Christ, who is the principal minister. However, the personal witness of the priest's holiness is a powerful example and serves to attract the faithful to Christ (unfortunately in the same way that the counterwitness of a priest can turn people away from Christ). This teaching also reminds us that the minister of the Church needs to look nowhere but into his ministry to find his raison d'être and his way of living the Gospel. The priest does not have another occupation, nor does he occupy another place in the City. Other than in exceptional cases determined by the bishop, a minister of the Church must only announce the Gospel, celebrate the sacraments, and guide the community. This is what transmits Christ's holiness to the Church, and it is the seat of the priest's personal holiness.

The council then mentions Christian spouses and parents. This is another important form of holiness in the Christian community because it is through spouses and parents that the new generations will most readily reach the Gospel. The fecundity of a family is not confined to itself. The council points out that households cooperate with the very fecundity of the Church. The same idea as that of the ministers is taken up again: It is not in addition to one's tasks in life that one is sanctified; rather, one's sanctification occurs in the very accomplishment of these tasks. The same logic of charity must animate widows, widowers, and single people, in whom love must be just as alive as in others. This charity must penetrate all aspects of human life, and this is why the council also mentions workers, especially those who engage in hard labor, and gives them as an example the One who was "the carpenter's son." Going still further, Vatican II mentions that those who are poor, have an infirmity, are sick, or are suffering in any way are also configured to Christ by the same charity. In sum, no state, no situation, and no context in life would not favor manifesting this love. One sees here that Christians, if they are saved by the free generosity of God's love, become equally in Christ a savior for others. This is the depth of the holiness of Christ—the Saint and the Sanctifier (Heb 2:11)— that makes Christians saints and sanctifiers for others.[3]

THE WAYS AND MEANS OF HOLINESS (LG 42). The vocation to the perfection of charity has been presented thus far in its fundamental principles: assimilation to Christ and the Gospel's penetration of all aspects of life. The council has not accentuated what used to be called "practices of piety and asceticism," by which the faithful were exhorted to sanctify themselves. That is not to say that such practices have not kept their entire value (quite the contrary). However, the council made an effort to put them in their rightful place. In the past one assumed an actual risk when practicing one's religion in a ritualistic way, thinking that that would suffice to be "following the rules." There was a rather contractual conception of holiness that risked becoming a caricature rather than the real thing. We have heard criticisms on this subject for forty years! However, the current situation may not be an improvement. In the hopes of abandoning this juridical concept, many people abandoned all practices of piety and asceticism and as a result also abandoned religion altogether. There is, therefore, a precise relationship between these practices and holiness that we must find again and deepen. The council made a point to do so. What follows is a strong, concrete application of the doctrine of the ecclesial mystery-sacrament: Holiness, which is the reality of grace, is inseparable from the sign-instruments that bestow and express it.

Recalling that holiness is charity, Vatican II teaches that devotions, practices of asceticism, reading of the Word of God, participation in the sacraments, and perseverance in prayer are all justified by the care of the *growth* of charity: "For charity, as the bond of perfection and the fullness of the law (cf. Col 3:14; Rom 13:10), rules over all the means of attaining holiness and gives life to these same means. It is charity which guides us to our final end." When one says that charity is sufficient, one does not mean that the other virtues are in vain—in particular the virtue of religion. On the contrary, charity gives rise to and animates the other virtues by giving them their true goal: holiness.

Having placed charity in its true place, the council finishes its teaching by recalling the ancient doctrine of the excellence of charity. As such, charity has no measure, in the sense that one need not fear having too much charity because we can never love too much. Recalling the example of the heights that Christians achieved in charity, Vatican II emphasizes this "measure without measure."[4] Here the council restates the theology of the martyr, which clarifies our Christian condition on this important point. If all are not called to the supreme witness of charity, "nevertheless all must be prepared to confess Christ before men. They must be prepared to make this profession of faith even in the midst of persecutions, which will never be lacking to the Church in following the way of the cross." The council then mentions virginity or celibacy consecrated to the Lord. The excellence of this form of life does not in any way denigrate marriage, but Vatican II recalls the doctrine of St. Paul (1 Cor 7), according to which the consecrated state powerfully favors a complete charity for God and in him for everyone. The other advice, poverty and obedience, which can be lived in all states in life, are also recalled for the same reason: They liberate the heart to make it capable of loving more and better.

Chapter 5 concludes by recalling the common vocation of all Christians to charity. This does not turn us away from the world. On the contrary, it is the saints who are the most active in the world because they situate the world in its true place as God created and redeemed it. It is in the world that God, in Christ, gives himself to the very life of the faithful, and this life must transfigure the world and orient it toward the consummation of the Kingdom of God, which transcends it. The correct conception of holiness does not empty out the world with its constraints and its demands but refuses to be limited by the world: "For the form of this world is passing away" (1 Cor 7:31), while charity will never pass away (1 Cor 13:8).

Eschatological Nature of the Pilgrim Church

The full title of chapter 7 is "Eschatological Nature of the Pilgrim Church and Its Union with the Church in Heaven." At the end of *Lumen gentium*, Vatican II recalls the teachings of the first two chapters. It does not limit our regard for the Church on earth. When we contemplate its mystery-sacrament present both today among us and already in eternal glory, we see not two Churches (one that is earthly and visible and one that is celestial and invisible) but a single Church that is both on pilgrimage here on earth and already extant in heavenly glory. How can we grasp this new aspect of the mystery?

THE THEOLOGICAL PLAN OF HOPE (LG 48). The opening paragraph is of particular importance because it strongly situates the true nature of the Christian life on earth: Eternal life has *already* begun. After death, at the definitive entry into God's glory, it is not another life that will begin; rather, we will find the fulfillment of the life given us to live here on earth: "The promised restoration which we are awaiting has already begun in Christ." We are already in the final age (I Cor 10:11).

The theological virtue that enables us to live this already-begun fullness of eternal life is hope. This virtue is not well known; it risks being lived minimally or badly. Nonetheless, it enables us to live in the Kingdom while we are still on earth. Latin has only one word for this virtue (*spes*, which means "hope" in English), as do many languages, to designate two realities that should not be confused. There is, on the one hand, hope (in French, *espoir*), which is the waiting for a good thing to come (for example, a student's expectation of school vacation). On the other hand, there is hope (in French, *espérance*), which is waiting for the accomplishment of something that one already possesses (for example, when one says in French that a woman has "espérances," this means that she is pregnant; her child already exists in her womb, but she is waiting for its birth at the end of her pregnancy). Christian life possesses a hope (espoir) of knowing the return of Christ, but that which will come on the last day is not a completely new coming because Christ is already in the womb of the Church, directing it from the inside to the consummation of history: espérance. This paragraph is a solid reminder of the eternal life, which has already begun and enhances the value of our time on earth; it is our eternity that plays out today in time.

COMMUNION IN THE LIFE OF ALL CHRISTIANS (LG 49). This hope (espérance) puts us in profound communion with all those who live in the grace of Christ because everyone shares in the same life—growing here on earth or achieved in heaven. *Lumen gentium* pursues its teaching here by underlining the communal aspect of hope (espérance). The mystery of the Church gathers together in one community those who are still on earth, those who are still in purgatory after death, and those who have already come to the glory of God. Those who must still hope and those who have already found the term of their hope live in the same charity that unites every member of this unique body. In this way, a profound solidarity links those who journey toward God with those who are already face to face with God. It is the *communion of holy people* that is thus realized and is the very definition of ecclesial reality.

In the pilgrim Church on earth, nothing has importance except in the degree to which it serves this communion of divine life. The proclamation of the Gospel, the celebration of sacraments, and the service of pastors have value because they effect this communion, make it grow, heal it when injured, and spread it to the ends of the earth. If one distinguishes rightly in the mystery of the Church that which is a *means* of grace from that which is the very *reality* of grace, it would be disastrous to separate these two aspects: The reality of grace is first present in the means of grace to be manifested and sown. For this reason the intercession of the saints exists to facilitate our access to grace and to help us to receive its fruits.

THE PRESENCE OF THE CHURCH IN HEAVEN AND THE CHURCH ON EARTH (LG 50). The council did not want to forget this union with heaven and earth for the benefit of the deceased who are still in purgatory before being admitted to God's vision. It is a strong expression of the charity of the saints and the Christians who are still on pilgrimage on earth to pray for the deceased. Vatican II further emphasizes the presence of the huge procession of the saints with the Lord. They form the part of the only Church that, because it is already in glory, is very close to us. We are walking toward them, and they accompany us toward this glory. From the beginning of the Christian community, the cult of saints blossomed in honoring the apostles, the martyrs, the Virgin Mary, and the holy angels. This cult then grew by also honoring the consecrated faithful and, more generally, men and women who shone by the excellence of their virtues. This ecclesial practice, which profoundly witnesses to the faith and hope of Christians, clearly states that saints exercise a significant influence on the daily life of the community. Not only do they ask for and obtain from Christ many graces that we need, but they are also a shining example for us to follow. They attest that holiness is possible, and through them we can contemplate the face of Christ.

All of these considerations underlie the cult of the saints in the Church. The council developed this point to clarify the nature of this cult so as not to incur the reproach of our Protestant brothers and sisters, who fear that the unique holiness of God will be veiled by the cult of the saints. For this reason, Vatican II restates very clearly that the cult is an expression of our veneration of the saints, which always "tends toward and terminates in Christ and . . . through him in God who is wonderful in his saints and is magnified in them."

The justness and uprightness of the cult of the saints (i.e., the correct expression of the close union between the Church on earth and that in heaven) is principally assured by the liturgy. The liturgical action of the people of God, gathered together by Christ, is first the glorification and praise of God. It is always with the Church in heaven that the Church on earth accomplishes the liturgical service that culminates in the Eucharistic celebration. This is the place par excellence where we are united with the cult of praise and thanksgiving, which the Church of heaven never ceases to give to God in Christ.

PASTORAL RECOMMENDATIONS (LG 51). The chapter concludes by giving directives of a pastoral nature. The council knows that this union of the Church on earth with that of heaven may be misunderstood. One may either underestimate this profound union by addressing oneself only to Christ or to God or focus excessively on the saints, while neglecting God.

The Christian life should always hold these different aspects together, and the way to do so is to recognize the order of charity and to see and respect the order that links us all. The love of God is always first, but it does not negate others; on the contrary, it brings us into communion with each other, according to the place that each of us occupies in this large family. The fervor of our love for God cannot help but spring forth to touch the lives of others and to guide us to love those who are still far from this love so that they may enter into it and inspire us to always practice charity. Christ is the supreme model of this strength of love, for it was out of love of the Father that he gave his life for the salvation of the world.

The Blessed Virgin Mary, Mother of God, in the Mystery of Christ and the Church

THE HISTORY OF CHAPTER 8 IN VATICAN COUNCIL II. This chapter, which concludes the teaching of the constitution, explains how the mystery of the Church is already realized in the Mother of God.[5] Classically, the magisterium concludes its doctrinal teachings with a Marian development. This is not only an indication of piety but also a constant reminder that the mystery of Mary is the most perfect illustration of the success of the design of salvation in Christ. It is in this light that many of the dogmatic affirmations are clarified for us. I briefly mention the debates on this chapter, which sparked significant tension in the conciliar assembly.

During the era of classical theology (from the seventeenth to the twentieth century), Marian theology was the center of two major preoccupations. First, it was considered important to counter Protestant positions. In effect, the doctrine of justification, its effects, and the collaboration of creatures in their salvation are all operative in Mary. It was also essential to develop the Marian teachings in the form of an exaltation of privileges, or "glories," of Mary. On the one hand, there was often a literature of controversy, which was not always serene. On the other hand, another literature was rather "exalted" in that it lacked limits and did not sufficiently respect the difference between a single savior—Christ—and those who are saved (everyone, including Mary). The council wanted to develop more wisdom on the subject. Some people currently distinguish between Mariology (classical theology) and Marian theology (the current situation).[6] However, in this major movement of the classical age were lodged the faith and expression of the Christians. They are marked by two dogmatic definitions (1854: the Immaculate Conception; 1950: the Assumption), which indicate that this period was extremely fecund. It is necessary, then, to clearly distinguish—and in Marian theology, this is particularly important—the faith of the people of God from its theological or pastoral expressions, which do not have the same value. Thus, Vatican II intended neither to object to this past (it is very recent) nor to marginalize the tradition

nor to cultivate a nostalgic return to the Middle Ages or to the fathers, as if
nothing had happened since then.

Moreover, the council did not believe that everything begins today with an
appropriation that is finally scientific and critical of the Gospel, as those who
are committed to a hermeneutics of rupture maintain. In theology, as Pope
Benedict XVI recently stated, one must learn to think *in continuity*; this is
essential. This is what can be called *tradition* with its dual aspect: a faithful
memory and a creative innovation; it is the ever-expanding knowledge of the
same subject. I will not emphasize this further and mention it only because it
expresses the manner in which we can best approach our study. With Vatican
II, we have the principal current discernment of Marian theology. Grasping
what the council says about the Virgin Mary will teach us how to distinguish between that which fundamentally belongs to Marian dogma and that
which emanates from its expression, which is proper to one period of time or
another.

On January 25, 1959, John XXIII announced the convocation of the universal council. On June 18 of that year Cardinal Tardini invited the bishops, the
superiors general of the orders, and the Catholic universities to present their
propositions to the council. Of the approximately two thousand responses,
nearly six hundred asked the council to speak about the Virgin Mary. Almost
half of the propositions asked that there be no more new Marian titles (ecumenical concerns were the principal reason for this request). The remainder
asked for a definition of Mary Mediatrix (only about thirty requests addressed
the definition of Mary as Coredemptrix). Here one can see the seed of the difficulties that arose during the conciliar debates. The preparatory project of the
schema, *De Ecclesia*, included an appendix with an outline on the Virgin Mary
titled "The Blessed Virgin Mary, Mother of God and Mother of Mankind."
Then John XXIII modified the title to "The Blessed Virgin Mary, Mother of the
Church." It was in the second conciliar session (1963) that the schema came
under discussion. Two factions then confronted one another in the council:
One (called "Christocentric") wanted to retain the traditional title of *Mater Dei;*
the other (called "ecclesiocentric") strongly advocated for *Mater Ecclesiae* (or
Mater Fidelium).

Clearly there is truth in both perspectives: Mary, by her unique relationship with Christ, possesses a superiority relative to other Christians. However,
she has a place in the mystery of the Church and not above it. The title of *Mater
Ecclesiae* carried with it the risk of honoring only the aspect of superiority, while
overshadowing Mary's ecclesiality.

During this session there arose a conciliar movement driven mainly by the
Spanish bishops, who promoted the title of *Mater Ecclesiae* and—inseparably—
a special schema consecrated to Mary; they thus advocated not placing the
Marian schema within the Constitution on the Church. However, the theological commission of the council decided (by a very weak majority) to include the
schema on the Virgin Mary within that of the Church. It is neither a separate
schema nor even an addendum to the schema on the Church; it is, in fact, fully

part of it. Clearly, therefore, Mary is a true member of the Church (indeed a supereminent one). The major debate on this took place on October 24, 1963.[7] The major arguments for a separate schema (general idea: the preeminence of Mary) were as follows:

- in relation to the Trinity: Mary is the only one to be fully glorified (Assumption).
- in relation to all of the other members of the Church: Mary is full of grace.
- in relation to the participation in the redemption: Mary lived the objective redemption before participating in the subjective redemption.
- in relation to Christ: Mary is with her Son in an intimacy without comparison.

For this conciliar movement, only a separate schema could honor these fundamental points. In opposition to this, another movement presented the following argument against the separate schema (principal idea: maintain the unity of all theology):

- Mary is, like the Church, a fruit of the redemption.
- Mary *personally* represents that which the Church is as a *community*, and in this sense she is Mother of the Church; she does not transcend it.
- ecumenical argument: Be careful not to widen the gap with Protestantism.

After the debates, voting took place on the following question: "Would it please the Fathers for the schema on the Blessed Virgin Mary, Mother of the Church, to be integrated into the schema *De Ecclesia?*" The result was 1,114 *placet* votes and 1,074 *non placet* votes—a difference of forty; a change in only twenty votes (of more than 2,188, or 1 percent of the votes) would have altered the outcome. This decision manifested the clearest division among the fathers (even more than the schema on religious liberty). Some fathers left the conciliar meeting room in tears: "They have dethroned the Virgin."

The question was sent to the theological commission so that it could propose a solution. The commission explained the matter in the following way:

1. Mary is on the side of Christ because she is not a sinner.
2. However, Mary is also on the side of men because she has also been saved, and in this she is truly a member of the Body of Christ, which is the Church.

To make an absolute of either tendency always contains an error: they are linked one to the other. Mary is beyond the Christians who we are, but is still within the Church. Conciliar unity was finally established. If the insertion of the schema *De Beata Virgine Maria* in the *De Ecclesia* had such an opposition, it was because it came from a very real danger: bringing the Virgin Mary to the rank of a simple member of the Church, without acknowledging her uniqueness and excellence. Two theologians of the theological Commission (Philips and Balic) attempted to write a synthesis. In the third conciliar session (1964), the schema on the Virgin Mary came back into discussion with the following title: *Of the Blessed Virgin Mary in the mystery of Christ and of the Church*. It was an accommodation that remained (with amendments). It is notable that the title of *Mother of the Church* had disappeared.[8]

If one says "Mother of the Church," then Mary precedes the Church; if one says "Mother in the Church," then Mary is with the Church. All of this engages an ecclesiology. If she is the Mother of the *members* of the Church, can one say that she is the Mother of the ecclesial *institutions*? Certainly not. Nonetheless, the title was excluded from the schema. Paul VI, in his closing speech of the third session, proclaimed Mary to be the Mother of the Church, which received ovations from nearly all of the fathers.[9] As for the *textus emandatus*, it holds to that which all Catholics communally admit.[10] This text was submitted to a vote of the fathers. The result was *placet* 2,180,[11] *non placet* 10. Next, the final text, which became chapter 8 of *Lumen gentium*, was put to a vote on November 19, 1964; the outcome was as follows: *placet* 2,096, *non placet* 23 (and 1 abstention). Finally, the entire *Lumen gentium* constitution was approved almost unanimously, with the exception of 5 *non placet* votes, on November 21, 1964.

At the conclusion of this long and painful conciliar beginning, it was established that the Virgin Mary is *in* the Church, like her crowning. Not only is she the classic example of the Church, but she is also—and this is important—the eschatological icon of the Church: Mary is the beginning and the end of the Church (not in the same way, of course). In the Church, the Mother of God is its crowning, just as she is the crowning of the *Lumen gentium* constitution.[12] Mary, without losing any of her privileges, is the perfect illustration of the glory of the Christian vocation and of holiness when it is completely realized. On the other hand, if Mary, who is without sin, is a virgin and Mother of God, it is *for* the Church and the salvation of mankind. This integration of the schema *De beata* in *De Ecclesia* is an essential step in both Catholic Marian piety and the ecumenical process. The explanation in this chapter thus situates the mystery of the Virgin Mary in relation to the mystery of both Christ and the Church, manifesting in this way the strong link between the two. This conciliar history clearly explains the contents of chapter 8.

THE CONTENTS OF CHAPTER 8. The introduction situates Mary as *Mother of our God and Lord Jesus Christ* (LG 52) and as *Mother of the members of Christ* (LG 53). It also indicates that the council's intention is to shed light on her role without, however, going into the still-disputed questions. It offers an ample explanation of Marian doctrine that states the faith of the Church precisely and fervently.

The first developments present Mary in the mystery of her son by a biblical, theological explanation (LG 55–59). Mary is depicted in Christ's life in the days when he was in flesh among us, from the annunciation to the ascension. The idea that dominates these developments is the perfect union of Mary with the person of Jesus and his work of salvation. Her faith and the charity are unceasingly affirmed. As the mother of Jesus, Mary is his first and most perfect disciple; she follows her son in his mission; she intercedes for sinners (Cana); she is associated with the passion; and she knows the glorification of her whole being in completing her life on earth by an assumption without compare.

From Mary's personal relationship with Christ follows her association with all of those who become brothers and sisters of Jesus (*LG* 60–65). The council focused wholly on correctly situating her in the Church, while underlining the uniqueness and eminence of her place; nonetheless, her position is completely subordinate to Christ, and in this way it illustrates our own Christian condition. In this perspective, the most delicate question was that of Mary's role as Mediatrix. Taking up the faith of the Church, Vatican II underlines the unique mediation of Christ (1 Tim 2:5–6) and explains how it does not negate but instead favors Mary's participation.

One encounters here a primary teaching of Catholic (and Orthodox) theology that the council wanted to recall because it constitutes a major subject of debate (perhaps the principal one) with our Protestant brothers and sisters and also concerns the question of sacerdotal ministry:

> For no creature could ever be counted as equal with the incarnate Word and Redeemer. Just as the priesthood of Christ is shared in various ways both by the ministers and by the faithful, and as the one goodness of God is really communicated in different ways to his creatures, so also the unique mediation of the Redeemer does not exclude but rather gives rise to a manifold cooperation which is but a sharing in this one source. The Church does not hesitate to profess this subordinate role of Mary. It knows it through unfailing experience of it and commends it to the hearts of the faithful, so that encouraged by this maternal help they may the more intimately adhere to the Mediator and Redeemer. (*LG* 62)

It is, in effect, by an absolutely free disposition and not by necessity that it pleased God, by pure goodness, to associate creatures to the gift of his grace. Mary is the highest realization of this cooperation by her intercession, but she is not the only one. I have already noted, in the theology of holiness, that Christians are not only *saved* but also, according to the degree to which they are unified with Christ, *saviors*. Mary, cooperating with the gift of grace, illustrates to perfection the vocation of all men. This precision is of capital importance because it grounds the two themes by which chapter 8 concludes these developments: Mary, icon, perfect example of the Church (*LG* 63), and Mary, model for the virtuous life of each and every Christian (*LG* 65).

As an icon of the Church, Mary personally illustrates what the Church is as a community. What is principally concerned here is the constancy of faith, hope, and charity. In the person and life of Mary, the Church contemplates its mystery of a faithful and fruitful union with the Spouse, who is Christ. The personal holiness of Mary, Virgin and Mother, refers to the mystery of the Church, which is also without blemish or wrinkle, engenders all men into the life of grace. That which we believe in the holiness of the Church, we first contemplate in the mystery of the Mother of God. As Cardinal Journet said, the *Church is Marian.*[13]

Mary is the living example of the perfectly Christian life; consequently, by her life she bears witness to the perfection of virtues. In this, all Christians can contemplate in Mary that to which grace calls them to be, not only personally but also in their apostolic actions to collaborate in the salvation of all men.

Chapter 8 concludes with some very useful reminders concerning the Marian cult (*LG* 66–67). Considering Mary's exceptional place as Mother of God in the mystery of her Son and the Church, Christians venerate her in a special way. This cult states the faith and the love of those who acknowledge the Son of Mary. The council recalls that a cult reserved for God (cult of *latrie*) because it is a cult of adoration is reserved strictly for God alone.[14] There is also a cult of the saints (cult of *dulie*), which venerates these great witnesses. Although it is addressed to the saints, it terminates in God, who is the author of all holiness. It is legitimate to devote a cult to the saints because their holiness—it is indeed a gift from God—is also a work of their cooperation under grace. The cult of Mary (*hyperdulie*), then, is a part of the cult of the saints, but it has a unique place because of the excellence of her holiness. Vatican II, knowing that this question was and remains a great ecumenical difficulty with our Protestant brothers and sisters, wanted to make a clear distinction between the cult given to God and those that venerate Mary and the saints. Therefore, in ecclesial practice, we are invited, on the one hand, to not neglect the cult of the Virgin and, on the other hand, to not fall into excesses that would blemish the expression of faith in the mystery of the Mother of God.

Conclusion

These chapters of *Lumen gentium* are of great importance for an understanding of the mystery of the Church. The community of the grace received from Christ by his Spirit according to the design of the Father. The Church is the great work of the Trinity, which restores creation, which fell into sin.

A strict doctrine of the mystery of salvation resides in a correct understanding of several elements that must be held together. The modern spirit holds these as paradoxes, antitheses, and oppositions, while authentically Christian wisdom prefers to speak of *complex realities* in contemplating the profound unity of God's work.[15]

In the mystery of salvation, everything is a *free gift* from the Triune God. To save the world, the Trinity revealed itself by communicating the interior life of Father, Son, and Holy Spirit. At the same time, revelation and salvation call for people to receive these gifts, engage their lives, and seek to bear fruit in good works. While the first chapter of the constitution concentrates on the gift of God, chapter 2 highlights the point that this grace is at the heart of Christian life, which best deploys it by the exercise of the authentic baptismal priesthood. If *all is grace*, the grace that is in us fosters a virtuous life, by which the holiness given to us becomes truly ours. And this holiness configures us so deeply to Christ that we are saved and also become participants in the work of our salvation in Christ.

In the mystery of salvation, the reality of the kingdom of God is *already here* because the life of grace is eternal life, which will not pass away. At the same time, this life is *not yet* complete; it waits for its individual and community fulfillment, which will be the completion of the gift of God when Christ returns in glory. Consequently, the Church is visibly in this world, and the Kingdom of God is growing toward its eschatological completion.

In the mystery of salvation, the *reality* of grace reaches us by the *means* of grace, and the union of these two is such that they form one reality, one Church. This is at the same time a sign-instrument of salvation *and* salvation itself, wherein the visible and invisible, human and divine, temporal and eternal, transcendent and immanent are unified in the mystery of the Word incarnate, of whom the Church is the pure and faithful Spouse.

Holiness is the reception of this mystery of grace, which configures us to Christ. It is present in the profound life of this mystery of unity of the invisible, the divine, and the eternal, toward which all that is visible, human, and temporal is ordered and subordinated (*SC* 2). This holiness is the great family mark that is already uniting us with the citizens of heaven and among whom the Virgin Mary shines with a brightness without compare.

Truly, the entry into such a mystery, which is beyond us in every way, is not reserved for an elite. This is the final "complex reality" of the mystery of holiness: that which is the highest, the most excellent, and of the greatest price is intended for everyone, is accessible to everyone, and is the true good of everyone. Contrary to our way of life in civil society, where everything is measured by power and money, all of the goods of God are offered generously to everyone in the community, of which Christ is the head. Our religion is not a religion of heroes but of saints, that is to say, humble men and women who, each day, allow themselves to be loved by Christ and, by the power of the Holy Spirit, walk—slowly or quickly, depending on the person and on the particular time—toward the destination of hope, which does not deceive: God Himself, *Christ who is all and in all* (Col 3:11), the Church in glory.

NOTES

1. It is necessary, however, to make the connection with the preceding chapter (ch. 2, "The People of God"). In deliberately placing the development of the people of God before that of the hierarchy, the council specifically intended to speak first of Christ's faithful ones before mentioning any distinction. The expression *Christi fideles* is more encompassing; it is the common quality of all of God's children: Baptism is the true treasure. Thus, before studying the distinctions among the members of the Body of Christ, we must remember that what is most important is to be a member.

2. In *L'église du verbe incarné*, vol. 1 (Paris, 1954), 670–71, Charles Journet expresses this idea as follows: "The hierarchy is a cause of the Church. . . . However, there is an aftershock, in the sense that the fortune of the hierarchy, the precise state of its historic development, the choice perhaps of its declarative terms, and above all the nature and quality of its canonical decisions, is explained in an important way by the interior state of the charity of the Church in different ages of its existence."

3. The teaching on the apostolate of the lay faithful (*Apostolicam actuositatem*) develops a particularly important point that is not mentioned here: the holiness of the baptized in spreading the Gospel by participation in evangelization. However, in light of this passage one can understand the degree to which this apostolate is a necessity of charity and not an occupation reserved only for specialists. See chapter 13, this volume.

4. Cf. St. Bernard of Clairvaux, *De diligendo Deo* (I, 1; *PL* 182, col. 974).

5. For chapter 7 on the religious life, see chapter 12 of this volume.

6. This distinction has been widely adopted in some current thinking. Mariology dates from the time of Father Suárez (fifteenth and sixteenth centuries).

7. Fifty-fifth general congregation; cf. *Acta synodalia* II/3, 338 s. (trad. fr. partielle, Doc. catho. 1963, col. 1574 s).

8. See *Acta synodalia* III/I, 541–43: The reasons given for this change are interesting. First, it is neither traditional nor even very recent (John XXIII, maybe Leo XIII); second, it is not known in the East (ecumenical); third, it is not theologically clear (Mother *of* or *in* the Church?). Furthermore, the pastoral explanation is complex, and it would be difficult to see the link with the constitution *Lumen gentium*, which is Christ centered.

9. This is a good example of a conciliar decision by acclamation (see Doc. catho. 1964, col. 1544).

10. See the *relatio* (Roy) in *Acta synodalia* III/6, 23 (trad. fr. Doc. catho. 1964, col. 1253).

11. Of which 521 *placet juxta modum*, reduced to ninety-five propositions, of which twenty-six were retained (cf. *Acta synodalia* III/8, 151–71).

12. This expression is from Paul VI, Doc. catho. 1964, col. 1543.

13. Cf. our study "L'église est mariale," in *Actes de la semaine théologique* (Fribourg, Switzerland: 2002); *Charles Journet: Un témoin du XXe siècle*, ed. Guy Boissard (St. Maur, France: Parole et Silence, 2003), 137–46.

14. Cf. Dt 6:13.

15. The adjective *complex* does not necessarily signify "difficult to understand." Rather, because it comes from the Latin verb *complector* (to hold together, to embrace), it means "composed of parts," in contrast to "simple" or "not composed of parts." This complexity implies two things: on the one hand, the mystery of the Word incarnate, who unifies in himself God and people (one reality: the Savior, but complex); on the other hand, the nature of our intelligence, which understands by divisions and compositions.

3

Revelation and Its Transmission

Francis Martin

Background

The dogmatic constitution *Dei verbum* was promulgated on November 18, 1965. The final vote that day on what was the seventh form of the document was 2,344 *placet* and 6 *non placet*: a major accomplishment for a constitution that twice required papal action in order to facilitate an impasse on the council floor.[1] It is not my intention to trace the "text production" process of *Dei verbum*; there are excellent historical studies of *Dei verbum* that the reader may consult.[2] I wish rather to offer a theological commentary on the document as it stands, with particular attention to its power for renewal, a power it possesses precisely because of its fidelity to tradition.

Perhaps the greatest accomplishment of *Dei verbum* was to have remained faithful to the teaching of tradition on key issues such as revelation itself, the inspiration and truth of the scriptures, and the relation of scripture, tradition, and magisterium, while setting the stage for an integration of modern historical work within the tradition. Future theological commentary must base itself on the ground thus established and try to further the integration inaugurated at the council. It is, after all, not a council's role to embark on new speculative teaching but rather to clarify and substantiate the Church's traditional teaching and to elucidate the way in which it is a light to the pilgrim Church of the present and the future.

In this chapter I comment briefly on the preamble and the paragraphs of chapters 1, 2, and 3. I follow this with some remarks on how, in the light of these paragraphs, the various elements of *Dei verbum* can move us to an integration of some aspects of modern historical, philosophical, and theological advances with the tradition that has preceded us.

A Commentary on the First Part of *Dei Verbum*

The Preamble

There are two parts to the preamble.[3] First, the council describes itself and its understanding of the task entrusted to it. Then, after stating that it intends to follow in the footsteps of the two preceding councils, it uses a text from Saint Augustine that is addressed to those who wish to instruct people in the Christian faith to describe its own desire to "catechize" the whole world and bring it to faith, hope, and finally love.[4]

The first sentence sets forth the rhythm involved in any teaching of the word: first, to listen to the Word as he speaks in the scriptures to the heart of the Church and to receive his message with reverence. Then, to proclaim that word with confidence: *religiose audiens et fidenter proclamans.* This same attitude is expressed again in article 10, where the magisterium is described as not above the word of God but rather as serving it. The magisterium thus "lovingly [*pie*] listens, keeps in holiness, and faithfully expounds" the word of God. Both of the expressions "confidently proclaims" and "faithfully expounds" allude to a New Testament theme, that of *parrēsia*, a term that evokes the notion of speech that is truthful, confident, public, courageous, and candid. In so describing itself, the council acknowledges that it is conscious of acting in obedience to the Holy Spirit and provides us with a hermeneutic for interpreting its statements. These are intended to follow in the footsteps of preceding councils and to be in conformity with the New Testament.

The council fathers then indicate the exact direction of this obedience by describing themselves as "obedient to the words of St. John." The prologue to the First Letter of John, to which the text makes reference, not only presents the principal theme of chapter 1 of the document but, because of the role of this chapter, also places the whole of *Dei verbum* under the aegis of the rhythm we have already seen ("experience—proclaim") and goes on to declare that the goal of this proclamation is *communion* with each other within the communion of the Father and the Son.[5] We must bear in mind this initial statement of purpose as we enter into the theological intricacies of the document: It is presented as the way to communion with the Trinity and the joy that inevitably follows from such a fellowship.

As already mentioned, the second part of the preamble announces that, as it sets forth "authentic teaching on Divine Revelation and its transmission," the council expresses its indebtedness to the two preceding councils. While *Dei verbum* moves ahead and thus contributes to the advancement of the apostolic tradition (*DV* 8), we must take this statement seriously: Those who present this teaching are aware of their debt to the work of the Holy Spirit within the Church for nearly two millennia. It is for this reason that they describe themselves as being at the service of the "summons to salvation" (*salutis praeconium*), echoing New Testament phrases such as "word of salvation" (Acts 13:26) and "the word of truth, the good news of your salvation" (Eph 1:13), thus linking God's self-manifestation with human salvation.

Chapter 1, On Revelation Itself: The Nature and Object of Revelation

REVELATION AND COMMUNION. God is described as acting from "his goodness and wisdom," and his action is "to reveal himself and . . . the mystery of his will." In contrast to the similar statement in Vatican I, God is expressly the agent here, and the reference to Ephesians 1:9 moves the consideration to "the mystery of his will" (*to mystērion tou thelēmatos autou/sacramentum voluntatis suae*) with all that the Greek and Latin terms evoke in regard to the biblical teaching about God's personal counsel and its created manifestation.[6] In the document, the mystery of his will is described by alluding to Ephesians 2:18 and 2 Peter 1:14:[7] God the Father wills that we have access to him in the Holy Spirit through Christ, the Word of God made flesh, and that we become sharers in the divine nature. As Aquinas noted, this plan of God made it absolutely imperative that he reveal both himself and this goal of our existence since we could never know God as a dialogue partner or come to grasp the gift that he makes (and then restores) to us unless he himself makes it known.[8]

In a way, the most significant aspect of the opening sentence of article 2 is the statement (which repeats Vatican I) that God reveals *himself*. Because of God's action in Christ, anticipated in the Old Dispensation and perfected in the New, he addresses himself to the very depth of the human person. This makes of revelation a speaking and an answering of a profoundly unique kind: It is a friendship and a dialogue.[9] The theme is continued and magnificently expressed in the second sentence of this paragraph, a passage that has few counterparts in ecclesiastical documents and seems to be inspired by article 70 of *Ecclesiam suam*.[10]

ACTIONS AND WORDS. The second part of article 2 enters into the actual mode of dialogue by looking at the divine initiative. The "economy" or working out of revelation takes place in actions (*gestis*) and words (*verbis*) "intrinsically connected with each other" in such a way that they illumine one another. This statement sets forth what may be called the sacramentality of revelation. It is the same word (*dabar*) of God present as both action and verbal expression by which the action/event is transposed into language. The word that gives language expression to the action ensures that God's act be rendered more intelligible and be continually present to God's people. Thus, the biblical expression in "words" has a unique capacity to transpose, express, and mediate the action, the *res*, or the *mysterion*. Hans Urs von Balthasar expresses it thus: "The gradual clothing of the events within the folds of Scripture is not only an inevitable drawback (because the people of the Orient of that time did not know, in fact, an historiography in the modern understanding of the term), but assuredly also this corresponds unqualifiedly to a positive intention of the Spirit."[11]

It is easy to see how this understanding of the biblical mediation of the events wrought by God in a mysteriously unique manner challenges our temptation to use the event as reconstructed by the historical-critical method as the norm by which to judge ("critical") the text rather than serve it. How then do we understand the event as mediated by the sacred text in comparison with the event as reconstructed by historical critical methods? How is it true that "the works accomplished by God in the history of salvation manifest and confirm both the teaching and the realities signified by the words, while the words proclaim the works and bring to light the mystery contained in them"? The integration of historical methods within the whole theological task of biblical interpretation occupies the council in article 12, and I reserve my remarks for that later discussion.

PREPARATION OF THE GOSPEL REVELATION. The text outlines four stages in God's plan to prepare mankind for the Gospel, that is, for the full manifestation of salvation in Jesus Christ. There is, first, God's witness to himself in creation, to which the document returns in article 6. Then there is God's self-manifestation, which makes known "the mystery of his will" to our first parents. Then, after their fall, there is God's continual care, in some mysterious way, for the entire human race, which moves them toward eternal life through perseverance in good works. Finally, he called Abraham and began an economy of covenant, moving his chosen people ever closer to the penultimate, though definitive, stage of that economy: the incarnation of his Son, along with his redemptive life, death, and resurrection, and the forming of his Body, the Church, through the action of the Holy Spirit. This is to be brought to its consummation when God declares: "Behold, I make all things new" (Rev 21:6).

Despite suggestions that the text include references to other passages that link Christ and creation (for example, Col 1:16–17; 1 Cor 8:6; Rom 11:36; Heb 1:2), the council fathers opted to refer only to the classical text, which speaks of God's continual creating and conserving action as being effected "per Verbum." The wording implies that he also presents (*praebet*) his witness to himself in the same way. The question of the Christological dimension of other texts, particularly Colossians 1:16–17, is left open, and creation itself appears as part of a saving economy of revelation.[12] In its present form, then, the paragraph presents a biblical view of God's way of relating to the human race by clearly distinguishing between a "testimony" in created reality, which God constantly provides (the verbs are present participles), and a "self-manifestation" to the first humans. In modern Western theological thought the distinction is made rather between nature and grace. The document, while not denying this perspective, distinguished between nature and history and thus complements an intellectualist understanding of revelation with one that is more interpersonal. Such a viewpoint strengthens the description in article 2, which, as we have seen, describes revelation as coming from God's love, involves speaking as a friend, and calls mankind to communion with him, thus making grace the fruit of revelation.

The revelation made to our *protoparentes* and their fall is simply stated as a fact on the basis of Genesis 1–3 and subsequent tradition. God's care for the whole of humanity before and outside of Israel is placed under the teaching of Romans 2:6–7, which speaks of God rendering to each one according to his works (Prov 24:12; Ps 62:12) and then goes on to state: "To those who, by perseverance in good work, seek glory, honor and immortality, [he will give] eternal life. To those characterized by self-seeking and who resist the truth, going along with injustice, [there will be] wrath and fury." Paul, by mentioning those who persevere in doing good (literally, "good work") and in seeking (not deserving) the eschatological goods promised to Israel, implies that they are justified through some connection with Christ since in no other way would they attain "eternal life." Thus, though the exact manner of Christ's preincarnational presence is not discussed, the council's choice of biblical texts and its own terminology turn us in the direction of the ancient patristic understanding of key New Testament texts.[13]

The text moves on to discuss what I earlier called the "economy of covenant."[14] Bypassing the covenant with Noah,[15] the council begins with the call of Abraham and the promise to him. While it is possible to situate Abraham plausibly within the culture and times of the Levant of the second millennium BC,[16] the reality and spiritual impact of God's word to him are experienced most profoundly in his spiritual children.[17] The working out of the plan in regard to Abraham's immediate spiritual heirs is then mentioned briefly by speaking of what Israel learned from the patriarchs, Moses, and the prophets about God Himself and about a "promised Savior." The paragraph ends with the mention of Christ, who, in Augustine's phrase, "lies hidden" not only in the prophecies but also in the events recorded in the Old Testament, whose relation to the future is unique.

CHRIST, THE CONSUMMATION OF REVELATION. This key article makes four statements that build on one another. The first, based on Hebrews 1:1–2, speaks of the overall economy of revelation and unites its two parts by the analogous use of the word "speak." The second describes the definitive revelation in Christ, the incarnate Word, who "speaks the words of God" and accomplished the divine plan of salvation. The third statement sets forth the sacramental nature of the revelation effected by Christ by means of his "presence and manifestation" and by all of his actions, which efficaciously testify to the fact that "God is with us" to free us and to bring us to eternal life. The final part of the article states that this revelation in Christ is unsurpassable and unrepeatable and will be completed at the "glorious manifestation of our Lord Jesus Christ."

By citing the opening lines of the Letter to the Hebrews, the council invokes one of the solemnest assertions concerning the true reality of the One in whom God's revelation takes place. It is worth reflecting on this text for the light it sheds on the nature of revelation. A literal translation of these lines runs as follows:

> On many occasions and in many ways in times past God, having spoken to the fathers by the prophets, at the end of these days, spoke to us in a Son whom he established as heir of all things through whom he also made the ages who, being the radiance of his glory and the imprint of his being, and sustaining all things by the word of his power, having brought about purification of sins, sat down at the right hand of the Majesty on high; having become as superior to the angels as different from them is the name he has inherited. (Heb 1:1–4)

The subject of the first four verbs ("having spoken," "spoke," "established," "made") is *Theos*, God: The Father is the author and source of revelation. At first, all of the verbs that describe the Son are present participles that express his eternal reality ("being," "sustaining"). Then, in a breathtaking move, this eternal and perfect image, the Sustainer of the universe, is described as the agent of an activity within time ("having brought about," referring to the Cross) who is given a new honor ("sat down at the right hand of the Majesty") and even "becomes" superior to the angels. Thus, the eternal God and his eternal and coequal Son are first presented, and then the Son's temporal activity is described as the fulfillment of God's speaking and initiating dialogue. If this were not the case, revelation would result in little more than the dutiful acceptance of theological formulae and a set of moral norms, a far cry from Aquinas's description of faith as consisting "essentially in an act of knowing, that is its formal or specific perfection; this is clear from what its object is."[18]

The document then describes this economy of revelation in Christ by speaking of his presence, his manifesting activity (especially his death and resurrection), and the sending of the Holy Spirit. These acts complete revelation and are accomplished by the "sacramental" reality of the Word made flesh, who joins in himself the divine and the human and also the visible and the invisible.[19]

The question remains, then, as to how this economy is continued after the ascension. The basic answer is given in 1 John 5:6, which speaks of Christ, who "came," and the Spirit, who "is bearing witness." The locus of this witness is the Church, whose liturgical action as effective revelation is described by Saint Leo: "All those things which the Son of God both did and taught for the reconciliation of the world, we not only know in the account of things now past, but we also experience in the power of works which are present."[20]

Another dimension of revelation is highlighted in article 8, which speaks of the faithful as having an "intimate understanding of the spiritual realities which they experience." The final sentence of article 4 mentions the "new and definitive covenant" and the fact that "no new public revelation is to be expected." This salutary statement leaves intact the question raised by John Paul II, who remarked that the Old Covenant has never been revoked,[21] as well as that of the public destiny of revelations such as those at Lourdes, Fatima, and

Paray le Monial: In the first instance we must strive to understand how the former revelation is completed and yet has a fruit of its own, while in the second we must learn to distinguish between public effect and public authority.[22]

REVELATION MUST BE RECEIVED BY FAITH. The description of faith given here corresponds to the "dialogue of salvation" described by Paul VI in *Ecclesiam suam*, articles 70–79. Revelation, therefore, consists in a movement not unlike that in "doctrina" or "teaching," as described by Thomas Aquinas, in that God offers himself and a knowledge of his plan of salvation and also supplies the light by which this can be understood, yielded to, and embraced.[23] An extremely important aspect of the response to revelation concerns the role of the will in the act of faith. In the following statement the light of revelation is described as appetible: "So also in the faith by which we believe in God there is not only the accepting of the object of assent, but something moving us to the assent. This is a kind of light—the habit of faith—divinely imparted to the human mind. It is more capable of causing assent than any demonstration.... It is clear, then, that faith comes from God in two ways: by way of an interior light that leads to assent and by way of the realities that are proposed from without and that had as their source Divine Revelation."[24]

What has been entrusted to the Church is actually presented to human beings, along with the attraction of the light, so that believers yield to what God works in them; it is a faith informed by love or "the obedience of faith," "by which a human being offers his whole self to God." This notion that faith is essentially a work of God is in fact the leitmotif of John 6.[25] So far, what has been said applies to faith in both the Old Dispensation and the New: In both there is entrustment of oneself and an intellectual content. The fact of the Incarnation, however, means that faith in Christianity includes a creed that consists mostly of historical facts, in which the fundamental realities made known to us in Christ can be articulated in a way not usually explicit in Judaism.

This description of faith, along with the use of the term "experience" (which we encounter in article 8), marks a courageous return to a more traditional understanding of faith, many of whose aspects had been misused in Modernism.[26] Again, the articles of faith are not considered to be merely intellectual statements but, as we have seen, are rather the means of coming into faith contact with divine reality, "a perception of divine truth that leads us to that truth itself."[27] The final statement in this paragraph prepares the way for considering the progress of the apostolic preaching (no. 8). Here we begin to catch a glimpse of the work of the Holy Spirit, who finally effects and confers an ever-deeper knowledge of revelation through his transforming action, thereby uniting the believer to Christ (see, among other New Testament texts, 1 Jn 4:7–5:21).[28]

REVELATION AND CREATION. These two paragraphs treat, first, of those realities that surpass human understanding and, then, those that can be known by reason but, in our present condition, are not fully attained. The first paragraph resumes what was already said in article 3. The second paragraph asserts the biblical teaching on the attainability of knowledge about God by considering creation.[29]

The biblical tradition is clear: God can be known in, by, and through his creation. For some, who first come to know God as Savior of his people, source of instruction, and respondent to their prayers, creation is a means by which God is *recognized* as also being the exclusive Author of the world. For those outside this dispensation, God and his uniqueness and rights can be *discovered* in his work of creation, in nature, and in the longings of the created heart. While it is true that this discovery can be made by human reason, the "imprint of the divine light in us,"[30] it is also true that, in the present state of the human race, both individually and culturally, this de jure ability requires, as the council reiterates, a special help in order to achieve its goal.[31] This is also attested to by the earliest Church fathers. For instance, Origen states: "We affirm that human nature is not sufficient in any way to seek God and find him with purity unless it is helped by the one who is the object of the search."[32]

It is helpful, in considering this teaching, to bear in mind some basic notions. First, knowing is an act of the person and not only of the mind. This is clearly seen, for instance, when we compare various kinds of knowing. The lowest type is that enshrined by the positive sciences and unconsciously taken over in other disciplines, namely, knowledge caused by "compelling evidence." This knowledge strives for an ever-increasing elimination of the human factor, though the ideal has been subverted by the famous principle of indeterminacy. The second level is that of appreciating a work of art: Here the human factor is absolutely necessary since art demands of the receiver an active openness, a movement of receptivity. The third level is that of interpersonal knowledge, which is impossible without both active receptivity and self-gift. This last type reaches a unique level and an intensity in the personal knowledge of God, something achieved only by divine initiative. The principle is, therefore, that the higher forms of knowledge demand a greater self-involvement on the part of the knower, who must also finally become a lover.

Chapter 2, *The Transmission of Divine Revelation*

THE APOSTLES AND THEIR SUCCESSORS, BEARERS OF THE GOSPEL. As René Latourelle remarks in regard to this chapter, "This is the first time that any document of the extraordinary Magisterium has proposed such an elaborate text on the nature, object and importance of Tradition."[33] After an initial general statement to the effect that God has governed history in such a way that all generations have access to his revelation, article 7 goes on to develop this in three stages. The first of these is the presence and activity of Jesus himself as consummating the revelatory activity of God in the Old Testament and commissioning the Apostles to continue making the Gospel known to the whole world. The second stage describes the manner in which the Apostles carried out this commission, including the activity of "apostolic men," who committed the message of the Apostles to writing. The final stage describes the ongoing process of tradition entrusted to the bishops as teachers and, under their guidance, to the whole Church until its pilgrimage is complete.

Underlying all of this presentation is once again a view of revelation as an *interpersonal* reality and not merely an intellectual occurrence. This can be seen first of all in the ways in which the article differs from the comparable presentation in the Council of Trent, upon which it depends and to which it refers in footnote 2. After pointing out several significant differences, Joseph Ratzinger describes their general import. Far from wishing merely to play off salvation history theology with its accent on deed as well as word against a more pronounced word theology, the goal is rather "to open up a comprehensive view of the real character of Revelation which—precisely because it is concerned with the whole man—is founded not only in the word that Christ preached, but in the whole of the living experience of his person, thus embracing what is said and what is unsaid, what the Apostles in their turn are not able to express fully in words, but which is founded in the whole reality of the Christian existence of which they speak, far transcending the framework of what has been explicitly formulated in words."[34] Such a view of revelation implies a different understanding of the act of knowledge, as well as the act of expressing it in language. Let it suffice here to point out that this different understanding underlies previous expressions in the document such as the description of God the Father "speaking to men and women as friends" (*DV* 2).[35] The same understanding of communication is reflected in the article's wording as it describes the second stage, namely the transmission by the Apostles, who "by oral preaching, examples and institutions handed on that which they received from Christ, whether from his speech, way of life and works, or that which they learned from the inspiration of the Holy Spirit." The added remark about "apostolic men" receiving from the Holy Spirit the grace to commit the message to writing elevates scripture to a unique position, but it can be understood only in the light of the whole communicative process, especially the action of the Holy Spirit. A remark of Thomas Aquinas is enlightening in this regard:

> After the level of those who receive revelation directly from God, another level of grace is necessary. Because men receive revelation from God not only for their own time but also for the instruction of all who come after them, it was necessary that the things revealed to them be passed on not only in speech to their contemporaries but also as written down for the instruction of those to come after them. And thus it was also necessary that there be those who could interpret what was written down. This also must be done by divine grace. And so we read in Genesis 40:8, "Does not interpretation come from God?"[36]

The grace of interpretation is conferred on the subject of revelation, namely, the Church itself, and that is why those who are charged with the task of interpretation must share in the Church's life, especially its liturgical life, if they are to understand the whole life communicated in revelation since "It pleased God in his goodness and wisdom to reveal *himself* and to make known the mystery of his will" (*DV* 2). Such a faith vision is the basis of Aquinas's position, which is not nearly as "intellectualistic" as is often thought. For him, "the teaching of the Church" is more than verbal and dogmatic pronouncements; it is the whole life of the Church insofar as it is under the aegis of the Holy Spirit, and it is in this Spirit that we receive the apostolic tradition in all its fullness. Here is one example of many expressions: "Faith adheres to all the articles of faith because of one reason [*medium*], namely because of the First Truth proposed to us in the Scriptures understood rightly according to the teaching of the Church [*secundum doctrinam Ecclesiae*]."[37]

SACRED TRADITION. Article 8 provides a clear indication of the distance the document *Dei verbum* traveled since the introduction of its first draft on November 14, 1962.[38] What Joseph Ratzinger says of chapter 2 as a whole is particularly true of article 8: "It is not difficult to see the pen of Y. Congar."[39] Many aspects of revealed reality come together to shed light on the nature of tradition. Three of these are the following: (1) the nature of the Church as both visible and invisible, as is stated in *Lumen gentium*;[40] (2) the nature of revelation as "brought about by actions and words intrinsically connected with each other" (*DV* 2) and the fact that this is true as well, though in a different manner, of the transmission of revelation; and (3) just as God has chosen to manifest and communicate both *himself* and the eternal decrees of his will by revelation (*DV* 6), so too tradition, by which this revelatory act is made present to all generations, "is a real, living self-communication of God";[41] it is "the Epiclesis on the history of salvation, namely the theophany of the Holy Spirit without which the history of the world is incomprehensible and Sacred Scripture remains a dead letter."[42]

The first assertion in this section is that the apostolic preaching, expressed in a "special manner in the inspired books," needed (*debebat*) to be preserved by a continuous succession (of designated men), and that is why the Apostles exhort their addressees to be faithful contenders for the traditions, either written or oral, which they have received. Further, by speaking of the content of the apostolic tradition as constituting all that contributes to the life of the Church and describing this transmission as taking place in its "teaching, life and worship," we return to the ample understanding of tradition, which is one of the defining characteristics of *Dei verbum*.

The second statement, which includes all of the second paragraph, is one of the most significant of the whole document. It has to do with what is explicitly called the "progress" (*proficit*) and "growth" (*crescit*) of tradition. The assertion that tradition "makes progress" is immediately explained by saying that what "grows" is an "understanding" (*perceptio*) "both of the realities and of the words that have been handed on."[43] This introduces the cognitional questions, what is understanding and how does it grow? The short answer is that understanding is both an awareness of being modified by something or someone else and the ability to assert that fact and to speak about the object of the knowledge. Growth in understanding occurs as the knowing subject is increasingly modified by the object: There is a growth in conformity, which takes place as a result of a willingness to be so modified. Thus, in all forms of knowledge growth in understanding takes place through a conversion.[44]

The second way that understanding grows is by an intimate knowledge of the realities that the believers experience. With this mention of experience we cross a threshold that, given the specter of Modernism, had appeared impassable.[45]

The final way in which the apostolic tradition makes progress is "by the preaching of those who have received with Episcopal succession the sure charism of truth." This implies, at least ideally, that the bishops are themselves involved in the two previously mentioned activities of study and contemplation and possess an intimate knowledge of divine realities gained by experience. It also implies (and indeed requires) that they are listening to the faithful, guiding their ongoing penetration of the word in scripture and tradition, and confirming what God's people are authentically learning as they experience divine realities. In this manner the whole Church advances the effective power of what is revealed, expressed in scripture, mediated by tradition, and proclaimed and celebrated in the liturgy.

THE MUTUAL RELATIONSHIP BETWEEN SACRED SCRIPTURE AND SACRED TRADITION. This article and the following are, in the nature of things, among the most controversial in the whole document. Indeed, John Paul II, in his encyclical *Ut unum sint* (no. 79), puts first in his list of "areas in need of fuller study before a true consensus of faith can be achieved," "the relationship between Sacred Scripture, as the highest authority in matters of faith, and Sacred Tradition, as indispensable to the interpretation of the Word of God." The challenge offered by Protestant objections to the Catholic understanding of tradition, along with a more nuanced understanding of the history of tradition, led the fathers at Trent to propose a formula in which revelation would be viewed as being contained "partially" in scripture and "partially" in tradition. For reasons not made clear in the *acta* of the council, the *partim...partim* terminology was dropped in the final draft of session 4, though much subsequent Catholic theology continued to treat of the scripture-tradition relation in these terms as though it were the teaching of Trent.[46]

On the other hand, the Protestant Reformation, with its insistence on *sola scriptura*, gratefully accepted the promise of the historical methods to produce an understanding of the sacred text that would not stand in need of any interpretation from tradition. This position was still held out as a future possibility by some Protestant commentators on *Dei verbum*, though other Protestant commentators firmly reject the idea of a text in need only of the right use of the historical critical method.[47] Centuries of debate and discussion have matured the terms of the argument, but, as John Paul II has reminded us, the relationship between scripture and tradition still ranks as the primary theme in need of clarification in Protestant-Catholic dialogue.[48] I discuss this further in the context of the following article.

THE RELATION OF SCRIPTURE AND TRADITION TO THE WHOLE CHURCH AND TO THE MAGISTERIUM. In article 10 two aspects of tradition are mentioned and distinguished from one another. There is, first, the whole body of understanding that bears the revelation transmitted in the sacred text along and includes in some way the discerning of which books belong in the canon. This also includes the liturgical interpretive context given to the books, along with a wide stream of preaching and theological elaboration over the centuries. The second aspect of tradition is called the magisterium, or the teaching office of the Church, which, at least in Catholic faith and practice, relies on this millennial "handing on" of the scriptural text with its broad understanding and yet has the authority by the gift of the Holy Spirit to define certain aspects of the biblical tradition in such a way that other opinions are declared wrong.

All Christian groups accept the first aspect of tradition either implicitly or explicitly, with greater or lesser authority accorded to it. Most theologians acknowledge the fact that some form of tradition plays a role in the interpreting of any text; Hans Georg Gadamer has conclusively established this.[49] In regard to scripture there is a growing consensus that the Holy Spirit exercises causality in the handing on of the experiential understanding of what is mediated by scripture, as well as in the sacraments.[50] This is summed up in the phrase in I John 5:6, which refers to the work of redemption effected by Jesus by saying that "he came" (aorist participle), while the action of the Holy Spirit is that he "is bearing witness" (present participle), that is, making the words and work of Jesus permanently available and life giving to and through the Church. The locus of this action is, therefore, primarily the Church.

Such a position challenges the opinion that the scriptures can be understood from within any context, provided that the correct methods are rigorously applied. This challenge is multiform. It comes from those who appeal to the Rule of Faith as the ultimate interpretive norm,[51] or, more generally, to the role of the Holy Spirit in the Church,[52] or finally to the multiform presence of the Word in the Church.[53]

Many Protestant commentators correctly pointed out that *Dei verbum* did not directly address the problem of correcting tradition itself, though the council's very documents reformed or laid the foundation for the reform of many aspects of Church life that required change. One need only think of the liturgy, ecumenism, the role of the laity, and the position on religious liberty as examples. These are instances of how "the ecclesial Magisterium making use of Scripture and tradition" reformed and advanced key areas of the Church's life and thought.

The achievement of *Dei verbum* here, as in many other dimensions of doctrine, consisted in restating the whole of the tradition, preserving what risked being lost, and modifying excesses. Articulating more profoundly the way in which scripture, tradition, and magisterium, "each one in its own way under the action of the Holy Spirit," preserves and develops the apostolic heritage requires those very qualities of familiarity, faith experience, intellectual acumen, and fidelity to the Holy Spirit that the document calls for. It must also be a Catholic, that is, an authentically ecumenical, effort.

Chapter 3: The Divine Inspiration of Sacred Scripture and Its Interpretation

THE INSPIRATION AND TRUTH OF SACRED SCRIPTURE. The major contribution of article 11 is that of preserving all of the aspects of the traditional understanding of the divine origin of sacred scripture, its dual authorship, and its truth.[54] Given the state of theological thinking at that time, this was a considerable achievement and has preserved for further thought and investigation the task of pursuing each of these topics in greater depth. Unfortunately, little progress has been made in answering this theological challenge, posed principally by the fact that the historical sciences have greatly changed the "model" that underlies the ancient and medieval understanding of the relation between narrative and event, as well as the whole process of successive redactions of a text within a long, ongoing tradition; this latter factor is more prominent, of course, in the composition of the Old Testament. The solution lies in a retrieval of the ancient principles and their application to our understanding of the whole process of text production and text reception as we now understand it. It will also involve a profound reassessment of our modern and postmodern understanding of cognition, history, and language.[55]

HOW SACRED SCRIPTURE SHOULD BE INTERPRETED. After having asserted that the human authors, writing as true authors, "consigned to writing everything and only those things which God wanted" and that this activity "transmits without error the truth which God, for the sake of our salvation, wanted put into the sacred writings," the council fathers had now to explain how the sacred text is to be interpreted. One of the primary purposes of the latter section of article 11 had been to rescue the discussion about inerrancy from its previously fruitless debates by introducing the concept of *veritas*, which God, *nostrae salutis causa*, wished to communicate. This eliminates many of the problems of the inerrancy debate and allows a simple acknowledgement of the inaccuracies (historical, textual, and so forth) that appear in the sacred text.[56] This same notion of the mode of expression now underlies the ensuing discussion of literary genre, culture, and so on in an attempt to understand the human authors on their own terms.

The opening lines of article 12 place the accent on grasping what "the sacred writers really intended." This introduces a cardinal principle already enunciated by Saint Athanasius and quoted in *Divino afflante Spiritu*: "Here, as indeed is expedient in all other passages of Sacred Scripture, it should be noted, on what occasion the Apostle spoke; we should carefully and faithfully observe to whom and why he wrote, lest, being ignorant of these points, or confounding one with another, we miss the real meaning of the author."[57] This basic rule governing the interpretation of all texts takes on a particular importance when the interpreters are removed linguistically, culturally, and geographically from the text they are studying. There is also a danger in this manner of expression, and it lies in the two dimensions of the verb "to intend." The work of establishing cultural sympathy can result in a reasonably successful attempt to understand the correct tenor of the author's work (i.e., what the author intended to say). However, the statement is about *something*, and that too is what the author intends—some reality, some aspect of being; thus, interpreting a text includes participating in the knowledge that the author is communicating. "The one who does not understand the reality cannot draw the meaning out of the words."[58]

In the second paragraph, which describes the historical work of the exegete, the accent is placed, as I have noted, on grasping what the document calls the author's "intention."[59] It is impossible to exaggerate the benefit that has accrued to the study of the Sacred Page and thus to the Church by the correct application of the methods this paragraph describes. We must bear in mind the earlier statement of this document, which speaks of the *oeconomia revelationis* taking place "gestis verbisque intrinsece inter se connexis" (*DV* 2). In this context we may say that in order to participate more fully in the reality mediated by the words—*intentio* understood metaphysically—it is imperative that we grasp what, in terms of his own context, the author "wants to say"—*intentio* understood psychologically. This will ultimately involve a deeper understanding of the nature of language.

The third paragraph of article 12 begins with a long sentence, whose opening phrase changes the direction of thought and is followed by statements that point successively to the fact of the canon of scripture, the tradition of the Church, and the "analogy of faith." This sentence is succeeded by remarks regarding the magisterium and the way in which biblical interpretation both serves this function and is subject to it.

Three procedures are listed in this text as part of reading and interpreting holy scripture in the same Spirit in which it was written, and these are necessary "in order rightly to draw out the meaning of the sacred texts." There is, first, attention "to the content and unity of the whole of Scripture," what may be called "canonical criticism." There is then an account of "the living Tradition of the entire Church." This must refer to the fathers and liturgies of both East and West, as well as the living faith practice of the members of the Church. Finally, there is "analogia fidei," a traditional phrase that emphasizes two facts: that the Bible is a whole with a multifaceted but consistent message and that each part of the sacred text must be understood as compatible with others in the canon, indeed as deriving from and contributing to an understanding of the whole.[60]

The final two sentences of article 12 discuss the relationship between exegetical work and the Church's teaching office and function. The first sentence urges exegetes to work according to the "rules" just elaborated so that the judgment of the Church "might mature." Because the documents of Vatican II are the fruit of the biblical, liturgical, patristic, and theological work of the previous 150 years, especially that of the *ressourcement* movement, they are themselves a good example of such collaboration. The final sentence enunciates the principles that the Church has the divine mandate and ministry of preserving and interpreting the scriptures and that other efforts are subject to the authority of the Church's judgment. These principles are well expressed by Thomas Aquinas: "Faith adheres to all the articles of faith because of one reason [*medium*], namely, because of the First Truth proposed to us in the Scriptures understood rightly according to the teaching of the Church [*secundum doctrinam Ecclesiae*]."[61]

GOD'S CONDESCENSION. This text puts the accent on the *sugkatabasis* (condescension) of God.[62] It is shown in the way Almighty God "comes down" to our level in order to communicate. This is then compared to the Incarnation: The comparison is loose, but a foundation exists for it. To take seriously the teaching on inspiration means to understand that, in some mysterious way, the Word enters into a culture and a linguistic grid: He becomes "flesh" in language.

Much work remains to be done in order to elaborate a Christian theology of language, but it is necessary in order to complete the integration I have been describing. It will not be achieved without a deep sense of the poetic quality of language—the fact that it reveals rather than represents. The beginnings of such a theology are implicit in the writings of some of the fathers and Medieval theologians I have cited here. I close this section with a text that offers a foundation for the continuation of this line of thought. It is from Aquinas's commentary on the Prologue of John: "Though there be many participated truths, there is but one absolute Truth which by its own essence is Truth, namely the Divine Being itself, by which Truth all words are words. In the same way there is one absolute Wisdom, raised above all, namely the Divine Wisdom by participation in whom all wise men are wise. And in the same way the absolute Word by participation in whom all who have a word are said to be speaking. This is the Divine Word, which in Himself is the Word raised above all."[63]

Concluding Reflections

Dei verbum yields its intelligibility to those who, entering into its spirit, embrace what Benedict XVI called its "hermeneutic of reform," that is, "the renewal in the continuity of the one subject-Church which the Lord has given to us. She is a subject which increases in time and develops, yet always remaining the same, the one subject of the journeying People of God."[64] As I pointed out earlier, the apostolic constitution, with all of its multiform aspects, stayed faithful to the teaching of past centuries while finding a way to allow for the legitimate development that the Holy Spirit effects through the ages. Examples would be the more personal context within which the giving and receiving of revelation is appreciated; the awareness (in article 7) of a more sophisticated understanding of biblical authorship achieved in modern historical study; a sensitivity to Protestant views regarding scripture and tradition;

and the role of study, contemplation, and experience on the part of the faithful in contributing to the progress of the apostolic tradition (*DV* 8).

One of the most significant positions, however, was the reiteration and development of the teaching of *Divino afflante Spiritu* regarding the use of the historical and literary methods available today in the study of the sacred text. In this crucial matter the task before us is clear; its immense importance was already accented when, in 1988, Joseph Ratzinger reminded us that "the exegetical problem is identical in the main with the struggle for the foundations of our time. Such a struggle cannot be conducted casually, nor can it be won with a few suggestions. It will demand, as I have already intimated, the attentive and critical commitment of an entire generation."[65]

NOTES

1. B.-D. Dupuy ends his history of the document in the council by commenting on the final vote: "Thus ended, with a near unanimity what was doubtless the most decisive and difficult debate of the Second Vatican Council." B.-D. Dupuy, ed., *La révélation divine: Unam sanctam*, 70a, 70b (Paris: Cerf, 1968), 117.

2. One of the finest can be found in the opening and closing sections of ibid. One may also consult the introductory remarks by Joseph Ratzinger, as well as historical studies of some of the chapters in *DV* in *Commentary on the Documents of Vatican II*, vol. 3, ed. Herbert Vorgrimler (New York: Herder and Herder, 1969). The study by Giuseppe Alberigo, *Breve storia del concilio Vaticano II* (Bologna: Mulino, 2005), as well as its massive predecessor, begin from an ideological stance and are also subject to an approach to history writing that concentrates on what I have called "text production" rather than text interpretation. See Agostino Marchetto, *Il Concilio Ecumenico Vaticano II: Controppunto per la sua storia* (Vatican City: Libreria Editrice Vaticana, 2005).

3. See Saint Augustine, *On the Catechizing of the Uninstructed*, 4, 8 (*PL* 40, 316). Translations of *Dei verbum* are my own.

4. "With this love, then, set before you as an end to which you may refer all that you say, so give all your instructions that he to whom you speak by hearing may believe, and by believing may hope, and by hoping may love." Saint Augustine, *The First Catechetical Instruction* [De catechizandis rudibus], trans. Joseph P. Christopher (Westminster, Md.: Newman Bookshop, 1946), 24.

5. See Henri de Lubac, "Commentaire du préambule et du chapitre I," in *La révélation divine*, vol. 1, ed. B.-D. Dupuy (Paris: Cerf, 1968), 157–304.

6. Commentators have noted these differences and pointed out that Vatican I *first* mentions that God is knowable from created realities "by the natural light of human reason" and then goes on to speak in more abstract terms: "It pleased his wisdom and goodness to reveal to the human race by another and supernatural way both himself and the eternal decrees of his will." Dogmatic constitution *Dei Filius*, Denziger-Schönmetzer, 33d ed., no. 3004.

7. There is also the use of Jn 1:14, "the Word became flesh," but the council did not include that reference.

8. *Summa theologiae* (*ST*) I, q. 1, a. 1: "I answer that, it was necessary for man's salvation that there should be a knowledge revealed by God besides philosophical science built up by human reason. Firstly, indeed, because man is directed to God, as to an end that surpasses the grasp of his reason: 'The eye has not seen, O God, besides you, what things you have prepared for those who wait for you' (Isaiah 64:4 Vulg.). But the

end must first be known by men who are to direct their thoughts and actions to the end. Hence it was necessary for the salvation of man that certain truths which exceed human reason should be made known to him by Divine Revelation."

9. Note how the Letter to the Hebrews sums up the whole of Christ's action on earth and his continued activity now by describing it as a speech of God: "On many occasions and in many ways in times past God, having spoken to the fathers by the prophets, at the end of these days, *spoke to us in a Son*" (Heb 1:1–2).

10. "Indeed, the whole history of man's salvation is one long, varied dialogue, which marvelously begins with God and which He prolongs with men in so many different ways." Pope Paul VI, encyclical letter *Ecclesiam suam* (Washington, D.C.: National Catholic Welfare Conference, 1964). The whole of article 70 deals with the theme of "dialogue."

11. Hans Urs von Balthasar, "Il senso spirituale della scrittura," *Ricerche Teologiche* 5 (1994): 7.

12. See the ample discussion in André Feuillet, *Le Christ sagesse de Dieu d'après les épitres pauliennes, études bibliques* (Paris: Gabalda, 1966), 202–17. Also, Jean-Noël Aletti, *Colossiens 1:15–20; Genre et exégèse du text: Fonction de la thématique sapientielle* (Rome: Biblical Institute Press, 1981), 115–40.

13. See the remarks by de Lubac, "Commentaire du préambule et du chapitre I," 202–205. "The Son of God has been sown everywhere throughout the Scriptures [of Moses]. Sometimes He speaks with Abraham, sometimes with Noah, giving him the measurements of the ark; He looks for Adam, brings judgment on the Sodomites. There are times when He is actually seen, guiding Jacob on his way, speaking with Moses from the bush." Irenaeus, "Against the Heresies," IV, 10, 1, in *The Scandal of the Incarnation: Irenaeus against the Heresies*, ed. Hans Urs von Balthasar, trans. John Saward (San Francisco: Ignatius Press, 1990), 50–51 (no. 90).

14. See Rolf Rendtorff, " 'Covenant' as a Structuring Concept in Genesis and Exodus," *Journal of Biblical Literature* 108 (1989): 385–93.

15. Genesis 6 and 9, where the term "covenant" (b^erît in Hebrew) occurs eight times.

16. See K. A. Kitchen, *On the Reliability of the Old Testament* (Grand Rapids: Eerdmans, 2003), ch. 7, "Founding Fathers or Fleeting Phantoms—the Patriarchs."

17. For an older but still valuable collection of studies on Abraham, see "Abraham, père des croyants," in *Cahiers sioniens* 5(2) (1951).

18. *De veritate*, 14, 2, ad 10. Or again, "Such an act [of faith] does not have a proposition as its term, but a reality, since just as with scientific knowledge, so also with faith, the only reason for formulating a proposition is that we may have knowledge about the real" (*ST* II–II, q. 1, a. 2, ad 2).

19. In this sense, revelation, all of which shares in the economy of the Incarnation, is "art," as described by Flannery O'Connor: "a delicate adjustment of the outer and inner worlds in such a way, that without changing their nature, they can be seen through each other." Flannery O'Connor, *Mystery and Manners: Occasional Prose* (New York: Farrar, Straus, and Giroux, 1969), 34–35, as cited in Susan Srigley, *Flannery O'Connor's Sacramental Art* (Notre Dame, Ind.: Notre Dame University Press, 2004), 16.

20. *On the Passion*, 12 (*Sources chrétiennes* 74, 82); see also *On the Resurrection*, 1 (*Sources chrétiennes* 74, 123); *On the Epiphany*, 5 (*Sources chrétiennes* 22, 254); and *On the Passion*, 5 and 18 (*Sources chrétiennes* 74, 41, 112). For the references to these citations see Dom Marie-Bernard de Soos, "Le mystère liturgique d'après Saint Léon le Grand" (Münster: Aschendorffsche Verlagsbuchhandlung, 1971).

21. "The encounter between the people of God of the Old Covenant, which has never been revoked by God (cf. Rom 11:29), and that of the New Covenant is also an

internal dialogue in our Church, similar to that between the first and second part of its Bible." Eugene Fisher and Leon Klenicki, eds., *Spiritual Pilgrimage: Texts on Jews and Judaism 1979–1995: Pope John Paul II* (New York: Crossroad, 1995), 13.

22. For more on this latter point see the *Catechism of the Catholic Church*, nos. 66–67.

23. "So we should consider that one man manifests something to another by explaining his concept through some external signs, either by speech or by writing; but God manifests something to man in a twofold manner. In one way, by infusing an interior light through which man knows: Psalm 42:3 (Vg): 'Send forth your light and your truth.' In another way by setting forth external signs of his wisdom, that is creatures perceivable to the senses: Sir 1:10 (Vg): 'He poured her (wisdom) out over all his works.'" *Ad Romanos, Lectura VI*, in *Super epistolas S. Pauli lectura* (Roma: Marietti, 1953), no. 116, I, 22. Aquinas uses the same example of "teaching" in regard to prophecy in *ST* II–II, q. 173, a. 2, c.

24. In Boethius, *De Trinitate*. 3, 1, ad 4, trans. Armand Maurer, St. Thomas Aquinas, *Faith, Reason, and Theology: Questions I–IV of His Commentary on the De Trinitate of Boethius* (Toronto: Pontifical Institute of Medieval Studies, 1987), 69.

25. Albert Vanhoye, "Notre foi, oeuvre divine d'après le quatrième évangile," *Nouvelle revue théologique* 86 (1964): 337–54.

26. See Joseph Ratzinger, "Die Debatte über das Offenbarungsschema," in *Die erste Sitzungsperiode des Zweiten Vatikanischen Konzils: Ein Rückblick* (Cologne: J. P. Bachem, 1963).

27. *Perceptio divinae veritatis tendens in ipsam* (*ST* II–II, q. 1, a. 6, sc).

28. See Francis Martin, "1 John," in William Farmer, ed., *The International Bible Commentary* (Collegeville, Minn.: Liturgical Press, 1998), 1823–1832. See esp. 1830–1832, which treats 1 Jn 4:7–5:21.

29. For a longer treatment of the biblical tradition's teaching on the knowability of God from creation, see Francis Martin, "Revelation as Disclosure: Creation," in *Wisdom and Holiness, Science and Scholarship: Essays in Honor of Matthew L. Lamb*, ed. Michael Dauphinais and Matthew Levering (Naples, Fla.: Sapientia Press, 2007), 205–47.

30. Thomas Aquinas, *ST* I–II, q. 91, a. 2.

31. For a discussion of this point, see Stanislas Lyonnet, "La connaissance naturel de Dieu," in Stanislas Lyonnet, ed., *Études sur l'épître aux Romains* (Rome: Editrice Pontificio Istituto Biblico, 1989); Hans Urs von Balthasar, *The Theology of Karl Barth*, trans. Edward Oates (San Francisco: Ignatius, 1992), pt. 3, "The Form and Structure of Catholic Thought."

32. *Against Celsus*, 7, 42; 3, 47. In Robert Wilken, *The Spirit of Early Christianity: Seeking the Face of God* (New Haven, Conn.: Yale University Press, 2003), 18. In the same place we find these words of Irenaeus: "The Lord taught us that no one is able to know God unless taught by God. God cannot be known without the help of God" (*Against the Heresies* 4, 6, 4). This is further developed by Aquinas, who comments on 1 Cor 1:21 ("For since, in the wisdom of God, the world did not know God through wisdom, it pleased God through the folly of what we preach to save those who believe."): "The divine wisdom when making the world, left his marks on the things of the world as it says in Sir 1:10, 'He poured her (wisdom) out over all his works.' Thus, creatures themselves, made through the wisdom of God have a relation to God, whose marks they bear, like the words of a man relate to his wisdom which they signify. And as the disciple arrives at knowing the wisdom of the teacher through the words that he hears, so man can arrive at knowing God's wisdom through the creatures made by him as it says in

Rom 1:20.... But man, because of the futility (*vanitatem*) of his heart, has gone astray from the rectitude of the knowledge of God as it says in John 1:10: 'He was in the world and the world was made by him and the world did not know him.' Therefore God led the faithful to a saving knowledge of himself by certain other means which are not found in the specific natures (*rationibus*) of creatures. For this reason these means are considered folly by worldly men who consider only the natures of human things. These other means are the teachings of the faith."

33. René Latourelle, *Theology of Revelation* (New York: Alba House, 1966), 476.

34. Joseph Ratzinger, "The Transmission of Divine Revelation," commentary on chapter 2 of *Dei verbum*, in *Commentary on the Documents of Vatican II*, vol. 3, ed. Vorgrimler, 182.

35. For a development of this notion, see Franz Jozef van Beeck, "Divine Revelation: Intervention or Self-communication?" *Theological Studies* 52 (1991): 199–226.

36. *Summa contra gentiles* 3, 154.

37. *ST* II–II, q. 5, a. 3, c, and ad 2. A full development of this theme would require a treatment of Christ himself as "*auctor doctrinae*" both as God, the First Truth, and as man, the privileged manifestation of that truth. See Yves Congar, "Tradition et 'sacra doctrina' chez Saint Thomas d'Aquin," in Johannes Betz and Heinrich Fries, eds., *Église et tradition* (Lyon, France: Xavier Mappus, 1963), 173–74.

38. For an idea of the conflicting currents of thought in the preconciliar Church regarding the nature of tradition, see Brian Daley, "The *nouvelle théologie* and the Patristic Revival: Sources, Symbols, and the Science of Theology," *International Journal of Scientific Theology* 7 (2005): 362–82.

39. Ratzinger, "Transmission of Divine Revelation," 184.

40. See *Lumen gentium* 4, which states that "Ecclesial communion is at the same time both invisible and visible."

41. "For Congar, tradition is a real, living self-communication of God. Its content is the whole Christian reality disclosed in Jesus Christ, including the implicit contents of that disclosure. The Holy Spirit is the transcendent subject of tradition; the whole Church is its bearer." Avery Dulles, in the introduction to the reprint of Yves Congar, *The Meaning of Tradition*, trans. A. N. Woodrow (San Francisco: Ignatius Press, 1964, 2004), ix.

42. Neophytus Edelby in *Acta synodalia Sacrosancti Concilii Oecumenici Vaticani II*, vol. 3, pt. 3 (Vatican City: Typis Polyglottis Vaticanis, 1974), 306–307. The Latin phrase that is translated "Epiclesis on the history of salvation" reads "*Epiclesis historiae salutis*," but this can mean only that the tradition is the enlivening action of the Holy Spirit upon the history of salvation and renders both the history and the inspired expression of it in the scriptures intelligible and life giving.

43. Recall the *gestis verbisque* of no. 2.

44. For a development of this, see Bernard Lonergan, *Method in Theology* (New York: Herder and Herder, 1972).

45. For an excellent study of this concept in *DV*, see Alessandro Maggiolini, "Magisterial Teaching on Experience in the Twentieth Century: From the Modernist Crisis to the Second Vatican Council," *Communio* 23 (1996): 225–43.

46. See Avery Dulles, *The Craft of Theology* (New York: Crossroad, 1992), 88–89.

47. For conflicting Protestant notions on this point, see Ratzinger, "Transmission of Divine Revelation," 188–93. Ironically, this same insistence on the independent clarity of the sacred text led as well in the other direction, namely, to an unwitting installation of reason as the arbiter in the case of unclear biblical texts. For a development of this point see Klaus Scholder, *The Birth of Modern Critical Theology: Origins and Problems of*

Biblical Criticism in the Seventeenth Century, trans. John Bowden (London: SCM Press, 1990).

48. For an excellent treatment of the current state of the discussion, see Telford Work, *Living and Active: Scripture in the Economy of Salvation* (Grand Rapids: Eerdmans, 2002), 261–301.

49. Hans George Gadamer, *Truth and Method*, trans. Joel Weinsheimer and Donald Marshall (New York: Seabury, 1989).

50. See, for instance, Ignace de la Potterie, "Parole et esprit dans S. Jean," in *L'évangile de Jean: Sources, rédaction, théologie*, ed. M. de Jong, *Bibliotheca Ephemeridum Theologicarum Lovaniensium*, vol. 44 (Gembloux, France: Duculot, 1977), 179–201.

51. See Robert W. Wall, "Reading the Bible from within Our Traditions: The 'Rule of Faith' in Theological Hermeneutics," in *Between Two Horizons: Spanning New Testament Studies and Systematic Theology*, ed. Joel B. Green and Max Turner (Grand Rapids: Eerdmans, 2000), 88–107.

52. David S. Yeago, "The Bible, the Church, and the Scriptures: Biblical Inspiration and Interpretation Revisited," in *Knowing the Triune God: The Work of the Spirit in the Practices of the Church*, ed. James J. Buckley and David S. Yeago (Grand Rapids: Eerdmans, 2001), 49–93.

53. Leo Scheffczyk, "Sacred Scripture: God's Word and the Church's Word," *Communio* 28 (2001): 26–41.

54. Some of the material in the commentary on ch. 3 of *DV* has appeared in Francis Martin, "Some Aspects of Biblical Studies since Vatican II: The Contribution and Challenge of *Dei Verbum*," in *Sacred Scripture: The Disclosure of the Word* (Naples, Fla.: Sapientia Press, 2006) 227–47. It is used here with the permission of the publishers.

55. For a beginning in this direction, see Olivier-Thomas Venard, " 'La Bible en ses traditions': The New Project of the École biblique et archéologique française de Jérusalem Presented as a 'Fourth Generation' Enterprise," *Nova et Vetera* (English) 4 (2006): 142–58; also see the chapter by Denis Farkasfalvy in this volume.

56. At times discrepancies appear between the present state of our historical knowledge and the statements in the sacred text. Thus the worldwide "census" under Caesar Augustus in Lk 2:1, the discrepancy in dating between Dan 1:1 and the Chronicle of King Nebuchadnezzar regarding the siege of Jerusalem, and so on. There are also mistaken attributions: Mk 27:9 names Jeremiah, while in fact the text adduced in regard to Judas's death is Zech 11:12.

57. *Contra Arianos* I, 54; *PG* 26, col. 123 (*Divino Afflante Spiritu*, no. 34). The phrase translated "real meaning" (*alēthinēs dianoias*) also evokes nuances of a "real understanding" of the author's text.

58. "Qui non intelligit res non postest sensum ex verbis elicere." Martin Luther, *Tischreden*, Weimarer Ausgabe 5, 26, no. 5246.

59. Note the number of times the notion of author's intention is invoked: "Ad hagiographorum intentionem eruendam" [attention must be paid to literary forms]; the interpreter must investigate what the author "exprimere intenderit et expresserit"; finally, due attention must be paid to common styles of speech in order to attain a correct understanding of what the sacred Author "scripto asserere voluerit."

60. The *Catechism of the Catholic Church* (no. 114), commenting on this passage of *Dei verbum*, defines the analogy of faith this way: "By 'analogy of faith' we mean the coherence of the truths of faith among themselves and within the whole plan of Revelation."

61. *ST* II–II, q. 5, ad 2. For a judicious account of the way in which the Church asserts the meaning of a biblical text see Maurice Gilbert, "Textes bibliques dont l'Église

a défini le sens," in *L'autorité de l'écriture*, ed. Jean-Michel Poffet (Paris: Cerf, 2002), 71–94.

62. John Chrysostom, *On Genesis* 3, 8 (Homily 17, 1 [*PG* 53, 134]). The Greek term used here for "adaptation" is *sugkatabasis*.

63. Thomas Aquinas, *Super evangelium S. Joannis lectura* (Roma: Marietti, 1952), no. 33.

64. Address to the Roman Curia (Dec. 22, 2005), *L'Osservatore Romano* (English) (Jan. 4, 2006), 5. See Benedict XVI, "A Proper Hermeneutic," in this volume.

65. Statement made at the Ratzinger Conference on Bible and Church, held in New York, January 1988; Josef Ratzinger, "Biblical Interpretation in Crisis: On the Question of the Foundations and Approaches of Exegesis Today," in *Biblical Interpretation in Crisis: The Ratzinger Conference on Bible and the Church*, ed. Richard John Neuhaus (Grand Rapids: Eerdmans, 1989), 16.

4

Inspiration and Interpretation

Denis Farkasfalvy, O.Cist.

The dogmatic constitution *Dei verbum* was the product of a lengthy "struggle," and even the final version is not the "mature conclusion" of the process that produced it.[1] Here I neither discuss its detailed history nor trace the path that the theology of revelation and inspiration has traveled between the two Vatican councils. Instead, I undertake a historical inquiry to demonstrate a double thesis:

1. For the theology of inspiration, inerrancy, and the ecclesial use of scripture, *Dei verbum* has successfully restored the proper context in which tradition developed and nurtured them.
2. In chapters 3–5 *Dei verbum* applied a renewed theology of revelation, to which the aforementioned topics belong, but the effort of synthesis resulted in an incomplete text that is still awaiting full development.

The Place of Biblical Inspiration in *Dei verbum*

Obtaining the Proper Context

The original schema of what later became the dogmatic constitution *Dei verbum* was the product of a certain "Roman theology" that was well known from theological manuals used in Rome at pontifical universities in the first half of the twentieth century. These were textbooks assigned to compulsory courses called *Introductio generalis in sacram scripturam*.[2] The famous encyclical *Divino afflante* by Pius XII was basically a product of the same Roman school of theology in its final and best phase. A comparison of the topical outline of this encyclical with the leading textbooks is instructive. Their common point of departure is a proof of the "existence of inspiration," which presents the Bible as essentially a collection of texts written under the inspiration of the Holy Spirit.[3] This is followed up in two directions. First, the "extent" of inspiration is discussed to show that it includes every text of the Catholic Bible.[4] Second, the "essence" or "nature" of inspiration is treated as a divine influence on the sacred writers of the biblical books,[5] the hagiographers, to engage their minds and wills so that the literary works they produced could be truly characterized as both "authored by God" and written by human authors, the latter as instruments of God. To conclude the first part of the treatise, this double authorship, human and divine, is discussed in terms of the scholastic concept of "instrumental causality," which is borrowed from the treatise of the *Summa* of Saint Thomas about prophecy and then applied to literary authorship.[6]

The second part continues with the study of inerrancy as the "most important effect of inspiration" and covers every text in its entirety, including those with a nonreligious content (e.g., history, geography, natural sciences, descriptive observations).

The encyclical *Divino afflante*, published in 1943, was rightly hailed for two decades as "the Magna Charta of Catholic biblical scholarship." It encouraged linguistic, archeological, and critical studies of texts and focused on the literal sense while also emphasizing the importance of the Church fathers' exegetical tradition. It kept the theology of inspiration and inerrancy, however, locked in a narrow perspective of the Roman textbooks. *Divino afflante* was issued on the fiftieth anniversary of Leo XIII's encyclical *Providentissimus Deus* and closely reiterated the main theses of that papal document. *Divino afflante*, nevertheless, projected admiration of and enthusiasm for modern biblical studies and, in support of the patristic renewal slowly expanding in the 1930s and 1940s, encouraged the study of ancient exegesis, though without proposing any specific guidance for combining the two trends.[7]

High hopes were connected with the novel concept of the "literary genre," which *Divino afflante* strongly promoted. The importance of this cannot be underestimated. Catholic exegetes began to emphasize that, due to their specific literary genres, most biblical texts could not be held to standards of modern science and historiography. In both the pulpit and the classroom, this brought badly needed relief.

The study of the literary genre provided further benefits. Catholics began to realize that the majority of the biblical texts constituted religious poetry. What is in prose, moreover, often follows ancient literary conventions of persuasive, ethical, or legislative texts. For many of the biblical texts, therefore, a rationalistic application of "inerrancy" (in the sense of "historicity" and modern historiography) began to appear pointless. *Divino afflante* successfully opened the doors for a Catholic "biblical movement" that quickly gained momentum.[8]

The first preparatory schemas of the council on biblical matters (inspiration and inerrancy), however, offered little hope for significant progress. Trying to deal with the considerable backlog of the Councils of Trent and Vatican I, the first five schemas (A through E) tried in vain to place tradition (and thus the magisterium) above scripture by controlling its interpretation and thus to resolve the potential conflicts between the "two sources of Revelation," scripture and tradition, by subordinating the former to the latter.

In their response, the council fathers rejected the documents prepared by the preparatory committee and soon brought the conciliar debate to the brink of a stalemate. Thereafter, a papal intervention (in November 1962, by John XXIII) removed the project from the agenda. Almost two years passed until an initiative issued by Pope Paul VI (March 7, 1964) brought these topics back under a new title, *De revelatione*, and with a newly appointed subcommittee in charge.[9] This group began to draft a new schema with fresh insights.

Now for a second time the "theology of revelation" took center stage in the council, integrated some of the topics treated previously, and marginalized others. The new schema approached revelation according to the patristic perspective of a comprehensive "economy of salvation."[10] This appeared successful, for the new schema easily transcended the dualism of "scripture vs. tradition," which had marred all post-Tridentine debates about this issue. *Dei verbum* set out to state at its beginning that "The divine economy is realized by deeds and words" (I, no. 2). In this perspective not even the "verbal" form of revelation appears central and primary. Revelation becomes a comprehensive concept: It includes all forms and means of communication by which God has chosen to manifest Himself to the human race. Most importantly, *Dei verbum* rectified the approach by which the papal encyclicals of Pius XII, *Divino afflante* and *Humani generis*, had begun their discourse by speaking of the inspired authors (*hagiographi*) of the sacred books. In the first place, *Dei verbum* correctly emphasized that, because revelation takes place as history (and not just *in* history), it cannot be reduced to verbal and conceptual expressions, let alone to written texts. Second, *Dei verbum* did not allow the notion of "revealed truth" to be reduced or restricted to propositional statements. Instead, it means the complex historical events and developments that, in fact, have certain cognitive aspects and obtain expression in narratives, texts, and theological statements but also include other aspects of the religious experience and give birth to alternative forms of verbal expression, such as poetry, legislation, prophecy, and prayer, all of which appear in the Bible.[11]

The conciliar document's opening paragraph contains a summary sketch of "sacred history" in the way the Bible deals with history, narrating the biblical past. Such treatment of the past is frequently repeated in patristic authors with no regard to modern historical consciousness. By this procedure the document was allowed to integrate further patristic doctrine on revelation and inspiration easily. On the other hand, *Dei verbum* made no attempt to bridge the gap separating the precritical view of history from contemporary thought. On matters such as human evolution, hominization, and the emergence of culture and religious practices in prehistorical times, it never even tried to integrate biblical content with contemporary categories of history, as was done, for example, in the terms of William Albright's classic, albeit outdated, work, *From the Stone Age to Christianity*.[12] The document cautiously preferred to repeat traditional language and avoided a confrontation between biblical history and modern anthropology.[13]

Biblical Inspiration in the New Context of Revelation

The final version (text F) of *Dei verbum* inserted the traditional doctrine of biblical inspiration into the context of a renewed notion of revelation. Although this traditional doctrine remained basically unchanged, the new context almost automatically enriched it. This appears most clearly in chapter 2, where the text moves from the notion of the "divine economy"—events and experiences happening to God's people (meaning both Israel and the nascent Church)—to the topic of "the Transmission of Divine Revelation." The concept of "transmission" was sufficiently wide as to include both the oral and the written transmission of God's self-disclosure; thus, from the beginning, the unity of (rather than the distinction between) scripture and tradition was emphasized. Yet, by a curious though intentional shortcut, the document quickly passes over in one sentence the first phase of sacred history and, with regard to the Old Testament, does not even distinguish between oral and written traditions: "In his gracious goodness, God has seen to it that what He had revealed for the salvation of all nations would abide perpetually in its full integrity and be handed on to all generations" (*DV* 7).

One might even be led to think that this sentence wants to include, right from the beginning, the transmission of revelation through Christ and his apostles, for without mentioning the scriptures of the Jewish people it continues immediately with the following: "Therefore, Christ the Lord in whom the entire Revelation of God the most high is summed up (cf. 2 Cor 2 1:20, 3:16–4:6) commanded the Apostles to preach the Gospel which had been promised beforehand by the prophets and which He Himself has fulfilled in his own person and promulgated with his own lips." In any case, the concept of revelation presented here is strongly Christocentric. All revelatory instances are summarized as "the Prophets" in a comprehensive sense, those who have preceded and anticipated Christ until He, at the peak of revelation, pronounced the Good News "with his own lips" and transmitted it thereafter through his chosen Apostles to all future generations. In this scheme, the longitudinal or temporal dimension of the salvation-history outline is complemented by a scheme of mediation, in which there is but one mediator and revealer, the Son, who engages further spokesmen and mediators in every age and time. Christ's omnipresence in every phase of the economy of salvation makes each one transcend its historical limitation in two ways, by overcoming finiteness and receiving temporal extension and by becoming released from the locksteps of temporal succession. By their theandrical constitution, that is, since Christ is both human and divine, his actions obtain a supratemporal relevance and availability; they even exercise supratemporal causality (most clearly in the sacraments, but analogously in every kind of proclamation of the word) by bringing about and endowing with efficacy the salvific encounters between God and man always and everywhere.

Christ, the "prophets" of the Old Testament, and the Apostles form a sort of "triptych," a triple structure of revelatory mediation with the terms "prophets" and "Apostles" taking a generalized and quasi-technical meaning.

The term "prophets" signifies the recipients of revelation in Israel, ultimately the authoritative sources of the Old Testament scriptures, while the term "Apostles" refers to the immediate recipients of Jesus' mission, chosen eyewitnesses who took the word of revelation from his mouth and became the fountainhead of the apostolic tradition from which the scriptures of the New Testament also originate. Understood in this way, the economy of salvation cannot be reduced to "a historical process" conceived as a one-dimensional accumulation of subsequent installments. Rather, it is a chain of anticipations that lead to their peak in Christ, which happens all at once at the incarnation of the Logos, but then are extended and distributed to all subsequent times and places.

Only at this point does *Dei verbum* introduce "the Scriptures." Although the document previously referred to "Moses" (*DV* 3) and "the prophets" (also in no. 3 and later in no. 7), these were mentioned in a role of "speaking" God's word as if by an oral message.[14] Scripture as such is mentioned explicitly for the first time in article 7, in reference to the full message of Christ's revelation: "the Apostles and those apostolic men who, under the inspiration of the Holy Spirit, have put into writing the message of salvation" (*DV* 7).[15]

It is no accident that, in this way, the first mentioning of scripture and biblical inspiration takes place in reference to the apostolic tradition, so that the document begins its theology of inspiration in reference to the New Testament. Throughout its entirety the document understands all of the scriptures as derived from Christ, their fountain. Thus later, in chapter 4, the texts of the Old Testament are treated as "the economy of salvation *fore-announced, narrated and explained*" (*praeannuntiata, enarrata atque explicata, DV* 14). We might be dealing here with one of the least understood and appreciated aspects of the document. As the patristic heritage has always maintained, the purpose and meaning of the Old Testament lie in its prophetic character. Only by pointing to Christ does it possess permanent value for mankind's universal salvation history. The economy of salvation of the Old Testament has its raison d'être chiefly in this (*in hoc potissimum disposita erat*), that it might "prophetically announce and typologically signify the coming of Christ as the Redeemer of all and his messianic Kingdom" (*DV* 15).[16]

Because it is based on a patristic theology of revelation, the concept of biblical inspiration presented in *Dei verbum* stands head and shoulders above that of *Divino afflante* and the Roman textbooks of the 1950s. The latter usually started with a chapter "De exsistentia inspirationis," in which arguments taken from scripture and tradition were listed in order to "prove" that *scripture was inspired.* This method did not involve (the textbooks argued) logical fallacy because, at this point, the Bible was used only as a historical source without any supposition of its inspired character. However, using the Bible as a historical source to prove that it was *believed to be inspired* was a confusing procedure. At best it illustrated that different passages in the biblical books referred to other passages of the same collection of books as inspired and that both Judaism and Christianity accepted a general concept of "the scriptures"—the precise content of which remained unclear until the completion of the canon by the Church's magisterium.

Dei verbum used a different approach, one that began, like many other documents of Vatican II, with the self-understanding of the Church. From its beginnings, the Church as a "community of salvation" understood itself to be in possession of "the scriptures," due to its belief that Christ's life, message, death, and resurrection had taken place "according to the scriptures" (cf. 1 Cor 15:3–4). The authentic Pauline texts provide the earliest witness to this specifically Christian development: "Whatever was written previously was written for our instruction, so that by endurance and by the encouragement of the scriptures we might have hope" (Rom 15:4). This awareness was linked with the apostolic tradition, itself conceived as a received teaching "about what was there from the beginning (ἀπ᾽ ἀρχῆς ἀπ᾽)" (cf. 1 Jn 1:1) and transmitted by those who were original eyewitnesses: again "ἀρχῆς" (Lk 1:1).[17] This understanding of "the scriptures" implies faith in their inspiration. However, this faith is, with regard to both context and content, quite different from what one can glean from scattered and casual remarks about various biblical passages that assert or allude to the existence of inspiration.[18]

In the textbooks that preceded *Dei verbum* the relationship of tradition and scripture, as well as their connection to the magisterium remained unclarified. In the system that the preconciliar textbooks projected, the only sufficient and truly efficient criterion of truth was the magisterium. For it was not clear whether either scripture or tradition was definable without recourse to decisions by the magisterium. In the vision that *Dei verbum* proposes, a clear effort is made to tip the balance in favor of the "apostolic Church." The apostolic Church is seen as a historically closed and unchangeable reality, enshrined in the twenty-seven books of the New Testament as a divinely created literary depository of revealed truth but extended into time through the ministry of the Church, which continues dispensing the salvific treasures of Christ's teachings, his sacrificial death, and everlasting risen life. In this vision, revelation is conceived as a broad, multidimensional reality, and scripture constitutes only one component of this reality. Scripture is the written documentation of salvation history, which in the ongoing ministry of the Church coexists with the flow of tradition and the ecclesial expansion of Christ's presence on earth.

After the first two chapters with a basically patristic orientation, chapter 3 of *Dei verbum* delineates a theology of inspiration that becomes increasingly entangled in a set of modern concerns that lie outside the patristic perspective. This is the reason we need to examine this chapter next before we turn to two sets of statements about the two testaments (chapters 4 and 5). These chapters constitute a skillful summary of traditional doctrine, yet appear to be incomplete and unfinished.

Inspiration and Interpretation

The Concept of Inspiration in Chapter 3

While chapters 1 and 2 of *Dei verbum* masterfully succeeded in *replacing* the opening chapter of the textbooks on "the existence and essence (or nature)" of revelation, chapter 3 treats the issues of the manuals under the heading "De extensione inspirationis"—and repeats them for the most part. These problems had been left unresolved by Vatican I and were revisited by the encyclicals that followed (*Providentissimus Deus, Spiritus paraclitus,* and *Divino afflante*). Various theologians attempted to limit the extent of inspiration to certain parts of the Bible by carving out texts and/or topics that would not have been authored by God and thus would not be covered by inerrancy. These included Cardinal Newman's famous proposal to eliminate the inspiration of the "obiter dicta"—statements unessential to the purpose of the biblical authors because of their lack of religious relevance. Yet the magisterium insisted that the biblical text was covered by inspiration in its entirety and thus was fully endowed with inerrancy.

Chapter 3 begins with an insistence on the true authorship of the human writers who produced the biblical texts. That they were *veri auctores* excludes any mechanistically conceived authorship in which the human author would have no freedom of decision, authorial purpose, or goal but would be just a blind instrument that follows the Divine Author. The human authors' conscious and free participation in the process of inspiration had already been highly emphasized in *Divino afflante*, which advised caution in the interpretation of many patristic and medieval images that compared the human authors to inanimate instruments (pen, flute, pipe). At the publication of *Divino afflante*, Augustinus Bea (who was probably the ghostwriter of the encyclical) published the view that the phrase "Deus auctor scripturae" constitutes the most important formula for inspiration.[19] A decade thereafter, Rahner raised serious objections to the indiscriminate use of this metaphor and argued that God cannot be called a "Verfasser" (literary author) but only the "Urheber" (originator) of a book, while admitting that the Latin term "auctor" is ambiguous. Rahner's proposal was received positively by many (German) theologians, yet *Dei verbum* did not follow up on his remarks about "divine authorship." There was good reason for that: Rahner never examined whether tradition had called God "auctor scripturae" in a literary sense.[20] Even now, forty years after *Dei verbum*, it is not quite clear to what extent and in what sense tradition speaks of "Deus auctor scripturae."[21]

Ironically, the authors of the first schema on revelation and the new subcommittee that replaced them easily agreed on the concept of a "double authorship," human and divine, for the Bible. One may ask, however, why the term "veri auctores" for the human authors went unmatched by a reference to God as *verus auctor*. It seems that insistence on the hagiographers as *true* authors was so much the focus of attention that God's role as "auctor scripturae" was never questioned.

In a book published too late to influence the council,[22] Luis Alonso Schökel showed that in patristic texts God is said to be "the author of Scripture" much less abundantly and unanimously than modern authors had assumed.[23] Do we know with more precision what the medieval theologians thought about it? Saint Thomas Aquinas provides a rather stable usage when he speaks about God as the "auctor principalis" and the hagiographer as the "auctor instrumentalis" of scripture.[24] One cannot, however, identify this Thomistic usage as speaking of a double literary authorship. What Saint Thomas had in mind is probably the very same distinction between *Verfasser* (*auctor instrumentalis*) and *Urheber* (*auctor principalis*), for which Rahner argued.[25] It seems that this usage of the term "auctor" applied *analogously* to God, and the hagiographer has given rise to the concept of a "double authorship." In this sense did the council of Trent call God the "auctor" of scriptures: "Omnes libros tamen Veteris quam Novi Testamenti, cum utriusque unus Deus sit auctor... pari pietatis affectu ac reverentia [concilium] suscipit et veneratur" (from the year 1546; D 83).[26]

The texts of the councils of Florence and Trent emphasize the *one* divine author of the *two* testaments. At Vatican II this emphasis shifts. Originally, insistence on *both testaments* came from a very ancient, anti-Gnostic, and specifically anti-Marcionite tradition, formulated for the first time by Irenaeus and Tertullian.[27] Tertullian uses the word "auctoritas" and leaves no doubt that the issue is not "literary authorship" but the one and same divine *authority* by which both testaments are endowed. However, "auctoritas" in Tertullian corresponds to the same "origin" in Irenaeus, and thus the councils of Florence and Trent probably spoke of both an equal authority and an identical authorship or source for both testaments. Yet none of these statements affirm that God, to equip his salvation plan with written records, took up the métier (trade) of a writer and "wrote a letter to Philemon," compiled wise sayings (Proverbs), or became a poet of love songs (Song of Songs) or a humorist (Jonah).[28]

Then in a peculiarly convoluted sentence (the third sentence of no. 11), the conciliar text combines this double authorship (human and divine) of sacred scripture. The commission's intention was to show the two authors undiminished in their respective roles and nature and thus joining forces to produce (that is, to author) a common product. There was no way of avoiding a tension between the notion of "true authors," who are in full possession of their talents yet were being "employed" (one could even say "used"), so that, while writing as free agents, they would write exactly that—no more or less—which the Divine Author wanted *them* to put down in writing.

This scheme encountered, to some extent, Karl Rahner's concerns: The Divine Author is not said to "commit to writing" anything and is never said to be a "literary author." He makes the human writers produce exactly what He intends *them* to write. Only the hagiographer is a "literary author," or "Verfasser," yet the Divine Author is specifically responsible for everything the text says or, more correctly, for the whole of the resulting text. The problem created by this model should not be underestimated: The human being whom God employs is fully and specifically predetermined to do what God wants the person to do. Can we still say that the human writer is making fully free decisions? Yes, we can as long as we understand that the transcendental divine cause does not reduce or restrict human freedom but rather constitutes and neither diminishes it nor becomes diminished by it.[29] While the language of the document fully incorporates the use of "author" and "authorship" for both God and human beings, the text carefully avoids stating that God is a literary author and refuses to employ the Thomistic categories of "causa principalis" and "causa instrumentalis."

In spite of its nuanced restraint, this first paragraph of article 11 of *Dei verbum* failed to make a major impact on post–Vatican II Catholic biblical scholarship. It was perceived as a statement locked in a traditional framework, irredeemably out of touch with contemporary scholarship's projections about the origins of the biblical books. In fact, the threefold scheme "God—hagiographer—inspired text" may well be applicable to the origins of certain texts, like the (authentic) Pauline letters. But for books like the Gospels or the Pentateuch this scheme appears to be too simplistic. The (transcendental) Divine Author coordinates a flow of events in which the text is shaped, transformed, and undergoes redactional changes and corrections in successive mental, oral, and written phases, all of which are accomplished with the participation of various human beings who may not even know each other but influence each other's work. Who are the veri auctores, the "true (literary) authors"? Here a serious gap appears, separating *Dei verbum*'s concept of inspiration from the modern scholar's conception of the birth of biblical texts. However, the ultimate problem may stem from the fact that the modern concept of a literary author is too closely linked with the way modern literary works are produced, while the traditional doctrine was formulated in a cultural milieu that had the liberty of speaking of Moses, David, or Solomon in the Old Testament and the four evangelists or Peter, Paul, and John in the New Testament, as hagiographers or sacred writers in some sense but always in a different, analogous sense. For ancient tradition, the concept of the hagiographer was *never sufficiently concretized;* thus the door remained open to broad factual divergences.

In *Dei verbum* the term "hagiographer" is used sparingly, and the document prefers to speak of "authors" rather than "writers" in order to avoid conflicts with the meaning of literary authorship as used in modern biblical scholarship. All of this caution, however, had little impact on Catholic biblicists, who needed a concept of inspiration applicable to the process in which they learned to assess the origin of the biblical texts. Critical scholarship kept on moving to an increasingly anonymous model of the (literary) authors, merging more and more with the concept of "redactors" and "compilators," even with the image of so-called traditionalists (the preachers, teachers, and church leaders of various times), most of whom had no personal intention to produce lasting documents. Which of these people should we then identify with "the chosen persons" envisaged in *Dei verbum?* Which are the men God selected to put into writing "those and only those things which God wanted to be put in writing?"[30] Thus, understandably, the carefully crafted sentences of *Dei verbum* had a weak impact on post–Vatican II biblical scholarship.

Dei verbum also failed to address the issue of verbal inspiration.[31] One can only guess that the general trend at the council was to be cautious with the idea that God determined every iota in the Bible. As a result, however, the traditional formulas about verbal inspiration faded in an aura of respectable retirement. At the end, most readers of the documents of Vatican II were likely to retain little more from the council's doctrine of inspiration than the notion that, after Vatican II, Catholics stopped thinking that the characteristics of the biblical *text* were divinely authored and failed to notice that the double authorship influenced not only the meaning of the scriptural text but also sacred scripture itself.

The Treatment of Inerrancy in Dei Verbum

The topic of inerrancy made history at Vatican II. Since the First Vatican Council it had sat like a time bomb waiting to explode; when it did, it probably created more noise than damage. The manuals treated "inerrancy" as the chief and most important effect of inspiration, a misperception caused by the many rationalist efforts in trying to find erroneous statements in the Bible. In Christian apologetics, the concept of "inerrancy" became an exercise in blind denial by excluding any formal error from the canonical text. The "progressive wing," which during the first session of the council soon emerged as a mighty force, soon set out to terminate this anxious clinging to the concept of inerrancy and replace it with a more relaxed view, one that allowed readers to question the historical, geographic, and scientific accuracy of the Bible. Was it, after all, essential for the Bible to be absolutely free of human error? It may even be appropriate for the human authors as veri auctores to show their limitations and be fallible in matters that would not compromise the transmission of divine truth into human concepts and language. The theologians who rewrote the first draft of *Dei verbum* soon eliminated the term "inerrancy" and replaced it with "truth," claiming to introduce a "positive" approach to the topic, an approach more consistent with the theology of revelation presented in chapters 1 and 2. This, of course, achieved little.

The question was inevitable: *What kind of truth* is meant? At this point the shadows of the past returned. The debates of Vatican I, the positions taken by Leo XIII in his *Providentissimus Deus*, and the rejected formulas of theologians such as Franzelin and Cardinal Newman were recalled as earlier attempts to materially limit the extent of inspiration to certain topics or assertions of the biblical text. Finally it happened: Franz Cardinal König of Vienna—a cardinal facing an ecumenical council—asserted publicly that the Bible contains errors. In retrospect, this intervention appears as a relatively minor event and barely a scandal. By now, Cardinal König's authority as an expert in Oriental studies has considerably faded, and his samples of "biblical errors," which had been known for a long time, were at best inconclusive. The veneer of his tactfully elegant Latin phrase (*a veritate deficere*) has also worn off. All that is remembered is that he admitted that "The Bible contains errors."

At the time, of course, the procedures went off track, and John XXIII stalled the document by taking it off the agenda. Ultimately, the topic was given a new chance. At the last session of the council, as a new debate took shape, the question of inerrancy resurfaced. This time, a new schema specified the truth that the Bible teaches unfailingly as "veritates salutares," or "truths which belong to (that is, which promote or effect) salvation." A significant minority reacted adversely, thinking that the formula was ambiguous. The objections raised in the first session reappeared: The new draft text limits inerrancy (and thus inspiration) to religious and moral statements. This time, however, the progressives were in sure majority, and the committee to which the issue returned stuck to its guns. It hoped that "veritates salutares" would eventually pass into the final text. It was, again, the papacy that saved the council from itself. Paul VI, admitting his own "perplessità" on the issue, ordered further study and reflection and asked for a new formulation.

The result was a phrase that won almost unanimous approval: "veritatem quam Deus nostrae salutis causa litteris consignari voluit," meaning: "truth that, for the sake of our salvation, God wanted to be put [namely, by the biblical authors[32]] in writing." This saved the document from ambiguity and possibly error as well. It has ultimately provided, however, no significant insights or true advancement for the issue under debate. On the one hand, the concept of "truth" in the document still remains undifferentiated and unspecified. Moreover, since the phrase "sine errore" was eventually reinserted into the text, "inerrancy" in its traditional sense also returned. Therefore, those who refused to accept Cardinal König's contention that the biblical texts are sometimes "deficient in truth" had every reason to agree with the amended text.[33] On the other hand (and this is no small matter for the postconciliar era), in some ambiguous translations and interpretations, *Dei verbum* misleadingly appears to teach that inerrancy covers only those statements that regard *our salvation*. One may say that this misinterpretation caught on early in the reception of the council and is being propagated even by recognized and first-rate scholars.[34]

Despite more than a century of bickering over the Bible's antiquated notions about the physical world and events of history as errors, the experts of the council did not manage to reformulate the issue of inerrancy. For the Church fathers and their medieval followers, the truth of the Bible was its Christological content, that is, a revealed truth offered to the reader, who was to embrace it with faith. In their precritical approach to history and science, they easily embraced a biblical view of reality. The first two chapters of *Dei verbum* improved this view by regarding biblical history as an "economy of salvation." Yet a number of issues remained obscure. To see how the Christological truth of the Bible extends itself to each and every part of its text (as the chief result of inspiration) would have demanded a new hermeneutics, for which the theologians of Vatican II were not yet prepared. The way in which this kind of revealed truth, the truth of the Bible, relates to the notion of scientific and historical truth that we pursue by modern scholarly research was not successfully explained. In this respect, the conciliar document constitutes no breakthrough. At best, it manages to diffuse some of the rationalistic challenges about "veritates profanae" by proposing a new *point of view*, maybe even a new method, for us to apply when probing the truthfulness of the Bible's propositional statements. *Dei verbum* might have indicated some paths by which the rationalist approach to the "truth of the Bible" may be transcended. It failed, however, to squarely confront the problem (implied in the "double authorship" of holy scripture) as it is rooted in the very structure of the economy of salvation: God chose to descend into the realm of human imperfection, where the light of truth is sparse and must exist in the penumbra of partial knowledge mixed with partial ignorance.

Inspiration and Incarnation

The patristic outline of salvation history puts into its center the incarnation of the Son as the peak of God's self-disclosure, which essentially achieves the divine plan and creates the highest and most intimate union between God and man. All previous anticipations (like the institutions and texts of the Old Testament) and later extensions (like the sacraments and the apostolic writings of the New Testament) draw their meaning and validity from this central event of "God becoming flesh." It is not quite clear when and with what clarity the ancient church saw an analogy between "God made man" (the incarnation) and "the Divine Logos becoming human word" by means of biblical inspiration. Is it in the "inspired author" (and the reader) or in the "inspired text" that human and divine elements are linked? And in what sense is this linkage analogous to the hypostatic union, so that we may speak of biblical Monophysites and Nestorians?[35] It seems that the Church fathers applied the analogy mostly to the inspired text,[36] pointing out its quasi-sacramental qualities.[37] Due to a broader prescholastic use of the word "sacramentum," we find explicit texts all the way up to the twelfth century, in which the biblical written word is said to be "a sacrament."[38] However, on the level of the inspired author, parallelism between the grace of incarnation and the charism of inspiration can be established only with more difficulty. Even if *Dei verbum* makes use of the patristic idea of divine "condescension" (*synkatabasis*),[39] it is unclear how this analogy operates. Does this parallelism illustrate God's humility to assume the *appearance* of human words or rather the permanent union between Himself and the physical world? In either case, does this truly mean proper analogy with the hypostatic union (the Word becoming flesh), or is it just a metaphor externally related to the Word made flesh who dwelt among us?[40]

Rahner's use of the term "Schriftwerdung" might throw light on the difficulties that arise from a direct comparison between inspiration and incarnation. For a correct understanding of the statement "the Word became flesh" (Jn 1:14), one needs to make clear that "the Logos" had meant the Son, the second divine person, and "flesh" meant Jesus' individual human nature and, thus, that the "Menschwerdung" took place on the personal level. But Schriftwerdung does not mean uniting the divine and the human authors in a similar process. Rather, it means that divine revelation becomes perceptible as a human message proclaimed, and at the end of the process it becomes written word, fixed and preserved with stable and unchangeable canonicity. Further reflection leads us to discover that the process of Schriftwerdung is not so much a parallel to Menschwerdung as it is the *continuation* and extension of the latter into the former. Schriftwerdung is not a parallel or an alternative mode for the Logos to plunge into the human realm (as if by an additional "katabasis") but a mode of transmitting Christ, the one and only incarnate Word, by means of spoken and written words. While in Menschwerdung the immutable God *enters history* in a flux of events that peak with a human being's individual life, in Schriftwerdung something of an opposite movement takes place: This flow of history becomes crystallized, solidified, and codified in a fixed text and canon. The latter event resembles the resurrection of Jesus more than his conception and birth. Schriftwerdung belongs to the objective side of inspiration, which modern treatises of biblical inspiration, those that focus only on the use of Saint Thomas's treatment of prophecy in the *Summa*, tend to lose sight of.

The Theology of the Old Testament

Some irony exists in the fact that chapter 4 of *Dei verbum*, a surprisingly short summary of the Christian outlook on the Jewish scriptures, was accepted and integrated into the document without major controversies or crises. The content of the chapter reflects, once again, a largely patristic point of view, which modern biblical scholarship, both inside and outside Catholic circles, has not been able to fully integrate into contemporary exegesis. In fact, while the preconciliar patristic ressourcement proclaimed the "unity of the two Testaments" as central, Old Testament scholars were much less enthusiastic to join ranks with a "Christian reading" of the Bible.[41]

Moreover, chapter 4 of the document is based almost entirely on the most ancient layers of Christian tradition about the Bible, which, due to the rise of critical scholarship, lost much ground and was eventually ignored by modern exegetes. Its medieval reception was resurrected in the monumental volumes of Henri de Lubac's *Exégèse médiévale* starting in 1959, just about the beginning of the council, but they never gained much attention in the postconciliar Catholic renewal. The English translation of these volumes had to wait for more than thirty years.

Dei verbum's approach to the Old Testament is best rendered in the first sentence of article 15: "The salvation plan of the Old Testament has been ordered for the main purpose of preparing the coming of Christ, the Redeemer of all and of the messianic kingdom, to announce prophetically this coming (see Lk 24:44; Jn 5:39; 1 Pet 1:10) and to set up for it signs through various types (see 1 Cor 10:12)." This approach results in an almost exclusively Christian view of the Old Testament books. The text continues: "The books of the Old Testament, in accordance with mankind's condition before the time of salvation inaugurated by Christ, make manifest to all the knowledge of God and of man, as well as the way in which God, being both just and merciful, deals with the human being" (*DV* 15).

It is remarkable how this document, when we view the Old Testament as *books*, focuses exclusively on its universal and ongoing relevance. The text offers no word about the role of Jewish exegesis or the meaning of these texts for their original or contemporary addressees. Equally astonishing is the fact that the Pontifical Biblical Commission's document of 2002, titled *About the Jewish People and Their Sacred Scriptures in the Christian Bible*, signified a full return of the pendulum to its opposite extreme by showing only minimal esteem for mainstream patristic exegesis and settling for a double track of meaning, one Jewish and one Christian, for the Old Testament, the latter being set up side by side with a Jewish reading of scripture, which can still be carried out from a perspective of mere expectation. In the Christian reading, Jesus is "for us still the One to come." Nonetheless, when He comes, "He will have the traits of the Jesus who has already come and is already present and active among us."

This effort of combining a positive appreciation of present-day Jewish exegesis with a Christological fulfillment of the Old Testament is hardly present in *Dei verbum*. After explaining the *historical* role of the scriptures for the Jewish people of old, the conciliar text grounds the "permanent value" (*perennem valorem*) of the Old Testament texts in a Christological perspective. Originally they prophetically anticipated the economy of salvation, but then this history *came to its term and end*, yet exhibited no resources for justifying a Jewish reading of the Bible. Moving in the opposite direction, the Biblical Commission's document states that such a "Jewish reading of the Hebrew Bible is both possible and necessary." Such a reading stands "in continuity with the Jewish Sacred Scriptures from the Second Temple period, a reading analogous to the Christian reading which developed in a parallel fashion." While I cannot fully discuss the Biblical Commission's document here, I must point out the basic features of its divergence from *Dei verbum* in this study:

1. The Biblical Commission made no attempt to integrate its new approach to the Jewish interpretation of scripture into the Catholic and especially patristic exegetical tradition. It is perplexing how new paths for dealing with Jewish exegesis may be opened without first studying patristic and medieval tradition on the rather complex issue of the "Judaica interpretatio."

2. The Biblical Commission's document might not have meant to say that both Jewish and Christian exegetical traditions are equally legitimate or should be embraced on equal footing. Actually, by referring to two different "faiths" (and stating in the same paragraph that the rabbinical traditions exclude faith in Jesus), its puzzling statements about "two irreducible" readings of the Old Testament may lead us to understand that by "readings" the document deals with nothing more than the literal sense, without engaging the reader's faith. The ancient sense of "littera," however, cannot be identified with either the modern literal sense or "the historical and critical meaning" that modern exegesis aims at.

3. The possibility remains that the Biblical Commission pursued a more pragmatic than theological goal. In that case, one must point out, also pragmatically, that Jewish-Christian cooperation in achieving a literal *reading* of the Bible spans a tradition of two thousand years. Its future cannot be meaningfully discussed without awareness of such a long-standing history and without exploration of the common elements of Jewish and Christian *faiths*, which, in the past and on both sides, transcended the positivistic historico-critical method of modern exegesis.

The last paragraph of chapter 4 (no. 16) is surprisingly and regrettably short. Using well-known and old formulas, it states the relationship of the two Testaments: The New Testament is hidden (*latet*) in the Old, while the Old shows its meaning (*patet*) in the New. Accordingly, the text continues, the proclamation of the Gospel recapitulates and resumes the texts of the Old Testament so that they both acquire a new meaning and obtain *their own* full meaning. In doing so, the two Testaments enlighten and explain each other.

In spite of its simple grammar, the meaning of this paragraph is complex and convoluted. It also leaves a number of questions unresolved. In particular, it lacks clarity about the sense in which the New Testament texts achieve the "fulfillment" of the Old. How do texts obtain a full meaning (*completam significationem*) in *other texts* so that this full meaning is indeed their own and is therefore neither added nor superimposed? Forty years later the Biblical Commission appeared rather perplexed about this "fulfillment" and stated that it is "an extremely complex notion" (no. 21, p. 48). Then, in a lengthy development, it took issue with various failed schemes, all termed "fundamentalist" and thus unacceptable.

At this point we realize why *Dei verbum* is incomplete: It should have provided more specific guidelines about the relationship of the two testaments, probably by appealing generally to Christology and specifically to the theandric nature of the acts of Christ. As acts performed by the Incarnate Son of God, they transcend the limitations of history and equally impact past and future. Having as their subject the divine Logos, they become retroactively and anticipatorily effective; this fact can validate their anticipatory and retrospective reading in the framework of a universal salvation economy.

The Treatment of the New Testament

The fifth chapter of *Dei verbum* is again short and profoundly steeped in patristic thought. It begins by extolling the superiority of the New Testament as that part of the Bible that presents God's word and salvific power in a preeminent way (*praecellenti modo*). The text does not hesitate to assert that Christ alone has "words of life eternal" (cf. Jn 6:68), as he came at the "fullness of time" (Gal 4:4), and the mystery he revealed may not be approached in any other way (cf. Eph 4:4–6).

Moreover, among the writings of the New Testament *the four canonical Gospels* are preeminent, for they give first-rate witness to the life and teaching of the Word incarnate. The scriptures are put on three different levels of dignity and importance, based on their closeness to Christ. On the highest level we find the four Gospels, then the rest of the apostolic writings, and finally the books of the Old Testament in two subcategories: law and prophets. This grouping of the Bible as a *graduated collection of books* is explicitly present in the patristic heritage. In his *Commentary on John*, Origen asks in what sense all scripture may be called "Gospel" and ends up with a similar hierarchy of biblical books. By this system, Origen subsumes all scripture under the one term "Gospel," meaning the proclamation of Christ in the humility of his Incarnation and in his glorious risen life.

The conciliar document also asserts the "apostolic origin of the four Gospels" (*DV* 18). The statement is nonambiguous: "The Church always held and everywhere holds" (*semper tenuit et ubique tenet*) this conviction, and it leaves little doubt that the council meant to affirm the apostolic origin of the Gospels as a tenet of faith taught by the consensus of all of the Church fathers and the magisterium.

The rest of article 18 further explains this statement. It uses the term "apostolici viri," which Tertullian used to express that the apostolic authorship of the Gospels does not necessarily imply literary authorship by one of the Twelve. The term, however, does mean that each Gospel takes its origin from apostolic preaching and is correctly attributed to either a specific apostle (Matthew or John) or one of the collaborators of the apostles (Mark and Luke). This is also the sense in which Saint Irenaeus understood the canonical gospels.[42]

In spite of *Dei verbum*'s statement to the contrary, the majority of leading Catholic biblical scholars in the postconciliar period began to call the canonical Gospels anonymous works. It became customary to regard the so-called superscriptions in the ancient manuscripts ("Gospel according to N.") as later additions without historical foundation. Martin Hengel's studies on the "Überschriften" of the gospels are still not known well enough in Catholic literature,[43] while the popularity of Raymond Brown's writings discouraged contrary opinions.[44] All of this happened because of the postconciliar shifts in Catholic scholarly positions on the authorship of the four Gospels, which the following points summarize:

1. The credibility of Papias's witness has decreased because of a curious alliance between modern critical scholarship and Eusebius's antimillenarist bias, which led Eusebius to make derogatory comments about Papias. Eusebius himself, however, never doubted Mark's ties to Peter's preaching or the fourth Gospel's Johannine origin. He criticized Papias only with regard to the attribution of the Book of Revelation to the apostle John, claiming that he was uninformed and had poor judgment. Similarly, by suggesting that perhaps *all* second-century sources on the Gospels (Justin, Irenaeus, Clement of Alexandria, Tertullian, and others[45]) depended on Papias, modern critics questioned all of the patristic evidence about the apostolic origin of the gospels.[46]

2. By adopting the two-source hypothesis and assuming that Matthew's Gospel depended on Mark, scholars judged it improbable that Matthew, an eyewitness, could have written a Gospel that relied on Mark, who was not an eyewitness. In addition, the early tradition (represented also by Papias) about an original Aramaic form of the Gospel of Matthew was ruled out by linguistic arguments that showed that the Greek text was not a translation from a Semitic original.

3. The identification of Luke's Gospel with "that of the Apostle Paul" was declared critically pointless since Paul knew very little about the historical Jesus. Furthermore, the Church fathers' tendency to identify Luke's work with

Paul's εὐαγγέλιον μοῦ was thought to be based on an anachronistic understanding of the word εὐαγγέλιον for in the first century εὐαγγέλιον meant an
oral message of salvation, and only in the second century did it begin to
connote a literary composition. The Pauline link in Luke's Gospel was also
discredited by showing that the image of Paul in Acts was historically inac-
curate, and thus neither Acts nor Luke's Gospel could be attributed to an
author who knew Paul. After that there was no reason left for considering
Luke's Gospel as apostolic.

    4. The "Quaestio Johannaea"—the debate on the authorship of the Fourth
Gospel—has been solved, or rather dissolved, by identifying "the beloved
disciple" with an anonymous figure of the early Church and the "John" of the
Johannine writings with one or several early church figures, presbyters, and/or
prophets but certainly not the son of Zebedee. On this point a claim was
introduced that John the Apostle suffered early martyrdom. Using old liturgical calendars and the assumption that Jesus' prediction of the martyrdom of
the sons of Zebedee must have been based in the synoptic tradition as a
vaticinium ex eventu, scholars began to assume that the early church preferred
to suppress the tradition about John's martyrdom rather than accept a non-
apostolic authorship for the fourth Gospel.

    These four points permeate the present state of research as a whole. They
summarize a definite tendency in Catholic biblical scholarship that runs
contrary to *Dei verbum*. The document abstained from discussing the shades of
meaning for the concept of literary authorship in antiquity and intended to
keep an open mind about the role of further redactors and editors. Unfortunately, in the postconciliar climate, the open-ended approach of the
document was misinterpreted as a signal that the doctrinal guidelines of the
past have lost their validity; thus, denial of the apostolic origin of the canonical
gospels apparently became *opinio communis* in Catholic publications.[47]

    An even more damaging conflict between *Dei verbum* and its Catholic
reception concerns the historicity of the canonical Gospels, which the document addresses in article 19. This text is largely based on the introductory
verses of the Lukan double work, Luke 1:1–4 and Acts 1:1–4. Without making
explicit statements about the literary genre of a gospel, it focuses on the process
by which the apostolic preaching about Jesus was shaped and solidified into
stable forms of a mostly oral tradition and was eventually channeled into four
literary works that later became the canonical Gospels. The document emphasizes that this tradition pays equal attention to "deeds and words" (*fecit et
docuit, fecerat et docuerat*). This view has been widely contradicted by scholars
who use the Gospel of Thomas as a "fifth gospel" and overlook the fact that this
writing does not contain narratives and lacks interest in Jesus' "deeds," including his passion and resurrection. Rejecting the Gnostic trend, *Dei verbum*
cannot recognize the apocryphal gospels as gospels, either in the form of
revelatory discourses or dialogues between Jesus and his disciples; yet with a
fairly tolerant attitude, it did not exclude the possibility that, at the composition
of the canonical Gospels, collections of sayings (the so-called Testimonia) had

been preserved either in the oral or written form and eventually influenced the composition of the canonical Gospels.

Dei verbum insists that if and when the authors of the canonical Gospels participated in the process that leads from oral to written forms of tradition, they selected only a portion of the available material, which they then recorded in writing (*auctores conscripserunt quaedam . . . seligentes*). The document recognizes the possibility that the original Gospel writers used a mixture of oral and written sources (*e multis aut ore aut iam scripto traditis*), yet it clearly asserts that the composition of the Gospels relies merely on the memories of eyewitnesses and also on a fuller understanding (*pleniore intelligentia*) provided by the disciples' postresurrection encounters with Jesus and enlightenment by the "Spirit of truth" (*eventibus gloriosis Christi instructi et lumine Spiritus veritatis edocti*).

Indeed, *Dei verbum* collects a number of insights formed by recent scholarship about the process of redactional activities that accompanied the formation of the Gospels. The model that *Dei verbum* presents includes compositional changes of the material either for the sake of topical or doctrinal synthesis (*quaedam in synthesim redigentes*) or accommodation to the needs of the local communities (*vel statui ecclesiarum attendendo explanantes*) or even for retaining an exhortative focus of preaching and teaching (*formam denique praeconii retinentes*).

One can confidently state that the document provides a balanced methodology by which the transmission of the Jesus tradition appears as a possibly complex and protracted process that allows a number of alternative hypothetical scenarios and prescribes no particular source theory. It certainly does not impose a specific synoptic source theory; it does not even mention Matthean or Marcan priority. It avoids references to both ancient and recent theories about the chronological order of the Gospels. But, equally important, *Dei verbum* does not speak about the evangelists' "creative" expansion of tradition, the "retrojection" of postresurrection prophetic utterances into the activities of the earthly Jesus, or the formation of Dominical sayings from christologically rewritten Old Testament material and apocryphal texts. No mention is made of a possible accretion to the Jesus tradition from creative prophecy and exegesis for the sake of solving doctrinal or moral problems for the early church. Yet it allows much room for the activities of the Paraclete teaching the apostolic communities the "fullness of truth" (cf. Jn 16:13), without allowing the insertion of fictional narratives or the invention or exaggeration of miraculous happenings and gratuitous biographical details. While abstaining from drawing a concrete division between authentic and apocryphal (oral) tradition, the document consistently embraces the whole canonical Jesus tradition as historical and normative and refuses to allow the revision of the Church's understanding of Jesus through extracanonical sources.

Concluding Remarks

A present-day review of the theological content of *Dei verbum* leads us back to a list of satisfactory gains and accomplishments, as well as to a set of *desiderata*,

that is, goals to be reached by further study and renewed emphasis on introductory disciplines for the study of the Bible:

1. By its most significant impact on the theological thinking of the Church,
Dei verbum has restored the outlook of patristic and medieval tradition by
demanding that scriptural inspiration be handled in the context of revelation
and that revelation be looked at in the context of a salvation economy. This approach opened up for modern times a wealth of traditional theological thinking: texts of patristic exegesis, preaching, catechesis, liturgical texts and rites,
as well as the whole world of ancient spirituality, including monastic theology.

2. The discrepancies that divide modern historical consciousness from the
biblical outline of history became more apparent, requiring a new approach.
We face more acutely than ever before the need to reconcile the current history
of religions, the philosophy of religion, the theology of culture and history, or
simply the theology of "man" and of "time" with those precritical assumptions
in which Christian theology has been embedded throughout its development.

3. Recent decades have seen renewed efforts at a modern attempt of returning to the unity of the Bible as a framework of interpretation. Often called
"canonical interpretation" or "canonical criticism," this new approach is
connected most importantly with Brevard Childs and his vision of biblical
interpretation. The theology of *Dei verbum* has much to learn from and much
to offer this trend. Both the views expressed in *Dei verbum* and the foundational
ideal of canonical interpretation are honestly committed to the use of historical
criticism and the reading of the Bible in the framework of Christian faith, but
they also steer clear of the agnostic or skeptical presuppositions of the Enlightenment. At the same time, canonical interpretation has not yet confronted
the fullness of the patristic heritage in terms of the Rule of Faith, the context of
sacred tradition, and the magisterium.

4. *Dei verbum* initiated a new synthesis of biblical inspiration, but the
postconciliar years were unable to follow up on these initiatives in any significant way. Our understanding of the patristic tradition of inspiration is still
fragmentary and obscure. We cannot tell with clarity what the Church's tradition *really* taught about the divine authorship of the biblical books, how the
divine and human sides of biblical authorship are related, and how the human
intermediaries of revelation are to be seen in their multiple functions of initiating and furthering the written records of divine revelation. In this regard we
may list the following specific needs:

a. We must see how the formation of the Bible transmits the charism of
the prophets and the Apostles as intermediaries of the divine Word to
hagiographers, the biblical authors constituting written records of revelation for the ongoing spiritual nourishment of God's people.

b. We need to see how the "subjective inspiration" that affects the hagiographers has resulted in biblical texts (sacred or inspired books in the
sense of an "objective inspiration") and, finally, in the Church's firm
possession of the canon.

c. We must revisit the issue of "verbal inspiration," which transcends both precritical naiveté and critical arrogance with a postcritical theological sobriety that recognizes the importance of the canonical text's accuracy and the Church's ongoing vigilance over the scriptural text.

d. We must explore the ecumenical relevance and potential of the New Testament canon, one of the few elements of the Christian heritage that, in the course of church history, has survived most of the storms of disunity and disintegration.[48] It may be of importance to investigate the causes that made this collection of twenty-seven books resistant to every force of division so that today all Christian schools of theology are able to use the same critical text of the New Testament. We should see whether we can find paths that lead to common avenues of interpretation and theological methodology beyond a common canon and canonical text.

NOTES

1. J. Ratzinger, "Origin and Background," commentary on *Dei verbum*, in *Commentary on the Documents of Vatican II*, vol. 3, ed. H. Vorgrimler (New York: Herder, 1969), 155.

2. One of the best representatives of such books is H. Höpfl and B. Gut, *Introductio generalis in sacram scripturam* (Rome: Arnado, 1950), further expanded and edited first by A. Metzinger, then by L. Leloir, and used until the late 1960s. Similar books were compiled by J.-M. Lagrange, A. Merk, J.-M. Vosté, A. Bea, S. Tromp, and others. Bea and Tromp played a major role in writing the first schema of *Dei verbum*.

3. "De exsistentia inspirationis" begins on p. 1 of Höpfl and Gut, *Introductio generalis*. The same content appears in nos. 1 and 2 of *Divino afflante*.

4. This issue follows in the encyclical under no. 3. In Höpfl and Gut, *Introductio generalis*, the chapter "De extensione inspirationis" begins only on p. 63, as this textbook gives logical priority to the nature of inspiration.

5. The section "De natura inspirationis" begins in Höpfl and Gut, *Introductio generalis*, 40, while the encyclical begins speaking of the influence of the Holy Spirit on the authors in no. 5.

6. Cf. Höpfl and Gut, *Introductio generalis*, 49. In the encyclical *Divino afflante*, Saint Thomas's doctrine of instrumental causality is markedly absent. Instead, quotations from the Church fathers illustrate the idea of "divine words in human language" (no. 41) and the concept of "divine condescension."

7. It explicitly speaks of "theological" and "spiritual" (even "mystical") interpretation built upon the "analogy of faith" (no. 24).

8. Cf. R. Aubert, *La théologie catholique au milieu du XXe siècle* (Paris: Aubier, 1956).

9. This new group included, among others, Lucien Cerfaux, Carlo Colombo, Yves Congar, Aloys Grillmeyer, Charles Moeller, Karl Rahner, Joseph Ratzinger, and Otto Semmelroth.

10. The alliance of two powerful intellectual trends in the Church, the "biblical movement" and the "patristic movement," became chiefly responsible for animating the theology of Vatican II. They enabled the church to participate in the modern-day advances of historical and linguistic studies. One may also say that the rediscovery of the Greek Church fathers (among them most importantly Irenaeus, Origen, and the

Cappadocians) made the most powerful and longest-lasting impact on modern Catholic theology, including specifically the theology of revelation and a new outlook on exegesis. It became clear that as early as the second century a brilliant vision of Christian theology began to unfold: a vision of a "sacred oeconomia" (history of salvation and revelation), capable of presenting a "gradual development" of revelation in which both the element of human imperfections and the feature of God's gracious condescension appear to be components of God's self-disclosure.

11. Of course, this way of transcending *Divino afflante* the same time, a fruit of the study of the literary genres, which the same encyclical strongly encouraged.

12. Baltimore: John Hopkins, 1957.

13. One might say that the council's caution was eventually vindicated if we recall the enthusiasm that surrounded the works of Teilhard de Chardin, which reached their peak of popularity just before and during the council but soon lost their appeal.

14. One must admit that both the biblical text and tradition frequently use verbs like "says" or "said" when quoting a written text. Nevertheless, it appears intentional that the concept of inspiration is brought up only after surveying the whole of revelation, including its fullness in Christ.

15. The division of the authors into "apostoli" and "(viri) apostolici" comes as early as Tertullian, who referred to the four Gospels in his *Adversus marcionem* and named Matthew and John "apostoli" and Luke and Mark "apostolici": "Denique nobis fidem ex apostolis Johannes et Matthaeus insinuant, ex apostolicis Lucas et Marcus instaurant." *Adversus marcionem* IV.2.2 (*Sources chrétiennes*, 456, 68).

16. In his book *Inspiration in the Bible: Quaestiones disputatae* (New York: Herder and Herder, 1961), Karl Rahner states: "It follows that by willing and creating the Apostolic Church and its constitutive elements with a formal, absolute, salvation-historic and eschatological will, God wills and creates the Scriptures in such a way that He becomes their inspiring originator and author (50). Immediately after the formulation of this thesis, Rahner makes it clear that this "definition of inspiration" applies to the Old Testament just as well. He does not mean that scripture would become scripture only in retrospect by canonization (as if canonicity could *replace* the notion of inspiration) but that the process by which scripture comes about ("Schriftwerdung") integrally extends itself to the formation of the canon. Therefore, also in the case of the Old Testament, the fact of biblical inspiration is revealed with certitude and full clarity only at the coming of Christ. Only then does the prophetic message that prepares his coming become manifest, and the identity of the inspired books become established by the ministry of the Church.

17. These two uses of the expression ἀπ' ἀρχῆς in the New Testament well express what the original apostolic message meant for Luke and John. That this foundational preaching needs to be written down so that the church may obtain solid certainty (ἀσφάλεια) is emphasized by Luke (1:4).

18. *Dei verbum* has therefore succeeded in pointing out the specific characteristics of the Christian belief in the scriptures, which helps us to better understand that Christian theology about God's Word necessarily differs in some essential points from Jewish thought. Nor can Jewish and Christian canons coincide in content and meaning.

19. A. Bea, "'Deus auctor S. scripturae.' Herkunft und Bedeutung der Formel," *Angelicum* 20 (1943): 16–31.

20. Nor did he examine the shades of meaning that "auctor" possessed or, most importantly, what the corresponding terms meant in the Greek tradition.

21. Two aspects are usually overlooked in the discussion. First, the word "auctor" connotes authority, and the Bible is certainly endowed with divine authority. Second,

ancient usage (and spelling) has mixed the words "auctor" and "actor." For example, in Saint Bernard's fifty-sixth sermon on the Song of Songs (*SCC* 56, 1, *Leclercq* II, 114), Christ is said to be the "auctor" of the scriptural text, but the meaning of the word is "actor." Cf. Denis Farkasfalvy, *L'inspiration biblique dans la théologie de saint Bernard* (Rome: Herder, 1964), 34.

22. Luis Alonso Schökel, *The Inspired Word: Scripture in the Light of Language and Literature* (New York: Herder, 1967). This English edition, prepared by Francis Martin, is more complete than the original Spanish text, *La palabra inspirada* (Barcelona: Herder, 1966).

23. Alonso Schökel even observes that the "literary analogy" of a "divine author" is fairly absent from ancient Church fathers, with the possible exception of Justin Martyr, whose text, however, does not fit the modern-day concept of "someone writing through an intermediary." In ancient texts, reference to God as an "author" is at best a mixed metaphor, for the divine "author" is usually described as someone *speaking* but not necessarily "dictating," just communicating or declaring certain statements while the writing is done only by the *human* author. In all of these texts it is not clear to what extent a patristic witness would impute literary authorship to both the divine and human agent. Moreover, when God is said to be "dictating" to a person who then writes the text, it is not clear at all how far this metaphor is meant to go and to what extent the word *dictare* is meant to convey the sense of a modern dictation or only a wider sense of authorship as in the German verb "dichten." All of these considerations add up to the realization that we need many more detailed studies in order to answer the question, "What did the Church fathers really say about God as the *auctor* of the Scriptures?"

24. *Summa theologiae* I, q. 110; *Quaestiones Quodlibet* 6, 16; 14 ad 5.

25. H. Urs Von Balthasar, *Summa theologica: Die deutsche Thomas, Ausgabe*, vol. 23 (Vienna: Herder, 1958), 359.

26. This text, which closely repeats the statement of the Decree of the Jacobites given at the Council of Florence in 1441 (D 706), has also found its way into *Dei verbum*.

27. I quote only a few examples:

Quoniam autem dictis nostris consonat praedicatio apostolorum et Domini magisterium et Prophetarum adnuntiatio, et Apostolorum dictatio et Legilatoris ministratio, unum eundumque Deum Patrem laudantium. (Irenaeus, *Adversus haereses* II, 58, 2)

How could the Scriptures have testified of Him (= the Logos), unless all are from the one and same Father? (ibid. IV, 20, 1)

Tam enim apostolus Moyses quam apostoli prophetae, aequanda est auctoritas utriusque officii ab uno eodem domino apostolorum et prophetarum. (Tertullian, *Adversus marcionem* IV, 24, 8–9)

28. These examples are meant to illustrate Rahner's statement: "If God is to be the literary author of the Scriptures, He is, if we may formulate it in this way, a categorical and not a transcendental cause" (*Inspiration in the Bible*, 15).

29. Rahner has a few well-formulated sentences about the correct application of the concept of instrumentality to inspiration: "It is precisely not a question of the instrumentality of a secretary in regard to the author, but of a human authorship which remains completely and absolutely unimpaired, which is permeated, embraced but not diminished by the divine authorship. Only in this sense is it an instrument of God.

And it is an instrument in such a way that the instrumentality of the writer, linked with the divine authorship, does not only tolerate, but also demands the human authorship, and that there would be no point in divine authorship if man were but a secretary" (ibid., 15).

30. Paragraph 11. *Dei verbum* contains no attempt to further a collective concept of inspiration, not even in the form in which Karl Rahner presented it in *Inspiration in the Bible*.

31. By definition, if a text is produced under the influence of divine inspiration, then God's influence on the writer must trickle down all the way to the text and affect the very words of scriptures. And, in fact, the time and effort spent on critical textual issues seems to indicate a conviction that every bit of verbal nuance in the biblical texts matters.

32. This is the meaning of a last-minute change of the active *consignare* into the passive *consignari*.

33. Vorgrimler's commentary translates it as "lacking accuracy," but the expression *deficit a veritate* is much stronger, for it contains the noun meaning "truth."

34. See, for example, Raymond E. Brown in his most influential *The Critical Meaning of the Bible* (New York: Paulist Press, 1981), 18–19. He suggests that the ambiguity came from a conscious "juxtaposition of more conservative older formulations with more open recent formulations." A vicious footnote (18n41) ridicules those "for whom it is a doctrinal issue that the Church never changes" and recalls Galileo, who, when told that it was a doctrinal issue that the earth does not move, officially changed his position while whispering sotto voce "E pur si mouve (Nevertheless, it moves)." This is a sad performance. The legend quoted about Galileo is correctly "Eppure si muove" (so much for the author as a linguist), but the statement is widely recognized as apocryphal: It never happened (so much for the author as a critical historian.) The charge that the council was purposely misguiding the faithful may be best left without any comment.

35. Cf. Alonso Schökel, *Inspired Word*, 52–53, with bibliography on p. 88.

36. One of the early studies was by J. H. Crehan, "The Analogy between *Dei Verbum incarnatum* and *Dei Verbum scriptum* in the Fathers," *Journal of Theological Studies* 6 (1955): 87–90.

37. Among the first to point out that Origen has initiated this parlance was H. de Lubac, who greatly influenced most of the Church fathers and the monastic Middle Ages. Cf. the chapter "Les incorporations du Logos," in H. de Lubac, *Histoire et esprit* (Paris: Aubier, 1953), 336–63.

38. So, for example, Saint Bernard comments on the first verse of the Songs of Songs as *"sermonis huius profundissimum sacramentum"* (*SCC* I, 4, *Leclercq* I, 4).

39. The text quotes Saint John Chrysostom, *Hom in Gen 3:1*, 16, 2 (*PG* 53, 134).

40. In fact, in Origen and his followers we find texts that compare the letter of the scriptural word to the Flesh of the Word, but in the sense of a tool of manifestation or appearance (his vestments), and not nature taken up as his human nature was. See the following texts: *"Secundum litteram quae tamquam caro verbi est et indumentum divinitatis eius." Hom in Lev 1:1* (*PG* 12, 405a–b). By Ambrose: *"Et fortasse vestimenta verbi sunt sermons scripturarum." Hom in Lc 8:13* (*CCL* 14, 219); by Bernard: *"Vestimentum profecto spiritus littera est et caro Verbi." Ad milites Templi* VII, 13 (*Leclercq* III, 226).

41. Cf., for example, the approach proposed by Célestin Charlier, *La lecture chrétienne de la Bible* (Maredsous: Editions de Maredsous, 1950).

42. The short paragraph in Irenaeus (*Adv. haer.*, III, 1) expresses such a clear logical sequence:

(1) Matthew preached the gospel and put it in writing in Aramaic—during that time Peter and Paul preached in Rome—
(2) After their death (= ἔξοδος) Mark gave written form to Peter's preaching, and
(3) Luke, a companion of Paul, wrote another gospel—
(4) Finally John, the Lord's disciple who rested on his breast, wrote a gospel in Ephesus of Asia Minor.

43. *Studies in the Gospel of Mark* (London: SCM Press, 1985).

44. *The Critical Meaning of the Bible* (New York: Paulist Press 1981), 69–71.

45. The anti-Marcionite prologues and the Muratorian Canon could be included as well.

46. It is routinely overlooked that Papias *quotes another older tradition*, and thus the hypothesis of making Papias the "creative" source of all of this tradition is absurd. Moreover, Hengel has shown that the superscriptions and Papias's source ("the presbyter") must have been contemporaries; hence we have multiple attestations of an older tradition.

47. See, for example, Daniel J. Harrington, *The Gospel of Matthew* (Collegeville, Minn.: Liturgical Press, 1991), 8. However, the pendulum might have begun to move back in support of the position of *Dei verbum*, as, for example, in a new German publication by Hans-Joachim Schulz, *The aspostolische Herkunft der Evangelien* (Vienna: Herder, 1995).

48. The canon of the New Testament is essentially a product of the second century's anti-Gnostic battle, in which, among other things, the Apostle's Creed also obtained its shape. In spite of the controversies that later enveloped Revelation and Hebrews, all Christian Bibles today have the same table of contents, and no proposals of altering the New Testament canon have received significant support.

5

Theology of the Liturgy

Pamela E. J. Jackson

The constitution on the sacred liturgy *Sacrosanctum concilium* became the first document promulgated by the Second Vatican Council on December 4, 1963, having been approved by a vote of 2,147 to 4. Those who drafted the schema of *Sacrosanctum concilium* believed that it was necessary for the constitution to be built on a solid theological foundation.[1] Citing the 1947 encyclical *Mediator Dei*, they affirmed that the sacred liturgy did not consist merely in the outward aspect of worship, nor could it be reduced to a list of ecclesiastical laws for proper performance of the rites; rather—as exercise of the priesthood of Christ in his Mystical Body, the Church—the liturgy had profound theological significance.[2] The theology of the liturgy in *Sacrosanctum concilium* has been described as its principal part, which will last for centuries.[3] From this theology, *Sacrosanctum concilium* then derived the principles, or norms, on which the renewal of the liturgy in accord with the council's purposes should be based;[4] on the basis of these norms, the constitution decreed specific changes in the celebration of the liturgy.

Sacrosanctum concilium's theology of the liturgy is thus the key to understanding both what the council fathers believed the liturgy to be and how they envisioned it being celebrated. This chapter first summarizes this theology and then considers the sources that informed it, its relationship to the theological tradition that preceded it, and how this theology was intended to serve as basis for renewal. The constitution's theology of the liturgy is found primarily in article 2 of the introduction and at the beginnings of its first five chapters: articles 5–13 of chapter 1 (General Principles for the Renewal and Fostering of the Sacred Liturgy);[5] articles 47–48 of chapter 2 (The Most Holy Mystery of the Eucharist); articles 59–61 of chapter 3 (The Other Sacraments and Sacramentals); articles 83–85 (The Divine Office); and articles 102–106 (The Liturgical Year).[6] In chapter 1, after the theological exposition of the nature of the liturgy, *Sacrosanctum concilium* provides norms for the renewal of the liturgy. In chapters 2–5 the theological summary is followed by decrees for particular reforms.

As the first document promulgated by the council, *Sacrosanctum concilium* begins by summarizing in its first article the purposes Pope John XXIII gave for calling the council and affirming that the renewal and fostering of the liturgy have a role in accomplishing these purposes.[7] To explain why attention to the liturgy will help the council achieve these goals (such as deepening the Christian life of the faithful), the constitution's second article provides a preliminary summary of the ecclesiological significance of the liturgy. The liturgy, above all the Eucharist, is the outstanding means whereby the faithful can "by vital activity enter into," and manifest to others, the mystery of Christ and the real nature of the true Church.[8] This nature is simultaneously human and divine, visible and endowed with invisible realities, fervent in action and free for contemplation, present in this world and in pilgrimage to the next—all in such a way that the human is subordinated to the divine, the visible to the invisible, and so on.[9] Because the work of redemption is made present in the liturgy, the liturgy builds those within it into a dwelling place for God in the Spirit, while strengthening their power to preach Christ, and thus manifests the Church as a sign to the nations.[10]

The primary exposition of the theology of the liturgy in *Sacrosanctum concilium* is found in the opening section of chapter 1. Here the constitution explains "the nature of the liturgy and its importance in the Church's life" (as this section is titled) by showing the liturgy's place in the ongoing drama of salvation history.[11] The God who wanted all to be saved and know the truth called a people, did mighty works to deliver them, made a covenant with them, and spoke to them by the prophets—all as preparation for the culmination of his saving work in his Son, Jesus Christ, who made it possible for human beings to be reconciled to God. Christ "achieved his task of redeeming humanity and giving perfect glory to God, principally by the paschal mystery of his blessed passion, resurrection from the dead, and glorious ascension."[12]

In order to communicate the redemption and reconciliation he won to those he won it for, Christ sent the apostles empowered by the Holy Spirit, even as he himself had been sent by the Father. The apostles not only preached the gospel of Christ's saving work but also brought it into effect through the sacrifice and the sacraments, around which all liturgical life revolves. Thus, in baptism Christians are inserted into the Paschal mystery; united with Christ in his dying and rising, the baptized receive the Spirit of Adoption, which enables them, now reconciled, to call upon God as Father and be true worshippers. Similarly, from the very beginning the Church has "never failed" to come together to celebrate the Paschal mystery by celebrating the Eucharist, "in which 'the victory and triumph of his death are again made present.'"[13]

By presenting the liturgy of the Church in the context of salvation history, *Sacrosanctum concilium* demonstrates that "the liturgy is in fact the economy of salvation prolonging itself through ritual and sacramental acts. It is Jesus who passes in the midst of his own and continues his redemptive work. . . . The liturgy actualizes salvation in all times and places."[14] Far from being merely a set of outward actions, the liturgy is "the point at which the mystery of Christ continues to operate" and thus the heart of the Church's life.[15]

Sacrosanctum concilium, article 7, explains that in order to accomplish this, "Christ is always present in his Church, especially in its liturgical celebrations," in four ways: (1) at Mass, both in the person of his minister, the priest, who presides *in persona Christi*, and above all under the Eucharistic elements; (2) in the sacraments; (3) in his word, through the proclamation of scripture in the liturgy; and (4) when the Church prays and sings, as he promised in Matthew 18:20.[16] Christ unites the Church to himself through the liturgy, in which God is perfectly glorified and worshippers are made holy (*SC* 7.1–2).

The liturgy, then, is an exercise of Christ's priestly office, where "by means of signs perceptible to the senses, human sanctification is signified and brought about in ways proper to each of these signs," and the whole public worship is performed by the Mystical Body of Jesus Christ, head and members.[17] Therefore, "every liturgical celebration, because it is an action of Christ the priest and of his Body which is the Church, is a sacred action surpassing all others," compared to which no other action is as efficacious for human sanctification and the glorification of God.[18]

Since in the liturgy, Christ the high priest is present uniting his Body to himself in giving perfect glory to the Father, the liturgy has an eschatological dimension; those worshipping in the liturgy participate in a "foretaste of that heavenly liturgy celebrated in the holy city of Jerusalem toward which we journey as pilgrims."[19] Having situated its explanation of the nature of the liturgy in the context of salvation history, beginning with God's mighty works under the Old Covenant to draw his people back to himself, *Sacrosanctum concilium*, in article 8, brings the narration of salvation history to its eschatological culmination: "The liturgy is the continuation of the work which Christ, on ending his visible presence on earth, committed to the Church and which remains her commission till he comes again. Thus it is at the same time the beginning of participation in the eternal liturgy of the City of God."[20]

Sacrosanctum concilium, articles 5–8, also throw into relief the Trinitarian character of God's work in salvation history focused in the liturgy. The Father sends the Son, who sends the Holy Spirit to indwell believers, to draw them to himself and lead them back to the Father so that they may praise him forever in the heavenly Jerusalem; through the sensible signs of the liturgy, Christ pours out the Spirit, unites believers to himself, and "renders perfect worship to God by bringing everything back to the Father."[21]

Having described how the liturgy functions as means through which Christ's saving work is mediated to his disciples until his return, the constitution acknowledges that the liturgy by itself does not make up the entire activity of the Church.[22] *Sacrosanctum concilium*, article 9, explains that the Church must preach the gospel of salvation to unbelievers, so that they can believe and repent in order to enter into the liturgy.[23] The Church also prepares believers for the sacraments and teaches them how to live as faithful disciples of Christ.

However, *Sacrosanctum concilium*, article 10, affirms, "the liturgy is the summit toward which the activity of the Church is directed; at the same time it is the fount from which all the Church's power flows." It is the *summit* because the ultimate goal of the apostolic works described in *Sacrosanctum concilium*, article 9, is that all who are reconciled to God in baptism should come together and praise him in the Church and participate in the Paschal sacrifice and feast. The liturgy is the *source* of the Church's power because the renewal of the Lord's covenant with his people in the Eucharist draws the faithful into the compelling love of Christ, and thus "grace is poured forth upon us as from a fountain; the liturgy is the source for achieving in the most effective way possible human sanctification and God's glorification, the end to which all the Church's other activities are directed."[24]

In order for the liturgy to be fully effective in the lives of the faithful, they must have the proper dispositions to enter into it with integrity and be able to cooperate with the grace poured forth in it; this means pastors should take care that worshippers understand what God is doing in the liturgy, are actively giving themselves to that, and are bearing fruit from the grace that is given.[25] In addition to communal liturgical prayer, Christians are called to "pray to the Father in secret," to "pray without ceasing," and to "bear in their bodies the dying of Jesus."[26] Further, popular devotions that are approved are strongly commended; they should "harmonize with the liturgical seasons, accord with the sacred liturgy, [be] in some way derived from it, and lead the people to it, since, in fact, the liturgy by its very nature far surpasses any of them" (*SC* 13).

Within *Sacrosanctum concilium*'s treatment of the nature and importance of the liturgy in articles 5–13, article 7 on the presence and action of Christ in the liturgy has been described as the key article:[27] The articles preceding article 7's affirmations concerning the nature of the liturgy and its special efficacy are understood as leading up to and preparing for those affirmations, while the articles following (which treat the importance of the liturgy and its place in the life of the Church) are seen as flowing from them.[28] This exposition of the nature of the liturgy in general at the beginning of chapter 1 is complemented by summaries of the theology of various aspects of the liturgy at the beginnings of chapters 2–5.

In articles 47–48 *Sacrosanctum concilium* expands on its central way of speaking of the Eucharist: as the sacrifice of Christ and his Church (clergy and laity) in its relation to the Paschal mystery.[29] The language employed (Eucharistic sacrifice of the body and blood of the Savior, Paschal banquet, table of the Lord's body) makes clear that, as a sacrificial meal, the Eucharist culminates with consuming the victim.[30] *Sacrosanctum concilium* affirms that because Jesus instituted the Eucharist to perpetuate the sacrifice of the cross throughout the ages and to entrust to the Church, his bride, a grace-filled memorial of his death and resurrection, when the faithful are present at this mystery of faith, they should not be like strangers or silent spectators. Rather, through a good apprehension of the mystery through the rites and prayers, they should participate in the sacred action "conscious of what they are doing, with devotion and full involvement."[31] They should experience learning from God's word and being nourished by Christ's body. They should give thanks to God, and, "offering the immaculate Victim, not only through the hands of the priest, but also with him, they should learn to offer themselves as well";[32] and, day by day, through Christ the Mediator, they should be brought together in union with God and each other until finally God is all in all.

The constitution develops its teaching on the sacraments at the beginning of chapter 3. Article 59 explains that while the purpose of the sacraments is to make people holy, build up the body of Christ, and give worship to God, because they are signs they instruct. Sacraments both require faith, and also, by words and objects, they "nourish, strengthen and express it."[33] Not only do they impart grace, but the very act of celebrating them best disposes the faithful to receive that grace fruitfully, to worship God fittingly, and to exercise charity. Because such grace is given through these sacred signs, it is of the highest importance that the faithful easily understand the signs, and frequent with greatest eagerness the sacraments that were instituted to nourish the Christian life. *Sacrosanctum concilium*, article 61, concludes that for the faithful who are well disposed, the effect of the sacraments and sacramentals[34] "is that almost every event in their lives is made holy by divine grace that flows from the paschal mystery of Christ's passion, death and resurrection," from which all of the sacraments and sacramentals derive their power; there is almost no proper use of material things that cannot be directed to human sanctification or the praise of God.

The theological character of the Liturgy of the Hours is treated at the beginning of chapter 4. *Sacrosanctum concilium* presents the Liturgy of the Hours as being a continuation of the priestly work of Christ, the High Priest, in which he joins the Church to himself in unceasingly praising God and interceding for the salvation of the world (*SC* 83). When Christ became incarnate, he brought to earth the hymn of praise sung eternally in heaven so all humanity could sing it with him (*SC* 83); the Church arranged the Liturgy of the Hours so the whole course of day and night could be consecrated by the praise of God. When priests (and certain designated others) pray the Liturgy of the Hours, "it is the very prayer that Christ himself, together with his Body, addresses to the Father" (*SC* 84). Those who are responsible for praying the Liturgy of the Hours are both fulfilling a duty of the Church and participating in the highest honor of the Bride of Christ, "for by offering their praise to God they are standing before God's throne in the name of the Church, their mother" (*SC* 85). Praying the Liturgy of the Hours is also a way for priests to heed Saint Paul's exhortation to "pray without ceasing," and to unite their minds and hearts to Christ the true Vine so their pastoral work can bear fruit, since "apart from me you can do nothing."[35]

Sacrosanctum concilium fleshes out the theological meaning of the liturgical year in articles 102–106. The constitution explains that the Church celebrates Christ's saving work by means of liturgical commemorations on fixed days throughout the year (*SC* 102). "By a tradition handed down from the apostles and having its origin from the very day of Christ's resurrection, the Church celebrates the paschal mystery every eighth day, which, with good reason, bears the name of the Lord's Day, or Sunday" (*SC* 106). This weekly coming together on the Lord's Day to hear God's Word and participate in the Eucharist and thus make memorial of the passion, resurrection, and glorification of the Lord Jesus, is the foundation and nucleus of the entire liturgical year (*SC* 106). Once a year, the Church commemorates the passion and resurrection of the Lord with the greatest solemnity—on Easter. Throughout each year, the Church "unfolds the whole mystery of Christ" from his incarnation to the expectation of his return (*SC* 102). These liturgical celebrations are not simply occasions for thinking about things that happened in the past; rather, "Recalling thus the mysteries of redemption, the Church opens to the faithful the riches of the Lord's powers and merits, so that these are in some way made present in every age in order that the faithful may lay hold on them and be filled with saving grace" (*SC* 102).

Since Mary is inseparably joined with the saving work of her Son, the Church venerates her in a special way throughout the yearly cycle, rejoicing in her as the most excellent fruit of redemption and the image of what the Church hopes to be (*SC* 103). Also, by celebrating the anniversaries of the martyrs and other saints, the Church proclaims the Paschal mystery accomplished in those who have suffered and been glorified with Christ, offers them as examples, and pleads for God's favors through their merits.[36] In the liturgical seasons the Church completes the formation of the faithful through instruction, prayer, and works of penance and mercy (*SC* 105).

The Sources of *Sacrosanctum Concilium*'s Theology of the Liturgy

The theological sections of *Sacrosanctum concilium* make extensive use of scriptural texts, both direct quotations noted within the body of the constitution, and references to ideas found in scripture, which are identified in the footnotes. In addition, *Sacrosanctum concilium* draws on material from the fathers of the Church, liturgical texts, and the Council of Trent, as seen in the notes, as well as on other traditional theological material and Church documents, which are not explicitly mentioned in the notes.

The very first sentence of *Sacrosanctum concilium*'s treatment of the theology of the liturgy (article 2) quotes the prayer of the *Roman Missal* that describes the liturgy as "making the work of our redemption a present actuality" (*opus nostrae Redemptionis exercetur*),[37] and this becomes the foundation for the theological exposition that follows. This prayer had also been cited in the discussion of the nature of the Eucharistic sacrifice in *Mediator Dei* (1947), the first encyclical ever dedicated entirely to the liturgy;[38] from the very beginning, *Sacrosanctum concilium* is signaling its continuity with both the venerable liturgical tradition of the Church and the magisterial documents that were the fruit of the scholarly work of the liturgical movement.

Sacrosanctum concilium's treatment of the nature of the liturgy as best understood from the perspective of salvation history in which Christ acts as, in a sense, sacrament of salvation, is grounded in the understanding of fathers of the Church such as Augustine.[39] One of the scholars involved in drafting the text, Cipriano Vagaggini, notes that although *Sacrosanctum concilium* does not explicitly refer to Christ as "sacrament," it uses biblical and patristic texts that convey that understanding, speaking of Christ as "the Word made flesh, anointed by the Holy Spirit... 'the physician, being both flesh and of the Spirit.'"[40] What Ignatius of Antioch was affirming in describing Christ as *medicum carnalem et spiritualem*, was that Christ has "both human nature, including a body (*sarx*), and divine nature (*pneuma*), and that he heals in us both the spirit, to which he communicates the Holy Spirit, and the body, which he will resurrect."[41] *Sacrosanctum concilium* continues, "For his humanity, united with the person of the Word, was the instrument of our salvation" (*SC* 5), and Vagaggini elucidates that the understanding that "in Christ, his human nature, body included, was and is a conjoint and living instrument by which his divinity worked and works our salvation, is the common doctrine of the Greek Fathers. This same doctrine then often recurs in St. Thomas."[42]

Therefore, *Sacrosanctum concilium* affirms, quoting the fifth-century *Verona Sacramentary*, that in Christ "the perfect achievement of our reconciliation came forth and the fullness of divine worship was given to us."[43] This means that since the first source, human and divine, of the salvation of the world is in Christ, whether for human sanctification *by* God or giving perfect worship *to* God, therefore, all salvation of humanity and all worship of God must be a "certain participation" in what exists most perfectly in Christ.[44] *Sacrosanctum concilium* explains that Christ made this possible through his Paschal mystery, through which, in the words of the *Roman Missal*, " 'dying he destroyed our death and rising, he restored our life.'[45] For it was from the side of Christ as he slept the sleep of death on the cross that there came forth the sublime sacrament of the whole Church."[46] Here, in order to describe how Christ's work is continued in the Church, especially in the liturgy, *Sacrosanctum concilium* draws on patristic reflections on the Church as born from the side of Christ as Eve came from Adam, which Pius XII had referred to in *Mystici Corporis* (1943).[47]

From these patristic and liturgical texts, *Sacrosanctum concilium*, article 5, is describing how Christ's saving work is continued in the Church, which functions as a kind of general sacrament derived from Christ, the primordial sacrament.[48] Article 6 describes how this occurred through the ministry of the apostles: how people were inserted into Christ's Paschal mystery through baptism and how they celebrated it in the Eucharist, where, in the words of the Council of Trent, "the victory and triumph of his death are again made present."[49]

Article 7's reflection on how Christ is present in the liturgy draws heavily on *Mediator Dei*. To *Mediator Dei*'s affirmation that Christ is present in the Mass through his minister, *Sacrosanctum concilium* adds the declaration of Trent, "the same now offering, through the ministry of priests, who formerly offered himself on the cross."[50] *Sacrosanctum concilium* then repeats *Mediator Dei*'s affirmations of how Christ is present above all under the Eucharistic elements, in the sacraments, and when the Church prays together (Mt 18:20); when describing how Christ is present to act in the sacraments, the constitution substitutes a reference to Saint Augustine for the technical language of *Mediator Dei*.[51] While *Sacrosanctum concilium* also adds that Christ is present in his word proclaimed in the liturgy, most of this section on the ways Christ is present in the liturgy is taken almost verbatim from *Mediator Dei*;[52] the statement that follows, that Christ associates the Church with himself in the work of human sanctification and glorification of God in the liturgy, was based on three different sections of the encyclical.[53]

Further, when *Sacrosanctum concilium*, article 7, then declares that the liturgy is rightly considered as "an exercise of the priestly office of Jesus Christ," it is using the very words *(sacerdotalis muneris exercitatio)* of *Mediator Dei*.[54] The affirmation that "in the liturgy the whole public worship is performed by the Mystical Body of Jesus Christ, that is, by the head and his members," is also found in *Mediator Dei* and was repeated in "De musica sacra" (1958).[55] Article 7 concludes that the liturgy is a "sacred action surpassing all others" *(actio sacer praecellenter)*, which is a quotation from Pius XI's apostolic constitution *Divini Cultus*,[56] and that it is uniquely efficacious, which is taken from the teaching of *Mediator Dei*.[57] The description of the heavenly liturgy in *Sacrosanctum concilium*, article 8, weaves together five scriptural texts, which are cited in the notes.

After explaining in article 9 how the liturgy does not "exhaust the entire activity of the Church,"[58] *Sacrosanctum concilium* goes on in article 10 to speak of the liturgy as the "summit [*culmen*] toward which all the activity of the Church is directed...the fount from which all the Church's power flows." Those who wrote this section in the schema cited several texts of Thomas Aquinas,[59] as well as the teaching of the *Catechism of the Council of Trent* that the Eucharist is "truly and necessarily to be called the fountain of all graces" since it contains "the author of all the sacraments, Christ the Lord."[60] Leo XIII in *Mirae caritatis* (1902) had spoken of the Eucharist as the "fount and most important gift of all God's gifts"[61] and stated that from it, "the Church draws and possesses all its power and glory, all divine charisms that adorn it, and every good thing."[62] In *Mediator Dei*, the Eucharist had been called the "font and center of Christian piety," "the chief action of divine worship," and the "culmination and center...of the Christian religion."[63] In illustrating the power of the liturgy, *Sacrosanctum concilium* quotes prayers of the *Roman Missal* stating that the liturgy "moves the faithful, filled with 'the paschal sacraments,' to be 'one in holiness,'" and praying that "they may hold fast in their lives what they have grasped by their faith."[64]

The reason *Sacrosanctum concilium* gives for this preeminence of the liturgy is that the end to which all the activity of the Church is directed is the glorification of God and human sanctification and that the liturgy is the most efficacious source for the grace to pursue these ends; this idea may also be found in *Mediator Dei*.[65] Article 10's affirmation of the liturgy as font and summit of the Church's life—which was repeated in *Lumen gentium* 11—is ultimately grounded in scripture and the fathers of the Church.[66]

According to those who drafted the schema, the purpose of *Sacrosanctum concilium*, articles 11–13, was to solemnly affirm the teaching of *Mediator Dei* on the relationship between the liturgy and the spiritual life of individual Christians.[67] In article 11, the constitution declares the necessity that liturgical participation be combined with sincere internal piety in order to be fully efficacious (and therefore the need for pastors to foster that). In article 12, *Sacrosanctum concilium* uses scriptural texts to describe the aspects of spiritual life outside of liturgical celebrations that make fruitful liturgical participation possible, and illustrates the need for the baptized to give every aspect of their lives to God by quoting the *Roman Missal:* "This is why we ask the Lord in the sacrifice of the Mass that 'receiving the offering of the spiritual victim,' he may fashion us for himself 'as an eternal gift.' "[68] In affirming the value of popular devotions, as long as they are in harmony with the liturgical seasons, are "in some way derived from" the liturgy, "and lead the people to it," article 13 draws on the 1955 instruction on the restored rite of Holy Week, as well as *Mediator Dei.*[69]

The second chapter of *Sacrosanctum concilium* was titled "The Most Holy Mystery of the Eucharist" so that the title would include the memorial of the passion and communion, as well as the sacrifice of the Mass; the word "mystery" is used in the sense it had for fathers of the Church such as Ambrose.[70] According to Salvatore Marsili, article 47 "presupposes the eucharistic doctrine defined by the Council of Trent, and makes generic reference to it, condensing into a few words the matter treated in the 'Decree on the Most Holy Sacrament of the Eucharist' (sess. 13, October 11, 1551) and in the 'Doctrine of the Most Holy Sacrifice of the Mass' (sess. 22, September 17, 1562)."[71] In stating that Christ's purpose in instituting the Eucharist was to "perpetuate" (*perpetuaret*) the sacrifice of the cross, *Sacrosanctum concilium* employs a term very close to that used by the Council of Trent (*repraesentaretur*);[72] *Sacrosanctum concilium* took the word "*perpetuaret*" from Leo XIII's encyclical *Caritatis studium*.[73] Augustine's reference to the Eucharist as "sacramentum pietatis, signum unitatis, vinculum caritatis," which is quoted in article 47, had been cited in part by Trent.[74] Similarly, article 47 quotes from the *Roman Breviary* to describe the Eucharist as a Paschal banquet "in which Christ is eaten, the heart is filled with grace, and a pledge of future glory is given to us;" Trent had also alluded to this text.[75]

Article 48 begins by borrowing the exhortation that the faithful should not be "strangers or silent spectators" at the Eucharist from Pius XI's *Divini cultus*.[76] The phrase "they should be instructed by God's word" was based on language found in fathers such as Origen on the faithful being nourished at the table of the word; this idea is seen clearly in the reference to *mensa verbi* in article 51 and in *Dei verbum*, article 21.[77] The statement that the faithful are "offering the immaculate Victim, not only through the hands of the priest, but also with him," is very close to *Mediator Dei*'s affirmation that they "not only offer the sacrifice through the hands of the priest, but also, in a certain sense [*quodammodo*] with him."[78] In article 48's reference to the faithful learning to offer themselves to God through the offering of the sacrifice there is a resonance of Augustine's teaching on Eucharistic sacrifice in *City of God*;[79] *Sacrosanctum concilium* explicitly cites Cyril of Alexandria in speaking of the faithful being drawn into unity with God and each other through Christ the Mediator.[80]

The opening statement of chapter 3 on the purpose of the sacraments is based on Thomas Aquinas's teaching that the purpose of the sacraments is divine worship and human sanctification.[81] The affirmation that "being signs, they also have a teaching function" is also taken from Thomas; [82] the sign character of the liturgy in general had been mentioned in *Sacrosanctum concilium*, articles 7 and 33. The declaration in article 59 that because, as signs, the sacraments instruct and also "nourish, strengthen, and express" faith, "it is of the highest importance that the faithful should readily understand the sacramental signs" is reminiscent of Trent's insistence that the faithful be instructed in the meaning of the rites of the Mass and the sacraments so that they are prepared to receive the grace given there.[83] Further, the constitution's speaking of Christ's Paschal mystery as the source "from which all sacraments and sacramentals draw their power" is derived from the understanding of Paul, the fathers, and Thomas.[84]

Sacrosanctum concilium's theology of the Liturgy of the Hours at the beginning of chapter 4 draws substantially on the teaching on the Divine Office in *Mediator Dei*. Most of its first article, 83, is in fact a verbatim quotation from the encyclical.[85] Similarly, article 87 speaks of the reforms that are grounded in this theology as a continuation of the renewal of the office already "happily begun" by Pius XII.

The theology of the liturgical year in articles 102–106 is drawn from the same sources that inspired the renewal of the liturgy of Holy Week and Easter from 1951 to 1955; the understanding of the nature of Christian commemoration in these mainly patristic sources is that it is rooted in and centered on the Paschal mystery.[86] Easter has special prominence, as the "most solemn" celebration of the Paschal mystery; so does Sunday, as the "Lord's Day" (as it is called in Revelation 1:10) and the "eighth day" (as it is known as early as the Epistle of Barnabas), when Christ's resurrection opens up the possibility of entering into the new creation.[87] Patristic understanding, as well as the influence of *Mediator Dei*,[88] is seen in the affirmation in article 102 that "the riches of the Lord's powers and merits" are "in some way made present" in the celebration of the liturgy for the faithful to encounter them.[89]

The Relationship of *Sacrosanctum Concilium* to the Theological Tradition

Having considered the principal articles in which *Sacrosanctum concilium*'s theology of the liturgy is articulated, and the sources on which these articles were based, it is possible to offer some reflections on the relationship between the constitution and the earlier theological tradition. In studying *Sacrosanctum concilium*'s theology of the liturgy, it is immediately apparent that, as one of the members of the Preparatory Commission has written, there is an effort to break away from formulations that are too speculative, and to speak "the language of the Fathers."[90] It is clear that the constitution "speaks the language of the Fathers" in the sense that, even as the theological writings of the fathers have an immediacy that comes from being directly rooted in scripture, so too, much of *Sacrosanctum concilium*'s theological "vocabulary" is drawn directly from the sacred text. But, even more important, *Sacrosanctum concilium* develops its theology of the liturgy within the conceptual world of the fathers: It views all aspects of the Christian faith from the perspective of the economy of salvation. Using this wide-angle lens reveals the continuity of God's work throughout revelation and thus allows *Sacrosanctum concilium* to illuminate the connections between God's saving work at different stages of salvation history. It also brings into clearer focus and restores to prominence certain important dimensions of God's work in the liturgy.

As seen in articles 5 and 6, *Sacrosanctum concilium* grounds its exposition of the theology of the liturgy in the patristic vision of reality as centered in God's revelation of Himself through his interventions throughout human history, from Creation through the time before Christ, Christ's earthly ministry, and the life of the Church until its eschatological culmination.[91] For the fathers, this revelation is made up of *mysteria* or *sacramenta* (persons, events, or other elements in scripture that are seen to point beyond themselves to reveal something about God and his saving work), and the fathers understand the liturgy within this framework.[92] Patristic writings on the theological meaning of the liturgy are thus made up of explanations of the "mysteries" or "sacraments" it contains: The fathers attempt to discover, for each aspect of the liturgy, why and in what sense it is a "mystery"—how it reveals, communicates, and enables participation in divine realities.[93]

One aspect of the theology of the liturgy that is thrown into relief by *Sacrosanctum concilium*'s situating its discussion of the liturgy within the context of the economy of salvation, is the understanding of the celebration of the liturgy as a continuation of God's saving work begun in scripture. While this concept had not been at the forefront of theological discussion in recent centuries, the constitution reaffirms the fathers' insight that "today the history of salvation is really focused in the prism of the liturgy, even if its rays come from the Old Testament and especially from Christ, and reach out toward the heavenly Jerusalem."[94]

Approaching the liturgy from the perspective of salvation history also results in a theology of the liturgy that gives great prominence to the Paschal mystery, which is the "pivotal concept" of salvation history.[95] Henri Jenny, one of the drafters of the schema, emphasizes that since the Paschal mystery is the center of the economy of salvation, it is the center of the liturgy (which is the celebration of the Paschal mystery daily, weekly, and annually) and the center of all Christian life.[96] At the same time, *Sacrosanctum concilium*, article 47's referring to the Eucharist as a "memorial" (*memoriale*) of the Savior's death and resurrection tends "to establish that the Eucharist is the center and synthesis of the *paschal mystery* of Christ, or of that mystery which the liturgy in general and the Eucharist in particular continue to memorialize in the Church."[97] The centrality of the Paschal mystery in every aspect of the liturgy is constantly affirmed in the constitution.[98]

Further, since *Sacrosanctum concilium* adopts the patristic framework in which God reveals Himself through sacramenta—from events and prophecies under the Old Covenant, through the words and deeds of Christ, and then through sacred signs in the Church—the constitution, like the fathers, speaks of the Church itself as "sacrament."[99] Vagaggini explains that this term was used to affirm a profound truth: "namely, the intimate, indissoluble bond between Christ, the Church and the liturgy in the present order of salvation," a bond that is

> a close structural connection which has its prototype in Christ himself, in whose image the Church is fashioned, and the Church in turn reflects its manner of being principally in the liturgy.
>
> And this structure is exactly that of the *sacrament* or *mystery*, namely a sensible and visible thing which somehow contains and communicates to the well-disposed an invisible, holy and divine reality in the order of salvation, a reality which at the same time shows itself to those who have faith and hides itself from those who have not.[100]

Sacrosanctum concilium, article 5, thus envisions Christ as primordial sacrament, from whose side came forth the *mirabile sacramentum* of the whole Church, which then expresses itself most fully in the "sacrament" of the entire liturgy, particularly in the seven rites known today as the sacraments.[101] The underlying idea may be summarized in a classic text of Leo the Great: "What was visible in the life of the Redeemer, has passed over into the sacraments."[102]

Articulating a theology of the liturgy from within the patristic conceptual world necessarily brings into focus the importance of all liturgical rites as *signs*. In the theology of Thomas Aquinas, each of the seven sacraments is a sign that efficaciously causes that which it signifies, and "the explanation of the individual sacraments hinges wholly upon the sign proper to each as the expression of the particular grace which it confers."[103] When, from the sixteenth century, theology devoted itself more to discussion of the efficacy of the seven sacraments, there was less reflection on their sign-aspect (and that of the liturgy as a whole).[104] *Sacrosanctum concilium*'s retrieval of the patristic context for explaining the theological nature of the liturgy highlights the importance of the sign-character of the liturgy.

Thus, presenting the celebration of the liturgy as a continuation of salvation history and locus within which God communicates and reveals Himself through sacred signs, and emphasis on the centrality of the Paschal mystery, are distinguishing marks of *Sacrosanctum concilium*'s theology, but they are not innovations. Rather, adopting the patristic perspective of the economy of salvation enables the constitution to restore to prominence insights into the nature of the liturgy that had not been receiving the attention they deserved.

Sacrosanctum concilium's reappropriation of the patristic vision of the theological nature of the liturgy cannot, however, be construed as a repudiation of the teaching of the Council of Trent in regard to the liturgy; Trent approached liturgical matters from a different angle because its purpose was different. The Protestant Reformation presented specific challenges to traditional Catholic doctrine and practice concerning the sacraments. In order to address these, Trent needed to consider the individual parts of the sacramental system and analyze the specific nature of each sacrament, whereas *Sacrosanctum concilium* was able to "return to a more synthetic view of the liturgy."[105] Those who drafted *Sacrosanctum concilium* saw themselves as building on the teaching of Trent and deepening it; in presenting the articles on the Eucharist to the council fathers, the relator explained that there was no need to repeat everything that the Council of Trent had already stated so well.[106]

When explaining the kinds of changes in the outward form of the Mass that were understood to flow from *Sacrosanctum concilium*'s theology, article 50 refers to Pius V's expressed ideal in promulgating the *Roman Missal* of 1570 that some rites be restored "to the original norm of the holy Fathers."[107] The preamble to the *General Instruction of the Roman Missal* (1970) explains: why this had not been possible in 1570; how *Sacrosanctum concilium* has made it possible finally to fulfill Pius V's desire; and how "the liturgical norms of the Council of Trent have certainly been completed and perfected in many respects by those of the Second Vatican Council."[108] The theological understanding of the liturgy in *Sacrosanctum concilium* thus does not contradict that of Trent; rather, it situates Trent's teaching on the sacraments in a broader context to enable a richer understanding of the mystery of God in Christ made present in the liturgy, and facilitate participation in it.

The constitution's theology of the liturgy also reflects more than half a century of the work of the liturgical movement, which was itself informed by the renewal in biblical scholarship and the study of the writings of the fathers by the ressourcement theologians.[109] The scholars of the liturgical movement were inspired by the faith of the early Church, and wanted to recover its awareness of the Paschal character of the Christian cult and the importance of the whole Mystical Body of Christ in the celebration of the liturgy.[110] Many years of international scholarly meetings (such as the 1956 Assisi Congress) had prepared those who worked on the text of the constitution, so that *Sacrosanctum concilium* could be described as a "blessed rich harvest... which had been ripening along in the last decades under the breath of the Holy Ghost."[111]

Many of the ideas of the liturgical movement were articulated in Pius XII's groundbreaking 1947 encyclical, *Mediator Dei*. In addition to all of the individual phrases or sentences that *Sacrosanctum concilium* quoted from *Mediator Dei*, the constitution also drew from it in more general ways. Bernard Capelle had affirmed that the doctrine of *Mystici Corporis* (1943) was central to *Mediator Dei*'s understanding of the liturgy; later Vagaggini would add that in the two encyclicals "liturgy and ecclesiology are inseparable. And they remain inseparably linked in the present constitution."[112] *Mediator Dei*'s Christological focus and its emphasis on the liturgy as exercise of the priesthood of Christ are also seen in *Sacrosanctum concilium*.[113]

Pius XII himself had stated that it was Pius X who gave the liturgical movement "a decisive impetus" in his 1913 *motu proprio Abhinc duos annos*, in which he listed goals for liturgical reform that he did not live to accomplish.[114] In 1948 a commission for liturgical reform (which became known as the Pian Commission) was appointed, and during the next twelve years was responsible for reforms such as the restoration of the Easter vigil and Holy Week, and new editions of the *Breviary* and the *Pontifical*.[115] The document that had provided the basis for the work of the Pian Commission was given to each of the members and *periti* of the Conciliar Commission, and what many in the liturgical movement hoped for from the council was a completion of the work begun under Pius XII.[116] Herman Schmidt, who helped draft the schema, wrote in 1965 that it was no exaggeration to say that *Sacrosanctum concilium* was the crowning of Pius XII's labors because the spirit that animated his pontificate shone through all of its articles.[117]

Sacrosanctum Concilium's Theology of the Liturgy as Basis for Renewal

The general norms for the renewal of the liturgy and the specific changes based on those norms called for by *Sacrosanctum concilium* are the logical result of its theology. For example, that Christ "is present in his word" is the basis for the norm that "Sacred Scripture is of the greatest importance in the celebration of the liturgy," which leads to the decree that there be more readings from scripture proclaimed at Mass and that they be taken from a broader range of biblical books.[118] Because "in the liturgy the whole public worship is performed by the Mystical Body of Jesus Christ, that is the head and his members," therefore, communal celebrations with active participation are to be preferred as far as possible, and one way for this to be realized is in the restoration of the Prayer of the Faithful.[119] Since "in the liturgy by means of signs perceptible to the senses, human sanctification is signified and brought about in ways proper to each of these signs," it is therefore very important that signs be intelligible so that worshippers can understand the sanctification God is offering and dispose themselves to receive it; this leads to the principle that rites be characterized by "noble simplicity" and to the possibility for use of the vernacular and adaptations to culture, especially in mission lands.[120] Finally, the principle to be considered first in liturgical reform—the full, conscious, and active participation "called for by the very nature of the liturgy"—derives from the theological "nature of the liturgy" as source and summit of the Church's life.[121] It is because the Eucharist is the sacrifice of Christ and the *whole* Church, which is the "sacrament of unity," that *Sacrosanctum concilium* places such emphasis on the importance of the full, conscious, and active participation (internal and external) of the faithful.[122]

While those who wrote the schema of *Sacrosanctum concilium* derived the norms and specific changes decreed from its theology, they were also careful to note when those norms and decreed changes could also be found in earlier sources. For example, the crucial distinction in article 21 between divinely instituted elements in the liturgy, which may not be changed, and elements that may be modified had been made by Pius XII,[123] and the acknowledgement of the usefulness of the vernacular in the liturgy is taken from a statement in *Mediator Dei*.[124] The rationale for openness to adapting the liturgy to other cultures was drawn from Benedict XIV's *Summi Pontificatus*.[125] The affirmation of the bishop as center of the liturgical life of the diocese is based on extensive citations from Ignatius of Antioch.[126] The article that praises the liturgical movement as a work of the Holy Spirit quotes Pius XII.[127] Article 45's call for the establishment of diocesan liturgical commissions reiterates Pius XII's desire in *Mediator Dei*; article 46's recommendation that dioceses also have commissions for music and art is based on Pius X's 1903 *motu proprio* on sacred music and other earlier documents.[128]

As to specific reforms, the requirement for a homily on Sundays and holy days cites the precedent of early Roman practice described by Justin Martyr, as well as *Mediator Dei's* inclusion of the homily in a list of liturgical acts.[129] Article 53's call for the restoration of the Prayer of the Faithful is based on testimonies of several early fathers.[130] The schema provides a lengthy list of precedents for the practice of Eucharistic concelebration[131] and refers to Cyprian's discussion of the imposition of hands in the sacrament of penance.[132] The strong recommendation in *Sacrosanctum concilium*, article 55, that the faithful be given communion consecrated at the Mass in which they are participating is inspired by the theological concern that the Church must "do everything that may clearly manifest at the altar the living unity of the Mystical Body,"[133] but it had already been commended by Pius XII, who had cited Benedict XIV.[134] A careful reading of the entire schema and its notes reveals that a significant number of what are sometimes assumed to be *Sacrosanctum concilium's* "new" norms and reforms in fact point to the example of earlier precedents.[135]

In considering the major themes of *Sacrosanctum concilium*, it is important to understand them within the context of the constitution's theology and relationship to the earlier theological understanding of the liturgy, rather than as independent concepts susceptible to continual reinterpretation. In order to illustrate this, the remainder of this chapter offers brief reflections on four of *Sacrosanctum concilium's* characteristic emphases: the sign-aspect of the liturgy, the importance of the Word of God in the liturgy, the pastoral character of the liturgy, and the call for active participation.

Sacrosanctum concilium's attention to the sign-aspect of the liturgy is not aimed at advancing particular aesthetic preferences but comes from awareness of the theological reality that it "pertains to the essence of the liturgy that it takes place in sensible signs."[136] In his commentary on *Sacrosanctum concilium*, Jungmann describes how, while the need to counteract the Reformation had led to emphasis on the minimum required for sacramental validity and efficacy in liturgical celebrations, now "the sense and the sign should again fully assume their proper place. The forms should be intelligible. The form and the content should be in accord with each other. The form should express what is really meant (cf. Article 69), and the reality should correspond to the form."[137] Since sacramental signs effect the grace they signify, they need to clearly represent that grace so that worshippers know what is being communicated to them and are therefore able to receive it and cooperate with it.[138]

Shortly after chapter 1 was approved, Vagaggini, who helped draft it, explained: "If the liturgy is a set of signs, in order that it fulfill well the exigency of its nature, it is necessary that these signs express what they are meant to signify in such a way that the people can easily understand them in order to be able to participate fully at the celebration of the supernatural reality that is at the same time veiled and revealed (no. 21). This is the principle of principles of every liturgical reform."[139] It is this intention—to enable worshippers to "participate fully in the supernatural realities"—that informs *Sacrosanctum concilium*'s decrees that change specific liturgical rites, not a desire to strip the liturgy of any sense of transcendence, nor a preference for the minimalist, simplistic, or merely didactic.

Similarly, the constitution's emphasis on the important role of the Word of God in the liturgy[140] and its call for more scripture lessons and preaching rooted in scriptural sources are much more than ecumenical good-will gestures. The liturgical movement had been inspired by the importance of the Word in the patristic Church and the way the Word proclaimed in the liturgy had formed the spiritual life of the early Christians, and it wanted to recover this; in the decades preceding the council there were various proposals for more scripture lessons at Mass to be taken from a wider representation of biblical books.[141] Article 51's call for an expanded lectionary was thus intended "to give nourishment to a biblically based and deepened piety by means of a more richly covered table of the Word, the proclamation of which was now to be really directed towards the people."[142]

Sacrosanctum concilium's presentation of the liturgy as locus where salvation history continues provided a strong rationale for adding an Old Testament lesson to Sunday Mass[143] and led to its call for the kind of preaching that was "a proclamation of the wonderful works of God in the history of salvation, or in the mystery of Christ that is always present in us, and is working especially in liturgical celebrations."[144] This preaching was envisioned as the "living word of proclamation—and this not in the sense of just any instruction, but as the vivification of the mystery, to which the celebration in question is devoted."[145] The desire of the drafters of the schema was that the whole liturgical celebration should be imbued with meditation on the Word of God.[146]

Sacrosanctum concilium is also known for its appreciation of the pastoral character of the liturgy, but it is important to understand what the council fathers meant when they used the word "pastoral" in regard to the liturgy. After the council, in some circles the word "pastoral" applied to the liturgy came to mean less demanding, more interesting and enjoyable, and perhaps even entertaining. This is not the vision of a renewed liturgy hoped for by those who drafted the schema, nor by the bishops who approved *Sacrosanctum concilium*'s final text.

In the only place that provides an explicit rationale for the council's mandated reforms, *Sacrosanctum concilium* states, "In order that the Christian people may more surely derive an abundance of graces from the liturgy, the Church desires to undertake with great care a general reform of the liturgy itself" (*SC* 21). The council believed the faithful would receive these graces through "the source of the true Christian spirit": the "full, conscious, and active participation in liturgical celebrations" *called for by the liturgy's very nature* as exercise of the priestly office of Jesus Christ, perpetuation of his sacrifice, and whole public worship of the Mystical Body of Christ, head and members.[147] *Sacrosanctum concilium* provides a description of a "pastoral" liturgy in article 48. Because worshippers understand the rites and prayers, they are able to participate in them sincerely and reverently. They learn from the proclamation of God's word, join the priest in offering the sacrifice and offer themselves with it, receive spiritual strength from the Body of Christ in communion, and are drawn into ever deeper union with God and Christ's Body, the Church. This is what *Sacrosanctum concilium* means by "pastorally effective," and the changes in the liturgy's outward form, which it then mandates in article 49 "in order that the sacrifice of the Mass, even in its ritual forms, may become pastorally effective to the utmost degree," are intended to result in a liturgy that, as much as possible, enables the description of article 48 to be a reality.[148] As Jungmann explained, "What above all is urgently necessary at the beginning of this new epoch is to facilitate access to the riches of the mystery of Christ to the faithful and to strengthen their bond of union with the altar."[149] Further, if the faithful were better able to understand how God was working through the liturgy and forming them into his Church, they would be better able to live a life of discipleship and Christian witness in the world.[150]

It was this understanding of what it meant for the liturgy to be renewed on the basis of pastoral concerns that had informed the liturgical movement, and had been the reason for the restoration of Holy Week.[151] The purpose of the 1956 Assisi Congress, held in honor of Pius XII in his eightieth year, was to "pass in review the admirable initiatives of Pope Pius XII in the field of pastoral liturgy,"[152] and the pope told the Congress that the liturgical movement was a "sign of the movement of the Holy Ghost in the Church to draw men more closely to the mysteries of the faith and the riches of grace which flow from the active participation of the faithful in the liturgical life."[153] Speaking at that congress, Cardinal Antonelli affirmed that the true purpose of liturgical renewal went far beyond outward expression and "wants to reach the soul, in order to work in its depths and incite a spiritual renewal in Christ, the High Priest from whom every liturgical action acquires its value and efficacy."[154]

When the schema of *Sacrosanctum concilium* cites in its notes the concerns expressed by the bishops of the world in their responses to the consultation of the Antepreparatory Commission, the bishops' desiderata for liturgical change are often pastoral in this sense of wanting to enable the faithful to enter into deeper union with God through the liturgy. When *Sacrosanctum concilium* addresses the pastoral character of the liturgy, it envisions rites where "the faith of those taking part is nourished and their minds are raised to God, so that they may offer him their worship as intelligent beings and receive his grace more abundantly."[155]

Jungmann describes the pastoral end of the liturgy as worshippers becoming a living sacrifice,[156] and this way of thinking about what the ultimate pastoral purpose of the liturgy is leads to another characteristic emphasis of *Sacrosanctum concilium:* the active participation of the faithful. As Marsili explains,

> The Eucharist really implies interior *dynamic* movement, since it is not a form of worship expressed by human religiousness, but an *action* ("do this"), which brings us infinite vitality within the reality of the mystery that is in Christ, the only Priest of the New Testament: "Behold, I come to do thy will, O God" (Heb 10:7). This interior movement, which is a separation from oneself and an adhering to God, is the natural requisite for the eucharistic "mystery of worship," and at the same time a justification for that external action of the Christian assembly which is being rightly called "active participation."[157]

While active participation is a prominent theme of *Sacrosanctum concilium*,[158] the council fathers intended that this should be understood above all as an interior participation, "that is, a conscious participation elevating the heart and soul, which also expresses itself in—is aided by—the exterior rite."[159] To ensure that this was absolutely clear, Cardinal Bea proposed an amendment to the schema, which the council accepted. While the schema text had stated only that the faithful should "know the rites and prayers well," the cardinal urged that the text add that the faithful should know the mystery which is communicated through the rites and prayers."[160]

Conclusion

In treating *Sacrosanctum concilium*'s theology of the liturgy, this chapter has sought to illustrate the extent of the constitution's indebtedness to a great number of earlier sources that included discussion of the liturgy's theological nature. Those who drafted the schema or worked on the editing of the final text of *Sacrosanctum concilium* clearly acknowledged their desire for continuity with the preceding theological and liturgical tradition.[161] *Sacrosanctum concilium*, article 23, requires that there be careful study before any changes in rites are made, that no changes be made unless they are required for the good of the Church, and that any new forms should grow organically from those that already exist.[162] *Sacrosanctum concilium*, article 50, reiterates Pius V's desire for elements of the liturgy, when necessary, to be restored to the *pristinam normam*

THEOLOGY OF THE LITURGY

of the holy fathers; *Missale Romanum*, the 1969 apostolic constitution promulgating the new missal, describes how four centuries of preparation since
Trent had made this possible.[163]

At the end of the first session of the council, Pope John XXIII stated that
"It was no accident that the first schema to be considered was the one dealing
with the sacred liturgy. The liturgy has to do with man's relationship with God.
This relationship is of the utmost importance. It must be based on the solid
foundation of Revelation and apostolic teaching, so as to contribute to man's
spiritual good; and that, with a broadness of vision which avoids the superfi-
ciality and haste so often characterizing relationships between men."[164]

Thus, in *Sacrosanctum concilium*, the council began by taking seriously the
principle that "the salvation of souls is the highest law";[165] the liturgical renewal it envisioned was not an end in itself but a means toward the spiritual
renewal of the Church.[166] In order to provide a secure basis for spiritual renewal, *Sacrosanctum concilium* had to be built on a solid theological foundation
grounded in the tradition, as was in fact provided at the beginning of its first
chapter: "In fact, how else is the liturgy to be understood in these articles if not
as a concrete actualization through sacred signs of the history of salvation centered on the mystery of Christ, present and active in us? For that is the mystery
which the Bible announces, dogma systematically and synthetically presents
in its depth, spiritual theology teaches to be lived and pastoral theology transmits to its own. If this is true, the liturgy is nothing else than dogma experienced
in its most sacred moments, the Bible prayed, the spirituality of the Church in
its most characteristic act, the summit and font of pastoral activity."[167]

This theological understanding of the liturgy, rooted in the vision of the
fathers, incorporating the teaching of Trent, and drawing on the insights of the
liturgical movement and magisterial documents of several popes, was intended
to inform a renewed liturgy that would better enable the faithful to live out the
call to holiness soon to be affirmed by the Council in *Lumen gentium*.

NOTES

1. Pierre Jounel, "Genèse et théologie de la constitution '*Sacrosanctum concilium*,'"
Ho Theológos, n.s., 1(3) (1983): 354; Josef Jungmann, "Constitution on the Sacred Li-
turgy," in *Commentary on the Documents of Vatican II*, vol. 1, ed. Herbert Vorgrimler
(New York: Herder and Herder, 1967), 11.

2. The final draft of the schema of *SC* approved by the Preparatory Commission
and sent to the council's Central Commission included throughout the text of the
schema sections titled *Declarationes*, which provided reasons for its content, further
explanations of how statements made in the schema were to be understood, and extensive documentation of sources on which the schema was based. When the Central
Commission sent the schema to the future council fathers, these declarationes were
omitted; they are, however, useful for determining what those who wrote *SC* were
basing it on.

The verbatim citation of *Mediator Dei* as rationale for the theology of the liturgy in
the first part of *Sacrosanctum concilium* is found in a *declaratio* in the schema in *Acta et
documenta Concilio Oecumenico Vaticano II Apparando*, series 2, vol. 3, pt. 2 (Rome:

Typis Polyglottis Vaticanis, 1969), 12. Subsequent references to the schema will refer to this as *Sacrosanctum concilium* schema. The section of *Mediator Dei* cited is found in *Acta apostolicae sedis* 39, series 2, vol. 14 (1947), 532.

3. Cipriano Vagaggini, O.S.B., "De sacrae liturgiae natura," in *Constitutio de sacra liturgia cum commentario.* Bibliotheca *"Ephemerides liturgicae,"* sectio pastoralis 2 (Rome: Edizioni Liturgiche, 1964), 50; cf. Vagaggini, "Fundamental Ideas of the Constitution," in *The Liturgy of Vatican II*, vol. 1, ed. William Baraúna (Chicago: Franciscan Herald Press, 1966), 97. Vagaggini goes on to say that this theology is at the service of liturgical renewal; he also describes chapter 1 of the constitution, which contains most of its theology, as like "the soul" of *Sacrosanctum concilium,* in "I principi generali della riforma liturgica approvati dal Concilio," in *L'osservatore romano* (Dec. 8, 1962).

4. *Sacrosanctum concilium* schema, "Declaratio," 12; cf. Jounel, "Genèse et théologie," 358–59.

5. "Renewal and fostering" are used here to translate *"instaurandam et fovendam."* *Instaurandam* refers to renewing or restoring; *fovendam* means cherishing or fostering. English translations sometimes render this as "reform and promotion," which can create the impression that *Sacrosanctum concilium*'s main purpose was to change the outward form of the liturgy. However, the commentaries on *Sacrosanctum concilium* written by those on the subcommission that actually drafted the text of chapter 1 (e.g., Vagaggini, Schmidt, Jenny, Jungmann) convey the sense that the primary intention was to increase the faithful's understanding of the liturgy and love for it, and their participation in the supernatural realities mediated by it, so that they could better receive grace through it—and that changes in the liturgy's outward form were intended to enable this.

6. *Sacrosanctum concilium,* AAS 56 (1964): 97–138. All of the quotations of the Latin text of *Sacrosanctum concilium* in this chapter are taken from this volume. Since this chapter considers *Sacrosanctum concilium*'s theology of the liturgy, which is not specifically addressed in chapters 6 (on sacred music) and 7 (on sacred art), these chapters are not treated here.

7. The pope stated these purposes in his first encyclical, *Ad Petri cathedram* (June 29, 1959), AAS 51 (1959): 497–531.

8. According to Vagaggini, "actu quodam vitali penetrent" is the council's intended meaning for *vivendo exprimant;* the mystery of Christ means all that Christ is in himself and for the world and that which he communicates to us through the Church, above all in the sacraments. Vagaggini, "De sacrae liturgiae natura," 48.

9. SC 2. (Here and elsewhere, due to the theological density of *Sacrosanctum concilium,* it has been necessary to offer an English summary or a paraphrase of the Latin text, always with references.) For discussion of how the Church's theandrism in its nature and structure reflects that of Christ, since it is his Body, and continuation and expression in the world, see Vagaggini, "De sacrae liturgiae natura," 48.

10. Vagaggini provides extensive commentary on the four paragraphs of the introductory section of *Sacrosanctum concilium,* including comprehensive and detailed analysis of SC 2. "De sacrae liturgiae natura," 47–52.

11. For the rationale for situating the discussion of the liturgy in the context of salvation history, see *Sacrosanctum concilium* schema "Declaratio," 13. Jungmann explained, "It was to be manifested that in the celebration of the liturgy the history of salvation is carried forth" (Jungmann, "Constitution on the Sacred Liturgy," 11). Further, it is impossible to grasp the true nature of the liturgy except within the perspective of the history of redemption; see Herman Schmidt, S.J., *La constitution de la sainte liturgie* (Brussels: Editions Lumen Vitae, 1966), 154.

12. *SC* 5. Unless otherwise noted, all of the direct quotations of *SC* in English are from the translation by the International Commission on English in the Liturgy in *Documents on the Liturgy 1963–1979: Conciliar, Papal, and Curial Texts* (Collegeville, Minn.: Liturgical Press, 1982), 4–27.

13. *SC* 6 (ICEL), quoting the Council of Trent, sess. 13 (Oct. 11, 1551), decr. *De ss. Eucharist.*, cap. 5.

14. Henri Jenny, introduction to *Constitution de la sainte liturgie* (Paris: Editions du Centurion, 1964), 16. "In fact, what is the liturgy except the actuality, under the veil of sacramental signs, of the Sacred History of Christ present and working among us?" Vagaggini, in "Father Vagaggini's Article on the Liturgy Document," in *Council Daybook, Vatican II: Sessions 1 and 2*, ed. Floyd Anderson (Washington, D.C.: National Catholic Welfare Conference, 1965), 124.

15. Jungmann, "Constitution on the Sacred Liturgy," 12.

16. For discussion of how Christ is present in word and sacrament see Schmidt, *La constitution de la sainte liturgie*, 182–84.

17. *SC* 7.3. For further discussion of the liturgy as Christ's priestly act, see Jungmann, "Constitution on the Sacred Liturgy," 14.

18. For the uniqueness of Christ's presence in the liturgy see Vagaggini, "Fundamental Ideas of the Constitution," 103. For a technical discussion of *eodem titulo* ("by the same title") see Vagaggini, "De sacrae liturgiae natura," 59–60.

19. *SC* 8; cf. Vagaggini, "De sacrae liturgiae natura," 61.

20. Jungmann, "Constitution on the Sacred Liturgy," 14.

21. Vagaggini, "Fundamental Ideas of the Constitution," 113. For a more extensive discussion of *SC*'s treatment of the Trinitarian setting of the liturgy see 112–13.

22. For the rationale for including discussion both of the importance of missionary activity and of the liturgy as "summit and font," see *Sacrosanctum concilium* schema, "Declaratio," 14; Jungmann, "Constitution on the Sacred Liturgy," 14–15.

23. Vagaggini comments on how *SC* mentions the connection between the Church's missionary activity and the liturgy in articles 2, 5, 9, 10, 11, 33, 34, 41. Vagaggini, "De sacrae liturgiae natura," 49.

24. For specific ways the Church receives power from the liturgy see also *SC* 2.

25. *SC* 11. For further commentary on this article see Vagaggini, "De sacrae liturgiae natura," 62–63.

26. *SC* 12, referring to Mt 6:6, 1 Th 5:17, 2 Cor 4:10–11.

27. Schmidt, *La constitution de la sainte liturgie*, 154.

28. For much more detailed exposition of the structure of *SC* 5–13 see Vagaggini, "De sacrae liturgiae natura," 53–61.

29. Vagaggini provides more thorough treatment of this in "Fundamental Ideas of the Constitution," 115–16.

30. For a detailed discussion of the theological concerns at issue in the composition of this part of the schema and of the revisions that resulted in the final text of *SC* 47–48, see Jungmann, "Constitution on the Sacred Liturgy," 31–35.

31. The Latin text is "conscie, pie, et actuose" (*SC* 48).

32. *SC* 48 (ICEL); the rest of this sentence is a word-for-word translation from *SC* 48.

33. "That is why they are called sacraments of faith" (*SC* 59).

34. *SC* 60 describes sacramentals as sacred signs instituted by the Church that signify effects obtained through the Church's intercession and dispose people to receive the chief effect of the sacraments.

35. *SC* 86, quoting 1 Th 5:17 and Jn 15:5.

36. *SC* 104; cf. *SC* 8.

37. The prayer ("quoties huius hostiae commemoratio celebratur; opus nostrae Redemptionis exercetur") was the secret (offertory prayer) for the ninth Sunday after Pentecost in the *Missal of Pius V*. For the use of liturgical texts as authoritative sources in *SC* see Jordi Pinell, O.P., "I testi liturgici, voci di autorità nella Costituzione 'Sacrosanctum concilium,'" in *Costituzione liturgica "sacrosanctum concilium": Studi*, ed. Congregation for Divine Worship (Rome: Edizioni Liturgiche, 1986), 321–51.

38. *AAS* 39 (1947): 551.

39. For example, Augustine writes: "When our Mediator was manifested, he willed to be a manifest sacrament of our regeneration.... In fact there is no other mystery of God except Christ, in whom it is given to those who have died in Adam to be restored to life" (*Epistle* 187, 34).

40. *SC* 5, citing Ignatius of Antioch, *Ad Eph.*, 7, 2. Much of the discussion of the sources of *SC* 5–13 is based on a summary of Vagaggini's commentary "De sacrae liturgiae natura." For treatment of all of the patristic texts cited in *SC* see Achille Triacca, "L'uso dei 'Padri' nella Costituzione 'Sacrosanctum concilium,'" Asterischi metologici," in *Costituzione liturgica "Sacrosanctum concilium": Studi*, 353–81.

41. Vagaggini, "De sacrae liturgiae natura," 54.

42. Ibid., 54-55. As examples Vagaggini offers John Damascene, *De fide orthodoxa*, ch. 15, 19; and Thomas Aquinas, *Summa theologiae* III, q. 34, a. 1, ad 3.

43. *Sacramentarium veronense* (ed. Mohlberg), no. 1265, as quoted in *SC* 5 (ICEL). The formularies in the *Verona Sacramentary* date from the fifth and sixth centuries, though some may be older.

44. Vagaggini, "De sacrae liturgiae natura," 55.

45. *Missal of Pius V*, Easter preface, as quoted in *SC* 5 (ICEL).

46. *SC* 5 (ICEL), citing Augustine, *Ennar. in Ps.* 138, 2; and the oration after the second lesson of Holy Saturday in the *Missal of Pius V* before the restoration of Holy Week; "sublime sacrament" is ICEL's translation of *mirabile sacramentum*. Odo Casel uses this *typos* and the patristic commentaries on it (especially Augustine, *Tract. on John*, 120, 2) as part of his explanation of how the mystery of Christ is actualized in the mystery of worship. Odo Casel, *The Mystery of Christian Worship* (Westminster, Md.: Newman Press, 1962), 38–39.

47. *AAS* 35 (1943): 204. Vagaggini notes that *Mystici Corporis* quotes Leo XIII's discussion of this in *Divinum illud* (*Acta sanctae sedis* 29 [1896–1897]: 649); Vagaggini, "De sacrae liturgiae natura," 56.

48. Vagaggini, "De sacrae liturgiae natura," 56.

49. Council of Trent, sess. 13, *Decree on the Holy Eucharist*, ch. 5, as quoted in *SC* 5 (ICEL). For a much more detailed and extensive exposition of the theology of *SC* 5 and 6 see Vagaggini, "De sacrae liturgiae natura," 53–57.

50. Sess. 22, "On the Sacrifice of the Mass," ch. 2, as quoted in *SC* 7 (ICEL).

51. Augustine, *In Ioannis evangelium tractatus* VI, 1, no. 7; cf. Vagaggini, "De sacrae liturgiae natura," 57–58.

52. *AAS* 39 (1947): 528.

53. Ibid., 522, 528, 573.

54. Ibid., 529; cf. 522.

55. Ibid., 528–29; "De musica sacra," *AAS* 50 (1958): 632. For a discussion of how *Mediator Dei*'s definition of the liturgy as "the integral public worship of the Mystical Body of Jesus Christ" originates in the theology of *Mystici Corporis* (1943), see Bernard Capelle, O.S.B., "The Pastoral Theology of the Encyclicals *Mystici Corporis* and *Mediator Dei*," in *The Assisi Papers: Proceedings of the First International Congress of Pastoral Liturgy, Assisi-Rome, September 18–22, 1956* (Collegeville, Minn.: Liturgical Press, 1957).

56. *AAS* 21 (1929): 33.

57. Vagaggini explains why *Sacrosanctum concilium*'s teaching on the liturgy's special efficacy needs to be understood in light of *Mediator Dei* (532), although *Sacrosanctum concilium* does not use the terms *ex opere operato* and *ex opere operantis*, which are used in *Mediator Dei*. He also provides documentation that the reality expressed by the term *opus operantis Ecclesiae* was familiar to Thomas Aquinas; Vagaggini, "De sacrae liturgiae natura," 59–60.

58. Vagaggini notes Pius XII's discussion of this at the Assisi Congress (*AAS* 48 [1956]: 714); ET in *Assisi Papers*, 226–27; Vagaggini, "De sacrae liturgiae natura," 61.

59. *Sacrosanctum concilium* schema, "Declaratio," 26n24, cites: Aquinas, *In IV Sent.*, d. 8, q. 1, a. 1; *ST* III, q. 65, a. 3; q. 79, a. 1, ad 1; q. 63, a. 6. Vagaggini cites also Aquinas, *ST* III, q. 73, a. 3; q. 83, a. 4; q. 72, a. 12, ad 3; *De veritate*, 27, a. 4. Vagaggini, "De sacrae liturgiae natura," 62; idem, "Fundamental Ideas of the Constitution," 129.

60. *Catechism of the Council of Trent*, pt. 2, ch. 4, no. 47, in *Sacrosanctum concilium* schema, "Declaratio," 26n24. According to Vagaggini, "It is perfectly valid to say that the liturgy in its actual being is the summit and font of the activity of the Church, even though it may not equally be so in every part but only formally by reason of the Eucharist. For the Eucharist pertains to the liturgy not merely accidentally but substantially as the heart, the center or determining part in relation to its other components" (Vagaggini, "Fundamental Ideas of the Constitution," 106); this is part of a lengthier explanation on pp. 106–108.

61. "Horum omnium fons et caput bonorum," *Acta Sanctae Sedis* 34 (1901–1902): 644.

62. *Acta sanctae sedis* 34 (1901–1902): 642, translated in Vagaggini, "Fundamental Ideas of the Constitution," 106.

63. *Fons et centrum* and *praecipua actio* in *Mediator Dei* IV, 2 (*AAS* 39 [1947]: 592); *caput et veluti centrum* in II, 1 (*AAS* 39 [1947]: 547).

64. *SC* 10, quoting the *Roman Missal*, postcommunion prayer for the Easter vigil and Easter Sunday, and the collect for Easter Tuesday.

65. *Mediator Dei*, AAS 34 (1947): 532; cf. Schmidt, *La constitution de la sainte liturgie*, 139. Note also *Divini cultus*, AAS 21 (1929): 33.

66. See the extended exposition in Vagaggini, "Fundamental Ideas of the Constitution," 107–108, including his reference to "a fundamental teaching of St. Paul, St. John, St. Ignatius of Antioch, St. Irenaeus, Tertullian, St. Gregory of Nyssa, St. Cyril of Jerusalem, and especially of St. Cyril of Alexandria, St. John Damascene, and St. Thomas, without which the liturgy is unintelligible, namely, the doctrine of the principal and *ever-actual* role of the humanity of Christ in the history of salvation, and especially that of his most sacred and now glorious Body and Precious Blood" (107).

67. *Sacrosanctum concilium* schema, "Declaratio," 15; cf. relevant sections of *Mediator Dei*: AAS 39 (1947): 532–37, 583–87. The *Declaratio* specifically mentions *Mediator Dei*'s commendation of pious devotions such as the Way of the Cross and the Rosary.

68. *Roman Missal*, prayer over the gifts for the Monday in the octave of Pentecost, in *SC* 12.

69. *Sacrosanctum concilium* schema, 26n31. The *Declaratio* also refers to the 1958 instruction of the Sacred Congregation of Rites, *De Musica sacra et liturgia*, *Sacrosanctum concilium* schema, "Declaratio," 15.

70. Jungmann, "De Sacrosancto Eucharistiae Mysterio: Proemium," in *Constitutio*, 109.

71. Salvatore Marsili, O.S.B., "The Mass, Paschal Mystery, and the Mystery of the Church," in Baraúna, *Liturgy of Vatican II*, vol. 2, 4.

72. Jungmann, "De sacrosancto eucharistiae mysterio," 109; cf. H. J. Schroeder, O.P., *Canons and Decrees of the Council of Trent: Original Text with English Translation* (St. Louis: Herder, 1950), 418. (This is in sess. 22, ch. 1, "On the Sacrifice of the Mass").

73. Marsili, "Mass, Paschal Mystery," 19n1.

74. "Sacrament of love, sign of unity, bond of charity." Trent had not included *sacramentum pietatis, Canons and Decrees of the Council of Trent*, 355 (sess. 13, ch. 8).

75. This is the *Magnificat* antiphon for Second Vespers for Corpus Christi. Trent states that Christ wished the Eucharist to be "a pledge of our future glory," sess. 13, ch. 2, in *On the Holy Eucharist: Canons and Decrees*, 355. For more thorough exposition of the sources drawn on in *SC* 48 see Marsili, "Mass, Paschal Mystery," 4–25.

76. *AAS* 21 (1929): 40.

77. The idea of "the table of the word" is also used in Thomas à Kempis, *The Imitation of Christ*, and was cited from there by Cardinal Lercaro in his address to the 1953 liturgical congress in Lugano and by future Cardinal Augustine Bea at the Assisi Congress in 1956. For an explanation of how and why the word *mensa* was omitted from *SC* 48 see Jungmann, "Constitution on the Sacred Liturgy," 34.

78. *AAS* 39 (1947): 555–56.

79. *City of God*, bk. X, 5–6, 20.

80. *Commentary on the Gospel of John 11*, chaps. 11–12, cited in *SC* 48.

81. *SC* 59. The schema cites *ST* III, q. 62, a. 5, and q. 63, a. 6; *Sacrosanctum concilium* schema, 46. *SC* adds a further purpose: "to build up the Body of Christ."

82. The schema cites *De veritate*, 27, a. 4. That the sacraments are signs is "the first thing established by St. Thomas in his treatment" of them in the *Summa theologiae* (*ST* III, q. 60) (Liam Walsh, "Sacraments and Sacramentals," in *Vatican II: The Liturgy Constitution*, ed. Austin Flannery [Dublin: Scepter Books, 1964], 46).

83. Sess. 22, ch. 8, "On the Sacrifice of the Mass"; sess. 24, ch. 7, "Decree concerning Reform."

84. *SC* 61; see Vagaggini, "Fundamental Ideas of the Constitution," 114–15.

85. *AAS* 39 (1947): 573.

86. Cf. Vagaggini, "Fundamental Ideas of the Constitution," 113–14.

87. *SC* 102, 106; see the *Epistle of Barnabas*, 15, 8–9.

88. *AAS* 39 (1947): 580–81; cf. Schmidt, *La constitution de la sainte liturgie*, 158–59.

89. This draws from Odo Casel's research into patristic sources; see also Jungmann, "Constitution on the Sacred Liturgy," 71. Another example of *SC*'s borrowing from the fathers is the schema's reference to Tertullian in its explanation of the Paschal fast; *Sacrosanctum concilium* schema, 56n8.

90. Jounel, "Genèse et théologie," 359.

91. Cf. Cipriano Vagaggini, *The Theological Dimension of the Liturgy* (Collegeville, Minn.: Liturgical Press, 1976), 599–600.

92. See Vagaggini, *Theological Dimension*, 598. For discussion of how the concept of *mysterion* is employed by New Testament authors, especially Paul, and in Justin, see ibid., 600–601. For the meaning of *mysterion* in Origen, "which is afterwards common to all subsequent patristic literature," see ibid., 601–604. A summary of the use of the terms *sacramentum* and *mysterium* in the Leonine and Gelasian sacramentaries may be found on p. 66n64.

93. For further discussion of the positive and negative aspects of patristic focus on the liturgy's value as *mysterion*, see Vagaggini, *Theological Dimension*, 622, 625.

94. Vagaggini, "Fundamental Ideas of the Constitution," 112. Vagaggini here advocates the need for all disciplines of theology to consider their objects from the perspective of salvation history and argues that "to view this perspective in its natural setting, the liturgy is indispensable."

95. Ibid., 113.

96. Cf. Gal 2:20; see Jenny, introduction to *Constitution*, 17. According to Jounel (himself a member of the Preparatory Commission), Jenny's presence on the sub-commission that was responsible for chapter 1 ensured that the Paschal mystery, "which he spoke about constantly and with competence and passion, would be presented as the nucleus of the entire liturgy" (Jounel, "Genèse et théologie," 354).

97. Marsili, "Mass, Paschal Mystery," 5. Marsili explains that the use of the word *memoriale* indicates "the intention of accentuating the concrete and objective character of Christ's words, 'Do this in memory of me.'" Cf. Vagaggini, "De sacrae liturgiae natura," 57, who comments on how patristic Eucharistic prayers understood the Eucharist as *anamnesis* (memorial) of Christ's death *and resurrection*.

98. See *SC* 5, 6, 12, 47, 61, 81, 102, 104, 106, 107, 109. Vagaggini documents this in detail in "Fundamental Ideas of the Constitution," 114; cf. Schmidt, *La constitution de la sainte liturgie*, 154. Vagaggini claims that the only way to "rediscover that concrete and unitary sense of all of history and of the entire life of the Church and individual souls *in the dead and risen Christ*" is to "follow the spirit of the liturgy according to the wish of the council" (Vagaggini, "Fundamental Ideas of the Constitution," 115).

99. See above, 107.

100. Vagaggini, "Fundamental Ideas of the Constitution," 101–102. Vagaggini holds that this truth had not been receiving the attention it merited.

101. Ibid., 102.

102. *Sermo* 74, 2; cf. Vagaggini, "De sacrae liturgiae natura," 57.

103. *ST* III, q. 62; Vagaggini, *Theological Dimension*, 575. For a more detailed exposition of Thomas's theology of the liturgy, much of which is implicit in *SC*, see Vagaggini, *Theological Dimension*, 574–75. Note also that the schema's discussion of the stages of salvation history explicitly cites *ST* I–II, q. 101, a. 2; III, q. 60, a. 3, *Sacrosanctum concilium* schema, "Declaratio," 13n19.

104. For discussion of how the lack of attention to sign affected the theology of the liturgy see Vagaggini, *Theological Dimension*, 587; cf. 610–11.

105. Walsh, "Sacraments and Sacramentals," 44.

106. Jungmann, "Constitution on the Sacred Liturgy," 33. While both Jungmann and Marsili strongly affirm the continuity between Trent and *SC*, they also note ways that *SC* has developed the teaching of Trent.

107. Apostolic constitution, *Quo primum*, as cited in the *General Instruction of the Roman Missal* 6, 3d typical ed., trans. ICEL (Washington, D.C.: U.S. Conference of Catholic Bishops, 2003), 9.

108. *General Instruction of the Roman Missal*, 6–15; the direct quotation is from 15, p. 14, in the U.S. Conference of Catholic Bishops edition.

109. Cf. Schmidt, *La constitution de la sainte liturgie*, 58. See also Bernard Botte, O.S.B., *Le mouvement liturgique: Témoinage et souvenirs* (Paris: Desclée, 1973), 97–101.

110. Joseph Jungmann, "The History of Holy Week as the Heart of the Liturgical Year," in *Studies in Pastoral Liturgy*, ed. Placid Murray, O.S.B. (Maynooth: Furrow Trust, 1961), 21–24; Jounel, "Genèse et théologie," 350.

111. E. Lengeling, cited by Jungmann, "Constitution on the Sacred Liturgy," 7; see also Botte, *Le mouvement liturgique*, 102–109.

112. Capelle, "Pastoral Theology," 35, cf. 39; Vagaggini, "Fundamental Ideas of the Constitution," 100. See also Capelle, "Pastoral Theology," 39, for *Mediator Dei*'s treatment of the communal dimension of the liturgy, which is also important in *Sacrosanctum concilium*.

113. Cf. Salvatore Marsili, "La teologia della liturgia nel Vaticano II," in *Anàmnesis*, vol. 1, *La liturgia, momento storico della salvezza*, ed. S. Marsili et al. (Rome: Casa Editrice Marietti, 1974), 80ff. For discussion of the ways *Sacrosanctum concilium* developed the thought of *Mediator Dei* see Vagaggini, "Fundamental Ideas of the Constitution," 104.

114. "Allocution to the Assisi Congress," in *Assisi Papers*, 223.

115. Annibale Bugnini, *The Reform of the Liturgy, 1948–1975* (Collegeville, Minn.: Liturgical Press, 1990), 9–10; cf. Jounel, "Genèse et théologie," 350.

116. This document was the 342-page *Memoria sulla riforma liturgica* and its four supplements; Nicola Giampietro, O.F.M. Cap., *Il. Card. Ferdinando Antonelli e gli sviluppi della riforma liturgica dal 1948 al 1970 (Analecta liturgica 21)* (Rome: Centro Studi S. Anselmo, 1998), 52; Bugnini, *Reform of the Liturgy*, 7–8; Schmidt, *La constitution de la sainte liturgie*, 58.

117. Schmidt, *La constitution de la sainte liturgie*, 57. Vagaggini explains that, in stating the goal of providing norms *"de fovenda atque instauranda liturgia,"* the word *instauranda* refers to completing the task of renewing liturgical books and legislation begun under Pius XII. "De sacrae liturgiae natura," 50.

118. *SC* 7; 24; 51 (ICEL).

119. *SC* 7; 27; 53 (ICEL).

120. *SC* 7 (ICEL); cf. 33, 34; 36.2; 37. Note that when *SC* 37 speaks positively of qualities of various cultures, it employs phrases from Pius XII's encyclical *Summi pontificatus (AAS* 31 [1939]: 428f.).

121. See Vagaggini, "De sacrae liturgiae natura," 62.

122. *SC* 7, 10, 11, 14, 19, 26, 47–48. Cf. Vagaggini, "Fundamental Ideas of the Constitution," 115.

123. *Sacrosanctum concilium* schema, 18n41, cites *Mediator Dei, AAS* 39 (1947): 541–42, and the *Allocution to the Assisi Congress, AAS* 48 (1956): 723–24.

124. Schema contains a verbatim quotation from *Mediator Dei, AAS* 39 (1947): 545; part of this is used in *SC* 36. For a summary of permissions to use the vernacular in various parts of the liturgy by Pius XI and Pius XII see Pierre Gerlier, "Bilingual Rituals and the Pastoral Efficacy of the Sacraments," in *Assisi Papers*, 48ff.

125. *Sacrosanctum concilium* schema, "Declaratio," 20–21.

126. *SC* 41; see *Sacrosanctum concilium* schema, 28n64.

127. The schema cites the *Allocution to the Assisi Congress, AAS* 48 (1956): 712; *Sacrosanctum concilium* schema, 28n65; 29,n66. This is quoted in *SC* 43.

128. *Sacrosanctum concilium* schema, "Declaratio," 25, cites *Mediator Dei, AAS* 39 (1947): 562; *motu proprio, Acta sanctae sedis* 36 (1903–1904): no. 24.

129. *Sacrosanctum concilium* schema, "Declaratio," 31; cf. *SC* 52.

130. *Sacrosanctum concilium* schema, "Declaratio," 31, n18, n19. Cf. Jungmann, "Constitution on the Sacred Liturgy," 37. Jungmann also notes that the statement that preaching may draw its content from liturgical as well as scriptural sources has a precedent in Trent's urging pastors to explain aspects of the Mass to the faithful (sess. 22, ch. 8), Jungmann, "Constitution on the Sacred Liturgy," 24.

131. *Sacrosanctum concilium* schema, "Declaratio," 33–34; cf. *SC* 57, 58.

132. *Sacrosanctum concilium* schema, "Declaratio," 42n13.

133. Capelle, "Pastoral Theology," 41 (regarding *Mediator Dei*).

134. *Mediator Dei, AAS* 39 (1947): 564n108.

135. Among many further examples, note *SC* 100's call for pastors to celebrate Sunday vespers in church, drawn from *Mediator Dei, AAS* 39 (1947): 575 (*Sacrosanctum concilium* schema, 51); cf. the explanation of *SC* 108's affirming the precedence of feasts of the Lord over feasts of the saints in Henri Jenny, "De proprio de tempore," in *Constitutio*, 183; and Jounel, "De cultu sanctorum," in *Constitutio*, 186–87. Salvatore Famoso's commentary on the general norms (articles 21–34), in *Constitutio*, 71–86, provides many sources for the norms.

136. Vagaggini, "De sacrae liturgiae natura," 58.

137. Jungmann, "Constitution on the Sacred Liturgy," 23.

138. Cf. Marsili, "Mass, Paschal Mystery," 7: "The Mass is in the order of signs, or rather it is something whose meaning, the thing *signified* which is then its *content*, is not understood if one does not understand the sign."

139. Vagaggini, "I principi generali della riforma liturgica," (quotation trans. by Matthew Lamb). Cf. Vagaggini, "Fundamental Ideas of the Constitution," 116.

140. Note especially *SC* 6, 7, 9, 24, 35, 48, 52, 56.

141. As early as 1942 Romano Guardini called for adding a two- or three-year lectionary cycle; Josef Jungmann, *The Mass of the Roman Rite: Its Origins and Development*, vol. 1 (New York: Benziger Brothers, 1951), 403. At the Assisi Congress in 1956 Bea spoke of a three- or four-year cycle in "The Pastoral Value of the Word of God in the Sacred Liturgy," in *Assisi Papers*, 85–86. Cf. Jungmann, "Constitution on the Sacred Liturgy," 37.

142. Jungmann, "Constitution on the Sacred Liturgy," 37.

143. Similarly, one of the arguments for three readings was that the council wanted the history of salvation to be the basis of theology and Christian life, Bugnini, *Reform of the Liturgy*, 415.

144. *SC* 35.2 (trans. by the author).

145. Jungmann, "Constitution on the Sacred Liturgy," 24.

146. *Sacrosanctum concilium* schema, "Declaratio," 19; cf. 22.

147. *SC* 14; 7; 47.

148. Jungmann explains that this is what it means to revise the liturgy according to its pastoral aspect, as opposed to an archeological, historical, or aesthetic aspect ("De Sacrosancto Eucharistiae Mysterio," 110). After describing the council's highest priority in regard to the liturgy as (not reform but) fostering the liturgical life of the faithful in full and active participation, internal and external, appropriate to a community, and affirming that any outward reforms were simply a means to this end, Vagaggini concluded that the intention of the council was therefore clearly above all pastoral ("De sacrae liturgiae natura," 50).

149. Josef Jungmann, "A Great Gift of God to the Church," in Baraúna, *Liturgy of Vatican II*, vol. 1, 66. Jungmann was the relator of the subcommission that drafted the section of the schema on the Mass. See also Jungmann, "Constitution on the Sacred Liturgy," 35.

150. Cf. Jungmann, "Constitution on the Sacred Liturgy," 9.

151. *Liturgicus hebdomadae sanctae ordo instauratur, AAS* 47 (1955): 838–47. See esp. 842 for a description of the pastoral purpose of the reform.

152. Gaetano Cicognani, "Opening Address," in *Assisi Papers*, 6.

153. "Allocution," in *Assisi Papers*, 224.

154. Ferdinando Antonelli, O.F.M., "The Liturgical Reform of Holy Week: Importance, Realizations, Perspectives," in *Assisi Papers*, 162. Cardinal Antonelli was the Relator General of the Sacred Congregation of Rites.

155. *SC* 33 (ICEL). Cf. Carlo Rossi's explanation of the pastoral purpose of the revisions in the rites of the sacraments, "De ceteris sacramentis et de sacramentalibus," in *Constitutio*, 129.

156. Jungmann, "De Sacrosancto Eucharistiae Mysterio," 110.

157. Marsili, "Mass, Paschal Mystery," 15.

158. The word "participatio" or words derived from it appear in sixteen articles of *SC*: nos. 11, 14, 19, 21, 26, 27, 30, 41, 48, 50, 53, 55, 79, 114, 121, and 124. Lengeling believes that this call to active participation results from a renewed understanding of the Church. E. J. Lengeling, *Die Konstitution des Zweiten Vatikanischen Konzils über die heilige Liturgie* (Münster: Regensberg, 1964), 82.

159. Jungmann, "Constitution on the Sacred Liturgy," 35.

160. "Dicitur 'ut ritus et preces atque mysterium, quod per ea exprimitur, bene intelligant': non tantum ritus et preces, sed etiam ipsum mysterium; non tantum res externa." Augustine Cardinal Bea, in *Acta synodalia*, vol. 1, pt. 2, 22. Jungmann considers this change in the text as having far-reaching importance, in "Constitution on the Sacred Liturgy," 35. Participation is thus understood not as an end in itself but as a means through which the mystery itself is understood (Jungmann, "De Sacrosancto Eucharistiae Mysterio," 110).

161. On the eve of the council Jungmann wrote of the need for, "as far as possible, pious conservation and faithful tradition in the outward form of the liturgy," *Pastoral Liturgy* (New York: Herder and Herder, 1962), 372. Shortly after the council he explained how even the new "forms" of active participation were actually recovery of earlier tradition; see "A Great Gift of God to the Church," 67.

162. *SC* 4, in providing for the reform of other (i.e., non-Latin) rites "where necessary," calls for them to be "revised carefully in the light of sound tradition," as well as being renewed to better meet the needs of present times.

163. *Missale Romanum*, in *Vatican Council II*, vol. 1, *The Conciliar and Post-Conciliar Documents*, ed. Austin Flannery, rev. ed. (Northport, N.Y.: Costello, 1992), 138.

164. "Toward a New Pentecost," address of Pope John XXIII to the council fathers at the close of the council's first session (Dec. 8, 1962), *The Pope Speaks* 8 (1963): 400.

165. Vagaggini, "Fundamental Ideas of the Constitution," 118.

166. Jungmann comments that the liturgical movement had been concerned, ultimately, "with the renewal of Christian thought and life out of the sources which flowed into the liturgy" ("Constitution on the Sacred Liturgy," 8).

167. Vagaggini, "Fundamental Ideas of the Constitution," 110–11.

6

The Sacraments of the Church

Romanus Cessario, O.P.

This chapter complements that by Dr. Pamela Jackson, a recognized scholar on the liturgy of the Catholic Church, whose professional expertise qualifies her to write authoritatively on the history and reception of the conciliar text on the sacred liturgy.[1] The objective of the present chapter is more narrowly conceived to focus on the sacraments of the Church and their presentation in *Sacrosanctum concilium*. I maintain that the constitution on the sacred liturgy should be read within a hermeneutic of continuity with previous Catholic teaching on worship and sacraments, especially with what the Church teaches about the sacraments in the documents of the sixteenth-century Council of Trent.[2]

To argue that the constitution on the sacred liturgy is to be read in continuity with the overall tradition of the Church is not a fancy of twenty-first century revisionism. Cardinal Avery Dulles has reminded us that the 1985 Synod of Bishops had identified continuity and complementarity as the guiding principles of interpretation to employ when reading the documents of the Second Vatican Council.[3] In order to signal the agreement among the contributors to this volume on the hermeneutics of continuity as the preferred way to read the documents of the Second Vatican Council, the editors have chosen as the title for the volume: *Vatican II: Renewal within Tradition*. It is true, of course, that the liturgical modifications seem to afford, both for those who are old enough to remember the Church's ceremonies before 1964 and for those who have cultivated an appreciation for the preconciliar liturgical forms, one of the best illustrations of the claim made by some authors that the Second Vatican Council introduced a moment of discontinuity and even of dramatic change into the life and tradition of the Catholic Church.[4] The correct way of looking at the history, however, is to accept *Sacrosanctum concilium* as a milestone in the Church's divinely mandated effort to give the world authoritative instruction about Christian existence, in which the members of Christ's Body join him in offering due worship to the eternal Father.[5] To employ a phrase found in the first chapter of the constitution, *Sacrosanctum concilium* aims to ensure that Catholics render an *integer cultus publicus*.[6]

Some of the misunderstanding that informs contemporary beliefs and exchanges about the sacraments and liturgical practices arises from the false assumption that *Sacrosanctum concilium* is meant and therefore able to sustain a new constitutive account of Catholic teaching on the sacraments. One clear sign that this assumption is false appears in a close examination of the *Catechism of the Catholic Church*, part two, "The Celebration of the Christian Mystery," which cites the Council of Trent approximately the same number of times as it does *Sacrosanctum concilium*. In the *Catechism of the Catholic Church* we find the intended complementarity at work in the authoritative text that Pope John Paul II describes as "a statement of the Church's faith and of catholic doctrine, attested to or illumined by Sacred Scripture, the Apostolic Tradition, and the Church's Magisterium."[7]

This chapter further argues that *Sacrosanctum concilium* should be read as a corrective to liturgical irregularities that, since the late modern period, had become associated with the execution of Catholic liturgy. Leave it to sound liturgical theologians to sort out chaff from wheat. What matters is that one read the conciliar text as a corrective to liturgical discipline and practice, not as an invitation to construct a new theology of worship and sacraments. To put it differently, the Second Vatican Council presumes and presupposes what the Council of Trent had to say about the nature, number, and several effects of the sacraments, while *Sacrosanctum concilium* is concerned principally with showing how to live the sacraments, especially how to guide the members of the Church to enter prayerfully into the Holy Sacrifice of the Mass.

To discuss the sacraments as they are found in *Sacrosanctum concilium* I develop three considerations adapted to the overall purposes of this volume: first, some occasional remarks about the formation of the constitution on the sacred liturgy and about the liturgical movement in the Catholic Church that preceded it; second, an observation on the structure and the contents of the constitution, especially as they shape the presentation of the sacraments in the *Catechism of the Catholic Church;* and third, a suggestion for students who want to ensure that their studies in both sacramental theology and liturgy are done in a manner that respects the overall achievement of the Second Vatican Council as the Church urges us to understand it, specifically, that the council be interpreted in continuity with the great tradition of the Church, including the teachings of earlier councils.[8]

History

One way to emphasize the continuity of *Sacrosanctum concilium* with what went before is to recall the evolution of liturgical studies, especially in Europe, that preceded the drafting and the issuance of the conciliar constitution. Experts in the field of liturgy know that a variegated consensus had been developing since the beginning of the twentieth century, at least among a professional class of liturgists and catechists, on many of the specific provisions that found expression in *Sacrosanctum concilium*. It should come as no surprise to discover that the constitution passed the conciliar scrutiny with a practical unanimity.[9]

A Pastoral Council

In Germany, shortly after the promulgation on December 4, 1963, of the constitution on the sacred liturgy, then Father Joseph Ratzinger published the first of a series of reports about the work of the Second Vatican Council. Later, these essays were collected and published together in English under the title *Theological Highlights of Vatican II*.[10] At the end of his section on the liturgical schema, Father Ratzinger includes the following observations about a preliminary vote on the text that would become known as *Sacrosanctum concilium*: "The liturgical debate that many thought had dragged on too long ended on November 14, 1962, with a vote for the basic adoption of the schema, with the necessary changes left up to the commission. Even the optimists could not have expected the result of the voting—2,162 in favor, 46 opposed (with 7 invalid votes). And so the adoption was a decision that both looked to the future and showed encouragingly that the forces of renewal were stronger than anyone would have dared hope."[11] The practical unanimity with which the council fathers accepted the liturgical schema may be interpreted to suggest that they found the contents familiar and so judged the essential emphases and directives framed by the constitution as exhibiting continuity with what they had come to understand both to constitute the teaching of the Catholic faith and to govern the sound practice of the Catholic religion.

In order to understand why the fathers overwhelmingly accepted the composition of *Sacrosanctum concilium*, we can choose from many of the 130 articles that make up this first of the four constitutions promulgated at the Second Vatican Council. Let one example suffice. Consider a text in the constitution's first chapter, one that even today would easily be recognized as a standard expression of both classical and postconciliar theology: "Rightly, then, the liturgy is considered as an exercise of the priestly office of Jesus Christ. In the liturgy the sanctification of man is signified by signs perceptible to the senses, and is effected in a way which corresponds with each of these signs; in the liturgy the whole public worship is performed by the Mystical Body of Jesus Christ, that is, by the Head and his members."[12]

It would be difficult to point out where in this emblematic paragraph a serious break occurs with the antecedent theological tradition, such as that embodied in the teaching of Saint Thomas Aquinas. Again, it is fair to assume that the reference to the Mystical Body of Christ would have reminded the bishops of those encyclicals on the Church and on the sacred liturgy issued in the 1940s by Pope Pius XII, who, during his pontificate between 1939 and

1958, would have appointed many of the prelates present at the Second Vatican Council.

In short, nothing in *Sacrosanctum concilium* seems to have raised theological warning signs. The bishops, one may assume, understood the constitution as a way of purifying the existing sacramental practice of the Church. Moreover, in some places a brittle juridicism may have developed that was associated with the administration of the sacraments, especially of penance. After the irrational excesses of World War II, a punctilious juridic outlook no longer suited the religious temper of the times. The academic practice of associating instruction in the sacraments with instruction in canon law surely contributed to developing this juridical and somewhat restricted view of sacramental efficacy. Furthermore, the pastoral application of sacramental practice had introduced into Catholic life certain theological questions that seemed less urgent in a period nourished by modern studies in biblical, historical, and ecumenical theology. To cite one example, one may point to the sometimes overwrought post-Tridentine controversies among seventeenth- and eighteenth-century scholastic theologians that centered on specifying the difference between attrition and contrition. These theological debates sought to determine how the dispositions required in the penitent for a fruitful reception of the sacrament of penance worked to create a clean heart in the one who approached the sacred tribunal.[13]

Curiously, it was not questions of doctrine or discipline but of language that provoked the greatest number of exchanges among the fathers on the floor of the Vatican Basilica. Again, as Father Ratzinger noted, "the subject that preempted by far the most discussion during the first session was, oddly enough, the debate over the language of the liturgy."[14] Those who are old enough to remember the introduction of the vernacular languages into the Church's liturgical actions, especially during the Sunday Mass, will recall that the gradual removal of Latin from the Mass of the Roman Rite signaled for most ordinary Catholics that change if not renewal was about to seriously affect the way they practiced their religion. That the question of the use or disuse of the Latin language gripped the period of the immediate reception of *Sacrosanctum concilium*, may be gleaned from a remark made by that distinguished student of the liturgy, French Oratorian Louis Bouyer (1913–2004). In a book that he published in 1964, indeed within a year after the promulgation of the conciliar constitution, Father Bouyer reflected on a certain tension that he observed among Catholic intellectuals and faithful: "Just as a fanatical and exclusive attachment to Latin may be unreasonable and opposed to the good of souls, so, a desire to suppress any possible use of an ancient language appears equally unreasonable."[15] In any event, provision for some use of the vernacular in the liturgy of the Mass did not keep the fathers from almost unanimously endorsing the proposed constitution on the sacred liturgy, which (one may infer from Father Boyer's remark) they did in order to be useful to "the good of souls."

The Perils of Ressourcement

The historical background that explains the shape of the original draft and, one may argue, the almost unanimous acceptance of the liturgical schema is found in a twentieth-century phenomenon generally referred to as the "liturgical movement." Several recent and important accounts of the history of the liturgical movement in the Catholic Church, such as the widely acclaimed study by Father Alcuin Reid, are available.[16] There is some advantage to be had, however, in returning to an account that was written before 1962 (see Louis Bouyer's 1955 book, *Liturgical Piety*, which inaugurated the series titled Liturgical Studies).[17] Since the lectures that formed the basis for this book were delivered several years before the announcement of the Second Vatican Council, they were not influenced by the sometimes tendentious debates that have occurred among Catholics of the postconciliar period, although the book's contents clearly reveal a specifically Gallic outlook on liturgical renewal that initially exercised considerable influence on postconciliar liturgical attitudes.

In the first chapters of *Liturgical Piety*, Father Bouyer explores a rich and interesting period in the life of the Church, especially when one considers that the liturgical activities, both intellectual and pastoral, which collectively are considered to constitute the movement, took place during a period in European history that witnessed two world wars fought mainly within the countries where this liturgical movement enjoyed its most significant development, namely, Holland, Belgium, France, Germany, and Austria. This scholar from France presents to an audience in the United States, *continent de l'imaginaire*, as René Rémond describes French outlooks on the United States in the mid-nineteenth century, a spirited account of developments in the European world of Catholic liturgy.[18] Father Bouyer's constructive critique of the direction that liturgical theory and practice had taken during the post-Tridentine period is expressed with a typical French *clarté*: "Nothing of lasting value, then, can be achieved without a preliminary criticism of both the Baroque and the Romantic mentality, since the false notion of the nature of the liturgy has been formed by both periods."[19] Today we would describe the temper of this opinion as overly influenced by a preferential option for the primitive.

Other professionals of his generation shared Father Bouyer's evaluation of the Baroque and Romantic periods, which include the seventeenth, eighteenth, and nineteenth centuries. So it became fashionable to criticize Dom Propser Guéranger (1805–1875) for his restoration of "all the pomp characteristic of the later days of Cluny" and to praise primitive Benedictinism instead.[20] Saint Francis de Sales (1567–1622) was wrong to tell his beads when he presided at but did not celebrate the Mass. And so forth. Liturgists came to prefer the very remote past to the more immediate past. Modern biblical studies and historical theology, especially patristic studies, began to shape the approach that professionals took to liturgy. Critical views of scholastic and Thomist theology also emerged.

One result of the approach adopted by mid-twentieth-century liturgical scholars is evident: For the Catholic world afterward, liturgy would no longer mean only rubrics and ceremonies. A much-criticized formalism, enforced with juridical sanctions, gave way to the search for personal experiences of prayer in the liturgy and active participation by all in liturgical actions. This project was thought, rightly or wrongly, moreover, to be enhanced by a return to sources that took the form of recovering the monuments of the Church's liturgy. We have now learned, however, that it is not always easy to recover the remote past. Consider, for example, what was taken to be the restoration of an ancient practice and which now has become one of the most notable features of the postconciliar Roman Rite, the offertory procession. Some liturgists claimed that in the Middle Ages power-grabbing monks had abusively suppressed this expression of the congregation's active involvement and prayerful self-offering in the Mass. Recently, Eamon Duffy has stated convincingly that "there is in fact no warrant for supposing that an offertory procession . . . was ever a feature of the Roman Mass."[21]

It is beyond the scope of this chapter to discuss the many details of the "constructive critique" that Father Bouyer and others mounted against those figures in the liturgical movement that preceded him and his generation.[22] No effort is made, moreover, to give an account of the accomplishments in the fields of spirituality and liturgy that may be attributed to both him and other authors broadly identified with ressourcement theology. At the same time, one thing should be apparent. The integration of historical retrievals and perspectives into the overarching divine science that Thomists call the *sacra doctrina* has not always been successful. Put simply, liturgical theology requires more than historical research. Consider, for instance, the hubristic claim made by Josef Jungmann (1889–1975) in his 1959 book, *The Early Liturgy to the Time of Gregory the Great*: "History is a precious corrective of mere speculation, of subjective hypothesis. True knowledge of our present liturgy is knowledge based on the solid rock of historical facts; it is by studying the past that we can best learn how to shape the future."[23] This headiness now appears even a bit ironic when one recalls that the introduction of the offertory procession into the Roman Mass is said to owe a great deal to the initiative of Jesuit Father Jungmann.[24]

The liturgical movement owed its strength not only to theological lecture series and scholarly monographs but also to the dedicated lives of large numbers of monks and nuns, as well as to occasional laypersons who seriously committed themselves to the promotion of the *opus Dei* as found in the Rule of Saint Benedict. Liturgical renewal often accompanied social and religious reform movements. In the United States, Dorothy Day and her Catholic Worker Movement offer one example of how liturgical practice and social activism can combine to promote new emphases in Catholic lay life.[25] Mention also should be made of St. Benedict's Center at Harvard Square in Boston, Massachusetts, which drew students to the Catholic faith through the study of Thomism and an introduction to Benedictine spirituality adapted to the needs of laypersons.[26] I mention these notable examples from preconciliar Catholic life in the United States in order to illustrate that some partisans of liturgical renewal found their enthusiasm compatible with the styles of classical, indeed even of neoscholastic, theology.

From the start of the twentieth century, the liturgical movement attracted many participants. In his edition of and commentary on the constitution on the sacred liturgy, Herman Schmidt, S.J., onetime professor at the Pontifical Gregorian University in Rome, identifies some of the key events and figures that shaped the twentieth-century liturgical renewal.[27] He begins his short account with the 1903 *motu proprio* of Pope Pius X, *Tra le sollecitudini*, and then reports on the theological polemics that accompanied developments in biblical, liturgical, and ecumenical studies before Word War I.[28]

Father Schmidt further remarks on the boost that Pope Pius XI gave to liturgical renewal by the issuance of his 1928 apostolic constitution on divine worship, *Divini cultus*, and goes on to describe the pastorally oriented liturgical initiatives that arose mainly in Germany and Austria before World War II. The author continues with an account of the reprise of these initiatives that took place as early as 1946 at the Maestricht congress held under the direction of the German Benedictine Dom Odo Casel (1884–1961). He also notes with pleasure the November 20, 1947, encyclical *Mediator Dei* and observes certain affinities between this encyclical on the sacred liturgy and the two encyclicals of Pius XII issued in 1943, namely, *Mystici Corporis Christi* (June 29) and *Divino afflante Spiritu* (September 30). This triad of encyclicals, one may argue, reflects the theological agenda for students, who, especially in Europe, began their theological studies during the immediate postwar period: liturgical, biblical, ecclesiological, and ecumenical studies.[29] Lastly, Father Schmidt reminds his readers that Pope Pius XII also enacted practical reforms of the Church's liturgical celebrations, especially those in the early 1950s that altered the way that monasteries and parishes throughout the Catholic world observed the liturgical ceremonies of Holy Week. It is easy to imagine that the whole life of the Church during the decades immediately preceding the early 1960s was accustoming the future participants in the Second Vatican Council to see that shepherding liturgical renewal is part of the everyday routine of episcopal governance.

Other activities also shaped the outlook of bishops and priests in the period immediately preceding the January 25, 1959, announcement of the Second Vatican Council by Blessed Pope John XXIII. From the early 1950s, international congresses were held throughout Europe that galvanized the interest of both clergy and laity in realizing aesthetically heightened celebrations of the Mass and the other sacraments. The emphases of twentieth-century liturgical and theological research, writing, and teaching were formed in part by scholars who, having been named experts to assist the prelates of the Second Vatican Council, gathered as early as October 1963 around the archbishop of Bologna, Giacomo Cardinal Lercaro (1891–1976). Cardinal Lercaro was one of the principal (albeit controversial) figures at the Second Vatican Council and was also known to have been especially active in promoting what was then referred to as liturgical renewal.[30] The official *periti* at the council included E. Bonet; A. Dirks; J. A. Jungmann; A.-G. Martimort; H. Schmidt; C. Vagaggini; J. Wagner;

Frederick McManus, a Boston priest; and, after the first session, the American Benedictine Godfrey Diekmann.[31] After the close of the council, these scholars continued to implement the renewal.

Sacraments

The constitution on the sacred liturgy that was promulgated in December 1963 comprises an introduction (nos. 1–4), seven chapters (nos. 5–130), and one appendix. The introduction states the purposes that lie behind the issuing of a constitution on the sacred liturgy and concludes with an expression of pastoral urgency on the part of the fathers: The council "sees particularly cogent reasons for undertaking the reform and promotion of the liturgy."[32] The companion chapter in this volume discusses the overall structure of the constitution.[33] Of special interest to the topic at hand, however, is chapter 3, which addresses the sacraments other than the Eucharist and sacramentals: *De ceteris sacramenta et de sacramentalibus.* The relationship of the Eucharist to the other sacraments is adumbrated in article 6 of the constitution, where it is said that the apostles were sent both to preach and "to enact what they were announcing through sacrifice and sacraments, the things around which the whole of the liturgical life revolves."[34] The twenty-four articles of chapter 3 support the view that, at least with regard to the sacraments other than the Eucharist, the fathers of the council aimed to correct liturgical practices that they believed (for whatever reason) should be corrected and at the same time they were not concerned with making fundamental adjustments to the theology of the sacraments. As Liam Walsh points out in a commentary published in 1966, the vast majority of the articles (nos. 63–82) are devoted to matters of liturgical discipline.[35]

The commentatorial literature that aims to interpret the constitution on the sacred liturgy is, as I have already suggested, both ample and diverse. Those authors who read the document within the context of the theological emphases present in the other constitutions and in light of the sound theological work that had been developed in old Europe during the first half of the twentieth century wrote by and large edifying discourse.[36] Take for example the themes that the aforementioned Father Schmidt identified as those that illuminate the theological spirit behind *Sacrosanctum concilium*. He orders his materials under the following headings: Emmanuel; Jesus Christ is the same yesterday and today, he will be so forever; sacred signs; the word of God; the People of God. Similar themes, it is true, emerge also in the commentaries of Fathers Louis Bouyer and Josef Jungmann, to name two *periti* whom I cite in this chapter.[37] Father Schmidt, however, appears to have observed one of the principles that would later find expression in the 1985 extraordinary assembly of the Synod of Bishops: Each passage and document of the council must be interpreted in the context of all the others, so that the council's integral teaching may be rightly grasped.[38] Complementarity with what has gone before is assumed. In his 2005 article, "From Ratzinger to Benedict," Cardinal Avery Dulles, summarizing the present pope's view about what *Sacrosanctum concilium* was meant to accomplish, excludes one option: "The council fathers, [Ratzinger] insists, had no intention of initiating a liturgical revolution."[39]

The sixteenth-century Protestant Reform wreaked much havoc on the liturgical life of the Catholic Church, as any informed persons will recognize when they visit European cathedrals now in the hands of other religious denominations. Indeed, lamentable signs of liturgical revolutions, often iconoclastic in spirit and effect, are found throughout ancient Christendom, both Eastern and Western. As far as we know, however, the liturgical reforms implemented after the Council of Trent did not create commotion within the ranks of the faithful. Historians, for example, do not record dissatisfaction in the immediate wake of the liturgical provisions that Michael Ghislieri (1504–1572), who reigned as Pope Pius V from January 7, 1566, to May 1, 1572, imposed in the late sixteenth century. One noted historian of the period, Nicole Lemaître, a biographer of Pius V, has ventured to explain the motivation that fueled the pope's resoluteness in implementing the post-Tridentine liturgical reforms by appealing to his holiness and personal character. She explains that Saint Pius V lived his life with such an ardent and conscious expectation of the return of Christ the Lord that the thought never entered his mind that any liturgical changes would be required before the Parousia.[40] In other words, the immutability of the eternal liturgy set the standards for the Church's liturgy on earth. It may be interesting to observe that, in his aforementioned article, Cardinal Dulles also reports that "Ratzinger in several places laments the abruptness with which the Missal of Paul VI was imposed after the council, with its summary suppression of the so-called Tridentine Mass."[41]

The Council of Trent, and by extension the *Roman Missal* promulgated by Pope Pius V in 1570, appears in an opening article of the Second Vatican Council's liturgy constitution, which, in connection with presenting the causality at work in the sacraments, cites the second chapter of the "Teaching on the Mass, of the Council of Trent, session 22 of September 17, 1562."[42] Pius V effectively reformed more than the *Roman Missal* and *Breviary*. Earlier, on September 24, 1566, he published the catechism of the Council of Trent, the so-called *Roman Catechism*.[43] It is useful to compare the structure of the second part of this sixteenth-century catechism with the parallel section of the *Catechism of the Catholic Church* issued by Pope John Paul II on October 11, 1992, thirty years after the opening of the Second Vatican Council. In the *Roman Catechism*, which was addressed to pastors, the word "liturgy" does not appear in the introductory section of part two, chapter 1, which is titled "De sacramentis in genere." Instead, we find an exhortation addressed to parish priests on the importance of the sacraments: "The exposition of every part of Christian doctrine demands knowledge and industry on the part of the pastor. But instruction on the Sacraments, which, by the ordinance of God, are a necessary means of salvation and a plenteous source of spiritual advantage, demands in a special manner his talents and industry."[44]

In complementary contrast, the introductory section to part two of the *Catechism of the Catholic Church* begins with the question, "Why the Liturgy?" Ten paragraphs are devoted to explicating what the Church means by "liturgy."

In one of them, a quotation from *Sacrosanctum concilium*, article 7, which mentions "full public worship," helps to answer the question, what does the word "liturgy" mean?[45] Although the contrast is evident, the complementarity of the two approaches can also be discerned. Instead of an encouragement to priests to teach people about the sacraments, the bishops (to whom the *Catechism of the Catholic Church* is addressed) are given an outline to explain what the liturgy is within the Church of Christ. Within this overarching context, instruction on the sacraments in general and in particular is located.

What conclusions may we draw from the comparison of the diverse introductory texts on the sacraments that are found in two of the authorized catechisms that have been published in the Church since the late sixteenth century? First of all, in its second article, "Arrangement of Material," the apostolic constitution *Fidei depositum* adverts to the structural differences that exist between the catechism of Saint Pius V and that of Pope John Paul II. The apostolic constitution notes that the *Catechism of the Catholic Church* follows the same ordering of the main parts, creed, sacraments, commandments, and prayer as that followed by the *Roman Catechism*. At the same time, the *Catechism of the Catholic Church* offers something "new" in the presentation of the sacraments that responds "to the questions of our age." The following text from *Fidei depositum* illustrates the overall emphasis that one finds in the new presentation of doctrinal materials: "The Liturgy itself is prayer; the confession of faith finds its proper place in the celebration of worship. Grace, the fruit of the sacraments, is the irreplaceable condition for Christian living, just as participation in the Church's Liturgy requires faith. If faith is not expressed in works, it is dead (cf. Jas 2:14–16) and cannot bear fruit unto eternal life."[46]

The liturgy occupies a key place in the presentation of the Christian life and of the faith that sustains it. This introduction of liturgy as such into a general description of the Catholic life is innovative, or "new," as the apostolic constitution itself avows. Furthermore, the claim is made that this innovation responds to "the questions of our age."[47] The great figures of the liturgical movement would have agreed wholeheartedly.

To grasp what is different about the "new way" of presenting the sacraments that one finds in the *Catechism of the Catholic Church*, it is useful to compare what is said in the *Roman Catechism* about the rites that accompany the sacraments. The introductory section to the second part (where the word "liturgy" is not found) contains a section titled "ceremonies." Here is what is said under the heading of "Caeremoniae," which approaches one meaning of the preconciliar use of the word "liturgy":

> To (the matter and form) are added certain ceremonies. These cannot be omitted without sin, unless in case of necessity; yet, if at any time they be omitted, the Sacrament is not thereby invalidated, since the ceremonies do not pertain to its essence. It is not without good reason that the administration of the Sacraments has been at all times, from the earliest ages of the Church, accompanied with certain solemn rites. There is, in the first place, the greatest propriety in manifesting

such a religious reverence to the sacred mysteries as to make it appear that holy things are handled by holy men. Secondly, these ceremonies serve to display more fully the effects of the Sacraments, placing them, as it were, before our eyes, and to impress more deeply on the minds of the faithful the sanctity of these sacred institutions. Thirdly, they elevate to sublime contemplation the minds of those who behold and observe them with attention, and excite within them faith and charity. To enable the faithful, therefore, to know and understand clearly the meaning of the ceremonies made use of in the administration of each Sacrament should be an object of special care and attention.[48]

This section occurs within a summary discussion of basic sacramental theology that is broadly based on the order of the topics found in the *tertia pars* of the *Summa theologiae*.[49] One emphasis from this text is clear: Liturgy understood as the decorous performance of the external rites is ordered to serve the sacraments. The sacraments themselves, that is, precisely as sign-causes of divine grace, are not considered an instance of enacting the liturgy.

Whatever one may say about the way the liturgical handbooks of the early twentieth century defined liturgy as the official form for the external worship of the Church, it is evident upon comparing the previously mentioned texts that different but complementary emphases are represented in the two catechisms. The question Father Bouyer formulated about pre-1950s' liturgical outlooks is "whether we could find in the liturgy any training in prayer, or whether, indeed, we could consider the liturgy itself to be a prayer in any proper sense of the word."[50] One could argue that the *Catechism of the Catholic Church*, which takes up the teaching of *Sacrosanctum concilium*, reflects the influence of the liturgical movement, at least as it was understood by an author like French Oratorian Louis Bouyer. The question that remains to be asked is whether the retrieval of what is considered a more ancient understanding of the liturgy of the Church has helped accomplish the corrective work of *Sacrosanctum concilium*. One does not have to be a Baroque bishop or a Gothic-revival monk or even a punctilious rubricist to harbor the suspicion that Catholics would better appreciate the sacramental causality at work in the Church's liturgy were celebrants given to pay careful, indeed prayerful, attention to the prescribed rubrics. On the other hand, today's widespread liturgical informality and even slovenliness can hardly be attributed to *Sacrosanctum concilium*. An attentive reading of this constitution reveals that the fathers were intent upon making the causal efficacy of the sacraments more attractive and comprehensible to the Catholic people, not reducing the sacraments to empty symbols of a creature-centered religious ritualism.

Suggestions for Further Study

While Fathers Bouyer and Josef Jungmann were spending the summers lecturing at the University of Notre Dame in South Bend, Indiana, Father Bernard

Leeming, S.J., was carrying on the trade of the sacramental theologian as it had been practiced more or less since the publication of the *Roman Catechism*. In 1956 he published an article that gives a sort of state-of-the-union report to sacramental theologians.[51] Father Leeming, who in his day was an acknowledged expert in sacramental theology, reported the following about sacramental theology: (1) the method of doing sacramental theology has been affected by the renewal of biblical studies and a new emphasis on the study of words and language; (2) there exists accelerated theological inquiry into questions such as the objective efficacy of the sacraments, the nature of sacramental grace (which had been a disputed question among the classical theologians), the manner of the dominical institution of the sacraments, the requirements of the minister, the nature of the priesthood of all of the faithful, specifically whether the notion is mystical, metaphorical, or analogical, and the intention required of the minister, specifically whether mistaken beliefs (such as may be found among non-Catholic ministers) create a defect of intention, the concept of the validity of the sacraments as it was discussed within what may now be described as the nascent ecumenical movement, and, lastly, debates on questions associated with the sacrament of confirmation; (3) "wider trends" also continue to develop in the theology, which include the bourgeoning antischolastic spirit (which favors what the author describes as an "inclusive" trend, occasioned by the return-to-the-sources movement),[52] the status of Odo Casel's "mystery-presence" theory, which he identifies with the Southern German liturgical renewal,[53] discussions about what the sacraments permanently accomplish in the life of the Christian, and, finally, the relationship of the sacraments to the Church. This tally sheet of theological discussion topics gives us some idea of the state of the discipline of sacramental theology on the eve of the Second Vatican Council.

I conclude this chapter on the sacraments in *Sacrosanctum concilium* by offering a brief survey of the present state of sacramental theology. In the middle of the first decade of the twenty-first century, the study of sacramental theology remains almost exclusively subordinated to the programs in liturgical studies. Although one may find some exceptions to this general rule, perhaps in the ecclesiastical faculties in Rome, students, especially in the United States, who express an interest in studying the sacraments are confided to the care of professional liturgists. One effect of this transposition is that the topics discussed in the discipline reflect the interests of the professional liturgists. To identify the explanatory factors behind this evolution requires further research. Such an inquiry would need to include an analysis of the philosophical preferences, such as anthropology, phenomenology of symbol, sociology, and philosophy of language, that emerge in studies that aim to elucidate the nature of social groups and their cohesion. The inquiry should also probe the reasons many theologians consider metaphysics less likely to be useful in sacramental theology than did the classical scholastic theologians.[54] Few would contest that while the majority of the seminarians enrolled in programs of formation in the United States are able to air views on sacramental symbolism, very few are trained to give accounts of sacramental causality or even efficacy.

More than a few pastoral situations have become apparent over the past decade that suggest the failure of the theological community to teach the classical theses on the sacraments and thus arguably betray the pastoral objectives of *Sacrosanctum concilium*. One may point to the widely publicized reports from the bishops of the United States that indicate that only a small percentage of American Catholics have been taught about the Real Presence, or to the waning interest in receiving (and in some cases, sadly, of administering[55]) the sacraments of healing, or, again, to the dramatic drop in priestly vocations that is reported in many parts of the country. Also, there are the cultural challenges to Christian marriage to consider, including the high rate of divorce among Catholics. Finally, there are the reported abuses of the Holy Eucharist, the redress of which occupies the lengthy *Instruction on Certain Matters to Be Observed or to Be Avoided regarding the Most Holy Eucharist*, issued by the Holy See in 2004 under the Latin title *Redemptionis sacramentum*. It is not my purpose to suggest causal connections between the documented, depreciated state of Catholic sacramental practice in the life of the Church, especially in Western Europe and North America, and the preconciliar liturgical movement or what is worthy in postconciliar liturgical programs and studies. One must, however, conclude that present-day sacramental theology requires a new kind of ressourcement, one that draws heavily on the *tertia pars* of Saint Thomas Aquinas's *Summa theologiae* and the commentatorial tradition (including the authors of the Baroque period) that follows upon it.[56]

Some resources are available for the student who wishes to stand back and, with the help of Saint Thomas Aquinas, take a fresh look at sacramental theology. A recent example is Dominican Liam Walsh's 2005 essay, "Sacraments," published in *The Theology of Thomas Aquinas*.[57] Allow me especially to warmly recommend two volumes by another member of the Irish Dominican Province, Father Colman O'Neill, O.P., who at his death was teaching dogmatic theology at the University of Fribourg in Switzerland. These are *Sacramental Realism*[58] and his earlier *Meeting Christ in the Sacraments*.[59] The second of these books is a complete course of sacramental theology developed around the time that *Sacrosanctum concilium* was being drafted. The revised version takes into account important developments that occurred through the 1980s, especially the publication of the 1983 *Code of Canon Law*. The first book, *Sacramental Realism*, offers a solid account of the principles of sacramental theology, with special attention to the question of sacramental causality. This book contains material not easily available elsewhere about Catholic teaching on the sacraments. Among the new generation of postconciliar theologians is the prolific Matthew Levering, whose *Sacrifice and Community* aims to retrieve both "what is new and what is old" (see Mt 13:52) by exploring the character of the Eucharist as communion in and through sacrifice.[60]

In *Summa theologiae* III, question 62, article 5, Saint Thomas reminds us that, by his passion, Christ inaugurated the rites of the Christian religion ("per suam passionem initiavit ritum Christianae religionis"). Religion is a virtue that belongs to the cardinal virtue of justice. Justice prescribes what is due to another. "Clearly, then," writes Aquinas, "religion is a virtue because it pays the debt of honor to God."[61] Even Father Schmidt acknowledges that the bishops thought that the early drafts of *Sacrosanctum concilium* relegated *la glorification de Dieu* to a second level of importance. As a result, the phrase was added, he reports, in different articles.[62] Perhaps the time has come to examine the sacramental instruction and practice that exist in the Church in order to see whether they conform to the truth that Aquinas recalls when discussing the necessity of the sacraments in *Summa theologiae* III, question 61, article 1: "Now it is necessary for human salvation that men should be united in one denomination constituted by true religion."[63]

The sacraments of the new law create communion on earth. The various implications of the already-mentioned axiom, which Aquinas adapts from the writings of Saint Augustine, will best be discovered by a careful return to the sources of theology (the new ressourcement) that these two great Western doctors have put at the disposal of the whole Church. Only true religion creates communion. The renewal of sacramental theology should proceed on the assumption that the Holy Spirit guided what the fathers of the Second Vatican Council had to say about the sacraments of the Church. This conciliar voice is clear enough to enable readers of *Sacrosanctum concilium* to resist the proposals of those sacramental theologians who today legitimate their own real ruptures with the Catholic sacramental tradition by appeal to the first document issued by the Second Vatican Council.

NOTES

1. For example, see Pamela Jackson, *An Abundance of Graces: Reflections on Sacrosanctum concilium* (Chicago: Hillenbrand, 2004).

2. Father F. Antonelli, O.F.M., who served as secretary of the conciliar commission on the liturgy, makes a point of noting the "complementary character" of Trent and Vatican II. See his article in the Dec. 8, 1963, issue of *L'osservatore romano*.

3. Avery Dulles, "Vatican II: The Myth and the Reality," *America* (Feb. 24, 2003), succinctly summarizes the principles that should govern a Catholic reading of the documents of the Second Vatican Council. "To overcome polarization and bring about greater consensus, Pope John Paul II convened an extraordinary assembly of the Synod of Bishops in 1985, the 20th anniversary of the close of the [Second Vatican] council. This synod in its final report came up with six agreed principles for sound interpretation, which may be paraphrased as follows: 1) Each passage and document of the council must be interpreted in the context of all the others, so that the integral teaching of the council may be rightly grasped. 2) The four constitutions of the council (those on liturgy, church, Revelation and church in the modern world) are the hermeneutical key to the other documents—namely, the council's nine decrees and three declarations. 3) The pastoral import of the documents ought not to be separated from, or set in opposition to, their doctrinal content. 4) No opposition may be made between the spirit and the letter of Vatican II. 5) The council must be interpreted in continuity with the great tradition of the church, including earlier councils. 6) Vatican II should be accepted as illuminating the problems of our own day" (8–9).

4. For example, Jesuit John W. O'Malley advances a nuanced but firm argument for this position in his "The Style of Vatican II," *America* (Feb. 24, 2003): 12–15; and again in "Vatican II: Official Norms," *America* (Mar. 31, 2003): 11–14.

5. See *Sacrosanctum concilium* 7: "Christ indeed always associates the Church with Himself in this great work wherein God is perfectly glorified and men are sanctified. The Church is his beloved Bride who calls to her Lord, and through Him offers worship to the Eternal Father [*Aeterno Patri cultum tribuit*]." The English version of the constitution is that of the official Vatican translation.

6. *Sacrosanctum concilium* 7: "In the liturgy the whole public worship [*integer cultus publicus*] is performed by the Mystical Body of Jesus Christ, that is, by the Head and his members."

7. See the Oct. 11, 1992, apostolic constitution *Fidei depositum*. "On the Publication of the *Catechism of the Catholic Church* prepared following the Second Vatican Ecumenical Council," no. 3.

8. See Synod of Bishops, "Final Report," *Origins* 15 (1985): 445–46: "Moreover, the council must be understood in continuity with the great tradition of the church." See also Avery Dulles, "Vatican II: The Myth and the Reality," *America* (Feb. 24, 2003): 9.

9. See *Acta synodalia sacrosancti Concilii Oecumenici Vaticani II*, vol. 2: *Periodus secunda; Pars V: Congregationes generales LXV–LXXXIII* (Rome: Typis Polyglottis Vaticanis, 1973), 767: The final vote on the schema was taken on Nov. 22, 1963: *placet* 2,158; *non placet* 19; *placet iuxta modum*: 1. There was a solemn and public approval on Dec. 4, 1963, with a vote of 2,147 *placet* and 4 *non placet*.

10. Joseph Ratzinger, *Theological Highlights of Vatican II*, trans. Henry Traub, S.J., et al. (New York: Paulist Press Deus Books, 1966). The original German reports were published after each of the four periods of the council by the Cologne firm J. P. Bachem.

11. Ratzinger, *Theological Highlights*, 19, 20. For the later and contrasting views of the same author see Joseph Ratzinger, *The Spirit of the Liturgy*, trans. John Saward (San Francisco: Ignatius Press, 2000).

12. *Sacrosanctum concilium* 7: "Merito igitur liturgia habetur veluti Iesu Christi sacerdotalis muneris exercitatio, in qua per signa sensibilia significatur et modo singulis proprio efficitur sanctificatio hominis, et a mystico Iesu Christi corpore, capite nempe eiusque membris, integer cultus publicus exercetur."

13. For further information see *Dictionnaire de Spiritualité*, vol. 12, cols. 986f.

14. Ratzinger, *Theological Highlights*, 17.

15. Louis Bouyer, *The Liturgy Revived: A Doctrinal Commentary of the Conciliar Constitution on the Liturgy* (Notre Dame, Ind.: University of Notre Dame Press, 1964), 96.

16. Alcuin Reid, O.S.B., *The Organic Development of the Liturgy* (London: St. Michael's Abbey Press, 2004), has been well received by distinguished Catholic theologians. For present-day views of the liturgical movement by some American authors see the report of the 1999 meeting of the Society for Catholic Liturgy by Lauren Pristas in *Antiphon* 4.3 (1999): 48–51.

17. Louis Bouyer, *Liturgical Piety* (Notre Dame, Ind.: University of Notre Dame Press, 1955).

18. See René Rémond, *Les États-Unis devant l'opinion française, 1814–1852*, vol. 1, Cahiers de la fondation nationale des sciences politiques, no. 117 (Paris: Armand Colin, 1962), 58ff.

19. Bouyer, *Liturgical Piety*, 5.

20. Ibid. For another view of the celebrated restorer of French monasticism in the nineteenth century see Louis Soltner, O.S.B., "Dom Guéranger et la liberté monastique," in *Lacordaire, son pays, ses amis, et la liberté des ordres religieux en France*, ed. Guy Bedouelle (Paris: Les Éditions du Cerf, 1991), 205–15.

21. Eamon Duffy, "Worship," in *Fields of Faith: Theology and Religious Studies for the Twenty-first Century*, ed. David F. Ford, Ben Quash, and Janet Martin Soskice (New York: Cambridge University Press, 2005), 120.

22. In 1956 an abridged French translation, with the addition of a subtitle, *La vie de la liturgie: Une critique constructive du mouvement liturgique*, was published by the Dominicans at their distinguished Paris publishing house, Les Éditions du Cerf.

23. Josef A. Jungmann, *The Early Liturgy to the Time of Gregory the Great*, trans. Francis A. Brunner (Notre Dame, Ind.: University of Notre Dame Press, 1959), 8, as cited in Duffy, "Worship," 124.

24. Duffy, "Worship," 120.

25. See her tribute to Benedictine educator and liturgist Father Virgil Michel (1890–1938), "Fellow Worker in Christ," *Orate Fratres* 13 (1939): 139–41. Also see Mark Zwick and Louise Zwick, "Dom Virgil Michel, OSB, the Liturgical Movement, and the Catholic Worker," in *The Catholic Worker Movement: Intellectual and Spiritual Origins* (New York: Paulist Press, 2005), 58–74.

26. For instance, see the obituary "Leonard Feeney: In Memoriam" that then Father Avery Dulles, S.J., published in *America* (Feb. 2, 1978) and which was republished in *They Fought the Good Fight: Orestes Brownson and Father Feeney*, ed. Thomas Mary Sennott (Monrovia, Calif.: Catholic Treasures, 1987).

27. Herman Schmidt, S.J., *La constitution de la sante liturgie: Texte–Genèse–Commentaire–Documents* (Brussels: Editions Lumen Vitae, 1966), 49–59.

28. For the contemporary significance of this document see Jonathan Gaspar and Romanus Cessario, "'Worthy of the Temple': Liturgical Music and Theologal Faith," *Nova et Vetera* (English) 3 (2005): 673–88.

29. In this context it is useful to recall what then Cardinal Joseph Ratzinger said upon being received into the Pontifical Academy of Sciences during its plenary session (Nov. 8–11, 2002): "I did my philosophical and theological studies immediately after the war, from 1946 to 1951. In this period, theological formation in the faculty of Munich was essentially determined by the biblical, liturgical and ecumenical movement of the time between the two World Wars." For the complete text of his remarks see Pontifical Academy of Sciences, *Scripta Varia* 105, *The Cultural Values of Science* (Vatican City, 2003), 50–52.

30. The website of the Archdiocese of Bologna comments as follows about this notable and controversial figure of the Vatican II period: "Fu anche un indiscusso protagonista del Concilio Vaticano II, prima come animatore e moderatore della commissione liturgica, poi come presidente del "Consilium ad exsequendam constitutionem liturgicam."

31. For documentation on all but the last name see Reiner Kaczynski, "Toward the Reform of the Liturgy," in *The Mature Council: Second Period and Intersession, September 1963–September 1964*, vol. 3 of *History of Vatican II*, ed. Giuseppe Alberigo (English version, ed. Joseph A. Komonchak) (Maryknoll, N.Y.: Orbis, 2000), 238. Diekmann was nominated by Archbishop Paul Hallinan for the second, third, and fourth sessions of the council. For further information see Kathleen Hughes, *The Monk's Tale: A Biography of Godfrey Diekmann* (Collegeville, Minn.: Liturgical Press, 1991).

32. *SC* 1: "Suum esse arbitratur peculiari ratione etiam instaurandam atque fovendam liturgiam curare."

33. For the convenience of the reader I provide a schematic overview of the constitution: The first chapter (5–46) stipulates the general principles that should govern the restoration and the promotion of the sacred liturgy. Here only the main subdivisions are given: (1) the nature of the sacred liturgy and its importance in the Church's life

(nos. 5–13); (2) the promotion of liturgical instruction and active participation (nos. 14–20); (3) the reform of the sacred liturgy, which is subdivided into four sets of norms that the council stipulates for the carrying out of the mandated changes (21–40); (4) promotion of liturgical life in diocese and parish (41–42); and (5) the promotion of pastoral-liturgical action (43–46). The second chapter (47–58) treats the most sacred mystery of the Eucharist. The third chapter (59–82) treats the other sacraments and sacramentals. The fourth chapter (83–101) treats the divine office. The fifth chapter (102–111) treats the liturgical year. The sixth chapter (112–121) treats sacred music. The seventh chapter (122–130) treats sacred art and sacred furnishings. Lastly, the appendix (1–2) contains a declaration made by the council on the revision of the calendar.

34. *SC* 6: "Sed etiam ut, quod annuntiabant, opus salutis per sacrificium et sacramenta, circa quae tota liturgica vertit, exercerent."

35. See Liam Walsh, O.P., "Sacraments and Sacramentals" in *Vatican II: The Liturgy Constitution*, ed. Austin Flannery, O.P. (Dublin: Scepter, 1966), 44.

36. For some interesting observations about theological developments in Europe *entre les deux guerres* see my article titled "An Observation on Robert Lauder's Review of G. A. McCool, S.J.," *Thomist* 56 (1992): 701–10. It is possible to inquire whether certain emphases developed during the twentieth century, especially by European theologians, in biblical, historical, and even ecumenical studies, eventually contributed to some of the controversies about the Church's liturgy that have prompted some theologians and church members to call for a reform of the liturgical renewal.

37. See Bouyer, *Liturgy Revived;* and Jungmann's essay "Constitution on the Sacred Liturgy," in *Commentary on the Documents of Vatican II*, vol. 1, ed. Herbert Vorgrimler, trans. Lalit Adolphus, Kevin Smyth, and Richard Strachan (New York: Herder and Herder, 1967–1969).

38. See note 3.

39. Avery Cardinal Dulles, "From Ratzinger to Benedict," *First Things* (Feb. 2006), 26.

40. On this opinion and for details of the liturgical renewal that took place under Saint Pius V, see Nicole Lemaître, *Saint Pie V* (Paris: Librarie Arthème Fayard, 1994), 198, and ch. 10, "Imposer ou unifier la liturgie?"

41. Dulles, "From Ratzinger," 26. The 7 July 2007 "Litterae Apostolicae Motu Proprio Datae" of Pope Benedict XVI, "Summorum Pontificum," addresses this historical circumstance by authorizing the use of the 1962 Missal as a *Forma extraordinaria* of the Roman Rite.

42. See *SC* 7n20.

43. *Catechismus romanus, seu catechismus ex decreto Concilii Tridentini ad parochos Pii Quinto pont. max. iussu editus*, ed. Petrus Rodríguez (Rome: Liberia Editrice Vaticana, 1989).

44. *Roman Catechism*, pt. II, ch. 1 (Rodríguez, ed., p. 153, lines 1–4).

45. See note 6.

46. Apostolic constitution, *Fidei depositum*, no. 2.

47. Ibid.

48. *Roman Catechism*, pt. II, ch. 1 (Rodríguez, ed., pp. 165–66, lines 286–300).

49. This should come as no surprise inasmuch as the theological consultants responsible for the Council of Trent's decrees on the sacraments were drawn mainly from the ranks of Spanish Dominicans, whose native land it was thought had not been compromised by the introduction of Lutheran theology. For further information see Angelo Walz, *I Domenicani al Concilio di Trento* (Rome: Herder, 1961).

50. Bouyer, *Liturgical Piety*, 1.

51. Bernard Leeming, S.J., "Recent Trends in Sacramental Theology," *Irish Theological Quarterly* 23 (1956): 195–217.

52. To quote Father Leeming's opinion at the time: "The trend is genial, but sometimes results in a lack of clearness and blunt facing of the problems" (ibid., 204).

53. Father Leeming aired the view that "the word 'mystic' may perhaps sometimes be used to cover up poverty or confusion of thought" (ibid., 206). After the council Johann Auer, *A General Doctrine of the Sacraments and the Mystery of the Eucharist* (Washington, D.C.: Catholic University of America Press, 1995), wrote that "the central concerns of the mystery theology of O. Casel, which seemed to have been somehow rejected by the encyclical *Mediator Dei* (1947), were now incorporated rather globally by both the language and the intention of the council" (174).

54. In his address titled "Current Challenges for Sacramental Theology," *Antiphon* 5 (2000): 44, 45, Cardinal Godfried Danneels concedes that the theses that deal with sacramental causality require reworking: "Classical theologians have worked out a wide array of theories in response to this question [how do the sacraments bring forth their effects?], but most of them are extremely difficult to uphold today" (44).

55. For some reflections on this phenomenon see my "Walk according to the Light: An Illustration from North America," in *Camminare nella luce: Prospettive della teologia morale a partire da 'Veritatis splendor,'* ed. Livio Melina and José Noriega (Rome: Lateran University Press, 2004), 401–407.

56. For further information on Thomism see my book titled *A Short History of Thomism* (Washington, D.C.: Catholic University of America Press, 2005).

57. Liam G. Walsh, O.P., "Sacraments," in *The Theology of Thomas Aquinas*, ed. Rik Van Nieuwenhove and Joseph Wawrykow (Notre Dame, Ind.: University of Notre Dame Press, 2005), 326–64.

58. Colman O'Neill, O.P., *Sacramental Realism* (Chicago: Midwest Theological Forum, 1998).

59. Colman O'Neill, O.P., *Meeting Christ in the Sacraments*, rev. ed., Romanus Cessario, O.P. (New York: Alba House, 1991).

60. Matthew Levering, *Sacrifice and Community: Jewish Offering and Christian Eucharist* (Malden, Mass.: Blackwell, 2005).

61. See *Summa theologiae* II–II, q. 81, a. 2: "Cum ergo ad religionem pertineat reddere honorem debitum alicui, scilicet Deo, manifestum est quod religio virtus est." For further discussion, see my *Virtues, or the Examined Life* (New York: Continuum, 2002), 145–46.

62. See Schmidt, *Constitution*, 144.

63. *ST* III, q. 61, a. 1, sc: "Sed necessarium est ad humanam salutem homines adunari in unum verae religionis nomen."

7

Doctrinal Perspectives on the Church in the Modern World

J. Brian Benestad

The Pastoral Constitution on the Church in the Modern World (*Gaudium et spes*) is divided into two parts. Preceded by a preface and a brief introduction, part I primarily lays out doctrinal principles, but not without suggesting pastoral applications. Part II has mainly a pastoral orientation but on the firm ground of doctrinal principles; therefore, it has both contingent and permanent elements.[1] *Gaudium et spes* is a constitution and stands as one of the four pillars of the council, along with *Lumen gentium, Dei verbum,* and *Sacrosanctum concilium,* respectively the Dogmatic Constitution on the Church, the Dogmatic Constitution on Revelation, and the Constitution on the Liturgy, which is also a doctrinal document but without "dogmatic" in the title. *Gaudium et spes* develops the council's doctrine on the nature of the Church and must be understood in the light of *Lumen gentium* and not vice versa. The title of the constitution mentions "the Church in the world of this time" so as not to give the impression that the Church stands over against the world but, like every other institution, is just a presence *in* the world of today.

Ten years after the publication of *Gaudium et spes,* Joseph Ratzinger wrote an article that explained that the preface (*GS* 1–3) of this council document had been used in Europe, especially in the Netherlands, to justify a close identification with the concerns of the world. Ratzinger criticized the preface for its astounding optimism. "An attitude of critical reserve with respect to the formative forces of the new age was to be given up through a decisive involvement in its movement."[2] Otherwise stated, the preface of *Gaudium et spes* did not show sufficient awareness of the tension between the Catholic tradition and the modern philosophy, which exercises a strong influence in the contemporary era. For example, it had nothing to say about moral relativism, the invocation of rights for bad ends, or the growing influence of historicism. It did not sufficiently warn people "of the perilous frailty of human nature which has been a threat to human progress in all the periods of history."[3] Despite the limitations of the preface, it does not seem to me that a careful reading of this brief text justified any kind of secularization.

In the same article Ratzinger also mentioned his opinion that the rest of *Gaudium et spes* after the preface did purify and deepen the heritage of the Catholic tradition.[4] In a recent address to the Roman Curia, Pope Benedict XVI said that Vatican Council II has to be rediscovered today by paying close attention to the text of its documents. Those documents cannot be properly interpreted, he argues, with "a hermeneutic of discontinuity and rupture" but only with a "hermeneutic of reform." The real council is found in the texts, not in some vague "spirit" of the council that would constitute a rupture with the deposit of faith. With this focus I reflect on the introduction and part I.[5]

Articles 4–10 are titled "Introductory Statement, the Human Condition in Today's World." This introduction purports to be a phenomenological description of the world at the time of the council. The council undertakes this project because "in every age it is the duty of the Church to scrutinize the signs of the time and to interpret them in the light of the Gospel" (no. 4, modified translation). Much of this introductory statement is not particularly illuminating, with a few very noteworthy exceptions.

Most notable is the council's observation that "the change in mentality and structures frequently calls into question the *bona recepta*, especially among the young" (*GS* 7, modified trans.). Those Latin words are translated as "accepted values" or "traditional values." In my mind, a more accurate translation would read something like "long-accepted religious beliefs and practices, as well as the traditional virtues." At this point in time the *bona recepta* have been further called into question. A second related conciliar observation is that "growing multitudes are abandoning religion in practice" (*GS* 7, modified trans.). People are profoundly shaken by the denial of God or religion found in the areas of philosophy, literature, the arts, humanities, history, and the civil laws. Not rarely are such denials presented "as a requirement of scientific progress or of a new type of humanism" (*GS* 7, modified trans.). The Catholic Church is still reeling form this phenomenon.

After listing various imbalances in the world without any incisive commentary (*GS* 8), the council says that "it devolves on humanity to establish a political, social, and economic order which will to an ever better extent serve man and help individuals as well as groups to affirm and *perfect* the dignity proper to them" (ad dignitatem sibi propriam affirmandam et *excolendam*, *GS* 9, modified trans. and my emphasis). This notion of various communities playing a role in refining, ennobling, and perfecting human dignity is an extremely important contribution of *Gaudium et spes* both to the Catholic Church and to the whole world. Part I has a lot to say on the foundation, meaning, permanence, and *perfecting* of human dignity. The last theme has yet to be integrated into most presentations of Catholic social doctrine in the United States.

The rest of section nine contains examples of affirming and perfecting human dignity. The council mentions the provision of material goods to people in the developing nations, greater freedom for citizens in many parts of the world, the possibility of more people participating in the political and cultural life of their nations, equality for women before the law, greater opportunity for laborers and farmers to develop their talents, the extension of the benefits of culture to everyone, and greater brotherhood within and among nations. Most of these examples are readily accepted as ways to show respect for human dignity. What is not so readily understood is the conciliar teaching in part I that the education of the mind, the purification of the heart, and greater unity among human beings, based on truth, are important ways to elevate and perfect human dignity.

The last article of this section contains several very important points. First, the council affirms that there is a close connection between the disorder in the soul and that in society, echoing on this point the grand Catholic tradition, represented especially by St. Augustine, St. Thomas Aquinas, and St. Thomas More. Here are the council's words: "Indeed, as a weak sinful being, man not rarely does what he would not, and fails to do what he would. Hence, he suffers from internal divisions, and from these flow so many and such great discords in society" (GS 10). This means that the Church and society must pay attention to the formation of the character of citizens in order to make possible the bringing about of a just social order. This conciliar position is opposed to that strain of modern political philosophy that holds that justice is best sought by establishing the most appropriate structures and passing the best laws, with scant or no attention paid to the virtues and vices of individuals.

The council fully recognizes both the difficulty of addressing contemporary problems faced by humanity and of finding answers to the grand questions about the purpose of human existence and the shape of the best political and social order. In order to be of some assistance to the world the council proposes, "in the light of Christ . . . to speak to all in order to illuminate the mystery of man and to cooperate in finding a solution to the principal problems of our time" (GS 10, modified trans.). The council explains that it is the Church's belief "that Christ, who died and was raised up for all, can through his Spirit offer man the light and the strength to measure up to his supreme vocation" (ibid., modified trans.).

The Church and the Vocation of Human Beings

Part I begins with a prefatory article (GS 11) that explains that the Church will have a dialogue with unbelievers "on the question who and what man really is."[6] To this end the Church, "moved by faith" under the guidance of the Holy Spirit, "seeks to discern [discernere replaces animadvertere (to take notice of) from an earlier draft[7]] the true signs of God's presence and purpose" (GS 11). The emphasis on discernment calls to mind the traditional Catholic teaching on the discernment of spirits so prominent in the Spiritual Exercises of

St. Ignatius. *Gaudium et spes* expresses the Church's belief that discernment and action under the influence of faith will lead to a true humanism.[8]

The Nature and Basis of Human Dignity

The next eleven articles, which make up chapter 1 (*GS* 12–22), address subjects that pertain to the dignity of the human person. I first briefly discuss the prevailing view of human dignity and then present the contrasting view of *Gaudium et spes*, which focuses on the *perfecting* of human dignity. This goal has enormous implications for ethics and social ethics and exercises an influence on the subjects treated in part II. Later in this section I take up the other subjects discussed in relation to human dignity. Because of the greater significance of chapter 1 on human dignity, I devote more space to it than to chapters 2, 3, and 4, respectively, on people in community, human activity in the world, and the mission of the Church in the contemporary world. Pope Benedict's first encyclical, *Deus caritas est*, further clarifies the text of *Gaudium et spes* on the mission of the Church in the world by discussing her contribution to justice.

Liberal regimes dispose citizens to have an incomplete understanding of human dignity. People are said to have dignity because they are autonomous and capable of making choices. According to the commonest opinion in contemporary society, the dignity of the human person is especially secured by ensuring the protection of rights. The initial and primary emphasis on rights is, of course, a logical step since the autonomous exercise of choice requires the possession of rights. Catholic social doctrine certainly agrees that the dignity of the human person needs the protection of rights but stresses that people have to exercise their rights in the light of moral law; otherwise, they will diminish their dignity. This kind of emphasis is nearly absent in a liberal democracy.

Another consequence of understanding dignity as constituted by human autonomy is linking the assessment of human dignity to a person's quality of life, especially the capacity to make autonomous choices. It is now commonly thought that people's dignity diminishes with their declining quality of life. Some argue that they are not entitled to the same rights as healthy individuals. The Terri Schiavo case showed that the courts and many people gave their approval to the withdrawing of food and water from her because of her poor quality of life.

Pope John Paul II refers to the contemporary assault on the traditional understanding of human dignity in his *Evangelium vitae*: "We must also mention the mentality which tends to *equate personal dignity with the capacity for verbal and explicit*, or at least perceptible *communication*. It is clear that on the basis of these presuppositions there is no place in the world for anyone who, like the unborn or the dying, is a weak element in the social structure, or for anyone who appears completely at the mercy of others and radically dependent on them, and can only communicate through the silent language of a profound sharing of affection."[9]

This way of understanding the human person is highly individualistic, even tyrannical, and fails to appreciate the rhythm of life, in which a person moves from the weakness and dependence of the unborn, to the strength of adulthood, to the weakness of old age. Even during the time of people's strength, they are dependent in various ways for their physical, intellectual, and spiritual care. In the Catholic mind, human beings retain their dignity when they are receiving care and may even grow in dignity. Think of those who accept their dependance and suffering as a way of identifying with the passion of Christ.

The liberal understanding of dignity is a challenge to the Catholic Church both in the area of ordinary catechetics and Catholic social thought. Careful education is necessary for Catholics to understand that the dignity of the human person is not essentially constituted by the ability to make choices. According to Catholic teaching, people have dignity for three reasons: They are created in the image and likeness of God, redeemed by Jesus Christ, and destined for eternal life in communion with God.[10]

This threefold foundation for human dignity (creation, redemption, and the call to communion with God) is both unshakable and instructive. No act of the human person can remove this foundation. Even when people commit the worst sins and crimes and suffer diminished physical and spiritual capacities they retain human dignity. While informed Christians often acknowledge and emphasize this Christian teaching about the permanent character of human dignity, rarely do Catholics hear that human dignity is also a goal or an achievement. But this perfection of human dignity is the clear implication of the threefold foundation of human dignity.

Given the foundation of human dignity and the reality of sin and error, it logically follows that all, with the help of God's grace, will have to strive and strain to reach their ultimate goal, communion with the triune God. All human beings are able to do this, argues Pope John Paul II, because God "willed to leave man 'in the power of his own counsel' [cf. Sir 15:14], so that he would seek his Creator of his own accord and would arrive at full and blessed perfection by cleaving to God" (GS 17, modified trans.).[11] Christians continually achieve or *perfect* their dignity by seeking the truth, resisting sin, practicing virtue, and repenting when they succumb to temptation. In other words, dignity is not just a permanent possession that is unaffected by the way we live. In one sense, dignity may also be diminished by a life of sin or continuously appropriated over a lifetime by seeking perfection, as John Paul II said.

In *Rerum novarum* Pope Leo XIII made the same point using language characteristic of Thomas Aquinas: "True dignity and excellence in men resides in moral living, that is, in virtue."[12] Saint Leo the Great's famous Christmas sermon states this point in a memorable way: "Christian, recognize your dignity, and now that you share in God's own nature, do not return by sin to your former base condition."[13] It is significant that this quotation stands as the first sentence in the section on morality in the new *Catechism of the Catholic Church*. It immediately directs attention to the necessity of achieving or perfecting human dignity by living a moral life.

Gaudium et spes has a number of passages that indicate the perfection that dignity requires of an individual. In its section on the theology of the body, the text says, "But the very dignity of man requires that he glorify God in his body and does not permit the body to serve the perverse inclinations of his heart" (*GS* 14, modified trans.). So, the use of the body to engage in adultery, fornication, or any other bodily sin is a failure to respect the requirements of human dignity and the glory of God. To commit sins with the body is to act beneath one's dignity and therefore is an assault on human dignity.

The next article makes the point that "the intellectual nature of the human person is perfected by wisdom and needs to be. For wisdom gently attracts the mind of man to a quest and a love for what is true and good" (*GS* 15). In addition to doing what is good, it is the seeking and finding of the truth that "maintains the dignity of man," as Cardinal Ratzinger has pointed out.[14] The corollary is also true. Failure to seek the truth endangers the maintenance of one's dignity. In article 16, which is on conscience, the text says, "Man has in his heart a law written by God. To obey that law is his very dignity and according to which he will be judged" (modified trans.). In other words, disobedience of God's law is synonymous with acting beneath one's dignity, and God's favorable judgment of human beings depends on fidelity to the dictates of their conscience. Otherwise stated, obeying their formed conscience perfects the dignity of human beings.

Gaudium et spes further adds these thoughts: "Man's dignity demands that he act according to a knowing and free choice.... Man achieves [the perfection of his dignity] when emancipating himself from all captivity to passion, he pursues his goal in a spontaneous choice of what is good, and procures for himself through effective and skillful action, apt means to that end. Since man's freedom has been damaged by sin, only by the help of God's grace can he bring such a relationship with God into full flower" (*GS* 17).

Finally, in the last two articles of part I the text reads, "The Church holds that the recognition of God is no way hostile to the dignity of man, since this dignity is rooted and perfected in God" (*in ipso Deo fundatur et perficiatur*, *GS* 19). It is communion with God that perfects the dignity of human beings, which can come about only through cooperation with God's grace. In the last article the text says that "Christ fully reveals man to himself and makes clear his most high vocation" (*GS* 22, modified trans.), namely, communion with God and with others through union with Christ. Pope John Paul II may have quoted this sentence from Vatican II more than any other conciliar text. Finally, *Gaudium et spes* makes clear that the perfection of human dignity is a gift made available to all through the death and resurrection of Jesus and the mysterious action of the Holy Spirit, who "in a manner known only to God offers to all the possibility of being associated with this paschal mystery" (*GS* 22, modified trans.).

Pope John Paul II goes so far as to say that martyrdom is "the supreme glorification of human dignity."[15] This statement makes eminent sense because martyrs achieve the summit of human dignity by laying down their lives

DOCTRINAL PERSPECTIVES ON THE CHURCH IN THE MODERN WORLD   153

for God and neighbor. This is the reason Christians hold martyrs in such high regard.

Having discerned the essential elements of human dignity, let us now go back to the beginning of chapter 1 and consider some of the other subjects discussed in relation to this concept. Article 13 discusses sin, the reality of which is revealed to us not only by revelation but also by the experience common to all. Sin causes disorder in our soul and disrupts our relationship with others and with God. "Therefore man is split within himself. As a result, all of human life, whether individual or collective, shows itself to be a dramatic struggle between good and evil, between light and darkness" (*GS* 13). This is one of several places in *Gaudium et spes* where the council mentions the influence that personal sin or vices can have on society and political life. This is a very important point since it is not readily appreciated in the contemporary world, even in many Catholic circles.[16]

Article 14 discusses the constitution of man. He is "one in body and soul." Thus, he may not show disrespect for his body in any way as it is an integral part of his person. Yet, "by his interior qualities [*interioritas*] he outstrips the whole sum of things." He comes into contact with God in the depth of his heart and perceives the truth when he recognizes an immortal and spiritual soul in himself. In these thoughts Ratzinger discerns two Augustinian influences: "the distinction between the 'homo interior' and 'exterior,' and the 'philosophia cordis.' As compared with the corpus-anima schema, this [first distinction] introduces a greater element of personal responsibility and decision regarding the direction of life. It therefore analyzes man more on historical and dynamic than on metaphysical lines. The second is the concept of the 'philosophia cordis,' the biblical concept of the heart which for Augustine expresses the unity of interior life and corporeality."[17] The presence of these Augustinian themes is one of the many indications that *Gaudium et spes* is in continuity with the grand tradition of the Church; this council document is in no way a break with traditional teaching.

The next three articles are a logical follow-up to the previous one on the constitution of man because they "expound what human spirituality is under three aspects: as intellect (that is, as man's capacity for truth), as conscience (that is, as man's capacity for good), and as freedom."[18] The council first notes that great progress has been made in the empirical sciences, as well as in the technical and liberal arts, but then draws a striking contrast between the knowledge drawn from these sciences and arts and the wisdom that perfects the intellect by inclining it "to seek and to love what is true and good" and thus to pass "through visible to invisible realities" (*GS* 15, modified trans.). Then the council makes a dramatic statement about the importance of wisdom, which is even more obvious today because of the new things made possible by biotechnology. "Our age, more than previous centuries, needs such wisdom, so that whatever new things are discovered by man become more human. The future destiny of the world stands in peril unless wiser men and women are forthcoming" (*GS* 15, modified trans.). This statement surely means that the council has no faith in automatic progress through scientific advances. Recently some wise scholars have pointed out that we run the risk of dehumanizing ourselves if we do not have the wisdom to step back from cloning and the destruction of human embryos for research purposes.

Of course, to understand what the council means by wisdom would require a familiarity with the grand tradition of classical Catholic learning. The council mentions one very important traditional observation on the acquisition of wisdom. Acquiring certain wisdom is difficult because of the consequences of sin, while the acquisition of scientific knowledge labors under no such handicap. In looking at this article together with the previous one Ratzinger comments, "The affirmation of metaphysics which articles 14 and 15 formulate with regard to the question of man and of God, is one of the fundamental positions of the schema."[19] To affirm the reality of metaphysics is to affirm the possibility of attaining the kind of overarching wisdom of which the council speaks.

The article on conscience affirms that people discern in the intimate recesses of their conscience or heart a law inscribed by God, one that calls everyone to love God and neighbor. All Christians and non-Christians are united by following their consciences in their search for what is true and for solutions both to their own personal dilemmas and to the pressing problems of the day. If their conscience does not err, people will be following "objective norms of morality" (*GS* 16). Despite the existence of the law written in the heart by God, conscience, according to the council, "not rarely errs from invincible ignorance without losing its dignity" (*GS* 16, modified trans.). The reason such frequent erring can occur in the presence of God's interior call is left unexplained.

Ratzinger holds that the dialogue between Christians and non-Christians hinges ultimately on their common recourse to conscience: "Fidelity to conscience unites Christian and non-Christians and permits them to work to solve the moral tasks of mankind, just as it compels them to both humble and open inquiry into truth. In this essential kernel the 'objectivism' of the schema is certainly right and not vulnerable to critical thought."[20] What the future Benedict XVI found wanting in the article was insufficient attention to the difficulties that modern men and women experience in finding what is true and good.

In the article on freedom the council first mentions that people often understand freedom as license and use it to pursue evil ends. The proper use of freedom is knowingly and willingly to realize one's dignity by "emancipating oneself from all captivity to passion" and by seeking the good under the influence of God's grace. Joseph Ratzinger found this article to be "one of the least satisfactory in the whole document," mostly because of what it does not address and for using Pelagian terminology in speaking of man as "sese ab omni passionum captivitate liberans finem suum persequitur et apta subsidia . . . procurat." Ratzinger believed it should have done three things: (1) explained the New Testament teaching on freedom, (2) addressed "that overshadowing of freedom of which psychology and sociology at the present time inform us in such a disturbing way," and (3) discussed the difficulty of exercising freedom properly because of "the discord which runs through man and which is described so dramatically in Romans 7:13–25."[21] Despite these limitations the text still distinguishes between liberty and license and makes crystal clear that man "obtains" dignity by using his freedom well ("Talem vero dignitatem obtinet homo cum ... finem suam in boni libera electione persequitur").

Article 18 on death explains that people would not have to die if Adam and Eve had not sinned. Death, however, is overcome by the death and resurrection of Jesus. Christian faith relieves believers' anxiety by promising life with Christ after death and by giving them the power to communicate with their deceased loved ones in Christ. Ratzinger's most important comment on this article is this: "In a positive sense, the Christological promise is expounded in three directions: as a promise of eternal community of man with God, as a promise of the new communication of men with one another in Christ, and finally as a reference to Christ's community with us in death, which at the same time guarantees and includes our communion of life with him. Here for the first time the Easter mystery appears as the center of Christology and the center of personal life."[22]

The next three articles constitute a dialogue with contemporary atheism. The council attempts to discern the kinds and causes of atheism, as well as the remedies the Church can offer. I must omit commentary on this section.

The chapter on "The Dignity of the Human Person" in *Gaudium et spes* culminates in a Christocentric theology. "The truth is that only in the mystery of the incarnate Word does the mystery of man take on light.... Christ, the final Adam, by the Revelation of the mystery of the father and his love, fully reveals man to himself and makes his supreme calling clear" (*GS* 22). Christ's life and death reveal to all human beings that they have very great dignity and are called to eternal union with God. *Gaudium et spes* logically adds that "All this holds true not only for Christians, but for all men of good will in whose hearts grace works in an unseen way. For, since Christ died for all and since the ultimate vocation of man is in fact one, and divine, we ought to believe that the Holy Spirit in a manner known only to God offers to all the possibility of being associated [*consocientur*, not *se conscient*, as stated in a previous draft of *Gaudium et spes*] with this paschal mystery" (*GS* 22, modified). The passive form of the verb indicates that God is the agent who associates all people to the paschal mystery. Joseph Ratzinger comments, "We cannot bring about the paschal mystery for ourselves; as the mystery of death and resurrection, by its very nature it can only be received."[23] The dignity to which all are called is God's gift, which we do not achieve merely by our own efforts.

Persons in Community

Chapter 2 of *Gaudium et spes*, "The Community of Mankind," simply reviews "some of the more basic truths" of Catholic social doctrine on human society in the light of revelation. It calls to mind the constant teaching of the Church about the social nature of the human person. In John 17:21–22 Jesus "implied a certain likeness between the union of the divine Persons and the union of God's children in truth and charity. This likeness reveals that man ... cannot fully find himself except through a sincere gift of himself" (*GS* 24, modified trans.). In other words, men and women can attain their perfection only by loving God and their neighbor in the proper way. Just as loving oneself badly is possible, so people can love each other in a harmful way. The union among human beings, therefore, can be realized only if they love each other in accordance with the *truth* about God and man.

The protection and perfection of human beings depend to a very large extent on the communities of which they are members: the family, voluntary associations,[24] the Church, and the political community. The protection of people's rights and the development of their personal qualities or virtues are the two great advantages of all social life. Without rights people's lives, liberties, and property are in danger. Having rights, however, is not enough to be a good human being. That requires a good character brought about by the practice of the virtues. In addition, only people with a virtuous character will definitely respect the rights of others. Those with a bad character will choose to respect rights only when it is in their self-interest.

Although not going into much detail, the council points out that the development of the human person depends on the health of the family, associations, and the state. In other words, individuals are influenced for good or ill by the regime. The council makes this point by arguing that the quality of social life can even help people realize the religious dimension of their vocations in life but quickly adds that "men are often diverted from doing good and spurred toward evil by the social circumstances in which they live and are immersed from their birth" (*GS* 25). In other words, the community's way of life has deep effects on the lives of individuals. In the United States, for example, the culture or regime induces many young people to bow down before the dictatorship of relativism. Those with a strong religious faith are capable of escaping the pervasive influence of a bad regime, but they often have to struggle. That is probably why Pope John Paul II kept asking bishops in Rome for their *ad limina* visits what they had done to change the culture of their countries.

The council further adds that the defects of the social order, manifested in private associations and government, originate primarily in the pride and egoism of individual citizens. It is, then, sin that perverts the culture or the regime. Once the regime is perverted by the effect of individual sins, as a whole it then coaxes individuals to do more evil. In the council's words, "When the order of things is affected by the consequences of sin, man, born with an inclination toward evil, thereafter finds new inducements to sin, which cannot be overcome without strenuous efforts and the assistance of grace" (*GS* 25, modified trans.). The council is actually highlighting the deep and pervasive influence of the regime in a manner reminiscent of Plato and Aristotle. These philosophers also recognized the important role of individuals' virtues and vices in bringing about a particular regime and the role of the latter in determining the kind of character individual citizens would acquire.

In arguing that individuals must be good if society is going to be good, the council is really siding with the ancients in their quarrel with the moderns about the main source of justice in a society. Kant argued in his *Perpetual Peace* that a just society is possible even in a nation of devils, provided people intelligently organize the order of things in social and political life.[25] Marx said that injustice could be overcome by doing away with private property and establishing communism. Plato, Aristotle, Augustine, Aquinas, and Thomas More contended that the attainment of justice in society always depends on the wisdom and virtue of individual citizens.

The kind of regime or social order the council favored is one that makes possible the attainment of the common good, that is, "the sum of those conditions of social life which allow social groups and their individual members to attain their proper perfection more fully and more quickly" (*GS* 26, modified trans.). For this to happen a continual effort must be made to establish a social order respectful of freedom, "founded on truth, built on justice and animated by love" (*GS* 26). This project, of course, requires educating citizens to virtue so that they will fulfill their duties and respect rights. It also requires establishing the kind of society where families and religious groups can effectively pursue their mission.

One cannot overestimate the importance of the council's statement on the common good. Its correct interpretation shows that the Catholic Church has not abandoned a substantive understanding of the common good in favor of something like a procedural republic. In other words, the council is not saying that the common good should be limited to things like a flourishing economy, the protection of rights, good health care, a clean environment, and other similar goods. The Catholic Church keeps trying to persuade people that seeking the common good requires attention to truth, justice, love, virtue, and duty in the social order. What specific initiatives the various elements of the social order, such as the family, the church, and the various levels of government, should take are not specified, but they are addressed in chapter 4 of part I and in part II of *Gaudium et spes*.

In part II the council document does say that the political community exists on account of the common good (*GS* 74). Thus, the government should try to make possible the attainment of the common good, substantively understood, through its own action and by relying on the various elements of the social order. In a liberal society governments will have a limited role in promoting the virtues, but one nonetheless. For example, public schools necessarily inculcate diligence and teach students to respect one another and not to cheat on exams. The law prohibits murder, rape, and robbery. It may properly give people incentives to stay married, erect obstacles to divorce, and pass laws that protect the life of the unborn, forbid euthanasia, and even teach that marriage can take place only between a man and a woman. By making use of the "bully pulpit" the president may invite citizens to volunteer services to their country, as John Kennedy famously did.

One of the reasons that many have not grasped the full teaching of *Gaudium et spes* is that the council does not sufficiently clarify its definition of the common good. When it gives specific examples of the common good, it lists things that would be the object of any procedural republic: "food, clothing, and shelter; the right to choose a state of life freely and to found a family, the rights to education, to employment, to a good reputation, to respect, to appropriate information, to activity in accord with the upright norm of one's conscience, to protection of privacy and to rightful freedom in matters religious" (*GS* 26). The requirements of human dignity and therefore of the common good require much more than this list indicates, as I have previously indicated. The council did, however, spell out what the dignity of the human person requires in and from the social order, as we have seen, thereby shedding more light on the shape of the common good.

Because of the dignity of the human person, *Gaudium et spes* implies that the mores should not support, and the law should not allow, any of the following:

> any type of murder, genocide, abortion, euthanasia, or voluntary suicide; whatever violates the integrity of the human person, such as mutilation, torments inflicted on body or mind, attempts to coerce the will itself; whatever offends human dignity, such as subhuman living conditions, arbitrary imprisonment, deportation, slavery, prostitution, the selling of women and children; as well as ignominious working conditions . . . and other disgraceful things of this sort. (*GS* 27, modified trans.)

While this list is obviously not meant to be exhaustive, it is sufficiently inclusive to indicate the kinds of things that should receive no support from the law or the mores. The obvious reason is that the practice of these things is an assault on human dignity. The less obvious reason is that "such behavior defiles those who do them more than those who suffer the injustice" (no. 27, modified trans.). In other words, the doers of evil deeds act beneath their own dignity. This fact indicates that the common good must include concern for the character of citizens. In some instances, then, the law should not only protect citizens from being the victims of injustice but also prevent others from being perpetrators of injustice. This approach of the council brings to mind a statement of St. Augustine on the justification for the use of force against evildoers: "He whose license for wrongdoing is wrested away is usefully conquered, for nothing is less prosperous than the prosperity of sinners, which nourishes punishable impunity and strengthens the evil will, which is, as it were, an enemy within."[26]

After reading the last section of the chapter on community, one cannot but notice that the council fathers leave the realm of politics and civil society and focus on the life of the Church. While most of the chapter emphasizes the common good of civil society, this last section exclusively discusses sanctification, solidarity, and social unity in the Church. The Church, whatever the state of civil society and the political order, must always pursue these goals. When things are going well, the life of the Church will make significant contributions to the common good of civil society. Even when civil society fails to be a place of solidarity among citizens, the Church can still provide a haven for its members who seek sanctification in a community bound together by solidarity.

Human Action in the World

The council injects a note of realism in pointing out that human action will always be engaged in a "monumental struggle against the powers of darkness" (no. 37). People will always encounter opposition when they work for peace and justice. The only solution is for human beings, constantly threatened by pride and disordered self-love in their activity, to be "purified and perfected by the power of Christ's cross and resurrection" (GS 37) and to be nourished by the body and blood of Christ, the viaticum for the journey back to God.

The council teaches that "a man is more precious for what he is than for what he has. Similarly, all that men do to obtain greater justice, wider brotherhood, and a more humane ordering of social relationships has greater worth than technical advances" (no 35). The council is surely implying that it is not science and technology that will bring about a just society but the new commandment of love Christ taught us, which is "the basic law of human perfection and, therefore, of the world's transformation" (GS 38). This latter statement is still another way the council expresses its agreement with the teaching of Augustine and Aquinas: The common good of society depends on the perfection of individual souls.

The Mission of the Church in the Contemporary World

The fourth and last chapter of part I is titled "The Mission of the Church in the Contemporary World." To read this chapter correctly readers must keep in mind that it presupposes everything said in the first three chapters on human dignity, community, and human activity, as well as in the entire constitution of *Lumen gentium*. This is important because some have argued that *Lumen gentium* must be interpreted in the light of *Gaudium et spes*.

While exercising its proper salvific and eschatological mission, the Church also acts "as a leaven and a kind of soul for human society" (GS 40). In communicating divine life to humanity and teaching the truth of revelation, the Church also "heals and elevates the dignity of the human person, strengthens what holds society together and imbues everyday human activity with a deeper meaning and signification" (GS 40, modified trans.). The Church promotes human dignity, as we have seen, by making clear that it is not only a given but also a goal to be sought by avoiding sin and seeking holiness. This teaching corresponds to people's sense that they can act beneath their dignity or in accordance with it. The Church helps keeps society together by forming consciences, teaching the meaning of justice, and putting love into practice in so many ways. It also helps people to see that all of their good actions, however ineffective in a worldly sense, build up the kingdom of God. The Catholic Church further recognizes and appreciates the good done by other Christian churches for the individual and various communities and openly acknowledges that the "world" can prepare the ground for the preaching of the gospel. This seems to mean that the laws and customs of society facilitate the perception and reception of the gospel teaching.

The council fathers next take up the question of human rights and note that the Church proclaims the benefits of human rights "by virtue of the gospel entrusted to her" (*GS* 41, modified trans.). They applaud people's growing recognition and vindication of their rights but offer a caveat and a criterion for the evaluation of rights. The caveat is that the movement to promote rights must be protected against a "false autonomy," one that does not take its bearings by an objective moral standard. "For we are tempted to think that our personal rights are fully ensured only when we are exempt from every requirement of divine law. But in this way, the dignity of the human person is not saved, but rather perishes" (*GS* 41, modified trans.). I believe this statement is extraordinarily important. It is one of the clearest statements in Catholic social doctrine regarding the necessity of an objective criterion for the exercise of rights. Without a common objective standard, rights can become loose canons that shoot down elements of both divine and natural law that stand as guides for the exercise of human freedom. In addition, this text says that the preservation of human dignity requires obedience to the divine law.

While the Church's mission is not to take on the responsibility of establishing justice in the political order; it will, however, necessarily benefit the state and society as it pursues its proper mission. As Congar noted, "the Church at the very moment in which it is least *of* the world, can be most *for* the world."[27] By teaching the truth about Jesus Christ and putting love into practice the Church, as an institution and through its individual members, helps "to construct and consolidate society [*communitas hominum*] according to the divine law" (*GS* 42, modified trans.). In his first encyclical Pope Benedict XVI says that the Church contributes to the realization of justice in a society by forming consciences, putting forth rational arguments to clarify the meaning of justice, and reawakening people's spiritual forces for the great tasks facing humanity. The clarification of the meaning of justice is crucial since practical reason has difficulty discerning its meaning because the love of power and interest inhibit disinterested perception. Echoing *Gaudium et spes*, Pope Benedict reiterates the point that the Church has no political mission. Establishing a just social order is the work of politics, to which the laity of the Church in their role as citizens are invited to make concrete contributions. The Church, however, can have a very great impact on the establishment of just social order if it stimulates "greater insight into the authentic requirements of justice as well as greater readiness to act accordingly."[28]

Because of her religious mission, the Church is not bound to any particular economic, social, or political system. The Church can be at ease with any government that respects her religious liberty and the rights of individual citizens, although Catholic social doctrine seeks to persuade people that some form of constitutional democracy seems to work best in contemporary society. The kind of democratic government favored by Catholic social doctrine is one in which the civil law is in conformity with the moral law, as Pope John Paul II reiterated in his 1995 encyclical *Evangelium vitae* (*GS* 72).

Gaudium et spes encourages all of the lay faithful to let their faith influence every aspect of their lives. The council fathers make this exhortation in the light of their conviction that the "split between the faith that many profess and their daily lives must be counted among the more serious errors of our age" (*GS* 43). In 1998 Cardinal Avery Dulles addressed this problem with his usual clarity: "Any effort by the Church to say what is morally permitted, required or prohibited by the law of God in the spheres of politics, medicine, business or family life is resented as an intrusion into alien territory.... Anyone who sees religion as determinative for secular activities is likely to be regarded as a fanatic. Teachers, businessmen, politicians, or judges who let religion impinge in a major way on their professional activities are considered eccentric."[29] In more recent times Catholic senators have demonstrated this split between faith and life by their proud and untroubled advocacy of maintaining the constitutional right to abortion established by *Roe v. Wade*. Of course, there are also many Catholics who let their faith affect the way they do their work and live their family life.

In order to convince the lay faithful that the integration of faith and life is crucial for them *Gaudium et spes* adds: "The Christian who neglects his temporal duties neglects his duties toward his neighbor and even God, and jeopardizes his eternal salvation" (*GS* 43). This surely means that people's religious beliefs must inform their professional, family, and social lives. In other words, with a well-formed conscience, the laity are to ensure that "the divine law is inscribed in the life of the earthly city" (*GS* 43).

In carrying out their tasks the laity can properly look to priests for instruction in the faith and for spiritual strength but should not expect them to have specific answers to concrete problems. "The Church guards the heritage of God's Word and draws from it religious and moral principles, without always having at hand the solution to particular problems" (*GS* 33). For example, priests can teach laypeople who work in hospitals to make sure that patients receive proper, loving care, but they cannot usually tell them what changes would have to be made there to improve patient care. The lay faithful need to acquire the competence to figure that out for themselves. While laypeople have the primary responsibility to be a leaven in all of the seams of society, bishops and priests can also have an enormous impact on political and social life by their teaching and their activities.

Distinguishing the duties of clergy from those of the laity has been difficult since the end of Vatican Council II. Right at the beginning of his papacy Pope John Paul II told bishops to pursue justice through evangelization,[30] to communicate Catholic social doctrine,[31] and to avoid anything that "resembles political party spirit or subjection to this or that ideology or system."[32] "Secular duties and activities belong properly although not exclusively to laymen" (*GS* 43). These duties include the prudent application of Catholic social principles to public policy. In making such prudential judgments on the basis of shared goals, "it happens rather frequently, and legitimately, so," says Vatican II's *Gaudium et spes*, "that with equal sincerity some of the faithful will disagree with others on a given matter" (*GS* 43). These disagreements can arise when Catholics apply doctrinal and moral principles to public policy or to the vast domain of civil society. For example, Catholics may disagree on the best way to run a Catholic school, a Catholic hospital, or town-sponsored athletic teams for children. In the political arena, differences of opinion are inevitable because of the complexity of issues (for example, taxes, welfare, and economic policy). Where there is legitimate disagreement, no individual or group "is allowed in the aforementioned situations to appropriate the Church's authority for his opinion" (*GS* 43).

Some theologians have improperly invoked the passage in article 43 or the one in article 33 that address the inability of bishops and priests to give specific answers to particular problems as a directive to be silent in areas where they in fact have the knowledge and duty to speak. Bishops and priests should never be silent about the principles of Catholic social teaching even if those principles have a direct bearing on the political issues of the day. For example, bishops rightfully argue in the public domain against the cultural and legal acceptance of abortion, euthanasia, same-sex "marriage," and the death penalty with the qualifications outlined in the *Catechism of the Catholic Church*, no. 2267. They can also tell Catholic politicians they are wrong to support clear evils such as abortion. On the other hand, bishops should be hesitant to speak when the possibility exists of legitimate disagreement among the Catholic faithful. They should provide principles to serve as guidelines for decision making but not put their apostolic authority behind debatable policy options.

Another significant misinterpretation of article 43 is to invoke the expertise and "experience" of the laity as a ground for denying the continuing validity of Church teaching on certain moral matters. For example, not a few theologians believe the laity make an irrefutable point when they "ask whether the official church can continue to reject the relevance of lay experience in its moral teachings on sex, contraception, the role of women and the response to the HIV/AIDS crisis, even as the church also teaches that democratic participation and openness to dialogue are essential to good governance in secular political life."[33]

The next-to-last article of this first part of *Gaudium et spes* says that the Church has gained much from its interaction with cultures and regimes over the centuries, For example, the Church has been able to present Christ's teaching "with the help of the concepts and the languages of diverse peoples and has tried to clarify it especially with the wisdom of the philosophers, to the end of adapting the Gospel, as was appropriate, to the grasp of all and to the requirements of the wise" (*GS* 44, modified trans.). One immediately thinks of

Augustine's use of Cicero and the Platonists and Thomas Aquinas's use of Aristotle. In his commentary on this article Yves Congar notes, "it is well-known that the unity of the Roman Empire was favorable to the spread of Christianity."[34]

In conclusion, the council ends part I by reiterating the teaching of *Lumen gentium* that the Church is " 'the universal sacrament of salvation,' simultaneously manifesting and exercising the mystery of God's love for man" (*GS* 45, citing *Lumen gentium* 15). In continuity with the constant Catholic teaching across the ages, *Gaudium et spes* states that the purpose of the Church is still—and always will be—to work for the salvation of the whole human race. In summarizing the basic teaching of Vatican II on the purpose of the Church, Cardinal Avery Dulles, S.J., wrote: "The council repeatedly and emphatically taught that the procurement of salvation is the most important task of the church."[35]

NOTES

1. Cf. first footnote in *Gaudium et spes* for more details. I sometimes quote exactly from *Documents of Vatican II*, ed. Walter Abbott and trans. Joseph Gallagher (New York: America Press, 1966). More often than not I modify the Gallagher translation in the light of the official Latin text.

2. Joseph Ratzinger, "Der Weltdienst der Kirche: Auswirkungen von *Gaudium et spes* im letzten Jahrzehnt," *Internationale Katholische Zeitschrift* 4 (1975): 441.

3. Pope Benedict XVI, "Address of His Holiness Benedict XVI to the Roman Curia Offering Them His Christmas Greetings" (Dec. 22, 2005) at the beginning of this volume.

4. Ratzinger, "Der Weltdienst der Kirche," 440.

5. See Pope Benedict XVI, "To the Roman Curia Offering Them His Christmas Greetings."

6. Joseph Ratzinger, "The Dignity of the Human Person," in *Commentary on the Documents of Vatican II*, vol. 5, *Pastoral Constitution on the Church in the Modern World*, ed. Herbert Vorgrimler (New York: Herder and Herder, 1969), 118. Ratzinger, now Pope Benedict XVI, notes that the Church unfortunately describes the dialogue as taking place between the Church and the human race, as if the Church somehow stood apart from humanity in its own private world.

Ratzinger did the commentary on chapter 1 of part I in the pastoral constitution. Throughout this chapter I refer to Joseph Ratzinger, and not Pope Benedict XVI, when quoting his commentary.

7. The commentary of Joseph Ratzinger alerted me to the change from *animadvertere* to *discernere*.

8. Ratzinger comments, "What is to be demonstrated, therefore, is that precisely by Christian faith in God, true humanism, i.e., man's full development as man is attained, and that consequently the idea of humanism which present-day atheism opposes to faith can serve as the hinge of the discussion and a means of dialogue" ("Dignity of the Human Person," 118).

9. Pope John Paul II, *Evangelium vitae*, no. 19.

10. See Pope John Paul II, *Christifideles laici*, no. 37: "The dignity of the person is manifested in all its radiance when the person's origin and destiny are considered: created by God in his image and likeness as well as redeemed by the most precious

blood of Christ, the person is called to be a 'child in the Son' and a living temple of the Spirit, destined for eternal life of blessed communion with God."

11. Pope John Paul II, *Veritatis splendor*, no. 34, quoting *Gaudium et spes*, 17.

12. Pope Leo XIII, *Rerum novarum*, no. 37.

13. *Catechism of the Catholic Church*, no. 1691.

14. Joseph Cardinal Ratzinger, *Truth and Tolerance: Christian Belief and World Religions* (San Francisco: Ignatius, 2004), 193.

15. *Dominum et vivificantem*, no. 60.

16. Ratzinger also makes note of a verb-tense change in the next-to-last paragraph of this article, which indicates to him too optimistic an account of things. See "Dignity of the Human Person," 126: "But the Lord himself came to free and strengthen man, renewing him inwardly and casting out that prince of this world (cf. Jn 12:31) who held [*retinebat* instead of *retinet*, meaning retains] him in the bondage of sin" (no. 13). In other words, the present tense is more appropriate because the prince of this world is still going about like a roaring lion seeking someone to devour.

17. Ratzinger, "Dignity of the Human Person," 128.

18. Ibid., 130.

19. Ibid., 133.

20. Ibid., 136.

21. Ibid., 138.

22. Ibid., 142.

23. Ibid., 162.

24. *Gaudium et spes* and other Church documents refer to the gathering of men and women into private and public associations as "socialization." The word also refers to all the social ties people have, as well as the various ways they are dependent upon each other.

25. Cf. Immanuel Kant, *Perpetual Peace and Other Essays* (Indianapolis: Hackett, 1983), 124.

26. "Letter 138 to Marcellinus," in Augustine, *Political Writings*, ed. Ernest Fortin and Douglas Kries (Indianapolis: Hackett, 1994), 209.

27. Yves Congar, "The Role of the Church in the Modern World," in Vorgrimler, ed., *Pastoral Constitution on the Church*, 218.

28. Pope Benedict XVI, *Deus caritas est*, no. 28.

29. Avery Dulles, "Orthodoxy and Social Change," *America* 178 (June 20–27, 1998): 10.

30. John Paul II, *John Paul II in Mexico* (London: Collins, 1979), 80.

31. Ibid., 82.

32. John Paul II, *Journey in the Light of the Eucharist* (Boston: St. Paul Editions, 1980), 349.

33. David Hollenbach, S.J., "Joy and Hope, Grief and Anguish—*Gaudium et Spes* 40 Years Later," *America* 193 (Dec. 5, 2005): 13.

34. Congar, "Role of the Church in the Modern World," 220.

35. Avery Dulles, *The Reshaping of Catholicism: Current Challenges in the Theology of Church* (San Francisco: Harper and Row, 1988), 141.

8

Pastoral Perspectives on the Church in the Modern World

Matthew Levering

Part two of *Gaudium et spes* flows from the pastoral constitution's goal, stated at the outset of the document:

> This sacred synod, proclaiming the noble destiny of man and championing the godlike seed which has been sown in him, offers to mankind the honest assistance of the Church in fostering that brotherhood of all men which corresponds to this destiny of theirs. Inspired by no earthly ambition, the Church seeks but a solitary goal: to carry forward the work of Christ under the lead of the befriending Spirit. And Christ entered this world to give witness to the truth, to rescue and not sit in judgment, to serve and not to be served. (*GS* 3)

Gaudium et spes takes as a guiding principle, then, that human beings have a "noble destiny" of "brotherhood," communion in the triune God. This destiny comes from Christ, who in word and deed witnessed to the truth of God's merciful love for human beings. Christ has rescued us, who have rebelled against God, and he has done this by laying down his life and taking the humblest place, so that we might be reconciled to God and attain the graced fulfillment that God intends for us. Guided by Christ's spirit, the Church, according to *Gaudium et spes*, seeks to imitate Christ's action in the world and to lay down her life so as to serve the graced fulfillment of human beings. The key theme of *Gaudium et spes* thus is that the Church's teachings do not oppose human development, as many modern thinkers have postulated, but rather that the Church, knowing the glorious destiny of human beings and following the path of Christ, has as her very mission authentic human development.[1]

Given this mission, part two of *Gaudium et spes* identifies five loci that, if human beings are to proceed toward their destiny of union with Christ, require configuration to the image of Christ. These five loci are marriage and the family, culture, economics, politics, and the use of coercive military force. In each of these areas, inadequate understanding of the dignity and destiny of the human person can lead to a dehumanization that obscures the truth that Christ has revealed about each and every human being.[2] Dehumanization—the fruit of the *libido dominandi*, in Augustine's phrase—is the very opposite of Christ's saving work. The Church therefore, on each of these five fronts, serves human beings by calling upon individuals and societies to act in ways that accord with the truth of Christ's love.

Focusing upon part two of *Gaudium et spes*, then, this chapter asks whether its teachings constitute a moment of discontinuity rather than legitimate development and prudential application in the Catholic Church's doctrinal tradition regarding these five areas. I briefly summarize the teachings of the second part of *Gaudium et spes* with the goal of showing that its conclusions are not discontinuous with the prior Catholic magisterial teaching.[3]

Marriage and the Family

Gaudium et spes observes that "this institution is not everywhere reflected with equal brilliance, since polygamy, the plague of divorce, so-called free love, and other disfigurements have an obscuring effect" (*GS* 47). Among these other disfigurements are "excessive self-love, the worship of pleasure and illicit practices against human generation" (*GS* 47). In addition to these internal problems, the full truth of marriage faces difficulties also due to social, psychological, demographic, and economic pressures. While some of these pressures, *Gaudium et spes* suggests, have increased in recent times, clearly the problems have not changed. Does *Gaudium et spes* propose solutions that break with previous teaching on these matters? Its covenantal language differs from that of *Casti connubii*, Pius XI's 1930 encyclical on marriage and the family, but the two documents insist upon the same key elements as integral to marriage and the family.

Before entering into the specific problems and pressures, *Gaudium et spes* reflects upon the nature of marriage as a "conjugal covenant of irrevocable personal consent" and "a mutual gift of two persons" (*GS* 48). This covenantal account of "mutual gift" indicates how *Gaudium et spes* intends to renew the Church's teaching on marriage and the family, namely by meditation on the interior dynamism described by *Casti connubii*: "By matrimony, therefore, the souls of the contracting parties are joined and knit together more intimately than are their bodies, and that not by any passing affection of sense or spirit, but by a deliberate and firm act of the will; and from this union of souls by God's decree, a sacred and inviolable bond arises" (ch. 1).[4] *Gaudium et spes* reflects upon this profoundly intimate "knitting together" that takes place by the man's and the woman's "deliberate and firm act of the will" and in so doing manifests more deeply the truth of Saint Paul's comparison of marriage to the union of Christ and the Church.

Just as Christ gives himself to the Church, so also is the union of man and woman in marriage an irrevocable "mutual self-bestowal" (GS 48). Because marriage is inscribed within God's self-giving love in Christ, marriage embodies the dynamism of fruitful self-gift: "Authentic married love is caught up into divine love and is governed and enriched by Christ's redeeming power and the saving activity of the Church, so that this love may lead the spouses to God with powerful effect and may aid and strengthen them in the sublime office of being a father or a mother" (GS 48). The "mutual self-bestowal" flows into the gifting that is procreation; understood in this way, the unitive and the procreative are inseparable because both belong to the dynamism of "mutual self-bestowal." The family should image the self-giving of the man and the woman in Christ.

Carrying forward this biblical image of marital self-giving as reflecting the communion of divine self-giving, Gaudium et spes observes, "Such love, merging the human with the divine, leads the spouses to a free and mutual gift of themselves, a gift providing itself by gentle affection and by deed; such love pervades the whole of their lives: indeed by its busy generosity it grows better and grows greater" (GS 49). The dynamism of self-giving love requires the indissolubility of marriage since the "equal personal dignity of wife and husband" (GS 49) means that once the total marital gift of self has been bestowed and reciprocated, it cannot be renounced (without becoming its opposite, the illegitimate using of another person). All marital actions, including but hardly limited to sexual intercourse, should be configured to this dynamism of totally self-giving love.

For Gaudium et spes, the self-giving character of marital love ordains it to a "supreme gift": children (GS 50). Without discounting other aims of marriage, Gaudium et spes teaches that the "true practice of conjugal love, and the whole meaning of the family life which results from it, have this aim: that the couple be ready with stout hearts to cooperate with the love of the Creator and the Savior, Who through them will enlarge and enrich his own family day by day" (GS 50).[5] In the "mutual self-bestowal" that imitates the divine love, marital love has as its aim the generative self-giving that imitates and participates in God's generative self-giving. Like Casti connubii, in short, Gaudium et spes gives children a unique place in its account of marriage: They are the procreative gift that flows from and manifests the unitive gift of "mutual self-bestowal" that belongs to marriage as characterized by the fruitful self-giving pattern of Christ's divine self-gift.[6]

This fruitful self-giving, as would be expected, is a matter of intelligence as well as will. Just as God in his wisdom lovingly and freely generates creatures, so also the dynamism of self-gift in human beings involves the exercise of intelligence. This exercise of intelligence consists in two primary aspects: first, judgments about "their own welfare and that of their children, those already born and those which the future may bring" in light of "the material and spiritual conditions of the times as well as of their state of life" as members of the family, the society, and the Church; and second, recognition that such judgments, to be true, must share in the authoritative wisdom of God's law of self-giving love, which well-formed conscience knows to be authentically interpreted not by autonomous individuals but by Christ's mystical Body (*GS* 50). Only in this way will judgments about human welfare truly order persons to fulfillment. It is this law of self-giving love that reveals most fully that fulfillment cannot be reasonably attained without "trusting in divine Providence and refining the spirit of sacrifice" (*GS* 50). The reasonableness of a large family flows, in part, from the reasonableness of self-gift as the mode of human fulfillment in Christ.

At times, due to various circumstances, increasing family size will not be reasonable even within the law of self-gift. During such times, *Gaudium et spes* recognizes, illicit methods of birth control and even abortion and infanticide threaten to distort marriage's reasonableness (that is, the truth of mutual self-bestowal) into its opposite, violent dehumanization of other human beings. Problems arise when the emphasis on "mutual self-bestowal" is interpreted solely in terms of human intentionality abstracted from the composite reality of the person. As *Gaudium et spes* says, the pattern of mutual self-bestowal, while requiring a decisive act of the will, involves the whole body-soul person. Thus:

> the sexual characteristics of man and the human faculty of reproduction wonderfully exceed the dispositions of lower forms of life.... Hence when there is a question of harmonizing conjugal love with the responsible transmission of life, the moral aspects of any procedure do not depend solely on sincere intentions or on an evaluation of motives, but must be determined by objective standards. These, based on the nature of the human person and his acts, preserve the full sense of mutual self-giving and human procreation in the context of true love.[7]

Gaudium et spes goes on to warn again against interpreting "mutual self-bestowal" solely in worldly terms rather than in the light of Christ. The chapter concludes by sketching the various duties of the husband and the wife in the education and upbringing of children and proposing that in the performance of these duties the spouses will together grow in "mutual sanctification." While not repeating *Casti connubii*'s biblical language of the husband's headship, *Gaudium et spes* comes to similar conclusions about the complementary roles of father and mother in the family (*GS* 52).[8]

On the key points regarding marriage and the family, therefore, *Gaudium et spes* stands in continuity with the Church's prior doctrinal teaching.

Cultural Development

Human culture, *Gaudium et spes* suggests, depends upon human nature:

> Man comes to a true and full humanity only through culture, that is through the cultivation of the goods and values of nature. Wherever

> human life is involved, therefore, nature and culture are quite inti-
> mately connected one with the other. The word "culture" in its general
> sense indicates everything whereby man develops his many bodily
> and spiritual qualities. (GS 53)[9]

This development occurs in history and thus takes many forms, although "culture" cannot be seen as fully coterminous with "customs." The pastoral constitution briefly sketches the present historical state of human culture. Here it emphasizes particularly the technological advances of the nineteenth and twentieth centuries, as well as the view that these developments make possible more potential for cultural creativity in the lives of human beings. In this vein, the pastoral constitution sounds a strikingly optimistic note:

> Throughout the whole world there is a mounting increase in the sense
> of autonomy as well as of responsibility. This is of paramount im-
> portance for the spiritual and moral maturity of the human race. This
> becomes more clear if we consider the unification of the world and the
> duty which is imposed upon us, that we build a better world based
> upon truth and justice. Thus we are witnesses of the birth of a new
> humanism, one in which man is defined first of all by this responsi-
> bility to his brothers and to history. (GS 55)

One may justly wonder how such optimism could be expressed two decades after the Holocaust. Perhaps this optimism flows from the hope that the horror of the Holocaust has opened human minds, at least for a time, to appeals to "build a better world based upon truth and justice." One thinks also of the optimistic enumeration in *Quadragesimo anno* of the blessings that have flowed to human culture due to the contributions of *Rerum novarum*.[10]

Whatever the case may be, *Gaudium et spes* is aware of the difficulties of the contemporary cultural situation.[11] In accord with Catholic understanding of human nature, *Gaudium et spes* affirms developments in the arts and sciences as expressive of humanity's vocation to theoretical and practical wisdom. The knowledge of truth and ability to perform the good cannot be opposed to human fulfillment and, as history has shown, can serve the message of the gospel. The Church has made use of the cultural fruits of each historical epoch (*GS* 58). Yet, as *Gaudium et spes* recognizes, "Today's progress in science and technology can foster a certain exclusive emphasis on observable data, and an agnosticism about everything else.... Indeed the danger is present that man, confiding too much in the discoveries of today, may think that he is sufficient unto himself and no longer seek the higher things" (*GS* 57). A false sense of autonomy, devastating to the human person, is not the only possible negative fruit of contemporary cultural developments. A second problem to which *Gaudium et spes* points is the idea that the Church herself is an outmoded manifestation of a particular culture whose time has come and gone (cf. *GS* 58).

In depicting the "birth of a new humanism," therefore, *Gaudium et spes* cautions that if this newborn humanism is to grow to true maturity, then culture must "be subordinated to the integral perfection of the human person, to the good of the community and of the whole society" (*GS* 59). While human culture requires "the legitimate possibility of exercising its autonomy according to its own principles" (*GS* 59), it cannot function autonomously: It has a "proper end" toward which it tends.[12] Knowing this "end" requires understanding human nature and its vocation in grace so as to apprehend "the meaning of culture and science for the human person" (*GS* 61). As *Gaudium et spes* says, "It remains each man's duty to retain an understanding of the whole human person in which the values of intellect, will, conscience and fraternity are preeminent. These values are all rooted in God the Creator and have been wonderfully restored and elevated in Christ" (*GS* 61). According to *Gaudium et spes*, learning this "end" occurs primarily in the family.

Without knowledge of this proper end, human culture becomes destructive; *with* that knowledge, however, human culture participates in the fulfillment of human beings in Christ. The "end" is understood in Christ. Thus *Gaudium et spes* urges that Christians seek to imbue cultural activities with the wisdom that comes from knowing the end of the human person, thereby ensuring that human "religious culture and morality may keep pace with scientific knowledge and with the constantly progressing technology" (*GS* 62). Otherwise, this technological development may serve, as *Gaudium et spes* has already warned, false ends distorted by the lack of recognition of the Creator and Redeemer. *Gaudium et spes* clearly fears that if Christian theology does not inform contemporary cultural expressions more deeply, these expressions will become suffused with a rejection of God. To avert this situation *Gaudium et spes* urges: "Theological inquiry should pursue a profound understanding of revealed truth; at the same time it should not neglect close contact with its own time that it may be able to help those men skilled in various disciplines to attain to a better understanding of the faith" (*GS* 62).[13] For similar reasons *Gaudium et spes* hopes that many of the laity will undertake theological study.

By rejecting a "false autonomy" of culture and tempering its optimistic appraisals, then, *Gaudium et spes* maintains continuity with the Church's long-standing approach to the works of human reason (culture).

Economic Development

In line with the tradition of Catholic teaching, *Gaudium et spes* argues that economic development, in order to be true growth, must conform to the true nature and "end" of human beings: "In the economic and social realms, too, the dignity and complete vocation of the human person and the welfare of society as a whole are to be respected and promoted. For man is the source, the center, and the purpose of all economic and social life" (*GS* 63). While praising technological advances in production, *Gaudium et spes* repeatedly expresses the concern that economic practice have as its "fundamental finality" not profit but "the service of man, and indeed of the whole man with regard for the full range of his material needs and the demands of his intellectual, moral, spiritual, and religious life" (GS 64).[14] As in its chapter on culture, it is the end, the *telos* or goal, that concerns *Gaudium et spes*.

Certain principles follow from this teleological account of economics, which is rooted in an understanding of the human person. First, the end, embedded as it is in the created dignity and vocation of all human beings, becomes obscured when economic power belongs only to a few, whether individuals or nations. Second, neither absolute individualistic laissez-faire nor absolute governmental control should order economic activity since government control displaces the dignity of individual initiative, and individualism neglects the common good. Third, human beings must be respected as such, and not simply in terms of their utility; human beings must be treated "not as mere tools of production but as persons" (GS 66) whose fulfillment comes not solely through work, and the ill and aged members of the community must be cared for. On the basis of these principles *Gaudium et spes* treats matters such as just wage (sufficient for a family), labor unions, private property,[15] the monetary system, and the distribution of land.

In all of these areas, *Gaudium et spes* follows *Rerum novarum* as developed by *Quadragesimo anno* and *Mater et magistra*. This section concludes with an implicit response to Marx's notion that religion is the "opiate" of the masses: "Whoever in obedience to Christ seeks first the Kingdom of God, takes therefrom a stronger and purer love for helping all his brethren and for perfecting the work of justice under the inspiration of charity" (GS 72).

Political Development

In discussing politics, as in the chapter on culture, *Gaudium et spes* begins on a highly positive note: "The present keener sense of human dignity has given rise in many parts of the world to attempts to bring about a politico-juridical order which will give better protection to the rights of the person in political life" (GS 73). As indicated by the list of rights that follows, *Gaudium et spes* has in view primarily movements against communist and totalitarian repression and for civil rights.[16] Expressing as much a *hope* as a reality, *Gaudium et spes* again highlights the nature and "end" of human beings: "There is no better way to establish political life on a truly human basis than by fostering an inward sense of justice and kindliness, and of service to the common good, and by strengthening basic convictions as to the true nature of the political community and the aim, right exercise, and sphere of action of public authority" (GS 73). The most important of these "basic convictions" is that human beings are political because of the reality of a common good, ultimately God, toward which human nature is directed. To enter into political community is not a matter of mere choice, as if human beings were autonomous individuals. Human beings cannot attain the common good outside of community. *Gaudium et spes* states, "The political community exists, consequently, for the sake of the common good, in which it finds its full justification and significance, and the source of its inherent legitimacy" (GS 74).

While political communities can legitimately be structured in different ways, truly human life, as established by God, requires a political community. In other words, political authority derives ultimately from God's ordering rather than from individual consent because the reality of the common good is prior to individuals' consent to it.[17] As *Gaudium et spes* puts it, "It is clear, therefore, that the political community and public authority are founded on human nature and hence belong to the order designed by God, even though the choice of a political regime and the appointment of rulers are left to the free will of citizens" (GS 74).

Once this crucial (Pauline) point is understood, then *Gaudium et spes* has no hesitation in particularly encouraging democratic forms of political community. It observes that "It is in full conformity with human nature that there should be juridico-political structures providing all citizens in an ever better fashion and without any discrimination the practical possibility of freely and actively taking part in the establishment of the juridical foundations of the political community and in the direction of public affairs, in fixing the terms of reference of the various public bodies and in the election of political leaders."[18]

Similarly, on the basis of this account of the common good, *Gaudium et spes* speaks of the "rights" and "duties" of citizens. On this view rights are not markers of autonomy but flow from what is necessary for the attainment of the common good. Not only the political community but also the family and other "intermediate bodies or organizations" serve the attainment of the common good, and so again we find the principle of subsidiarity. While encouraging democratic polities, *Gaudium et spes* grants a role to governmental intervention, though not to the extent of dictatorial or totalitarian control.

Gaudium et spes also takes up here the relationship of the political community and the Church.[19] Both the political community and the Church serve the common good, but in different ways. The former cannot bring about the Kingdom of God; instead, the political community, while it should be imbued through its members by Christian truths and virtues,[20] aims at temporal goods—ideally rightly ordered to eternal goods, but not themselves eternal goods. In contrast, the Church, without neglecting the temporal good of human beings, primarily aims at the Kingdom of God, which, though as yet imperfectly realized, she herself is. For this reason, the Church is not merely a distinctive political community alongside other political communities: "The Church, by reason of her role and competence, is not identified in any way with the political community nor bound to any political system. She is at once a sign and a safeguard of the transcendent character of the human person" (GS 76). By her union with Christ in the Holy Spirit, the Church leads human beings to the ultimate end, union with the Trinity, whereas political communities can only lead human beings to proximate temporal ends that ideally are ordered to the ultimate end revealed in the Church.

This distinction of the Church from merely this-worldly political communities has various repercussions. For one, some means that political communities legitimately use to attain temporal goods are not legitimately used by the Church to attain spiritual goods. For another, while the Church may accept privileges from the political community that assist in the accomplishment of her mission, she may equally renounce them. In the final analysis the Church requires (for herself) from political communities only that "at all times and in all places, the Church should have true freedom to preach the faith, to teach her social doctrine, to exercise her role freely among men, and also to pass moral judgment in those matters which regard public order when the fundamental rights of a person or the salvation of souls require it" (GS 76).[21]

As is clear, these requirements, along with the presence of practicing Christians in the citizenry, will profoundly challenge the political community to live up to the order of justice in advancing temporal goods, and yet this challenge ultimately redounds to true peace among human beings. *Gaudium et spes* recognizes that the Church's effort "to foster and elevate all that is found to be true, good and beautiful in the human community"—an effort that, like all good deeds, will not (as the proverbial saying goes) go unpunished—in fact "strengthens peace among men for the glory of God" (GS 76). Peace in Christ conduces to temporal peace, and vice versa.

In short, by ordering its account of politics, including democratic politics, around the common good (ultimately Christological), as well as by insisting that the Church is not a mere this-worldly association, *Gaudium et spes* establishes its continuity with earlier Catholic political theory, even though its treatment also goes beyond what some earlier popes had taught.

War and Peace

Not surprisingly, *Gaudium et spes* is opposed to war. Rightly describing war's "frightfulness," it observes,

> Even though recent wars have wrought physical and moral havoc on our world, the devastation of battle still goes on day by day in some part of the world. Indeed, now that every kind of weapon produced by modern science is used in war, the fierce character of warfare threatens to lead the combatants to a savagery far surpassing that of the past. Furthermore, the complexity of the modern world and the intricacy of international relations allow guerrilla warfare to be drawn out by new methods of deceit and subversion. In many causes the use of terrorism is regarded as a new way to wage war. (GS 79)

This opposition to war, however, does not lead to accepting peace at the cost of justice. The end of human nature, the common good, requires justice. In accord with the tradition of Catholic thought on war and peace, the pastoral constitution insists that "peace is not merely the absence of war" and explains, in contemporary context, that this means that peace is neither "brought about by dictatorship" nor "the maintenance of a balance of power between enemies" (GS 78). Furthermore, true peace, given the fallen human condition, is something that cannot actually be achieved by human power. Christ alone, in charity, can achieve the justice that is "peace"; Christ gives this charitable justice to us. *Gaudium et spes* teaches, "That earthly peace which arises from love of neighbor symbolizes and results from the peace of Christ which radiates from God the Father. For by the cross the incarnate Son, the prince of peace reconciled all men with God. By thus restoring all men to the unity of one people and one body, He slew hatred in his own flesh; and, after being lifted on high by his resurrection, He poured forth the spirit of love into the hearts of men" (*GS* 78). The Church therefore has an indispensable element to offer to seekers of temporal peace. Without the justice made possible by charity, the human quest for peace will be fruitless.[22]

Gaudium et spes does not adopt pacifism. It might seem that the standards for peace are so high—not merely justice but indeed a justice grounded in supernatural charity—that the best one can do is refuse, in all circumstances, to employ violence, thereby at least witnessing eschatologically to "peace." *Gaudium et spes* has the following to say in this regard: "We cannot fail to praise those who renounce the use of violence in the vindication of their rights and who resort to methods of defense which are otherwise available to weaker parties too, provided this can be done without injury to the rights and duties of others or of the community itself" (*GS* 78).

Without rejecting individuals' practice of pacifism, in short, *Gaudium et spes* cautions that human beings, in justly defending the temporal good of individuals and the community, may in certain circumstances use violence; otherwise human beings, especially the poor and the weak, would be left entirely at the mercy of the violent assaults of oppressors while others stood by and refused to offer effectual assistance. An example that *Gaudium et spes* gives is "the methodical extermination of an entire people" (*GS* 79)—here thinking no doubt of the Holocaust. Those who killed the Jews, even under orders, committed heinous acts; those who used violence to defend and save the Jews acted rightly.[23]

Clearly, then, *Gaudium et spes* provides no absolute plan to free human beings from violence, beyond the urgent evangelistic task of conversion of hearts: "Insofar as men are sinful, the threat of war hangs over them, and hang over them it will until the return of Christ. But insofar as men vanquish sin by a union of love, they will vanquish violence as well and make these words come true: 'They shall turn their swords into plough-shares, and their spears into sickles. Nation shall not lift up sword against nation, neither shall they learn war any more' (Is 2:4)" (*GS* 79). Beyond the call to evangelize and general encouragement to peacemakers, however, does *Gaudium et spes* have anything else to offer to the quest for peace and the desire to end war?

It does, beginning with the stricture that war must be undertaken for "just defense" as opposed to "subjugation of other nations" (*GS* 79). Furthermore, war must be conducted justly, which excludes (with Hiroshima and Nagasaki no doubt in mind) "any act of war aimed indiscriminately at the destruction of entire cities of extensive areas along with their population" (*GS* 80). *Gaudium et spes* goes on to warn that the arms race in weapons of mass destruction "is an utterly treacherous trap for humanity" and to propose that an international political authority be developed so that war might be "outlawed" (GS 81). While one can argue that *Gaudium et spes* does not inquire sufficiently into the possibility that the international body might itself become an instrument of oppression, it is fully in line with the advocacy of earlier twentieth-century popes for strong international political organizations to complement the system of nation-states and reduce the likelihood of war.[24] The Church's role within these international organizations is to establish "the fraternal exchange between men on solid ground by imparting knowledge of the divine and human law" (GS 89). Since she is able to teach the "end," the Church merits a formal place within the deliberations of the community of nations, and her members should also seek to play an important role through Catholic and ecumenical associations.

On the grounds that war often stems from economic pressures, at the center of *Gaudium et spes*'s recommendations for assisting the avoidance of war is a lengthy discourse on how to improve international economic cooperation, especially with regard to imbalances between developing and technologically advanced countries. Here, in the context of a broader discussion of the need to assist in alleviating poverty in undeveloped countries (in regard to which *Gaudium et spes* proposes a new organ of the Church specifically aimed at international service to the poor), the issue of population growth appears.[25] While recognizing that population growth could legitimately require governments to address the issue by "social and family life legislation" (GS 87) and educatory steps, the pastoral constitution cautions that only the husband and wife have the right to determine how many children they have and that regulation of births must accord with the moral law, which, as we have seen, is the law of "mutual self-bestowal" in each person's body-soul unity.

The political teaching of *Gaudium et spes*, in sum, attempts to balance the recognition that the injustice that breeds war will continue until the return of Christ, with the truth that efforts to avert war and to insist upon its just limitations can have significant salutary effect. And yet *Gaudium et spes* offers no mere instruction in realpolitik—it ultimately offers the call to conversion: " 'Behold, now is the acceptable time for a change of heart; behold! now is the day of salvation' " (GS 82). It also offers, as an eschatological sign of the unity-in-diversity of the human race, the Church herself (GS 92).[26]

By retaining the Augustinian account of "peace," as well just war doctrine, then, *Gaudium et spes*'s presentation of war and peace displays continuity with the Catholic tradition.

Conclusion

Gaudium et spes's final paragraphs are devoted to expressions of ecumenical hope for full unity among Christians and of optimism for ever-deepening dialogue with all non-Christians that takes as its starting point the unity of the human race. This hope for brotherhood manifests itself in love. Quoting John 13:35, *Gaudium et spes* points out that Christians will be known by how they love and serve each other. If "the Father wills that in all men we recognize Christ our brother and love Him effectively" (*GS* 93), then Christians are called to the task of serving the world. Such service means participating in the development of all human beings' potential for the true and the good—development that includes, within the eternal "end," temporal goods. In seeking to undertake such loving service, Christians must rely upon the Holy Spirit, not upon their own power, as *Gaudium et spes* makes clear by ending with Ephesians 3:20–21.

As we have seen, *Gaudium et spes* identifies five major areas in which such loving service is particularly needed: marriage and the family, culture, economics, politics, and the quest for world peace. To each area the pastoral constitution applies the Catholic understanding of the nature of human beings as ordered to the end of charitable union with God. In so doing, it offers a vision for the five areas that both renews and stands in continuity with the key positions of earlier Catholic teaching:[27] in marriage, indissolubility and the combination of the unitive and procreative ends (now articulated around the concept of "gift"); in culture, Christian humanism as a measure of growth in theoretical and practical wisdom; in economics, the "end" of the body-soul person rather than mere profit; in politics, the derivation of political authority from God (the common good) rather than from individual human choice; and in the quest for world peace, the insistence upon justice, as well as the doctrine of just war and an international thrust consonant with the unity of the human race.

NOTES

1. Norman Tanner, S.J., drawing upon remarks that Edward Schillebeeckx, O.P., made near the end of the council at a Dutch Center of Documentation conference, argues that the debates over the schema on the Church in the world in the council's third session (1964) represented a pastoral shift that, by its nature, fostered a new understanding of the magisterium: "The knowledge, moreover, that the issues in question concerned the present historical situation and therefore were of their very nature contingent, made the council's declarations about them also contingent. In this way there came about a notable change in the traditional idea that a general council, precisely because it is an extraordinary organ of the Church's Magisterium, must deliberate within the framework of absolute and timeless truth and that its teachings must be valid for all eternity" (Tanner, "Chapter V: The Church in the World (*Ecclesia ad extra*)," in *History of Vatican II*, vol. 4, *Church as Communion: Third Period and Intersession, September 1964–September 1965*, ed. Giuseppe Alberigo (English version ed. Joseph A. Komonchak [Maryknoll, N.Y.: Orbis, 2003]), 270; for Schillebeeckx's remarks, 327–28). Yet the issues addressed by part two of *Gaudium et spes* required, as we will see, certain principles that are "absolute and timeless truth" and thus "valid for all eternity." Tanner's historical survey tends to be shaped by his view, similar to F. X. Murphy's (Xavier Rhynne's), that "in the council hall there was quite a sharp divide between those fathers who thought the schema did not state clearly enough what they considered to be the traditional teaching of the Church and those who wanted to update this teaching: *Conservatives* (or *traditionalists*) and *progressives* (or *liberals*) are quite apposite terms, though they were never used in the speeches in the council hall" (308). These terms, however, are misleading since all of the bishops accepted Catholic commitment to

authoritative tradition. The terms should be replaced by ones that indicate more fully the common bond that the bishops, even in disagreeing, shared.

2. *Gaudium et spes* has frequent recourse to the concept of "human dignity." In questioning this concept, Ernest L. Fortin, A.A., has pointed out that "John Paul II's unprecedented insistence on the more or less Kantian notion of the 'dignity' that is said to accrue to the human being, not because of any actual conformity with the moral law, but for no other reason than that he is an 'autonomous subject of moral decision' ([*Centesimus annus*] no. 13). The more usual view, which Kant was rejecting, is that one's dignity as a rational and free being is contingent on the fulfillment of prior duties. That dignity could be forfeited and was so forfeited by the criminal who had no respect for and no desire to abide by the moral law. One's goodness or dignity was not something given once and for all; it was meant to be achieved. Its measure was one's success in attaining the end or ends to which one was ordered by nature. The Rousseauean and Kantian notion of the sovereign or sacred individual had yet to make its appearance. To be and to be good were two different things" (Fortin, "From *Rerum novarum* to *Centesimus annus*: Continuity or Discontinuity?" in Fortin, *Collected Essays*, vol. 3, *Human Rights, Virtue, and the Common Good: Untimely Meditations on Religion and Politics*, ed. J. Brian Benestad [Lanham, Md.: Rowman and Littlefield, 1996], 229). While agreeing that Fortin's understanding of "dignity" as measured by "attaining the end or ends to which one was ordered by nature" is a primary and neglected meaning of "dignity," I nonetheless maintain that there is also a "dignity" that belongs to human beings as the *imago Dei* and that is not erased by sin. Thomas Aquinas makes a helpful distinction between the imago as "a natural aptitude for understanding and loving God" and the imago as "the conformity of grace" and as "the likeness of glory": *Summa theologiae* I, q. 93, a. 4. Cf. Lawrence J. Welch, "*Gaudium et spes*, the Divine Image and the Synthesis of *Veritatis splendor*," *Communio* 24 (1997): 794–814.

3. For a helpful summary of Archbishop Karol Wojtyla's influence on the final form of *Gaudium et spes* see George Weigel, *Witness to Hope: The Biography of Pope John Paul II* (1999; New York: HarperCollins, 2001), 166–69. A little more than a decade later Wojtyla and Joseph Ratzinger met for the first time at the conclave that elected John Paul I. As Weigel relates, "Ratzinger, one of the intellectual fathers of *Lumen gentium* (the Dogmatic Constitution on the Church), and Wojtyla, one of the architects of *Gaudium et spes* (the Pastoral Constitution on the Church in the Modern World), found themselves in what Ratzinger later recalled as a 'spontaneous sympathy' for each other's sense of what was needed to secure the legacy of Vatican II. Most concisely, *Gaudium et spes* had to be reread through the prism of *Lumen gentium* so that the Church could engage the modern world with its own unique message" (ibid., 244).

4. Bernhard Häring, who became a leading dissenting moral theologian, wrote in 1968 about the preparation of this chapter of the document: "Before the council, the bishops had been sent a schema on 'Marriage, Family, and Chastity.' Taken as a whole it was timeless and unproblematic. It was intended to perpetuate the negative and rigorist casuistry of the standard textbooks" (Häring, "Fostering the Nobility of Marriage and the Family," in *Commentary on the Documents of Vatican II*, vol. 5, *Pastoral Constitution on the Church in the Modern World*, ed. Herbert Vorgrimler, trans. W. J. O'Hara [New York: Herder and Herder, 1969], 225). Häring pictures the debate that occurred at this stage as between the "conservative group" and the "open-minded bishops" (225). The key for Häring is the priority of love (the unitive aspect of marriage), even though he grants that "the text makes it equally plain that procreation and upbringing are not incidental" (234). Typical of Häring's commentary are comments like the following: "There is no trace here of the self-assurance of the deductive philosophical way of

thinking about natural law which appeared to arrive by its syllogisms at absolutely certain metaphysical solutions and so failed to understand the problems raised by a new age and its new difficulties" (229). He likewise argues for a reading of the text that corresponds to a "fundamental option" theory: "In the text at this point [no. 48], however, it is not the single act but the whole community of life and love which is viewed as mutual self-giving" (233). Regarding no. 48, Häring observes appreciatively that "the 151 fathers who wished to teach that conjugal love is taken up into divine love 'by fecundity,' were not followed. It is noteworthy that they did not even receive an answer here. Their perpetually repeated amendments one-sidedly stressing fecundity were frequently answered by reference to the unqualified worth of a childless marriage when there is a right attitude in other respects" (235–36). Häring also reads *Gaudium et spes*'s section on marriage and the family as rejecting the Augustinian view of sexual intercourse as affected by lust and thereby needing to be re-ordered toward self-giving. At the time of writing Häring was engaged in "the current controversy about ways of responsible birth regulation" (238). Due to the influence and the representative nature of the *Commentary on the Documents of Vatican II*, ed. Vorgrimler, in which Häring's commentary appears, I make frequent recourse to this commentary in the footnotes to this chapter in order to shed light on the basic approach of scholars who see discontinuity in *Gaudium et spes*.

5. Häring states that "the council teaches extremely clearly in the first sentence of article 50 that marriage and married love, *regarded as a whole*, are essentially and intrinsically ordained to the creation of life" (239). He adds his interpretation: "This turning away from a narrow and at the same time incorrect analysis of the marriage act to a view of the married vocation as a whole is momentous" (ibid.). In Häring's view the key is that individual acts of marital sexual intercourse do not receive their "moral 'justification' from other 'goods' of marriage" (240).

6. Norman Tanner, S.J., comments, "Regarding the two ends of marriage—the procreation and bringing up of children and, second, the mutual help that spouses give to each other and the remedy for concupiscence—which had provoked sharp debate in 1964, both are mentioned in a discreet way and without entering into the thorny issue of the priority of one over the other" (Tanner, *The Church and the World: Gaudium et Spes, Inter Mirifica* [New York: Paulist Press, 2005], 51). I suggest instead that the priority of children is placed carefully within the whole framework of married love and therefore no longer risks appearing as an extrinsic priority.

7. GS 51. In "Fostering the Nobility of Marriage" Häring observes: "The subtitle of article 51 expresses clearly and frankly a problem which is still largely unsolved. How is the harmonious cultivation of conjugal love to be meaningfully reconciled with responsible regulation of births? The council had the courage frankly to state the difficulties and even the dangers of an over-simplified solution. A long period of continence in marriage, even if undertaken by mutual agreement, can represent a danger to marital fidelity, as the apostle of the gentiles himself pointed out (1 Cor 7:5)" (242). He also notes as regards abortion: "The request of three council fathers for a precise definition of 'abortus' was not granted (*Responsum* 101c). There are in fact marginal cases where no unanimity as yet prevails whether an 'abortus' is involved or not, for example, when the fetus certainly has no further prospect of life, while the mother's life can still be saved" (243). Even when appealing to natural law, *Gaudium et spes* does so, Häring emphasizes, from a "personalist viewpoint" that understands "the immense difference between merely animal structure and human sexuality" (ibid.). He finds "a dynamic conception of the Church's teaching on the question of birth control. The reference to *Casti connubii* stands in conjunction with Pius XII's address to Italian midwives in 1951 in which for

the first time the idea of consciously responsible procreation clearly appeared in a pronouncement of the Magisterium. Both texts must also be understood in the light of Paul VI's address of June 1964, according to which certain questions were to be submitted to thorough study in view of the new situation and new scientific knowledge. The Magisterium is viewed as functioning within the history of redemption. This also points to an understanding of natural law which more consciously takes into account the temporal, historical character of man than was done by the purely static doctrine of natural law which prevailed with the advent of rationalism" (244).

8. Häring points out that, "As opposed to one-sided older tendencies to describe the role of the wife exclusively as that of housewife and mother, stress is laid on the presence of the father and his importance for the children's upbringing, as well as on the legitimate social progress of women" (ibid., 245). His discussion of this chapter of *Gaudium et spes* concludes: "Unenlightened Christians who cling stubbornly to past modes of life and fight doggedly for secondary matters which are often not specifically Christian but only things of the day before yesterday, have no influence on the course of history" (ibid.).

9. In his commentary on this chapter of *Gaudium et spes* ("The Proper Development of Culture," in Vorgrimler, *Pastoral Constitution on the Church in the Modern World*), Roberto Tucci proposes with regard to no. 53: "The animal finds what it needs ready-made; it only has to search, collect, or, as the case may be, hoard. Man, on the other hand, has to make what he needs by means of the specifically human activity which we call 'work.' 'Nature' is the material and object of man's work; man applies mind and hand to it and adapts it to himself, transforms it according to his requirements, makes it provide what he needs. But while acting upon nature, man also transforms himself" (255). *Gaudium et spes*, however, does not conceive "nature" as merely "the material and object of man's work." See Matthew L. Lamb, "Nature Is Normative for Culture," *Nova et Vetera* (English) 3 (2005): 153–62.

10. Tucci remarks on this text: "It is indubitable that this shows a very favourable conception of one absolutely decisive aspect of contemporary culture, which after starting with Faustian or Promethean pride, is gradually being inspired by an increased sense of responsibility and universal solidarity. 'Man who is the author of culture' becomes a synonym for man capable of making a better world on the ethical plane itself, that is, in truth and justice, and consequently capable of a new humanism characterized precisely by moral commitment through corporate responsibility of all for each. Precisely because of this initial favorable judgment, the text met with opposition from various fathers who detected in it an exaggerated and dangerous optimism" (260). For helpful discussion see, for example, Larry S. Chapp, "The Retrieval of *Gaudium et spes*: A Comparison of Rowland and Balthasar," *Nova et Vetera* (English) 3 (2005): 118–47; Hans Urs von Balthasar, "The Council of the Holy Spirit," in *Explorations in Theology*, vol. 3, *Creator Spirit* (San Francisco: Ignatius Press, 1993), 245–67; David L. Schindler, "Christology and the *Imago Dei*: Interpreting *Gaudium et spes*," *Communio* 23 (1996): 156–84; Walter Kasper, "The Theological Anthropology of *Gaudium et spes*," *Communio* 23 (1996): 129–40.

11. As Tucci rightly says regarding the effect of no. 56, "The optimism of the previous article is quickly reduced to just proportions by consideration of the many contradictions which confront modern man in his project of achieving a 'new humanism' fraught with great hopes" ("Proper Development of Culture," 260). However, Tucci quickly adds, "But even here the positive note is the stronger, for the contradictions are not regarded as insuperable obstacles, but as pointers to corresponding moral obligations which present themselves to the conscience of people today who want to be

lucidly responsible for their task of building a truly human culture" (260–61). Tucci's focus is on highlighting the positive aspect.

12. Tucci states, "Having affirmed the autonomy of culture in relation to faith, and unfolded the essential content of that autonomy, the last paragraph goes on to vindicate the independence of culture in the face of political and economic power" (ibid., 270–71). It is this kind of emphasis on "autonomy" that Tracey Rowland ably critiques in *Culture and the Thomist Tradition: After Vatican II* (New York: Routledge, 2003).

13. As Tucci says appreciatively: "It may be noted in passing that one father complained that this passage in article 62 did not pay due heed to the dangers which threaten young seminarians from modern culture. The Commission replied that the text refers to the professors, and indicates precisely how to safeguard effectively the young men entrusted to them from such dangers" ("Proper Development of Culture," 284–85). Tucci concludes by emphasizing "the new spirit which the council has introduced into the Church. In the field of culture, as in others, it is true that the council did not mark the end of a journey but the opening of new roads by which Christians must courageously travel, in a spirit of initiative and invention, in a climate of fruitful liberty, with humility and courage" (287).

14. In contrast, Oswald von Nell-Breuning, in his commentary on this chapter ("Socio-economic Life: Commentary," in Vorgrimler, *Pastoral Constitution on the Church in the Modern World*), observes: "There is no trace here of that skeptical, critical attitude to economic life, so frequently found in ascetical writings and in official ecclesiastical pronouncements, which asserts that it diverts men's minds from higher things and attaches them to lower things. The optimistic attitude of John XXIII (*Mater et magistra*, nos. 246, 254ff.) has prevailed" (292). Nell-Breuning also contrasts Leo XIII's teaching in *Rerum novarum* that "inequalities in the economic and social situation are unavoidable because authority and subordination are indispensable, an integral part of the divinely willed order of things, and have to be borne with submission" with *Gaudium et spes*'s "definitely critical attitude to economic and social inequalities" (293–94). It is clear that *Gaudium et spes* does not call for the rooting out of all inequalities.

15. Nell-Breuning observes, "It is a matter for satisfaction that unfortunate expressions about property being an extension of the personality into the world of things, and others of that kind, have not found their way into *Gaudium et spes*" ("Socio-economic Life: Commentary," 310).

16. The question of whether the Church's doctrine on political life is best expressed in the language of "rights," while not a question originating with Vatican II, is an important one. For the medieval understanding of "ius" (translated as "right"), particularly in canon law, see Charles J. Reid Jr., *Power over the Body, Equality in the Family: Rights and Domestic Relations in Medieval Canon Law* (Grand Rapids, Mich.: Eerdmans, 2004); Brian Tierney, *The Idea of Natural Rights: Studies on Natural Rights, Natural Law, and Church Law* (Grand Rapids, Mich.: Eerdmans, 2001 [1997]). For criticism of "rights" language, especially as found in the political philosophy of Jacques Maritain and in the encyclical tradition influenced by his approach, see, for example, G. J. McAleer, *Ecstatic Morality and Sexual Politics*, chapters 7–9; Rowland, *Culture and the Thomist Tradition*; and especially Ernest L. Fortin, A.A., "Human Rights and the Common Good," "Sacred and Inviolable: *Rerum novarum* and Natural Rights," and "From *Rerum novarum* to *Centesimus annus*: Continuity or Discontinuity?" in Fortin, *Human Rights, Virtue, and the Common Good*, 19–28, 191–222, and 223–29.

17. As Nell-Breuning rightly remarks in his commentary on chapter 4 ("The Life of the Political Community: Commentary," in Vorgrimler, *Pastoral Constitution on the Church in the Modern World*), "In complete accordance with the traditional line and

appealing to Romans 13:1–5, the council describes the *communitas politica* as grounded in human nature and therefore as belonging to the divine order of the world" (319).

18. *GS* 75. Nell-Breuning comments: "When Pius XII in his Christmas message in 1944 praised the advantages of democracy, people tended to regard this merely as reflecting the world situation created by the imminent victory of the democratic powers. In fact, the official Church had long shown great reserve in regard to democracy. It is sufficient to read Leo XIII's encyclicals on the State to realize that the Pope is not addressing the people (except to exhort them to obedience) but the princes, whom Leo XIII in a certain sense treats as his equals. On the other hand, Catholic theologians, in particular the great Spanish scholastics (Vitoria, Suárez, etc.) as early as the sixteenth century, maintained the principle of the sovereignty of the people, if properly understood. . . . This ancient and venerable doctrine of the sovereignty of the people was suspected for a time of being incompatible with Leo XIII's doctrine of the State, and was not extolled as the Church's official teaching on the State even by Pius XII in his famous address to the Roman Rota on October 2, 1945, though he showed himself very well-disposed towards it, which at all events was a big step forward. Until then, the tendency was to assimilate the structure of the secular State authority as closely as possible to the divinely appointed hierarchical structure of the Church, thus exhibiting State and Church as closely akin in social structure, and mutually complementary. Pius XII, on the contrary, pointed out that the doctrine of sovereignty of the people has the particular merit of bringing out clearly the fundamentally different structure of authority in State and Church. Authority in the State flows, so to speak, from below upwards; issuing from the people, it extends to the government as the highest *organ* of the State. In the Church, it flows from above downwards" ("Life of the Political Community: Commentary," 320). Yet Nell-Breuning has to admit that "*Gaudium et spes* does not go as far as formerly in endorsing the doctrine of the sovereignty of the people or, to put it another way, the principle of the intrinsically democratic structure of the State," even if for Nell-Breuning *Gaudium et spes* "tacitly assumes that principle as a starting point which it takes for granted as a matter of course" (321). To my mind, the key is *Gaudium et spes*'s affirmation that political authority flows ultimately from God, not from the people or from individuals.

19. As Nell-Breuning points out, "When Leo XIII dealt with the relation between the two, he assumed that the State was Christian or, more precisely, a Catholic denominational State. What variations ensue if the State does not correspond to this conception, one has to work out on one's own responsibility; Leo XIII did not discuss this situation which, ideally, should not exist, nor the consequences to be drawn from it. His successors also remained, in all essentials, true to that line, Pius XII, for example, in his teaching on tolerance: As such and by rights, the State professes the Catholic faith as the State religion and therefore promotes and supports the Catholic Church and defends it against the incursion of other religious denominations and, of course, of non-religious ideologies; where this condition is unfortunately not realized, it may be appropriate for the sake of the common good for the State to permit non-Catholic religious societies and non-religious ideological associations on its territory and to grant them protection. The council starts from a fundamentally different assumption. It accepts the ideologically pluralistic society not as the ideal case but as normal in present-day conditions" ("Life of the Political Community: Commentary," 323–24). This point seems right.

20. Tanner notes that this section of *Gaudium et spes* "appears strongly influenced by the separation of church and state in the United States and seems to eschew the ideal of a Catholic state that was close to the heart of many in Europe and South America"

(Tanner, *Church and the World*, 57–58). Much depends, however, upon what one means by "the separation of church and state."

21. Nell-Breuning comments that "here a very definite turning point is passed, not so much in doctrine as in practice. The council proclaims that the Church does not put its trust in privileges granted by the State.... Today the Church knows what harm was done by its close links with the upper classes of society and particularly with the State (alliance of Throne and Altar) to its credibility in the eyes of the broad masses of the population, the less fortunate, the oppressed and the exploited. Much too late, only after the Church had lost the greater part of the workers, has this realization prevailed; everything will depend now on translating it into practice. The council has drawn a cheque; it must be honoured" ("Life of the Political Community: Commentary," 326–27). Certainly the council teaches here the minimum that the Church requires from political communities, but whether it is best to keep to the minimum is not here decided.

22. René Coste rightly observes in his commentary on chapter 5 ("The Fostering of Peace and the Promotion of a Community of Nations: Commentary," in Vorgrimler, *Pastoral Constitution on the Church in the Modern World*): "Without actually quoting it, the council refers to the famous Augustinian definition which has repeatedly figured in Catholic theology and official pronouncements: *Pax omnium rerum tranquillitas ordinis.* Peace is understood here in Augustine's sense" (348).

23. Coste's commentary is instructive with regard to the difficulties that can arise: Inspired by Gandhi and Martin Luther King Jr., he wants to affirm nonviolence as a Christian principle and yet also to agree with Augustine. He states, "We have deliberately left aside one basic gospel maxim, that of nonviolence. Is it not self-evident, though too often forgotten, that renunciation of force is always both condition and consequence of charity and peace? Can it be doubted that for Christians non-violence, both collective and individual, is the norm?... A plain commitment to non-violence to the very limits of possibility is called for. The content of this principle must, however, be precisely understood. It must not be reduced to a particular scholastic opinion or a special technique, nor should it be limited to absolute non-violence" (ibid., 350). It must be nonviolence, yet not "absolute." At this stage Coste asks rhetorically, "Does the gospel not oblige us to acknowledge absolute non-violence as a universal principle, and consequently to reject every recourse to legitimate defense even in the most tragic and generally recognized cases? This is an extremely difficult problem, for at first sight the interpretation of the gospel seems to point in this direction.... Though we cannot justify our opinion in detail here, we concur with Vatican II, with the unanimous tradition of Catholic doctrine since Augustine (who for his part reflects the view of the major part of the early Church) and with the great majority of theologians, in holding that Christ did emphatically propound his dynamic ideal of non-violence but did not mean it absolutely to forbid Christians any recourse to legitimate defense, especially when this appears absolutely necessary for the defense of the innocent. He was aware, of course, that God's witnesses under the old covenant interpreted the Decalogue precept 'Thou shalt not kill' as condemning murder but not resistance to unjust violence. Neither his words nor his behavior prove that he rejected this interpretation or replaced it by a law that admits of absolutely no exception. The apostolic Church which made such efforts to be perfectly faithful to his teaching, indubitably accepted the right of legitimate defense, at least against common law crimes (for example, Rom 13:1–7; 1 Pet 2:13f.). Love for our brethren must be active" (350–51). Having said this, Coste goes on to emphasize the priority of nonviolence as the basic stance of the Christian even while accepting, insofar as he understands it, just war doctrine.

24. On this point see, for example, Robert John Araujo, S.J., and John A. Lucal, S.J., *Papal Diplomacy and the Quest for Peace: The Vatican and International Organizations from the Early Years to the League of Nations* (Naples, Fla.: Sapientia Press, 2004).

25. Coste affirms in his commentary on no. 87: "The problem of the increasingly rapid growth of world population has become one of the gravest of our time.... Demographers regard it as not at all unlikely that by the year 2000 the world population will be 6,000 million. Even leaving out of account the fantastic problems created by the simultaneous presence of so many human beings on the earth, this demographic growth immediately involves direct and terrible consequences in conjunction with underdevelopment" ("Fostering of Peace," 365–66).

26. In summarizing the contribution of this part of *Gaudium et spes* Coste observes, "Even if it adds little that is new to the teaching of recent popes, that fact itself is of great importance. The continuity of doctrine must be emphasized. The same fundamental line of thought and the same spirit persists from Pius XII who took over the important themes from his predecessors and whose teaching retains its full importance, whatever some may say about it, through John XXIII whose two great encyclicals attracted so much attention, down to Paul VI whose teaching on international problems is already so substantial, and so to Vatican II. The Christian has surely a right to regard this as a sign of the special assistance of the Holy Spirit" ("Fostering of Peace," 368).

27. With an eye to those who rejected the Second Vatican Council, Tanner observes that while Archbishop Lefèbvre "refused to endorse the decree with his signature at the time of the council," his "formal opposition was reserved more for other decrees, principally those on the liturgy (*Sacrosanctum concilium*), ecumenism (*Unitatis redintegratio*), and religious liberty (*Dignitatis humanae*)" (Tanner, *Church and the World*, 61).

The Decrees

9

The Decree on the Bishops' Pastoral Office in the Church, *Christus Dominus*

Brian Ferme

Christus Dominus was approved on October 28, 1965, by a vote of 2,139 *placet*, 2 *non placet*, and 1 invalid vote and was approved immediately by Paul VI. The decree was the result of the integration of two schema: *De cura animarum* and *De episcoporum munere pastorali* and reflected the work of the commission *De episcopis*.[1]

Unlike the other documents of Vatican II, *Christus Dominus* 44 concludes with a specific reference to the proposed revision of the *Code of Canon Law*: "This most sacred synod prescribes that in the revision of the Code of Canon Law suitable laws be drawn up in keeping with the principles stated in this decree." This general directive underscores not only the particularly practical nature of *Christus Dominus* but also its essential link with the revision of the Church's canon law. On January 25, 1959, John XXIII, after a solemn celebration in the Patriarchal Basilica of Saint Paul outside the walls, announced his intention of holding a synod for the diocese of Rome, of celebrating an ecumenical council, and of revising the (1917) *Code of Canon Law*.[2] It is thus not without some historical relevance that the present *Code of Canon Law* was promulgated on January 25, 1983. In the apostolic constitution *Sacrae disciplinae leges*, with which John Paul II promulgated the code, the pontiff stated that "In so doing, my thoughts go back to the same day of the year 1959 when my predecessor of happy memory, John XXIII, announced for the first time his decision to reform the existing corpus of canonical legislation which had been promulgated on the feast of Pentecost in the year 1917."

An appreciation of the importance and subsequent impact of *Christus Dominus* is intimately linked not only to various postconciliar norms that put into legal effect many of the issues that *Christus Dominus* touched on but also to the revision and promulgation of the

1983 *Code of Canon Law,* along with the various legislative documents that followed it with respect to the topics treated in the decree: the role of bishops within the universal Church and their relationship with the Apostolic See; the role of the diocesan bishop in their particular (diocesan) Church; and the co-operation between bishops for the good of various particular churches. Each of these general themes necessarily involved a series of more specific and generally canonical questions dealt with by *Christus Dominus*: the Synod of Bishops; a bishop's *potestas* (authority) in his diocese; a bishop's faculty to dispense; the role and competence of the Roman Curia, especially with respect to the office of the diocesan bishop; intradiocesan questions (e.g., the diocesan curia, the diocesan pastoral council, the diocesan clergy [especially pastors of souls], religious within the diocese); extradiocesan questions; episcopal conferences; the boundaries of ecclesiastical provinces and regions; and bishops with inter-diocesan offices.

It is arguably no exaggeration to claim that *Christus Dominus* is an especially canonically oriented decree, and a glance at the 1983 code confirms the extent to which it was the source for the canons that were fashioned as a response to what it contained. In effect, the 1983 code and subsequent legislation were the natural complements to *Christus Dominus*.[3] Many of these issues demanded a considerable reworking of the 1917 code as established canonical institutions were legally reconfigured and new ones were legally formed. Given that, a number of these institutions both during and after the council were the object of considerable theological and canonical discussion, the result not only of diverse understandings of the council texts but often also of the practical difficulties involved in implementing *Christus Dominus*. In the forty years from the promulgation of *Christus Dominus* the major questions have been resolved through the publication of a number of key documents that specifically answered critical themes raised in the decree and which thereby determined the Church's mind on issues that in turn reflected the proper understanding of the council.

In his first address to the Roman Curia on December 22, 2005, Pope Benedict XVI considered a proper understanding of the council and its texts. The pontiff made the significant point that the implementation of the council had been difficult due to an incorrect interpretation resulting from a hermeneutics of discontinuity and rupture instead of one of reform or renewal within continuity: "The hermeneutics of discontinuity risks ending in a split between the preconciliar Church and the postconciliar Church. It asserts that the texts of the council as such do not yet express the true spirit of the council. It claims that they are the result of compromises in which, to reach unanimity, it was found necessary to keep and reconfirm many old things that are now pointless. However, the true spirit of the council is not to be found in these compromises but instead in the impulses toward the new that are contained in the texts."

The postconciliar process of the legal application of *Christus Dominus* reflects an important element in the hermeneutics of reform understood as the necessary and ongoing translation into legal language of the doctrines proposed by the council and in a particular fashion by *Christus Dominus*. At the same time it also reflects continuity with respect to the Church's constant teaching on these doctrines. The 1983 code is intimately connected with and dependent upon Vatican II: A considerable number of canons are taken directly from its documents; many are new, a result of the council's teaching (e.g., canons on the Synod of Bishops and episcopal conferences). Others were reworded to reflect conciliar thought, and the code itself was restructured to reflect the threefold *munera* (duties) of teaching, sanctifying, and ruling. In *Sacrae disciplinae leges*, John Paul stated:

> The instrument which the code is fully corresponds to the nature of the Church, especially as it is proposed by the teaching of the Second Vatican Council in general and in a particular way by its ecclesiological teaching. Indeed, in a certain sense this new code could be understood as a great effort to translate this same conciliar doctrine and ecclesiology into canonical language. If, however, it is impossible to translate perfectly into canonical language the conciliar image of the Church, nevertheless the code must always be referred to this image as the primary pattern whose outline the code ought to express insofar as it can by its very nature.

In a very real sense the 1983 code and subsequent legislation reflect what might be termed an "authentic interpretation" of the council, or in the words of the pontiff a "hermeneutics of reform," with which the council is most adequately understood and correctly implemented. This is especially obvious with *Christus Dominus*, and the link between Vatican II and legislative enactments remains critically important for a correct understanding of the conciliar texts themselves.

The decree *Christus Dominus* is conveniently divided into three general areas: bishops in the universal Church (chapter 1), bishops and their dioceses (chapter 2), and the cooperation among bishops (chapter 3). Each area includes various questions, all of significance, but some of greater direct importance not only on the practical life of the Church but also for a proper understanding of its essential structure.

Bishops in the Universal Church

Christus Dominus begins with a brief preface that offers no new insights and whose purpose is clear enough, namely to demonstrate how the decree corresponds to the ecclesiology presented in *Lumen gentium*. It is impossible to understand the theological foundations for the practical working out of the office of bishop, particularly the diocesan bishop, without a proper and profound understanding of the doctrine (especially concerning the Roman pontiff and bishops), which is found in this foundational council document. The concise paragraphs of *Christus Dominus* reiterate the doctrinal foundations of the pastoral office of bishops within both the universal and the particular church. Specifically, it underlines that the Roman pontiff, successor of Peter, "by divine institution enjoys supreme, full, immediate and universal authority over the care of souls." As "pastor of all the faithful" the pope has a particular mission, namely to provide for the common good of the universal Church and the good of individual particular churches, which is founded on the task of building up the body of Christ (Eph 4:12).

The essential interdependence between the universal and the particular church is further clarified and expanded in consideration of the office of bishops, who are the "successors of the apostles as pastors of souls," an understanding already established at Vatican I in its dogmatic constitution on the Church.[4] It logically follows that, "together with the supreme pontiff and under his authority, they have been sent to continue throughout the ages the work of Christ, the eternal pastor." The work of Christ is understood to be accomplished through the bishop in the unfolding of the threefold *munera sanctificandi, docendi, regendi.*

The fundamental doctrinal foundation upon which the common pastoral mission of the bishop is exercised is highlighted by *Christus Dominus.* A bishop can exercise his episcopal office (*munus*) only through valid episcopal ordination and hierarchical communion; namely, he must be in communion with and under the authority of the supreme pontiff and in communion with the other bishops, all of whom are united in a college, *collegium episcoporum.* It is only within this college, *uniti in Collegio,* that the bishop properly exercises the *tria munera,* even if individual bishops practically exercise their office "individually over the portion of the Lord's flock assigned to them, each one taking care of the particular Church committed to him." The same doctrinal logic necessarily applies also to those occasions when bishops might jointly decide on certain issues as in synods, councils, or conferences of bishops.

A bishop's exercise of the tria munera is always done as part of the College of Bishops—in hierarchical communion with the pontiff and the other bishops. While the practical consequences of that exercise are open to development and varied forms, the foundational doctrine must be the center of a bishop's activity. Pastoral action by bishops, while generally lived out within a specific particular church, can never be undertaken in isolation from membership in the College of Bishops. Any idea of some sort of political balance of powers in the exercise of their office, especially between the episcopate and the papacy, is clearly excluded. Rather, as members of the college, all bishops must have a profound sense of being successors of the Apostles, charged with the same solemn mission.

Given these doctrinal foundations, chapter 1 turns to a consideration of the relationship of bishops to the universal Church developed by means of their role within it and their relationship to the Apostolic See.

The College of Bishops, in which the apostolic college continues without break, together and never without its head, the Roman pontiff, is the subject of supreme and full power over the universal Church.[5] This power is exercised in a solemn manner in an ecumenical council,[6] and an important and logical consequence of the doctrine of the College of Bishops is enunciated by *Christus Dominus,* specifically that "all bishops who are members of the episcopal college have the right to be present at an ecumenical council." This is an important clarification with respect to the former legislation, which listed those besides bishops who participated with a deliberative vote at an ecumenical council: cardinals, even not bishops, nonconsecrated residential bishops, abbots or prelates *nullius*, abbots primate, abbots superior of monastic congregations, and supreme moderators of exempt clerical religious. Titular bishops called to a council had deliberative vote, unless otherwise stated in their convocation.[7]

Christus Dominus makes it clear that all bishops have a right to be present at an ecumenical council, though it did not concern itself specifically with the question of deliberative vote. The present code clarified any doubts on that question by stating that "All the bishops and only the bishops who are members of the College of Bishops have the right and duty to take part in an ecumenical council with a deliberative vote."[8]

This same supreme and full power of the college can also be exercised by bishops who live in various parts of the world, provided that the head of the college either calls them to collegiate action or freely accepts their united action.[9] Clearly this includes legislative, judicial, and executive power (namely, the power of governance). Under specific circumstances it also includes the power of teaching authentically (namely, the exercise of the authentic and authoritative magisterium, a doctrine highlighted in *Lumen gentium*, article 25, and canonically determined by the addition of new canons to the present *Code of Canon Law*).[10] *Christus Dominus* also mentions this particular function of the College of Bishops (*CD* 2, 12, 13), and the understanding of the ordinary and universal magisterium exercised by the college remains a noteworthy example of one of the significant fruits of the council's "hermeneutics of reform."[11]

One practical, important, and relatively new institutional expression of the bishops' relationship with the universal Church and in a particular manner their assistance to the ministry of the Church's Supreme Pastor was called for by *Christus Dominus*, article 5, the creation of the Synod of Bishops. Despite discussion both before and during the council suggesting the establishment of a kind of permanent council whereby bishops might exercise their authority over the universal Church, once the doctrinal understanding of the College of Bishops was determined, especially in *Lumen gentium*, discussion turned to the most effective means of expressing not only the authority of the college but also the participation of all the bishops in solicitude for the universal Church (*omnes Episcopos sollicitudinis universae Ecclesiae participes esse*).

While considerations also turned on the establishment of a type of *coetus* (ecclesiastical assembly) of bishops, the precise nature of such a body was never clearly resolved, and the issue was determined when Paul VI announced on September 14, 1965, his intention of creating the Synod of Bishops, which he formally instituted the following day.[12] The synod was a means by which the bishops were to assist the pope in the exercise of his ministry and not one by which the bishops would exercise their supreme authority over the Church, which clearly was institutionally exercised in an ecumenical council as *Christus Dominus* itself had stated. Paul VI's *Apostolica sollicitudo* stated that by its very nature the task of the synod is to inform and give advice. The general aims of the Synod of Bishops were threefold: to encourage close union and valued assistance between the pontiff and the bishops of the entire world; to ensure that direct and real information is provided on questions and situations that touch upon the internal action of the Church and its activity in the contemporary world; and to facilitate agreement on essential points of doctrine and on methods of procedure in the life of the Church.

Christus Dominus (no. 5) underlines the same general thrust: "Bishops from various parts of the world, chosen through ways and procedures established or to be established by the Roman pontiff, will render especially helpful assistance to the Supreme Pastor of the Church in a council to be known by the proper name of Synod of Bishops." The 1983 code not only spells out the practical structure of the synod but also indicates its specific aim in canon 342: "The Synod of Bishops is a group of bishops who have been chosen from different regions of the world and meet together at fixed times to foster closer unity between the Roman pontiff and bishops, to assist the Roman pontiff with their counsel in the preservation and growth of faith and morals and in the observance and strengthening of ecclesiastical discipline, and to consider questions pertaining to the activity of the Church in the world."

Chritus Dominus and *Apostolica sollicitudo* also stated that the synod "will be acting in the name of the entire Catholic episcopate," a concept not found in the 1983 code. The Code Commission argued that this concept was omitted because of the nontechnical nature of the term and its ambiguity, as representation of the College of bishops, in its legal sense, could not be attributed to the synod.[13] In fact, the synod is an institution that manifests *collegialis affectus* (namely, the bond of communion between the pope and his brothers in the episcopate) and offers a structure that reflects the bishops' concern "for the good of the entire Church." This collegialis affectus, *sub specie iuris* (the synod's legal institution), is expressed in the bishops' solidarity and joint solicitude for the Church; the synod cannot be conceived as a type of representative parliamentary assembly; rather, it is a juridical expression of hierarchical communion.

A further consequence of the bishops' *sollicitudo* for the Church is illustrated by *Christus Dominus*'s concern for those parts of the world in which the Word of God has not yet been proclaimed or where, as a result of a small number of priests, the people's faith is endangered. Consequently, bishops should promote works of evangelization and the apostolate. One specific means of such work is highlighted in the decree (namely, that bishops should ensure that sacred ministers and laity be prepared for the missions and that attention be directed and help given to those areas that suffer from a lack of clergy). In addition, *Christus Dominus* calls on bishops to come to the aid of needy churches and to extend brotherly help to bishops, "who for the name of Christ are oppressed by false accusations and harassment, are detained in prison or forbidden to exercise their ministry" (*CD* 7).

The other critical element in the bishops' pastoral ministry within the universal Church concerned their relationship with the Apostolic See, and

Christus Dominus proposed a number of very important practical changes in this area.

Dispensations

As successors of the apostles the bishops automatically (per se) have all of the ordinary, proper, and immediate authority necessary for the exercise of their pastoral office in their dioceses. Given that the diocesan bishop has *potestas propria* for the exercise of his ministry, it was clear that the former system of granting faculties to bishops (the system of concession), which the Council of Trent understood as *tamquam sedis apostolicae delegatus*, needed revision. Practically, this was resolved by authorizing the diocesan bishop to dispense from the Church's general laws, except in those matters reserved to the supreme authority of the Church.[14] In other words, the system of concession was replaced by one of papal reservation, founded on the doctrine established by *Lumen gentium* (no. 18), which states that the bishop's power comes through episcopal ordination (*LG* 21) and becomes exercisable through canonical mission (*LG* 24). In this sense, a diocesan bishop possesses *omnis potestas* necessary for exercising his *munus pastorale*, and his dispensatory power flows from this understanding. There are limits to this dispensatory power. One has already been mentioned (namely, he cannot dispense from those things reserved to the supreme authority, as, for example, dispensation from clerical celibacy).[15] In addition, *Christus Dominus* places another important limit. The granting of a dispensation must be for the spiritual benefit of the faithful. In fact, the spiritual benefit of a Christian determines the scope of the dispensing power.

The 1983 code is understandably more precise as to the bishops' dispensatory powers. While underlining the connection between dispensation and the spiritual good of the faithful and establishing that a diocesan bishop cannot dispense from matters reserved to the Apostolic See, canon 87, §1, also inhibits the bishop from dispensing from procedural or penal laws. In addition, the canon clearly states that only universal and particular *disciplinary* laws can be dispensed. In other words, laws that determine the constitutive elements of acts cannot be dispensed. Thus, a diocesan bishop, for the spiritual good of the faithful, can dispense with the disciplinary law requiring canonical form for the marriage of a Catholic, but he cannot dispense from the law that requires valid consent to be given in marriage, as this is a constitutive element of marriage as understood by the Church.[16]

The Roman Curia

The schema *De rationibus episcopis inter se et sacrae curiae Romanae congregationes* (1961) examined relations between diocesan bishops and the Curia, suggested the co-opting of local bishops as members, and proposed the creation of episcopal conferences in every nation.[17] The latter would be taken up by *Christus Dominus* in articles 37–38, while articles 9–10 would deal with the Roman Curia. The decree acknowledges the outstanding service that the Curia has rendered to the pope and the bishops, but it asks in general that it be reorganized and better adapted to the needs of the times and of various regions and rites. Practically, *Christus Dominus* requests that the task of reorganization and adaptation be effected by "special thought to their number, name, competence, and particular method of procedure, as well as to the coordination of their activities" (*CD* 9). Further, given that the Curia is for the good of the universal Church, *Christus Dominus* asks that officials, members, and consultors "be drawn more widely from various geographical areas" and "that into the membership of these departments there be brought other bishops, especially diocesan ones, who can more adequately apprise the supreme pontiff of the thinking, the desires, and the needs of all the Churches" (*CD* 10). In addition, it suggests that "it would be of service if these same departments would give a greater hearing to laymen who are outstanding for their virtue, knowledge and experience." The reforms of the Roman Curia established by Paul VI and John Paul II have met these requests.[18]

Legates of the Roman Pontiff

Article 9 devotes one sentence (added in the final draft) to legates of the Roman pontiff: "The fathers also earnestly desire that, in view of the pastoral role proper to bishops, the office of legates of the Roman pontiff be more precisely determined." This was a logical consequence of the principle established in the previous article concerning the proper, ordinary, and immediate power of diocesan bishops in their dioceses and the fact (already established in the 1917 code [canon 269 §1]) that legates were not to interfere with the free exercise of the jurisdiction of local ordinaries. This request was met in 1969 by Paul VI in his *motu proprio sollicitudo omnium Ecclesiarum* on papal legates and representatives, which was further clarified in the 1983 code (cc. 362–67).[19]

Bishops and Their Dioceses

It was not the intent of *Christus Dominus* to offer a comprehensive description of the tasks of diocesan bishops or to provide a complete description of the organization of a diocese, even though article 22 suggested "a fitting revision of diocesan boundaries be undertaken prudently and as soon as possible." Rather, the council fathers wished to underscore a number of critical and practical points that they felt were centrally important to an understanding of the *Ecclesia particularis* or diocese, which is described as "that portion of God's people which is entrusted to a bishop to be shepherded by him with the cooperation of the presbyterate."[20] Thus the division of chapter 2 offers a framework within which *Christus Dominus* is written and upon which further questions would be treated after the council's closure. The chapter is divided into three sections: diocesan bishops (*CD* 11–21); diocesan boundaries (*CD* 22–24); and those who cooperate with the diocesan bishop in his pastoral office (*CD* 25–35). This final section deals with coadjutor and auxiliary bishops, the diocesan curia and councils, diocesan clergy, and religious working within the diocese.

Within his diocese the bishop exercises his office through his teaching, as well as priestly and pastoral activity, and the decree summarizes texts taken from the schema *De cura animarum*. Given that *Christus Dominus* is expressly concerned with the bishop's pastoral office, we do not find an extensive or exhaustive treatment of the *tria munera—docendi, sanctificandi, et regendi*—that the council used to describe and center the office of bishop. Rather, we have a number of brief, concise, and concrete descriptions that are based particularly on *Lumen gentium*.

Articles 11–15 deal with the teaching and sanctifying office of bishops. Eminent among their chief duties is announcing the gospel of Christ, which involves the presentation of the whole mystery of Christ. A number of consequences arise from this particular task: While Christian doctrine must be adapted to the needs of the times and to the situation of individuals, bishops have a responsibility to safeguard doctrine; they are responsible for the proper catechetical training of both children and adults; they are to use various means for making Christian doctrine known; they are to ensure the presentation of doctrine in schools, academies, conferences, and writings; and they are to use the mass media in their teaching office. In fulfillment of their *munus sanctificandi*, bishops, "who have been taken from among men and appointed their representatives before God in order to offer gift and sacrifices for sins," are "the principal dispensers of the mysteries of God." As the promoters and guardians of the diocese's entire liturgical life, they are held to cultivate holiness among their clerics, as well as to foster priestly, religious, and missionary vocations.

The following articles (*CD* 16–21) turn directly on the bishop as "father and pastor" and deal with a number of more practically oriented themes. Thus, the bishop, understood as one who serves, should have a special love for priests since he is concerned for their spiritual, intellectual, and material well-being. The same concern is also directed to others: to the laity, who share in the life of the Church in the manner proper to their state, and to separated brethren and nonbelievers.

Clearly, as pastor, the bishop in fulfillment of his pastoral office not only must encourage various forms of the apostolate but also is responsible for their coordination. Thus, the bishop is to encourage the faithful to carry out the apostolate according to their state of life and ability. Further, the bishop should have a special concern for those whose condition of life requires different pastoral services: migrants, exiles and refugees, mariners, airline personnel, and gypsies.

This section concludes with reference to a number of practical questions. Article 19 reiterates a principle on relations between Church and state. Nothing new is said, but even given the Church's readiness to enter into dialogue with the world, the office of bishops is to be exercised independently of any secular power. "Hence, the exercise of their ecclesiastical office may not be hindered, directly or indirectly, nor may they be forbidden to communicate freely with the Apostolic See, with ecclesiastical authorities, or with their subjects." This independence of the Church from secular interference has an important consequence, unambiguously stated by *Christus Dominus*: "This most sacred ecumenical synod declares that the right of nominating and appointing bishops belongs properly, peculiarly, and of itself exclusively to the competent ecclesiastical authority." The statement reflects a question burdened with a long and complex history, and *Christus Dominus* requests that those rights or privileges of election, nomination, presentation, or designation no longer be granted to civil authorities, who are asked to make a voluntary renunciation of their rights in the nominating of bishops.

Finally, the decree turns to the question of bishops' resignation from office (*CD* 21). As a matter of fact, the decree did not decide whether a diocesan bishop should be appointed for life or whether an age limit should be imposed. It did, nevertheless, request that "when diocesan bishops and others, regarded in law as their equals, have become less capable of fulfilling their duties properly because of increasing burden of age or some other serious reason, they are earnestly requested to offer their resignation from office either on their own initiative or upon invitation from the competent authority."

Paul VI, in his *moto proprio Ecclesiae sanctae*, cleared up the question by determining that all diocesan bishops would voluntarily offer their resignation on completion of their seventy-fifth birthday and that, in the case of diocesan bishops, the pontiff would have the discretion to decide whether to accept the resignation. The 1983 code follows this norm.[21]

Cooperation within the Diocese

The final part of chapter 2 considers individuals and institutions central to the pastoral office of the diocesan bishop: coadjutor and auxiliary bishops, the diocesan curia and councils, and the diocesan clergy and religious.

The question of coadjutor and auxiliary bishops had been treated by the 1917 code, which had distinguished between personal coadjutors, who were attached to the diocesan bishop with or without the right of succession, and diocesan coadjutors, who were appointed for the needs of the diocese (*CIC* 17, canon 350). *Christus Dominus* provides a clearer legal picture by establishing more precise terminology: The coadjutor bishop is distinguished from the auxiliary bishop by virtue of the fact that the former has the right of succession, a distinction found in the 1983 code.[22]

Articles 25 and 26 then consider various practical legal issues. Thus, article 25 deals with reasons for the appointment of an auxiliary or coadjutor bishop, and article 26 states that when the good of souls demands, the diocesan bishop should not hesitate to ask for one or more auxiliaries. Auxiliary bishops might be appointed if the extent of the diocese or the number of faithful is too large, a reason similar to that given for the possible partition of a diocese (*CD* 22–24). The decree does not determine which measure might be taken in the case of a diocese characterized by a large number of the faithful or geographically too large: the appointment of auxiliary bishops or dismemberment. Clearly this must be left in the final analysis to the Holy See, which will take into account the overall demands of the diocesan bishop's effective pastoral ministry "because the diocesan bishop cannot personally fulfill all his episcopal duties as the good of souls demands" (CD 25). On the other hand, the decree offers no specific reason for the appointment of a coadjutor bishop except the general statement that a particular need sometimes requires it. Clearly, there is a connection with article 21 concerning the resignation of bishops, as the appointment of a coadjutor, as distinct from an auxiliary, is always directly connected with the actual person of the diocesan bishop, who may be burdened with problems associated with age or health.

A single article (CD 27) considers a number of individuals and institutions that the council fathers regarded as important to the bishop's pastoral office. Chief among them (*officium eminens*) is the vicar general, who is the alter ego of the bishop in general diocesan administration. *Christus Dominus* also established the possibility that diocesan bishops could, if the diocese requires it, appoint one or more episcopal vicars for a certain part of the diocese, to a specific department of the curia, or for certain groups in the diocese. This was an important development as it would offer greater flexibility to the diocesan bishop's pastoral initiatives, especially given the fact that it is the diocesan himself who determines the precise duties of the episcopal vicar. The decree also asks bishops to look to the reorganization of councils and the diocesan curia in light of needs and the work of the apostolate. In this context *Christus Dominus* asked that pastoral councils be established in each diocese, whose function "will be to investigate and to weigh matters which bear on pastoral activity, and to formulate practical conclusions regarding them."

A considerable number of articles are devoted to the diocesan clergy and religious (CD 28–35) and treat several interrelated questions: the freedom of bishops in the appointment to ecclesiastical offices; cooperation and harmony between the bishop and the clergy; unity within the diocesan presbyterate; priests charged with supraparochial apostolic work. A significant portion is given over to the special role pastors play in the diocese, "for as shepherds in their own right they are entrusted with the care of souls in a certain part of the diocese under the bishop's authority" (CD 30). As for the general description of the role of bishops, *Christus Dominus* understands the exercise of the pastoral office of pastors as teaching, sanctifying, and being shepherds of their flock. The decree makes it clear that in the appointment of pastors the bishop is to take into account not only his knowledge of doctrine but also his piety, apostolic zeal, and other apposite gifts and qualities. Again, following upon the request that the rights of the civil authority in the appointment of bishops are to be given up, so also with respect to the appointment of pastors, "all rights whatsoever of presentation, nomination, reservation are to be suppressed." The basis for this clear norm is found in the fact that the parish exists only for the good of souls, and the suppression of rights of nomination will enable the bishop to provide for that more easily.

One legal question that *Christus Dominus* considered concerned the stability of the office of pastor. The stability of the parish priest is still confirmed but is considerably limited. Thus the distinction between parish priests who cannot be removed and those who can is abolished, and the procedure for the transferal and removal of pastors is to be reexamined and simplified. Here is a further example of the general principles enunciated by *Christus Dominus* that require the more detailed determination that would be ushered in by the 1983 code. The latter has established precise norms concerning stability in office (canon 522) and procedures for transferal and removal. As for bishop, "pastors who are unable to fulfill their office properly and fruitfully because of the increasing burden of age or some other serious reason are urgently requested to tender their resignation voluntarily or upon the invitation of the bishop" (*CD* 31), a point reflected in the new code (canon 538 §3).

A final series of articles (*CD* 33–35) concerns religious and their work in the diocese. Religious priests, though technically not incardinated into the diocese, "in a certain genuine sense [they] must be said to belong to the clergy of the diocese inasmuch as they share in the care of souls and in carrying out works of the apostolate under the authority of the sacred prelates" (*CD* 34). A series of principles is laid down with respect to the apostolic work of religious in the diocese with a view to ensuring harmonious cooperation and the maintenance of unity within the diocese. While the institution of exemption is maintained, *Christus Dominus* makes it clear that all religious, exempt and nonexempt, are subject to the authority of local ordinaries in those things that pertain to the public exercise of divine worship, the care of souls, preaching for the people, the religious and moral education of the faithful, catechetical instruction, and liturgical formation. The bishop's authority is also extended to the various works of the apostolate in the diocese, which includes Catholic schools directed by religious at least with respect to general policy and supervision (*CD* 35).

The Cooperation of Bishops

The possible initiatives that might have been listed in the decree on the cooperation of bishops for the common good of various particular churches is extensive, but the decree limited itself to underlining three it considered particularly important. Hence the division into three sections: synods, councils, and especially episcopal conferences; the boundaries of ecclesiastical provinces and the establishment of ecclesiastical regions; bishops with an interdiocesan office. While all have had importance after the council, there is no doubt that the establishment of episcopal conferences has had a marked impact on the postconciliar Church.

Section I, devoted to synods, councils, and episcopal conferences, is based on an understanding of the synodal element in the constitution of the Church, and article 36 states that from the very first centuries of the Church bishops were conscious of the fellowship of fraternal charity and zeal for the universal mission entrusted to the apostles. "Thus there were established synods, provincial councils, and plenary councils in which bishops legislated for various churches a common pattern to be followed in teaching the truths of faith and ordering ecclesiastical discipline." Given this, the council earnestly desires that "the venerable institution of synods and councils flourish with new vigor," in order that the faith will be spread and discipline preserved.

The synodal element among the particular churches is not to be understood as a formal participation in the supreme power of the Church but rather as a special and vital form of cooperation of bishops for the common good of several churches. While the formal collegiality of the bishops concerned the universal Church and in this sense exercised supreme power, the council, in *Lumen gentium* (no. 23), did not intend to deny an expression of collegial unity "in the mutual relations of individual bishops with particular Churches and with the universal Church."

The first section in fact says very little on synods and councils and limits itself to article 36. Rather, *Christus Dominus* emphasized episcopal conferences, which (though not legally a council or synod) are to be considered as an expression of the synodal element of the Church. In fact, the institution of the episcopal conference has become one of the most significant and important developments of Vatican II and to all extent and purposes has become the expression of the synodal element of the Church, thereby replacing the more formal council or synod. Articles 37–38 treat episcopal conferences, which actually is the central subject of the first section of chapter 3.

Episcopal Conferences

Already in the nineteenth century, bishops of various nations began meeting regularly to confront questions that arose as a result of significant social changes: the rise of secular liberalism, revolutions, and economic changes. The problems posed by these changes required the bishops to seek common solutions to meet the task of evangelization in new and developing situations. The growth of these meetings of bishops, often supported by the Holy See but without a clear institutional form, explains why the fathers of Vatican II devoted attention to them: "Nowadays especially, bishops are frequently unable to fulfill their office suitably and fruitfully unless they work more harmoniously and closely every day with other bishops. Episcopal conferences, already established in many nations, have furnished outstanding proofs of a more fruitful apostolate. Therefore, this most sacred synod considers it supremely opportune everywhere that bishops belonging to the same nation or region form an association and meet together at fixed times" (*CD* 37).

Christus Dominus not only recognized the reality and significance of these meetings of bishops but also determined their institutional structure. Meetings of bishops were transformed from what might be termed ad hoc, even if regular, meetings into a juridical institution that became part of the constitutional law of the Church. The meetings were no longer voluntary assemblies but rather became obligatory. Moreover, their clear juridical structure no longer simply wielded moral authority but also was capable of issuing juridically binding decisions.

The decree describes an episcopal conference in the following manner: "An episcopal conference is a kind of council in which the bishops of a given nation or territory jointly exercise their pastoral office by way of promoting that greater good which the Church offers mankind, especially through forms and programs of the apostolate which are fittingly adapted to the circumstances of the age" (*CD* 38).

While the 1983 code repeats *Christus Dominus* almost word for word, canon 447 includes some important variations that mirror the ongoing reflection on the nature and scope of the episcopal conference: "The episcopal conference, a permanent institution, is the assembly of the bishops of a country or of a certain territory, exercising together certain pastoral offices for Christ's faithful of that territory. By forms and means of apostolate suited to the circumstances of time and place, it is to promote, in accordance with the law, that greater good which the Church offers to mankind."

The code underlines the permanence of episcopal conferences, which distinguishes them from other juridical institutions of a synodal character, such as provincial and plenary councils (cc. 439–46). In fact, they have juridical personality *ipso iure* (canon 449 §2), and they have a permanent organization whose scope is to ensure the proper coordination of pastoral activities for the greater good. Further, while *Christus Dominus* states that the bishops in conferences "jointly exercise their pastoral ministry," the code expressly limits that joint exercise to "certain pastoral functions," though it does not specify what they are.

This limitation is meant to stress that the diocesan bishop's exercise of the pastoral ministry is strictly personal and not collegial as it arises precisely because of the nature of his office (already expressed in the earlier part of *Christus Dominus*). The joint exercise refers to those areas that necessitate cooperation among pastors to adequately meet the demands that the greater good of the Church requires. There is no doubt that in the contemporary world pastoral action must often confront problems that affect an entire nation or territory, and this necessarily requires study and guidance in order to lead the faithful and avoid confusion and division. Given this, even after the promulgation of the 1983 code,[23] considerable debate still took place as to the nature of episcopal conferences: What precisely was the link between the eminently pastoral ministry of the diocesan bishop and the joint pastoral activity of bishops in a conference; what was the theological status of the conference; and what teaching authority did the conference enjoy? There was concern that conferences might limit a bishop's authority within his own diocese, an authority derived from divine law.

In light of these pressing and important questions, the final report of the second Extraordinary Synod of Bishops (1985) called for further study on the nature and authority of episcopal conferences: "It is hoped that the study of their theological status and above all the problem of their doctrinal authority might be made explicit in a deeper and more extensive way." The Congregation of Bishops prepared a working paper that was circulated in 1988, and consideration of this and connected questions continued for some ten years until, on May 21, 1998, the instruction on episcopal conferences, *Apostolos suos*, on their theological and juridical nature, was published.[24] In a very real sense this instruction, along with the 1983 code, fleshes out in both theological and legal terms the general request of *Christus Dominus* that episcopal conferences be established.

In article 38, §4, *Christus Dominus* mentioned the legally binding decisions of episcopal conferences, and the 1983 code gave them more detailed expression.[25] On the other hand, the inadequacy of *Christus Dominus* (and even of the 1983 code) as to the theological nature of conferences was met by *Apostolos suos*. It stated that "when the bishops of a territory jointly exercise certain pastoral functions for the good of their faithful, such joint exercise of the episcopal ministry is a concrete application of collegial spirit [*affectus collegialis*]" (*CD* 12). On the other hand, *Apostolos suos* was careful to explain the nature of the application of collegial spirit in relation to the exercise of the episcopal ministry in a formal collegial sense: "The exercise of the episcopal ministry never takes on the collegial nature proper to the actions of the order of bishops as such, which alone holds the supreme power over all the Church. . . . Episcopal collegiality in the strict and proper sense belongs only to the entire College of bishops, which as a theological subject is indivisible" (*CD* 12).

In light of this understanding of the pastoral action of conferences and the understandably broad scope of conference activity,[26] it was inevitable that conferences would have to concern themselves with doctrinal questions, especially with regard to the common good of the particular churches and the pressing needs of contemporary problems that included doctrinal issues. *Apostolos suos* acknowledges that "the joint exercise of the episcopal ministry also involves the teaching office," (*CD* 21) but it makes the important point that such pronouncements of the conference must be kept within precise limits because "while being official and authentic and in communion with the Apostolic See, these pronouncements do not have the characteristics of a universal Magisterium" (*CD* 22). Further, given that the doctrine of the faith is a common good of the Church and a bond of her communion, "the bishops, assembled in episcopal conference, must take special care to follow the Magisterium of the universal Church and to communicate it opportunely to the people entrusted to them" (*CD* 21). While *Apostolos suos* recognized that episcopal conferences could teach authentically, it set legal limits to its exercise in article 22:

> Taking into account that the authentic Magisterium of the bishops, namely what they teach insofar as they are invested with the authority of Christ, must always be in communion with the Head of the College and its members, when the doctrinal declarations of episcopal conferences are approved unanimously, they may certainly be issued in the name of the conference themselves, and the faithful are obliged to adhere with a sense of religious respect to that authentic Magisterium of their own bishops. However, if this unanimity is lacking, a majority alone of the bishops of a conference cannot issue a declaration as authentic teaching of the conference to which all the faithful of the

territory would have to adhere, unless it obtains the *recognition* of the Apostolic See, which will not give it if the majority requesting it is not substantial.

Christus Dominus finally deals with two areas of practical significance for the Church: The first treats of the possible restructuring of ecclesiastical provinces and the establishment of ecclesiastical regions; the second, with bishops who hold an interdiocesan office with a specific article (*CD* 43) dedicated to the care of military personnel.

The decree bases its concern for the potential restructuring of provinces and the establishment of regions on the fact that "the welfare of souls requires appropriate boundaries not only for dioceses but also for ecclesiastical provinces." While the diocese is the ordinary locus for the care of souls, to which in fact all of the Church's activities are directed, the council recognized that provinces and regions could take a certain responsibility for tasks that either could not be accomplished by a diocese or would be even better addressed regionally. The approach reflects the reality that a diocese is to be considered not only in its essential relationship to the universal Church but also in its connection with neighboring particular churches. In fact, ecclesiastical circumscriptions should reflect the necessary cooperation between particular churches, and this is especially the case in the often complex and delicate relations between bishops and civil authorities, a point made in the final sentence of article 39.

The section on bishops who hold an interdiocesan office addresses those tasks that cannot be effectively carried out within a single diocese and necessarily require special legislation. These tasks, which might be accomplished for all or several dioceses of a certain territory, clearly need to be carefully determined in order not to encroach upon the legitimate tasks of the dioceses themselves. It is then no particular surprise that *Christus Dominus* requests that the Church's common law define the relationships between bishops who serve in the interdiocesan offices, diocesan bishops, and episcopal conferences.

Finally, in a brief paragraph *Christus Dominus* discusses the spiritual care of military personnel, an area in which the proper relationship between the bishop entrusted with the pastoral care of such personnel and the local bishop is clearly an exemplification of what immediately preceded in article 42. To meet this need, John Paul II in 1986 published *Spirituali militum curae*.[27]

Conclusion

In his address to the Roman Curia in 2005, Pope Benedict XVI pointed to the fact that the proper understanding of the council and its texts has "silently but more and more visibly...[borne] and is bearing fruit." This is eminently verified in the forty years that separate us from *Christus Dominus*. Based on the foundational doctrinal insights of *Lumen gentium*, it offered the essential parameters for the fulfillment of the pastoral office of bishops and in the process pointed the way to the renewal of a considerable number of canonical institutions. This was effected in a singular fashion by a significant number of legislative documents that included the 1983 *Code of Canon Law*. These legal texts not only determined the precise structures of canonical institutions but also reflected, albeit in legal language, the proper understanding of the council texts, especially as they pertained to the right ordering of the Church, both universal and particular, in the pastoral office of bishops. The council has produced rich fruit in its multifaceted postconciliar legislation.

NOTES

1. For the history of *Christus Dominus* see Klaus Mörsdorf, "Decree on the Bishops' Pastoral Office in the Church," in *Commentary on the Documents of Vatican II*, vol. 2, ed. Herbert Vorgrimler (New York: Herder and Herder, 1968), 165–97; Luigi Maria Carli, "Genesi storico dottrinale del decreto 'Christus Dominus,'" in *Ufficio pastorale dei vescovi e chiese orientali cattoliche* (Turin: Elle Di Ci, 1967), 11–59.

2. John XXIII, *Primus concilii oecumenici nuntius* (Jan. 25, 1959), *AAS* 51 (1959): 65–69.

3. Mörsdorf, "Decree on the Bishops' Pastoral Office," 197, remarked in 1968: "The Decree on the Bishops' Pastoral Office affects the legal order of the Church much more than any other document of the council, especially as regards the Latin Church; hence it is understandable that it will become fully effective only with the reform of canon law."

4. Denzinger, no. 3050.

5. See canon 336.

6. See canon 337.

7. *CIC* 17, canon 223.

8. Canon 339, §1. The same canon in paragraph two states that others who are not bishops can be called to an ecumenical council by the supreme authority of the Church, to whom it also belongs to determine their roles in the council.

9. See canon 337, §§2–3.

10. The relevant new canons were mandated by John Paul II in the *motu proprio ad tuendam fidem* (May 18, 1998), *AAS* 90 (1998): 457–61.

11. In general see B. Ferme, "Developments in Church Magisterium: The Pontificate of John Paul II," *Periodica* 90 (2001): 45–83.

12. Paul VI, *moto proprio apostolica sollicitudo*, *AAS* 57 (1965): 775–80.

13. *Communicationes* 14 (1981): 93.

14. *Christus Dominus* 8: "Except when it is a question of matters reserved to the supreme authority of the Church, the general law of the Church gives each diocesan bishop the faculty to grant dispensations in particular cases to the faithful over whom he exercises authority according to the norm of law, provided he judges it helpful for their spiritual welfare."

15. See canon 291.

16. Canon 86: "Laws are not subject to dispensation to the extent that they define those things which are essentially constitutive of juridic institutes or acts."

17. *Acta synodalis*, series 2, vol. 3, pt. 1, 286–90.

18. Paul VI, apostolic constitution *Regimini ecclesiae universae* (Aug. 15, 1967), *AAS* 59 (1967): 885–928; John Paul II, apostolic constitution *Pastor bonus* (June 28, 1988), *AAS* 80 (1988): 841–930.

19. *AAS* 61 (1969): 473–84.

20. Canon 369 offers the same description.

21. Canons 401, 411.

22. Canons 403ff.

23. The relevant canons on episcopal conferences are 447–59.

24. *AAS* 90 (1998): 641–58.

25. *Christus Dominus*, no. 38, 4: "Decisions of the episcopal conferences, provided they have been made lawfully and by the choice of at least two thirds of the prelates who have a deliberative vote in the conference, and have been reviewed by the Apostolic See, are to have juridically binding force in those cases and in those only which are prescribed by common law or determined by special mandate of the Apostolic See, given spontaneously or in response to a petition from the conference itself." See in general *CIC* 83, cc. 447–59.

26. *Apostolos suos* (no. 15) remarks that "it is not possible to give an exhaustive list of the issues which require such cooperation," though it does mention issues that require action on the part of conferences: "relations with civil authorities, the defense of human life, of peace, and of human rights, also in order to ensure their protection in civil legislation, the promotion of social justice."

27. *AAS* 78 (1986): 481–86.

10

The Decree on the Ministry and Life of Priests, *Presbyterorum Ordinis*

Guy Mansini, O.S.B., and Lawrence J. Welch

In this chapter we show the continuity of the Decree on the Ministry and Life of Priests with prior, principally doctrinal tradition. Therefore we focus especially on *Presbyterorum ordinis*, article 2. We recall some of the history of the composition of that key article and interpret it against the background of prior Catholic tradition. Although the decree is novel in conception and expression relative to much modern theology of the priesthood, this originality functions to assert more important continuities with the greater breadth of scripture, the ancient liturgy, and the fathers.

The history of the Decree on the Ministry and Life of Priests, *Presbyterorum ordinis*, is as long as the Second Vatican Council itself and therefore hard to summarize.[1] From envisioning a purely disciplinary decree that dealt with practical matters of ministry and spiritual life, the fathers gradually came to realize the necessity of saying something about priests comparable in dignity and fundamentality to what the council said of bishops and laity. In other words, the decree would have to address doctrine in some measure.[2] This realization, however, was tardy (witness the late date of the rejection of the draft schema *De vita et ministerio sacerdotali*, which followed from it—October 19, 1964).[3] Only one more session of the council remained.

Remarkably, in little more than one month, the Commission for the Discipline of the Clergy and the Christian People, charged with drafting a new text, was able to distribute a draft of a new schema to the council fathers on November 20, 1964. One of the important differences from previous drafts was the title, *De ministerio et vita presbyterorum*, which signaled that the subject was not the priesthood in general (*sacerdotium*), inclusive of the bishops, but the presbyterate (*presbyteratus*), priests of the second order. Moreover, the reversal in the order of "life" and "ministry" reflects the fact that it treats the ministry first (part two) and makes it determinative of what priestly life should be like (part three).[4] At this pass, it was natural for the commission to take guidance from previous conciliar work and look back to the Dogmatic Constitution on Church, *Lumen gentium*, article 41, for a word about priestly spirituality, and to *Lumen gentium*, article 28, for the all-important first doctrinal word. It was over the content of this doctrinal word that the council fathers divided. After they sent in their written comments to the commission in January of 1965, the schema was revised. The modified text was transmitted to the fathers on May 28, 1965, but was not publicly debated until the 148th general congregation on October 14, 1965. After several days of discussion, the fathers voted overwhelmingly (1507 to 12) on October 16 to accept it as the *textus recognitus*, that is, the basis for the final version. Still, important work remained.

Article 2 and the "Two Conceptions" of the Priesthood at the Council

Because of its indebtedness to *Lumen gentium*, the very first draft of *Presbyterorum ordinis* inserts the priest into the theology of mission, proceeding from Christ to the apostles, and from the apostles to the bishops, and it did so at the express request of 124 fathers.[5] This did not, however, satisfy those with an allegiance to other ways of understanding the priesthood, especially that cultivated by the French School. At the distribution of the first emendation of the first draft text of *Presbyterorum ordinis*, just after acceptance of this emended text as the textus recognitus, Archbishop François Marty famously summarized the divergence of views:

> As to the specific nature of the ministry and life of presbyters. On this matter, there have been expressed two conceptions which seem to differ at first glance. For one of them insists more on the consecration of the presbyter worked by the sacrament of Orders, and on the personal union of the presbyter with Christ, who is the font of holiness and spiritual efficaciousness. The other conception, however, insists on the mission of the presbyter, which mission he receives from Christ through the sacrament: that is, the presbyter, since he becomes a member of the Order of presbyters, by that fact becomes a helper of the Order of bishops, so that he acts in the person of Christ unto the building up of the Church.
>
> In fact, each of these two conceptions puts in light an aspect of great importance in the ministry and life of presbyters. Therefore, our commission will take care to show how these two conceptions combine with one another harmoniously and indeed complete each other, so that they go together in the unity of presbyteral ministry.[6]

It is easy to illustrate Marty's summary. So, on the one hand, responding to the first draft, Archbishop Darmajuwana thought the text should emphasize more the priest's service to humanity, and Archbishop Garrone wanted a text more concordant with *Lumen gentium*, where episcopal priesthood has its origin in the mission given by Christ and a scope that is the entire world.[7] Bishop Gufflet criticized the first draft for maintaining a conception of priesthood that is "purely cultic" and in contradiction to Saint Paul, while Archbishop de Provenchères wanted more emphasis on the ministry of the word.[8] On the other hand, Bishop de Langavant wanted a more theocentric text that expressed the priest's service to God; furthermore, "the sacrifice of the cross, and therefore also the sacrifice of the Mass, has for its first end the glory of God. This is also the most excellent function of the priest. As Christ became incarnate and was immolated on the cross 'on account of the glory of God,' the priest is consecrated in the first place to render glory to God in offering the sacrifice of the Mass, and also in interceding, in praying, in adoring in the name of all humanity."[9]

So also in the speeches of October 13–15, 1965, to which Marty especially refers, we find Cardinal Döpfner praising the emended text for not viewing the presbyterate solely under its "cultic aspect," according to which it is ordered to offering sacrifice and administering the sacraments but extending it to the threefold *munera* (functions) of Christ.[10] For Cardinal Richaud, on the other hand, it was not sufficient to think of priesthood solely under the heading of a mission to humanity; "the first response to priestly vocation lies in a greater love for Christ." This found expression in the text, he noted, but should have been more prominent. Further, "the primordial function of presbyters, which lends value and inspiration to their zeal and ministry, rests in the consecration of the priest to the exterior and interior worship of God."[11] In the same vein, Bishop Henríquez Jiménez located the "essential reality" of the priesthood "wholly in the ontological configuration to Christ the Priest as well as in the real participation in his own unique and eternal priesthood."[12]

These two positions came in large part to coalesce around the question of whether the document should emphasize the ministry of sanctification (especially in saying Mass) or the ministry of the word and evangelization. The three munera were in fact prominent in the text from the first draft at the express request of 116 fathers.[13]

The commission therefore set itself the task of combining two lines of understanding the priesthood: the priest as conformed to Christ and consecrated unto the service of God; the priest as sharing in the apostolic mission of the bishops, itself a share in the mission of Christ, for the salvation of men. This task can also be understood as a call to insert the Tridentine view of the priest as the one who offers the Eucharistic sacrifice within the larger framework of an earlier and more ecclesiologically oriented concept of priesthood, where the functions of preaching and ruling are brought to the same level of articulation as that of sanctifying.[14]

At this distance, one may wonder what the great difficulty was. Marty himself says carefully (and we think accurately) of the positions only that they "seem to differ" and that only "at first glance." One might say that it was a difficulty more of temperament or spirituality than of doctrinal synthesis. As Yves Congar remarked long before the council, defining the priesthood in terms of consecration to God is not so much a theological definition as a spirituality.[15] But it is a spirituality that has had powerful and very practical effect. It is the spirituality, for instance, whose working out could be seen in the monasteries and convents of male religious of the 1950s and 1960s with many priests, where ten or twelve altars might be packed into one oratory, so that each priest, assisted by one server, might discharge the duty of offering daily sacrifice to God.

Doctrinally, on the other hand and to repeat, the synthesis is not difficult. Congar notes resources within the French School itself, citing Saint Vincent de Paul, who gives due attention to mission, functionality, and ministerial finality at one stroke: "The priest is a man called by God to share in the priesthood of Jesus Christ in order to extend the redemptive mission of Jesus Christ in doing what Jesus Christ did, in the way in which he did it."[16] Congar observes as well that if Saint Thomas's definition of priesthood ties it to the Eucharist, his enumeration of the acts of the priest firmly characterize the priesthood as a prolongation of apostolic mission.[17]

Congar for his own part and commenting on the text of *Presbyterorum ordinis* finds a solution in the Christian cult. His remarks, moreover, are the more weighty as he helped produce the text he comments on.[18] The Christian's worship of God, Congar tells us, is in the first place the interior self-sacrifice of the person to God, a sacrifice that both finds achievement in fraternal charity and care of the poor and depends on and is expressed by the Eucharistic sacrifice.[19] Both sacrifices, however, the personal and the liturgical, absolutely presuppose the word of the gospel accepted in faith, and so they presuppose the call to and articulation of faith, which is preaching. Therefore, the apostolic, evangelical aspect of priestly ministry can never be forgotten and is a presupposition of the other aspects.[20]

After the council, synthesis of the two views took the form of picking one or another of the three munera of the priest and making it architectonic or deriving the other two from it, and there were many essays in this vein.[21] Joseph Ratzinger, for example, notes that the scope and intention of the word of the gospel includes sanctifying and ruling.[22] Therefore, baptism and Eucharist cannot be thought to be alien to the word of the gospel; word and Eucharist cannot be opposed to one another.[23] Rather, the Eucharist is the fulfillment of the word, where the word wants to lead us, and even what it wants to become. It is not just that sanctifying and ruling presuppose faith and so preaching, as Congar points out, but that the word of the Gospel of its nature passes over to the sacrament of the Word made flesh.[24] Karl Rahner similarly privileged the priest as proclaimer of the word, the supreme degree of which makes present what it proclaims in sacrament and for a rightly ordered community.[25] Walter Kasper proposed to unify the conception of priestly ministry in the notion of leadership in teaching, worship, and community relations, and this seems, in fact, to privilege the *munus regendi*.[26]

While the relation of the munera to one another is doubtless important, it is only one part of the synthesis of *Presbyterorum ordinis*, our own view of which we present shortly.

Juxtaposition or Synthesis?

After the acceptance of the textus recognitus, three substantive changes were made to the section on the nature of the priesthood. First, there is a return to the first draft's introduction, which speaks of the entire people of God as sharing the mission of Christ and in his threefold munus. Second, there is the addition of article 2d, on the spiritual and existential sacrifice of the faithful, which is treated as finding sacramental consummation through the ordained priesthood. Third, there is the addition of article 2e, on the ultimate purpose of the priesthood, specified as the salvation of men and the glory of God. With various other emendations of the text, the council approved these important additions on December 2.[27] This reworking of what was to become article 2 of the final text was principally Congar's work.[28] On December 7, 1965, the decree was overwhelmingly approved in public session, 2,390 to 4.

Did *Presbyterorum ordinis* succeed in producing an organic doctrinal statement that brought together the two views, that of the priest as consecrated by the sacrament of orders for the worship of God (preeminently in offering the sacrifice of the Mass) and that of the priest as sharing in apostolic mission, which itself is fully participated only by the bishop?

It is sometimes said that the missionary perspective ended up encompassing the cultic one, which was absorbed into it. In this way, the missionary view would be the view of the council and *Presbyterorum ordinis* simply speaking, within which a place is found for the other (but now relativized) view. In the Herder commentary Friedrich Wulf remarks on the decree: "The one-sided cultic character of the Catholic priesthood has been absorbed into the wider apostolic ministry, which has found expression above all in the doctrine of the three offices of Christ."[29] On the other hand he laments the characterization of the priest (in article 2) as facing the Church, representing Christ the head, as "one-sided"—he wants the priest to represent the priestly church, too—and recognizes that the "sacerdotal-cultic idea" of the priest, the concept of the priest as determined by the power of orders, "predominates" in the second and third sections of article 2. He finds better the fourth section of article 2, which "brings into the foreground the missionary aspect, the commission to preach and to sanctify addressed to the New Testament ministry."[30]

Basically, therefore, Wulf treats the text as if its unity were that of a bag containing two cats. Sometimes one "predominates," and at other points the text is "one-sided." In this way, the text would illustrate the "juxtaposition" of views, old and new, that Hermann Pottmeyer finds in the production of the council. For him, synthesis on matters such as the relation of pope and episcopal college, the unity of revelation, and the theological relation of the Catholic Church to other churches was not reached but is the part of theologians to achieve.[31] Even so, Pottmeyer expressly forbears accusing the production of incoherence. With regard to *Presbyterorum ordinis*, this is left to Christian Duquoc.[32] He can say that "a rather classic theology of the priesthood" is "meshed with a quite untraditional presentation of ministerial activity."[33] He thinks the decree suffers from "indecisiveness" and that a "latent opposition" exists between the old and the new views.[34] The theology of sacrifice found in article 5 can be read as either subsumed into the theology of mission or at odds with it and therefore, according to Duquoc, as an obstacle to the democratic reformulation of office that the new view of priesthood, which is present but not everywhere controlling in the text, aimed at.[35] Daniel Donovan, too, thinks the council "had to sacrifice consistency" in order to meet the demands of both views; sometimes the mission view predominates, but at other times "priesthood," *sacerdotium*, reabsorbs all of the presbyteral munera into itself.[36]

For our part, we think the decree is unfairly criticized as incoherent and as achieving nothing more than a juxtaposition of views. Moreover, in our opinion the nature of the synthesis is not a simple matter of picking one of the munera and declaring it architectonic. Evidently, if there is a synthesis of a part of the deposit of faith, it will be discerned only against the background of prior theological and dogmatic tradition.

Mission, Munera, Mediation

It is true that the function of sanctifying, which culminates in the presidency of the Eucharist, is said to be but one of three functions or munera for which the priest or apostolic minister is sent.[37] In this way, the accent is formally on mission, and cultic priestly activity is but one thing within a greater whole, as a part of it, in addition to the other two offices or functions.

The text, however, does not leave the three munera with identical roles in our understanding of the priesthood, as if they contributed to it in the same way and on the same footing. Article 5, which Duquoc finds ambiguous, is decisive. First, the priest's ministry as a whole and all the works of his apostolate are said to be ordered to the Eucharist (no. 5b). This is new with respect to the textus recognitus. It is repeated substantially in article 13, where priests "fulfill their highest office"—*munus suum praecipuum adimplent*—in the Eucharist (no. 13d), which phrase is also new relative to the textus recognitus.[38]

Second, in a striking phrase, the munus of preaching has its origin in and finds its summit in the Eucharist, *fons et culmen totius evangelizationis* (no. 5b). This, too, is new with respect to the textus recognitus and must likewise be understood to be responding expressly to the desire to synthesize the two views. Article 5 is at this point doing nothing but paraphrasing article 2d, the whole of which is an addition and where the Eucharistic sacrifice, to which the spiritual sacrifice of Christians is joined, is the goal to which priestly ministry "tends" and that in which it is "consummated." Here, too, the ministry of priests "begins from the proclamation of the gospel" but "draws its force and strength from the sacrifice of Christ," to which, once again, it is said to be directed. As to the particular discussion of the ministry of the word in article 4, it makes Congar's point that, since the sacraments are sacraments of faith, the ministry of the word is presupposed to the sacramental ministry and is even intrinsic to it, as the text states explicitly with regard to the Mass (*PO* 4c).

Of priestly rule, finally, the fathers teach in article 6 that "no Christian community can be built without being rooted in and turning on the celebration of the most holy Eucharist" (*PO* 6e). The Eucharist leads to works of charity (*PO* 6e), and the law of the community is said to be the law of charity (*PO* 6c). Union in charity, of course, is nothing but the *res* of the sacrament of the Eucharist. If the *archê* is the end, then we may well say that this last function (ruling in and for charity) rules the other two munera. On the other hand, since the sacraments of the New Law—and especially and preeminently the Eucharist—contain what they signify, they cannot be thought of as indicators of something utterly distinct from them or as instruments extrinsic to what they accomplish. Therefore, it is reasonable to conclude that, if formally the mission view is primary, as introducing and framing the presentation, substantively, the cultic, Eucharistic view is primary.

In this, the text is faithful to the New Testament. For apostolic mission originates with Christ, who is made present in the Eucharist and makes himself present precisely as enacting the Paschal mystery. But it is from the fullness of the Paschal mystery that the mission arises (John 21). Therefore, whatever participation there may be in apostolic mission originates in the Eucharist, which is the sacramental availability of the Paschal mystery.[39]

Further, the priestly mission is to bring the laity, those who consecrate their lives to Christ in consecrating the world to him, to a share in Christ's own consecration of himself to the Father.[40] The Eucharist is therefore also the terminus of the mission in this world. If the word of the gospel does not pass over to sacramental reality, moreover, and if our action in the world does not join up with Christ's action, then one must wonder whether Christian life is more than just one of many other social constructions of reality.[41] Rather, Eucharist means that Christianity, our union with Christ, is not just a matter of saying and doing, a moral reality, but lands us in a reality deeper than our own by a saying and a doing that is more than our own.[42] So, yes, in the order of generation, so to speak, preaching must be first, and the council explicitly says so (no. 4a); however, in the order of perfection, as containing the reality that preaching is about, sanctification is first.[43] This is, in fact, the synthesis article 2d presents to us.

Consideration of the mediations at stake in the munera shows how the "two conceptions" are mutually inclusive. If sanctification is taken quite narrowly to mean performance of and presidency over the cult, then the missionary mandate of the New Testament minister includes that as but one activity to be taken with two others. On the other hand, saying that the New Testament minister is one who is sent adverts to only one side of a double mediation, the side that goes from God to man. In the same way, "preaching" and "ruling" are also similarly one sided and move from God toward man. Priesthood, on the other hand, classically signifies both sides of the mediation, from God to man and from man to God.[44] The downward mediation is prior, for it brings both the word of divine instruction and interior grace.[45]

However, the other side, whereby men arrive in the heavenly sanctuary with their sacrifice, is also signified by "priest," as it is not by "apostle." The question, then, is what is meant by the Christian cult.[46] If we mean very narrowly the service of the altar in the sanctuary, then saying that sanctifying is but one of three functions of the one sent breaks open priestly activity to include preaching and ruling. But if the cult of Christians is "existential"[47] and if the altar of sacrifice is cosmic,[48] then "priest" once again regains its capacity to be the comprehensive appellation of Christian ministry, which gathers a community by preaching, orders it in charity, and consummates its spiritual sacrifice in the sacrament of the sacrifice of Christ.

Moreover, if we consider the munera in their original and paradigmatic deployment by Christ, then the office of Christ's priesthood must be preeminent.[49] For it conveys more fully the mediation of Christ, downward and upward, both Son of God and Son of man, than either kingship or prophecy of themselves can do. So, the name Christ receives, according to Hebrews 1:4, summing up his divine dignity as Son, King, Lord, and Creator (1:5–14) and his solidarity with us as Son of man, the pioneer of salvation, and brother (2:1–16), is "high priest" (2:17).[50] Priestly concept and reality have also died and been raised in the triumph of the cross, with the same continuity and discontinuity of the buried and glorified body, of the Old Testament and the New. Downward, priestly mediation consists in the teaching of a new law and its infusion into the heart and of the forgiveness of sins; upward, it is the offering of a sacrifice that achieves salvation because it places the offerers in the heavenly sanctuary sacramentally and in hope so that at death the members may be where their Head has preceded. On the contrary, to make of Christian ministry a ministry only of the word or so to emphasize it when conceiving Christian ministry as a share in apostolic mission as to fail to see any antecedent foreshadowing in the priesthood of the Old Testament is to confine the Church to the synagogue and to refuse to enter into the Body that is the temple.[51]

The Synthesis of Article 2

It is important to see that the synthesis of article 2 occurs within the context of the great themes of the council's ecclesiology, for it is made possible by the council's faithfulness to these themes. This faithfulness is declared from the outset, in article 1, where the treatment of the priesthood is related to these themes in a single sentence that forms as it were an ecclesiological preface to the decree: "For, by the sacred ordination and mission they receive from bishops, priests are promoted to the service of Christ the teacher, priest and king whose ministry they share, the ministry by which the Church is unceasingly built up here on earth into the people of God, the body of Christ and the temple of the holy Spirit."[52]

First, the mission of priests evokes the missions of Christ and the Church. Second, priestly mission is ordered to build up the Church as the communion of the people of God, whose Christological and pneumatological dimensions are immediately brought forward, since communion in the Church is communion with the persons of the Trinity. Third, this mission of Christ and the Church that priests share in is given the same threefold articulation as in *Lumen gentium*. Fourth, the ministry of priests, already situated between Christ, who sends them, and the people to whom they are sent is tied to the ministry of the bishops, to which it has been a principal goal of the council to give adequate treatment.[53]

The reconciliation and synthesis of the two views occurs at three places, especially in the attention at article 2a and 2d to the spiritual sacrifices of the faithful, at article 2b, and at 2e. Article 2a affirms that all of the faithful are a royal priesthood, offering spiritual sacrifices to God.[54] This looks forward to article 2d, where the synthesis occurs in terms of the relation of priesthoods, in that the ministerial priest is sent to enable the exercise of the baptismal priesthood of the faithful.[55] The Christian's sacrifice, which is the whole offering of all of one's life and of every human action to the Father, is rendered possible through the apostolic ministry of priests, which by preaching calls the faithful to this sacrifice and is consummated in being sacramentally united to the sacrifice of Christ in the Eucharist. Article 2 as a whole shows, as it were, how the spiritual sacrifice of the whole body is to be enabled and sacramentally accomplished in the Eucharistic sacrifice of the Head through the ministry of priests. "This is the goal of the whole ministry of priests, and in this it is consummated." Moreover, their ministry, "which begins from the proclamation of the Gospel, draws its force and strength from the sacrifice of Christ."[56]

Before this, article 2b repeats the doctrine of Trent, which states that within the body of Christ there are ministers who in virtue of their sacred power offer sacrifice and forgive sins. These ministers, however, are to be understood in the line of the great sending: Christ to the apostles, the apostles to the bishops. As the bishops are appointed "to share his [Christ's] own consecration and mission," first mentioned at the beginning of article 2a, so by implication do priests, who are delegated to collaborate with the bishops "in carrying out the apostolic mission." Consecration and mission are united in that consecration is for mission.[57]

The last paragraph, article 2e, also reconciles the two views. It shows the unity of the theocentric, "consecratory" view with that of the "anthropocentric," apostolic view. Underneath the text is the recollection of Saint Irenaeus's dictum that the glory of God is the life of man and that the life of man is the knowledge of God.[58] So, as the text has it, priests are certainly devoted to the glory of God, but "that glory [of God] consists in this, that human beings consciously, freely and thankfully accept the work of God that was brought to perfection in Christ, and manifest it in their whole lives." The entire life and activity of priests, including preaching, sanctifying, and ruling, as well as most notably the very prayer and adoration of the priest, therefore "contribute both to increasing the glory of God and to advancing men in the divine life." The theocentric intent of priesthood, comprising the worship of God, is consummated in the sanctification of man.

This leaves us with article 2c, the middle section of the article, where the originality of the council comes to light as it presents its summary and controlling dogmatic view of the priest. The text articulates how the priest discharges his apostolic mission by recalling the threefold munera, and it explains the nature of the consecration for mission in terms of the sacrament of orders. Presbyteral office is conferred by a distinct sacrament, whereby priests are "patterned to the priesthood of Christ [*Christo sacerdoti configurantur*], so that they may be able to act in the person of Christ as head of the body [*ita ut in persona Christi Capitis agere valeant*]."[59] Here let us quote Henri Denis apropos of that last phrase: "It seems to us that it is on this little phrase in fact that the *specificity* of the hierarchical minister in general and that of the presbyteral minister in particular rests. Indeed, if one looks for what is *original* in the task of the priest in relation to that of the Christian, one is referred to this sign which is essential to the Church: the sign of Christ the Head for his Body. In other words, there is a ministry in the Church in order that the work of Christ in the work of the Church may be signified."[60]

We report the story of the composition of this text shortly. For now, we wish to make an observation on another sense in which article 2 is synthetic. The allusion to Saint Irenaeus in article 2e reminds us how deeply rooted the entire article is in the tradition. The text is synthetic, not just conceptually, relative to the "two views," but relative to scripture and tradition, too.

At the outset, in article 2a, the text joins consecration and mission in the citation of John 10:36, which speaks of Christ as "consecrated and sent into the world." It is right to recall here, too, the Letter to the Hebrews, where Christ is in one breath both the apostle and the high priest of our faith (3:1). Thus, his priestly work includes his authoritative declaration of the content of our profession of faith,[61] while his consecration as priest consists in his obedient death,[62] which Christians make actual in their own obedient sacrifice of daily life and charity (13:1–6) and memorialize in the Eucharist and indeed proclaim until he comes again.[63] The linkage of consecration and mission therefore picks up the original connection of these things in the Christology of the New Testament, which itself builds on the commissioning narratives of the Old. "Before I formed you in the womb I knew you, and before you were born I consecrated you; I appointed you a prophet to the nations" (Jer 1:5). "The Spirit of the Lord is upon me, because he has anointed me [consecrated me] to preach good news to the poor; he has sent me to proclaim release to the captives" (Lk 4:18, citing Is 61:1–2).[64] Returning to John's gospel, finally, we recall that Christ's priestly invocation in chapter 17 declares not just his own consecration, which is at the same time the achievement of his mission, but also that of those who in chapter 20 are sent as he was sent (20:21).

The threefold character of the mission of Christ collects the anointings of prophet, priest, and king in the Old Testament, bespeaks the unity of the workings of word and spirit, of history and grace, and thus illustrates the inseparability of Christology and pneumatology in the Incarnation itself. For the fathers, the trilogy does not move beyond Christology, the explanation of the name "Christ." It is the liturgy of initiation, the postbaptismal anointing, that makes the Christian (as well as Christ) prophet, priest, and king.[65] The ancient liturgies of ordination collectively attest that ordination enables a man to teach, sanctify, and rule, and although they do not pick out these functions as three, Congar thinks they come "very close to our trilogy."[66] In Saint Thomas, the munera are invoked for both Christ and his ministers.[67]

The nature of the ministerial priest as representative of Christ is patristic, though one has to look to the citations of *Lumen gentium*, article 21, for a witness to this tradition in the council's texts. The assertion of the sacramentality of orders repeats Trent, of course, but Trent itself, in repeating the common theology of the thirteenth century on orders and the character imparted by orders does nothing but bring forward the twelfth century's ordering and labeling of the patristic and especially Augustinian inheritance. Best of all, all the foregoing is poured into understanding the priest's place between the sacrifice of the faithful and the sacrifice of Christ, just where Saint Paul places his own ministry, the Apostle who knew nothing for the Corinthians "except Jesus Christ and him crucified" (1 Cor 2:2) so that they might be God's temple (3:9, 16) and present their bodies "as a living sacrifice to God" (Rom 12:1).[68]

The Christological view of priesthood to which the text orients us in article 2c, where priests are "patterned to the priesthood of Christ, so that they may be able to act in the person of Christ, the head of the body," exactly reflects our epistemic situation. Not only is Christ the mediator of grace by his action, but, in the order of our very thinking about him, he is also the mediator of a new concept of mediation and of priesthood. His priesthood, a "better priesthood," is exercised in his death, in the Paschal mystery; the priesthood of the faithful, for its part, is achieved in the transformation of life in the power of and as uniting themselves existentially to Christ; ordained priests render the mediation of Christ present, especially in the Eucharist, which makes the Paschal mystery present and unites the spiritual sacrifice of the faithful to that of Christ. Vanhoye maintains that "If...we consider the texts of the New Testament which describe the characteristics of the apostolic or pastoral Christian ministry, we observe that these texts present the ministers of the Church as the living instruments of Christ the mediator and not as the delegates of the priestly people."[69] And again, the specific function of the priest is "the manifestation of the active presence of Christ the mediator...[and] of Christ the priest, in the life of believers in order that they may explicitly welcome this mediation and by its means transform their whole existence."[70]

Presbyterorum ordinis, article 2, is synthetic, therefore, not in the way of some theological encyclopedia but in the way a magisterial text as at Trent or the First Vatican Council is synthetic. It would have us think of the foundational realities necessary to understand priesthood: the plan of God, revealed in Christ, set in motion by Christ's mission, a mission continued in apostolic and episcopal ministry, and directed toward the consummation of all things at Christ's return. Within this, the true "frame" offered by the council, lies the sacramental priesthood of priests of the second rank, a priesthood deriving from and representing Christ's by the consecration of orders, a priesthood that enables the Eucharistic consummation of the existential priesthood of Christians, which presupposes both faith and evangelization and flowers in a community ordered by charity and awaiting the Lord's return. That, by any fair stretch of the word, is a "synthetic" view.

Doubtless, not everything is said in one article of the decree. The subsequent unfolding of the text, however, is organically related to this second article. In the second part of the decree, on the ministry of priests, articles 4–6 take up the munera of preaching, sanctifying, and shepherding mentioned in article 2c, as well as keeping the order of the munera among one another established in article 2d. Articles 7–9 develop the priest's relations to bishop, other priests, and the faithful by spelling out the ecclesial references of article 2b.

The third part of the decree, the life of priests, takes as its point of departure the consecration of priests, first mentioned in article 2b; according to article 13, moreover, the holiness of priests is a holiness that is learned and lived within the discharge of the munera mentioned in article 2c. The unity and harmony of the life of priests (article 14) finds adumbration in the last lines of article 2e. In article 15, the priest finds an example of the virtues of humility and obedience in the Christ he represents, which harks back to article 2c. Finally, in article 16, celibacy shows the priest as friend of the bridegroom, betrothing the faithful to Christ, just as in article 2d the ministry of priests is to lead the faithful to the banquet of the Lamb, which we can also characterize as the *wedding* banquet of the Lamb.

Nova in Veteris: The Doctrinal Novelty of Article 2

The text of article 2 is novel relative to previous magisterial teaching by its combination of a theology of mission and consecration, of word and sacrament, by the very comprehensiveness of the framework in which it inserts priesthood, and in the detail with which it lists the priest's relations to others. Still, none of this touches its most important novelty, one that was not seen at the time for what it was and that, if we think it good, must be attributed solely to the accidents of the composition of the text, which is to say, solely to the providence of God and the guidance of the Holy Spirit, which, as we believe, governed the proceedings of the council.

Taking up *Lumen gentium*, article 28, for the text of the second section of *Presbyterorum ordinis* meant also (indirectly but more basically) taking up *Lumen gentium*, article 21. For *Lumen gentium* understands priests in the first instance as helpers of the bishops such that priests are of the same kind of minister as are bishops but of lesser degree. If, however, priests are to be understood ecclesiologically in relation to bishops, then the definition of the priesthood and of priestly ministry follows from that of episcopal office and ministry.[71]

In the formation of *Lumen gentium*, article 21, which asserts the sacramentality of episcopal ordination, there is repeated the teaching of Trent that ordination imparts a character.[72] And in accord with the standard understanding of the effect of orders and the permanence of the character, the preliminary draft asserted that a bishop could neither be reduced to the lay state nor become again a simple priest. The fathers, however, desired a positive expression of the effect of the sacrament. Responding to this wish, the doctrinal commission offered in place of the negative characterization of the effect of ordination the statement that, in virtue of ordination, grace was given and a character imparted in such wise that bishops take the place of Christ himself and represent him or act *in eius persona* as teacher, shepherd, and priest.

The text means to connect ordination with all three munera or offices— teaching, ruling, and sanctifying. Ordination equips a bishop, as the ancient ordinals witness, for all three *ministeria*, for the whole and every part of his properly episcopal ministry. In this way, the text implies the unity of the three powers; ordination gives the radical wherewithal for all, for each is essential to episcopal functioning and is a nonalienable part of episcopacy.

The authors of the text have therefore invoked a quite traditional phrase, *in persona Christi*, by which to express the effect of orders for all three functions. In doing so, however, they extend the range of this phrase and modify its prior usage. If they are not saying something new, they are saying the old in a new and quite succinct and powerful form. For Saint Thomas, for example, the priest or bishop acts *in persona Christi* only when consecrating the Eucharistic elements.[73] *Mediator Dei*, less than twenty years before the council, respected this usage.

Lumen gentium, article 28, the text immediately in the background to *Presbyterorum ordinis*, article 2, seems to have fallen back to this older usage. Expressly, it speaks of the priest acting *in persona Christi* only in the sacrifice of the Mass, and its reference to *Mediator Dei* likewise takes us back to the old usage. Implicitly, however, *Lumen gentium*, article 28, expands the sense of representing Christ to all three munera. This is clear from outside the text from the *relatio* of Henríquez Jiménez.[74] However, the text itself also implies it in several ways. First, by the power of the sacrament of orders, priests are consecrated "in the image of Christ (*ad imaginem Christi*), the high and eternal priest ... to preach the Gospel and pasture the faithful and celebrate divine worship." But doing something to or in or after the image of Christ is representing Him in doing it, and representing Christ is acting in his person. Second, sharing "in the *munus* of Christ the one mediator" for evangelizing and exercising "the *munus* of Christ the shepherd and head" in pastoral care are functionally equivalent in the text to "acting in the person of Christ" in the Eucharistic cult.[75] The text could as well have said for the last that the priest shares in the munus of Christ the Priest and for the former that he acts in the person of Christ the Mediator and Shepherd.

Presbyterorum ordinis, therefore, follows *Lumen gentium*, article 28, in giving *in persona Christi* a broader sense for priests, as *Lumen gentium*, article 21, does for bishops, and it did so from the first draft, with very general approval of the fathers. It follows article 28 also in saying expressly, as article 21 did not, that the representation is of Christ as *head* of the Church, an uncontested and unremarked precision whose importance emerged only later.[76]

At *Presbyterorum ordinis*, article 2, it is true, where it is a matter of the priest acting *in persona Christi* for all his presbyteral functioning, the council appeals to *Lumen gentium*, article 10, which asserts the priest so acts only in the Eucharist. And at article 6, speaking of the pastoral or ruling function of the priest, the council harks back to *Lumen gentium*, article 28, which has the phrase again in a Eucharistic context and which itself appeals to *Mediator Dei*, correctly and narrowly, for this point. However, it is quite certain that *Presbyterorum ordinis* means to assert that the priest acts in the person of Christ and indeed in the person of Christ the head in discharging all three functions. This is clear from the context, for article 2c speaks of building up (that is, gathering by teaching), sanctifying, and ruling the body of Christ. It is also clear from the *Acta*. The second draft has it in article 2 that the priest acts *in persona Christi* expressly for all three *munera*. To a *modus* after the third draft, which drops the express listing of all three, requesting the restoration of the earlier text, the answer is that the text evidently enough supposes that all three are in question. The commission answers that "presbyters are always said to share in the *munera* of the bishops, which indeed are the ones mentioned."[77] So we are to understand that they share them as to exercise them all, as do the bishops, in the person of Christ.

Furthermore, as *Mediator Dei* spoke of the priest acting in the person of Christ the *head* in sanctifying and in offering the sacrifice of the Mass, so the council at *Presbyterorum ordinis*, article 2, means that for all three functions, the priest acts in the person of Christ the Head.[78] The representation, in each function, is of Christ precisely in his distinction from the Church his body, "facing" the Church, as we might put it.[79] Where the *munera* are named, the representation of Christ in distinction from the Church goes without saying: The teacher is not one of the taught; the shepherd is not one of the sheep; and the high priest enters into the sanctuary alone. Article 2 does not at this point name the *munera*, however, and so the specification of Christ as head is suitable. While *Presbyterorum ordinis* neither reproves the denial of this nor insists that this representation is true exclusively of the priest, in keeping with the positive and irenic tone of the entire production of the council, *Mediator Dei* does.[80]

It should be noted that spokesmen for both of the "two views" of Marty's *relatio* strongly approved speaking of the priest's acting in the person of Christ for all three *munera*.[81] For partisans of the theology of mission, this way of speaking seems to break the hold of the cult on the priesthood and to break open its hitherto exclusive connection to the Eucharist and sanctification. The others, too, liked this high view of priesthood. It extends the way of expressing the priest's role in the cult to expressing his functioning in whatever he does and with the same weighty accent; it ties whatever the priest does, and not just in "saying Mass," to the presence, the action—the person—of Christ himself. Both sides came together on the high ground—that is, on a high view of the priesthood. Both sides came together, and this is a sign and reminder that, in the council, the mind of the whole Church comes to expression.[82] On the other hand, it is to be denied that it is a new view relative to the tradition as a whole. *Petrus baptizat, hic [Christus] est qui baptizat,* Saint Augustine says; and again, *Nos Christum praedicamus . . . Christus autem Christum praedicat, quia seipsum praedicat.*[83]

What is new in the synthesis of article 2, then, is the enlargement of the reference of acting in the person of Christ the head as compared with prior, especially Thomist, usage. Now, not just in quoting the words of institution (as for Saint Thomas, *Mediator Dei, Lumen gentium* 28, and *Presbyterorum ordinis* 5) but for all three munera, the priest represents Christ. This makes the entire ministry of the priest something that before was by the customary language usually said only of his activity in the sanctuary. It heightens the worth—or our appreciation of the worth—of the other functions. Is this part of the mission view or the cultic view of the priest? It transcends both and seems to be a happy accident of the production of the text. It takes what once was used to express the priest's agency in the Eucharist and makes it express his whole ministry and activity. This occurs in article 12 even more strongly, perhaps, where priests, acting in the person of Christ, are said also to be "the living instruments of Christ the eternal priest" and to take the place of Christ.

Because the priest represents Christ in his entire ministerial activity, the objective call to a complete holiness of life that priesthood makes becomes obvious, as in article 12, and the prosecution of this holiness within the discharge of the munera also becomes evident, as with article 13, and yet the unity of priestly life and holiness in Christ, since the discharge of all of his duties has to do with the actions and representation of Christ, also follows naturally in the text at article 14.

It is wonderful that an expression of such power and unexpected consequence for the future should be produced as it were almost by accident and yet find universal approval. As to unforeseen consequence, yes, the newly expressed synthesis of article 2 (and especially this happy twist of fate in the production of the text whereby the priest represents Christ generally in his ministry and not just at the altar) of ancient tradition, medieval and Tridentine doctrinal precision, and Baroque piety provided the wherewithal to meet postconciliar challenges to the Church's understanding and practice.

This should not surprise us. As Jean Frisque remarks, "carried along as it was by the dynamism of the council, a document like our decree in some measure escapes from its redactors; it no longer belongs to them."[84] Because the council expresses the mind of the whole Church and does so under the inspiration of the Holy Spirit, we can speak with B.-D. de La Soujeole of a certain "openness" of the conciliar teaching, by which he means that the doctrinal richness "contained in the documents could not have been clearly—at least explicitly—present to the mind of the fathers and could not appear but much later."[85]

Conclusion

We conclude by asking where the legacy of *Presbyterorum ordinis* is to be found. This depends very much on whether its view of the nature of priesthood is coherent, a true synthesis of the two dominant views with which the council started, or whether it is a juxtaposition of pieces that cannot go together. In the latter case, the legacy is a choice between two unsynthesizable pieces. As one popular hermeneutic of the council would have it, we could pursue a recon- stituted post-Tridentinism, a sort of resupernaturalizing and resacerdotaliza- tion of ecclesial ministry (bad things), as some claim to see in the 1971 Synod and the Letters to Priests of John Paul II. On the other hand, still according to this hermeneutic, the course is forward, to the democratic and declericalized, egalitarian, charismatic, and collaborative style of ministry toward which the council took but a few hesitant and indecisive steps.

A seemingly more moderate hermeneutic (and one critical of the forego- ing) would see the decree, as it sees the production of the council generally, as a juxtaposition of views, but a not incoherent one. Rather, according to this view, "Fidelity to the council requires that both juxtaposed theses be taken seriously and that an attempt be made through a more penetrating theological reflection and a renewed ecclesial praxis to reconcile them in a synthesis that will allow further advances."[86] So, the council bequeathed to the Church and theology the task of working for a synthesis that the council itself could not or did not effect.

We believe that neither of these approaches is helpful for interpreting *Presbyterorum ordinis*. The textual history of the decree and the speeches and discussions that are part of that history show that it was certainly not the council fathers' intention to do nothing more than juxtapose two theses or viewpoints. The October 16, 1965, *relatio* of Archbishop Marty gave voice to that intention, which the fathers accepted. Further, we think it is no great feat of interpretation to see the fulfillment of this intention in article 2 of the decree. Interpreting *Presbyterorum ordinis* therefore cannot be a matter of weighing or balancing two masses of material, the theses of a progressive council majority on one side and of a conservative council minority on the other. We are to see, rather, that consecration is for the purpose of extending the mission of Christ, whose own end is the glory of the Father in a redeemed humanity. The priest-presbyter is sent forth as one consecrated *in persona Christi capitis* authoritatively to proclaim the Gospel to the world, to extend the offer of sal- vation in the sacraments, and to build up the Church.

Determining the legacy of *Presbyterorum ordinis* depends also on whether the decree is read against the background of prior Catholic tradition, the great democracy of the diachronic voices from Scripture, itself read as *Dei verbum*, article 12, teaches us to read it, to the Fathers, from the Fathers to the theo- logians of the twelfth and thirteenth centuries, and very much including past conciliar and papal teaching. The Synod of Bishops urged this way of inter- pretation on the council's twentieth anniversary.[87]

We think that, if read in that way, the synthesis of the views and the adequacy of the one view arrived at become manifest. If the priesthood was framed in the theology of mission, it remained the ministry that culminated in the Eucharistic sacrifice, where the Christian's sacrifice of life passes over sacramentally into the eternal sacrifice of the Lamb. Precisely because it was framed in the theology of mission, both its historical institution by Christ, as well as its sacramental enablement, now, by Christ through the Spirit, were affirmed. If the priest was not hailed as an *alter Christus*, he was described as acting *in persona Christi capitis* no longer merely at the Eucharist but also across the length and breadth of his ministry. The decree put it that the priest was to find holiness within the very exercise of his ministry—teaching, sanctifying, ruling. Still, that is what he was to find—holiness. The relation of the priest as minister to bishop, to fellow priests, to the laity, and including to the laity in their own apostolic labor (in other words, the concrete ecclesial context into which the priest is inserted) was affirmed expressly and in detail. Still, he remained a "man apart," both by reason of his consecration and in order to have something to bring to the people in whose midst he lived and worked.

If read in this way, furthermore, where the truly synthetic character of the decree becomes manifest, then it is possible to answer the question of its legacy, which appears to be the 1992 apostolic exhortation, *Pastores dabo vobis*. This is true for the ecclesiological presuppositions of the priesthood, which were spelled out by Pope John Paul II as the mystery, the communion, and the mission of the Church; it is true for the centrality of the priest as representing Christ the head; it is true for the priority of this representation relative to priestly representation of the Church; and it is true for the clarity with which celibacy is also linked to this representative character of the priest. All of these things, some more or less developed by the council, are brought fully to expression by the pope, especially in relation to the human and ecclesial situation, the signs of the times, at the beginning of the third millennium. In this way, *Pastores dabo vobis* shows us a privileged way forward in the task of receiving the synthesis of *Presbyterorum ordinis*.

NOTES

1. See Jean Frisque, "Le décret 'Presbyterorum Ordinis': Histoire et commentaire," in *Les prêtres: Décrets "Presbyterorum ordinis" et "Optatam totius,"* ed. J. Frisque and Y. Congar (Paris: Cerf, 1968), 123–89; Joseph Lécuyer, "History of the Decree," in *Commentary on the Documents of Vatican II*, vol. 4, ed. Herbert Vorgrimler (New York: Herder and Herder, 1967), 183–209; René Wasselynck, "Histoire du décret," in *Les prêtres: Élaboration du décret de Vatican II; commentaire* (Paris: Desclée, 1968), 15–34; Paul Cordes, *Sendung zum Dienst: Exegetische-historische und systematische Studien zum Konzilsdekret vom Dienst und Leben der Priester* (Frankfurt am Main: J. Knecht, 1972). Lécuyer played a principal role in the production of the decree; Frisque, too, collaborated.

2. Lécuyer, "History of the Decree," 193–94.

3. Frisque, "Le décret 'Presbyterorum ordinis,'" 125, 128–29. Norman Tanner summarizes the speeches of Oct. 13–15, 1964, critical of the schema in *History of Vatican*

II, vol. 4, ed. Giuseppe Alberigo, English version ed. Joseph A. Komonchak (Maryknoll, N.Y.: Orbis, 2003), 347–53.

4. Lécuyer, "History of the Decree," 195.

5. *Acta synodalia sacrosancti Concilii Vaticani II*, vol. 4, pt. 4 (Rome: Typis Polyglottis Vaticanis, 1970–), 863. Or see Francisco Gil Hellín, *Decretum de presbyterorum ministerio et vita, presbyterorum ordinis: Concilii Vaticani II synopsis in ordinem redigens schemata cum relationibus necnon patrum orationes atque animadversiones* (Vatican City: Libreria Editrice Vaticana, 1996), 10, note to the first draft. Hellín's synopsis comprises the last four drafts of the decree. The same synopsis, but without Hellín's references to the interventions of the fathers and the explanatory reports of the responsible commission, appears in René Wasselynck, *Les prêtres: Élaboration du décret presbyterorum ordinis de Vatican II, Synopse* (Paris: Desclée, 1968).

6. Concluding *relatio* of François Marty, archbishop of Rheims, Oct. 16, 1965, presenting the "textus recognitus," in *Acta synodalia*, vol. 4, pt. 5, 70–71.

7. Darmajuwana, in *Acta synodalia*, vol. 4, pt. 4, 916; and Garrone, in ibid., appendix, 660.

8. Gufflet, in ibid., 929; and de Provenchères, in ibid., 918.

9. Ibid., appendix, 653–54; but from this worship, it is to be noted, will come the priest's "zeal for the apostolate" (654).

10. Ibid., 764.

11. Ibid., 732.

12. Ibid., 747; it is therefore too little to say that the priest shares in the mission of the bishop (748).

13. Ibid., 864.

14. For the relation of *Presbyterorum ordinis* to Trent, see the comprehensive study by Henri Denis, "La théologie du presbytérat de Trente à Vatican II," in Frisque and Congar, *Les prêtres*, 193–232.

15. Yves Congar, *Lay People in the Church*, rev. ed., trans. Donald Attwater (Westminster, Md.: Newman Press, 1967), 154.

16. Yves Congar, "Le sacerdoce du Nouveau Testament: Mission et culte," in Frisque and Congar, *Les prêtres*, 237.

17. Ibid., 234–35.

18. See Ricardo Burigana and Giovanni Turbanti in *History of Vatican II*, vol. 4, 566–67; and see Yves Congar, *Mon journal du concile*, vol. 2 (Paris: Les Éditions du Cerf, 2002), 202 (Oct. 15, 1964). In pointing to the importance of Congar's commentary we do not mean it is weighty as an author's comment is weighty. In the first place the council is the author of the final text. Congar's role was rather that of a gifted secretary helping his master find his own voice. Second, Congar was very aware of this, that the text belonged to the council fathers, not to the *periti*; see, for example, *Mon journal*, vol. 2, 255 (Nov. 11, 1964); 447 (Oct. 22, 1965); and 451 (Oct. 25, 1965).

19. Congar, "Le sacerdoce," 254–55. Note the dependence, 254: "Before being latreutic, and in order to be latreutic, the Christian sacramental cult is theurgic and soteriological: it does not consist at first in offering, in making something rise up from us to God, but in receiving the effective gift of God."

20. Ibid., 256. So also Hellín Cardinal Alfrink, 625.

21. See Avery Dulles, S.J., *The Priestly Office: A Theological Reflection* (New York: Paulist, 1997), who canvasses some of the more important of these essays, 20–22, 47–51.

22. Joseph Ratzinger, "Priestly Ministry: A Search for Meaning," *Emmanuel* 76 (1970): 495–96, 498.

23. In the same vein see the International Theological Commission, "The Priestly Ministry," in *International Theological Commission: Text and Documents, 1969–1985*, ed. Michael Sharkey (San Francisco: Ignatius Press, 1989), 61–62. This text was published in 1970.

24. In addition to Ratzinger's "Priestly Ministry," see his "Life and Ministry of Priests," a paper given on Oct. 24, 1995, for a symposium on the thirtieth anniversary of the decree. It can be found at the Vatican website, under the Congregation for the Clergy.

25. Karl Rahner, "The Point of Departure in Theology for Determining the Nature of the Priestly Office," *Theological Investigations*, vol. 12, trans. David Bourke (New York: Seabury, 1974), 31–38.

26. Walter Kasper, "A New Dogmatic Outlook on the Priestly Ministry," in *The Identity of the Priest* (New York: Paulist Press, 1969), 20–33.

27. Changes included the revised word order of the title, *Latinitatis causa*, to *De presbyterorum ministerio et vita*.

28. Congar, *Mon journal*, vol. 2, 443 (Oct. 20, 1965) and 511 (Dec. 7, 1965). Congar rewrote articles 1–3, wrote the first redaction of articles 4–6, and revised articles 7–9 and 12–14 and part of the conclusion. He said the text was three parts the work of Joseph Lécuyer, Willy Onclin, and himself. Lécuyer oversaw the crucial section on celibacy. On the commission's acceptance of Congar's draft of number two, see *Mon journal*, vol. 2, 457 (Oct. 29, 1965): "Ils épluchent le texte sur quelques expressions, ils ne s'attachent guère au fond. De sorte que le texte passé sans coup férir. C'est inouï! C'était inespéré."

29. Friedrich Wulf, "Commentary on the Decree: Articles 1–6," in Vorgrimler, *Commentary on the Documents of Vatican II*, vol. 4, 224. Wulf worked on the decree as a *peritus* toward the end, especially on number 16; see Congar, *Mon journal*, vol. 2, 442–43 (Oct. 20, 1965).

30. Wulf, "Commentary," 222.

31. Hermann J. Pottmeyer, "A New Phase in the Reception of Vatican II: Twenty Years of Interpretation of the Council," in *The Reception of Vatican II*, ed. Giuseppe Alberigo, Jean-Pierre Jossua, and Joseph A. Komonchak (Washington, D.C.: Catholic University of America Press, 1987), 37.

32. Christian Duquoc, "Clerical Reform," in Alberigo, Jossua, and Komonchak, *Reception of Vatican II*, 297–308. Duquoc seems to assume that the reform of the theology of the priesthood the council aimed at was also a general "reform" of the manners, ministry, and life of priests.

33. Ibid., 298.

34. Ibid., 299.

35. Ibid., 300, 303–305.

36. Daniel Donovan, *What Are They Saying about the Ministerial Priesthood?* (New York: Paulist Press, 1992), 11; see also 19.

37. For the priest as sent, sharing in apostolic ministry, see *Presbyterorum ordinis* 2b, 2d; for a share in the *triplex munera* see nos. 1b, 4, 5, 6, 7a, and 13.

38. The interpretation of this text (which Wulf gives in "Commentary on the Decree," 271)—that the Eucharist is preeminent relative only to other sanctifying functions but not to the other munera—is contrary to the text, as well as to the sense of the council to be discerned in the "Response to Modus 26" to number 13 (*Acta synodalia*, vol. 4, pt. 7, 198), and is contrary to *Presbyterorum ordinis* 5 and to *Lumen gentium* 28.

39. For the Eucharist as the origin of mission see Joseph Ratzinger, "Eucharist and Mission," *Irish Theological Quarterly* 65 (2000): 247, 262.

40. See *Lumen gentium*, no. 33, and *Apostolicam actuositatem*, no. 2.

41. See John Paul II, *Veritatis splendor*, nos. 19–21.

42. See Ratzinger, "Eucharist and Mission," 241, 262.

43. For the same in Saint Thomas see B.-D. de la Soujeole, "Les *tria munera Christi*: Contribution de saint Thomas à la recherche contemporaine," *Revue Thomiste* 99 (1999): 71–72; the ordering is the same as that for faith (preaching), hope (ruling), and charity (sanctification).

44. See, for example, Thomas Aquinas, *Summa theologiae*, III, q. 22, a. 1; and Raymond Brown, *Priest and Bishop: Biblical Reflections* (New York: Paulist Press, 1970), 10–13.

45. Congar, "Le sacerdoce," 254 (our translation): "Before being latreutic, and in order to be latreutic, the Christian sacramental cult is theurgic and soteriological: It does not consist at first in offering, in making something rise up from us to God, but in receiving the effective gift of God." See also Gisbert Greshake, *The Meaning of Christian Priesthood*, trans. Paeder MacSeumais (Westminster, Md.: Christian Classics, 1989), 82–83.

46. Ibid., 251–56.

47. Ibid., 254–55.

48. Ratzinger, "Eucharist and Mission," 261–62.

49. According to Saint Thomas, Christ as Head has the perfection of all of the graces, which, in the body, are distributed one to a priest, another to a king, and still another to a giver of the law, as was Moses; see Aquinas, *ST* III, q. 22, a. 1, ad 3; *In Rom.* 1:1, no. 20. Since the grace of Christ's Headship is one with his personal grace, moreover, it is in virtue of the same reality that Christ is Prophet, Priest, and King; see Aquinas, *ST* III, q. 8, a. 5. This is not to say that teaching means sanctifying and sanctifying means ruling, else the question of which is preeminent could not arise. It is, however, to say that his kingship is his priesthood, and his priesthood is his messiahship. So also in the doctrine of God, we say that the divine justice is the divine mercy, though justice and mercy do not mean the same thing, and thus there remains the question of which attribute is preeminent.

50. Albert Vanhoye, *Old Testament Priests and the New Priest according to the New Testament*, trans. J. Bernard Orchard (Petersham, Mass.: Saint Bede's, 1986), 85–87.

51. See Joseph Ratzinger, who correctly resists the tendency to dismiss the Old Testament as having anything to say about Christian priesthood and ministry; see his "Life and Ministry of Priests."

52. This sentence is substantially that of the draft of Nov. 20, 1964.

53. For more on this ecclesiological context of the decree see Archbishop Julian Herranz Casado, "The Image of the Priest in the Decree *Presbyterorum Ordinis*: Continuity and Projection toward the Third Millennium." This paper was delivered in 1995 at the symposium on the priesthood for the thirtieth anniversary of the decree and can be found on the Vatican website, under the Congregation for the Clergy. With Alvaro del Portillo, Herranz formed the secretariat of the commission *De disciplina cleri et populi christiani*, which was responsible for drafting the decree.

54. Neither *Lumen gentium* nor *Presbyterorum ordinis* characterizes the priesthood of the faithful as metaphorical, as did Pope Pius XII, *Magnificate Dominum*, *AAS* 46 (1954): 669. When the commission responsible for *Presbyterorum ordinis* was reproved for treating the "metaphorical" priesthood of the faithful before the ministerial priesthood, it merely noted that *Lumen gentium* did not so characterize the priesthood of the faithful and that the finality of the ministerial priesthood terminates in the universal priesthood (*Acta synodalia*, vol. 4, pt. 7, 118, "Response to Modus 15").

55. Spiritual sacrifice is the reason for exterior sacrifice; see Aquinas, *ST* II–II, q. 85, aa. 1 and 2; *In Hebr.* 2:3, no. 157. More originally, see Saint Augustine, *The City of God*, bk. 10, ch. 5.

56. In this way the text moves from mission (no. 2a and 2b) to cult, in which cult the existential sacrifice of the faithful is joined to the Eucharistic sacrifice of Christ; see Frisque, "Le décret 'Presbyterorum ordinis,' " 140–41.

57. See Congar's remark on Marty's "two conceptions of the priesthood," *Mon journal*, vol. 2, 443 (Oct. 20, 1965): "Deux conceptions du sacerdoce: Comme consécration (union personnelle au Christ), comme envoyé! Précisément, le concile a redécouvert l'unité de consecration et mission!"

58. *Adversus haereses* 4.20.7.

59. Tanner translates the last clause as a purpose clause, but it is rather a result clause (signaled by the *ita ut*) and should read "such that [or "in such a way that"— Flannery edition] they can act in the person of Christ the head." It is a question of stating the certain effect—the result—of the sacrament of orders, not a hope that may be impeded.

60. Henri Denis, "La théologie du presbytérat de Trente à Vatican II," 215–16 (our translation): "Il nous semble que cette petite phrase est en fait celle sur laquelle repose *la spécificité* du ministère hiérarchique en général et du ministère presbytéral en particulier. Si l'on cherche, en effet, en quoi la tâche du prêtre est *originale* par rapport à celle du chrétien, on est renvoyé à ce signe essentiel à l'Église: le signe du Christ-Tête, pour son corps. Autrement dit, il y a un ministère dans l'Église, pour que soit signifiée l'oeuvre du Christ dans l'oeuvre de l'Église."

61. Vanhoye, *Old Testament Priests*, 97–98. And for ruling see 230.

62. Ibid., 73, 83, 132–33, 137, 157.

63. Ibid., 223–24, 228–29.

64. See especially Congar, "Le sacerdoce du Nouveau Testament," 242–46, for a short discussion of this linkage.

65. Yves Congar, "Sur la trilogie: Prophète, roi, prêtre," *Revue des sciences philosophiques et théologiques* 67 (1983): 100. Congar makes more of the patristic witness to the trilogy than does J. Fuchs, "Origines d'une trilogie ecclésiologique à l'époque rationaliste de la théologie," *Revue des sciences philosophiques et théologiques* 53 (1969): 194–97.

66. Congar, "Sur la trilogie," 100. The consecration of the Holy Oil in the apostolic tradition invokes the three as three (99–100). See also Bernard Botte, "Holy Orders in the Ordination Prayers," in *The Sacrament of Orders* (London: Aquin Press, 1962), 21.

67. De la Soujeole, "Les *tria munera* Christi," 61–66. It should be noted that to say with Saint Thomas that preaching is "secondary" is not to say it is accidental; rather, flowing from the principal function of sanctifying, it is included in what is essential to priestly ministry (ibid., 71). Bishop Carli made much the same point at the council (*Acta synodalia*, vol. 3, pt. 4, 551). For the subsequent history see the articles by Congar and Fuchs. In English one may consult Peter J. Drilling, "The Priest, Prophet, and King Trilogy: Elements of Its Meaning in *Lumen gentium* and for Today," *Église et théologie* 19 (1988): 179–206. For further background on this subject in the decree see Cordes, the section titled "Die Darlegung der Presbyteraufgaben mit Hilfe des Schemas vom dreifachen Amt Christi," in Cordes, *Sendung zum Dienst*, 117–60.

68. For Saint Thomas on the spiritual sacrifice of Christians see M. Morard, "Sacerdoce du Christ and sacerdoce des chrétiens dans le *Commentaire des Psaumes* de saint Thomas d'Aquin," *Revue thomiste* 99 (1999): 119–42; and Gilles Emery,

"Le sacerdoce spiritual des fidèles chez saint Thomas d'Aquin," *Revue thomiste* 99 (1999): 222.

69. Vanhoye, *Old Testament Priests*, 316.

70. Ibid., 317.

71. For commentary on *Lumen gentium* 28 see Jean Giblet, "I presbiteri collaboratori dell'ordine episcopale," in *La Chiesa del Vaticano II*, ed. Guilherme Baraúna (Florence: Vallecchi, 1965), 872–95.

72. For what follows see Guy Mansini, "Sacerdotal Character at Vatican II," *Thomist* 67 (2003): 539–77.

73. Aquinas, *ST* III, q. 78, a. 1, c.

74. *Acta synodalia*, vol. 3, pt. 2, 213: "Munus quo sacerdos in persona Christi agit *speciatim* [emphasis added] in cultu Eucharistico exhibetur verbis Tridentini et Encyclicae *Mediator Dei* confirmatur; sed etiam participatio muneris sacerdotalis Christi in praedicatione verbi, in administratione sacramentorum, necnon in oratione et exemplo et, in gernere, in pascendo grege apparet." The participation in the other two munera, it seems, could also be expressed by saying the priest acts in the person of Christ.

75. *Presbyterorum ordinis* 6, on the shepherding role of the priest, practically quotes this line of *Lumen gentium* 28 verbatim.

76. See *Mediator Dei*, nos. 40, 84.

77. *Acta synodalia*, vol. 4, pt. 7, 121.

78. See also nos. 6 and 12 of the decree.

79. Which is how *Pastores dabo vobis* puts it.

80. See no. 84: "We deem it necessary to recall that the priest acts for the people only because he represents Jesus Christ insofar as [*quatenus*] He is Head of all his members.... The people, on the other hand, since they in no sense [*nulla ratione*] represent the divine Redeemer and are not mediator between themselves and God, can in no way possess the sacerdotal power."

81. Cardinal Döpfner, *Acta synodalia*, vol. 4, pt. 4, 874; Bishop de Cambourg, in ibid., appendix, 657; Cardinal Suenens, in ibid., 787, 788; and from the other side, Bishop Ndongmo, *Acta synodalia*, vol. 4, pt. 5, 67–68; Archbishop Perini, *Acta synodalia*, appendix, 671; commenting on no. 14, the unity of priestly life, Perini writes: "All things become one if the Presbyter, illumined and led by a *supernatural vision of things, acts always in the Person of Christ*: namely, if thinking, if preaching, if administering Holy Things, if visiting the sick, if comforting the afflicted and poor, if praying, if celebrating Mass: he feels in himself, as in the living instrument of Christ, Christ thinking, preaching, exercising charity, praying, offering sacrifice to the Father." See also the bishops of Argentina and France, *Acta synodalia*, vol. 4, pt. 5, 528, who suggest saying the priest acts "in the name of Christ" since acting "in the person of Christ" is more connected with the Eucharist; and Archbishop de Provenchères, *Acta synodalia*, vol. 4, pt. 5, 308, who says that priests are to preserve the "immediate and constant sacramental presence of Christ, Head and Shepherd, for all the faithful."

82. See Benoît-Dominique de la Soujeole, " 'En toute chose voir l'unité,' " in *Ordo sapientiae et amoris: Hommage au professeur Jean-Pierre Torrell*, ed. Carlos-Josaphat Pinto de Oliveira (Fribourg: Éditions Universitaires Fribourg Suisse, 1993), 438.

83. *In Ioannem*, 6.7, 47.3. See the citations at note 22 of no. 21 of *Lumen gentium*, and see Walter Kasper, "Priestly Office," in *Leadership in the Church*, trans. Brian McNeil (New York: Herder, 2003), 45–75, and the manifestation of the necessarily representative character of apostolic office in scripture, 49–55.

84. Frisque, "Le décret 'Presbyterorum ordinis,' " 133.

85. De La Soujeole, " 'En toute chose voir l'unité,' " 443; he finds an example of this is the conciliar teaching on the sacramentality of the Church.

86. Pottmeyer, "A New Phase in the Reception of Vatican II," 39.

87. See "The Final Report," no. 5, "A Deeper Reception of the Council," *Origins* 15 (1985): 445–46.

II

The Decree on Priestly Formation, *Optatam Totius*

Anthony A. Akinwale, O.P.

The Second Vatican Council remains pertinent forty years after its closing session. In a Church that is a communion of Churches, to use a phrase that Jean-Marie-Roger Tillard has brought to our attention (or, to use one coined by the Synod of the Church in Africa to deepen and express the conciliar ecclesiology of communion, in a Church that is the family of God), the council is teaching churches, old and new, what the Spirit has been teaching the Church.[1] Speaking in general terms, the council equipped the Church to face new challenges by taking her to her sources as she carries out her mission in the world. Speaking in specific terms, the Conciliar decree *Optatam totius* on priestly formation equips her to train priests who will be prepared to face the challenges.

Authentic Development of Christian Tradition in Modernity

In the history of the Church, councils do not cancel out each other. They amplify or emphasize what previous councils did not emphasize. Councils are instruments of the Holy Spirit put in the hands of the Church by the same Holy Spirit, instruments of transmission of the faith of the Church. Since the Holy Spirit is not subject to self-contradiction we can safely assume that councils do not substantially contradict each other.

The relationship between councils may be illustrated by recourse to John Cardinal Newman. Often celebrated as the absent but influential father of the Second Vatican Council, Newman postulates in his *Essay on Development of Christian Doctrine* that a living and vigorous idea develops when it modifies and is modified and that this occurs in a warfare of ideas, that is, in confrontation with other ideas. But in the process of the authentic development of an idea, Newman maintains, the original idea is preserved. Where there is no retention of the original idea, that is, where it is distorted, what is left is not an authentic development but a corruption of the original idea. In other words, authentic development occurs when, in its interaction with other ideas, the original idea transforms and is transformed but not conformed. If it were to conform it would lose its own identity and put on the identity of another idea. Newman applies his theory of the development of ideas to Christianity in order to defend Roman Catholicism against accusations that she had distorted Christianity. He explains his position by arguing that an idea is received within the universe of ideas of its recipients.

Newman's theory posits a certain reaffirmation of Thomas Aquinas, who, in his own account of how the human intellect understands (which was influenced by his reading of Aristotle), stated that whatever is received is received according to the mode of its recipient. And if Newman could be said to have reaffirmed Aquinas, Yves Congar, himself a disciple of Aquinas, has pointed out in the same vein, that whatever is transmitted is received by a living and therefore an active subject.[2]

In words that show the profundity of Newman's insight, Congar explained that the saving faith is received by minds who consider this faith not only as an absolute but also as a deposit given once and for all "since the Apostles," as a point of reference to which nothing is to be added and from which nothing is to be subtracted.[3] Yet, the minds that receive the faith receive it actively and not passively, according to the way these minds are. Arguing that historicity is an attribute of the human mind, Congar spoke of the actively receptive human mind with its discursive structure, successive and partial perceptions of reality, in interaction with other minds that exist within cosmic and biological duration. The once-and-for-all character of apostolicity is not negated by the historicity of its reception.[4]

With these thoughts on the transmission and reception that goes on between councils, I propose that, in order to read their teachings, Newman's eloquently articulated theory of the development of ideas be used as an interpretive key. This theory of the development of doctrine, anticipated by thinkers like Vincent of Lérins and Thomas Aquinas and further explained by Congar, sheds light on how the teachings of the Second Vatican Council are to be read and received within the ongoing story of the Church. In this specific instance, the theory should be borne in mind in reading the council's teachings on the life, ministry, and formation of priests.[5]

At Vatican II, the authentic development of Christianity took the form of tradition in modernity. It is difficult, if not impossible, to understand the council's teachings when they are not seen in these terms. Tradition is that which is handed on and received according to the mode of its recipients. The implication of espousing the Thomist stance that Newman echoes is that whatever is passed on wears the intellectual and spiritual garb of the giver's era. The recipient, who is anything but passive, needs to remove the garb and cast it in familiar terms. We must never distort that which is passed. The garb may change, but the wearer's identity may not. Tradition is a process whereby a changing Church, living in changing times, receives the unchanging message of the Gospel in apostolicity and transmits it in ways that change without altering the message.

The original idea of Christianity is found in Christ himself. In fact, Newman identifies this original idea in the Johannine affirmation of the incarnation: "The Word became flesh." But when he became truly human, the incarnate Word did not conform to human standards. Even as he manifested his human traits, those who saw him still wondered, "What manner of man is this?" (Mk 4:41). Derived from Newman's theory, this Christological principle of incarnation without conformation can also be applied to the Church and to the priesthood.

The irreversible match of history ensures that the Church always finds herself in new times and places. Finding that the Gospel message must be addressed to every new situation, she has to obey the imperatives of effective communication. She struggles to adapt the message to her audience, but she must not distort it. Not even the risk of losing the audience's affection must make her sacrifice the radicality of the message. It would be a caricature of the Gospel to set up apostolic tradition and modernity as antitheses. This tradition must be passed on to modernity in modernity without alteration.

Contrary to Archbishop Marcel Lefebvre, the council was no deviation from tradition but rather was in continuity with it. The fathers of the patristic era were largely present not only in the footnotes but also in the letter and the spirit of the council. The marvelous harmonization of theology, spirituality, and pastoral concerns in their writings needs to be rediscovered and retrieved if we are to arrive at a fruitful interpretation of Vatican II (in this specific instance, if we are to understand the council's idea of the life, ministry, and formation of priests).

When we consider Vatican II as a council in continuity with tradition, then we can come to understand that while the council represents an openness to modernity—the Church in the modern world—it is by no means an invitation to commit ecclesial suicide in an undifferentiated acceptance of modern culture (Western, Asian, or African). At Vatican II, the Church was acting like the wise scribe who brings out of his storeroom things both old and new (Mt 13:52). The Church may be in the modern world, but she is not of the modern world. And even as she seeks to collaborate with all men and women of good will— many of whom are found outside the Church, thanks to elements of sanctification dispersed throughout the world by the Spirit who blows where he wills—she cannot be dispensed from guarding a prudent relationship and critical friendship with culture. It is a risky but necessary relationship. The Church, transformed by the ideas and challenges of the modern world, must continue to prophetically challenge the modern world, that is, speak for God today by consistently calling the Church's attention to the ignorance and absence of the transcendental dimension, which tragically impoverishes the well-intentioned discourse of modernity in favor of human promotion.

However, before commenting on priestly formation according to the mind of Vatican II, I would like to discuss the council's ecclesiology. The ecclesiology of communion of the Second Vatican Council is not an innovation but a retrieval of New Testament and patristic self-understanding of the Church within the intellectual horizon of the modern world.[6] The Church is the sacrament of reconciliation and communion brought about by the prophetic message of the Gospel of Christ, his kingly service of his brothers and sisters, and the priestly sacrifice of his own body and blood on the Cross. Christ showed himself to be a servant of communion and reconciliation. "The Son of man came, not to be served but to serve, and to give his life as a ransom for many." He demonstrated this at the washing of feet as the hour approached when he who always loved his own loved them to the fullest. It was the hour when he gave the supreme demonstration of his service to his brothers and sisters.

The body of Christ, the Church, in imitation of her head, Christ, is to be at the service of communion. The priest, for his part, is to be formed to imitate Christ's service of communion through his imitation of Christ. He is to be formed to be the servant of communion through a life and ministry sacramentally configured to represent the *munus triplex Christi*. He represents Christ in a community that the author of the First Letter of Peter described as "the chosen race, the royal priesthood, the holy nation, a people set apart to sing the praises of God" (1 Pet 2:9–10). Far from describing the Church as an aggregate of priests, these words refer to the collective sacerdotal vocation of the entire Church.[7] The ministerial priesthood exists for the service of this collective vocation of the entire people of God. As Tillard has pointed out, the "ministry [of priests] exists in light of this priesthood of the *sacerdos* community. It is the servant of the Spirit of Christ for priestly and theocentric *communion* which is the local Church in its profound being and life. Also it could not be understood outside of the constant reference to this total community sense formed by the Spirit. . . . The ministry manifests its nature only in the act of the *whole* community where it is at work."[8]

The fact that it is the entire people of God that is sacerdotal in character does not remove the priestly character that comes with ordination. It only situates it within the communion of charisms and services that flow from the unique baptismal grace. Hence, Tillard adds, "Through ordination one enters into 'the portion of the people of God' destined for its service, 'a portion' whose honor consists of being of service for the *leitourgia*."[9] To examine the formation of priests according to *Optatam totius* is to examine how Vatican II proposes to form priests at the service of communion.

Formation for the *Munus Triplex* at the Service of Communion

The decree *Optatam totius* of the Second Vatican Council was not written ex nihilo. Josef Neuner helps to locate its starting point:

The starting point of the reform, therefore, was the existing seminary system that goes back to the fifteenth and sixteenth centuries and was solemnly confirmed as the form of education for the clergy on July 15, 1563, in the twenty-third session of the Council of Trent. The connection of the present reform with the seminary decree of Trent was underlined by the four hundredth anniversary of this very decree, celebrated during the third session on December 3, 1963, in Rome by a ceremony in Saint Peter's. The new decree was to be for the Church today what the seminary decree of Trent was for the stormy age of the Reformation.[10]

The Tridentine decree, as Neuner observes, was written with the intention of inculcating ecclesiastical discipline in candidates for the priesthood by shielding the same candidates from "the infectious spirit" of the age of the Reformation. *Optatam totius*, however, was written at a time when the Church adopted an attitude of openness to the world. This raises the question of the relationship between the Tridentine decree and *Optatam totius*. Neuner explains the problem in these terms:

> The Tridentine decree belongs to the age of the Counter-Reformation. It sought to isolate endangered youth from the dangers of the world and protect it, educate it and fortify it within the Church, in this way creating priests who would serve the Church free from the infections of the spirit of the age. The educational program was directed wholly towards the service of the Church, whereas hardly anything was said about the debate with the movements of the age. . . . The old seminary system ensured for the Church a reliable clergy, but it also increased their separation from the people and the growing estrangement of the Church from the new age. It not only educated people to obedience to Church authority, but also to a clerical mentality and closed thinking, and became combined with the one-sided institutional picture of the Church. If the Church at the council has now overcome the attitude of the Counter-Reformation, has moved out of a defensive attitude towards innovations and burst open clerical isolation, if she now understands herself in a new way as a sign of salvation for the world, in solidarity with the men of all ages, then this new orientation would inevitably affect the principles behind the training of priests.[11]

This question can be illustrated by way of a simple formulation: Can a document inspired by an attitude of openness be said to be in continuity with a preceding document inspired by a defensive attitude?

I believe that, while the change of orientation from defensiveness to openness may be undeniable, the Second Vatican Council did not abolish the substance of the theology of the priesthood conveyed by the Council of Trent. Denis Hurley's comments confirm my position: "In conformity with the principle of Catholic continuity, reference is made [in the decree] to the sound regulations of the past, on which the reforms of Vatican II are to be based. This is a salutary reminder of what we owe to the past, particularly to the Council of Trent. In a very real sense Trent made Vatican II possible through the clerical training that it inspired. This training was in need of reform to adapt it fully to the conditions of our times, but Trent had done its work well to produce the popes, bishops and theologians of Vatican II."[12] I find the seed of continuity between the two councils in the Tridentine portrayal of the priest as sacramental representation of Christ in his munus triplex of priest, prophet, and king. However, this portrayal of the priest has a history that did not begin at Trent.[13]

In the New Testament, the Synoptic Gospels contained the idea of the Apostles representing Christ in the munus triplex. First, the Eucharistic injunction "do this in my memory" and the mission to make disciples and to baptize represent Christ's authorization to lead the worship of the new covenant. Here Christ conferred the power to represent him in his priestly office. Second, the Markan account of the call of the Twelve makes it clear that he called them to be with him in order that they might proclaim the Gospel with authority (Mk 3:13–15). Two of the three Synoptic Gospels end with the evangelical injunction to the Apostles to go and preach to the whole world (Mt 28:16–20; Mk 16:15–17). In John's Gospel, he promised to send them the Paraclete, who would teach them all things and witness in them (Jn 16:7–15). And when, at his first appearance to them, he breathed the Holy Spirit on them, it was to equip them for their mission to preach (Jn 20:19–23). Here is the granting of the power to exercise the teaching office. Third, he gave them the power to govern the new Israel (Mt 19:28; Lk 22:28–30). However, this power to govern is the conferment of the office of servant-leader (Mt 24:24–28). The modality of exercising this power is taught by the example of the washing of feet, narrated in the Fourth Gospel (Jn 13:1–15). Hence, finally, as Nichols rightly observed, this portrayal of the Apostles as representing Christ in his munus triplex is not limited to the Synoptic Gospels. It can also be discerned in André Feuillet's analytical study of John 17, alongside the Songs of the Suffering Servant in the Book of Isaiah (42:1–4; 49:1–6; 50:4–9; 52:13–12).[14]

The Apostles' representation of the munus triplex of Christ passes from the New Testament through the patristic era, the Reformation, and Trent before it finds its way into *Presbyterorum ordinis* and the framework for the formation of priests in *Optatam totius*. In the ante-Nicene patristic period, for example, around 180 AD, Irenaeus reacted to the Gnostic claim of possessing a secret apostolic tradition by asking for adherence to the teaching of only those presbyters who have their succession from the Apostles. Others were to be treated with suspicion. As people who have inherited their ministry from the Apostles, these presbyters inherited the munus triplex, which the Apostles derived from Christ.[15]

This threefold office is reflected in the ordination prayers in Hippolytus of Rome's *Apostolic Tradition*. The intention of the prayers reveals an intention that the ordinandi exercise the ministry of the Word, the ministry of the sacraments, and the ministry of governance. John Chrysostom's treatise On the

Priesthood also spelled out the liturgical, pastoral, and teaching role of the presbyter. Nichols remarks that "Although the ministry of the Word is often conspicuous by its absence in medieval definitions of Order, ministerial preaching was understood as preparing people for a share in the Eucharistic banquet and sacrifice."[16] In medieval theology, order as a sacrament confers power to be at the service of others. Hence, one can still find traces of the threefold office in this era. Nichols further explains how this theology of the munus triplex found its way into the documents of Vatican II on the life, ministry, and formation of the priest. First, "In terms of the twentieth-century theology of priesthood which links in time the masters of the Catholic Revival to the Second Vatican Council, the French School's notion of the priest as continuator of the Word Incarnate retained a powerful subterranean influence. For the Catholic theology of the first fifty years of the twentieth century, the sacrament of Order is seen as a sacrament which re-presents, *represents* in the strongest possible sense of that term, the unique ministry of Jesus Christ himself."[17]

In speaking of the priest as one who represents Christ, some, such as Charles Cardinal Journet, spoke of a *munus duplex*—the priestly and the pastoral. But by virtue of a later development, the munus triplex would become predominant. Nichols explains:

> Although there are hints of this kind of Christological scheme in the patristic period, its systematic use is a Reformation development. It appears to have entered the mainstream of Catholic theology in two ways. The main channel was German-speaking Catholic theologians who borrowed it from their Lutheran counterparts in the course of the eighteenth century. The other vehicle of this type of Christological analysis was John Henry Newman, who himself seems to have taken it from Calvin's *Institutes*. Newman has applied it not only to the Church at large but, quite explicitly, to her ministry in particular. From the beginning of the twentieth century onwards, this threefold analysis of the representative task of the Church *vis-à-vis* the work of Christ grew in popularity until it finally swept the board by being incorporated into the two main ecclesiological encyclicals of Pope Pius XII: *Mystici Corporis Christi* of 1943 and *Mediator Dei* of 1947. It was from these encyclicals that it passed into the texts of the Second Vatican Council.[18]

The history that has just been traced is that of the fundamental understanding of the priest as representation of Christ. With what we have seen so far, while one may agree with Neuner that the Tridentine decree serves as the starting point of *Optatam totius*, such a statement of agreement is in need of nuance. *Optatam totius* was written within the ongoing conversation of the Christian tradition. While the Tridentine decree may be the proximate starting point, a theology of the priesthood, which can be traced back to scripture itself and crystallizes in the understanding of the priest in terms of the threefold office of

Christ, constitutes the ultimate starting point. Vatican II modified Trent in the light of the new landscape in which the Church found herself. For Vatican II, therefore, placing the priest in the modern world does not amount to changing the priest's identity. He will continue to be a priest—a representative of Christ in his threefold office in the world—without conforming to the standard of this world. Christ himself left the priest in the world to challenge (but not conform to) the world, even as it challenges the priest. That is why, unlike Trent, Vatican II did not quarantine the priest. Yet, the program of priestly formation it proposes is designed to equip the priest to engage the world without conforming to it.

Continuity between Trent and Vatican II in the area of priestly formation is evident in the fact that the Tridentine objective of forming priests who are in the world but not of it is continued at Vatican II. Trent hoped to accomplish this objective by isolating the priest from the world. Vatican II hoped to accomplish the same objective, not by isolating the priest from the world but by putting in place a program that prepared the priest to be challenged by the world and to challenge the world in prophetic nonconformism. There is therefore a continuity of objective although a discontinuity in strategy. In other words, the change of strategy does not justify any change of objective. The alternative will compromise the priest's identity, something Vatican II never intended. Like the idea in Newman's theory, the priest is inserted into the world not to lose but to affirm his priestly identity.

If what I have said thus far argues that *Optatam totius* was not written out of nothing and if, as a consequence, it is read with the immediate past represented by Trent in mind, it remains for me to affirm that *Optatam totius* should also be read alongside other documents of Vatican II. In concrete terms, although the Decree on the Formation of Priests, *Optatam totius*, was published before the Decree on the Life and Ministry of Priests, *Presbyterorum ordinis*, one should not be read without the other. *Optatam totius* provides a means for forming the priest (as described in *Presbyterorum ordinis*), which describes the life and ministry of priests in the light of the ecclesiology of communion and the understanding of the Church's mission in the modern world at the Second Vatican Council. At the council, the Church desired to renew herself by returning to the ecclesiology of communion rooted in scripture and in the writing of the Church fathers. This recourse to a scriptural and patristic ecclesiology points to the fact that the conciliar notion of renewal was a return to the sources, a dynamic retrieval and reappropriation of the wisdom of the past rather than a rupture with it. The vital role of the priestly ministry in implementing this desired renewal was accorded its due recognition in the opening sentence of *Optatam totius*: "The council is fully aware that the desired renewal of the whole Church depends in great part upon a priestly ministry animated by the spirit of Christ and it solemnly affirms the critical importance of priestly training."[19] Consistent with the desire for a renewal that is connected to continuity, *Optatam totius*, in laying down the fundamental principles of priestly formation, reaffirms regulations whose utility has been confirmed by experiences and introduces new regulations demanded by the same experience "in harmony with the constitutions and decrees" of the council. Furthermore, in a way that is consistent with an ecclesiology of communion, the directives concern diocesan priests immediately, but not solely. Nevertheless, there is room for adaptation to legitimate diversity (*OT* 1).

The council's clear and unambiguous affirmation of the necessity and objective of major seminaries ought to be given the utmost attention. Seminaries are loci for the formation of "true shepherd[s] of souls after the example of our Lord Jesus, teacher, priest and shepherd" (*OT* 4). This, as Hurley observes, is another statement that underlies the continuity between Trent and Vatican II. It is in reply to the opinion expressed in certain quarters that seminaries are no longer desirable:

> If, in the past, the seminary became an institution for isolating and protecting, we now run the opposite danger of over-emphasizing the importance of contact with reality. Contact alone does not train a man. If he is to make the most of his experience, he needs time and seclusion for study and reflection. And if his life is to demand a more than average degree of discipline, he must subject himself to methodical training to acquire the habit of it. The athlete and the soldier know this well. The tendency to exalt freedom and spontaneity must not lead us to forget that habits are not acquired without persistent effort and that sound habits are the indispensable springboard of spontaneity. The artist bears witness to this.
>
> It is a question of balancing discipline and experience. One must not be sacrificed for the other. When we remember what the clergy was before the Council of Trent, we can be grateful that Trent insisted on discipline. It was this discipline of the post-Tridentine clergy, the clergy of the seminaries, that made Vatican II possible.[20]

The importance of the affirmation of the need for seminaries is evident not only in its relation to Trent but also in view of the historical development of the theology of munus triplex, contained in the portrait of the priest in Vatican II's *Presbyterorum ordinis*: "Through the sacred ordination and mission which they receive from the bishops priests are promoted to the service of Christ the Teacher, Priest and King; they share in his ministry, a ministry through which the Church here on earth is unceasingly built up into the People of God, the Body of Christ and the Temple of the Holy Spirit."[21]

With these words, one can assert that implicit in the renewal the Church desired at the council is a theology that portrays the priest as the sacramental configuration of Christ. The priest has no identity apart from Christ and the Church. He is to be formed to serve Christ and the Church. He is neither a pop star nor a public relations officer of any ideology, ancient or modern, but the sacramental presence of Christ who is prophet, priest, and king in the Church and, through the Church, to the world. In the same way that the renewal the Church envisioned at the council was not meant to be a compromise of the Church's identity, the priest's identity is not to be compromised by his insertion in the world. Moreover, in order not to jeopardize this identity, he lives in the world without conforming to it.[22] His functions (which *Presbyterorum ordinis* describes beautifully) flow from his identity as the sacrament of Christ's redemptive presence to the Church and to the world: As Christ's redemptive presence he is the minister of God's word and of the sacraments and the Eucharist, as well as ruler of God's people.[23] The objective of priestly formation is to mold candidates who put on Christ in his munus triplex and, for that reason, do what Christ would do. This corresponds to the directive of *Optatam totius*:

> *They* [priests] *should be trained for the ministry of the Word,* so that they may gain an ever increasing understanding of the revealed Word of God, making it their own by meditation, and giving it expression in their speech and in their lives. *They should be trained for the ministry of worship and sanctification,* so that by prayer and the celebration of the sacred liturgical functions they may carry on the work of salvation through the Eucharistic sacrifice and the sacraments. *They should be trained to undertake the ministry of the shepherd,* that they may know how to represent Christ to men, Christ who "did not come to have service done to him, but to serve others and to give his life as a ransom for the lives of many" (Mk. 10:45; Jn. 13:12–17), and that, by becoming the servants of all, they may win over many (1 Cor. 9:19).
>
> Hence, all the elements of their training, spiritual, intellectual, disciplinary, should be coordinated with this pastoral aim in view, and all superiors and teachers should zealously cooperate to carry out this program in faithful obedience to the bishop's authority. (*OT* 4)

I have used italics to highlight the munus triplex in the quotation and to point out that each of the elements of priestly formation mentioned here corresponds with the being of the priest. The spiritual element corresponds to the sanctifying or priestly office and requires holiness; the intellectual element corresponds to the teaching or prophetic office and requires intelligence; and the disciplinary element corresponds to governing or kingly office and requires competence. In this respect, for priests, holiness, intelligence, and competence are all necessary but not sufficient. Consequently, priests are to be formed to be holy, intelligent, and competent. Each quality is necessary, but none is sufficient without the other two. Furthermore, the required competence is not just professional. The priest must be equally a man of moral competence and a man of good judgment and good character.

In addition, these elements—holiness, intelligence, and competence—reveal themselves in the lives and writings of the Church fathers. For this reason it is essential that candidates for the priesthood be familiar with the Church fathers. Despite what authors rightly describe as the fathers' eccentricities and excesses, the combined characteristics of profound spirituality, orthodox theology, and pastoral solicitude in patristic thought make the fathers good guides in the formation of holy, intelligent, and competent priests.[24]

It is evident that attention to these three elements of priestly formation constitutes the core of *Optatam totius*. Divided into seven sections (without counting the introduction and conclusion), these elements receive the greatest attention in sections IV–VI. While the first section contains brief remarks on priestly training in different countries, the second highlights the need for a more intense fostering of priestly vocation, the third looks at major seminaries, and the seventh provides guidelines on studies after the years of seminary training.[25]

Formation for Holiness

The goal of spiritual formation, which the council sees as inseparable from but closely associated with doctrinal and moral formation, is to develop priests who cultivate deep friendship with the Trinity.[26] The objective is to lead the student to "learn to live in intimate and unceasing union with God the Father through his Son Jesus Christ, in the Holy Spirit." The priest's life is to be lived with the Paschal mystery as a reference point so that he can initiate people into that mystery. The priest's spiritual formation (as envisioned at the council) should enable the priest to seek and find Christ. The list of where and in whom this is to take place is impressive: "They should be taught to seek Christ in faithful meditation on the Word of God and in active participation in the sacred mysteries of the Church, especially the Eucharist and the Divine Office; in the bishop by whom they are sent and in the people to whom they are sent, especially the poor, little children, the sick, sinners and unbelievers."

For Vatican II, priestly spirituality is not without its Marian component. Hence, "with the confidence of sons they should love and reverence the most Blessed Virgin Mary, who was given as a mother to the disciples by Jesus Christ as he was dying on the cross" (*OT* 8). This spirituality is meant to inculcate a sense of piety that does not reduce the priestly life to mere religious sentiment, a sense of the mystery of the Church expressed in "a humble and filial attachment to the Vicar of Christ," loyal cooperation with the bishop, harmony with fellow priests, devoted service to the people of God, and a life that conforms with the crucified Christ by "giving up willingly those things which are lawful, but not expedient" (*OT* 8–9).

In addition, conformity with Christ provides an intrinsic motivation toward the willingness to renounce lawful but nonexpedient things. This, no doubt, touches on training in priestly obedience, poverty, self-denial, and celibacy. The instinct of instant self-gratification is tempered by a life lived in constant reference to the Paschal mystery. Without a deep appreciation and an internalization of the mystery of the crucified Christ, it becomes difficult, if not impossible, even when the latest theories of the social sciences are deployed, to achieve the self-control that is required for holiness: Priestly obedience is perceived as unbearable bondage and an unacceptable violation of conscience, and celibacy is seen as nothing but an outdated, dispensable, and disposable ecclesiastical precept. The extent to which the disappearance of the Paschal mystery from the lives of contemporary Christians contributed to the crisis of fidelity (not just to celibacy but also to virtually every aspect of ecclesial life) is yet to be measured.

A diminished appreciation of Gospel values begins with a diminished sense of the Paschal mystery. A diminished sense of the Paschal mystery lessens motivation for the cultivation of virtues and the appreciation of asceticism. It amounts to a mistaken interpretation of Vatican II to see these as part of a Tridentine past that is to be discarded.[27] When the achievement of the past goes unrecognized, it becomes impossible to accomplish anything in the present. That is why the archives of a people should not be thrown into the refuse heap of history, especially when one is dealing with the people of God.

Formation for Intelligence in Holiness and Saint Thomas Aquinas

In the climate of renewal at Vatican II the formation of priests in holiness takes seriously the achievements of the biblical, patristic, and liturgical movements of the era. While the emergence of these movements helped to check the temptation to reduce intellectual formation to scholastic philosophy, it did not amount to doing theology by ignoring philosophy. Neither is it a question of saying farewell to Thomas Aquinas. *Optatam totius* counseled that candidates for the priesthood be introduced to theology "with St. Thomas as teacher [*S. Thoma magistro*]" (*OT* 14). Josef Neuner points out that the redaction of this article was preceded by a vigorous debate between "two sharply opposed views":

> Some considered that St. Thomas was not accorded a sufficiently important place in the decree, whereas his teaching had been recommended in more than one hundred papal documents (Cardinal Ruffini, Cardinal Bacci, Cardinal Caggiano, Archbishop Staffa), while others were against any special mention of St. Thomas (Cardinal Léger). Others again approved the moderate formula of the text (Cardinal Döpfner). The *modi* submitted on article 15 on philosophy were almost all concerned with the place of St. Thomas. Over one hundred fathers expressed in one form or another the desire that the system of *philosophia perennis*, as developed by St. Thomas, should be taught in the seminaries. Even after the first vote, 31 further requests for this were received up to January 31, 1965, the last official date for the submission of *modi*; after this date another 420 such requests were received. As against this, a *modus* signed by 117 fathers requested that no particular philosophical system be prescribed; St. Thomas should be taught to such an extent as was still valid today. With article 16 on the study of theology also over 200 *modi* asked that either the words "Sancto Thoma magistro" be left out of the text, or that it should be weakened by adding "praesertim," or else that other teachers of the Church should be recommended as well.
>
> In view of this conflict of opinions the original text, accepted by more than a two-thirds majority, was, in essentials, retained. It is in fact more than a compromise between two parties; it expresses in

broad terms the double duty of ecclesiastical instruction: to remain in the tradition and at the same time to be open to new questions and insights.[28]

Here again, Vatican II's openness to the present does not represent a break with tradition. Neuner's commentary provides a useful guide into the history and intention of the conciliar position: "St. Thomas is recommended as a teacher. He is not only the master who formulated in his time the contents of Revelation in the intellectual and linguistic forms of Aristotelianism (which was then modern) and hence became a model of the adaptation of theological research and language to contemporary life and culture—this was conceded by all, and many requested that the council should limit itself to recommending his method—but he is also a teacher in as much as he arrived at permanent insights which have to be taught in theological instruction."[29]

It is not merely a case of recommending Aquinas's method; it is also a case of asking those who provide theological formation, as well as those they are forming, to take the content of Aquinas's theology seriously. The competing modus submitted by 116 council fathers, to which Neuner refers, as well as the fact that the council did not accept it, buttresses the point that both the method and the content of Aquinas's theology are being advocated. Yet, nothing suggests that what has been adopted amounts to a canonization of every particular doctrinal position Aquinas espoused.[30] The old is not discarded; neither is the new rejected. There is, instead, a prudentially differentiated acceptance of the old and the new. Innovation is embraced within tradition and is thus a breakthrough within tradition, not a break away from it.

To ensure that innovation does not break from tradition presupposes a holistic view of priestly life and formation. It is to ensure that the priest's intellectual formation does not separate philosophy and theology as if the orders of nature and of grace (the natural and the supernatural) are to be separated. Being Catholic and a philosopher, a person of faith, and a person of intelligence—these are not contradictions. There is wisdom in the conciliar counsel to take Saint Thomas as teacher not just because of his method or content but, most importantly, because of his life, which exemplified an admirable combination of ardent pursuit of both holiness and intelligence.[31]

The priest is to be formed as a man of faith. But faith, contrary to what many think, is an intelligent act. The Catholic priest must be a man of faith who never trivializes the tedious task of tidy thinking. A priest can and must be a philosopher, that is, of the mode that Aquinas described in his reflection on the office of the wise man.[32] It is his duty to be at the service of God's people, who are searching for the universal source of things and the meaning of life. In this regard, good philosophy is presented as an indispensable instrument of doing good theology. In order not to separate faith and reason, the priest endeavors not to separate philosophy and theology. Such a separation would impede the possibility of a comprehensive understanding of the human person, of the person and office of the priest himself, of the world, and of the centrality of the mystery of Christ.[33] Good philosophy is needed to respond to the challenge of secularism in the north and to the challenge of sacralism and superstition in the south. The Second Vatican Council anticipated this need when it outlined the teaching method of philosophy: "The teaching method adopted should stimulate in the students a love of rigorous investigation, observation and demonstration of the truth, as well as an honest recognition of the limits of human knowledge. Careful attention should be paid to the connection between philosophy and the real problems of life, as well as to the questions which engage the minds of the students. The students themselves should be helped to perceive the connection between philosophical arguments and the mysteries of salvation which are considered in theology in the higher light of faith" (*OT* 15).

The priest must learn to be able to encounter people who, broadly speaking, pose two types of questions in matters of faith: those that seek to debunk faith as nonsensical and those that seek to understand faith. Good philosophy relates with faith not by asking the first type of question but by asking the second type. One who studies philosophy with the aim of placing it at the service of *intelligentia fidei* may subject faith to analysis, and that is contrary to what some cynics and even well-intentioned believers think. Philosophy is understood here not as the pursuit of fables and inventions of the zeitgeist but as the pursuit of wisdom. Philosophy is never too much because it is never too much to desire wisdom.

The priest's desire for wisdom, like that of any human, must be relentless. Karl Rahner described Aquinas as a man whose theology was his spirituality and whose spirituality was his theology. Taking my cue from this statement, I maintain that philosophy, when understood the way Aquinas described it in *Summa contra gentiles*, in a symbiosis of theology and spirituality, enables the priest to see Christ as the Wisdom of God, who is to be constantly desired. Captivated (or rather, captured) by this desire for the wisdom of God, the priest is able to speak about the wisdom he seeks. Today's priest must assume the office of the wise person who seeks to understand the mystery of Christ (for this is where true wisdom lies) and to explain that mystery to the people of God, who are entrusted to his care through the language of his lips and of his priestly life.

Aquinas's life, method, and doctrine portray him as a wise man who used philosophy to understand divine revelation and then employed both philosophy and divine revelation to understand the human condition. This enabled him to see the distinction—not a separation—between nature and grace. Grace sublates but does not suppress nature. Nowadays, with the collapse of Aquinas's wise distinction between the natural and the supernatural, the effect is the flight of the awareness of the nature, necessity, and availability of grace. Gone, too, is the possibility of a positive education for celibacy—something integral to Vatican II's program of priestly formation—in which a positive appreciation of marriage and of sex in marriage goes hand in hand with a positive appreciation of celibacy. However, where celibacy is denigrated and sexual pleasure is presented as indispensable and readily available, the crisis of both celibacy and marriage expresses the crisis of commitment and fidelity.

Where the power of grace to sublate nature is forgotten, there is no recourse to grace. Where there is no recourse to grace, it becomes a comfortable option to see fidelity as impossible, dispensable, and disposable.

Aquinas's use of philosophy and divine revelation to understand the human condition is reflected in what the council teaches on the sources, purpose, and method of teaching theology. The sources of good theology listed in article 16 of *Optatam totius* cannot be ignored without jeopardizing priestly life and ministry: biblical themes, Church fathers (of both the East and the West), later history of dogma in relation to the general history of the Church, Saint Thomas as teacher, the liturgy, and the whole life of the Church. The article makes a clear statement of the purpose and method of teaching theology, which converge to make theology the nourishment of spiritual life and a preparation for the priest to face real-life situations:

> Theological subjects should be taught in the light of faith, under the guidance of the Magisterium of the Church, in such a way that students will draw pure Catholic teaching from Divine Revelation, will enter deeply into its meaning, make it the nourishment of their spiritual life, and learn to proclaim, explain, and defend it in their priestly ministry. They should learn to seek the solution of human problems in the light of Revelation, to apply its eternal truths to the changing conditions of human affairs, and to express them in language which people of the modern world will understand.[34]

Our age, like every other age, seeks wisdom. Yet, we must not overlook the fact that the wisdom the priest seeks is different from that of the age, despite its good intention. Long before Vatican II, John Newman had pointed out that the goal of priestly formation is to train the future priest to deepen his desire for the wisdom that is Christ and to learn the truth about Christ. A homily Newman gave at the opening of Saint Bernard's Seminary, near Birmingham, in the United Kingdom, on October 2, 1873, somewhat anticipated *Optatam totius*'s description of the seminary as locus for the formation of "true shepherd[s] of souls after the example of our Lord Jesus, teacher, priest and shepherd": "This handing down of the truth [about Christ] from generation to generation is obviously the direct reason for the institution of seminaries for the education of the clergy.... Catholic doctrine, Catholic morals, Catholic worship and discipline, the Christian character, life, and conduct, all that is necessary for being a good priest, they learn one and all from this religious school, which is the appointed preparation for the ministerial offices."[35]

"The special peril of the time before us is the spread of that plague of infidelity, that the Apostles and our Lord Himself have predicted as the worst calamity of the last times of the Church. And at least a shadow, a typical image of the last times is coming over the world. I do not mean to presume to say that this is the last time, but that it has had the evil prerogative of being like that more terrible season, when it is said that the elect themselves will be in danger of falling away."[36] The recently uncovered cases of clerical sex abuse represent, in my opinion, a period of infidelity as bad as that described by Newman. He went on to speak of the underlying philosophy of his time:

> The elementary proposition of this new philosophy which is now so threatening is this—that in all things we must go by reason, in nothing by faith, that things are known and are to be received so far as they can be proved. Its advocates say, all other knowledge has proof—why should religion be an exception?[37]

> A seminary is the only true guarantee for the creation of the ecclesiastical spirit. And this is the primary and true weapon for meeting the age, not controversy. . . .

> In this ecclesiastical spirit, I will but mention a spirit of seriousness or recollection. We must gain the habit of feeling that we are in God's presence, that He sees what we are doing; and a liking that He does so, a love of knowing it, a delight in the reflection, "Thou God seest me." A priest who feels this deeply will never misbehave himself in mixed society. . . .

> And next, most important in the same warfare, and here too you will see how it is connected with a seminary, is a sound, accurate, complete knowledge of Catholic theology.[38]

Newman's words provide a good summary of what priestly formation ought to be. It is the development of holiness and intelligence in competence.

Formation for Holiness and Intelligence in Competence

A priest must be a competent pastor. His competence is not just professional but also moral. This, in my opinion, responds to the moral and human aspects of formation that *Pastores dabo vobis* explicitly mentions. It includes respect for the lay faithful and recognition of their charism in collaborative ministry without abdicating sacerdotal responsibility.

While the art of dialogue and of being a good listener, as well as the techniques of modern pedagogy, psychology, and sociology are necessary in priestly formation, we must bear in mind that, according to article 19, for the priest there is virtually no competence without holiness and intelligence. Competence without holiness reduces him to a mere ecclesiastical bureaucrat without pastoral solicitude or to a social activist who espouses and practices detranscendentalized values. Holiness without competence makes him socially irresponsible and insensitive to the needs of the least of Christ's brothers and sisters. Holiness and/or competence without intelligence—an intelligence acquired when the intellect is cultivated in faith—makes him incapable of internalizing and exposing the mystery of faith. These, in my opinion, can be avoided when *Optatam totius* is studied and implemented by all those who are directly or indirectly responsible for the formation of priests today. The situation of the priesthood at this point in history testifies to the importance of this implementation.

The recent scandal is a brutal reminder of the vital importance of priestly holiness not just in matters of sexuality but also in the whole of the priest's life. For throughout his life, the priest is called to conform to the image of Christ. Moreover, to require holiness, intelligence, and competence of the priest is to ask him to be an outstanding person. The priest is to be a man who strives for holiness. He does not become relevant because of what he does but because of who he is. His holiness cannot be separated from his solid theological formation. And that theological formation, according to Vatican II, is to be undertaken with Saint Thomas as teacher. Its ingredients must be the available intellectual tools of the time. For Aquinas, these were good philosophy, scripture, and patrology.

Today, apart from philosophy, one should also speak of the social sciences (hitherto areas of philosophy but today separated from philosophy). The importance of the Church fathers remains undeniable.[39] The priest is minister of a Church who is the authentic interpreter of divine revelation; hence, he is also custodian and teacher of tradition. On the strength of this fact, he is a custodian of Christian tradition and should be conversant with that tradition. He is aided in this regard by familiarity with scripture and the Church fathers. This familiarity with the Christian tradition and the culture of the place where he is pastor must go hand in hand. In this manner this he will be able to demonstrate his pastoral competence as one who sees inculturation as a two-way street—evangelization of culture and inculturation of the Gospel. What I have just said explains why, unlike Trent, Vatican II does not advocate priestly formation in isolation from the trials and challenges of today's culture.

Having lived and studied in North America, I write from my experience of ecclesial life in that part of the world. I also draw from my experience of ecclesial life in Nigeria, where I was born and where I now live and work. With this background I can say that the priest of today, in the older churches in North America and Europe, must be ready to be a priest in a Western world of secularism, religious indifference, or religious relativism that is often mistaken for religious pluralism. In the young churches in Africa, he must be ready to be a priest where a combination of superstition and poverty-induced pietism motivate an aggressive evangelism of faith without reason. The theological formation of the priest in the Western world must include a positive identification with and an appreciation of all that is noble and pro-Christian even in the militant secularism of our time.

In the same way, the theological development of the priest in Africa, in the face of the growing challenge of Pentecostalism, must include a positive identification with and an appreciation of the noble and pro-Christian values of African culture. Yet, wherever theology is pursued, the saying "all that glitters is not gold" is true. Not every philosophical, cultural, or religious category can assist in the task of priestly education. That is why inculturation is a two-way street. A competent pastor uses the resources of the Christian tradition—and in this respect he does not limit himself to the resources of philosophy or the social sciences—to address the existential questions that the men and women of today's culture struggle with on a daily basis.

Conclusion

I have argued in this chapter that there is continuity between the theology of the priesthood at Trent and that of the priesthood at Vatican II. Councils do not turn their backs on each other. What was implicit (by this I mean "silently present") in the Tridentine theology of the priesthood—the threefold office of Christ sacramentally represented in the life and ministry of the priest—is made explicit at Vatican II in *Presbyterorum ordinis* and in *Optatam totius*. To demonstrate that such is the case, I have presented *Optatam totius* as reflecting this threefold office in its program of priestly formation. This explication or amplification of an implicit Tridentine teaching warrants the affirmation of continuity between Trent and Vatican II even as the defensive posture of Trent's program of priestly formation is replaced by the new and open tendency of that of Vatican II. Because the Council of Trent based its theology of the priesthood on the indissoluble relationship between the Eucharist and the priesthood, the threefold office is an intrinsic component of that theology. By so doing, the council prolonged the medieval theology of the priesthood. The Eucharist is sacrifice of the New Covenant, whose celebration Christ made possible by the institution of the sacramental priesthood. This sacramental priesthood, which began with the Apostles, continues in the priests of today.[40]

Yet, even as it emphasized the indissociable link between the Eucharist and the priesthood, the Council of Trent did not limit priests to celebrations of the Eucharist. The priest is not just the "man of the Mass." He must also exercise the prophetic ministry in holiness through preaching. Consequently, while preaching is recognized as the principal duty of bishops, the council did not totally exclude priests from this office.[41]

I have also asserted here that the intention of Vatican II is to form priests who are holy, intelligent, and competent. Each of these three qualities is necessary, while none is of itself sufficient. I believe they correspond, respectively, to the priestly, prophetic, and kingly office of Christ, whose sacramental representation the priest is called to be. The development of the priest in holiness, intelligence, and competence does not end in the seminary. It is a lifelong project of both the priest and the Church. Regular organization of retreats, seminars, and lectures, as well as a well-articulated policy of ongoing education are needed to continue the work begun in the seminary so that the priest will always be ready to face the challenges of his life and ministry. When it comes to priestly formation, what begins in the seminary does not end there. That is why the candidate must prepare not merely for ordination but also for the priesthood itself.[42]

Faced with modernity in its Western expressions and the imperative of openness to non-Western cultures, neither Catholic nor priestly identity must be negotiated away. The impression ought not to be created that that was ever the intention of the Second Vatican Council. The Church can and must embrace the modern world without losing her identity. The priest derives his identity from Christ through the Church. That is why, to use Newman's words, the goal of priestly formation as presented by Vatican II is to inculcate an ecclesiastical spirit in those who will be priests, pastors, and prophets in the world of our time. Since the program of development outlined by *Optatam totius* reflects the munus triplex of Christ, I conclude that, consequent to this Christological referent and to the ecclesiology of communion of the Second Vatican Council, *Optatam totius* reflects the intention to form the priest to be the servant of communion by being the sacrament of the redemptive presence of Christ, who himself is primordial minister of communion. He is to be formed to be both minister and representative of the Church, which is the sacrament of communion in the world. Configured to Christ, the apostolic identity of the priest is not to be compromised.

However, all that has been said thus far about priestly education would amount to nothing but a pious wish if certain prerequisites were ignored. The council recognized that the program of priestly formation it introduced requires suitable seminary formators. Such superiors and professors can "cultivate the closest harmony of spirit and action" with one another and with the students: "The training of students depends not only on wise regulations but also, and especially, on competent educators. Seminary superiors and professors should therefore be chosen from among the best and should be carefully prepared in sound doctrine, suitable pastoral experience and special training in spirituality and teaching methods" (*OT* 5). While the availability of suitable formators is necessary for priestly formation, it is not sufficient. In other words, it takes more than good formators to develop good priests. Suitable and willing candidates are also required: "Each candidate should be subjected to vigilant and careful enquiry, keeping in mind his age and development, concerning his right intention and freedom of choice, his spiritual, moral and intellectual fitness, adequate physical and psychic health, and possible hereditary traits. Account should also be taken of the candidate's capacity for undertaking the obligations of the priesthood and carrying out his pastoral duties" (*OT* 6).

The council advised against compromising standards in the training of priests. Not even a shortage of priests should be used as an excuse for admitting or ordaining unsuitable candidates. "Notwithstanding the regrettable shortage of priests, due strictness should always be brought to bear on the choice and testing of student[s]" (*OT* 6). The task of implementing *Optatam totius* is the sacred responsibility of bishops, major superiors of clerical religious, rectors, and of all those involved in priestly formation whether as teachers or candidates. It is indeed the sacred responsibility of the entire people of God. For in matters of recruiting, formation, and discernment of suitability for priestly life and ministry, the whole Church is called upon to live her character as communion. This is clear in the rite of ordination. When the bishop asks the one who presents the candidates, "Do you judge them to be worthy?" he responds, "After inquiry among the people of God, and upon the recommendation of those in charge of their training, I testify that they have been found worthy." Those words place a heavy responsibility upon those charged with priestly formation. They will ultimately be called to account by Our Lord Jesus Christ, who is, as the fathers of the Church and the great scholars teach, both priest and victim.

NOTES

1. Cf. J.-M.-R. Tillard, *Church of Churches: The Ecclesiology of Communion* (Collegeville, Minn.: Michael Glazier/Liturgical Press, 1992); Anthony Akinwale, *The Congress and the Council: Towards a Nigerian Reception of the Second Vatican Council* (Ibadan, Nigeria: Michael Dempsey Centre for Religious and Social Research, 2003), where it is argued that the idea of the Church as the family of God, adapted at the 1994 synod of African bishops, even as it represents an African reception of Vatican II's ecclesiology of communion, takes it cue from tradition in the third chapter of the letter to the Ephesians.

2. Yves Congar, *La tradition et les traditions: Essai théologique*, vol. 2 (Paris: Le Signe/Librairie Arthème Fayard, 1963), 28–43 [28].

3. I use the phrase "since the Apostles" and not "from the Apostles" to emphasize the uniqueness and unrepeatable character of the ministry of the Apostles. Here there is an effort to understand the *vrai sens* of apostolic succession. On this notion, see J.-M.-R. Tillard, *L'Église locale: Ecclésiologie de communion et de catholicité* (Paris: Cerf, 1995), 181–82.

4. "La foi salutaire est reçue par des esprits qui doivent la considerer, non seulment comme un absolu, mais comme un dépôt donné une fois pour toutes depuis les Apôtres, et s'y référer en conséquence, 'sans y rien ajouter, sans en rien soustraire.' Mais, en même temps, ces esprits doivent le 'recevoir' de façon vivante et selon ce qu'ils sont. Or ce sont des esprits *humains*. Leur structure est celle d'esprits discursifs, à perceptions successives et partielles; donc, aussi, d'esprit qui s'accomplissent seulment dans le commerce d'autres esprits, en recevant et en échangeant; enfin d'esprits vivant dans une durée temporelle cosmique et biologique. L'historicité est un attribut de l'esprit humain." Congar, *La tradition et les traditions*, vol. 2, 30.

5. For a study of the history of the idea of doctrinal development see Aidan Nichols, *From Newman to Congar: The Idea of Doctrinal Development from the Victorians to the Second Vatican Council* (Edinburgh: T&T Clark, 1990).

6. On this assertion see the very important works of Yves Congar, *L'Église: De saint Augustine à l'époque moderne* (Paris: Cerf, 1970), and Jean-Marie-Roger Tillard, *Chair de l'Église, chair du Christ: Aux sources de l'ecclésiologie de communion* (Paris: Cerf, 1992).

7. Interpreting these words as describing the Church as an aggregate of priests can be helpful in elaborating a theology of the priesthood that ignores the conciliar distinction between the common priesthood and the ministerial priesthood. According to Vatican II, the two "differ essentially and not only in degree" (*Lumen gentium*, 10). Understanding and explaining this assertion is a double task for the theologian.

8. See Tillard, *Church of Churches*, 169–74 [171].

9. Ibid., 211–23 [212].

10. Josef Neuner, "Decree on Priestly Formation," in *Commentary on the Documents of Vatican II*, vol. 2., ed. Herbert Vogrimler (New York: Crossroad, 1989), 371. See *Concilium Tridentinum, sessio XXIII, de reformatione*, ch. 18. For an account of the history of the final text of the document, apart from Neuner's and those of many others, see

Denis Hurley, "The Training of Priests," in *Vatican II on Priests and Seminaries*, ed. Denis Hurley and Joseph Cunnane (Chicago: Scepter Books, 1967), 169–211.

11. Neuner, "Decree on Priestly Formation," 371–72.

12. Hurley, "Training of Priests,",182.

13. To trace the history of the theology of the priest as representing the munus triplex of Christ I have relied principally on Aidan Nichols, *Holy Order: Apostolic Priesthood from the New Testament to the Second Vatican Council* (Dublin: Veritas, 1990). See also J. Colson, *Ministère de Jesus et le sacerdoce de l'évangile* (Paris: Cerf, 1966); P. Grelot, *Le ministère de la nouvelle alliance* (Paris: Cerf, 1967); Ludwig Ott, *Le sacrement de l'ordre: Histoire des dogmes* (Paris: Cerf, 1971).

14. Cf. Nichols, *Holy Order*, 5–11; André Feuillet, *The Priesthood of Christ and His Ministers* (New York: Doubleday, 1975).

15. Cf. Irenaeus, *Against Heresies*, IV, 26.

16. Nichols, *Holy Order*, 85.

17. Ibid., 126.

18. Ibid., 127–28.

19. *Optatam totius*, introduction.

20. Hurley, "Training of Priests," 186–87.

21. *Presbyterorum ordinis* 1.

22. Ibid., 3. There is an echo here of the prayer of Jesus in the Gospel according to John.

23. See ibid., 4–6.

24. Cf. Aidan Nichols, *The Shape of Catholic Theology: An Introduction to Its Sources, Principles, and History* (Collegeville, Minn.: Liturgical Press, 1991), 200–206. See also Ibadan Archdiocesan Preparatory Committee, *"Go, Make Disciples of All Nations"*: Instrumentum laboris *of the First Archdiocesan Synod* (Ibadan, Nigeria: Claverianum Press, 2004), ch. 3, which describes bishops and priests as "leaders and learners in holiness and competence."

25. The elements of priestly formation identified in *Optatam totius* find an echo in the postsynodal exhortation *Pastores dabo vobis*, in which Pope John Paul II speaks of four aspects of priestly formation: intellectual, spiritual, moral, and human. These appear not to correspond to what Vatican II itemized. After all, there is a difference between three and four. While *Optatam totius* speaks of a "spiritual element," *Pastores dabo vobis* speaks of a "spiritual aspect," and while the former speaks of an "intellectual element," the latter speaks of an "intellectual aspect." The "moral and human aspect" of *Pastores dabo vobis* could be seen as belonging to what *Optatam totius* calls the "disciplinary aspect."

26. See *Optatam totius*, nos. 8–12.

27. "With these attitudes firmly embedded in the tradition of priestly formation, due mainly to the Tridentine achievement, Vatican II was able to move on and consolidate more recent acquisitions of Catholic thought and experience—theological depth and human concern." Hurley, "Training of Priests," 191.

28. Neuner, "Decree on Priestly Formation," 395.

29. Ibid., 398–99.

30. See ibid., 398n39. The 116 fathers proposed these words: "Ecclesia Catholica proponit S. Thomam ut magistratum et exemplar omnium eorum, qui scientias theologicas colunt."

31. Karol Jozef Wojtyla, Pope John Paul II, very rightly described by Joseph Cardinal Ratzinger in his funeral homily as "a priest to the core," represents an imitation—a felicitous one—of this wonderful combination.

32. See Thomas Aquinas, *Summa contra gentiles*, bk. I, chapters 1–9.

33. Cf. *Optatam totius*, no. 14.

34. *OT* 16. Hurley captures the incisive character of number 16: "Everything is here: faith, Magisterium, penetration of revealed truth, personal and apostolic dimensions, the supremacy of scripture, respect for tradition both Eastern and Western, the historical development of doctrine, the scholastic achievement, the recognition of the divine mysteries in the liturgy and life of the Church, concern for human problems and the search for solutions in the light of Revelation and finally communication. It is doubtful if in all the history of education so much was ever said in so few words. The intellectual is here, the spiritual and the pastoral. This is the magna carta of the Catholic priesthood of the future." Hurley, "Training of Priests," 202.

35. John Newman, "The Infidelity of the Future," in *Reason for Faith: Nine Sermons from the Cardinal's Autograph Manuscripts* (Trabuco, Calif.: Source Books/Anthony Clarke, 1995), 118.

36. Ibid., 121.

37. Ibid., 122.

38. Ibid., 132–33.

39. For an appreciation of the importance of the Church fathers see Johannes Quasten, *Patrology*, vol. 1, *The Beginnings of Patristic Literature: From Apostles' Creed to Irenaeus* (Allen, Tex.: Christian Classics, 1995), 1–22. See also Nichols, *Shape of Catholic Theology*, 200–20.

40. DS, no. 1764.

41. "Archpriests, curates and all those who in any manner soever hold any parochial, or other, churches, which have the cure of souls, shall, at least on the Lord's days, and solemn feast either personally, or if they be lawfully hindered, by others who are competent, feed the people committed to them, with wholesome words, according to their own capacity, and that of their people; by teaching them the things which it is necessary for all to know unto salvation, and by announcing to them with briefness and plainness of discourse, the vices which they must avoid, and the virtues which they must follow after, that they may escape everlasting punishment, and obtain the glory of heaven." J. Waterworth, *The Canons and Decrees of the Council of Trent* (London: C. Dolman, 1848), 27, quoted in Nichols, *Holy Order*, 101.

42. See *Optatam totius*, no. 22.

12

The Decree on the Appropriate Renewal of Religious Life, *Perfectae Caritatis*

M. Prudence Allen, R.S.M., and M. Judith O'Brien, R.S.M.

The large number of perpetually professed women and men religious who chose to leave religious life after the close of the Second Vatican Council led many people to conclude that the council's official teachings were in discontinuity with previous magisterial teachings about consecrated life. Yet, a careful study of magisterial documents does not support this conclusion.[1]

Tracing the Church's teaching on the essential characteristics of religious life, we discovered a clear pattern of development that built on previous magisterial foundations. The earliest papal writings concentrated on particular religious congregations or founders. Within these texts were also articulated fundamental principles of religious life. Later documents more directly stated general principles of religious life over the centuries, moving from a juridical approach, to its interior personal dynamisms, to its rich ecclesial and spiritual dimensions.

Within this dynamic unfolding of the significance of religious life, the apostolic constitution *Lumen gentium* (November 24, 1964) reoriented the focus of religious life from individual sanctification toward the perfection of the Church. *Lumen gentium* dedicates chapter 6 to religious life. While this brief chapter does not consider all of the characteristics of religious life, it both encourages religious in the life of holiness and describes the ecclesial purpose of this vocation: "Let all, then, who have been called to the profession of the evangelical counsels make every effort to persevere and make greater progress in the vocation to which God has called them, for the richer purity of the church and the greater glory of the one and undivided Trinity, which in Christ and through Christ is the source and origin of all holiness."[2]

Perfectae caritatis, the Decree on the Renewal of Religious Life (October 25, 1965), offered a roadmap by which individual religious institutes could revitalize in communion with the Church.[3] *Perfectae caritatis* also portrays the purpose of religious life beyond a means of individual sanctification; progress within the religious vocation enhances the holiness of the Church. Religious life is a visible representation of the human life of Christ, who was chaste, poor, and obedient. Addressing members of religious institutes, *Lumen gentium* (no. 44a) posits: "And this consecration will be more perfect in as much as by firmer and more stable bonds Christ is more clearly seen to be united to his bride the church by an indissoluble bond."

The Second Vatican Council links a vibrant religious life and a dynamic ecclesial life. Pope Pius XII, in 1947, had previously described the impact of consecrated apostolic service in *Provida Mater Ecclesiae*: "We have only to look at the glorious calendar of religious men and women through the ages to see how a canonical religious life is closely interwoven with the holiness and catholic apostolate of the Church itself. The relationship is integral to the Church and to the religious orders and congregations, which by the grace of the life-giving Spirit has grown gradually and steadily in deeper and firmer self-consistency and unity and in wonderful variety of forms."[4] While Pope Pius XII used words such as "interwoven" or "integral" to relate the apostolic service of religious life to the Church, by 1965 there was a clearer connection: Growth in the religious life augments the sanctity of the Church.

To manifest the Church more completely, *Perfectae caritatis* (no. 2b) encouraged religious institutes to rediscover the founding charisms proper to each religious institute: "It is to the church's great advantage that each religious foundation has its particular spirit and function. Each must, therefore, reverence and embrace the genius and directives of its founder, its authentic traditions, the whole heritage, indeed, of the religious body."

With these powerful magisterial teachings about the significance of religious life for the Church, one question lingers: Why did so many religious men and women chose to leave their form of consecrated life after the Second Vatican Council? Along with offering evidence for the coherent unfolding of religious life up to and including the council, we offer some suggestions about how to approach this persistent question.

The methodology for this research drew from ten essential elements of religious life, which were identified in 1983 by the Congregation for Religious and Secular Institutes.[5] We traced each of these elements from the twelfth century in council documents,[6] papal documents,[7] and documents and decrees of the Sacred Congregation for Religious and Secular Institutes up to the Second Vatican Council.[8] Then we examined the constitutions and decrees of the Second Vatican Council for the same characteristics of religious life.

Since the Second Vatican Council did not address all ten essential elements of religious life in depth, we selected the following three to provide the central focus of our chapter: relation to the Church; consecration by public vows of chastity, poverty, and obedience; and communion in community.[9] This methodology enables us to demonstrate that *Perfectae caritatis* is continuous with, and dynamically develops from, the foundation of previous Church teachings on religious life.

Relation to the Church

How has the Church articulated the significance of religious life over the centuries? Early pontifical writings reveal approval of religious orders and their rules. They also addressed the relation of religious and bishops. Consider the First Lateran Council in 1123, which consisted of nine hundred bishops and abbots who met in Rome under Pope Callistus II. The council stated: "We order by general decree, that monks be subject to their own bishops with all humility, and show due obedience and devoted submission to them in all things."[10] In the Fourth Lateran Council, in 1215, canon 12 stipulated how often chapters should be held and when visitations should occur. Furthermore, other responsibilities were assumed, such as papal resolution of disputes, which would demonstrate that religious orders were under the hierarchy's protection and sincere guidance. The council members also discussed the protection of monasteries from hostile laypersons and added that local ordinaries should "take care to reform the monasteries under their jurisdiction."[11]

In *Solet annuere* (1226) Pope Honorius III declared: "The Apostolic See is accustomed to grant the pious desires and to share her kind favor with the upright desires of those petitioning her. Wherefore...We confirm by Our apostolic authority your rule, approved by Our predecessor, Pope Innocent... and We strengthen it with the patronage of this present writing....I enjoin the ministers by obedience, to seek from the lord pope one of the cardinals of the Roman Church, who is to be the governor, protector, and corrector of this fraternity."[12]

In 1312 Clement V in *Exivi de paradiso* resolved questions pertaining to poverty for the Franciscan order. The congregation had appealed to the Church for clarification of their vow of poverty. Pope Clement V responded in order that the Friars Minor could live their rule "(all doubts having been driven away) with full clarity of conscience."[13] He desired to offer further clarifications to the consciences "which have not been entirely quieted" (no. 2).

Four hundred years hence, Pope Pius IX in his 1847 encyclical *Ubi primum* strengthened a pastoral approach in order "to embrace your religious families with fatherly love, giving them Our most zealous attention, support and protection, and planning and providing for their greater good and dignity."[14] He appealed to religious and secular clergy: "Now We earnestly hope that all who are soldiers in the camp of the Lord honor God with one mind and one tongue and strive to maintain the unity of the Spirit in the bond of peace" (no. 10).

Pope Leo XIII's 1900 letter, *Au milieu des consolations*, defended religious congregations in France against animosity by civil government: "To strike at the religious orders would be to deprive the Church of devoted cooperators: at home where they are the necessary auxiliaries of the bishops and clergy in the exercise of the sacred ministry and the function of Catholic teaching and preaching which the Church has the right and the duty of dispensing, and which is demanded by the conscience of the faithful."[15]

This way of life was fostered, and religious orders were depicted as "devoted cooperators." While encouraged and honored by the Church, religious life was perceived primarily as a private means of sanctification for its members.

Pius XII, whose 1947 apostolic constitution *Provida Mater Ecclesia* was mentioned at the beginning of this chapter, opened a new dynamism of purpose beyond the protection and support of the individual religious and the establishment of congregations: "This class, 'religious,' a state between the two [(that is, sacred orders and laity)] and compatible with either, was created for no other reason than that it is closely identified with the essential purpose of the Church" (no. 9). Religious had an important and close effect upon the Church and therefore were implicitly more than cooperators. Was this teaching of Pius XII entirely new? For continuity with four hundred years of Church tradition one could refer to Saint Thomas Aquinas: "The difference of states and duties in the Church regards three things. In the first place it regards the perfection of the Church. For even as in the order of natural things, perfection, which in God is simple and uniform, is not to be found in the created universe except in a multiform and manifold manner, so too, the fullness of grace, which is centered in Christ as head, flows forth to his members in various ways, for the perfection of the body of the Church."[16]

The Second Vatican Council recognized that a revitalized religious life has an effect on all persons in the Church. The apostolic constitution, *Lumen gentium* summarized this orientation with the often-quoted words: "This state, therefore, which is constituted by the profession of the evangelical counsels, although it does not belong to the hierarchical structure of the church, does, however, belong unquestionably to its life and holiness" (*LG* 44d).

Not only did the Second Vatican Council describe the significance of religious life for the Church but it also settled a long-standing tension regarding this "way of perfection." If it is the more perfect means, why are not all called to this life? The answer lies in part in the mystery of vocation and the universal call to holiness. In addition, while few are called to this form of religious consecration, the entire Mystical Body of Christ is enriched in holiness, especially when religious institutes *renew* their institutes under the Holy Spirit's influence and the Church's guidance. *Perfectae caritatis* resonates with the transformed attentiveness to the effect of religious witness in the Church: "The quality of their loving identification with Christ in a complete gift of self, embracing the whole of life, is the measure of the richness of the church's life and the remarkable creativity of its mission" (*PC* 1c).

The straightforward statement of the ecclesial influence by religious supports the universal call to holiness, depicted in chapter 5 of *Lumen gentium*, which emphasizes that each state of life aids in the purification of the Church. A reformulation of the significance of religious life provided the context for the renewal of all religious institutes. The ecclesial importance of religious life naturally produced an evolving description of the vows, as the following section describes.

Consecration by Public Vows

Perfectae caritatis describes the search for true charity or the perfection of charity embraced by those in religious life. A religious vocation expresses "more perfectly the dedication already implicit in baptism" (*PC* 5a). Religious profession is a "God-given vocation as primarily a call to practice the gospel counsels" (ibid.). *Lumen gentium* affirms that it is a "divine gift which the Church has received from its Lord and maintains always with the help of his grace" (*LG* 43a). This form of life is of divine origin and a response to God's initiative.

The value of the vowed life is expressed in *Lumen gentium* (no. 13b): "Many in the religious state, striving toward holiness by a stricter path, are a stimulus to their fellow Christians by their example." This *stricter path* is founded on the distinction between a command, required of all the faithful, and a counsel, required of religious. A command, stated as a restriction like "Thou shall not steal," necessitates the removal of anything contrary to charity. A counsel necessitates the removal of anything that would hinder the acts of charity.[17] Therefore, to refrain from violation of the commandments is just the beginning ground to fulfill the counsels.

Beyond individual determination that pertains specifically to chastity, poverty, and obedience, the counsels lead toward the sanctification of the whole person. The profession of the evangelical counsels expresses the intention of the person to act in charity, united with the prayers of the Church. Moreover, the counsels foster or stimulate holiness within the Mystical Body of Christ. Therefore, while leading toward union with God in heaven, religious institutes make present to the world the eschatological vision of the Church. "The people of God have here no abiding city; they seek rather one that is to come. Therefore, the religious state, while giving its followers greater freedom from earthly cares, also makes clearer to all believers the heavenly goods that are already present in this world" (*LG* 44c).

Citing Saint Thomas and Saint Bonaventure in a footnote, *Lumen gentium* (*LG* 44b) points out the duty of religious to seek the sanctity of God's people: "By the charity to which they lead, the evangelical counsels in a special way unite those who make profession of them with the church and its mystery. Consequently, the spiritual life of these persons must be dedicated to the good of the whole church."

Earlier ecclesiastical writings took a more juridic approach to the vows. In 1279 Pope Nicholas stated in *Exiit qui seminat* that the friars are bound by vow "to observe those things as evangelical counsels which are expressed in the rule itself as precepts or prohibitions or under equipollent words."[18] The law stipulated particular things that ought or ought not to be done. In 1312 Pope Clement V clarified these for the Friars Minor in the declaration *Exivi de paradiso*: "Friars are not only obliged merely and absolutely to those three vows ratified by the profession of their rule [namely, to live in obedience, in chastity, and without property], but they are bound even to fulfill all those [other regulations], pertaining to the aforesaid three, which are proposed by the Rule itself" (no. 4).

In 1324 Pope John XXII in *Quia quorundam* reconfirmed previous papal judgments concerning the vows.[19] Even in these early documents, the profession of and perseverance in the three vows were fundamental. The Church also recognized distinct characteristics of various religious orders encapsulated in vows such as the vow of stability in the Benedictine tradition. In 1563 the Council of Trent, in its twenty-fifth session, "On Regulars and Nuns," expanded papal pronouncements regarding vows for particular religious orders to include all religious: "that all regulars both men and women should order and arrange their lives according to the provision of the rule they profess; and that above all they should faithfully observe what belongs to the perfection of their profession, such as the vows of obedience, poverty and chastity, and any other special [vows and] precepts particular to any rule or order which belong to their essential nature."[20] The essential link between the evangelical counsels and the perfection of one's state was well articulated by the Church four hundred years before the Second Vatican Council.

In 1847 Pope Pius IX promulgated the encyclical *Ubi primum*, which was addressed to the superiors of all men's regular orders. He appealed to religious "to fulfill their vows" (no. 7). This document contains a magisterial appeal to interior renewal and conversion of religious (no. 4), which suggests that some deterioration may have begun. In 1900 in *Au milieu des consolations*, Pope Leo XIII defended "the sublime evangelical counsels" (495) when the civil government in France threatened them. Calling vows "sacred things and the sources of the rarest virtue" (496), he identified their double purpose in elevating those who take them to a higher degree of perfection and preparing them for apostolic work for broader society.

Conditae a Christo, an apostolic constitution promulgated by Pope Leo XIII in 1900, recognized nonclerical active religious institutes.[21] Until 1900, although nonclerical active religious institutes were tolerated, ecclesiastical pronouncements formally recognized solely the enclosed communities of men and women religious, as well as active clerical religious institutes. The norms following *Conditae a Christo* were promulgated by the Sacred Congregation for Bishops and Regulars[22] and provided that the superior accept religious vows "in the name of the institute."[23] As religious institutes were perceived to be personal means of sanctification approved by the Church, the relationship between members and a religious superior was by agreement, perhaps even contractual in nature. The members submitted to the authority of the superior and the superior, in turn, received the members' vows.

The 1917 *Code of Canon Law* described the authority of a nonclerical religious superior as *dominative power* (canon 501) over their subjects, which could be likened to parental authority.[24] The code distinguished the effects of solemn and simple vows. Solemn vows, pronounced by enclosed religious, provided that any acts to the contrary were invalid. Simple vows, pronounced by members of active women's religious congregations and by the extern members of contemplative communities, bound less strictly. Acts contrary to the simple vows were unlawful or illicit but not invalid unless the constitutions expressly stated to the contrary (canon 579). While each member of a religious institute was bound to faithfully observe the vows, rules, and constitutions and to tend toward the state of perfection (canon 593), simple vows retained a quality of incompleteness. In fact, the profession of simple vows did not provide for a full gift of self, as is apparent in the vow of poverty described below. Nevertheless, in contrast to the norms following *Conditae a Christo*, canon 1308 introduced the term "public vows," in which the vows were accepted by the legitimate superior "in the name of the Church" and signaled an evolving consciousness of religious life's ecclesial importance.

In 1964 Pope Paul VI, in *Magno gaudio affecti*, an address to the General Chapters of Religious Orders and Congregations, reaffirmed the central place of vows for religious: "Religious life...which receives its proper character from profession of the evangelical vows, is a perfect way of living according to the example and teaching of Jesus Christ.... The profession of the evangelical vows is a super-addition to that consecration which is proper to baptism.... The vows of religion must be held in the highest esteem, and the greatest importance must be placed on their function and practice."[25]

This defense of vows illustrates the dramatic challenges that religious faced during and after the Second Vatican Council. A controversy existed regarding the taking of temporary vows, with the suggestion that, since vows should be forever, these would be promises.[26] The possibility of religious not taking vows was not introduced by either *Lumen gentium* or *Perfectae caritatis* and in fact runs counter to the expressed significance of vows:

> Through the gospel counsels and their perfect practice, God calls many, with many different graces, to dedicate themselves more especially to the Lord. They follow Christ. Chaste and poor (see Mt 8:20; Lk 9:58), he redeemed humanity and made it holy by obedience, even unto death on a cross (see Ph 2:8). Fired by that love with which the holy Spirit fills their hearts (see Rom 5:5), they live ever more intensely for Christ and the church, his body (see Col 1:24). The quality of their loving identification with Christ in a complete gift of self, embracing the whole of life, is the measure of the richness of the church's life and the remarkable creativity of its mission. (*PC* 1c)

Lumen gentium and *Perfectae caritatis* recognized a public vow as more than simply a self-donation for individual sanctification; it includes a full self-offering or holocaust within a divine vocation for the sake of the Church. The phrase "embracing the whole of life" overcomes a prior understanding of simple vows that was incomplete or did not pertain to the full gift of the person. *Perfectae caritatis* adds: "Active, apostolic charity is integral to the character of such religious bodies; they perform their characteristic work of charity in the name of the church which entrusts it to them" (*PC* 8).[27]

Ecclesiae Sanctae II, promulgated in 1966, stated norms for implementing *Perfectae caritatis* and included the following sentence: "Experimentations in things against the general law, a matter to be done with prudence, will be gladly permitted by the Holy See as opportunity warrants."[28] In retrospect, certain experiments undertaken by religious institutes changed, quickly or within turmoil, the core way of living. This change reaped increasing unrest among the members. The period from immediately after the the Second Vatican Council through the promulgation of the new Code (1983) demonstrates the need of religious superiors, members of general chapters, and their advisers to be properly educated in ecclesiology and the theology of religious life.[29]

After this discussion of the relation of vows to religious life in general, we turn now to the history of each vow in ecclesial documents.

Vow of Chastity

Using the classic description of chastity as freeing one to dedicate oneself with an undivided heart, in *Perfectae caritatis* this vow is immediately linked to "God's service [*servitio divino*] and apostolic work" (PC 12a).

Earlier ecclesial writings on chastity dealt with difficulties by stating and restating fundamental principles. For example, during the First Lateran Council, canon 21 stated, "We absolutely forbid . . . monks to have concubines or to contract marriages," and canon 14 of the Fourth Lateran Council decreed that clerics especially should "live chastely and virtuously."

In 1226 the bull of Pope Honorius III, *Solet annuere*, stated that "The Rule of the Friars Minor is this, namely, to observe the Holy Gospel of Our Lord Jesus Christ, by living in obedience without anything of our own, and in chastity" (no. 1). Pope Clement V in 1312 (no. 4) and Pope John XXII in 1324 (no. 3) repeated this formula verbatim. Under the 1917 code, the distinction between solemn and simple vows pertained to the vow of chastity. It invalidated an attempted marriage for one in solemn vows but pronounced a marriage illicit but valid for one in simple vows.

In 1950 Pope Pius XII in *Sponsa Christi* expressed the Church's "maternal solicitude especially for those virgins who, choosing the better part, completely abandoned the world and embraced in its fullness, in monasteries, perfect Christian life, adding to the profession of virginity, strict poverty and total obedience" (nos. 19–20).[30] He noted as well that the Church protected their lives by prudence and by laws of the most severe enclosure. At the same time, there was a change in the sequence of the vows, with chastity or virginity now given the primary place, followed by poverty and obedience.[31]

In 1951 Pope Pius XII, in *Counsel to Teaching Sisters*, expressed the importance of the vow of chastity for members of active religious institutes: "Chastity and virginity (which imply also the inner renunciation of all sensual affection) do not estrange souls from this world. They rather awaken and develop the energies needed for wider and higher offices beyond the limits of individual families."[32] In 1964 Pope Paul VI, in his address *On Religious Life*, demonstrated how the teachings of the Church have evolved from a protective and perhaps pragmatic description of chastity to one more enhanced with theological content, yet consistent with prior descriptions: "Finally, religious must preserve *chastity* as a treasured gem. Everyone knows that in the present condition of human society the practice of perfect chastity is made difficult, not only by a depraved moral atmosphere but also by a false teaching which poisons souls by overemphasis on nature. An awareness of these facts should impel religious to stir up their faith more energetically—that same faith by which we believe the declarations of Christ when He proclaims the supernatural value of chastity that is sought for the sake of the kingdom of heaven."[33]

Religious are called to be inflamed with love for God and others and therefore to recall to "the minds of the faithful that wonderful marriage decreed by God and which is to be fully revealed in the future age in which the Church takes Christ as its only spouse" (*PC* 12a). *Lumen gentium* adds that the counsels "willingly undertaken in accordance with the personal vocation of each individual, contribute not a little to the purification of heart and to spiritual freedom; they keep ablaze continuously the fervour of charity, and, as is confirmed by the example of so many holy founders, are able to bring the Christian into greater conformity with that kind of virginal and poor life which Christ the lord chose for himself and which his virgin mother embraced" (*LG* 46b).

Implied within the depiction of chastity is the reminder that not only does one promise God a sacrifice or an oblation of the entire self but also that vows mold the consecrated individual in likeness to Christ. Public vows express for all time both God's love and the religious's response of love for God: "Religious chastity demonstrates to all Christian people an astonishing alliance, initiated by God himself, to be completed in the world to come, when the church has Christ alone for consort" (*PC* 12a).

Vow of Poverty

Again the earlier Church documents began with corrections, such as in 1170 in the Third Lateran Council, whose canon 10 provides, "Monks are not to be received in a monastery for money nor are they allowed money of their own."[34] The earliest papal documents on the rules of the Friars Minor emphasized the meaning of their vow of poverty. Pope Honorious (1226) and Pope Clement V (1312) used phrases such as "without anything of our own" and "without property" and forbade alms boxes and inheritances. "Friars however can acquire nothing for themselves in particular, or for their Order, even in common."[35]

Early magisterial documents focused almost entirely on the exact meaning of the vow of poverty, specifically for Franciscan friars. Appealing to his predecessors Pope Gregory IX and others, Pope Nicholas III, in *Exiit qui seminat*, wrote, "This [poverty] ought to be observed not only individually but also in common" (no. 7). Making a distinction between *ius domini* and *usus facti*, Pope Nicholas specified guidelines for the use of books, clothing, other moveable goods, and money. The guidelines also pertain to association with benefactors, contents of last testaments, and the requirement of labor (nos. 8–16). Pope

John XXII continued to shed light on the significance of this vow for the Friars Minor and reasserted previous papal teachings about poverty (no. 4).

In 1563 the Council of Trent qualified that the strict Franciscan poverty was appropriate for other kinds of religious: "No regular, therefore, whether man or woman, may possess or keep immovable or movable goods of whatever value or however acquired. . . . Superiors may, however, permit them the use of movable goods to a degree that befits the lowly state of poverty they have professed, and while there should be nothing superfluous in this, nor should anything necessary be denied them" (Twenty-fifth Session, Decree on Regulars and Nuns, II, Tanner, I, 775–77).

In 1679 Pope Innocent XI again addressed the practical aspects of their vow of poverty for Friars Minor in *Sollicitudo pastorali*, where he stated that the observation of the rule and the manner in which poverty was to be expressed was an obligation of conscience for each member.[36] In 1900 Pope Leo XIII defended in *Au milieu des consolations* the meaning of religious poverty in a context of civil unrest in France: "There is no need to give any more importance to the other reproach that is made against the congregations, of being too rich. Even if we admit that the value set upon their property is not exaggerated there is no contesting that they are in honorable and legal possession, and consequently to despoil them would be an attack upon the rights of property. It is, moreover, necessary to remark that they possess nothing for their personal interest or for the good of their individual members, but for works of religion, charity, and beneficence" (I, 8–9, *AAS* 33: 361).

Under the 1917 *Code of Canon Law*, those in solemn vows would have no capacity to own unless their constitutions stated otherwise (canon 580), although those who professed simple vows would keep the ownership of property (*usus domini*) but cede administration to another (canon 569). The right to receive additional property would be retained; only after death could a religious in simple vows give away this property. In effect, this meant that sisters in active religious institutes could not renounce ownership of goods. Should the sister later leave the institute, she would recover complete control of her property (canon 580) and of her dowry (canon 551). Therefore, there was a hypothetical quality of poverty for those in simple vows; in fact, they had access to none of their own property, but they could reobtain full access if they chose to leave the religious community.

At the beginning of the twentieth century, the Church began to unfold the significant interior dynamism of the vow of poverty by comparing it with the material poverty of the poor in the world. In 1926 Pope Pius XI elaborated an interior spirituality of poverty in his encyclical on Saint Francis of Assisi, *Rite expiatis*, within the historical context of Marxism and the Russian Revolution of 1917. Pope Pius XI compassionately depicted forced poverty: "Sad indeed was the fate of common people, while between lords and vassals, between the greater and the lesser, as they were called, between the owners of land and the peasants existed relations in every sense of the word foreign to the spirit of humanity. . . . Those who did not belong to that most unfortunate class of human beings, the proletariat, allowed themselves to be overcome by egotism and greed for possessions and were driven by an insatiable desire for riches.... They looked on poverty and the poor as something vile."[37]

In contrast to forced poverty, he referred to Saint Francis's vow of poverty in assisting in "the reformation of society" (no. 12) and springing from his "love of evangelical poverty [no. 13]... which consists in the voluntary renunciation of every possession for reasons of love and through divine inspiration, and which is quite the opposite of that forced and unlovable poverty preached by some ancient philosophers" (no. 15).

Compassion for those who are impoverished links religious life to the good of society. In 1964 Pope Paul VI exhorted in his address *On Religious Life*: "There must also be inculcated a love of *poverty*, about which there is a great deal of discussion in the Church today. Religious must surpass all others by their example of true evangelical poverty. Therefore, they must love that poverty to which they have spontaneously committed themselves" (700). In addition to this analysis of the interior disposition of a religious with respect to poverty, Pope Paul VI hints at the opposite reality, namely, that if poverty is not practiced, something dies inside the religious. "Let religious of their own will be content with the things that are needed for properly fulfilling their way of life, shunning those little extras and luxuries which weaken the religious life" (ibid.).

Not only should the religious purify their lives, but the religious institutes should also "avoid excessive ornamentation in their buildings and elaborate functions, as well as anything else that savors of luxury, always bearing in mind the social conditions of the people among whom they live" (ibid.). In this context he also mentions the needs of the worldwide community.

Beginning with a classic description of poverty as an expression of the following of Christ's example, *Perfectae caritatis* adds the deeper obligation that members be poor in fact *and* in spirit (*PC* 13a). In the context of poverty, members were enjoined to banish or expel all undue solicitude and trust themselves to the provident care of God the Father (*PC* 13b). Thus, there is an interior surrendering of oneself and the additional opportunity to change constitutions to permit members to renounce inheritances (*PC* 13d). This marks a change from the prohibition in the 1917 *Code of Canon Law* of the alienation of inheritances by those who professed simple vows and in continuity with the Church's growing awareness of evangelical poverty, in which a religious renounces personal ownership of all goods.

Vow of Obedience

Concern for the good of each monk was the basis of canon 12 of the Fourth Lateran Council (1215): "For just as we wish the rights of superiors to be upheld so we do not wish to support wrongs done to subjects" (Tanner, 241). In the bull of 1226 Pope Honorius III referred to obedience twice. His second mention amplified its meaning for Franciscan friars: "Having truly finished the year of probation, let them be received to obedience, promising to observe always this very life and rule. And in no manner will it be licit to them to leave this [form of] religious life, according to the command of the lord pope, since according to the Holy Gospel, 'no one putting hand to the plow and turning back is fit for the Kingdom of God' " (ch. 2).

In 1312 Clement V summoned the Friars Minor "to observe the Holy Gospel of Our Lord Jesus Christ by living in obedience" (no. 4). Then, in 1563 the Council of Trent in session 25 reaffirmed for regulars and nuns "that they should faithfully observe whatsoever belongs to the perfection of their professions, such as the vows of obedience" (ch. 1).

The 1917 *Code of Canon Law* described the authority of a nonclerical religious superior as dominative power (c. 501). There was no further magisterial discussion of the vow of obedience until Pope Pius XII, who, in *Sponsa Christi* (1950), advised hermits and monastic nuns (cenobites) to "strengthen their state ... by a most strict obedience."[38] In 1951 Pope Pius XII told teaching sisters that for apostolic work "your religious vocation is a powerful ally ... [through] the vow, not only of chastity, but especially that of obedience ... always supposing, of course, that you live up to your vocation" (256).

Up to and during the Second Vatican Council some religious communities experienced either a too broad assertion of dominative power or a too weak conformist living of obedience instead of the sought-for mature and grace-filled imitation of Jesus' obedience to the will of his Father. As a result, during the renewal the council called for, some of these religious dismissed authority altogether in their confusing of accidental with essential.[39] Some religious communities even began to question whether any or all of the vows should remain in religious life. Other religious understood that the vows are essential to religious life, but they considered magisterial teachings in the context of merely one opinion alongside others. Our consideration of Church teaching emphasizes both their fundamental place in religious life and developments in their meaning.

During this same time frame one of the factors that pertained to a developing crisis in living out religious obedience involved the promotion of degree-granting programs for sisters in the United States. In 1949 more than forty states were actively working to upgrade their teaching standards to fulfill the requirements of the National Educational Association (NEA). The National Catholic Education Association (NCEA) began to seriously consider how to do the same for Catholic schools. Some religious institutes preferred to have their members immediately obtain a four-year degree before teaching. However, the majority of institutes inserted their members into teaching experience first and then followed this with summer programs that led to a college degree, perhaps over a twenty-year period.[40]

In 1951 the NCEA passed a resolution that a four-year degree program was needed for both elementary and high-school teachers. In 1952 a survey of 255 women's religious communities demonstrated that most did not provide adequate education as preparation for their teaching sisters, according to NEA standards for accreditation. In 1954 the Sister Formation Conference (SFC) was approved as a standing committee of the NCEA. While this committee had a significant impact on religious communities, its directors were not major superiors, so the lines of obedience began to blur and at times conflicted.

Some of the religious institutes could not afford the costs of higher education for so many members,[41] nor could they release their members for education without cutting back radically on the number of schools they served. In addition, major superiors were concerned about the impact this would have on their own mentoring programs, on the institutes' common life when universities were at a distance, and on the overall formation program. The SFC had increasing influence on the governance of religious institutes even though the major superiors did not direct the SFC. The SFC even fostered the education of sisters in secular and ecumenical environments—a radically new experience for many sisters.

In 1957 hints of difficulties in following the vow of obedience were more pronounced in Pius XII's address *Sous la maternelle* (The States of Perfection).[42] Setting forth principles, he carefully wove a linkage between mistreatment by superiors and harmful acts by the members of religious institutes. For example:

> Subjects will observe, furthermore, that religious discipline, which prohibits them from arrogating to themselves what is invested in the competency of superiors, and from undertaking on their own initiative changes which they cannot attempt without the authorization of their superiors. (*The Pope Speaks*, 2, 267)

> The major superiors cannot decide it [the spirit of their community] according to their taste or their impression, even in all good faith and sincerity.... But where he is not the founder, he should have recourse to the idea of the founder as it is expressed in the constitutions approved by the Church. It is not sufficient for him, then, to have a subjective conviction, even one supported by an isolated passage from the constitutions. (ibid., 268)

Pope Pius XII attempted to go to the roots of these struggles by addressing the meaning of conscience, the evolution of the human personality, and the role of sound education associated with the proper practice of the vow of obedience. His aim was to overcome the charges of "hindering maturing of...personality" and "feeling of sadness. He countered the argument that dependence of religious on their superiors "is opposed to the supreme and direct dominion of God over the conscience."[43] Religious authority, described in the past as analogous to the relationship of a parent to a child, was modified. Pope Pius XII subtly directed the concept of vows beyond an individual contract that the Church closely monitored and that the consecrated person could withdraw even after perpetual vows. Then Pope Pius XII prepared the way for the Church's development of a balanced spirituality for complete sacrifice of the will offered to God by all religious: "The superior can command only in the name of the Lord and in virtue of the powers of his charge; and the subject should obey only through love of Christ and not for human motives of utility or propriety, still less through pure compulsion. In this way, he will preserve, in the most complete submission, the joyous eagerness of one who ratifies, by the concrete acts of each day, the total gift of himself to his one and only Master" (*The Pope Speaks*, 2, 270).

On May 23, 1964, Pope Paul VI, in his address *Magno gaudio affecti* to the General Chapters of Religious Orders, reasserted and strengthened Pius XII's teaching: "Accordingly, religious should cultivate *obedience* with the greatest diligence. This is and must remain a holocaust of one's own will which is offered to God. A religious makes this sacrifice of self by humble submission to lawful superiors, whose authority, of course, should always be exercised within the limits of charity and with due respect for the dignity of the human person, even though nowadays religious have to undertake many more burdensome offices and carry out their duties more quickly and more willingly" (700).

The "holocaust of one's own will" forecloses the concept of a partial self-offering or contract between the consecrated religious and the superior. *Perfectae caritatis* describes a full and permanent surrender of one's will as an oblation to God in which members subject themselves to their superiors, who hold the place of God: "Religious trust and court God's will; they obey their superiors, therefore, in humility and under the direction of constitutions and rules. They surrender their minds and hearts, their gifts of nature and grace in doing what they are told, in living a life under obedience. They realize the exercise of obedience develops the body of Christ in accordance with God's plan" (no. 14b).

Members "entrust their lives to superiors, led by the Spirit to find God's authority in them" (no. 14a). Superiors are admonished to recall that their exercise of office is to be responsive to God's will in the spirit of service (no. 14c). This terminology defeats the concept of dominative power. This is not the language of the family but an implicit recognition of the dignity and maturity of the gift of obedience, which emulates the obedience of our Lord Jesus Christ to the Father.

Communion in Community

"Common life," the living together of members with a religious superior in prayer and fraternal life, provides the foundation for communion in community. In 1226 Pope Honorius wrote eloquently of common life in *Solet annuere*: "And wherever the friars are and find themselves, let them mutually show themselves to be members of the same household. And let them without fear manifest to one another their own necessities, since, if a mother nourishes and loves her own son according to the flesh, how much more diligently should he ought to love and nourish his own spiritual brother?" (ch. 6).

The Council of Trent supported common life for religious when it restated the essential character of each rule or order: "Above all they should faithfully observe what belongs to the perfection of their profession . . . and any other special precepts particular to any rule or order which belong to their essential nature and to the preservation of common life, food, and clothing" (Tanner, ch. 1, 776). The Council of Trent determined that "Those sent to study at universities should live only in religious houses" (ibid., ch. 4, 777).

In 1679 living the common life became a prerequisite for being chosen as a religious prelate or superior. Pope Innocent XI in *Sollicitudo pastoralis* contrasted the lifestyle of one who does not attend to life in common: "defective in attending the community choir, refectory, and other places, as is prescribed in his constitutions . . . who in all the aforementioned things does not follow the common life" (2). These early descriptions of community life have a similar thread: They express the benefit of an interdependence and instructed on the worth of life among the members. Only with a full common life would the vows, especially that of obedience, be fully effective, as compared to a hypothetical or partial commitment by one who chooses a living situation based on a variety of factors.

In 1901 Pope Leo XIII defended the common life of religious in Portugal when he objected to "religious forcefully removed from their domiciles."[44] In 1923 Pope Pius XI noted in *Studiorum ducem* the humility of Thomas Aquinas: "How submissively he obeyed a lay brother in the course of their communal life."[45] In 1947 Pope Pius XII mentioned in *Fulgens radiator* that "The community life of a Benedictine house tempered and softened the severities of the solitary life . . . through prayer, work and application to sacred and profane sciences, a blessed peace knows not idleness or sloth."[46] In 1950 Pope Pius XII in *Sponsa Christi* summarized the early years of Christianity for consecrated virgins "united together in order to live a common life separate from the company of men . . . [and thereby] avoided the grave dangers of corrupt Roman society" (no. 17, our translation). He added that the Church required a common life of monastic nuns. While Pope Pius XII accented the safety or security from danger that common life provided, it would be unwarranted to believe that protection was the sole rationale for this way of life. Ecclesial writings linked monastic life to fraternal support and peacefulness of life.

In *Perfectae caritatis* are these words: "Religious are members of one another in Christ; they should vie with one another in ceding status" (no. 15a). Superiors were requested to make it easier for members to subordinate their wills by respect of their human dignity. Superiors are "to so lead their communities that a vital, conscientious obedience creates partnership in initiating and maintaining apostolic work" (*PC* 14c). Moreover, the decree states that "The quality of their loving identification with Christ in a complete gift of self, embracing the whole of life, is the measure of the richness of the Church's life and the remarkable creativity of its mission" (*PC* 1c). The fervent expression of religious life is acknowledged as a purifying element in the Church. The Church also saw the example of ecclesial communion within religious life as best depicted by one class rather than two separate classes such as choir sisters and extern sisters in institutes of women (*PC* 15b).

The little that was directly said about common life during the Second Vatican Council did not imply that the Church's previous claims should be ignored or that living in common was accidental to religious life. Subsequent documents verified the essential place of common life: *Religious and Human Promotion* (1978) asked religious to become "experts in communion";[47] *Essential Elements of the Church's Teaching on Religious Life* (1983) reasserted that "Religious should live in their own religious house, observing a common life" (II, no. 12); *Fraternal Life in Community* (1994) repeated the earlier call to religious to become "experts in communion" and added a clear mandate to live together in common;[48] and Pope John Paul II's postsynodal apostolic exhortation *Vita consecrata* (1996) directly linked the call of religious to become a living sign of communion with the teachings of Vatican II: "A great task also belongs to the consecrated life in the light of the teaching about the Church as communion, so strongly proposed by the Second Vatican Council. Consecrated persons are asked to be true experts of communion and to practice the spirituality of communion."[49]

Conclusion

After considering the needs of the Universal Church and of particular dioceses, each religious institute was to adapt apostolic works to the requirements of the time and to abandon those works "less in accord with the present character and genius of their foundation" (*PC* 20a). *Perfectae caritatis* provided specific suggestions to religious institutes. The manner of living, praying, and working were to be accommodated to modern physical and psychological circumstances, as required by the nature of each institute (*PC* 3), to the necessities of the apostolate and other factors. By the time *Perfectae caritatis* was promulgated, substantial changes were already occurring in religious institutes, especially those dedicated to apostolic works of the Church.

What happened after the council? One cannot restrict the Church's articulation of the significance of religious life to 1965, but there was a noted pause after *Ecclesiae Sanctae II* (1966), which was to guide religious communities during the time of trial and experimentation. Once begun, these experiments became difficult to monitor and assess. The Sacred Congregation for Religious and Secular Institutes, in anticipation of the promulgation of a revised *Code of Canon Law*, issued a series of interim norms that were to assist in the renewal. These norms addressed specific topics but could not capture the massive alterations occurring throughout the world.

In many ways, the continuity of the Church's teaching about religious life can be seen within the context of the continuity of her understanding of the human person. Nevertheless, religious life was unsettled at that time, and massive numbers of departures took place. Could it be that the words of stability could not be heard by some of these persons? Yet, those who heard the precious gift of stability in Church teaching about essentials renewed their religious life with energy and joy and thereby fulfilled the deep call of Vatican Council II.

NOTES

1. We are grateful to Michael Woodward, director of the Vehr Theological Library, for his generous help in locating magisterial documents and translations of some Latin passages and to Sister Mary Nika Schaumber, R.S.M, J.C.D., for suggestions for revision.

2. *Lumen gentium* 47, *Decrees of the Ecumenical Councils*, vol. 2, ed. Norman P. Tanner, S.J., English ed. (Washington, D.C.: Georgetown Press, 1990), 887.

3. *Perfectae caritatis*, in Tanner, *Decrees of the Ecumenical Councils*, 939–47.

4. Pope Pius XII, apostolic constitution *Provida Mater Ecclesia* (On the Canonical States and on Secular Institutes for Acquiring Christian Perfection) (Feb. 2, 1947), *AAS* 39 (1947): 114–24, no. 7, http://www.vatican.va/holy_father/pius_xii/apost_constitutions/documents/hf_p-xii_apc_1.

5. The Sacred Congregation for Religious and for Secular Institutes, *Essential Elements in the Church's Teaching on Religious Life as Applied to Institutes Dedicated to Works of the Apostolate* (Boston: Daughters of St. Paul, 1983).

6. Council documents reviewed include those of the First Lateran Council, ninth ecumenical council (1123); Second Lateran Council, tenth ecumenical council (1139); Third Lateran Council, eleventh ecumenical council (1179); Fourth Lateran Council, twelfth ecumenical council (1215); Fifth Lateran Council, eighteenth ecumenical council (1512–1563); and the Council of Trent (1545–1563), twenty-fifth session, "On Regulars and Nuns."

7. Papal documents reviewed include those of Pope Honorious III, *Solet annuere*, "On the Rules of the Friars Minor" (1226); Pope Nicholas III, *Exiit qui seminat*, "On the Rules of the Friars Minor" (1279); Pope Clement V, *Exivi de paradiso*, "On the Rules of the Friars Minor" (1312); Pope John XXII, *Quia quorundam*, "On the Rules of the Friars Minor" (1324); Pope Innocent XI, *Sollicitudo pastoralis*, "Fostering and Preserving the Orders of Men Religious" (1679); Pope Pius IX, *Ubi primum*, "On Discipline for Religious" (1847); *Cum nuper*, "On Care for Clerics" (1858); Pope Leo XIII, *Conditae a Christo* (1900); *Au milieu*, "On Religious Congregations in France" (1900–1901); *Gravissimas*, "On Religious Orders in Portugal" (1901); Pope Pius X, *Code of Canon Law* (1917); Pope Pius XI, *Rerum omnium perturbationem*, "On St. Francis de Sales" (1923); *Studiorum ducem*, "On Thomas Aquinas" (1923); *Rite expiatis*, "On St. Francis of Assisi" (1926); Pope Pius XII, *Provida Mater Ecclesia*, "Concerning Secular Institutes" (1947); *Fulgens radiatur*, "Brilliant Light of St. Benedict" (1947); Pope Pius XII, *Sponsa Christi*, "Spouse of Christ" (1950); *Ci torna*, "Counsel to Teaching Sisters" (1951); *Sacra virginitas*, "On Holy Virginity" (1954); *Sedes sapientae*, "On Religious Formation" (1956); *Sous la maternelle*, "The States of Perfection" (1957) ; Pope Paul VI, *Magno gaudio affecti*, "On Religious Life" (1964); *Motu proprio Ecclesiae sanctae II* (1966).

8. Documents and decrees of the Sacred Congregation for Religious and Secular Institutes reviewed include *motu proprio primo feliciter* (1948); instruction *Cum sanctissimus* (1948); instruction *Inter praeclara* (1950); instruction *Inter coetera* (1956); *Salutaris atque* (1956).

9. The seven other essential elements are evangelical mission, apostolate, and identity; prayer; asceticism; public witness; formation; government; and Mary as model.

10. First Lateran Council, decree 16, in Tanner, *Decrees of the Ecumenical Councils*, vol. 1, 193.

11. Fourth Lateran Council, canon 12, in Tanner, *Decrees of the Ecumenical Councils*, vol. 1, 2412, A second translation of this same passage by H. J. Schoreder, O.P., reads: "Strive to reform the monasteries subject to them," in *Disciplinary Decrees of the General Councils: Text, Translation, and Commentary* (St. Louis: Herder, 1937), 254.

12. Pope Honorius III, *Solet annuere:* "On the Rule of the Friars Minor" (Nov. 29, 1223), introduction and ch. 12, *Bullarum diplomatum et privilegiorum sanctorum romanorum pontificum,* vol. 3 (Luigi Tomassetti and Francesco Gaude, 1858), English translation from the Franciscan Archive, http://www.papalencyclicals.net/Hono3/regula-e .htm.

13. Pope Clement V, *Exivi de paradiso* (May 6, 1312), in *Bullarium franciscanum* V, ed. Johanne Hyacinthe Sbaralea (Rome: n.p., 1759–1768), 195; *Seraphicae legislationis textus originales* (Ad Claras Aquas [Quaracchi], Florence: Collegium S. Bonaventurae, 1897), 229–60; "On the Rule of the Friars Minor," no 2, http://www.franciscan-archive .org/bullarium/exivi-e.html. English translation from the Franciscan Archive from the Latin text in *Annales minorum* of L. Wadding, vol. 6, 202–11.

14. Pope Pius IX, *Ubi primum* (June 17, 1847), no. 1, *Acta Pii IX,* I 1: 46–54; "On Discipline for Religious," English text, *The Papal Encyclicals: 1740–1878,* vol. 1, ed. Claudia Carlen, I.H.M. (Raleigh: McGrath, 1981), 287.

15. Pope Leo XIII, *Au milieu des consolations* (Dec. 23, 1900); *Codicis iuris canonici pontes,* vol. 3, *Romani pontifices,* ed. Petri Card. Gasparri (Rome: Typis Polyglottis Vaticanis, 1933), no. 645, or *ASS* 33: 355–63, *Acta Leonis XIII,* 20: 337–51; English text, John J. Wynne, ed., "The Religious Congregations in France: Letter from the Pope to the Archbishop of Paris, December 23, 1900," in *The Great Encyclical Letters of Pope Leo XIII,* trans. from approved sources (New York: Benzinger Brothers, 1903), 501.

16. Saint Thomas Aquinas, *Summa theologica,* trans. Fathers of the English Dominican Province (Westminister, Md.: 1948), II–II, q. 183, a. 2. See also Janusz A. Ihnatowicz, "Consecrated Life in the Ecclesiology of Vatican II," *Faith and Reason* 17 (1991): 167–87, here referring to Saint Thomas: "And thus without an adequate vision of the consecrated life, the whole people of God, priest, religious, laity, will be poorer in the understanding of the Church and of their own vocation" (167–68).

17. See, for example, Aquinas, *ST,* II–II, q. 184, a. 3, where he gives the examples of marriage and worldly business as hindering (but not opposing) the act of charity.

18. Pope Nicholas III, *Exiit qui seminat* (Aug. 14, 1279), 6, Mansi Conc. XXIV, 946, 2, Augustus Potthast, *Requesta pontificum romanorum* (Berlin: Akademische Cruck-U. Verlagsanstalt, 1957), vol. 2, 1746. English text, "He Who Sows," available from the Franciscan Archive, 2, http://www.papalencyclicals.net/Nicholo3/exiit-e.htm. Translated from the Registers of Nicholas III, 232–42, no. 564.

19. Pope John XXII, *Quia quorundam* (Nov. 10, 1324), 3; *CIC* 2.4.5: Extravagantes, *Codex iuris canonicis,* vol. 2, tit. 4, cap. 5 (Leipzig, 1881), pp. 1230–36, http://www .papalencyclicals.net/John22/qquor-e.htm. English text from the Franciscan Archives.

20. *Documents of the Council of Trent,* "The Twenty-fifth Session" (December 1563), ch. 1; Tanner, *Decrees of the Ecumenical Councils,* vol. 2, 776. Tanner's translation from the Latin of *"ordinis peculiaria vota et praecepta"* as "special precepts particular to" leaves out the force of the vows. Another English translation, available at http://www .catholic-forum.com/saints/trentoo.htm, keeps the meaning by the phrase "other vows and precepts that may be peculiar to."

21. Pope Leo XIII, apostolic constitution *Conditae a Christo* (Dec. 8, 1900); *Acta Leonis XIII,* 20: 317–27; *ASS* 33: 341–47. Gasparri, *Codicis iuris canonici fontes* 3 (1933): no. 644, 562–66.

22. Sacred Congregation for Bishops and Regulars, *Normae secundum quas sacra congregatio episcoporum et regularium procedere solet in approbandis novis institutis votorum simplicium* (June 28, 1901), in T. Schaefer, *De religiosis ad normam codicis iuris canonici,* 4d cd. (Rome: Typis Polyglottis Vaticanis, 1947), 1102–35.

23. Ibid., *Sectio altera, schema constitutionum,* pars prima, cap. VIII, nos. 101, 1113.

24. *Codex juris canonici: The 1917 or Pio-Benedictine Code of Canon Law*, ed. Edward N. Peters (San Francisco: Ignatius Press, 2001).

25. Pope Paul VI, *Magno gaudio affecti* (May 23, 1964); *AAS* 56 (1964): 565–71; English text, *On Religious Life*, address to the General Chapters of Religious Orders and Congregations meeting in Rome, *Review for Religious* 23 (November 1964), 698–704, esp. 699–700. A different translation of the phrase "function and practice" from the Latin *"usui et exercitationi"* (Acta Pauli Pp. VI, *Commentarium officiale, AAS* 567, http://www.papalencyclicals.net/Paulo6/p6relig.htm) reads "to their religious foundation and practice."

26. "Replace temporary vows with bonds of some other kind" was recommended by the Congregation for Religious and Secular Institutes, *Renovationis causam* (Jan. 6, 1969), *AAS* 61 (1969): 103–20 (*RC*, I, no. 2). This bond or promise during a time of "public service" would be made to the institute but not to God. See E. L. Heston, "Temporary Vows and Promises," *Review for Religious* 28 (1969): 376–77. See a summary and critique of these developments by Sister M. Nika Schaumber, R.S.M., *The Evolution of the Power of Jurisdiction of the Lay Religious Superior in the Ecclesial Documents of the Twentieth Century* (J.C.D. diss., Santa Croce Pontifical University, 2003), 134. *Renovationis causam* spoke only about temporary vows. The controversy of temporary commitment was settled in 1983 in the *Code of Canon Law* by the reintroduction of temporary vows.

27. The Latin text states: "In istis institutis, ad ipsum naturam vitae relgiosae pertinet actio apostolica et benefica utpote sanctum ministerium et opus caritatis proprium ab ecclesia ipsis commissum eiusque nomine exercendum." The English text misses the description of sacred ministry. See Ihnatowicz, "Consecrated Life in the Ecclesiology of Vatican II," note 11, which states that "The council's careful use of 'ministerial' language should be noted. Vatican II used *ministerium* as a synonym of *officium* to denote a service where, if not ordination, at least official delegation is necessary. For other kinds of service in the Church, *ministratio* is preferred (ten times in various documents)."

28. Pope Paul VI, *Ecclesiae sanctae II* (Aug. 6, 1966), *AAS* 58 (1966): 757–87, II, I, 6a. English text *"Motu proprio* Implementing Four Council Decrees" (Aug. 6, 1966), *Review for Religious* 25 (1966): 958.

29. Did religious institutes have sufficient theological and canonical resources available to its members to comprehend the ecclesiological significance of the members' vocations and of the institutes themselves? Institutes at times became embroiled in changing constitutions, governance structures, apostolic works, and even community life, perhaps to the detriment of interior rejuvenation of the institutes' original charisms. In some instances, the suggestions of clerical and secular advisors, while well intentioned, may have distracted religious from the very heart of their vocation. Some religious institutes turned to psychological or sociological guidance, which may have inhibited the renewal desired by the participants in the Second Vatican Council.

30. Pope Pius XII, *Sponsa Christi*. Latin text *AAS*, 43 (1951): 6–7 (concerning the canonical status of nuns of strict contemplative life). Our translation is from the French text, http://www.vatican.va/holy_father/pius_xii/apost_constitutions/documents/hf_p-xii_apc_i.

31. *Perfectae caritatis* 12 pertains to the vow of chastity, and the following paragraphs describe poverty and obedience. *Lumen gentium*, in its opening sentence in chapter 6, states that "The evangelical counsels of chastity consecrated to God, poverty and obedience constitute a divine gift which the church has received from its Lord and maintains always with the help of his grace." The sequence of the vows reenforces the

full gift of self to our Lord enunciated by Pope Pius XII and later by the Second Vatican Council and other ecclesial documents.

32. Pope Pius XII, *Ci torna* (Sept. 13, 1951), *AAS* 43 (1951): 738–44, no. 13. English text "To Teaching Sisters," *Review for Religious* 14 (1955): 254.

33. Pope Paul VI, *On Religious Life*, 701.

34. Third Lateran Council, *Canons*, 1179, no. 10. Tanner, *Decrees of the Ecumenical Councils*, vol. 1, 217.

35. Pope Honorius, *Solet annuere*, 1; and Pope Clement V, *Exivi de paradiso*, 9–13.

36. Pope Innocent XI, *Sollicituo pastoralis* (Nov. 20, 1679), *Bullarum diplomatum*, vol. 19, 214–18. English text "Fostering and Preserving the Orders of Men Religious," 3, http://www.catholic-forum.com/churches/saintsindex/sti61001.htm.

37. Pope Pius XI, *Rite expiatis* (Apr. 30, 1926), *AAS* 18 (1926): 153–75; English text "On St. Francis of Assisi," *Papal Encyclicals*, no. 199 [3: 293–304], 8.

38. Pope Pius XII, *Sponsa Christi*, *AAS* 43 (1951): 4–24, no. 16. Our translation is from the French text.

39. By "accidental" is meant a characteristic that may be regularly or irregularly associated with religious life but which is not needed for its definition, as "essential" characteristics are. Another way to state this is to say that an accidental characteristic can be missing without destroying religious life, but when an essential characteristic is missing, religious life itself is missing.

40. See Marjorie Noterman Beane, *From Framework to Freedom: A History of the Sister Formation Conference* (Lanham, Md.: University Press of America, 1993), 8–11.

41. Ibid., 18–20.

42. Pope Paul VI, *Sous la maternelle* (Dec. 11, 1957), *AAS* 50 (1958): 34–43. English text, *The States of Perfection*, address to the Second General Congress of the States of Religious Perfection, *The Pope Speaks* 4 (1957–1958): 264–72.

43. *TPS*, 2, 269–70. A historical description of the authority of lay religious superiors is provided in Schaumber, *Evolution of the Power of Jurisdiction*.

44. Pope Leo XIII, *Gravissimas* (May 16, 1901), Acta Leonis XIII, 21: 79–81; English text, "On Religious Orders in Portugal," *Papal Encyclicals*, no. 155 [2: 487–88], no. 4, esp. 487.

45. Pope Pius XI, *Studiorum ducem* (June 29, 1923), *AAS* 15 (1923): 309–26; English text, "On the Sixth Centenary of the Canonization of Saint Thomas Aquinas," *Papal Encyclicals*, no. 194 [3: 249–57], no. 5, 250.

46. Pope Pius XII, *Fulgens radiatur* (Mar. 21, 1947), *AAS* 39 (1947): 137–55, no. 13; English text, "On the Fourteenth Centenary of the Death of Saint Benedict," *Papal Encyclicals*, no. 232 [4: 111–18], 113.

47. Sacred Congregation for Religious and for Secular Institutes, *Religious and Human Promotion* (Apr. 25–28, 1978), 24, http://www.vatican.va/roman_curia/congregations/ccscrlife/documents/re_con_ccscrlife_d.

48. Congregation for Institutes of Consecrated Life and Societies of Apostolic Life, *Fraternal Life in Community* (Boston: Pauline Books and Media, 1994), 10, 25.

49. John Paul II, *Vita consecrata*, "On the Consecrated Life and Its Mission in the World" (Sherbrooke, Quebec: Médiaspaul, 1996), 46.

13

The Decree on the Apostolate of the Laity, *Apostolicam Actuositatem*

Robert W. Oliver, B.H.

The Decree on the Lay Apostolate presented unique challenges to the conciliar fathers relative to the other documents of the Second Vatican Council. The president of the initial commission on the lay apostolate, Ferdinand Cardinal Cento, observed to the Central Preparatory Commission that Vatican II would be the first ecumenical council to systematically consider the topics assigned to his commission. In contrast to the "vast patrimony" available to the other commissions, the commission on the laity faced a special task in developing proposals in accord with the Church's tradition, doctrine, and legislation.[1]

Pope John XXIII indicated his own awareness of these challenges when he called this commission "the newest mark" of the council he had summoned.[2] The official name, *Commissio de apostolatu laicorum in omnibus quae ad actionem catholicam, religiosam atque socialem, spectant* (Commission on the Apostolate of the Laity in Everything That Concerns Catholic Action, Religious and Social Action), indicated the wide range of issues ultimately addressed in the conciliar decree *Apostolicam actuositatem*.[3] The titles of the decree's six chapters specified the main issues:

Introduction (*Prooemium*, no. 1)
Chapter 1. On the Vocation of the Laity to the Apostolate (*De vocatione laicorum ad apostolatum*, nos. 2–4)
Chapter 2. On the Objectives to Be Pursued (*De finibus assequendis*, nos. 5–8)
Chapter 3. On the Various Fields of the Apostolate (*De variis apostolatus campis*, nos. 9–13)
Chapter 4. On the Various Forms of the Apostolate (*De variis apostolatus modis*, nos. 15–22)

Chapter 5. On the Preservation of Due Order (*De ordine servando*, nos. 23–27)

Chapter 6. On Formation for the Apostolate (*De formatione ad apostolatum*, nos. 28–32)

Exhortation (*Adhortatio*, no. 33)[4]

This chapter examines ways in which the council's teaching on the lay apostolate reflects the continuity of Vatican II with Church doctrine and legislation, while developing areas that were not previously given detailed attention by the magisterium. The analysis follows the outline of the decree and begins with the theological foundations presented in chapter 1 in order "to intensify the apostolic activity of the people of God" (*AA* 1). The next section expounds on the different "objectives," "fields," and "forms" of the lay apostolate in chapters 2–4, all of which aim "to penetrate and to perfect the temporal order with the Gospel" (*AA* 8). Particular attention is given to sections in chapter 4 that illustrate in detail the council's desire for continuity with principles regarding associations of the faithful. Finally, the fifth and sixth chapters of the decree address important and at times controversial issues for incorporating the lay apostolate into the "apostolate of the whole Church according to a right system of relationships" (*AA* 23).

"To Intensify the Apostolic Activity of the People of God," *Apostolicam Actuositatem*, Articles 1–4

The introductory article indicates the purpose for which *Apostolicam actuositatem* was issued: the desire of the conciliar fathers "to intensify the apostolic activity of the people of God." The choice of the phrase "impensiorem reddere" was a clear signal that the council wished to affirm the apostolic activities in which the laity were already at work, activities that Church authority has praised and supported through the centuries. The opening lines of the decree emphasize that "the Church can never be without the lay apostolate," a participation in the mission of the Church that is "proper to them and indispensable" in the Church's mission. Sacred scripture shows this apostolate to have been present "from the very beginning of the Church."[5]

The council's desire to address the lay Christian faithful in a special decree was due to a conviction that "our own times require of the laity no less zeal; in fact, modern conditions demand that their apostolate be broadened and intensified." In continuity with the service of laypeople throughout the centuries, the Holy Spirit's "unmistakable work" in the contemporary Church was again to fashion a laity "more conscious of their own responsibility" and to inspire them "to serve Christ and the Church everywhere."[6]

In order to effectively intensify the apostolic activity of the laity, the fathers proposed "to describe the nature, proper character, and diversity of the lay apostolate, to set out its fundamental principles, and to give pastoral directives" (*AA* 1). The first chapter, "On the Vocation of the Laity to the Apostolate," established the first and foundational principle that "the apostolate of the laity is derived from their Christian vocation." Through baptism, the faithful are united with Christ, the head, and with his body, the Church. This union is the source of the lay vocation and affords laypeople a share in the mission of salvation, which flows from the Father to the Son and is continued in the world by the Holy Spirit (AA 1 and 3).

This theological point of departure was one of the important indicators of the connection of *Apostolicam actuositatem* with the other conciliar documents, especially the Dogmatic Constitution on the Church. It was in sharp contrast to the predominantly apologetic methodology of contemporary ecclesiology, which most often began with the visible, "horizontal" dimensions of the Church's life and mission. In *Lumen gentium*, the council returned ecclesiology to a properly theological, or "vertical," point of departure. As does the constitution on the Church, *Apostolicam actuositatem* presents the Church first as mystery, born of the Trinity and moving toward the fullness of Trinitarian communion.[7]

This starting point was developed in response to the many conciliar interventions that expressed a desire for improvements in the theological and ecclesiological principles upon which the decree on the lay apostolate was to be based, statements more in continuity with Church teaching on the vocation and mission of the lay faithful.[8] According to one commentator, the fathers were especially concerned that the schema was "imprisoned in the limits and by the conceptual difficulties of pre-conciliar thought on the so-called theology of the laity."[9] They preferred a broader perspective, one in line with previous statements of the magisterium, such as *Rerum novarum* (1891) and the social encyclicals of the twentieth century, together with the ecclesiology of *Lumen gentium*.[10]

The opening sentences of *Apostolicam actuositatem* emphasize that each member of the Church has an important role in building up the Church and in the Church's mission in the world. Because the baptized share fully in the priestly, prophetic, and royal functions of Christ, the lay faithful are to strive to sanctify the world from within, permeating each activity with the spirit of Christ by the witness of their lives. In baptism the faithful "are assigned" (*deputantur*) to the apostolate by Christ himself.[11] In confirmation, they receive from the Holy Spirit special gifts of grace for witnessing to the Gospel, gifts that are the inner force of their apostolate and the source of their "right and duty" (*ius et officium*) to build up the Church and to participate in the Church's mission in the world. In the Eucharist, the Spirit consecrates the faithful to offer the spiritual sacrifices of the royal priesthood and confers upon them the gift of charity, the "true soul of the apostolate" (AA 3–4).

Many textual references emphasize that these theological, sacramental, and ecclesial principles are rooted in scripture, tradition, and the magisterium. They refer, for example, to Acts of the Apostles, where the lay faithful are active in the Church's first missionary efforts, by proclaiming the Lord Jesus "as far as Phoenicia, Cyprus, and Antioch. . . . The hand of the Lord was with them and a great number who believed turned to the Lord" (Acts 11:19–21). The writings of Saint Paul are also cited, particularly references to his many "co-workers in

Christ Jesus," among whom Priscilla and Aquila are noted particularly for their collaboration with the Apostle and their role in preparing him for his evangelistic work.[12]

The foundation of these principles is also evident in magisterial teaching on the sacrament of baptism. The Council of Florence affirmed, for instance, that in baptism the faithful are fully incorporated into Christ and the Church.[13] The Council of Trent added that this incorporation is the source of the faithful's participation in the common priesthood of Christ.[14] During the discussions on *Apostolicam actuositatem*, frequent mention was also made in the conciliar *aula* to more recent acts of the papal magisterium, especially Pope Pius XI, *Quadregesimo anno* (1931); Pius XII, *Mystici corporis Christi* (1943); Pope John XXIII, *Mater et magistra* (1961); and *Pacem in terris* (1963); and Pope Paul VI, *Ecclesiam suam* (1964).

The desire for authentic development in continuity with previous expressions of ecclesial doctrine was underlined by the commission on the laity in its responses to *modi* that expressed concerns with texts on the gifts of the Spirit and on the laity's participation in the priesthood of Christ. The commission reminded the fathers on several occasions that the council had approved similar statements in *Lumen gentium* and that the basis for the conciliar teaching on the laity is the Church's traditional teaching on the sacrament of baptism.[15]

The theological point of departure for the decree and the principles presented in the initial chapters constitute an effective foundation for an approach that contrasted sharply with the notions that laypersons are primarily the passive recipients of the governing and teaching power of the clergy and that the clergy are solely responsible for the Church's mission. *Apostolicam actuositatem* frequently repeats that the Church's mission concerns each member of the body and that no one of the baptized can remain passive. Using the imagery of Saint Paul and Pius XII's encyclical letter *Mystici corporis Christi*, the decree exhorts the laity that "as no part of a living body is merely passive but each shares in the functions and the life of the body, so too in the body of Christ, which is the Church" (*AA* 2). The decree presents this active role in the context of the unity of the Church's one mission: "In the Church there is a diversity of service but oneness of mission." It is Christ himself who instituted diverse modes of participation in this mission by communicating to the Apostles and their successors the authority to guide and direct the Church's mission. This diversity is subordinated to the unity of the mission of salvation, which belongs to the Church as a whole: "The laity share in the priestly, prophetic and kingly offices of Christ and therefore play their own part in the mission of the whole people of God in the Church and in the world" (ibid.).

"To Penetrate and Perfect the Temporal Order with the Spirit of the Gospel," *Apostolicam Actuositatem*, Articles 5–17

The following three chapters present the "objectives," "fields," and "forms" of the lay apostolate. It is noteworthy that the way in which the drafts used the term "apostolate" was the subject of long discussions in the commission. Several members preferred to restrict the term to works directly aimed at evangelization and the sanctification of human persons. Others preferred a wider sense that included the Christian renewal of the temporal order together with evangelization and sanctification. Some of the drafts referred to the more restricted concept as the "direct apostolate," while the more inclusive was termed the "indirect apostolate."

The conciliar debates made clear the fathers' desire to adopt the wider meaning of the term "apostolate."[16] *Apostolicam actuositatem* defines the apostolate of the laity, therefore, as embracing not only works for the evangelization and sanctification of the world but also efforts to penetrate the temporal order with the spirit of the Gospel: "Christ's work of redemption, while of itself directed to the salvation of human beings, also embraces the renewal of the whole temporal order. Hence the mission of the Church is not only to bring the message and grace of Christ to men and women, but also to penetrate and perfect the whole order of temporal things with the spirit of the Gospel. Therefore laypeople, in carrying out this mission of the Church, exercise their apostolate in the Church and in the world both in the spiritual and temporal orders" (*AA* 5).

This definition was specifically chosen in light of the desired continuity with *Lumen gentium* and the long history of lay service in the spreading of the Gospel.[17] Chapter 2 lists many of the "innumerable opportunities" that exist for exercising the lay apostolate, beginning with the witness of a committed Christian life and the proclamation of the Gospel of Christ. This section also links *Apostolicam actuositatem* with the great social encyclicals of the papal magisterium and with the witness of laypeople who have been beatified and canonized for their life, apostolic work, and martyrdom. The Second Vatican Council exhorts the laity to continue their efforts at evangelization and to develop new forms of the apostolate, forms that address the issues posed by their own time and place. Guided by the Gospel of Christ and the mind of the Church, they are to act with full respect for the principles provided by the Church's pastors. These principles, enunciated over many centuries, show the apostolate to include social action and works of charity because these works are expressions of God's love and thus part of the work of orienting the temporal order to Christ (*AA* 6–8).

The third chapter lists many fields for the lay apostolate. The lay faithful are called to be active in the Church and in the Church's mission, particularly through their own parishes and dioceses. They should "collaborate in every apostolic and missionary initiative" sponsored by their own ecclesial family and with a "truly apostolic mind" offer their skills to the Church. Specific areas enumerated include the apostolate of married persons and families, young people, everyday life, and the national and international orders (*AA* 9–14).

Chapter 4 combines the importance of the individual apostolate with long sections on the apostolate in associations of the faithful, including Catholic Action. The council's emphasis in this section intentionally falls quite clearly on the individual apostolate. Many conciliar fathers felt that too much emphasis was given to the organized apostolate in early drafts of the decree and that more attention was needed on the call of every baptized member to be engaged in the Church's mission, even in places where they are unable to participate in associations. The decree highlights the individual apostolate as the origin and condition of the whole lay apostolate and the call of the laity "always and everywhere" to the individual apostolate (*AA* 15–17, 22).[18]

Among the more significant aspects of these chapters is the recognition of a diversity of means to exercise the apostolate, a mission that ultimately includes every effort of the Church to spread the kingdom of God in the world. The diversity of means is subordinated to a unity of purpose, that of offering to all people the good news of salvation. In emphasizing these aspects of Church teaching on the lay apostolate, the council again places the action of Christ and the Holy Spirit at the center of its vision for the Church's vocation and mission. The fathers also show that all aspects of the laity's life and mission are ordered to the communion that is offered to all humanity in and through the Church.

Again seen in the context of the then contemporary ecclesiology, these texts mark a dramatic departure from a primarily juridical approach to the lay apostolate. Participation in the Church's mission was not presented as arising from a juridical concession of power granted by ecclesiastical authority. Rather, in the sacrament of baptism and their common human and ecclesial dignity all of the faithful are summoned to participate actively in the communion and the mission of the Church.[19]

"To Participate in the Apostolate by Way of United Effort," *Apostolicam Actuositatem*, Articles 18–22

The majority of attention in chapter 4 is given to associations of the faithful, with special consideration of the Catholic Action movement. As in the first chapter, this section begins with theological and ecclesiological foundations, principally the notion that associations are in harmony with the nature shared by all human beings and with the nature of the Church. Because human beings are social by nature, associations provide men and women with common support, formation, and better organization of their apostolic work, "so that much richer harvests can be expected from their activity than if they worked as individuals." They are an effective means through which people unite their wills and energies to reach common goals. Associations are, more profoundly, a response to the divine will for the Church because "God was pleased to unite believers in Christ into one people of God and into one body," and associations of the faithful are a true "sign of communion and the unity of the Church in Christ" (*AA* 18).

The chapter presents associations in a quite positive tone and underscores that they manifest the unity of the Church. Reflecting the council's broad definition of the lay apostolate, *Apostolicam actuositatem* presents a "great variety" of different associations and missionary purposes within the Church. Some serve the general apostolic purposes of the Church, while others pursue particular purposes, such as evangelization, Christian animation of the temporal order, and works of mercy and charity (AA 18–19).[20]

Several texts in the remainder of the section were among the most debated issues at the council, principally those on the right of the faithful to associate in the Church and the relationship of associations to ecclesiastical authority. Other matters included a perceived lack of an apostolic spirit in some associations, proper coordination of activities, the proper vigilance of ecclesiastical authorities, and a criticism that valuable resources and energies were being drained away from the Church and its apostolate. The debates on these topics cannot be interpreted according to the familiar "traditional-progressive" hermeneutic of Vatican II. More than a few fathers who usually identified with one side or another were surprised to find themselves in quite different company on issues related to associations of the faithful. The commission on the laity opposed even including the topic of associations in Apostolicam actuositatem. Ferdinand Klostermann, a member of the commission, observed that the material on associations was eventually met with "resignation," but that the commission was pleased when most of it was later transferred to the commission revising the 1917 code.[21]

To understand these issues adequately, we must read them in the context of the continuity of Church doctrine and legislation on associations. The Second Vatican Council, like many councils and synods before it, wrestled with the complex issues encountered by bishops in ordering ecclesial rights within the communion of the Church. Centuries-old discussions were reprised at Vatican II, as the fathers sought to balance the legitimate freedoms of the faithful in exercising their proper vocation with the proper role of ecclesial authorities and their responsibility for the common good. A brief sketch of this history exemplifies the continuity of Apostolicam actuositatem with earlier resolutions of these issues and points to several important developments in ecclesial doctrine and discipline.[22]

Since the earliest days of the Church, the faithful have formed associations to respond to the needs of their fellow believers and to participate together in the mission entrusted to the Church. The New Testament and many patristic writings witness to the growth of associations in the early Church. The Apostle Paul wrote, for example, of the establishment of an association in Corinth for the collection of alms for poor churches (1 Cor 16:1). Prior to the fourth century, associations were an important means for Christians to obtain certain legal capacities in the Roman Empire because associations established for religious purposes were exempt from the law that prohibited the formation of an association without previous permission from civil authorities.[23] Members of the Church were thus able to gain legal standing for efforts such as the burial societies (e.g., the fossores and lecticarii) and societies for hospital workers (e.g., the parabalani).

The fourth through ninth centuries witnessed a great expansion of associations of the faithful, first in the Near East and later in Western Europe. Particularly important impulses for this expansion came from associations connected with monasteries, fraternities of prayer, and purgatorial associations.

In the early centuries of the second millennium the mendicant religious orders blazed a similar path by establishing numerous third orders and confraternities. Other associations encouraged devotion to the saints, especially the Blessed Virgin Mary, service to the poor and the sick, care of widows and orphans, visits to the imprisoned, and the repair of churches. Even associations formed primarily for civil purposes, such as the professional guilds, frequently included religious and pious works among their members' official duties.[24]

The first instances of ecclesiastical legislation on associations were occasioned by this rapid growth.[25] The acts of many local councils and synods presaged the debates at Vatican II, particularly issues like threats to ecclesiastical discipline and concerns that associations were draining valuable resources and energies away from the Church and its apostolate.[26] The Council of Montpellier (1215) ruled, for example, that an "urgent necessity and evident utility" must be manifested prior to establishing a new association and that prior authorization be obtained from the diocesan bishop. Soon thereafter Pope Gregory IX decreed that no association be established in the city of Rome without the express permission of the Apostolic See.[27]

For the next several centuries canonists debated the free establishment of associations by the faithful in the Church. The authoritative commentary of Pope Innocent IV was among the first to affirm a right of the faithful to establish associations in the Church, a position soon adopted by the influential canonists Hostiensis, Joannes Andreae, and Baldus de Ubaldis.[28] Although local legislation continued to place restrictions on the establishment of associations, the Council of Trent chose simply to strengthen the bishops' role of vigilance over associations, especially the ability to enforce ecclesiastical discipline and visit all associations of the faithful.[29]

Acts of the magisterium following Trent continued to reflect the same difficulties in resolving these questions, particularly in light of the issues bishops encountered in local churches. Pope Clement VIII's apostolic constitution *Quaecumque* (1604) strengthened ecclesiastical oversight of associations and extended the authority of local ordinaries over associations.[30] Over the next three centuries Roman dicasteries repeatedly invoked *Quaecumque*, especially concerning issues such as the relationship of associations to parishes and diocesan authorities.[31]

The first comprehensive treatment of associations in universal church law was contained in the 1917 *Codex iuris canonici*. The long debate concerning the right of association in the Church appeared to be settled by a canon that stated that only associations erected or approved by the hierarchy were recognized as existing in the Church. All associations were subject to the vigilance and jurisdiction of the local ordinary, even those erected by apostolic privilege, and an ordinary had the right and duty to supervise all associations within his territory unless an individual association had obtained a privilege to the contrary.[32]

The issue was complicated, however, only three years after the promulgation of the code. A response from the Congregation for the Council to a question from the bishop of Corrientes (Argentina) concluded that "lay associations" were not subject to the local ordinary in the same manner as "ecclesiastical associations." The canons of the 1917 code did not apply, therefore, to such associations.[33] This surprising statement was still cause for a spirited debate at Vatican II on whether associations exist in the Church without an explicit connection to ecclesiastical authority.[34] This debate was further complicated by the fact that several popes had officially recognized the right of association in civil society.[35]

This history points to the significance of the texts prepared for Vatican II on associations. In April 1962 a proposed decree, *De fidelium associationibus*, clearly recognized a right of association in the Church: "It is proper to human beings and a true natural right [*verum ius natura*]" to establish associations to pursue specific ends in the Church. As the decree *Apostolicam actuositatem* eventually did, the text distinguished between certain ends of the apostolate for which the faithful could freely establish associations and ends that pertain solely to associations that receive official approval from ecclesiastical authority. Among the former purposes were the perfection of piety, the exercise of Christian charity, and the fostering of social works. Among the reserved ends were promoting public worship, teaching or expounding Christian doctrine, and "other activities of this type."[36]

This early text and its subsequent development are indicative of the complexity of interpreting the history of the Second Vatican Council.[37] In contrast to the current Church law in the 1917 *Code of Canon Law*, the preparatory document on associations affirmed that the apostolic initiatives of the laity in associations of the faithful belonged fully to the life and mission the Church. Such an important theological and ecclesiological statement required much discussion over the subsequent four years, as the fathers sought to express these principles in continuity with the development of previous doctrine and legislation concerning the laity.[38]

The effect of this history is quite evident in the section on associations in *Apostolicam actuositatem*, which includes the following declaration: "If the right relation with ecclesiastical authority is preserved, it is lawful for laypeople to found and run associations and to join those that exist" (*AA* 19). This statement is then followed by several principles that address issues raised in this context by previous councils and by the fathers at Vatican II. The establishment of new associations should not cause, for instance, a dispersion of the Church's energies, especially by the undertaking of works of the apostolate without sufficient reason. Existing associations should not be maintained if they cease to have a useful purpose or employ out-of-date methods. Associations are not to be understood as an end in themselves, but in service to the mission of the Church throughout the world. Their apostolic work must conform to the ends of the Church and evidence the Gospel spirit of each member and of the association as a whole, for which reason the council gives "first consideration" to associations that unite the faith and practical life of their members (*AA* 19–22).

The council's position on Catholic Action also demonstrates a prudent balance of long-standing pastoral concerns. In the years leading up to Vatican II, a large number of the debates on associations focused on Catholic Action, an apostolic movement of laypeople begun in the late nineteenth century.[39] The distinctive feature of Catholic Action, according to Pope Pius XI (not infrequently called "Il Papa dell'Azione Cattolica") was the collaboration of the laity and the clergy in apostolic activities that properly belong to the hierarchy.[40] In the years immediately preceding the council, however, many pastors and theologians questioned whether this understanding sufficiently encompassed all works of the lay apostolate, and many advocated models that included more initiative and greater autonomy. These differences were particularly evident at the World Congress on the Lay Apostolate in 1957, when then bishop Léon Suenens opposed a "monopoly" exercised by Catholic Action over the lay apostolate.[41] Pope Pius XII, who was known as a supporter of Catholic Action, spoke soon thereafter of a "regrettable and widespread uneasiness" concerning Catholic Action.[42]

The resolution of these issues was one of the primary tasks entrusted to the commissions developing the decree on the lay apostolate.[43] In *Apostolicam actuositatem*, the council clearly expresses its support for Catholic Action and pointedly addresses these issues in an article dedicated entirely to this association, albeit within the same chapter as other forms of associations. The council "earnestly commends" Catholic Action for responding to the needs of the Church's apostolate in many countries but leaves individual bishops free to decide which type of associations corresponded best to the needs of their dioceses (*AA* 20).[44]

"To Be Incorporated into the Apostolate of the Whole Church according to a Right System of Relationships," *Apostolicam Actuositatem*, Articles 23–33

Several other issues regarding the relationship of associations to ecclesiastical authority were moved to a broader context in the reorganized fifth chapter, "On the Preservation of Due Order" (*De ordine servando*). This chapter was complemented in the final stages of drafting by a new sixth chapter on the formation of the faithful for the apostolate.[45]

One of the significant contributions of *Apostolicam actuositatem* is the explication of different forms of the relationship between works of the lay apostolate and ecclesiastical authority. Some forms are erected by the hierarchy to meet pressing needs in the Church, others are commended by ecclesiastical authority as especially appropriate to the particular needs of time and place, and others are formed and directed by the faithful, of which many are praised by ecclesial authorities as the best way for the Church to fulfill its mission in a particular area (*AA* 21–24).[46] The categories themselves were not as important as the criteria the council used for distinguishing different forms of the apostolate. In contrast to the 1917 *Code of Canon Law*, Vatican II did not base these distinctions solely on the goals of the particular work of the apostolate, but on the diverse forms of relationship between works of the apostolate and the hierarchy. These relationships arise from the concrete objectives of those engaged in the apostolate and the manner in which the apostolate is organized to achieve these ends.

It was particularly significant that the first form listed are apostolic initiatives in the Church "constituted by the free choice of laypeople and directed by their prudent judgment." In answer to many objections, the commission explained that the terms freely "constituted" (*constituuntur*) and "directed" (*reguntur*) were purposefully chosen to indicate, on one hand, that initiatives of the baptized belong fully to the Church and, on the other, that the hierarchy has a role of vigilance for all works of the apostolate.[47] Second are forms of the apostolate that the hierarchy explicitly recognizes. A closer relationship is established, thirdly, when ecclesiastical authority assumes responsibility for apostolic initiatives directly concerned with spiritual ends and when these are united with the apostolic functions of the hierarchy. Finally, some functions that are closely connected with the pastoral office can be entrusted by the hierarchy to laypeople, including teaching Christian doctrine, certain liturgical actions, and the care of souls (*AA* 24).[48]

The importance of these criteria can again be understood best in the context of continuity with previous doctrine and legislation on associations of the faithful. The original drafts of these articles were developed in the context of the relationship of associations with the hierarchy, as the commission strove to articulate a balance between freedom to associate in the Church and the hierarchy's role of ordering all apostolic works to the common good. Their location in chapter 5 of *Apostolicam actuositatem* extends the principles that underlie this approach to all works of the apostolate.

The emphasis in the final chapter of the decree is on maintaining the unity of the Church and on fostering an apostolic spirit among the laity. As had earlier Church councils and synods, the Second Vatican Council exhorts the faithful to increase the spirit of unity within different forms of the apostolate and to be open to cooperation with others. Ecclesiastical authorities, for their part, are charged with developing means to coordinate the different forms of the apostolate effectively, while respecting the distinctive character of each form.

Conclusion

The conciliar doctrine in *Apostolicam actuositatem* and its pastoral directives on the lay apostolate have had much influence on subsequent acts of the magisterium, particularly Pope Paul's *Evangelii nuntiandi* (1975), the revised codes of canon law (1983 and 1990), and Pope John Paul II's apostolic exhortation on the lay vocation and mission, *Christifideles laici* (1988). The decree contributes an understanding of the lay apostolate that rests firmly on the theological foundation of the union of the baptized with Christ, the source from which all apostolic activity flows. It offers many spiritual and practical principles for balancing issues that have continued to arise in the exercise of the lay apostolate, especially the organization, coordination, and relation to the hierarchy of different forms of the apostolate.[49]

The enduring contribution of *Apostolicam actuositatem* can be measured best by the quality of the desired "intensification" of the lay faithful's participation in the mission of the Church. The decades following the council have witnessed great and sustained efforts among the laity for the building up of the Church, especially through family life and the new forms of "lay ecclesial ministry." Following the 1987 Synod of Bishops on the Vocation and Mission of Lay Faithful, Pope John Paul II affirmed that, "In looking over the years following Vatican II the synod fathers have been able to verify how the Holy Spirit continues to renew the youth of the Church and how he has inspired new aspirations towards holiness and the participation of so many lay faithful" (*Christifideles laici*, no. 2).

Reading the Decree on the Lay Apostolate again, however, raises questions as to whether the full breadth of the council's understanding of the apostolate has been embraced by all members of the Church—lay, consecrated, and ordained. Vatican II's description of a "diversity of service but oneness of mission" (*AA* 2) points to a Church that is "missionary by nature" (*Ad gentes* 2). The conciliar vision points decidedly outward, to sustained and creative efforts for the evangelization and sanctification of the world and to efforts to penetrate and perfect the temporal order with the spirit of the Gospel. In contrast to an age-old temptation to focus primarily on intramural issues, *Apostolicam actuositatem* holds that all ministries and works of the apostolate are to be at the service of the one mission entrusted to the Church by Christ. The Holy Spirit imparts gifts to the laity for this mission in order that they fulfill their "special part in the mission of the whole people of God" (*AA* 2). The full extent of this mission summons the whole Church "to intensify" the apostolate and to permeate our world "with the spirit of the Gospel" (*AA* 1, 5).

NOTES

1. *Acta et documenta Concilio Oecumenico Vaticano II apparando*, series 2, *Praeparatoria* 2/4, 520–21. For the topics assigned to the first commission see Pope John XXIII, apostolic constitution *Superno Dei nutu* (June 5, 1960), *AAS* 52 (1960): 433–37; and the "Quaestiones Commissionibus Praeparatoriis Concilii Oecumenici Vaticani II positae," *Acta et documenta*, 2/1, 410–14.

2. Vincenzo Carbone reproduced an autograph note from Pope John in "Gli schemi preparatori del Concilio Ecumenico Vaticano Secondo," *Monitor Ecclesiasticus* 96 (1971): 78.

3. The commission's rather unwieldy name was soon shortened in common usage to the "commission on the apostolate of the laity" or simply "commission on the laity." The official name of the conciliar commission, *Commissio de fidelium apostolatu: De scriptis edendis et de spectaculis moderandis*, reflected a transfer of tasks previously assigned to the Secretariat for the Communications Media. *Acta synodalia sacrosancti Concilii Oecumenici Vaticani II*, vol. 5, pt. 1, 116, 132, 200.

4. *Apostolicam actuositatem* (Nov. 18, 1965), *AAS* 58 (1966): 837–64.

5. *AA* 1. For English translations of the conciliar documents I consulted *The Documents of Vatican II*, gen. ed. Walter M. Abbott, trans. ed. Joseph Gallagher (New York: Herder and Herder, 1966); and *Decrees of the Ecumenical Councils*, ed. Norman P.

Tanner and Giuseppe Alberigo (Washington, D.C.: Georgetown University Press, 1990).

6. *AA* 1. The commission on the laity attempted to maintain a consistent distinction between the terms "the lay faithful" and "the faithful"; the latter term included all baptized persons—lay, religious, or clergy. The commission vigorously opposed the change of its title to *Commissio de fidelium apostolatu*, but the central commission responded that the change was motivated by the perception of an anticlerical ring to the term "laity" and a desire to make "clear that the schema was to be addressed to the faithful in the Church and not to Christians of other confessions." Ferdinand Klostermann, "Decree on the Apostolate of the Laity," in *Commentary on the Documents of Vatican II*, vol. 3, ed. Herbert Vorgrimler (New York: Herder and Herder, 1968), 277–78.

7. Several members of the commission published commentaries on *Apostolicam actuositatem*, including Klostermann, "Decree on the Apostolate of the Laity," 273–302; Achille Glorieux, "Introduction générale sur le décret *Apostolicam actuositatem*," and "Histoire de décret *Apostolicam actuositatem* sur l'apostolat des laïcs," in *L'apostolat des laïcs: Décret* Apostolicam actuositatem, ed. Alain Galichon (Paris: Maison Mame, 1966), 11–40, 91–139; and Franz Hengsbach, *Das Konzilsdekret über das Laienapostolat* (Paderborn, Germany: Bonifacius, 1967). See also *L'apostolat des laïcs: Décret* Apostolicam actuositatem, ed. Yves Congar (Paris: Les Éditions du Cerf, 1970).

8. The first *Schema decreti "De apostolatu laicorum" propositum a commissione de apostolatu laicorum* (Apr. 2–8, 1962) was divided into four parts, with 272 articles that covered fifty-two folio pages (*Acta et documenta*, vol. 2, pt. 4, 468–520). The several drafts of the early months of 1963 alternated between two and four parts, until the 1963 *Schema* (Apr. 22, 1963) was published in two parts of ninety-two articles and almost ten pages of notes (*Acta synodalia*, vol. 3, pt. 4, 669–710).

9. Evangelista Vilanova, "The Intersession (1963–1964)," in *History of Vatican II*, vol. 3, ed. Giuseppe Alberigo and Joseph A. Komonchak (Maryknoll, N.Y.: Orbis, 1995), 390.

10. The tone for the conciliar debate was set by Bishop Francis Hengsbach in the *Relatio super schemi decreti de apostolatu laicorum* on Oct. 7, 1964 (*Acta synodalia*, vol. 3, pt. 4, 15–24), and by the first several interventions, each of which emphasized the necessary connection with *Lumen gentium* (*Acta synodalia*, vol. 3, pt. 4, 24–45).

11. The connection of *Apostolicam actuositatem* with *Lumen gentium* was highlighted by the use of the same term, *deputantur*, in *Apostolicam actuositatem* 3 and *Lumen gentium* 33.

12. Acts 18:26; Rom 16:1–16; Phil 4:3.

13. Council of Florence (Nov. 22, 1439), "Bulla unionis Armeniorum," in Tanner, *Decrees of the Ecumenical Councils*, vol. 1, 542–44.

14. Council of Trent (Nov. 25, 1551), "Doctrina de sacramento paenitentiae," in Tanner, *Decrees of the Ecumenical Councils*, vol. 2, 704.

15. The modi and the commission's responses are printed with the May 1965 *textus emendatus* (*Acta synodalia*, vol. 4, pt. 2, 305–63) and the October 1965 *textus recognitus* (*Acta synodalia*, vol. 4, pt. 6, 12–126).

16. Glorieux, "Introduction générale," 28–29; and Santo Quadri, "I fini dell'apostolato," in *Il decreto sull'apostolato dei laici* (Turin: Elle Di Ci, 1966), 171–212. The debate on *Apostolicam actuositatem* was delayed until 1964 because the 1963 debate on *Lumen gentium* lasted longer than expected (*Acta synodalia*, vol. 2, pt. 6, 367–71). There were 144 written or oral interventions from Oct. 6 to Oct. 13, 1964, which were

added to the more than five hundred responses the commission had already received (*Acta synodalia*, vol. 3, pt. 4, 24–272).

17. Klostermann, "Decree on the Apostolate of the Laity," 326–27.

18. The commission wished "to emphasize sufficiently the significance of the purely personal apostolate of the individual" and to respond to the criticism that the chapter represented an ideal of the layperson "who is organized in every respect." Klostermann, "Decree on the Apostolate of the Laity," 294, 346. See also Glorieux, "Introduction générale," 122–23.

19. Alvaro del Portillo, *Laici e fedeli nella Chiesa: Le basi dei loro statuti giuridici*, 2d ed. (Milan: Giuffrè, 1999); and "*Ius associationis* et associationes fidelium iuxta Concilii Vaticani II doctrinam," *Ius canonicum* 8 (1968): 6–13. Monsignor del Portillo played a significant role in the formation of *Apostolicam actuositatem* as president of the antepreparatory commission on the laity, secretary of the *Commissione de episcopis et dioeceseon regimine*, and as a consultor to the theological commission.

20. Different forms of associations are mentioned in several other documents of Vatican II, including *Gravissimum educationis* 4–10; *Ad gentes* 15, 39, 41; and *Gaudium et spes* 90.

21. Klostermann, "Decree on the Apostolate of the Laity," 281–83. On the debate within the commission see the 1965 *relatio* to the council, *Acta synodalia*, vol. 4, pt. 2, 344; and Glorieux, "Introduction générale," 100–102, 111–15.

22. The most comprehensive studies on the history of associations include two texts available to the conciliar father: Georges Vromant and L. Bongaerts, *De fidelium associationibus* (Bruges, Belgium: Desclée, 1955), and Seraphinus de Angelis, *De fidelium associationibus: Tractatus ratione et usu digestus*, 2 vols. (Naples: M. D'Auria, 1959).

23. Examples are contained in the *Digesta Iustiniani*, 47.22.1; *Novellae leges*, 43.1 and 59.2; and *Codex Theodosianus*, 16.2.42.

24. For a detailed list of the activities of contemporary associations of the faithful see the Council of Bordeaux (1255), ch. 30, in *Sacrorum conciliorum nova et amplissima collectio*, vol. 23, ed. Iohannes D. Mansi (Paris: Welter, 1901–1927), 865.

25. According to the Decretists, the first intervention of ecclesiastical authority regarding associations of the faithful was at the Council of Gangres (355). Gratian quoted this council (D. 42, c. 1) and referred to several others, including Attigny (762), Salzburg (799), and Freising (805).

26. A decree issued in 852 by Hincmar, the archbishop of Rheims, was especially influential in the Middle Ages (Mansi 15: 479). Concerns about behavior at the meetings of associations of the faithful were frequently voiced in local synods and councils, such as Bourges (1528), Sens (1528), and Avignon (1594).

27. Council of Montpellier (Jan. 6, 1214), ch. 45; and Gregory IX, *Ad nostrum* (Oct. 26, 1232).

28. Innocent IV, *In quinque libros decretalium commentaria*, 5.31.14.1–2; Henricus Hostiensis, *Summa aurea*, 1.39.4; Joannes Andreae, *In quinque decretalium libros novella commentaria*, 5.31.14.1, 6; and Baldus de Ubaldis, *Commentaria in codicis libris*, 1.2.14.12.

29. Council of Trent, *Decretum de reformatione* (Sept. 17, 1562), chapters 8–9.

30. Pope Clement VIII, *Quaecumque* (Dec. 7, 1604), in *Codicis iuris canonici fontes*, vol. 1, ed. Petrus Gasparri and Iustinian Seredi (Rome: Typis Polyglottis Vaticanis, 1933–1939), 366–70.

31. In the early 1700s, for instance, three decrees from the Congregation for Rites referred to tensions between associations and the pastors of their parishes. The congregation affirmed both the authority of pastors and the right of confraternities to hold

meetings in accord with the approved statutes (Jan. 12, 1704; Nov. 22, 1710; and July 9, 1718). Similar interventions were made by the Congregation for the Council (Dec. 14, 1889), the Congregation for Bishops and Regulars, *Resolutio romana* (Jan. 18, 1907), and the Congregation for the Consistory, *A remotissima* (Dec. 31, 1909).

32. The 1917 *Code of Canon Law*, canons 686 and 690. Forty-two canons on associations were contained in the third part of book two (*De personis*), in a section titled *De laicis* (cc. 684–725).

33. Congregation for the Council, *Resolutio Corrienten* (Nov. 13, 1920), AAS 13 (1921): 135–44. The congregation was asked whether the Society of Saint Vincent de Paul was to be considered subject to the regulations of the 1917 code. The response was that the canons could not be applied to the society because the code addressed only associations "which through erection by ecclesiastical authority become truly ecclesiastical associations."

34. Wilhelm Onclin, "Principia generalia de fidelium associationibus," *Apollinaris* 36 (1963): 68-109. Monsignor Onclin's influential article was published as the debate began in the commission on the laity. The author, who was a member of the commission, reviewed extensively the history of canonical opinions on the right of association in the Church.

35. Leo XIII, *Rerum novarum*, nos. 48–61, ASS 23 (1890–1891): 663–69; Pius XI, *Quadragesimo anno*, nos. 31–38, AAS 23 (1931): 186–89; Pius XII, *Sertum laetitiae*, AAS 31 (1939): 643; John XXIII, *Mater et magistra*, no. 22, AAS 55 (1963): 406–407; and idem, *Pacem in terris*, nos. 23–24, AAS 55 (1963): 262–63.

36. *Acta et documenta*, vol. 2, pt. 4, 284, 286. The proposed conciliar decree *De fidelium associationibus* was presented in April 1962 by the commission *De disciplina cleri et populi Christiani*.

37. The material on associations was further developed by the commission *De episcopis et dioeceseon regimine* for inclusion in the proposed decree *De cura animarum* (*Acta synodalia*, vol. 2, pt. 4, 774–75; and *Acta synodalia*, vol. 5, pt. 1, 323–89). When the Central Commission greatly reduced the proposed documents, some of the material on associations was transmitted to the commission on the laity and the reminder to the commission for the revision of the code.

38. Several members of the Central Preparatory Commission raised a concern that, since Church law stated that all pious and charitable works fall under the authority of the hierarchy, those who form associations for purposes of piety and charity must seek prior authorization from ecclesiastical authority (*Acta et documenta*, vol. 2, pt. 4, 298–336). The difficulties in the commission on associations mirrored those of the rest of the council (Glorieux, "Introduction générale," 34).

39. The first pope to use terminology similar to "Catholic Action" was Pius X, who exhorted all Catholics to take part in "Catholic social action" in his first encyclical letter. Pius X, *E supremi apostolatus cathedra*, ASS 36 (1903–1904): 129–39. See also *Il fermo proposito*, ASS 37 (1904–1905): 761–62.

40. Pius XI, *Quae nobis*, AAS 20 (1928): 384–85.

41. *Documents du deuxième Congrès mondial pour l'apostolat des laïcs* (Rome: Copecial, 1957). Suenens explained his position in "L'unité multiforme de l'Action Catholique," Nouvelle revue théologique 80 (1958): 3-21. Grootaers referred to the 1957 Congress on the Lay Apostolate as the moment in which the "powder keg was lit" concerning Catholic Action. Jan Grootaers, "The Drama Continues between the Acts: The 'Second Preparation' and Its Opponents," in Alberigo and Komonchak, *History of Vatican II*, vol. 2, 443.

42. Pius XII, *Six ans se sont*, AAS 49 (1957): 929-30.

43. See Pope John XXIII, *Superno Dei nutu, AAS* 52 (1960): 433–37; and the *Quaestiones Commissionibus Praeparatoriis Concilii Oecumenici Vaticani II positae, Acta et documenta,* vol. 2, pt. 1, 410–14.

44. Some of the well-known Catholic Action groups begun in Europe include the Jocist Movement, founded by Father (later Cardinal) Joseph Cardijn (1912), the Schönstatt Movement (1914), and Focolare (1943). Catholic Action groups were not as popular in the United States, but some better-known examples included the National Council of Catholic Men, the National Council of Catholic Women, the Christian Family Movement, and Serra International.

45. The new fifth chapter brought together material dispersed in earlier schemata on the relationship of the lay apostolate to the hierarchy and coordination of the apostolate. Several topics were greatly reduced, and separate sections on charitable and social action removed. The last major reorganization of the outline was in the 1964 *textus prior* (*Acta synodalia,* vol. 3, pt. 3, 368–84), which was reduced to twenty-one articles in five chapters.

46. The terms "mandate" (*mandatum*) and "canonical mission" (*missio canonica*) were the subject of much debate throughout the council but do not appear in the final text. Lengthy footnotes were added to the 1963 and 1964 drafts to explain these terms (*Acta synodalia,* vol. 3, pt. 4, 680–81; ibid., vol. 3, pt. 3, 383), and Bishop Hengsbach gave a detailed explanation of them in the 1964 *relatio* (ibid., vol. 3, pt. 3, 412–13). In the 1965 *relatio,* however, he stated that the commission would not try to settle the controversies surrounding these subjects (ibid., vol. 4, pt. 2, 354–55).

47. See *Acta synodalia,* vol. 4, pt. 2, 350; and *Acta synodalia,* vol. 4, pt. 6, 108–109.

48. These categories were changed and reordered in the various drafts of *Apostolicam actuositatem.* Perhaps for that reason there is some disagreement among commentators on the number of different options for the relationship between the lay apostolate and the hierarchy. According to Bishop Hengsbach's 1964 *Relatio circa rationem qua schema elabarotum est* there are four forms of this relationship (*Acta synodalia,* vol. 3, pt. 3, 389). However, for different enumerations see del Portillo, *Laici,* 123; Alfonso Díaz Díaz, *Derecho fundamental de asociación en la Iglesia* (Pamplona: EUNSA, 1972), 188; and Winfried Schulz, "Le norme canoniche sul diritto di associazione e la loro riforma alla luce dell'insegnamento del Concilio Vaticano Secundo," *Apollinaris* 50 (1977): 161.

49. The definitive vote on *Apostolicam actuositatem* was cast on Nov. 18, 1965. It received the fewest dissenting votes of any of the conciliar documents, 2 negative and 2,340 affirmative.

14

The Decree on the Church's Missionary Activity, *Ad Gentes*

Francis Cardinal George, O.M.I.

The Missionary Tradition

A great Catholic theologian of the twentieth century, Romano Guardini, said of the Church, "She stands in history and by the power of the Holy Spirit, she proclaims the Savior through her existence, her words and her actions. She translates him into the language of our human life, brings him into relation with its forces and structures."[1] The Church's intentions and actions, therefore, are as original as those of Jesus Christ.

The perfect word of the revelation of God in Christ contained in scripture and the tradition that is its context is made present and challenges every era in the Church's mission. The Church "lives by her mission";[2] "the history of the Church is the history of Christian mission."[3] From that history, one learns what the Church understands her mission to be; it is a story with many stages and shows an evolution in the thought and practice of mission in and to the world.

The story begins with the event of Jesus Christ, which, culminating in Pentecost, is the response of the Triune God to the need of human beings for salvation and for communion with God.[4] From the beginning there has been mission *ad gentes*. In no way did the original community at Jerusalem ever settle into being a peaceful congregation content to quietly enjoy the divine gifts given by Christ and await the coming of the Lord. Peter's sermon gave the missionary invitation "to you and to your children and to all those far off, whomever the Lord our God will call" (Acts 2:39). In that discourse he establishes the Christian missionary tradition.

Even when addressed primarily to the Christian community, the Gospels' missionary intent is clear. All the preaching of the early

Church, aimed though it is at those within the Church, has the stamp of the missionary commission of the risen Lord (Mt 28:18–20). There is a universal orientation from the outset, a drive beyond Israel to the gentile peoples. Missionary activity occasioned one of the first great problems of the Christian community. The call to the people of Israel was clear enough, but how was the nascent Church to bring the Gospel to the gentiles? The "council of Jerusalem" was a decisive step in giving effect to the clearly universal missionary mandate in Matthew, which was born of the conviction that "a new people of redemption had been constituted by the blood of Jesus."[5]

Paul became the theologian of missionary activity and, in Romans 10:14f, gave mission its basis as a "sending." He describes the role of the missionary beautifully in a liturgical image as "performing the priestly service of the Gospel of God so that the offering up of the gentiles may be acceptable, sanctified by the Holy Spirit" (Rom 15:16). Paul set out with a holy urgency to carry the Gospel of Christ, preaching it "from Jerusalem all the way around to Illyricum" (Rom 15:19). The connection between the spread of the Church and the preaching of the Apostles was revealed to them; they were to become coheirs in Christ of the same body and copastors of the promise (Eph 3:1–5). In time, "all Israel will be saved" (Rom 11:26). The Church, by the nature of her vocation as Christ's redeemed community, is, under the guidance of the Holy Spirit, always to be in mission.

Christ formed the Church with "a genuinely universal spirit which opened the door of salvation to all equally."[6] After having "addressed herself without distinction to the whole people of Israel and recruited adherents from all circles of that nation, the Church then disclosed herself to the world by bursting the bounds of the old chosen people in an intrinsically inevitable and God-guided process."[7] The universal nature of the Church demands constant mission. This ecclesial charge is an official function of the Church, a permanent task, a means by which God fulfills his salvific will for the human family.[8]

This mission has been shaped in practice by developments in the ecclesial life and in the situation of the Christian communities.[9] The great and inspiring flowering of the apostolic and postapostolic era was followed by the Constantinian and post-Constantinian periods; the new relation of ruler and people within the Church modified missionary activity. After the progressive Christianization of Europe and the Near East, the missionary impulse was increasingly marked by the stability of the medieval synthesis and its Eurocentric character. The next great movement in mission came with the Counter-Reformation, which, in bringing about a far-reaching renewal in the Catholic Church, revivified the thrust of missionary work.[10] The Indian missiologist Father Sebastian Karotemprel dates the modern age of mission from around the sixteenth century (missionary activity of the Reformed churches began somewhat later). Milestones for Catholic missionary concern were the foundation in 1622 of the Roman Congregation for the Propagation of the Faith with worldwide mission as its responsibility; early in the nineteenth century, missiology emerged as a science and was made possible by the study of cultural anthropology by the Society of the Divine Word, along with the Missionary

Oblates of Mary Immaculate and with notable developments on the Protestant side. Missiology can be described as "the systematic study of the evangelizing activity of the Church and of the ways in which it is carried out."[11]

A German Divine Word priest, Dr. Josef Schmidlin, is often considered the father of Catholic missiology and the founder of what is known as the Münster School of missiology.[12] He emphasized mission as the spreading of the faith among non-Christians with a view to the conversion of individual unbelievers; this was God's will for mission. The emphasis was later strongly criticized as presenting an incomplete idea of salvation; an integral understanding of salvation would promote mission by keeping together both the transcendent nature of the Gospel message and the well-being of people and the culture in which they live.

The other notable missiological approach was that of the Louvain School, founded by Father Pierre Charles, S.J. Its basic thesis was that the planting of the Church in each place is the concrete manifestation of God's will. God wills all to be saved, not just as individuals but also as members of the Church. Like the Münster School, Louvain understood mission primarily as an activity outside the country of the missionary that had as goal to establish the Church with her necessary structures in a given territory. Gradually the territory would cease to be considered missionary as the Church there became more self-sufficient. Also, it proposed a model of adaptation by which the Church would transform local cultures and inculturate the faith.

This Catholic debate on the meaning and scope of mission was made more acute by the work of Protestant missiologists and by growing concern that human development, inculturation, and the freedom of the human person should be major concerns of mission. All of this conditioned the thinking of the Second Vatican Council when it came to say that the Church by her nature is missionary. The decree on mission, Ad gentes, became both a point of synthesis and a launching pad for further debate. It has been described as the beginning of "a new age of mission."[13] Some words of Pope John Paul II, though uttered in another context, give a good perspective from which to assess what was happening: "It is not a question of altering the deposit of faith, changing the meaning of dogma . . . or accommodating truth to the preference of the particular age."[14] The meaning of mission, understood in light of the mystery of the Church, can be grasped only "by the adherence of all to the content of revealed faith in its entirety."[15] In the Second Vatican Council, the Church set out not to invent mission but to deepen fruitful understanding of it.

Ad Gentes: The Magna Carta of Mission

It was both the success, the enormous growth of Catholic missions, and the pastoral and theological questions that this burgeoning of missionary activity aroused that led Vatican II, after a certain hesitation, to make a substantial statement on mission. The terrain had already been mapped out by the papal magisterium in a series of documents issued by Popes Benedict XV, Pius XI,

Pius XII, and John XXIII.[16] By the 1960s the theological debate was in strong ferment, and missionaries everywhere were raising new questions of a pastoral nature. At first it had been suggested in the council that what other conciliar documents such as *Lumen gentium*, the Constitution on the Church, might say in passing about mission would be adequate. This idea finally aroused strong reaction from both missionary bishops and many others from Europe. Gradually various projects for a document were floated—at one point it was no more than a series of propositions with a theological introduction—but a common mind emerged on the need for a decree that would state the meaning and necessity of mission.[17]

The Mission of the Church

Mission had already been acknowledged as integral to the life of the Church in *Lumen gentium*.[18] Numerous and clear voices from the council floor insisted that more be said.[19] It was declared that a decree should intensify, not lessen, the importance of the Church's missionary aim of preaching the Gospel to all; it should be clearly stated that "the ordinary way to salvation is within the Catholic Church."[20] Strong council personalities, such as Cardinal König of Vienna, supported this: "Without the grace of Christ, nobody can be saved, and the visible Church constitutes in the world the sacrament of salvation for all."[21]

The decree, at the outset, describes the Church as "divinely sent to the nations to be 'the universal sacrament of salvation' "[22]; missionary activity flows immediately from the very nature of the Church. That divine commission is then developed in what the decree says about the Church. The Constitution on the Church (*Lumen gentium*) had spoken of mission in terms of sending the entire people of God to convert the world. The decree made fuller use of the images of the Church already mentioned in the constitution (16 and 17); it speaks of the mystical body of the Word incarnate and of the one temple of the Holy Spirit (*AG* 7). Even more important, by situating mission in the plan of the Father and the mission of the Son and the Holy Spirit,[23] the decree put mission in the theological context of the key ecclesiological image of the council.

The 1985 Extraordinary Synod of Bishops, in evaluating the significance of Vatican II for the life of the Church, described "the ecclesiology of communion as a central and fundamental idea in the documents of the council," necessary "for the correct relation between unity and pluriformity in the Church."[24] The relationship of communion between the Father, Son, and Holy Spirit, which is the eternal being of God, overflows in the love (*AG* 2) manifested in creation and redemption to bring the Church into being as a created participation in that divine communion. In God, communion is the interplay of processions or "sendings"; in the Church, communion is a projection in time of God's mission, which makes God's inner life present to the world in a new way by drawing all who will accept it to share in that communion.[25]

One might speak of an interplay of communion and mission in the very being of God, which originates the "sending" that is the work of salvation. The "sending" in time of persons of the Trinity presupposes their eternal processions and adds to God's life a new historical mode of divine presence in the created world: the Church in mission. Communion, then, is both the origin and goal of mission. The mission of the Church is always "mission on behalf of communion."[26]

The sending of Christ and the Spirit becomes, from age to age, the mission of the Church.[27] The joint mission of Son and Spirit is continued in the social organism, which is at once the Son's ecclesial body and the temple of the Spirit. It is in this sense that the Church is a kind of sacrament, a sign and an instrument of the conjoined sending of Son and Spirit. In receiving the Spirit, the Church comes to exist by announcing the work of the Son and testifying to him so as to spread and instantiate everywhere the mystery of participation in the Trinitarian life.

Mission, then, is to be understood theologically in light of the communion that is the inner life of God and the necessary participation in the visible communion which is the Church; the failure to take this truth and its consequences seriously enough inevitably creates a crisis in missiology. Charles Cardinal Journet and a number of other bishops in the council discussion insisted on the necessity of the Church and her mission, "not simply for the melius essere" but for the "simpliciter esse of salvation."[28] It is hard to see how a missiologist can acknowledge that "the perfect communication and self giving that is God's very self is the Church's deepest self" and then go on to say that "the Church is fully one, yet divided."[29] The unique communion that is the life of God and is thus the source of the Church in her spiritual and visible being requires that we know her under not one but the many images presented in the Constitution on the Church (LG 2). It is not possible after reading the constitution (LG 3) and Ad gentes to claim, according to another missiologist, that one finds only "some vestiges of the hierarchical understanding of the Church" in the ecclesiology offered by Vatican II.[30] The decree insists that mission, "proclaiming the faith in salvation which comes from Christ," is due to "the express command which the order of bishops inherited from the apostles, an obligation in the discharge of which they are assisted by priests and one which they share with the successor of St. Peter, the supreme pastor of the Church, and also by reason of the life which Christ infuses into his members" (AG 5).

If we understand the nature of the communion that is the being of the Church, then we see a divine givenness and a wholeness that allow neither a dialectical approach to her nature nor a downplaying of its visibility and tangibility (1 Jn 1:1), which are integral to her being as mystical body of the incarnate Word.

Jesus Christ, the Origin and Source of Mission

The decree describes the mission of the Church and its origin in the union of Jesus Christ and the Holy Spirit as willed by the eternal plan of God the Father for the salvation of the world; it says that the Holy Trinity is the ultimate source and foundation of the Church's mission (AG 2), but "only starting with Christology does the Trinitarian confession of faith become an imperative."[31]

The Trinitarian foundation of the Church's mission is linked necessarily with Christ's Paschal mystery. "We can only talk about the source of mission in the Triune God because he has intervened in history through the death and resurrection of Jesus Christ to change the fate of the world."[32]

At the outset, *Ad gentes* talks of "Jesus Christ sent into the world as the true mediator between God and the human family" in order to "snatch men from the power of darkness and of Satan," to "establish among men a relationship of peace and communion with God," to "make men sharers in the divine nature," and to make known "the universal plan of God for salvation of mankind" (*AG* 3). The council's Constitution on Divine Revelation adds to this: "God sent his Son to dwell among men and tell them about the inner life of God" (*DV* 4). Christ was sent to bring "the Divine Revelation by which God wished to manifest and communicate both himself and the eternal decrees of his will concerning the salvation of mankind" (*DV* 6).

Christ is our salvation. We are saved because the Son of God underwent his passion and died on the cross. The decree points out the dimensions that make up the Christian concept of salvation (*AG* 3). These are the Incarnation, which is the principle of God's salvific self-communication; the redemption, which liberates humanity from the power of sin and death into the friendship of God; and the deification, which raises human nature to a participation in the divine life of the Trinity.[33] This was indeed the council fathers' vision when they insisted that "God is fully glorified only when all men live consciously in the faith of Christ. This is the goal of all missionary activity."[34] "Our aim is not to confirm each one in his own religion as does Moral Rearmament but to preach the Gospel to every creature."[35] A lay auditor from Africa added, "The essential task is bringing Christ to the world and the world to Christ."[36]

Ad gentes is based on the clear conviction of the uniqueness and salvific universality of Jesus Christ (*DV* 2). In Christ alone is the fullness of salvation; outside Christ there is no salvation: "The words, works and entire historical event of Jesus, while being limited as human realities, still have the divine Person of the Incarnate Word as their source and therefore contain in themselves the definition and complete revelation of his saving ways and of the divine mystery itself."[37]

In his *Introduction to Christianity*, first published very soon after the council, Josef Cardinal Ratzinger outlined the ground for the Christian claim to absoluteness that underlay the council's commitment to mission: "Christian faith says that in Christ the salvation of man is accomplished, that in him the true future of mankind has irrevocably begun and thus, although remaining future, is yet also perfect, a part of our present.... What has happened in Christ remains simultaneously both end and beginning. Humanity cannot go beyond him."[38]

"The Person of Jesus Christ and his death and resurrection are decisive for the salvation of all, whatever may be the way that salvation is mediated and appropriated by different persons. There can be no Christian mission without the proclamation of Jesus Christ."[39] The event of Jesus Christ is universal and normative for all. Confusion about Jesus Christ and the revelation he is and the salvation he brings can result only in confusion about mission. Even for the worthy goal of dialogue with other faiths and cultures the Christian cannot relativize or limit the nature of the revelation and the saving grace of Christ and its necessity for salvation.

Ad gentes draws to our attention that "The fathers of the Church constantly proclaim that what was not assumed by Christ was not healed" (*AG* 3). It is "in manifesting Christ that the Church reveals to men their true salvation and calling since Christ is the head and exemplar of that renewed humanity... to which all men aspire" (*AG* 8). While acknowledging that the power of God to save is without limit in whatever unsuspected or hidden ways that power works or reaches out, the only salvation is that which is in Jesus Christ. The decree is gentle but unequivocal:

> "For there is one God and one mediator between God and men, himself a man, Jesus Christ, who gave himself as a ransom for all" (1 Tim 2:4–5), "neither is there salvation in any other" (Acts 4:12). Everyone, therefore ought to be converted to Christ, who is known through the preaching of the Church, and they ought, by baptism, to become incorporated into him, and into the Church which is his body. Christ himself explicitly affirmed the necessity of faith and baptism (cf. Mk 16:16; Jn 3:5), and thereby affirmed at the same time the necessity of the Church. (*AG* 7)

Pope John Paul II liked to cite the Constitution on the Church in the Modern World, which says that "the Holy Spirit offers to all the possibility of being made partners, in a way known to God, in the paschal mystery" (*GS* 22); yet it is always the Paschal mystery of Jesus Christ.

What has been called a "pluralistic Christology" finds little foundation in *Ad gentes*.[40] According to *Ad gentes*, "God decided to enter into the history of mankind in a new and definitive manner by sending his own Son in human flesh so that through him he might snatch men from the power of darkness and of Satan (cf. Col 1:13; Acts 10:38) and in him reconcile the world to himself" (*AG* 3). This is the foundational insight of an "exclusivist" Christology. At the same time the decree is "inclusivist" to the extent that it acknowledges that "in ways known to himself God can lead those who, through no fault of their own, are ignorant of the Gospel to that faith without which it is impossible to please him" (*AG* 7). The salvation found by those who do not know Christ is, of course, still that offered by Christ and no other.[41]

What Then Is Mission?

At a popular level the term "evangelization" appears to have almost replaced mission. For a good many years the words "mission," "evangelization," and "witness" have been used almost synonymously. *Ad gentes*, however, took the trouble to work out a defining description of mission that assumes considerable significance in the face of some attempts to eliminate both the word "mission" and the concept itself. The difficulty is compounded because the

English language, in a postmodern situation, has suffered loss of meaning when using particular words in an overextended sense that robs them of specific meaning. An example is the application of "mission" to God as in "missio Dei," understandable as a metaphor but not literally true.[42] The decree uses "mission" and "evangelization" in particular meanings. It says that " 'Mission' is the term usually given those particular undertakings by which the heralds of the Gospel are sent by the Church and go forth into the whole world to carry out the task of preaching and planting the Church among people and groups who do not yet believe in Christ.... The special purpose of this missionary activity is evangelization and the planting of the Church among those people and groups where she has not yet taken root." (*AG* 6).

Historically this is significant in its insistence on bringing together the approaches of the Münster and Louvain schools of missiology. The separation of evangelization and Church planting had been artificial, a battle of academics that could only harm missionary vision. Now the debate has to go on holding both concepts together and developing a synthesis in light of the theological and ecclesiological bases for mission offered by *Ad gentes*.

Evangelization, which in the sense of the decree is an integral part of mission, "is that activity through which, in obedience to Christ's command and moved by the grace and love of the Holy Spirit, the Church makes herself fully present to all persons and peoples in order to lead them to faith, freedom and the peace of Christ by the example of her life and teaching and also by the sacraments and other means of grace" (*AG* 5). It is through evangelization that Church implantation happens.[43]

In a Catholic understanding, "the proclamation of the Gospel and the conversion of mankind necessarily lead to the administration of the sacraments and the formation of a church. Conversely it would be utopian to found a church before the faith has been proclaimed and visible success has been had with conversions."[44]

Yves Cardinal Congar, who played a role in formulating the text of *Ad gentes*, agrees: "The planting of the Church cannot be interpreted in a purely juridical sense; it is the implanting of a people of God which derives its origin first of all from the faith and thus from proclamation."[45] There can be no opposition between what the Church teaches and the Good News of the Gospel. The two interpenetrate in the understanding of the Trinitarian communion, which is the ground of the Church's existence. Mission, given by God in Christ, necessarily and fully includes both, thus excluding mere expansionism or ecclesiocentricity.[46]

It is vital both in Catholic missiological discussion and in teaching the faith to hold to the term "mission" as *Ad gentes* presents it. It does not seem to foster theological clarity to say that the "Triune God is the primordial missionary"[47]—for who can "send" the Trinity? The danger is that when everything is mission, nothing is mission. Yet it is true that one of the key words of the Gospels is "sending." Jesus, the Son of God, is sent by the Father and in turn sends out the Twelve. In this context one can say that "all the salvific activity of the Church has to do with being sent and sending; this is what *Ad gentes* calls 'missio Ecclesiae.' "[48]

Since the beginning of the Church there has been mission *ad gentes*. The decree quite clearly directs missionary activity to those who do not yet know Christ. This means drawing individuals to the faith and enabling the Church to become part of social and cultural conditions that Christianity has not yet touched. Cardinal Journet had already anticipated the thrust of the decree when he wrote the following: "The goal of missionary activity is, 1) in the night of this world, everywhere the Church still exists only in potency or in initial, hindered act, 2) to establish the Church in her complete act, 3) according to the exigencies of Catholic charity, that is to say, under indigenous forms."[49]

Today some question the value of this kind of missionary activity and the Church's right to engage in it. They ask whether the goal of conversion is appropriate and whether it is necessary for salvation. The decree had been clear enough that one of the goals of missionary work is "that non-Christians, whose heart is being opened by the Holy Spirit, coming to belief, may freely be converted to the Lord."[50]

The decree raised but did not expand on a theme that has been much debated since the council: human promotion and development. The Gospel is to act as a leaven "in the interest of liberty and progress, a leaven with regard to brotherhood, unity and peace" (*AG* 8). The decree aligns itself with the thrust of the Constitution on the Church in the Modern World on the relationship between Church and world, so that Christ may be known as "the hope of the nations and their Savior" (*AG* 8). Postconciliar teaching encouraged Christians to see efforts on behalf of justice and peace as a constitutive dimension of the Gospel.[51] In the decades following the council an emerging globalization of economic, political, and cultural structures has often become the vehicle of a powerful secular force with a diminished sense of God. In this atmosphere some Catholics began to find it congenial to think of human development as the primary goal of mission. The decree teaches, however, that "the Church has a spiritual and transcendent mission which cannot be reduced to a socioeconomic or political agenda."[52]

In face of distractions from the true nature of the Christian mission, Yves Cardinal Congar insisted with *Ad gentes* 7 that the missionary activity of the Church is "founded a) on the way in which God realizes concretely his will on universal salvation; b) on the ontology of the Church, the mystical body of Christ; c) on the attainment of the end foreseen by God for his creation."[53] Congar notes that the council rejected any concept of mission as a "quest for mere 'melius vivere.' . . . The Church is missionary in terms of the exigencies of her very existence."[54]

The second sentence of *Ad gentes* is a quotation from Saint Augustine on the missionary activity of the apostles, who, "following the footsteps of Christ 'preached the word of truth and begot churches'" (*AG* 1). The Church's missionary task is "to reveal and communicate the love of God to all men and to all peoples" (*AG* 10). It is not enough, as some suggest, to limit one's missionary service to promoting human development and helping people preserve their own religious traditions. Confident proclamation of salvation in Christ flows from the conviction that he truly holds the answers to the deepest human longings.[55] "Today, as always, proclamation of Jesus Christ cannot be substituted by purely temporal and human programs; the Gospel continues to be the center of missionary activity."[56]

Proclamation and Dialogue

The council's Declaration on the Church's Relation to Non-Christian Religions at the outset stated clearly that the Church "proclaims and is in duty bound to proclaim without fail Christ who is the way, the truth and the life (Jn 14:6). In him, in whom God reconciled all things to himself (2 Cor 5:18–19), men find the fullness of their religious life" (*NA* 2).

"The explicit proclamation of the person and message of Jesus Christ, or at least the burning intention to do so, is what ultimately makes mission mission... without the practice or intention of introducing others into a relation with God through and in Jesus" mission does not exist.[57] Proclamation entails an invitation to commit oneself to Christ and to enter through baptism into Christ's Church. It takes various forms, but it always means introducing a person to Christ, to his truth, and to his community of faith and grace and awakening a response of acceptance.

Christ proclaimed the truth of what he had heard from and seen in the Father. He commanded his followers to proclaim his Gospel. Proclamation is at the heart of missionary activity, which is "nothing else than the manifestation of God's plan, its epiphany and realization in the world and in history, that by which God, through mission, clearly brings to its conclusion the history of salvation" (*AG* 9).

Some want to reduce proclamation to witness of life and charity, to programs of human promotion, or to the substitution of a certain type of interreligious dialogue as a new form of mission. Here the temptation has been to inflate dialogue to become a means of obtaining truth that is still beyond both Christians and those of other faiths. Yet the truth of the mission of the Catholic Church is that its priority is always proclamation, albeit done in a context of respectful dialogue.[58]

Dialogue has various forms and levels. We have, for example, dialogue that is mutual communication at a human level and dialogue that is an attitude of friendship and respect, leavening missionary activity; more profoundly there is the dialogue that, in the context of religious plurality, includes all positive and constructive interreligious relations with individuals and communities of other faiths and is directed at mutual understanding and enrichment.[59]

The Second Vatican Council took a new step in tracing the reciprocal connection between dialogue and missionary activity: "In order to bear witness to Christ fruitfully, Christians should establish relationships of respect and love with those (of the great religions); they should acknowledge themselves as members of the group in which they live and, through the various undertakings and affairs of human life, they should share in their social and cultural life. They should be familiar with their national and religious traditions and uncover with gladness and respect those seeds of the Word which lie hidden among them" (AG 11).

Dialogue is now an inseparable part of the missionary task. It implies a new way of relating to and taking account of those to whom the proclamation is made and their situation. It means fostering reciprocal knowledge and understanding, including toward the religions of those who hear the proclamation of the Gospel for the first time. The decree spells out this dialogical structure: "Just as Christ penetrated to the hearts of men and, by a truly human dialogue, led them to the divine light, so too his disciples, profoundly pervaded by the spirit of Christ should know and converse with those among whom they live, that, through sincere and patient dialogue, these men might learn of the riches which a generous God has distributed among the nations. They must at the same time endeavor to illuminate those riches with the light of the Gospel, set them free and bring them once more under the dominion of God the savior" (AG 11).

The decree recognizes, of course, that elements of truth and grace "can be found to exist—through a secret presence of God, as it were—among the peoples of the earth" and that something of good can be "found in the heart and mind of man or in the particular rites and cultures of peoples" (AG 9). Significantly, the decree, "when dealing with missionary work, mentions solidarity with mankind, dialogue and collaboration, before speaking about witness and the preaching of the Gospel (AG 11–13)."[60] One cannot proclaim Christ apart from human relationships, nor can one influence someone he does not love.

The council's Constitution on the Church raised the question of how those who have not yet received the Gospel relate to the Church. It declared that "those who through no fault of their own do not know the Gospel of Christ or his Church but who, nevertheless, seek God with a sincere heart, and, moved by grace, try in their actions to do his will as they know it through the dictates of their conscience—these too may achieve eternal salvation.... Whatever good or truth is found among them is considered by the Church to be a preparation for the Gospel and given by him to enlighten all men that they may all at length have life" (LG 16).

The constitution goes on, however, to insist that one cannot simply accept this precarious situation as unchangeable. Lacking "the truth of God," open to human weakness and the wiles of the devil, even despite what is positive in their own religions, "they are exposed to ultimate despair." The Church is obliged in her missions to bring the offer of Christ's salvation. "The Church is drawn by the Holy Spirit to do her part for the full realization of the plan of God who has constituted Christ as the source of salvation for the whole world" (LG 17).

The council truly fostered a new attitude toward the other world religions: "The Catholic Church rejects nothing that is true and holy in these religions. She holds in sincere esteem those ways of life and conduct, those precepts and doctrines which, though differing in many respects from what she herself holds and teaches, nevertheless often reflect a ray of that truth which enlightens all men, yet she proclaims and is daily moved to proclaim unceasingly Christ who is the way, the truth and the life (Jn 14:6). In him in whom God reconciles all things to himself, men find fullness of life" (*NA* 2).

That teaching was developed when Pope Paul VI in the postsynodal apostolic exhortation, *Evangelii nuntiandi*, which enlarged on *Ad gentes* and spoke of the other faiths as "natural religious expressions worthy of esteem." However, he contrasted them with the religion of Christ, which "effectively establishes with God an authentic living relationship which the other religions do not succeed in doing."[61] "They are attempts, efforts, endeavors. They are arms outstretched towards heaven, to which they seek to arrive; but they are not a response to the act by which God has come to meet man. This act is Christianity, Catholic life."[62]

The Christian tradition of dialogue necessarily includes the possibility of conversion to Christ. Christian missionaries cannot set their belief on the same level as that of the person to whom the proclamation or witness is made, even while making the encounter in a spirit of dialogue and personal, mutual acceptance.[63] Nor may a Christian missionary ask that dialogue partners bracket their own faith in order to enter into conversation.

Within this understanding one can say that "proclaiming Christ must always be done in a context of respectful dialogue; the permanent priority of mission is proclamation in dialogue."[64] Proclamation and dialogue are not two equal entities; dialogue can be and needs to be a part of proclamation As one who devoted much of his missionary life to dialogue has explained, "Proclamation presupposes and requires a dialogue method in order to respond to the requirements of those to be evangelized and to enable them to interiorize the message received."[65] This might mean, for instance, as *Ad gentes* suggests, "fraternal dialogue with those who are working for peace to bring them into the peace and light of the Gospel" (*AG* 12).

Paul Knitter, in his 1996 book, *Jesus and the Other Names: Christian Mission and Global Responsibility*, claims that "mission is dialogue," thereby reducing evangelization to dialogue and emptying the witness to one's faith that dialogue implies. "Proclamation as a distinct expression of evangelization is thereby done away with."[66] Knitter rejects a "Christology that insists that Jesus is the only cause of and the unsurpassable criterion for the salvation to be realized in the Kingdom."[67]

Father Jacques Dupuis, S.J., says well that "one may not, on the pretext of honesty in dialogue bracket one's faith, even temporarily against the expectation, as has been suggested, of eventually rediscovering the truth of that faith through the dialogue itself. On the contrary, honesty and sincerity in dialogue specifically require that the various partners enter and commit themselves to it, in the integrity of their faith. Likewise the integrity of dialogue forbids any compromise or reduction of faith."[68]

It is puzzling that Father Dupuis seems to draw back from "using the terms 'absolute' and 'absoluteness' for Christianity as a historic religion"[69] and that he espouses the possibility of a simultaneous "double belonging"[70] to

Christianity and another faith since, in the end, this posits the incompleteness of both.

Conversion

In the spirit that pervaded the council it was to be expected that anything that resembled proselytism or infringement of religious liberty would be excluded; it was natural, therefore, that a statement on mission would insist, as does *Ad gentes*, that "the Church strictly forbids that anyone should be forced to accept the faith or be induced or enticed by unworthy devices" (*AG* 13).

Yet the decree forthrightly uses the term "conversion." In the preconciliar missiological debate, one-sided interpretations had been given of both the Münster School and the Louvain School. So there were those who created a false opposition by insisting that the goal of mission was not conversion or the salvation of souls or rebirth as the children of God but extension of the borders of the visible Church in a work of expansion.[71]

Cardinal Journet had already made the point very clearly to the council: "It is not to be said that the task of the missionary will not be to save souls."[72] The mission of the Church is, in the first place, addressed to peoples, not countries and regions. "The Church is implanted in human beings; it is they who constitute the Church." The decree repeatedly designates as the object of mission "peoples, groups or individuals who do not yet know Christ, in whom the Church has not yet taken root."[73]

The decree is clear that the goal of mission is preaching the Gospel and assembling the people of God with a view to opening the hearts of those who are not yet Christians so that by believing they might freely turn to the Lord (*AG* 13). "This conversion is, indeed, only initial, sufficient however to make a man realize that he has been snatched from sin and is being led into the mystery of God's love, who invites him to establish a personal relationship with him in Christ." This "involves a progressive change of outlook and morals which should be manifested in its social implications" (*AG* 13). This is the program of mission the Church has set out for herself with the decree and has been striving to implement ever since.

Conversion, as *Ad gentes* describes it, is a first, fundamental, decisive turning to Christ and to his Church. It is first of all the action of God, whose grace brings a person to the faith and to conversion; the missionary is the instrument of God's purpose. This conversion has to be followed by a real change in the life of the person freed from sin into a life marked by the liberty of God's children. God calls these individuals, who must then say "Yes" and entrust themselves to Christ, who renews them in the depths of their being. The mission is the occasion of the conversion.[74] To seek to make converts is not proselytism, since the faith is offered freely in order to offer union with God, salvation in Jesus Christ, and participation in the blessings and tasks of God's kingdom—although it is also necessary that "the motives for conversion should be examined" (*AG* 13). "The Christian faith is above all conversion to Jesus Christ."[75]

From Ferment to Crisis

Ad gentes gave the Church a charter of mission drawn from the living tradition and missionary practice from the beginning, all now directed to the future development of mission. The decree was the fruit of the ferment of questions and ideas already present through the first part of the twentieth century; though it provided material for solid solutions and healthy development, it was to stimulate an even more intense discussion among the bishops of the Church, missionaries, and missiologists. This discussion, however, became notably affected by the growing secularism of Western society and, to some degree, elsewhere.[76]

In the Catholic Church, one outcome of confusing renewal with self-secularization has been a diminished sense of the transcendent, a denial of God's direct agency; out of this has come a progressive loss of faith and Christian identity, resulting in a loss of mission itself.[77] As a result, Christ and his missionary mandate disappear from the Church's life. Mistaken answers have too often been given to real questions that arise from missionary experience. Rejection of the colonization with which missions had historically gone hand in hand; the cry for liberation from unjust and corrupt structures in the societies where missionaries have been working; the scandal of poverty in numerous places; and the social and economic disparity between North and South are all challenges that must be met in terms of the Church's faith in Jesus Christ.

Taken out of the context of faith, valid questions spawned ideologies that destroyed mission, as missionaries and missiologists sometimes substituted a radical commitment to the world for the commitment of faith. In trying to rethink mission in the modern world, some opted to do so on the world's terms by emptying proclamation of its content and making missiology almost a secular science. With that development went a rejection of *Ad gentes* in practice and often in theory.

In this complex and trying situation, the 1974 Roman Synod of Bishops took up the question of mission. The discussion was rather dispersed, but the apostolic exhortation *Evangelii nuntiandi* (1975), which Pope Paul VI based on the synod deliberations, was significant. *Ad gentes* had already said that "missionary activity is intimately bound up with human nature and its aspirations," and it asserts that the Gospel calls us to be a leaven in the world in the interests of liberty and progress, fraternity, unity, and peace (*AG* 8). *Evangelii nuntiandi* enlarged the concept of mission by linking it now more closely to human promotion and giving a summary of holistic mission theology. At the same time it ruled out terms such as liberation, option for the poor, dialogue, and inculturation as possible replacements for the concept of mission, although all of these can be necessary parts of mission or consequences of it. The salvation that the Church announces cannot be reduced to material well-being.[78] The proclamation of the Gospel is tied to people's eternal salvation.[79] Though the teaching of *Ad gentes* and its insistence on mission in the specific and traditional sense is integral to *Evangelii nuntiandi*, some in the missiological debate have claimed *Evangelii nuntiandi* as justification for going in contrary directions.

It was left to Pope John Paul II to show a way that would be faithful to the tradition and the teaching of *Ad gentes* and yet speak effectively to today's situation. He proposed "a thoroughly modern alternative reading of modernity."[80] It is a Christian account of modernity, "a unified understanding of the human condition that begins in God's revelation."[81] This different way to be modern is what Vatican II after all had set out to offer. In full fidelity to that purpose, *Ad gentes* had read mission in the perspective of encounter with Jesus Christ, a Christ-centered mission for the world that can exist only in and through the Church. On that understanding, Pope John Paul II further elaborated the papal magisterium on mission in several notable documents.

The Encyclical Redemptoris Missio, 1990

Pope John Paul II wrote this encyclical letter to mark the twenty-fifth anniversary of *Ad gentes*. Its aim was to confirm the missionary fruits of the council and also to examine the diminishment of the missionary impulse in the Church. It is a doctrinal reaffirmation of the theological and spiritual foundations of mission *Ad gentes*:

1. The truth grounded in the God of Jesus Christ meets the deep need of the human spirit. "The search for the whole truth which is God reaches its goal with the acceptance of the Gospel, the bearer of absolute truth."[82] Each person has a right to know the riches of the mystery of Christ.[83] The Jesus of history, who is the Christ of faith, is uniquely the fullness of God, the center and goal of history in its absolute and universal significance.[84] Some missiologists have been saying that Christ's revelation is limited and has to find its complement in other religions because the truth of God could not be grasped and manifested in its totality by any historical religion, even Christianity. "This is contrary to the faith of the Gospel."[85]

2. Jesus Christ is the only mediator and redeemer, the only foundation of mission.[86] Christ, the only mediator, has become not simply one mediator among many in the world's religions.[87] *Ad gentes* admitted that "in ways known to himself God can lead those who, through no fault of their own, are ignorant of the Gospel, to that faith without which it is impossible to please him" (*AG* 7). "Yet no one can enter into communion with God except through Christ by the working of the Holy Spirit."[88] Christ is present in the salvific process of both Christians and non-Christians, and the call to conversion must be addressed to non-Christians.

There are no parallel salvific mediations,[89] nor can missionary service be limited to human development and helping peoples preserve their own religious traditions.[90] "Proclamation is the permanent priority of mission. The Church cannot elude Christ's explicit mandate nor deprive men and women of the Good News of their being loved and saved by God. . . . All forms of mission are directed to this proclamation."[91]

3. The Church is central to mission; in some sectors of the missiological debate there has been strong pressure to relativize the Church as though it were provisional, simply an instrument to usher in the Kingdom of God and then disappear. *Redemptoris missio* makes clear that a necessary relation exists between Christ, his Kingdom, and the Church.[92] Jesus taught that the Kingdom of God was present in himself and his ministry. "The Kingdom of God is not a concept, a doctrine or a program subject to free interpretation but a person with the name and face of Jesus of Nazareth, the image of the invisible God."[93] He inaugurated the Kingdom on earth, and the Church he founded is the sacred sign and sacrament of that Kingdom.[94] In her missionary work, she carries out a service to the Kingdom.[95] The Kingdom and the Church cannot be separated. In the glorious consummation at the end of time, the Kingdom will "come" when "all the just from the time of Adam, 'from Abel, the just one, to the last of the elect' will be gathered together with the Father in the universal Church" (*LG* 2). While surely not excluding the action of Christ and the Spirit outside the Church's visible boundaries,[96] "the Church is the ordinary means of salvation and she alone possesses the fullness of the means of salvation."[97]

Forms of Kingdom-centered missiology that separate the Kingdom from the Church and also from Christ, so that mission becomes "promoting the so-called 'values of the Kingdom' (peace, justice, freedom, fraternity) as well as dialogue between peoples, cultures and religions with the goal of mutual enrichment" are misleading and inadequate.[98] The mission of the Church is to announce a Kingdom already present within her.[99]

4. The one salvation in Christ is brought about by the action of the Holy Spirit. The encyclical acknowledges that "through dialogue the Church seeks to uncover the 'seeds of the Word,' a 'ray of that truth which enlightens all men'; these are found in individuals and in the religious traditions of mankind."[100] The Holy Spirit can move human hearts to conversion to Christ beyond the visible Church, yet the Holy Spirit does not at all act as "an alternative to Christ."[101] The same Spirit who was at work in the saving deeds of Christ is at work in the Church, impelling her to proclaim Christ; this is the Spirit who can implant and develop his gifts in all individuals and peoples.[102] The absolute revelation of God is mediated to the human situation in Christ by the power of the Holy Spirit.[103] Therefore the activity of the Spirit "serves as a preparation for the Gospel and can only be understood in reference to Christ the Word who took flesh by the power of the Spirit.... Nor is the universal activity of the Spirit to be separated from his particular activity within the body of Christ which is the Church."[104]

5. In the missiological debate, weakening the term "mission" and the idea of mission *ad gentes* has resulted in confusion in thought and practice. Yet the Church in her magisterium and her pastoral strategy continues to uphold the concept as given in the decree, *Ad gentes*.

Pope John Paul II in the encyclical *Redemptoris missio* defines mission and its goal in light of the three concrete situations in which the Church carries out her various activities: mission *ad gentes*; pastoral care; and new evangelization.[105] There is the one mission of the Church,[106] but these three activities of it have to be safeguarded in their specificity. This is especially true of mission *ad gentes.* "Care must be taken to avoid the risk of putting very different situations on the same level or of reducing or eliminating the Church's mission and missionaries *ad gentes.*"[107] "In the life of the Church mission *ad gentes* is at the center, at the very heart of the Church's missionary mandate."[108] The truth is that lack of missionary fervor may reveal a deeper problem, a crisis of faith in Jesus Christ.[109]

Reflections and Orientation: Proclamation and Dialogue

A document on proclamation and dialogue by the Congregation for the Evangelization of Peoples and the Pontifical Commission for Interreligious Dialogue was published in 1991, shortly after *Redemptoris missio.* It takes its stand on the themes of the encyclical and insists that "The permanent priority of mission is proclamation in dialogue."[110]

Further light can be cast on the relation between dialogue and proclamation and the relation of other religions to the Church. Jesus sent his disciples to proclaim the Gospel; the Church's work of proclamation continues that of Jesus.[111] "Christ is the Truth and the Way which the preaching of the Gospel lays open to all men" (*AG* 8). The content of the proclamation is God's Word, which infinitely surpasses the inner hopes of the human heart,[112] which is made to respond to truth.[113]

"Interreligious dialogue and proclamation are both authentic elements of the Church's evangelizing mission."[114] They are not however on the same level, not interchangeable. To be genuine "interreligious dialogue on the part of the Christian presupposes the desire to make Jesus Christ better known, recognized and loved; proclaiming Jesus Christ is to be carried out in the Gospel spirit of dialogue."[115]

The Declaration, Dominus Jesus

It all seems clear enough. Yet the crisis in mission and in interreligious dialogue occasioned another document, *Dominus Jesus,* which repeats what the council had already said clearly in *Ad gentes,* namely, Christianity's claim to absolute validity.[116] Jesus is the incarnate Word of God, not just "one of the many faces the Logos has assumed."[117] Jesus is "the exclusive, universal and absolute source of salvation for the world, not simply one way to salvation among many others."[118]

Jesus Christ is "the key, the center and the purpose" of the entire sweep of human history.[119] Unequivocally and in full fidelity to the teaching of Vatican II in *Ad gentes, Dominus Jesus* excludes any idea that revelation in Jesus Christ is "limited, incomplete and imperfect" or that it needs to be complemented in revelations found in other religions.[120] This does not contradict the need for dialogue among cultures in order to evangelize. If contacts made possible in an era of globalization give birth to genuine dialogue among cultures and religions, new paths for evangelization and new ways of mission could open up in the new global areopagus.[121] Could that mean "an opportunity to do Christian theology in a new way: through the careful study of the teachings of other religious traditions"?[122] Such a possibility and any other outcome could be helpful and needed, subject to discernment by and fidelity to the Church's missionary tradition embodied in *Ad gentes* and the subsequent magisterium.

The primary service the Church can render to the world is to direct the gaze of all toward Christ the redeemer, the center of the universe and of history, in whom God's love and mercy are fully revealed. This is the goal of mission in all of its forms and the goal to which *Ad gentes* unwaveringly directs our gaze.

Mission, Today and Always

Since the decree *Ad gentes*, the Church's Magisterium in the pontificates of Pope Paul VI and Pope John Paul II has taken an evangelical turn. This insistence on mission and evangelization, with its recurrent themes of inculturation and dialogue, on work for universal justice and charity is rooted in the Second Vatican Council's own purpose, expressed not just in *Ad gentes* but in all its documents. The council was called to that the Church might be the center and expression of the world's unity. The Church's purpose is to convert the world to Jesus Christ in his body, the Church.

The teaching on mission has addressed the historical obstacles to mission in the midst of economic and cultural globalization. The mission of the Church is challenged anew by the abandonment of the faith on the part of historically Christian people, and Pope John Paul II responded by calling for a new evangelization to address this phenomenon. Finally, however, the greatest challenge to the Church's mission is any reductionist interpretation of who Jesus Christ is and what he has given his Church the command and authority to carry out. A reductionist understanding of the Church's missionary activity will destroy motivation for mission and, eventually, weaken the Church's internal life. Spiritual gifts must be shared or they will be lost.

In Jesus' own age, his contemporaries had great difficulty in coming to terms with his uniqueness. They entertained many erroneous ideas about him, all of them partial. Who Christ really is was revealed definitively in his resurrection from the dead, for only then does it become clear that Christ has a right to call the world to conversion. Today as well, there are partial and therefore erroneous ideas about Jesus Christ. When the Church is tempted to reduce her faith to them, she risks losing her life and betraying the mission given her by her Lord.

The originality of Jesus Christ marks the proclamation of the Gospel by the Church. Often misunderstood and sometimes hated, neither triumphalistic nor co-opted, the Church makes her way through every age with an original voice, that of the Savior of the world, her head and Lord. The way is always a missionary path.

NOTES

1. Romano Guardini, *The Church of the Lord* (Chicago: Regnery, 1966), 73.
2. Ibid., 11.
3. Sebastian Karotemprel, S.D.B., *General Introduction in Following Christ in Mission* (Nairobi, Kenya: Paulines Publications Africa, 1996), xv.
4. Tomaso Federici, "Pneumatalogical Foundation of Mission," in ibid., 95.
5. Rudolf Schnackenburg, *The Church in the New Testament* (New York: Herder and Herder, 1965), 62. This par. [4] draws heavily on Schnackenburg.
6. Ibid., 136.
7. Ibid., 137.
8. Ibid., 139.
9. Christopher Dawson, *The Historic Reality of Christian Culture* (New York: Harper, 1960), 103. Dawson writes, "The Church as a divine society possesses an internal principle of life which is capable of assimilating the most diverse materials and imprinting her own image upon them. Inevitably in the course of history there are times when this spiritual energy is temporarily weakened or obscured, then the Church tends to be judged as a human organization and identified with the faults and limitations of her members. But always the time comes when she renews her strength and once more puts forth her inherent divine energy in the conversion of new peoples and the transformation of old cultures."
10. See *Dictionary of the Christian Church*, 2d ed., ed. E. A. Livingstone (New York: Oxford University Press, 2000), s.v. "Missions." See also Diarmaid MacCulloch, "The Counter-Reformation as World Mission in the Reformation," in *Reformation: Europe's House Divided, 1490–1700* (London: Allen Lane, 2003), 414–27. This book is written from a traditional Protestant perspective but on this point is interesting and informative.
11. Karl Muller, S.V.D., "Missiology: An Introduction," in Karotemprel, *General Introduction*, 26.
12. Ibid., 40.
13. Karotemprel, *General Introduction*, xv.
14. Pope John Paul II, *Ut unum sint* (1995), no. 18.
15. Ibid.
16. Pope Benedict XV, *Maxime illud* (1919); Pope Pius XI, *Rerum Ecclesiae* (1926); Pope Pius XII, *Summi pontificatus* (1939); idem, *Evangelii praecones* (1951); idem, *Fidei donum* (1957); Pope John XXIII, *Princeps pastorum* (1959).
17. Joseph Cardinal Frings, archbishop of Cologne, in *acta synodalia sacrosancti Concilii Oecumenici Vatican Secundi*, vol. 3, pt. 6, 374–75.
18. *Lumen gentium*, nos. 16, 17.
19. Johannes Schutte, S.V.D., in *Acta synodalia*, vol. 4, pt. 3, 701.
20. Bishop Paternus Geise, O.F.M., of Bogor, Indonesia, in *Acta synodalia*, vol. 3, pt. 6, 386–88, speaking for the bishops' conference of Indonesia: He said missionary activity should be more closely linked with the inner nature of the Church. It is necessary to show the bond between missionary duty and the salvific will of God. "Missionary activity aims to make present everywhere the Church as the community of salvation and so to make visible to all the means of salvation entrusted to her by Christ." See also his later intervention in *Acta synodalia*, vol. 4, pt. 4, 162, and that of Cardinal Frings in *Acta synodalia*, vol. 4, pt. 3, 739.
21. Francis Cardinal König, archbishop of Vienna, in *Acta synodalia*, vol. 4, pt. 4, 137.

22. *Ad gentes*, no. 1, quoting *LG* 48. All citations from documents of the Second Vatican Council are from *Vatican Council II*, vol. 1, *The Conciliar and Postconciliar Documents*, ed. Austin Flannery, new rev. ed. (Northport, N.Y.: Costello, 1975), unless otherwise indicated.

23. *AG* 2; see Adam Wolanin S.J., "Trinitarian Foundation of Mission," in Karotemprel, *General Introduction*, 47–64.

24. Final report in Jan P. Schotte, C.I.C.M., *The Second Vatican Council and the Synod of Bishops* (1986), 68.

25. Basil Meeking, "Evangelization, the Goal of the Church's Teaching," *Midstream* 40 (2000): 67, 68. See also M. J. Scheeben, in *The Mysteries of Christianity* (St. Louis: Herder, 1946), 157, where he suggests that mission can be regarded as a reproduction or even a prolongation of the eternal processions. Aidan Nichols, O.P., *The Splendor of Doctrine* (Edinburgh: T&T Clark, 1995), 10: "The eternal processions of the Son and the Holy Spirit are 'archetypal' events . . . prolonged in the missions of the same Son and Holy Spirit to the world of time and space."

26. Pope John Paul II, apostolic exhortation *Christifideles Laici* (1988), no. 32.

27. *Catechism of the Catholic Church*, no. 730.

28. Charles Cardinal Journet, in *Acta synodalia*, vol. 4, pt. 3, 743.

29. Stephen B. Bevans, S.V.D., and Roger P. Schroeder, S.V.D., *Constants in Context* (Maryknoll, N.Y.: Orbis, 2004), 298.

30. Ibid., 250; There is a failure here to give account to the ecclesial truth well described by Dominican ecclesiologist Benoît-Dominique de la Soujeole in *La sacrement de la communion* (Fribourg: Editions Universitaires, 1998), 382. The gifts of God are in this concrete community; the holy Church is indeed this visible community. There is no duality of communities (spiritual church and official church). Vatican II in the sum of its teaching was a kind of Chalcedon of ecclesiology; the Church is not two communities but one complex reality.

31. Adam Wolanin, S.J., ibid., no. 24, 58.

32. Muller, "Missiology," 26.

33. See Paul Joseph LaChance, "Christ Our Salvation," *Josephinum* 12 (2005): 4.

34. The Most Rev. Joseph Cordeiro, archbishop of Karachi, speaking in the name of fifty bishops from various regions in *Acta synodalia*, vol. 4, pt. 4, 150–53.

35. Leo Cardinal Suenens, archbishop of Brussels, in *Acta synodalia*, vol. 4, pt. 4, 179–80.

36. Eusebius Adjakpley, in *Acta synodalia*, vol. 4, pt. 4, 329.

37. Pope John Paul II, address to the Congregation for the Doctrine of the Faith (Jan. 26, 2006), *L'osservatore romano* (Feb. 2000), 3.

38. Joseph Ratzinger, *Introduction to Christianity* (San Francisco: Ignatius Press, 1969, 2004), 198–99.

39. Sebastian Karotemprel, "Christological and Soteriological Foundations of Mission," in Karotemprel, *General Introduction*, 65.

40. Bevans and Schroeder, *Constants in Context*, 40.

41. Francis Clark, *Godfaring* (Washington, D.C.: Catholic University of America Press, 2000), 93. The Christian faith confesses Jesus of Nazareth to be the Son of God made man and to be the way, the truth, and the life for all human beings in all religious cultures. No attempted application of the theological principle of "communicatio idiomatum" can validate a theory of a pluriform salvific act in the history of the transcendent Word/Spirit distinct from the uniquely salvific act of the incarnate Word, who is Jesus the Nazarene.

42. William Frazier, M.M., "Nine Breakthroughs in Catholic Missiology, 1965–2000," *International Bulletin of Missionary Research* 25 (2001): 9.

43. See Francis Anekwe Oborji, "Mission in Catholic Mission Theology since Vatican II," *Omnis terra* 353 (2005): 33.

44. Suso Brechter, "Decree on the Church's Missionary Activity," in *Commentary on the Documents of Vatican II*, vol. 4, ed. Herbert Vorgrimler (New York: Herder and Herder, 1967), 118–19.

45. Cited in Karl Muller, in *Mission Theology* (Nettetal, Germany: Steyler, 1987), 43.

46. Ibid., 45.

47. William Frazier, in ibid., 9.

48. Muller, "Missiology," 29.

49. Charles Cardinal Journet, *Theology of the Church* (1958), 339–40.

50. In this citation from the Flannery text of *Ad gentes* a slight amendment has been made in light of the original Latin text: "Ut non-christiani, Spiritu Sancto cor ipsorum aperiente, credentes ad Dominum libere convertantur."

51. Roman Synod of Bishops, *Justice in the World* (1971), 6.

52. Ramón Macías Alatorre, "Liberation and Human Promotion," in Karotemprel, *General Introduction*, 178.

53. Yves Cardinal Congar, "The Necessity of the Mission *Ad gentes*," *Studia Missionalia* 51 (2002): 159.

54. Ibid., 157–58.

55. Francis Cardinal George, "One Lord and One Church for One World," *Omnis terra* 317 (May 2001): 189.

56. Jesus López-Gay. S.J., "Proclamation," in Karotemprel, *General Introduction*, 132.

57. Bevans and Schroeder, *Constants in Context*, 358.

58. Ibid.

59. Congregation for the Evangelization of Peoples/Pontifical Council for Interreligious Dialogue (1991), 9.

60. Ibid., 75.

61. Pope Paul VI, apostolic exhortation *Evangelium nuntiandi*, no. 53.

62. Pope Paul VI, *L'osservatore romano* (Mar. 23, 1966), 1.

63. Brechter, "Decree," 128–29: "Genuine dialogue is more than trivial conversation; it is an opportunity for bearing witness. According to Martin Buber, genuine dialogue does not presuppose that the partners agree beforehand to treat their own convictions as relative, but [that] they accept one another as persons.... On both sides dialogue involves bearing witness.... It is not the case that Christians, convinced though they are of being in full possession of the truth have nothing to learn from people of other religious views.... From the start the Christian must stress the grace-given character of belief in Christ; this excludes all arrogance but imposes the obligation on believers of speaking gratefully about Christ to all who are willing to listen."

64. Bevans and Schroeder, *Constants in Context*, 358.

65. Marcello Zago, O.M.I., "The New Millennium and the Emerging Religious Encounters," *Missiology: An International Review* (Jan. 28, 2000): 17.

66. Paul Knitter, "Jesus and the Other Names: Christian Mission and Global Responsibility" (Maryknoll, N.Y.: Orbis, 1996), 134–135; also 125–164.

67. Ibid., 135.

68. Jacques Dupuis, S.J., "The Church's Evangelizing Mission," *Pastoral Review* 1 (2005): 23.

69. Ibid., 27–28.

70. Ibid., 28–29.

71. Muller, "Missiology," 41.

72. Journet, *Theology of the Church*, 340.

73. Brechter, "Decree," 120; *Ad gentes* 6. Further explanation is required of the statement of Walter Cardinal Kasper quoted in William McConville, O.F.M., in the *New Dictionary of Theology* (Wilmington, Del.: Michael Glazier, 1987), 667: "The Church's mission which is rooted in the absolute claims of Christianity is not so much to save the individual—who in principle can be saved outside the visible communion—as to represent and proclaim the love of God, to give testimony to hope, and so to be a sign among the nations."

74. Karl Muller, *Mission Theology*, 144–45.

75. *National Directory for Catechesis* (Washington, D.C.: USCCB, 2005), 48.

76. Ibid., 104, 160.

77. Adam Wolanin, in Karotemprel, *General Introduction*, 50.

78. George, "One Lord," 189.

79. *Catechism of the Catholic Church*, no. 851.

80. George Weigel, *The Cube and the Cathedral* (New York: Basic Books, 2005), 169.

81. Ibid., 170.

82. Manuel Urena, "The Missionary Impulse in the Church according to 'Redemptoris Missio,'" *Communio* 19 (1992): 95.

83. *Redemptoris missio*, no. 8.

84. Ibid., no. 6.

85. Pope John Paul II, address to the Congregation for the Doctrine of the Faith, *L'osservatore romano* (English) (Feb. 2, 2000), 3.

86. *Redemptoris missio*, nos. 4, 5.

87. Jacques Dupuis, "The Church's Evangelizing Mission."

88. *Redemptoris missio*, no. 5.

89. Pope Benedict XVI, address to the Roman Clergy, *L'osservatore romano* (May 2005). The Holy Father referred to the temptation of contemporary missiologists to say about people of other faiths: "Why do we not leave them in peace? They have their authenticity, their truth. We have ours. And so let us live together in harmony."

90. George, "One Lord."

91. *Redemptoris missio*, no. 44.

92. Bevans and Schroeder, *Constants in Context*, 319, 311–12. In his book, *Toward a Christian Theology of Religious Pluralism*, Father Jacques Dupuis, taking a negative attitude to several of the statements of Vatican II, sets up a model of "regnocentrism" that criticizes the "narrow ecclesiocentric perspective" of the encyclical *Redemptoris missio* and states that "the Church is provisional by nature and due to disappear when the fullness of the Kingdom is achieved." This is usefully assessed by Francis Clark in *Godfaring*, ch. 7. Father Francis Oborji, in *Omnis terra* 353 (Jan. 2005): 38, says, "The problem begins when the Kingdom of God replaces the mission of Jesus Christ and the present role of the Church. This school of thought... forgets that the Church is a 'mystery.'"

93. *Redemptoris missio*, no. 18.

94. Ibid.

95. Ibid., no. 20; see Paul Vadakumpadan, S.D.B., "Ecclesiological Foundation of Mission," in Karotemprel, *General Introduction*, 100, 102.

96. *Redemptoris missio*, no. 18.

97. Ibid., no. 55.

98. Urena, "Missionary Impulse," 99.

99. Avery Cardinal Dulles, S.J., makes the point that, while the Church is not to be identified fully with the reign of God, neither is it to be totally separated from it. "In the eyes of believers, it should be obvious that the Kingdom of God cannot be adequately realized apart from the Church" (cited in Bevans and Schroeder, *Constants in Context*, 344).

100. *Redemptoris missio*, no. 56, quoting respectively *AG* 11, 15, and *NA* 2.

101. Ibid., no. 29.

102. Ibid.

103. So a question must be put to the assertion of the late Father Dupuis, in *Toward a Christian Theology*, 28, when he says that "God alone is the absolute... the humanity of Jesus is the personal human being of the Son of God.... It remains by its very nature... contingent."

104. *Redemptoris missio*, no. 29; Urena, "Missionary Impulse," 102: "The human person is constitutively oriented to the God of Jesus Christ through the Creator and through the interior activity of the Spirit. Far from finding plenitude in his own immanence, he is open to Jesus Christ whom he searches for without realizing it, and is led to Christ completely by the Church in which Christ, through the activity of the Spirit, lives throughout the ages as the light of the nations."

105. *Redemptoris missio*, no. 33.

106. Ibid., no. 31.

107. Ibid., no. 32.

108. Oborji, 38.

109. *Redemptoris missio*, nos. 11, 36; George, "One Lord," 184, 189.

110. Bevans and Schroeder, *Constants in Context*, 358.

111. Congregation for the Evangelization of Peoples/Pontifical Council for Interreligious Dialogue, 55–59.

112. *Ad gentes* 13; Congregation for the Evangelization of Peoples/Pontifical Council for Interreligious Dialogue, 67.

113. *Dei Verbum* 7. In his book *Truth and Tolerance* (San Francisco: Ignatius Press, 2003), Josef Cardinal Ratzinger commented, "We may say that, according to its own understanding of itself, Christianity stands at one and the same time in both a positive and a negative relation to the religions of the world; it recognizes itself as being linked with them in the unity of the concept of a covenant relationship and lives out of the conviction that the cosmos and its myth, just like history and its mystery, speak of God and can lead to God; but it is equally aware of a decided No to other religions and sees in them a means by which man seeks to shield himself from God instead of leaving himself open to his demands" (21).

114. Congregation for the Evangelization of Peoples/Pontifical Council for Interreligious Dialogue, 77.

115. Ibid.

116. Bevans and Schroeder, *Constants in Context*, 383.

117. Congregation for the Doctrine of the Faith: Instruction, *Dominus Jesus* (2000), 9. In *Truth and Tolerance*, after describing a fourth-century Roman emperor's defense of paganism, Cardinal Ratzinger went on: "This is exactly what enlightenment is saying today. We do not know truth as such; yet in a variety of images we all express the same thing. So great a mystery as the Divinity cannot be fixed in one image which would exclude all others—to one path obligatory for all. There are many paths; there are many images; all reflect something of the whole, and none is itself the whole. He is practicing

the ethic of tolerance who recognizes in each one a little of the truth, who does not set his own above what is strange to him, and who peacefully takes his place in the uniform symphony of the eternally unattainable that hides itself in symbols, symbols that yet seem to be the only way we have to grasp in some sense the Divinity" (176).

118. *Dominus Jesus*, no. 15.

119. Ibid., no. 13.

120. Ibid., no. 6; George, "One Lord," 191.

121. George, "One Lord," 194.

122. James Fredericks, "The Catholic Church and the Other Religious Paths," *Theological Studies* 64 (2003): 225–54.

15

The Decree on Ecumenism, *Unitatis Redintegratio*

Charles Morerod, O.P.

Ecumenism before Vatican II

In order to grasp some understanding of *Unitatis redintegratio*'s continuity with tradition, one might of course consider how Church unity has been understood for two millennia.[1] That would be too broad for our purpose. The ecumenical question is actually rather recent. First of all, the consciousness of a somehow permanent division, after both the Eastern schism of 1054 and the Reformation of the sixteenth century, appeared only some time after the divisions themselves. Such a consciousness was certainly clear by the end of the sixteenth century: From then on to be a Christian has implied belonging to one particular denomination.

The meaning of the division was interpreted in different ways. Some theologians tried to justify the situation. For instance, French Reformed pastor Pierre Jurieu (1637–1713) affirmed that "The Catholic and universal Church contains all the Christian Societies that keep the fundamental truths."[2] He rejected as "papist" the necessity of one visible Church: "Once the minds will have entered that truth that the Church is not enclosed within one communion only, one can be assured that papism is lost. Because one will see that it is not true any more that the Roman Church be that only communion and that out of her there would be no salvation."[3]

The first council of the Vatican (1870) has a far less positive view of the divisions: "Everybody knows that those heresies, condemned by the fathers of Trent, which rejected the divine Magisterium of the Church and allowed religious questions to be a matter for the judgment of each individual, have gradually collapsed into a multiplicity of sects, either at variance or in agreement with one another; and by this means a good many people have had all faith in Christ destroyed."[4]

The 1917 *Code of Canon Law* considered its subject to be all baptized people who were able to use their reason[5]—except for those who belonged to Eastern Catholic churches;[6] therefore, all members of other Christian denominations were legally submitted to the Roman pontiff; since the 1983 *Code of Canon Law* this has no longer been the case.[7]

The contemporary ecumenical movement began toward the end of the nineteenth century and was stimulated by the contacts and concurrence in missionary activities. As some similar initiatives were beginning among non-Catholic Christians, Pope Leo XIII instituted a week of prayer for the unity with the "dissident brethren" during the week before Pentecost.[8] The first ecumenical assemblies were not warmly appreciated by the popes of the time. In 1928 Pius XI published his encyclical *Mortalium animos*, in which he criticized ecumenical meetings (such as the Faith and Order Conference of Lausanne, 1927) for ecclesiological reasons: "They understand a visible Church as nothing else than a Federation, composed of various communities of Christians, even though they adhere to different doctrines, which may even be incompatible one with another. Instead, Christ our Lord instituted his Church as a perfect society, external of its nature and perceptible to the senses, which should carry on in the future the work of the salvation of the human race, under the leadership of one head, with an authority teaching by word of mouth, and by the ministry of the sacraments."[9]

Even the non-Catholics who might recognize some role of the pope do it for insufficient reasons, and therefore Catholics must stay away from these ecumenical meetings:

> Among them there indeed are some, though few, who grant to the Roman Pontiff a primacy of honor or even a certain jurisdiction or power, but this, however, they consider not to arise from the divine law but from the consent of the faithful.... Meanwhile they affirm that they would willingly treat with the Church of Rome, but on equal terms, that is as equals with an equal: but even if they could so act, it does not seem open to doubt that any pact into which they might enter would not compel them to turn from those opinions which are still the reason why they err and stray from the one fold of Christ. This being so, it is clear that the Apostolic See cannot on any terms take part in their assemblies, nor is it anyway [*sic*] lawful for Catholics either to support or to work for such enterprises; for if they do so they will be giving countenance to a false Christianity, quite alien to the one Church of Christ. Shall We suffer, what would indeed be iniquitous, the truth, and a truth divinely revealed, to be made a subject for compromise?[10]

In 1957 archbishop of Milan Giovanni Battista Montini—who would approve *Unitatis redintegratio*, article 7, years later as pope—said that "The Catholic Church, obviously, cannot take part to such meetings ... because she has the divine certainty of being in truth, and therefore she cannot allow to herself the ambiguity of hundreds of persons who, while affirming different things, profess to be, all for themselves, absolute possessors of truth."[11] That official approach to ecumenical meetings lasted more or less until Vatican II. Still, a few aspects of a new attitude already appear before the council.

A 1949 Instruction of the Holy Office opened the door to limited participation of Catholics in ecumenical meetings:

> Ordinaries will need to employ altogether exceptional watchfulness and control as regards mixed conventions and meetings held between Catholics and non-Catholics, which in recent times have come into vogue in many places to foster "reunion" in the Faith. If in truth these offer a desirable occasion for spreading a knowledge of Catholic doctrine with which generally non-Catholics are not sufficiently conversant, on the other hand they also readily conjure up no slight danger of indifferentism to Catholics. Where some hopes of good results appear, the Ordinary will be solicitous to secure their proper direction by designating for them priests, who are best fitted for such gatherings and show ability to expound and defend Catholic doctrine in a suitable and competent manner. The faithful, however, shall not assist at such assemblies without a special permission from the ecclesiastical authority, which should be given only to those who are known to be well instructed and firmly established in the Faith.[12]

Pope John XXIII will look at ecumenical meetings from a new perspective:

> We have taken note that almost all those who are adorned with the name of Christian even though separated from Us and from one another have sought to forge bonds of unity by means of many congresses and by establishing councils. This is evidence that they are moved by an intense desire for unity of some kind.[13]

Pope John does not claim that the model of unity expressed in ecumenical meetings (like those of the World Council of Churches) is sufficient, but he looks first at what is good: They promote at least some kind of unity. From this starting point it will become possible to act together for a fuller unity.

Ecumenism was one of the main focuses of Vatican II, and Pope John XXIII inserted that dimension into the structure of the council. The Internet site of the Vatican summarizes the historical data:

> It was Pope John XXIII's desire that the involvement of the Catholic Church in the contemporary ecumenical movement be one of the council's chief concerns. Thus, on June 5, 1960, he established a "Secretariat for Promoting Christian Unity" as one of the preparatory commissions for the council, and appointed Augustin Cardinal Bea as its first president. This was the first time that the Holy See had set up an office to deal uniquely with ecumenical affairs.
>
> At first, the main function of the secretariat was to invite the other churches and world communions to send observers to the Second

Vatican Council. Already, however, from the first session (1962), by a decision of Pope John XXIII, it was placed on the same level as the conciliar commissions. The secretariat thus prepared and presented to the council the documents on ecumenism (*Unitatis redintegratio*), on non-Christian religions (*Nostra aetate*), on religious liberty (*Dignitatis humanae*) and, together with the doctrinal commission, the Dogmatic Constitution on Divine Revelation (*Dei Verbum*).[14]

Archbishop Montini of Milan, the future Pope Paul VI, also perceived ecumenism to be one of the council's main tasks.[15]

Short History of *Unitatis Redintegratio*

The history of the Decree on Ecumenism has been well presented, together with commentaries, in several valuable works published shortly after the council.[16] Here I briefly summarize these books. The first schema on ecumenism, *De Ecclesiae unitate*, "Ut omnes unum sint,"[17] was prepared by the Secretariat for Unity, together with the oriental and theological commissions, from January to March 1963.[18] The theologians involved in drafting the text were mainly Belgian, Dutch, and French. It was presented in May 1963, between the first and the second sessions of the council, shortly before John XXIII's death. After the opening of the second session by Paul VI, the schema *De oecumenismo* was discussed in November and December 1963.[19] In January 1964 the pope met Patriarch Athenagoras. Until the spring of 1964, what was to become an independent Declaration on Religious Freedom was an appendix to the Decree on Ecumenism.[20] In September 1964 the council received the new version of the schema favorably and suggested a few *modi*, which three subcommissions considered.[21] The additions were discussed in November 1964,[22] and the final text was approved on November 21, 1964, by 2,137 yes votes and 11 no votes.[23]

The Introduction of the Decree

In the first two drafts of the schema, the text spoke more generally about the Church, thus beginning on a positive note in the usual style of Vatican II. Some fathers suggested that such content was already to be found in the schema *De Ecclesia* (*Lumen gentium*).[24] A new article 1 was then added, which dealt more specifically with the problem that had to be addressed.

Article 1, which introduces the whole decree, also explains its relation to the council's other texts. It says first that "The restoration of unity among all Christians is one of the principal concerns of the second Vatican synod." This intention (expressed by John XXIII and Cardinal Montini before the beginning of the council) was borne in mind by the fathers throughout the council, and its importance reflects the fact that the purpose of the Church is to establish unity between the whole of humanity and God (cf. the programmatic first articles of the constitutions *Lumen gentium, Dei verbum, Sacrosanctum concilium,* and *Gaudium et spes*).

The decree gives three reasons for that desire for unity: "Such division is clearly contrary to Christ's will. It is a scandal to the world and damages the sacred cause of preaching the gospel to every creature" because "many Christian communions claim to be the true inheritance of Jesus Christ" (this is one of the few cases in which Christian denominations are called "communions,"[25] a practice that became common in ecumenical dialogues but is little used in the decree,[26] although John Paul II stated that it summarizes the content of Vatican II[27]). Christ's desire for unity and the necessity not to be divided in preaching Christ were the basis of the ecumenical movement and are still its center. The text of article 1 goes on to explain that such a purpose, present among Christians of all denominations, can be achieved "with the help of the grace of the holy Spirit" (*Spiritus sancti fovente gratia*). That desire for unity, which belongs to the Christian faith, has been present "in recent times more than before" (*novissime ... abundantius*). The newness is part of a providential purpose developed in what Saint Irenaeus would call the "economy": "The Lord of the ages works out with patience and wisdom the plan of his grace on our behalf, sinners though we are." Continuity and newness have the deepest common root, that is, the divine plan.

The ecumenical movement is carefully defined: "Participation in this movement, called 'ecumenical,' entails invoking the triune God and confessing Jesus Christ as Lord and Savior, not merely as individuals, but also as members of the corporate bodies in which they have heard the gospel." Ecumenism is distinguished both from interreligious dialogue and from a dialogue limited to individuals (although of course the individual dimension is also part of the divine plan; cf. no. 4). The text explains the meaning of ecumenism first of all to Catholics.

Chapter 1

Chapter 1 is not about ecumenism generally speaking but about "Catholic principles on ecumenism." For the reason also highlighted in *Dei verbum*, articles 1 and 2—namely that God loves us and is Himself unity—state that God wants our unity. That unity is the purpose of the work of Jesus Christ, who gave his life for the Church and bestowed upon her the Holy Spirit, "who brings about that wonderful communion of the faithful." The sacraments— above all the Eucharist and the one baptism—and the ministers of the Church edify that unity obtained by Christ, who remains forever the "shepherd of our souls." Speaking about the ministries in the Church, the decree summarizes what is more developed in *Lumen gentium* or *Christus Dominus* (*Unitatis redintegratio*, article 2, mentions the Petrine ministry in relation to Christ, who remains the cornerstone and shepherd; this is supported by a reference to Vatican I). That unity, whose "model and source" is the Trinity, will be fully achieved in "the homeland in heaven."

Some divisions have existed in the Church from the beginning. The origin of the present doctrinal and disciplinary divisions cannot be attributed only to "the others": all of us are sinners, and no sinner can feel innocent of the divisions. Still, this is not a reason to accuse contemporary divided Christians of committing by their very birth the sins of heresy or schism: "Those who are now born into these communities and who are brought up in the faith of Christ cannot be accused of the sin involved in the separation." This important statement expresses the traditional idea that only a voluntary and conscious act can be a sin.

Having dealt with the responsibility for the divisions, the text explains the present situation in terms of real but imperfect communion: "Those who believe in Christ and have been truly baptized are in some kind of communion with the Catholic Church, even though this communion is imperfect." This is one of the key points of the decree, and a few months before the opening of Vatican II, Cardinal Bea had described that question as one of the most important ones the future council would address.[28] The basis of that imperfect communion is both faith in Christ and baptism. All baptized people "are members of Christ's body," which means of the Church (or of the communion of the Church, at least imperfectly). The text does not say which kind of communion would arise from a faith in Christ without baptism (as in the case of Quakers or of people born into the Salvation Army), but the sacramental element used in the distinction between Eastern and Western communities in chapter 3 suggests that baptism establishes a much stronger communion than a nonsacramental faith in Christ.

The partial membership to the Church is fundamentally rooted in faith in Christ and in baptism. The text also discusses some means of grace that are present "outside the visible boundaries of the Catholic Church": Such a statement must be understood in the light of *Lumen gentium*, article 8; I do not think that it means "out of the Church" or that it suggests that the Catholic Church is one among others of the Church of Christ; the meaning is rather one of full or partial communion, that is, membership in the Church. If the expression used in the decree leaves a rather Bellarminian impression, the explanation is more of the patristic (medieval) kind: "All of these, which come from Christ and lead back to Christ, belong by right to the one Church of Christ."[29] These means of grace can be "the written word of God; the life of grace; faith, hope and charity, with the other interior gifts of the Holy Spirit, and visible elements too" (no. 4 adds that the riches present in other communities must be esteemed). Not all of these elements are present everywhere or in the same degree, as the decree explains later on. What the text does not say is how we can know that groups of Christians as such—the question here does not in the first place concern individuals—live in faith, hope, and charity: The traditional Catholic teaching is not warm to the possibility of knowing the state of grace of individuals,[30] and the text does not explain how it is possible to affirm the presence of the theological virtues in communities.[31] An element is of course given in article 4: Non-Catholic Christians "bear witness to Christ, even at times to the shedding of their blood"; still, the link between such individual acts and the affirmation of the presence of the theological virtues in communities is not explained.

Although they can have some means of salvation, the other Christian communions or individuals "are not blessed with that unity which Jesus Christ wished to bestow on all those who through him were born again into one body" because the fullness of the means of salvation is to be found only in the Catholic Church (that is, all of the sacraments and the doctrine, dispensed by the College of Bishops, which is united to Peter's successor). The following question arises: Since all Christian communities are divided, should we not say that the Catholic Church is also not blessed with "that unity which Jesus Christ wished to bestow"? During the 1964 week of prayer for Christian unity, Pope Paul VI said that Catholics have the privilege of not having lost unity.[32] In his encyclical *Ut unum sint* Pope John Paul II said, "The Catholic Church thus affirms that during the two thousand years of her history she has been preserved in unity, with all the means with which God wishes to endow his Church, and this despite the often grave crises which have shaken her, the infidelity of some of her ministers, and the faults into which her members daily fall."[33]

Catholic theologians must deal with a paradox: All Christians are divided, and Catholics are in this situation of division, but the Catholic Church alone has never lost full unity. The fullness of the means of grace of the Church of Christ is in her alone. Do only the non-Catholics have to work for ecumenism then? Or does ecumenical dialogue mean that the other Christians go back to Catholic fullness and that the Catholic Church just invites them and waits? Some answer to these questions is given in article 4.

Article 4

After a period in which Catholics were not allowed to take part in the ecumenical movement (at that time only experts—basically priests—could attend meetings), the article exhorted "all the Catholic faithful . . . to take an intelligent part in the work of ecumenism," "with the attentive guidance of their bishops." The participation of experts, who could work at a better and nonpolemical mutual understanding, was highlighted as particularly important. On that basis, several initiatives "for the common good of humanity" and common prayer are possible.

The question raised by article 3 has some answers. The fullness of the means of salvation—and therefore of unity—does not prevent the Catholic Church from making progress in perfection because this unity "subsists in the Catholic Church as something she can never lose; and we cherish the hope that it will go on increasing until the end of time."[34] The Catholic Church as such has not lost unity, but has to possess it always more, as part of an ecumenical process in which "all are led to examine their own faithfulness to Christ's will for the Church and accordingly to undertake with vigor the task of renewal and reform." Article 6 says the same in different words and show its central character: "Every renewal of the Church essentially consists in an increase of fidelity to the Church's own calling. Undoubtedly this is the reason for the movement towards unity." A complementary aspect of that necessary progress is individual development, which aims at more fervor for the sake of the edification of the Body of Christ; individual conversions are not excluded but distinguished from ecumenical dialogue.[35] All gifts really received from God by any Christian must be received as a help, that cannot destroy faith.

The common celebration of the Eucharist is presented as the sign of achieved unity. Of course one could see this gift from the negative side: "It would appear to us that the Eucharist is, in the light of ecumenism, above all a symbol of the lost unity of Christians."[36] Perhaps, but one could also say about the Eucharist what Pope Paul VI said about his ministry (another sign of unity, which can be seen as a sign of division): "Are there not those who say that unity between the separated churches and the Catholic Church would be more easily achieved if the primacy of the Roman pontiff were done away with? We beg our separated brothers to consider the groundlessness of this opinion. . . . It would be vain to look for other principles of unity in place of the true one established by Christ Himself."[37] Unity must be kept in essentials, freedom in various forms of spirituality, rites, discipline, and charity in all things, as Pope John XXIII had said in his programmatic encyclical *Ad Petri cathedram.*[38]

Chapter 2

After the general principles presented in chapter 1 and before their application to the specific communities in chapter 3, chapter 2 presents the main lines of the practice of ecumenism.

Article 5

Article 5 introduces the chapter and says that ecumenism, which is by definition a dialogue between Christians (to be distinguished from interreligious dialogue[39]), is a sign of the unity that already exists. It is that unity that ecumenical dialogue aims at perfecting.

Article 6

This article describes ecumenism as a "renewal" (*renovatio*) and as a "continual reformation" (*perennis reformatio*) of the Church's fidelity to Christ in all aspects of the life of the Church. A footnote mentions three medieval councils that worked for such a renewal: The councils are older than the Protestant Reformation, and two of them (Lyon II and Florence) had as their main purpose unity between East and West. These historical examples also affirm that a reform is always needed. The renewal is not only at the moral level but also at the level of the formulation of doctrine, which is "to be carefully distinguished from the deposit of faith itself." If the postconciliar magisterium warns about the danger of exaggerating the distinction between dogmas and their expression (an excessive distinction would make any confession of faith impossible since human words are always needed),[40] an adequate distinction between content and expression has been used in several agreements of different levels signed by Popes Paul VI and John Paul II with some Eastern and Oriental churches.[41]

Articles 7–8

In line with the previous statements about the reformation of the Church, article 7 insists on the necessity of an "interior conversion" (*interior conversio*), which leads above all to humility and generosity. That conversion has the double effect of making those who undergo such conversion more open to others and closer to the Father, the Son, and the Holy Spirit: Those who are with God are in communion with others who are also with God. Article 8 goes on in the same vein and speaks about spiritual ecumenism (a movement started by Abbé Couturier in the 1930s): "This change of heart and holiness of life, along with public and private prayer for the unity of Christians, should be regarded as the soul of the whole ecumenical movement, and merits the name 'spiritual ecumenism.'" Pope John Paul II insisted on that spiritual dimension in his encyclical *Ut unum sint*.[42]

The question of the common participation in the sacraments celebrated in divided churches (*communicatio in sacris*) is a delicate point for practical reasons (e.g., marriages, funerals), as well as for theological ones.[43] The decree shows the two conflicting principles: "There are two main principles governing the practice of such common worship: first, the bearing witness to the unity of the Church, and second, the sharing in the means of grace. Witness to the unity of the Church generally forbids common worship, but the grace to be had from it sometimes commends this practice" (no. 8).

The first principle is the reason the Catholic Church normally does not accept a common participation in the sacraments (and above all to the Eucharist): Receiving the Eucharist in a Catholic Church is the strongest affirmation of full communion with the Catholic Church, and if a non-Catholic consciously receives it (except in a situation of urgent necessity), that person in effect solemnly claims not to be a non-Catholic. According to Eusebius of Caesarea, a common celebration of the Eucharist had been the sign of full communion between Pope Anicetus and Saint Polycarp after a dispute on the date of Easter.[44] Orthodox and Catholics agree on this point: "The true faith is presupposed for a communion in the sacraments. Communion is possible only between those churches which have faith, priesthood and the sacraments in common."[45] John Paul II emphasized that point in his encyclical *Ecclesia de Eucharistia*:

> Precisely because the Church's unity, which the Eucharist brings about through the Lord's sacrifice and by communion in his body and blood, absolutely requires full communion in the bonds of the profession of faith, the sacraments and ecclesiastical governance, it is not

possible to celebrate together the same Eucharistic liturgy until those bonds are fully re-established. Any such concelebration would not be a valid means, and might well prove instead to be *an obstacle, to the attainment of full communion*, by weakening the sense of how far we remain from this goal and by introducing or exacerbating ambiguities with regard to one or another truth of the faith.[46]

The practical consequences of the second principle, namely that the sacraments (particularly the Eucharist) provide grace, have been the object of disciplinary rules that pertained to the council itself, above all in the 1983 *Code of Canon Law* and the 1993 *Ecumenical Directory*. On the basis of these developments,[47] John Paul II explained in which sense some "intercommunion" is possible: "While it is never legitimate to concelebrate in the absence of full communion, the same is not true with respect to the administration of the Eucharist *under special circumstances, to individual persons* belonging to churches or ecclesial communities not in full communion with the Catholic Church. In this case, in fact, the intention is to meet a grave spiritual need for the eternal salvation of an individual believer, not to bring about an *intercommunion* which remains impossible until the visible bonds of ecclesial communion are fully re-established."[48]

The text then quotes *Ut unum sint* with regard to the conditions in which the Eucharist, penance, and anointing of the sick can be administered to other Christians. It summarizes the main points: "These conditions, from which no dispensation can be given, must be carefully respected, even though they deal with specific individual cases, because the denial of one or more truths of the faith regarding these sacraments and, among these, the truth regarding the need of the ministerial priesthood for their validity, renders the person asking improperly disposed to legitimately receiving them. And the opposite is also true: Catholics may not receive communion in those communities which lack a valid sacrament of Orders."[49]

The specificity of the individual cases is explained by the *Ecumenical Directory*. The possibility is rather broad for Eastern Christians to receive the sacraments from Catholic ministers:[50] "Whenever necessity requires or a genuine spiritual advantage suggests, and provided that the danger of error or indifferentism is avoided, it is lawful for any Catholic for whom it is physically or morally impossible to approach a Catholic minister, to receive the sacraments of penance, Eucharist and anointing of the sick from a minister of an Eastern Church."[51]

The conditions are quite precise for Western Christians (that is, Protestants): "The conditions under which a Catholic minister may administer the sacraments of the Eucharist, of penance and of the anointing of the sick to a baptized person who may be found in the circumstances given above[52] are that the person be unable to have recourse for the sacrament desired to a minister of his or her own Church or ecclesial community, ask for the sacrament of his or her own initiative, manifest Catholic faith in this sacrament and be properly disposed."[53]

Article 9

Ecumenical meetings at different levels—especially at the theological level—presuppose a good preparation of the Catholic participants (also of the separated brethren, but the council does not explain whom they are supposed to send to a dialogue). Such meetings favor a better mutual understanding, which is precisely why the participants must be well prepared. The better knowledge of "the position of the Catholic Church" pertains not only to the non-Catholics but also to the Catholics, who deepen their self-knowledge through dialogue.[54]

The fact that partners in dialogue "treat with the other on an equal footing" does not imply an ecclesiological indifference but rather everyone's readiness to give full right to all of the participants to explain their thoughts. In practice, this is often made easier by the friendship that develops between partners in dialogue.

Article 10

Teaching of theology and history, especially, must be ecumenical, which means corresponding to "the truth of things" (*veritas rerum*). The too often polemical approach of the past was in fact not a service to truth. Even before Vatican II some Catholic theologians had tried to present a more precise image of the Reformation and the Reformers, for instance. After Vatican II, in many places, Catholic and Protestant scholars collaborated to create common histories of the sixteenth century, and ecumenical translations of the Bible were published. Thus John Paul II was able to say, almost twenty years after *Unitatis redintegratio*, "We have been able to discern that the efforts of Evangelical and Catholic research offer us a more complete picture of the person and teaching of Luther, as well as a more adequate view of the complicated historical events of the sixteenth century. All these are important elements in the reconciliation and growing together of Catholics and Lutherans."[55]

A better knowledge cannot but help a real reconciliation, although it cannot provide it alone because historical data must still be interpreted. A 1990 document of dialogue between Catholics and Reformed shows a balance between a new historical objectivity and an ongoing necessity of interpretation (which implies criteria other than a simple reconstruction of facts): "Historical scholarship today has not only produced fresh evidence concerning our respective roles in the Reformation and its aftermath. It also brings us together in broad agreement about sources, methods of inquiry and warrants for drawing conclusions. A new measure of objectivity has become possible. If we still inevitably interpret and select, at least we are aware that we do, and what that fact means as we strive for greater objectivity and more balanced judgment."[56]

Article 11

In line with the previous article, article 11 insists on a true presentation of Catholic doctrine. If a polemical approach must be avoided, a "false irenicism, in which the purity of Catholic doctrine suffers loss" is not less dangerous. These opposite dangers are equally opposed to truth, and a way must be found to avoid both. The point here is not so much about ecumenical methodology (which could apply to all Christians) but about how Catholic theologians must present Catholic doctrine in an ecumenical context. Catholic doctrine must be portrayed clearly and with charity in order to enable its communication to non-Catholic theologians.

Many fathers mentioned the danger of irenicism or indifferentism, and Cardinal Bea commented on that point in November 1963. He said that the remedy was not in avoiding action toward unity but in checking it carefully.[57]

One of the key points of the whole decree is the principle of the "hierarchy of truths." The expression was presented to the council in November 1963 by Archbishop Andrea Pangrazio of Gorizia (Italy);[58] the idea may have been suggested to him by one of the Protestant observers at the council.[59] Here are some elements of the second part of his speech:[60]

> It is a good thing to enumerate the many ecclesial elements which by God's grace have been preserved in the communities separated from us and which have salutary effects on them. But I frankly confess that it seems to me this enumeration is too "quantitative," if I may say so.... In my opinion some binding factor is required for these individual elements. There should be a centre to which these elements are to be related and without which they cannot be explained. This binding factor and this centre is Christ himself, whom all Christians confess as the Lord of the Church, whom undoubtedly Christians of all communities strive to serve faithfully and who condescends to work wonderful things even in the communities separated from us through his active presence in the Holy Spirit.... So that the unity already present among Christians, as well as their still existing differences may be properly distinguished, I think it is important to consider fully the hierarchical order of the revealed truths [*ordo, ut ita dicam hierarchicus veritatum revelatarum*] through which the mystery of Christ is expressed and the ecclesiastical elements by which the Church is established. Even though all revealed truths must be believed with the same divine faith and all constitutive elements of the Church have to be faithfully retained [*Etiamsi omnes veritates revelatae eadem fide divina credendae et omnia elementa constitutiva Ecclesiae eadem fidelitate retinenda sint*], yet they are not all of the same importance. There are truths that belong to the order of the end, such as the mystery of the most holy Trinity, of the incarnation of the Word and the redemption.... But there are other truths, which belong to the order of the means of salvation, as for example the truth of the seven sacraments, of the hierarchical structure of the Church, of the apostolic succession and others.... In fact the doctrinal differences among Christians are less concerned with the truths that belong to the order of the end, and more with those concerning

the order of the means, which are undoubtedly subordinate to the former.[61]

Before the hierarchy of truths was introduced, the secretariat explained the text to the council in *modus* 49 (attributed to Card. König of Vienna): "It seems most important for ecumenical dialogue, that the truths about which all Christians agree, as well as those about which they differ, be rather evaluated than enumerated. Without any doubt all revealed truths must be held with the same divine faith, but their importance and 'weight' differ in reason of their link with the history of salvation and the mystery of Christ."[62]

In these two texts we find two elements: (1) a hierarchy among truths as a result of their different relation to the center of revelation (that is, Christ and his mystery) and (2) a proposition that all revealed truths must be held because they are revealed, although some are more important than others. The text of the decree does not explicitly mention the second element, but the context of article 11 ("doctrine should be clearly presented in its entirety") implies it.

When Pope John Paul II visited Switzerland in 1984, the former general secretary of the World Council of Churches, Willem A. Visser't Hooft, suggested a common document on the meaning of the notion of "hierarchy of truths"; the pope accepted his proposal, and the document was published in 1990. The two apparently conflicting points are mentioned:

> First of all, the council's sentence does not mean that there is only a more or less incidental relationship between these truths and the foundation, so that a merely relative character stamps them, and one can consider them optional in the life of faith. Still less does the decree's sentence consider truths of faith as more or less necessary for salvation, or suggest degrees in our obligation to believe in all that God has revealed. When one fully responds to God's self-revelation in faith, one accepts that Revelation as a whole. There is no picking and choosing of what God has revealed, because there is no picking or choosing of what Revelation is—our salvation. Hence, there are no degrees in the obligation to believe all that God has revealed.[63]

That question of the hierarchy of truths is absolutely central to any understanding of Catholic ecumenism, but it can easily be misunderstood. For example, where is the Assumption of Mary in the hierarchy of truths? Certainly not at the center. Should post-Vatican II theologians therefore drop that dogma about which Pope Pius XII said, "If anyone, which God forbid, should dare willfully to deny or to call into doubt that which we have defined, let him know that he has fallen away completely from the divine and Catholic Faith"?[64] When he said that to refuse the dogma would mean that one no longer has faith, Pius XII certainly had in mind Saint Thomas Aquinas's theology of the formal object of faith: The believer accepts the object of faith because it is revealed by God and transmitted by the Church; those who refuse it follow their own opinion instead of divine revelation, and that attitude implies that even the articles of faith that they accept are only private opinions instead of an acceptance of revelation.[65]

This is the second element, and Archbishop Pangrazio had seen no contradiction between it and the hierarchy of truths; otherwise the council fathers would have noticed that their text would change the status of a dogma proclaimed fourteen years before, as all of them certainly remembered.[66] The hierarchy of truths simply means that any truth received from divine revelation must be connected to the central mysteries. For instance, the dogma of the Assumption depends on the dogma of Mary's divine motherhood, which implies the more central truth that Jesus is God and man. Theology should begin with the more central truth and then explain the others progressively.

If Pius XII's words must be maintained, what does the hierarchy of truths mean for non-Catholics, who do not accept what the Catholic Church holds about dogmas such as the Assumption and therefore seem to have "fallen away completely from the divine and Catholic Faith"? In fact, such words do not apply to them all because most of them never rejected the Church they belong to in order to follow only their own private opinion.[67]

Article 12

On the basis and as a testimony of the already existing unity, all Christians are called to a common proclamation of their faith in Christ and to a common service to the world, in line with the contemporary practice of social collaboration. The ideal of common testimony is one of the origins of the ecumenical movement, and the double dimension—expression of faith and practical collaboration—has been expressed in the two main streams of the movement, united in the World Council of Churches since 1948: Faith and Order, Life and Work. The text adds that a common practice is useful also at the more doctrinal level because "All believers in Christ can, through such cooperation, easily learn to acquire a better knowledge and appreciation of one another."

Chapter 3

Article 13

The decree turns to the specific questions of other Christian denominations by distinguishing two very different types of divisions: The first part of the chapter (nos. 14–18) is about the divisions in the East (those traditionally called Nestorian and Monophysite and the schism traditionally considered to have begun in 1054,[68] now also called Oriental Orthodox and Eastern Orthodox[69]), while the second part (nos. 19–23) addresses the divisions in the West, that is, those that began with the Reformation of the sixteenth century (the Anglicans are a specific case because of the greater [if partial] persistence among them of "Catholic traditions and institutions"[70]).

The purpose of chapter 3 is not so much to describe all aspects of other denominations as to propose some "considerations for prudent ecumenical action." The council's intention was not to present a historical overview of divisions.[71]

Certain words in this article were changed because of an important suggestion written by Archbishop George Beck of Liverpool.[72] The version distributed in September 1964 said, "Several Communions, national or confessional, separated themselves from the Roman See."[73] The English bishop suggested—as it actually happened—to substitute *se seiunxerunt* (separated themselves) with *seiunctae sunt* (were separated). His argument was that the whole point of the discussion (*punctum discordiae*) between Anglicans and Catholics in England was that both pretended to be in continuity with the Church established in England before the sixteenth century and that to say "separated themselves" would mean that the English Church as such went on in the "Church of England" and that the introduction of a Catholic hierarchy in the nineteenth century was an intrusion that should be suppressed.[74] The present text does not offer a historical judgment, but its more passive form tries to objectively describe the facts.

Article 14

Article 14 describes in general terms the relationship between East and West, beginning with the unity of the past and underlining the very rich Eastern contribution to the common patrimony of faith (therefore also to the present doctrine of the Catholic Church). If a good knowledge of the relations before the divisions is central to the solution of these divisions, the description in this article of the role of the bishop of Rome before the divisions would be in itself a point of disagreement (even the undisputed importance of Pope Leo the Great in the solution of Chalcedon is not universally seen as a recognition of his jurisdiction). The Eastern churches are described as local churches (which means, for instance, that there is not "one Orthodox Church" in the sense of the "Catholic Church"), organized around the ancient patriarchal churches. The divisions are due to cultural differences that lead to a lack of mutual understanding and of charity and external factors (primarily political factors).

Article 15

The riches of the Eastern churches are to be praised and received by Catholics: liturgy (including the veneration of the Mother of God and of the saints), spirituality, theology, and monasticism. Because these churches have kept the apostolic succession and all of the sacraments, some sacramental sharing is commended (the conditions are mentioned in my comments on nos. 7–8). The decree highlights the Eastern riches not only as legitimate but also as being "of supreme importance for the faithful preservation of the fullness of Christian tradition." Later on, John Paul II repeatedly stated that "the Church must breathe with her two lungs."[75]

Article 16

After having praised the riches of the East, the decree adds that "the churches of the east, while mindful of the necessary unity of the whole Church, have the right to govern themselves according to the disciplines proper to themselves," which add to the splendor of the Church. The council acknowledges that this respect has not always been practiced and alludes to the "latinization" of some churches of Eastern rite in the past (in Ukraine, Lebanon, southern Italy, etc.[76]). This is a very important point since history inspired in the Eastern churches the fear that unity would mean the loss of their identity. Of course, article 16 does not mean that nothing whatsoever would have to change in the organization of the Orthodox churches because the respect of different practices is possible "while mindful of the necessary unity of the whole Church."

Article 17

The doctrinal riches of the East are considered in their relation to the West. The decree says that these riches are already present in the West, but the text speaks about the "authentic theological traditions of the Eastern Church"; when asked whether there was no risk of forgetting dogmatic differences, the secretariat replied that that risk was ruled out by the precision: "authentic."[77] If "if from time to time one tradition has come nearer to a full appreciation of some aspects of a mystery of Revelation than the other," it does not mean that they are opposed but that they must be kept together in order to fully express the Catholicity of the Church. It does not seem unfair to say that Catholic theologians are open to the theological patrimony of the East (for instance, Saint Thomas Aquinas was already naturally eager to use it[78]); however, the openness of most Orthodox theologians to Saint Augustine, for example, or to the scholastics tends to be quite limited. Here is a legitimate ecumenical question: If the Church has two lungs ... ?

It is interesting to see that the decree speaks about doctrinal differences only in general terms, without mentioning any particular point. For instance, the *filioque* is not mentioned: Perhaps this denotes a Western approach because, while for many Orthodox the *filioque* is highly important, most Catholic theologians do not consider it to be a dividing issue.[79] The Christological questions that divide the Catholic Church and certain Oriental churches such as the Copts, the Armenians, and the Assyrians (which will be the object of future—at least partial—agreements) are not mentioned, either. In any case, the decree deals instead with principles and leaves the details to further dialogue.

Article 18

The part of the decree that specifically concerns the Eastern churches concludes with an invitation to prayer, dialogue, and charitable collaboration. The desired unity in Christ must be about "what is essential": This certainly expresses a desire to respect as much as possible the legitimate doctrinal and disciplinary identity of the Eastern churches, unlike what has sometimes been done in the past (as mentioned in no. 16).

At the end of this section one might ask about the implications of an ecumenical mindset for the present relations of the still-divided Catholics and Orthodox. On the basis of the fact that the Eastern churches have kept all of the sacraments (and many other riches), important voices such as Cardinal Kasper's exclude a Catholic "proselytism" toward the Orthodox churches: "Since the Catholic Church recognizes the Orthodox churches as true churches and their sacraments as true sacraments and therefore authentic means of salvation for their faithful, it is absolutely inappropriate to exercise a missionary activity towards the Orthodox faithful."[80] Pope John Paul II and Patriarch Demetrios I of Constantinople also said in Rome in 1987: "We reject any form of proselytism, any attitude that would be or could be perceived as a lack of respect."[81] In 1993, in Balamand (Lebanon), the Joint International Commission for the Theological Dialogue between the Roman Catholic Church and the Orthodox Church published a report titled "Uniatism, Method of Union of the Past, and the Present Search for Full Communion."[82] It stated that, "While the inviolable freedom of persons and their obligation to follow the requirements of their conscience remain secure, in the search for reestablishing unity there is no question of conversion of people from one Church to the other in order to ensure their salvation."[83]

The Orthodox churches are very much concerned about what they feel is a Catholic (and Protestant) proselytism, above all in the former Soviet Union: For instance, any Russian—even an atheist who has never been baptized and who becomes Protestant or Catholic—is considered to be pulled away from the Orthodox Church. The Catholic understanding of "proselytism" is more limited. Unitatis redintegratio excludes some aspects of a bad proselytism, such as misrepresenting the separated brethren[84] or considering them as rivals.[85] The declaration Dignitatis humanae by the same council also excludes certain kinds of proselytism: "In spreading religious faith and in introducing religious practices everyone ought at all times to refrain from any manner of action which might seem to carry a hint of coercion or of a kind of persuasion that would be dishonorable or unworthy."[86]

What Cardinal Kasper suggested was not that any conversion should be excluded but that the ecumenical way to unity is a deeper conversion of all to Christ:[87] "The goal of ecumenism cannot be conceived of as a mere return of the others to the heart of the Catholic Church. The goal of full unity [can] be reached only through the action of the Spirit of God and the conversion of all to the one Head of the Church, Jesus Christ."[88] Generally the Catholic Church does not require that other Christians agree to unite with or return to the exact type of Catholic Church that existed at the time of the separation (in some cases, such as the Methodists, the break was with Anglicanism rather than Catholicism per se). Not only has the Catholic Church changed through the centuries, but Unitatis redintegratio speaks of a permanent need for reformation, and John Paul II invited to a dialogue on the modes of exercise of his ministry.[89] Still, in its essential dimensions, the pope's ministry is a necessary part of the being of the Church, as Cardinal Kasper said to the Federation of French Protestant churches.[90] Therefore, even the sacramental fullness of the Orthodox churches, without the pope's ministry, is not identical to the fullness of the means of salvation, and some conversion might be required in conscience, as *Lumen gentium* says: "Whosoever, therefore, knowing that the Catholic Church was made necessary by Christ, would refuse to enter or to remain in it, could not be saved" (*LG* 14).

Article 19

Article 19 discusses the "Separated Churches and Ecclesial Communities in the West." In the previous version, the title was "About the Communities [That Have] Appeared since the Sixteenth Century";[91] Bishop Carli of Segni suggested changing the article because it did not include the Waldensians and the Hussites.[92] These communities are described as very different among themselves, "especially in the interpretation of revealed truth"—which is the reason the decree gives only general indications of a dialogue with them—and the main common point is that these communities "have retained a special affinity and close relationship with the Catholic Church as a result of the long centuries in which all Christendom lived together in ecclesiastical communion." This point is interesting, and it is the only one in which these Western denominations are described as especially similar to the Catholic Church, which means that they exhibit more similarity to her than do the Eastern churches. The fact is that, for instance, there has been a huge (if differentiated) Augustinian impact on Catholic and Protestant theologies but not on Orthodox theology.

The ecumenical movement has been strong among Protestants at least since the beginning of the twentieth century, but, as the text says, it is not present everywhere. Some Protestant currents were (and some still are) vividly opposed to the Catholic Church and occasionally to any kind of ecumenism (even among Protestants). The decree on ecumenism invites them as it invites Catholics to greet dialogue with some openness.

Article 20

Articles 20 to 23 have an organized structure. On October 7, 1964, Archbishop John Heenan of Westminster explained that the secretariat had decided to give a short description of the Western communities and would organize it according to four main elements: confession of Christ (no. 20), study of sacred scripture (no. 21), sacramental life (no. 22), and life with Christ (no. 23).[93]

One main point of the already existing unity between Catholics and the other Western Christian denominations is the Lord Jesus Christ; the text joyfully underlines that unity, which is the basis of the deeper unity it desires. In November 1964 the secretariat explained that it had agreed to add "God" in

"Jesus Christ as God and Lord" in order to avoid a confusion with regard to the communities that call themselves Christian but do not believe in the divinity of Christ.[94]

The main differences mentioned between the Catholic Church and some Western communities are certain points of the doctrine that concern Christ, the understanding of the redemption, the Church and her ministry, and the role of Mary.

With regard to Christ, the main Reformers accepted the Christology of the early Church councils, even though their reason for doing so was more an exegetical agreement than an affirmation of the Church's authority.[95] Thus the question of disagreements on the meaning of scripture (and even, in the case of divisions, Christ himself) remains. Father Congar suggested—in a book aimed at giving Catholics a more favorable image of Luther—that Luther's Christology had a Monophysite tendency because it attributed all salvific work only to the divinity of Christ, thereby leaving nothing to his humanity.[96] Still, there is no real division in Christological doctrine between the Catholic Church and the mainstream Protestant denominations. There would certainly be a huge disagreement about Christological and Trinitarian doctrine between both Catholics and "Orthodox Protestants" (for example, Barthians) on the one hand and liberal Protestants on the other.

The main point of divergence is certainly not Christology as such, but rather—as the text says, showing a logical sequence—"the work of redemption, and, consequently, concerning the mystery and ministry of the Church, and the role of Mary in the work of salvation." It is well known that for the Reformers the doctrine of justification by faith and grace alone was the central mark of Christian life. As a consequence, all human works in relation to God tend to be underestimated, and this diminishes the consistency of the Church: "While the 'old churches' do not hesitate to affirm that the Church is the agent—'sign and instrument,' sacramentum—of Salvation which it is the beneficiary of, communities which have sprung up from the Reformation prefer to avoid every formula which could conceal the great affirmation of the faith: Salvation comes from God alone."[97]

The *Joint Declaration on the Doctrine of Justification*, signed on October 31, 1999, between the Catholic Church and the World Lutheran Federation,[98] expresses a basic agreement on that central issue but leaves open the kind of consequences the decree expresses: "There are still questions of varying importance which need further clarification. These include, among other topics, the relationship between the Word of God and Church doctrine, as well as ecclesiology, authority in the Church, ministry, the sacraments, and the relation between justification and social ethics. We are convinced that the consensus we have reached offers a solid basis for this clarification."[99]

Even the agreement on justification could not solve some of the problems related to the question of justification. Perhaps one element of a solution could be the study of the philosophical presuppositions unconsciously present in the initial formation of the Protestant mindset.

Article 21

The decree praises the devotion to scripture, which has been at the very center of the Reformation, and sees it as alive in the Protestant communities of its time. This is a major instrument for dialogue.

The text adds that some difference exists between the Protestant and the Catholic approaches to scripture, the main point of which is "a special place in the interpretation and preaching of the written word of God" for "the [Church's] authentic teaching office." The point is not to oppose Bible and Church authority but to know the correct interpretation of the Bible on key issues, given the fact that the biblical text is not univocally clear. While the Catholic bishops were gathered at Vatican II, official delegates of most Protestant—and many Orthodox—churches and ecclesial communities took part in the Fourth World Conference on Faith and Order in Montreal (1963).[100] They published a document titled "Tradition, tradition, and traditions," which addressed the question of the criteria for the interpretation of scripture:[101] Most people agree about the importance of the apostolic tradition, the fact of a canon of the Bible, the necessity of a reading in the Holy Spirit, and so on, but such criteria are not enough to choose between incompatible interpretations, and no sufficient criterion could be identified.

As another document of Faith and Order stated in 1998, "Montreal helped to overcome the old contrast between 'sola Scriptura' and 'Scripture and tradition.' . . . It must be recognized that Montreal left open the vital question of how churches can discern the one Tradition."[102] This question is central to ecumenical dialogue because, if there is no way of acknowledging some interpretation of scripture as corresponding to faith, any visible unity of Christians will be impossible. In 2005 the ecumenical Groupe des Dombes presented that as an ecumenical challenge for the Protestants: How can unity be declared with moving structures without permanent authority?[103]

In ecumenical dialogue, the most striking result of Church unity has been achieved in the Anglican-Catholic dialogue, which dealt with it as a service to a unified reading of scripture: "In solemnly formulating such teaching, the universal primate must discern and declare, with the assured assistance and guidance of the Holy Spirit, in fidelity to Scripture and Tradition, the authentic faith of the whole Church, that is, the faith proclaimed from the beginning. . . . The reception of the primacy of the Bishop of Rome entails the recognition of this specific ministry of the universal primate. We believe that this is a gift to be received by all the churches."[104]

More than four decades after *Unitatis redintegratio*, a new question has arisen. At Vatican II several Latin American bishops had mentioned as a serious problem the proselytism by a kind of Protestantism that differed from that found in Europe;[105] this conversion effort later created a major division within Protestantism. Current developments in the mainstream Protestant churches insist less than before on the authority of scripture (more precisely, scripture is interpreted in a hermeneutical framework that not infrequently leads away from a literal reading). Meanwhile, Evangelical and Pentecostal groups became the main Protestant bodies and have a more "fundamentalist" or at least more literal reading of scripture and a moral approach that is more critical of contemporary society.[106]

This is a new situation for Catholic dialogue: The traditional Protestant partners are now a minority among Protestants; with the Pentecostals (who are more numerous than all of the faithful of the member churches of the World Council of Churches together), a dialogue is more difficult because there is no global system of representation among them and because many of them—but not all—are not interested in a theological dialogue. The dividing line between the two Protestant approaches—"fundamentalist" exegesis or use of modern biblical scholarship—need not be an insurmountable problem for Catholic theology: Thanks to a metaphysical understanding of the different levels of causality (which was developed in order to understand the Christian economy, in which "we are God's fellow workers"[107]), Catholic theology has no problem in recognizing that the biblical books "have God as their author," that some people that God has chosen are also the "true authors" of these books, and that divinely chosen collaboration with human beings is also at work in the preaching and interpreting of the Bible.[108] Cardinal Bea praised Saint Thomas Aquinas for his understanding of instrumentality in revelation, which opened the way to Vatican II's quiet solution;[109] such an understanding can be applied to the whole life of the Church and is a key to the remaining issues of justification.

In the ecumenical field, the Catholic Church could work at a rapprochement between different Protestant approaches by using the cultural, historical, and theological affinity mentioned in article 19.

Article 22

After the biblical element that was considered to be the main common point, the decree speaks about the sacramental dimension, which is the reason chapter 3 is divided into two parts: While in the Eastern churches, the sacraments serve as a basis of unity, this is not the case with the Protestant denominations, who did not keep the sacrament of order and therefore neither the "full reality" of the Eucharist (*genuina atque integra substantia mysterii Eucharistici*). The communities in which the sacraments have not been completely preserved (and who usually affirm the existence of only two or three of the sacraments[110]) are called "ecclesial communities" instead of "churches."[111] The reason the second section of the chapter (from no. 19 on) begins with the title "Separated Churches and Ecclesial Communities in the West" is not clear:[112] The most probable reason for the mention of "churches" in this title is the presence in the West of the Old Catholics[113] and perhaps the Polish National Church;[114] perhaps some also had in mind the Anglicans, but this is less likely.[115]

At the sacramental level, the decree insists on baptism, whose validity is ordinarily recognized in the Protestant communities that use water and the Trinitarian formula,[116] that is, the mention of Father, Son, and Holy Spirit (the diffusion of other formulas could lead to a reconsideration of the systematic recognition of baptism). Baptism must also be "received with the right disposition," which is more of an individual question. The text does not say whether people who have received baptismal grace keep it; this point would be important if baptism has to be a common foundation of unity since traditional Catholic teaching insists on the impossibility of our state of grace, as mentioned in my comments on article 3.

If baptism "establishes a sacramental bond of unity existing among all who have been reborn by it," this unity is only a beginning and calls for a greater fullness, which is "complete profession of faith, complete incorporation into the institution of salvation such as Christ willed it to be, and finally the completeness of unity which Eucharistic communion gives." Using words taken from previous articles, the article states that baptism is not the fullness of the means of salvation and that full unity is only Eucharistic unity. What is lacking is the object of dialogue, and this has been so ever since. One element of this dialogue is found in the text itself: Because "the Spirit of Christ has not refrained from using them as means of salvation" (*UR* 3), these communities and their liturgical actions may not have the "full reality" of the Eucharist, but it does not mean that their celebrations of the Last Supper cannot be occasions of grace.

Article 23

Since many elements of Christian faith and devotion remain in the separated communities, they have developed many charitable institutions. This social action stems from a desire to be disciples of Christ, and an ecumenical community of disciples appears in common works. This article takes into consideration the life-and-work kind of Protestant ecumenism.

Conclusion

The decree concludes with a call to ecumenical action, whose main characteristic must be "fully and sincerely Catholic": The partners in dialogue will be offered the possibility of having Catholic partners, so that the exchange of information the decree calls for will be facilitated.

Perhaps the most important point in *Unitatis redintegratio* is the idea of fullness. *Plenitudo* has a double meaning in the document. On the one hand, the "fullness of grace and truth" (*plenitudo gratiae et veritatis*) has been "entrusted to the Catholic Church," where "it is possible to get every fullness of the means of salvation" (*omnis salutarium mediorum plenitudo attingi potest*; *UR* 3).[117] On the other hand, "the divisions among Christians prevent the Church from realizing in practice the fullness of Catholicity [plenitudo catholicitatis] proper to her, in those of her sons and daughters who, though attached to her by baptism, are yet separated from full communion with her" (*UR* 4). Therefore, the present fullness has to be constantly developed "to

attain that fullness of unity [plenitudo unitatis] which Jesus Christ desires"
(*UR* 4) "until it shall happily arrive at the fullness of eternal glory [aeternae
gloriae plenitudo] in the heavenly Jerusalem" (*UR* 3). Catholic ecumenism
moves therefore from an existing fullness—nothing is missing in the means of
salvation of apostolic faith—toward an increased fullness, as this final article
summarizes: "fully and sincerely Catholic, that is to say, faithful to the truth
which we have received from the apostles and fathers, in harmony with the
faith which the Catholic Church has always professed, and at the same time
directed towards that fullness [*in eam plenitudinem tendens*] to which our Lord
wills his body to grow in the course of time."

Dei verbum says the same: The Christian dispensation is definitive (cf. *DV*
4), and the Apostles' successors must keep it intact (cf. *DV* 8), but at the same
time "there is a growth in the understanding of the realities and the words
which have been handed down" (ibid.). The way Catholics see their relation to
the other Christians is strictly parallel to the Catholic idea of tradition: Tradition is fully authentic but can also develop until Christ returns; the Catholic
Church has the fullness of the means of salvation, but a permanent reform and
an always fuller conversion to Christ are required. This way the Catholic
Church can avoid an idea of tradition or an ecclesial identity that would be
either relativistic or unable to change anything in previous modes of expression or of life.

Ecumenical activity requires some initiatives, but it is described above all
as a "holy objective" that "human powers and capacities cannot achieve" and
that requires most of all our prayers and our conversion: Ecumenism is spiritual or is not.[118]

NOTES

1. The text of the decree *Unitatis redintegratio* (Vatican II's Decree on Ecumenism,
Nov. 21, 1964) is quoted in Norman Tanner's translation (*Decrees of Ecumenical Councils*); when the translation is modified, either the Latin words are added or a footnote
mentions the modification.

2. Pierre Jurieu, *Le vrai système de l'Église et la véritable analyse de la foi, où sont
dissipées toutes les illusions que les controversistes modernes, prétendus catholiques, ont voulu
faire au public sur la nature de l'Église, son infaillibilité et le juge des controverses* (Dordrecht,
the Netherlands: Chez la Veuve de Caspar et chez Théodore Goris, 1686), I.X, 79. My
translation.

3. Pierre Jurieu, *Traité de l'unité de l'Église et des points fondamentaux, contre mon-
sieur Nicole* (Rotterdam: Chez Abraham Acher, près de la Bourse, 1688), second page of
the preface (no page number). My translation.

4. Vatican Council I, constitution *Dei Filius*, introduction, in *Decrees of the Ecumenical Councils*, vol. 2, ed. Norman P. Tanner, S.J., original text established by G.
Alberigo et al. (London: Sheed and Ward, 1990), 804.

5. Cf. *Codex juris canonici* (1917), canon 12.

6. Cf. ibid., canon 1.

7. Cf. *Code of Canon Law* (1983), canon 11: "Merely ecclesiastical laws bind those
who have been baptized in the Catholic Church or received into it, possess the efficient
use of reason, and, unless the law expressly provides otherwise, have completed seven

years of age." About this canon, cf. the Canon Law Society of Great Britain and Ireland and the Canadian Canon Law Society, *The Canon Law, Letter & Spirit: A Practical Guide to the Code of Canon Law* (London: Geoffrey Chapman, 1995), 9: "This canon is a major innovation, in respect not only of the 1917 code (canon 12) but also of the thinking behind the draft of the revision commission as late as 1980. It represents in fact a particularly significant appreciation of the theological and ecumenical reflections of Vatican II. It deals with those who are obliged by what are technically called merely ecclesiastical laws, that is, laws whose sole source is the legislative authority of the Catholic Church. These are distinguished not only from the divine law, be it natural or positive, but also from ecclesiastical laws which themselves are but declarations or interpretations of the divine law. It is this canon which has given the distinction a particularly practical significance: merely ecclesiastical laws bind those only 'who were baptized in the Catholic Church or received into it'; the other laws mentioned above bind also the unbaptized."

8. Cf. Leo XIII, litterae apostolicae *Provida matris caritate* (May 5, 1895), in *Leonis XIII pontificis maximi acta*, vol. 15 (Rome: Ex Typographia Vaticana, 1896), 184–88; we speak about "dissident brethren" because of the text of that letter; cf. 187: "de reconciliatione quam instituimus dissidentium fratrum provehenda." The novena of prayer was confirmed by the encyclical *Divinum illud munus* (May 9, 1897), nos. 12–14; cf. *The Papal Encyclicals 1878–1903*, ed. Claudia Carlen, I.H.M. (Raleigh: Pierian Press, 1990), 416. The Octave of Prayer for Christian Unity as it exists nowadays was founded in 1906 by the Reverend Spencer Jones (vicar of Moreton-in-the-Marsh) and Father Paul Wattson of the Friars of the Atonement (when still Anglicans); after the friars became Roman Catholic, the observance was extended to the whole Roman Catholic Church in 1916. *Unitatis redintegratio* 8 alludes to the week of prayer.

9. Pius XI, encyclical *Mortalium animos* (Jan. 6, 1928), no. 6, in Carlen, *Papal Encyclicals 1903–1939*, 314–15.

10. Pius XI, encyclical *Mortalium animos*, nos. 7–8, pp. 315–16.

11. Giovanni Battista Montini, "Discorso nel santuario di S. Antonio Abate," Milano (Jan. 1, 1957), in *Discorsi e scritti milanesi (1954–1963)*, 3 vols. (Rome: Istituto Paolo VI/Studium, 1997), 1169. My translation.

12. Suprema congregatio sancti officii, instructio ad locorum ordinarios "De motione oecumenica" (Dec. 20, 1949), translation in *Jurist* 10 (Jan.–Oct. 1950): 210 (the whole text is published in Latin and English in that article, 201–13; original and official text in *AAS* 42 [1950]: 142–47).

13. "Ad quandam saltem deveniendi unitatem." John XXIII, encyclical *Ad Petri cathedram* (June 29, 1959), no. 64, in Carlen, *Papal Encyclicals 1958–1981*, 11.

14. Pontifical Council for Promoting Christian Unity, "History," http://www .vatican.va/roman_curia/pontifical_councils/chrstuni/documents/rc_pc_chrstuni_pro _20051996_chrstuni_pro_en.html. A very interesting history of the Secretariat for Unity is presented in the doctoral dissertation of an American Passionist who worked for years in the secretariat (then council): Jerome-Michael Vereb, C.P., "The Ecumenical Endeavour of Cardinal Bea" (STD diss., Pontifical University of Saint Thomas Aquinas, Rome, 2003).

15. Cf. letter to Cardinal A. Cicognani, secretary of state (Oct. 18, 1962), appendix, in *Giovanni Battista Montini arcivescovo di Milano e il Concilio Ecumenico Vaticano II* (Rome: Istituto Paolo VI/Edizioni Studium Vita Nova, 1985), 422.

16. Cf., for instance, Lorenz Cardinal Jaeger, *A Stand on Ecumenism: The Council's Decree*, trans. Hilda Graef (New York: P. J. Kenedy & Sons, 1965), published in German in 1965; Gustave Thils, *Le décret sur l'œcuménisme: Commentaire doctrinal* (Paris: Desclée

de Brouwer, 1966); Bernard Leeming, *The Vatican Council and Christian Unity: A Commentary on the Decree on Ecumenism of the Second Vatican Council, Together with a Translation of the Text* (New York: Harper & Row, 1966), 19–30; Augustine Cardinal Bea, *The Way to Unity after the Council* (London: Deacon Books, Geoffrey Chapman, 1967), 35–39.

17. On Nov. 26, 1962, Fr. Athanasius Welkyj, O.S.B.M., explained that more than ten possible titles were considered; the title that was ultimately chosen explains the topic of the schema without "undue proselytism." Cf. *Acta synodalia sacrosancti Concilii Oecumenici Vaticani*, vol. 1, pt. 3 (Rome: Typis Polyglottis Vaticanis, 1973), 549–50.

18. The *Schema decreti de Ecclesiae unitate "Ut omnes unum sint"* is published in *Acta synodalia*, vol. 1, pt. 3, 528–45. With regard to the drafting and the consolidation of the texts, cf. the explanation by Cardinal Cicognani, president of the Commission for Eastern Churches (Nov. 18, 1963), *Acta synodalia*, vol. 2, pt. 5, 468.

19. The *Schema decreti de oecumenismo* is published in *Acta synodalia*, vol. 2, pt. 5, 412–41. Explanations of the changes in the text are found in *Acta synodalia*, vol. 2, pt. 5, 442–95.

20. Cf. Jérôme Hamer, O.P., "Histoire du texte de la déclaration," in *La liberté religieuse, déclaration "Dignitatis humanae personae,"* ed. J. Hamer and Y. Congar (Paris: Cerf, 1967), 73; cf. also Thils, *Le décret sur l'œcuménisme*, 21.

21. The *Schema decreti de oecumenismo* is published in *Acta synodalia*, vol. 3, pt. 2, 296–329.

22. Explanations of these changes are given in *Acta synodalia*, vol. 3, pt. 7, 11–49, 412–21, and 669–702.

23. Cf. *Acta synodalia*, vol. 3, pt. 7, 783: "Decretum vero de oecumenismo placuit Patribus 2.137, dissentibus 11."

24. Cf. modus 5 by eleven African fathers, *Acta synodalia*, vol. 2, pt. 5, 446.

25. A term suggested by Archbishop Maurice Baudoux of Saint Boniface in Alberta (Canada); cf. *Acta synodalia*, vol. 2, pt. 5, 444.

26. Thils, *Le décret sur l'œcuménisme*, 33, explains that the Secretariat for Unity would have liked to use this term more but instead had to use "communities," partly in order to avoid sentences like "communions not in full communion."

27. Cf. John Paul II, encyclical *Ecclesia de Eucharistia* (Apr. 17, 2003), no. 34: "The Extraordinary Assembly of the Synod of Bishops in 1985 saw in the concept of an 'ecclesiology of communion' the central and fundamental idea of the documents of the Second Vatican Council."

28. He described that point as important and very complex as being one that non-Catholics wanted the council to address. He added that the sacramental dimension was central to it. Cf. Augustinus Kardinal Bea, "Geleitwort," in *Unio Christianorum*, Festschrift für Erzbischof Dr. Lorenz Jaeger zum 70. Geburtstag am 23. September 1962, Herausgegeben von Othmar Schilling und Heinrich Zimmermann (Paderborn, Germany: Bonifacius, 1962), 26.

29. See Thomas Aquinas, *Summa theologiae*, III, q. 8. a. 1: "He has the power of bestowing grace on all the members of the Church, according to Jn 1:16: 'Of his fullness we have all received.' And thus it is plain that Christ is fittingly called the Head of the Church."

30. Cf. Aquinas, *ST*, I–II, q. 112, a. 5; Council of Trent, *Decree on Justification*, sixth session (Jan. 13, 1547), ch. 8 (Denzinger, no. 1534, *The Christian Faith*, 1936) and ch. 12 (Denzinger, no. 1540, *The Christian Faith*, 1940).

31. Or in all of the members of these communities, as Cardinal Bea suggested: "Although the decree feels bound to declare that non-Catholic Christians do not have

access to the fullest possible means of grace, it makes it quite clear that grace is nevertheless conveyed to each and every individual and community by the Holy Spirit in virtue of their original baptism." Bea, *Way to Unity after the Council*, 147.

32. Cf. Paul VI, general audience (Jan. 22, 1964), *L'osservatore romano* (Italian) (Jan. 23, 1964), 1.

33. John Paul II, encyclical *Ut unum sint* (May 25, 1995), no. 11.

34. The "in Ecclesia catholica subsistere" of article 3 echoes the "subsistit in Ecclesia catholica" of *Lumen gentium* 8.

35. At the time of Vatican II some feared that the number of individual conversions to the Catholic Church would decrease; cf. Kevin McNamara, "Ecumenism in the Light of Vatican II," in *Vatican II on Ecumenism*, ed. Michael Adams (Chicago: Scepter Books, 1967), 75.

36. Bea, *Way to Unity after the Council*, 150.

37. Paul VI, encyclical *Ecclesiam suam* (Aug. 6, 1964), no. 110.

38. Cf. John XXIII, encyclical *Ad Petri cathedram* (June 29, 1959), no. 72. The encyclical itself quoted without reference the following expression: "In necessariis unitas, in dubiis libertas, in omnibus caritas." Research published after the encyclical shows that the formula—whom some had attributed either to Augustine or to Luther because of its Augustinian flavor—arose in fact in the seventeenth century; cf. J. Lecler, "A propos d'une maxime citée par le Pape Jean XXIII," in "Necessariis unitas, in dubiis libertas, in omnibus caritas," *Recherches de sciences religieuses* 49 (1961), 549–60; and *Recherches de sciences religieuses* 52 (1964), 432–38.

39. Since 1974, a Commission for Religious Relations with the Jews has been connected to the Vatican Dicastery for Ecumenism (then called the Secretariat for Promoting Christian Unity and now called the Pontifical Council for Promoting Christian Unity), and not to the dicastery responsible for interreligious dialogue. That connection to ecumenism, although always distinct from ecumenism itself, shows the specificity of Judaism, in a Christian perspective, in relation to other religions.

40. Cf. Congregation for the Doctrine of the Faith, declaration *Mysterium Ecclesiae* (June 24, 1973).

41. Cf. above all, the agreements between Pope Paul VI and the Patriarch Mar Ignatius Jacob III (Oct. 25, 1971), between Pope Paul VI and the pope of Alexandria, Shenouda III (May 10, 1973), between Pope John Paul II and Moran Mor Ignatius Zakka I Iwas, patriarch of Antioch and all of the East and supreme head of the Universal Syrian Orthodox Church (June 23, 1984), between Pope John Paul II and Karekin I, supreme patriarch and Catholicos of All Armenians (Dec. 13, 1996). The distinction between Eastern and Oriental churches is explained in the present commentary in no. 13.

42. Cf. *Ut unum sint*, nos. 21–27.

43. "Communicatio in sacris" indicates in the first place a common participation in the sacraments and indirectly some participation in other kinds of worship; cf. the explanation of the schema by the secretariat on Nov. 11, 1964: "In libris theologicis communicatio in sacris communiter non est notio univoca: se refert directe ad participationem in sacramentis, in obliquo autem ad participationem in quolibet cultu. Non alio modo de communicatione in sacris loqui intendit decretum de oecumenismo" (*Acta synodalia*, vol. 3, pt. 7, 416). Eight fathers suggested excluding any *communicatio in sacris* as inviting indifferentism and as contrary to the secular praxis of the Church, but the secretariat rejected the proposal because the majority had accepted the text: "Modus non accipitur; textus enim a majore Patrum parte acceptus est" (*Acta synodalia*, vol. 3, pt.

THE DECREE ON ECUMENISM 337

7, 682). On that question, cf. George Tavard, "Praying Together: *Communicatio in sacris* in the Decree on Ecumenism," in Alberic Stacpoole, *Vatican II by Those Who Were There* (London: Geoffrey Chapman, 1986), 202–19.

44. Cf. Eusebius of Caesarea, *Church History*, V, 24.

45. International Joint Commission for Theological Dialogue between the Catholic Church and the Orthodox Church, *Faith, Sacraments, and the Unity of the Church* (Bari, Italy, June 1987), no. 21, *Information Service* 64 (1987/II), 85.

46. John Paul II, encyclical *Ecclesia de Eucharistia* (Apr. 17, 2003), no. 44. Cf. also ibid., no. 35: "The celebration of the Eucharist, however, cannot be the starting point for communion; it presupposes that communion already exists, a communion which it seeks to consolidate and bring to perfection."

47. *Ecclesia de Eucharistia*, no. 45, quotes the two codes of canon law. The question is more developed in the *Directory for the Application of Principles and Norms on Ecumenism*, published by the Pontifical Council for Promoting Christian Unity after its approval by Pope John Paul II (Mar. 25, 1993), above all in nos. 122–36.

48. John Paul II, encyclical *Ecclesia de Eucharistia*, no. 45.

49. Ibid., no. 46.

50. Cf. *Directory for the Application of Principles and Norms on Ecumenism* (Mar. 25, 1993), no. 125. At the council, several groups of bishops—Eastern and Western—insisted on a broader possibility of intercommunion with Eastern Christians, according to a rather common and old practice. Cf. *Acta synodalia*, vol. 2, pt. 5, 455–56; cf. also the intervention of the Melkite Basilians' Superior Father Hage in *Acta synodalia*, vol. 2, pt. 6, 330–31.

51. Pontifical Council for Promoting Christian Unity, *Directory for the Application of Principles and Norms on Ecumenism*, no. 123.

52. Ibid., no. 130, namely, the case of danger of death or "situations of grave and pressing need."

53. Pontifical Council for Promoting Christian Unity, *Directory for the Application of Principles and Norms on Ecumenism*, no. 131.

54. This point has been mentioned at the council in a text of the bishops of the apostolic region of Bordeaux, cf. modus 119, *Acta synodalia*, vol. 2, pt. 5, 458.

55. John Paul II, "From Commemorations to Luther Arises a New Impulse for Reconciliation," audience to the Joint Catholic-Lutheran Commission (Mar. 2, 1984), *L'osservatore romano* (English) (Mar. 12, 1984), 12. He also said the same at his meeting with the bishops of the Danish Lutheran Church, Roskilde, Denmark, on June 6, 1989.

56. Reformed–Roman Catholic International Dialogue, "Finalization of Final Report: 'Toward a Common Understanding of the Church,'" no. 14, *Information Service* 74 (1990/III): 93.

57. Cf. Cardinal Bea's speech, Nov. 25, 1963, in *Acta synodalia*, vol. 2, pt. 6, 15: "Remedium huic periculi tamen non in eo est, ut actio ad unitatem promovendam omnino omittatur, sed in eo est ut ab ipsis Sacris Pastoribus ei rite invigiletur."

58. Archbishop Pangrazio's Nov. 25, 1963, speech is in *Acta synodalia*, vol. 2, pt. 6, 32–34.

59. Peter Hebblethwaite, *In the Vatican* (Bethesda, Md.: Adler and Adler, 1986), 149, supposes that Swiss Protestant theologian Lukas Vischer (future director of Faith and Order) suggested the idea to Archbishop Pangrazio. Asked about it in 2003, Vischer denied having done so and suggested that in fact the hint came from Edmund Schlink, German Protestant observer at the council.

60. The first part of the speech is about salvation history.

61. Speech of Archbishop Pangrazio, Nov. 25, 1963, translated in Jaeger, *Stand on Ecumenism*, 114–15. I have added to the translation some elements of the original Latin text.

62. *Acta synodalia*, vol. 3, pt. 7, 419. My translation.

63. Joint working group of the Roman Catholic Church and the World Council of Churches, "The Notion of 'Hierarchy of Truths': An Ecumenical Interpretation," Faith and Order Paper no. 150 (Geneva: WCC Publications, 1990), no. 25, p. 20.

64. Pius XII, apostolic constitution *Munificentissimus Deus* (Nov. 1, 1950), no. 45 (Denzinger, no. 3904, cf. *Christian Faith*, 715).

65. About our object of faith, cf. especially his *Summa theologiae*, II–II, q. 5, a. 3. In the contemporary ecumenical context, what was evident for Saint Thomas—the role of the Church in the transmission of revelation—is what has to be agreed on. So that believers can receive divine revelation, it is necessary to determine the criteria of a recognition of the Church.

66. I agree with Giovanni Cereti, *Commento al decreto sull'ecumenismo* (Turin: Borla, 1966), 161, who affirms a continuity in principles, which prevents a radical opposition between the hierarchy of truths at Vatican II and Pius XI's *Mortalium animos*.

67. Cf. Charles Journet, *What Is Dogma?* (London: Burns and Oates, 1964), 101–102.

68. Historical research turns up more precise distinctions, for example, between Nestorius himself and "nestorianism," or about the rather symbolic meaning of the year 1054.

69. The usual ecumenical terminology nowadays distinguishes between Eastern Orthodox churches (that is, those usually united to Constantinople, like the Greek Orthodox Church and the Russian Orthodox Church) and Oriental Orthodox churches (e.g., Assyrian Church of the East, Coptic churches, the Armenian Orthodox Church, Syrian and Malabarese Jacobites). This terminology is useful but also confusing since the Oriental churches differ widely among themselves; for instance, the Assyrian Church of the East and the Copts have been divided for fifteen hundred years at the very center of what determined their identity.

70. As it had been suggested not to speak about the persistence of Catholic structures in the Anglican Communion because of the invalidity of its orders, the secretariat replied that there was no total absence of Catholic structures and that the indication "in part" was sufficient: "Non est verum dicere communionem anglicanam, ratione invaliditatis ordinationum, omnino carere structura catholica. Incisa 'ex parte' sufficit ad vitandam ambiguitatem." Modus 13 (Nov. 14, 1964), *Acta synodalia*, vol. 3, pt. 7, 673.

71. Cf. ibid., vol. 2, pt. 5, 473, where Archbishop Martin of Rouen quoted an allocution by Paul VI to the non-Catholic observers (Oct. 17, 1963).

72. His suggestion, written "after September 14, 1964" (and available before the discussion of November 1964), is published in *Acta synodalia*, vol. 3, pt. 2, 901–903.

73. Ibid., vol. 3, pt. 2, 310, no. 13, p. [19], lines 9–10. My translation.

74. Cf. ibid., vol. 3, pt. 2, 902: "Si versio Anglicana eventuum vera est, Ecclesia hodierna Anglicana nexum continuitatis habet cum Ecclesia Anglicana medii aevi—continuitas non mere externae, nominibus et formis debitae, sed vere constitutionalis et quodammodo essentialis. Archiepiscopus Cantuarensis dicendus esset verus successor Sancti Augustini qui primus a Sancto Gregorio Magno ad hoc officium nominatus est. Nova illa hierarchia a Pio IX a. 1850 restaurata intrusio quaedam supplantrix reputanda esset, ut multi acatholici saec. XIX de facto illam incriminaverunt."

75. John Paul II, *Ut unum sint*, no. 54 (there are many other occurrences of this expression).

76. During the council, several Eastern rite bishops complained about the past latinization; cf. Melkite Patriarch of Antioch Maximus IV Saigh (*Acta synodalia*, vol. 2, pt. 6, 170–73), Bishop Joseph Tawil, patriarchal vicar of the Melkites in Syria (*Acta synodalia*, vol. 2, pt. 6, 25), and Archbishop Georges Layek of the Armenians of Alep (*Acta synodalia*, vol. 2, pt. 6, 356). Archbishop Franjo Šeper of Zagreb mentioned the same point as one of the reasons for the divisions in the Church (cf. *Acta synodalia*, vol. 2, pt. 6, 231; Šeper became a cardinal in 1968 and was prefect of the Congregation for the Doctrine of the Faith from 1968 to 1981). Bishop Maksimilijan Držecnik of Maribor presented additional reasons for the divisions. Cf. *Acta synodalia*, vol. 2, pt. 6, 266.

77. Cf. modi 5 and 7, *Acta synodalia*, vol. 3, pt. 7, 686.

78. Cf. the list of the occurrences of the Eastern and Western fathers in Aquinas's main works, established by Leo J. Elders, S.V.D., "Santo Tomás de Aquino y los Padres de la Iglesia," *Doctor communis* 48 (1995): 65–66. Cf. also Gilles Emery, O.P., "Saint Thomas d'Aquin et l'Orient Chrétien," *Nova et vetera* (French) 74 (1999): 19–36.

79. A document that addresses this question will be published later on; Pontificium consilium ad unitatem Christianorum fovendam, *Les traditions grecque et latine concernant la procession du Saint-Esprit* [The Greek and Latin traditions regarding the Procession of the Holy Spirit] (Rome: Typis Polyglottis Vaticanis, 1996), text in French, with translations into Greek, English, and Russian.

80. Walter Kasper, "Le radici teologiche del conflitto tra Mosca e Roma," *La civiltà Cattolica* (2002), 538. My translation. During the council, the archbishop of Seville, Cardinal José María Bueno y Monreal, had already said, "Equidem dialogus oecumenicus, ex definitione, proselytismus excludit." *Acta synodalia*, vol. 2, pt. 6, 41–42.

81. John Paul II and Demetrios I, French original in *Acta Apostolicae Sedis* 80 (1988), 254. My translation.

82. *Information Service* 83 (1993/II), 96–99, with corrections in *Information Service* 84 (1993/III–IV), 149.

83. "Uniatism, Method of Union of the Past, and the Present Search for Full Communion," no. 15.

84. Cf. *Unitatis redintegratio*, 4.

85. Cf. ibid., 18.

86. *Dignitatis humanae*, 4. In 1995 the Joint Working Group between the World Council of Churches and the Roman Catholic Church published a document that also excluded unfair preaching ("The Challenge of Proselytism and the Calling to Common Witness," Study Document, *Information Service* 91 [1996]: no. 19). Moreover, since preaching truth is of course an inescapable necessity (no. 8), even churches that are not in full communion should try to give a common witness of God's love (no. 10).

87. Cf. Kasper, "Le radici teologiche," 539.

88. Walter Cardinal Kasper, intervention "Lasting Significance and Urgency of *Unitatis redintegratio*" (Nov. 11, 2004), *L'osservatore romano* (English) (Dec. 1, 2004), 8.

89. Cf. John Paul II, *Ut unum sint*, no. 95.

90. Cf. Walter Kasper, "L'engagement œcuménique de l'Église catholique" (conference at the General Assembly of the French Protestant Federation, Paris, Mar. 23–24, 2002), *Documentation catholique* 2270 (May 19, 2002): 489.

91. "De communitatibus inde a saeculo XVI exortis," *Acta synodalia*, vol. 2, pt. 5, 427.

92. Cf. modus 165, ibid., vol. 2, pt. 5, 464.

93. Cf. Archbishop John Heenan (who became a cardinal in 1965) in ibid., vol. 3, pt. 2, 14: "Aliorum communitatum descriptionem dare minime voluimus; potius

quattuor puncta in textu elaborate, scilicet Christi confessio (no. 20), Sacrorum Librorum studium (no. 21), vita sacramentalis (no. 22), vita cum Christo (no. 23)."

94. Cf. modus 2, in ibid., vol. 3, pt. 7, 691.

95. Cf. John Calvin, *Institutes of the Christian Religion*, bk. 4, ch. 9.

96. Cf. Yves Congar, *Martin Luther, Sa foi, sa réforme*, "Cogitatio fidei," vol. 119 (Paris: Cerf, 1983), 108–33.

97. J.-M. R. Tillard, O.P., *Church of Churches: The Ecclesiology of Communion*, trans. R. C. de Peaux (Collegeville, Minn.: Liturgical Press, 1992), 230.

98. The World Lutheran Federation represents most Lutherans.

99. Lutheran World Federation and the Catholic Church, *Joint Declaration on the Doctrine of Justification* (Oct. 31, 1999), no. 43.

100. Faith and Order, which began as an independent ecumenical movement dedicated to theological dialogue, merged with the World Council of Churches at its foundation in 1948. The Catholic Church, without belonging to the World Council of Churches, became a full member of Faith and Order in 1968. At the 1963 Montreal meeting, there were only some Catholic observers (as there were some non-Catholic observers at Vatican II).

101. Cf. Paul S. Minear, ed., "Faith and Order Findings: The Report of the Fourth World Conference on Faith and Order," Faith and Order Paper nos. 37–40 (London: SCM Press, 1963); or "Documentary History of Faith and Order," ed. Günther Gassmann, Faith and Order Paper no. 159 (Geneva: WCC Publications, 1993), 10–18.

102. Faith and Order, "A Treasure in Earthen Vessels: An Instrument for an Ecumenical Reflection on Hermeneutics," Faith and Order Paper no. 182 (Geneva: WCC Publications, 1998), nos. 16–18.

103. Cf. Groupe des Dombes, *"Un seul maître": L'autorité doctrinale dans l'Église* (Paris: Bayard, 2005), no. 463.

104. *"The Gift of Authority:* Authority in the Church III," an agreed statement by the Anglican–Roman Catholic International Commission (London: CTS, 1999), no. 47.

105. That question was quietly mentioned in the second session by Raul Cardinal Silva Henríquez of Santiago, Chile, in his Nov. 26, 1963, speech (cf. *Acta synodalia*, vol. 2, pt. 6, 72). It was more clearly mentioned in the third session in a common text by 259 bishops from most Latin American countries (among them 112 Brazilians, 41 Colombians, and 40 Mexicans). Other Latin American bishops mentioned the same point individually. In a different context, Archbishop Georges Layek of Alep (Armenians) complained about Protestant proselytism in his region (cf. ibid., vol. 2, pt. 6, 280; text signed by five other Armenian bishops).

106. As a clear example of dividing lines among Protestants, the ordination of Gene Robinson, an openly practicing homosexual, as Episcopal bishop of New Hampshire in 2003, was justified with a reading of scripture that was open to contemporary society and refused by other Anglicans on the basis of a more literal reading.

107. 1 Cor 3:9.

108. Cf. *Dei verbum*, no. 11.

109. Cf. Bea, *Way to Unity after the Council*, 92.

110. Most mainstream Protestant communities accept only baptism and the Eucharist (for the Catholic faith, there can be no Eucharist without the sacrament of orders). Certain Lutherans, because of article 11 of the *Augsburg Confession* (1530), may still consider confession (the sacrament of reconciliation) to be a sacrament.

111. This distinction is not well received in the ecclesial communities. At the council, in the name of the Episcopal Conference of Scotland, Archbishop Gordon Joseph Gray of Saint Andrews and Edinburgh (who became a cardinal in 1969) said that

Protestants would rightly be affected by the term and suggested a distinction between *ecclesia orientalis* and *ecclesia occidentalis*. Cf. *Acta synodalia*, vol. 2, pt. 6, 118–19).

112. However, it is not without importance because the distinction between churches and ecclesial communities is a structural element of the decree. Therefore, Bernard Leeming's argument does not seem very convincing: "The Decree on Ecumenism is a pastoral document and its whole tone indicates that its purpose is not to make judgments about others, but to lay down general principles to be followed by Catholics in the search for Christian unity. To have attempted to determine where the word 'Church' is properly applied would not have been either necessary or helpful to this purpose, and it may be doubted whether it would be proper in itself." Leeming, *Vatican Council and Christian Unity*, 211–12.

113. This is the explicit example given by the secretariat when it replied to a modus that asked for the word "churches" to be removed from the title of that section: "Etiam in Occidente exsistunt communitates quae communiter 'Ecclesiae' vocantur, ex. gr. Veteris-Catholici" (reply to modus 1 about no. 19, *Acta synodalia*, vol. 3, pt. 7, 689). The secretariat used a plural but gave only one example, which spoke about a common usage without explaining its theological meaning.

Divided from Rome after the First Vatican Council (1870), the Old Catholics united themselves with a community that had preserved the episcopate since a division that began with the pope's nonrecognition of an archbishop of Utrecht elected in 1697 and went on with the help of a French Gallican bishop in 1724 and 1725. At the time of Vatican II, the validity of the orders of the Old Catholics would have justified the mention of the separated Church in the West.

It was probably not his intention to introduce a new teaching on the ecclesial status of Protestant communities when Pope John Paul II, writing about religious life, spoke about "the churches and ecclesial communities which originated in the Reformation." Postsynodal apostolic exhortation *Vita consecrata* (Mar. 25, 1996), no. 2.

114. The Polish National Church has a membership of about twenty-five thousand in the United States, founded as such in 1904. Its first bishop was ordained by an Old Catholic bishop in 1907 in Utrecht.

115. It is less likely because of Leo XIII's bull *Apostolicae curae* (1896), which pronounced Anglican ordinations "absolutely null and utterly void." The fact that after 1931 many Old Catholics bishops took part in many ordinations of Anglican bishops has introduced a new element, but it is doubtful that this could have justified to the council the idea to call the Anglican communion a "church" or a communion of churches.

116. On June 5, 2001, the Congregation for the Doctrine of the Faith declared the baptisms of the Mormons invalid. The primary reason was the negation of the Trinity (and of the divinity of Christ).

117. My translation.

118. As future Cardinal Dulles said with regard to Father Congar, "All who live according to the Gospel by that very fact promote the cause of ecumenism." Avery Dulles, S.J., "The Decree on Ecumenism: Twenty-five Years After," in *Walking Together: Roman Catholics and Ecumenism Twenty-five Years after Vatican II*, ed. Thaddeus D. Horgan (Grand Rapids: Eerdmans, 1990), 25.

16

The Decree on the Eastern Catholic Churches, *Orientalium Ecclesiarum*

Khaled Anatolios

Introduction

On first impression, the Decree on the Eastern Catholic Churches seems to offer slight ground for substantiating the claim that the Second Vatican Council intended its pronouncements to be in organic continuity with established ecclesial tradition. To begin with, the very situation that it addresses, the existence of Eastern churches distinguished from their Orthodox counterparts by communion with Rome, is a phenomenon that dates back for the most part only to the sixteenth century.[1] Moreover, the document seems to be largely concerned with matters of church discipline rather than with doctrine integral to the deposit of faith; indeed, the decree legislates certain reversals of policy in these matters of discipline. Nevertheless, this document is best read as a strong statement of the council's commitment to ressourcement. This is centrally demonstrated by the fact that where the decree institutes changes in discipline with regard to the Eastern Catholic churches, these changes are made for the sake of the restoration of an older tradition. Even more significantly, the document situates the question of the relation of the Roman Church to the Eastern Catholic churches as a question of the Church's fidelity to tradition, rather than as merely an issue of ecclesial housekeeping. Indeed, the document shows some innovation in casting the matter in this form, but such innovation bespeaks the radicality of the council's commitment to ressourcement.

In this chapter I summarize the document and pay particular attention to the significant changes it introduces. After showing the impulse to ressourcement evident in these changes, I compare the opening statements of this document with analogous statements in

Pope Leo XIII's 1894 encyclical, *Orientalium dignitas*. This comparison will reveal essential lines of continuity, as well as development between the two documents, but it will be evident that such development consists in Vatican II's more radical approach to situating the question of relations with the Eastern churches as an exigency of the Church's fidelity to tradition. The document on the Eastern Catholic churches can thus be read as a significant example of the dialectic of *aggiornamento* and ressourcement in the Second Vatican Council and as representing not a schizophrenic vacillation of perspective but an integral effort on the part of the Church to reorient itself to a fuller appropriation of its tradition in order to face the modern world with authenticity.

Summary

The document begins with an appreciation of the heritage of the Eastern churches as an integral part of the tradition of the Universal Church (*OE* 1). It uses the image of the "Mystical Body" to refer to the unity of the Church, which comprises different "rites," both Eastern and Western (*OE* 2).[2] All such rites are of equal rank, and all are equally submitted to the authority of the Roman pontiff (*OE* 3). The well-being of the universal Church requires the flourishing of all of these "individual churches," as well as the awareness on the part of both hierarchy and laity of the existence of diverse rites within the Catholic Church (*OE* 4). After these introductory remarks, there follows the main body of the document, whose central theme is the necessity of preserving the integrity of the Eastern rites. Emphasis is placed on conservation; changes must manifest a continuity with established tradition: "All members of the Eastern Churches should be firmly convinced that they can and ought always [to] preserve their own legitimate liturgical rites and ways of life, and that changes are to be introduced only to forward their own organic development" (*OE* 6).[3] To this end, the decree rehearses the essential features of the Eastern rites. It acknowledges the institution of the patriarchate and stipulates that the rights and privileges of patriarchs be restored according to the pronouncements of the ecumenical councils (*OE* 7–11). Within this restoration, an explicit allowance is made for patriarchs to appoint bishops within their patriarchal territories (*OE* 9). Next, the document expresses appreciation of the sacramental discipline of the Eastern churches and recommends their restoration where these have lapsed through latinization (*OE* 12).

A significant item within this restoration is that priests are granted permission to administer the sacrament of chrismation (confirmation), in keeping with Eastern custom (*OE* 13–14). The Eastern Catholic faithful are exhorted to participate in liturgical worship (*OE* 15), and provisions are made for accessibility to the sacrament of confession by allowing Catholic priests of a given rite to administer this sacrament to Catholics of any other rite (*OE* 16). The document encourages the restoration of the order of permanent diaconate (*OE* 17) and relaxes the canonical norms for marriages between Eastern Catholics and Eastern Orthodox (*OE* 18). The churches of the various rites are granted authority to institute and suppress feast days, determine the date of Easter, and regulate liturgical language (*OE* 19–23). Finally, Eastern Catholics are reminded of having a special duty to foster unity with Eastern Orthodox churches (*OE* 24), and, under certain circumstances, *communicatio in sacris* between Eastern Catholics and Eastern Orthodox is permitted (*OE* 26). The document concludes by looking forward to the realization of full communion between the Catholic Church and "the separated Eastern Churches" (*OE* 30).

Areas of Development

Admittedly, this document makes several changes with respect to previous magisterial pronouncements and practice. Four significant developments are evident in this short document. To begin with, the tone throughout presumes the equality of the various rites within the Catholic Church, and this principle is made explicit in the opening paragraphs: "These individual churches both Eastern and Western . . . are of equal rank, so that none of them is superior to the others because of its rite [*Eaedem proinde pari pollent dignitate ita ut nulla earum ceteris praestet ratione ritus*]" (*OE* 3).[4] This statement, while having antecedents in previous papal pronouncements, also represents a development from an earlier perspective, in which the Latin rite was considered to be preferable to other rites. The latter notion appears, for example, in Pope Benedict XIV's encyclical, *Allatae sunt*, promulgated in 1755: "Since the Latin rite is the rite of the Holy Roman Church and this Church is mother and teacher of the other Churches, the Latin rite should be preferred to all other rites."[5] Another instance of development appears in chapter 9, where the patriarchs of the various churches are granted the right to establish eparchies, or dioceses, and appoint bishops within the traditional territories of their jurisdiction. This allowance represents a development from previous practice, in which patriarchal synods were allowed to make recommendations only to the Apostolic See, which would then make the final selection.[6] In chapter 13, Eastern Catholic priests are permitted to administer the sacrament of chrismation, as is the Eastern custom. This allowance represents an official reversal of the proscription issued by Pope Pius X in 1907, which forbad Ruthenian Catholic priests from administering this sacrament in the United States.[7] Finally, the decree acknowledges that *communicatio in sacris* constitutes a "more relaxed" regulation, which is justified by solicitude for the sacramental needs of both Catholic and Orthodox faithful and as a means to further union with the Eastern Orthodox churches.

Development and *Ressourcement*

Clearly, therefore, this decree does not merely reiterate previous magisterial pronouncement but makes some significant developments. Judgment as to the continuity of these developments with ecclesial tradition, broadly considered, requires situating these changes within the history of previous magisterial pronouncements on the subject. With regard to the first instance of development, the assertion of the equality of all rites, I have already mentioned the directly contrary statement of *Allatae sunt*. The latter statement occurs in the context of a prohibition of transfer from the Latin to the Greek rite, which is significantly complemented by discouraging the reverse phenomenon of transfer from the Greek to the Latin rite. However, as a bald statement of the superiority of the Latin rite, this assertion is relatively isolated. On the contrary, we find numerous examples of expressions of praise and honor directed at the Eastern churches. Vatican II's understanding was closely anticipated by Pius XII in his 1944 encyclical *Orientalis Ecclesiae*. There, the appellation of "Mother Church" was applied not to the Roman Church per se but rather to the communion of all of the rites. The context again had to do with the transference of rites, though this time the intent was to reassure Eastern Christians who desired communion with the Catholic church: "[They] should have full assurance that they will never be forced to abandon their legitimate rites or to exchange their own venerable and traditional customs for Latin rites and customs. All these are to be held in equal esteem and equal honour, for they adorn the common Mother Church with a royal garment of many colors."[8]

With regard to the reversals of disciplinary injunctions that had previously curtailed the powers of patriarchal synods to choose their own bishops and forbade priests from administering the sacrament of confirmation, the text leads us to see that the point in both cases is to recover the more authentic tradition of the Eastern churches. Thus, in both cases we find language of restoration to more ancient tradition: "Following the most ancient tradition of the Church [*secundum antiquissimam Ecclesiae traditionem*], special honor is to be given to the patriarchs of the Eastern Churches, since each is set over his patriarchate as father and head. Therefore this holy council enacts that their rights and privileges be restored in accordance with the ancient traditions of each Church [*instaurentur iuxta antiquas traditiones uniuscuiusque Ecclesiae*] and the decrees of the ecumenical councils" (*OE* 9).[9] Moreover, "the established practice with regard to the minister of Confirmation, which has existed among Eastern Christians from ancient times is to be fully restored [*disciplina . . . ab antiquissimis temporibus apud Orientales vigens plene instauretur*]" (*OE* 13).[10]

Finally, the significant development of allowing for *communicatio in sacris* between Catholic and Orthodox is foreshadowed in earlier pronouncements that stress the proximity of the two churches in matters of faith and ritual. So Leo XIII, in his encyclical *Praeclara gratulationis* of 1894, expresses hope for reestablishing communion with the Orthodox churches: "so illustrious in their ancient faith and glorious past. . . . We hope it all the more inasmuch as the distance separating them from us is not so great. Indeed, with some few exceptions, we agree so entirely on other heads, that in defense of the Catholic faith we often have recourse to reasons and testimony borrowed from the rites and customs of the East."[11]

What is striking about all of these developments is that they share a motivation to return to the sources of the Church's ancient tradition. The dignity of the Eastern churches is affirmed by special reference to the antiquity of its traditions, and initiatives are taken to restore these traditions to their original state. However, perhaps a more significant feature of the document is the way that it situates the whole question of the Eastern Catholic churches within a radical project of ressourcement. Here again, it is precisely the innovations within the document that reinforce its recovery of tradition. A comparison between the opening paragraphs of this document and Pope Leo XIII's encyclical of 1894, *Orientalium dignitas*, will clarify the dialectic of development and ressourcement that we find in this document. The opening statements of the two documents show a striking similarity, which suggests that the council fathers were making deliberate, subtle revisions to the encyclical of the previous century. As with the Vatican II decree, *Orientalium dignitas* begins with expressions of appreciation for the heritage of the Eastern churches:

> The Churches of the East are worthy of the glory and reverence that they hold throughout the whole of Christendom in virtue of those extremely ancient, singular memorials that they have bequeathed to us. For it was in that part of the world that the first actions for the redemption of the human race began, in accord with the all-kind plan of God. They swiftly gave forth their yield; there flowered in first blush the glories of preaching the True Faith to the nations, of martyrdom, and of holiness. They gave us the first joys of the fruits of salvation. From them has come a wondrously grand and powerful flood of benefits upon the other peoples of the world, no matter how far-flung.... It has most especially been the habit of the Roman Church, the head of all the Churches, to render to the Churches of the East a great degree of honor and love in remembrance of the Apostles, to rejoice in her turn in their faithful obedience. Amidst changing and difficult times, she has never failed in any way in farsightedness and acts of kindness to sustain them against the forces that would strike them again and again, to hold fast to those that were overwhelmed, to call back those in discord with her.[12]

Several motifs within this opening encomium are fairly representative of pronouncements on the Eastern churches prior to Vatican II.[13] The churches of the East are accorded special honor, which is specifically linked to the antiquity of the Eastern heritage. It is customary to provide an outline of the illustrious features of this ancient heritage, with special reference to the witness of sanctity and martyrdom. The beautifying influence of the Eastern heritage on the Catholic Church is typically described in poetic images; the Eastern churches are described as "jewels," "ornaments," "flower in first blush," and so on. While the Roman church rejoices in the ancient beauty of the Eastern churches, it is depicted as helper and guardian of the Eastern heritage. The relation of the Roman Church to the Eastern churches is generally depicted in terms of activity rather than receptivity; it is characterized as helper and guardian of the Eastern heritage, rejoicing in the latter's obedience.

In the opening statements of Vatican II's *Orientalium Ecclesiarum* we find a similar expression of the honor to be accorded to the Eastern churches, but there is also a significant development in the articulation of this praise. The document largely dispenses with the plethora of poetic images that appear in earlier documents in favor of doctrinal language that links the value of the Eastern churches specifically with the Church's task of holding fast to revealed tradition: "The Catholic Church values highly the institutions of the Eastern Churches, their liturgical rites, ecclesiastical traditions, and their ordering of the Christian life. For, in those churches, which are distinguished by their venerable antiquity, *there is clearly evident that tradition which has come from the apostles through the Fathers, and which is part of the divinely revealed, undivided heritage of the Universal Church [elucet ea quae ab Apostolis per Patres est traditio, quaeque partem constituit divinitus revelati atque indivisi universae Ecclesiae patrimonii].*"[14]

In light of this statement, the earlier lavish praise of Leo XIII's encyclical becomes conspicuous for falling short of saying outright that the Eastern churches are cobearers of the tradition [*traditio*] of the universal Church, speaking more evocatively and with less doctrinal force of "those extremely ancient, singular memorials that they have bequeathed to us [*pervetustis rerum monumentis eisque insignibus commendata*]." Moreover, anticipating *Dei verbum*, the Vatican II document considers this tradition of which the Eastern churches are bearers to be integral to the manifestation of Divine Revelation: "a tradition ... which is part of the divinely revealed, undivided heritage of the universal Church." With this situating of the issue of relations with the Eastern churches as pertaining directly to divine revelation, there is also a subtle but significant change in the expression of an ecclesiology.

As previously noted, earlier documents tend to depict the Roman Church as beautified by the "jewel" or "ornament" of the Eastern Church and in turn to be its guardian and benefactor. In this decree, however, the Roman Church stands alongside the Eastern churches as corecipients of an integral divine revelation. It is not so much an issue of the "Eastern tradition," which the Roman Church appreciates and protects, but an inalienable aspect of divine revelation, which is granted to the whole Church. This point is made even more forcefully a little later in the document: "History, tradition, and very many ecclesiastical institutions give clear evidence of the great debt owed to the Eastern Churches by the Church Universal. Therefore the holy council not merely praises and appreciates as is due this ecclesiastical and spiritual heritage, but also insists on viewing it as the heritage of the whole Church of Christ" (*OE* 5).[15]

The foregoing comparison of the opening statements of Pope Leo XIII's *Orientalium dignitas* and Vatican II's *Orientalium Ecclesiarum* illuminates the dialectic of continuity and development that runs through the latter document. As we have seen, the Vatican II document takes up a tradition of praise and esteem found in earlier magisterial pronouncements regarding the Eastern churches. However, whereas earlier documents expressed such praise in poetic terms, Vatican II sees the relationship between the Roman Church and the Eastern Catholic churches as a question that bears directly on the Universal

Church's reception of revelation in tradition. It is this fundamental insight that grounds the document's overarching project of effecting a restoration of the heritage of the Eastern Catholic churches. For this reason, it affirms the equality of Eastern and Western rites, and it does not shy away from reversing earlier practices and pronouncements that seemed to dilute the distinct integrity of the Eastern churches. The developments thereby introduced are consistently oriented toward a restoration of the traditions of the Eastern churches for the sake of a ressourcement that would enable the Universal Church to enjoy a more integral reception of divine revelation. *Orientalium Ecclesiarum* thus stands as a prime example of development—not away from but toward—a fuller recovery of the Church's tradition.

NOTES

1. With the exception of the Maronite Church of Lebanon and the Italo-Albanian Catholic Church, Eastern Catholic churches were constituted by the reestablishment of communion with Rome on the part of various groups that had been separated from Rome after the East-West split of AD 1054. Among the earliest instances of the latter phenomenon, we have the Chaldean Catholic Church (in present-day Iraq), established in 1553, and the Ukrainian Catholic Church, formed in 1595. On the other hand, the establishment of some Eastern Catholic churches dates only to the nineteenth and even twentieth centuries: the Coptic Catholic patriarchate was established in 1899, while the first bishop of the Greek Catholic Church of Greece was consecrated in 1911. See Ronald Roberson, *The Eastern Christian Churches: A Brief Survey*, 6th ed. (Rome: Edizioni Orientalia Christiana, 1999).

2. Cf. *Lumen gentium*, no. 7.

3. English translation: *Vatican II*, vol. 1, *The Conciliar and Postconciliar Documents*, ed. Austin Flannery (Northport, N.Y.: Costello, 1998).

4. Ibid., 442.

5. *Allatae sunt*, no. 20; English trans.: *Vatican Documents on the Eastern Churches: Papal Encyclicals and Documents concerning the Eastern Churches*, vol. 1 (Fairfax, Va.: Eastern Christian Publications, 2002), 16.

6. Cf. *Quartus supra* (Jan. 6, 1873), 24; also, Pius XII's *motu proprio cleri sanctitati* (1957), canon 395.

7. *Ea semper*, a. 14.

8. *Orientalis Ecclesiae*, no. 27; in *Vatican Documents on the Eastern Churches*, vol. 2, 13.

9. Flannery, *Conciliar and Postconciliar Documents*, 445.

10. Ibid., 447.

11. *Vatican Documents on the Eastern Churches*, vol. 1, 166–67. Similarly, Pius XI in his 1928 encyclical, *Rerum orientalium*, no. 18: "A special reason for this hope [for unity] is that among those nations a very great part of Revelation has been religiously preserved, since service is rendered to Christ our Lord, great piety and love are shown towards his sinless Mother, and devout use made of sacraments." Ibid., 249.

12. *Vatican Documents on the Eastern Churches*, vol. 1, 179.

13. For other typical examples of praise for Eastern churches prior to Vatican II see Pius X, *Ea semper* (1907), Pius XI, *Eccleisa Dei* (1923), and Pius XII, *Orientales Ecclesias* (1952).

14. Flannery, *Conciliar and Postconciliar Documents*, 441; emphasis added.

15. Ibid., 443.

17

The Decree on the Instruments of Social Communication, *Inter Mirifica*

Richard John Neuhaus

"The original language of Christianity is translation." So I was told by a missionary priest in Nigeria. The language of Judaism is Hebrew, and the language of Islam is Arabic. But what is the language of Christianity? While Catholicism has a particular, although now attenuated, attachment to Latin, the language of Christianity is the language most appropriate to communicating the gospel of Jesus Christ. This understanding is reflected also in *Inter mirifica*, the Decree on the Instruments of Social Communication.

The new curial dicastery called for by the decree is called the Pontifical Council for Social Communication. Some have remarked that "social communication" is an awkward construction. Isn't all communication, by definition, social? When the council adopted the decree, it was suggested that the document was something of a departure from earlier magisterial texts. The Church has always emphasized that human beings are by nature social, but the social groups that received attention were the family, work associations, national societies, and so on. The media "instruments" discussed by the decree, it was said, are creating something new: a communications society. Many years later, after the "digital revolution" began to take off in the 1990s, people would speak of this communications society as "the global village." One could argue that *Inter mirifica* was prescient in anticipating this development. There is some evidence in the text itself to support that argument.

For a decree that deals with the news media, *Inter mirifica* has generally received bad press. More often, it has simply been ignored. Certainly it does not figure prominently in most accounts of the council. That is understandable. It is one of the first two documents the council approved (with a vote of 1,960 to 164) at the final meeting of the second session, on December 4, 1963. The other document approved that day was the Constitution on the Sacred Liturgy.

Benedict XVI has spoken about the two hermeneutics of the council: one of rupture and one of continuity. According to the first, a great divide or rupture exists between the "pre-Vatican II Church" and the "post-Vatican II Church." That trope has dominated and bedeviled the interpretation of the council for four decades. I have written elsewhere that perhaps the greatest single achievement of the long pontificate of John Paul II was the establishment of a controlling hermeneutic of the council, and it is emphatically one of continuity.[1]

Yet the reception of *Inter mirifica* was marred in many circles by devotion to the hermeneutic of discontinuity. In these circles, the controlling rubric was very simple: Change is good, and continuity is bad. In the Abbott edition of the documents of the council, the introduction to this decree quotes the great ecumenist, Father Gustave Weigel, S.J. "The decree does not strike me as being very remarkable," said Father Weigel. "It is not going to produce great changes. It does not contain novel positions, but gathers and officially states a number of points previously stated and taught on a less official level."[2]

In the same volume, the response by Stanley I. Stuber, an American Baptist who was an official observer at the council, was even harsher: "Behind the puritanical and restrictive language [of the decree] there are outdated elements which, if forced to their ultimate conclusions, would condone censorship, favor management of news, and promote a purely 'Catholic' religious philosophy of pre-council isolationism." Moreover, "it also presents several propositions which, if taken seriously, would disrupt, if not curtail, the chief aspects of Pope John's *aggiornamento*."[3]

Clearly Mr. Stuber's judgment—shared by many, and especially by journalists, at the time—is unequivocal: "It is because the instruments of social communication are so vital to the advancement of the Christian cause in the world, where they are needed most of all, that, although we cannot accept this decree as it now stands, we do take courage in the fact that it is surrounded by the progressive spirit of the council. Therefore its inherent dangers may in practice be eliminated and its preachments may in reality be developed to the benefit of all concerned."[4] When translated, this would seem to mean that *Inter mirifica* may not do much damage if it is conscientiously ignored.

Needless to say, this is not a judgment easily squared with a faithful Catholic's assent to the Spirit-guided teaching of the council. But it is important to understand why some, including faithful Catholics, were so disappointed by the decree. In February 1964 Father John Sheerin, then editor of *The Catholic World*, published "The Communications Decree: Why the Dissent?" (At that time, the word "dissent" was not as theologically freighted as it would become after, for instance, the organized opposition to *Humanae vitae* in 1968.) Father Sheerin's tone was less one of dissent, as that term is commonly used today, than of disappointment at a missed opportunity. He and others were also worried that the decree could be misused to support the employment of social communications for the purposes of "propaganda," in the pejorative meaning of that term. (And there is almost no nonpejorative use of "propaganda" in contemporary discourse.)

The disappointment with the decree is not a great puzzlement. The media, with Xavier Rynne of the *New Yorker* in the lead, had carefully orchestrated expectations of novelty, even revolution, from the council. And here was the document on, of all things, the media, and it seemed in many ways to be the same old thing. Admittedly, when the decree was adopted, the tone of council documents had not yet developed in a more dialogical, rather than admonitory, mode. The council fathers speak in the voice of "Mother Church" and express their confidence that "all the sons of the Church will cordially welcome and religiously observe this program of precepts and guidelines" (*IM* 24). The title *Inter mirifica* suggests a sense of openness and wonder, while the diction of the decree seems at times more like a laying down of rules.

It is no part of Catholic orthodoxy that the Holy Spirit guarantees that the teaching of the truth will be done with literary grace and persuasive argument. What might be called the tonalities of the decree leave much to be desired. There is a certain defensiveness in speaking of the numerous problems and abuses connected with the instruments of communication. Obviously, such abuses abound, but one might have wished for more of an exploratory reflection on opportunities. Then too, it is said that the decree tends to speak of the Church as an institution concerned about protecting its own institutional interests, rather than the Church as a "sacrament" in service to the world, a theme developed so powerfully in the council's later deliberations.

Much of this is simply to say that *Inter mirifica* came early on in the development of the council's way of speaking. It was adopted before the council found its characteristic voice, so to speak. However, if the manner of expression reveals inadequacies, it is not so much a failure to reflect the theme of *aggiornamento* as a failure to fully reflect the twin—and, I suggest, the more important—theme of the council, ressourcement. In *Lumen gentium, Dei verbum*, and *Gaudium et spes*, to cite three notable examples, one witnesses the Church reappropriating the fullness of her tradition through the centuries in order to more boldly engage the challenges of the contemporary world. *Inter mirifica*, by comparison, sometimes has the feel of an extended memorandum produced by a curial committee.

All that having been said, however, the decree bears witness to abiding truths of which we need always to be reminded. The document begins with the assertion that, in all things, including the instruments of communication, the Church has the "duty to preach the news of redemption" (*IM* 3). The media are one means among others "for the formation of Christians and for every activity undertaken on behalf of man's salvation" (*IM* 3). Critics have seen in these opening passages a narrow, institutional self-interest in how the media can serve the Church. Communicating the gospel, however, is not institutional self-interest but the constituting mandate and raison d'être of the Church.

The bishops go on to say, "On religious shepherds devolves the task of so training and directing the faithful that by the help of these instruments [of communication], too, they may pursue their own salvation and fulfillment, and that of the entire human family" (*IM* 3). I do not think that the bishops are here claiming a special expertise in the employment of the media but are acknowledging their responsibility in spiritually forming Catholics in developing and exercising such expertise. This becomes more evident in the second chapter of the decree, in which the council fathers call for the establishment of programs of training in communications at Catholic institutions of higher learning. Four decades later, there are many such programs, although it seems doubtful that many of them are marked by the concern for evangelization espoused by *Inter mirifica*.

In article number 5, we are told that "there exists within human society a right to information about affairs which affect men individually or collectively, and according to the circumstances of each." This may seem to be a rather vague generalization, but it is worth remarking that we may have here for the first time in such an authoritative teaching document the affirmation of a "right to information." This is not a right to any and all information. First of all, the information must be true, and then it should be communicated in a manner "as complete as charity and justice allow" (*IM* 5).

In view of today's commercial and personal ambitions in attracting media audiences by any means, including ever more meretricious programming, one may think the bishops naive in speaking about holding the media accountable to the norms of truth, charity, and justice—or even elementary decency. But we remember that the bishops are here addressing themselves to the Catholic faithful, who are responsible for acting with an informed conscience. One might observe that the moral degeneration of the media, in the fields of both news and entertainment, in subsequent decades makes this teaching of the decree all the more urgent.

As with other documents of the council, *Inter mirifica* underscores that the chief responsibilities of the laity are in the temporal realm. "It is the laity's particular obligation to animate these instruments [of communication] with a humane and Christian spirit" (*IM* 3). It is a great irony that, in the aftermath of the council, many interpreted its teaching to turn the energies of the laity toward seeking a greater influence in the government of the Church. All too often, this ecclesiocentric turn quite eclipsed the council's bold call for the laity to be the Church in the world. That call is clearly evident in *Inter mirifica*.

Although the decree has been criticized for being excessively negative on the abuses of the communications media, one might better describe it as realistic about the distortions occasioned by the "base desires in man, wounded as he is by original sin" (*IM* 7). Realistic, too, is the recognition that in dramatic presentations "the narration, description, or portrayal of moral evil can indeed serve to make man more deeply known and studied," but always with the goal "to reveal and enhance the grandeur of truth and goodness" (*IM* 7). In subsequent years it has become all the more obvious that such an unapologetically moral purpose is required to challenge the media's obsession with the morally shocking, debased, and "transgressive."

In response to moral protests against offensive content, the contemporary masters of the media commonly respond that nobody is forced to watch or listen to such programming. The decree acknowledges the element of choice but further notes that choice is attended by duty. "Special duties bind those readers, viewers, or listeners who personally and freely choose what these media have to communicate" (*IM* 9). With the digital revolution bringing the Internet and unforeseeable possibilities in the future, communications have become much more interactive and less a matter of simply "receiving." Of the responsibility of parents to see that the faith and good morals of children are not jeopardized by degrading materials, the decree says, "Let them see that such things never cross the thresholds of their homes and that their children do not encounter them elsewhere" (*IM* 10). It is an admonition that parents beyond number struggle to implement—with increasing difficulty.

As for the responsibility of civil authorities, article 13 affirms the freedom of the press while, at the same time, calling for government to enact and energetically enforce laws against abuses that pose "serious danger to public morals and social progress" (*IM* 12). How this should be done is left undefined, which has given rise to complaints that the decree condones government censorship. Except, however, for libertarian absolutists, most would agree that the civil authorities have a necessary role (and in most countries they do exercise a role) in limiting some forms of expression, notably in the broadcast media. Even so, with changing technology and the proliferation of broadcast media, such limits are increasingly attenuated. Moreover, in "developed" societies, where the very idea of public morals is widely viewed as antiquated, one might be tempted to view the directives of the decree as well intended but futile. Nevertheless, such governmental responsibility and authority are established in principle, and Catholics are enjoined, no matter how adverse the circumstances, to press the possibilities of implementation.

The second chapter of the decree directs attention to the pastoral efforts of the Church and calls on the laity to generously support both a "Catholic press worthy of the name" (*IM* 14) and efforts by both laypeople and ecclesiastical authority to foster films, television, and other media in harmony with "the natural law and Catholic teachings and precepts" (ibid.). Now in place is the aforementioned pontifical council and, in the United States and elsewhere, the communications offices connected with episcopal conferences. Especially in this country, sundry media projects sponsored by ecclesiastical authority have not been conspicuously successful. In addition, the Catholic press has, in readership if not in quality, dramatically declined.

The decree concludes with the hope that "all the sons of the Church will cordially welcome and religiously observe this program of precepts and guidelines" and will thus "season the earth as its salt, and illumine the world as its light. The council further entreats all men of good will, especially those who control these instruments [of communication], to strive to apply them solely for the good of mankind" (*IM* 24). In view of the current state of the media, one may be forgiven for thinking that entreaty is more in the nature of a wan hope. Nonetheless, it is the Church's task to teach and entreat "in season and out of season," as Paul writes Timothy (2 Tim 4:2), and *Inter mirifica* is faithful to that mandate.

What some criticize as the narrow and cramped vision of the decree may also be understood as reflecting a certain modesty and clarity about the Church's distinctive role in the modern world. The decree calls for a world of communications that is very different from the one that we have. It envisions social communications in the service of morality, truth, charity, and the common good. But it also recognizes the limits of what the Church can do to bring about such a change—calling upon faithful Catholics to exercise their influence in trying to effect the transformation envisioned.

The decree affirms the specific and proper concern of the Church with respect to the media, namely, the "duty to preach the news of redemption" (*IM* 3). In its modesty and clarity, the decree is similar to Pope Benedict XVI's first encyclical, *Deus caritas est.* There the pope recognizes the daunting demands of justice in a world wracked by injustices beyond number; Catholics and others with a rightly formed conscience should, he says, work to remedy such injustices, according to their discernment of their own responsibilities and callings; however, nobody should be deluded into believing that a just world will be securely established short of the promised coming of the Kingdom of God. Meanwhile, Benedict writes, the specific and proper ecclesial mission of the Church—the mission of the Church qua Church—is to proclaim, exemplify, and eucharistically celebrate the radical truth that God is love—*Deus caritas est.*

Similarly, *Inter mirifica*, after surveying the complexities and challenges of social communications—complexities and challenges that have become only more daunting in the years since the council—is anchored in the truth that what is specific and proper to the mission of the Church is the proclamation of the redeeming gospel of Jesus Christ. Were ecclesial leadership and Catholics in the media focused on that task, many other ills might be remedied as well. By an imaginative engagement of the culture and its means of social communications, the Church can again demonstrate that the original language of Christianity is translation.

NOTES

1. See Richard John Neuhaus, *Catholic Matters: Confusion, Controversy, and the Splendor of Truth* (New York: Basic Books, 2006).
2. Gustave Weigel, S.J., speaking at the United States bishops' press panel session, Nov. 14, 1963, quoted in Thomas J. M. Burke, S.J., introduction to *Inter mirifica*, in *The Documents of Vatican II*, ed. Walter M. Abbott, S.J. (New York: Guild, 1966), 318.
3. Ibid.
4. Ibid.

PART III

The Declarations

18

The Declaration on Religious Liberty, *Dignitatis Humanae*

F. Russell Hittinger

When Pope John XXIII convened the Second Vatican Council in 1962, most observers understood that the council would need to address the issue of religious liberty in the civil sphere.[1] Early drafts of a statement on relations between Church and state were included in a schema on the Church. At the close of the council's first session, the subject was moved over to the schema on ecumenism. Finally, at the third session in the fall of 1964, after some 380 amendments, the schema on religious liberty had become an independent document. It was not so clear, however, whether to undertake a general reconsideration of principles or to confine its work to a policy statement. All of these questions—where to place the statement, what title to give it, the range of its content and mode of treatment—reflect the troubled history of Church and state in the modern period.

A century earlier, at the First Vatican Council (1869–1870), the question of the Church's liberty and authority *ad intra* was taken up and to some extent resolved. The council affirmed papal jurisdiction over the whole Church.[2] Such affirmation was deemed necessary because many of the European states asserted that local churches enjoyed civil liberty only in union with the state and that the state had power to superintend the offices and properties of the Church. The new governments born and reborn in the revolutions of the nineteenth century seized ecclesiastical properties, abolished monasteries and religious orders, liquidated or took over seminaries and parochial schools, controlled the flow of communication between Rome and dioceses, and, in many instances, asserted the right to veto, nominate, and even appoint ecclesiastical authorities. The new states used older ecclesiological doctrines of the supremacy of the local or national church vis-à-vis Rome. In France, for instance, this was called Gallicanism; in

Germany, Febronianism; in Austria, Josephetism; in Italy, Riccism.[3] The ecclesiologies of the ancien régime were restored in the late eighteenth and nineteenth centuries to express the power of the new nation-states.

Consequently, issues of ecclesiology were deeply interwoven in the mélange of disputes between the Church and the states. Vatican I rejected root and branch the ecclesiology of Gallicanism. In so doing, the council resolved a narrow but important part of the problem of the Church's authority and liberty—at least *ad intra*. Vatican I's basic proposition concerned whether the liberty of the Church had to be answered in terms of its unity and whether its unity required communion with the bishop of Rome. In short, Vatican I concluded that Catholic bishops were not functionaries of the state or of national churches.

Pastor aeternus, issued on July 18, 1870, infuriated the European powers. The Austrian government promptly cancelled its concordat with Rome and claimed that the papacy after July 19, 1870, was not the same government with which it had negotiated. In Prussia, Bismarck initiated the infamous Kulturkampf, during which time (1873–1887) more than half the Catholic hierarchy in Prussia were imprisoned for refusing to comply with laws that gave the state power over the ordinary Church government. Although the immediate effect of Vatican I was to exacerbate the suspicion—and sometimes the outright belligerence—of the European states toward the Church, the council saved the Church's internal structure one generation before the European powers committed a kind of international and cultural suicide in the trenches of World War I.

At Vatican I, some theologians and bishops lobbied for a conciliar statement that would specifically address the Church-state problem and perhaps even go so far as to doctrinalize various papal decrees against the new states. The Syllabus of Errors, issued in conjunction with the encyclical *Quanta cura* (1864),[4] listed erroneous propositions, many of which concerned matters of civil governance. In the first month of the council, a draft of *De Ecclesia Christi* was leaked to the German press.[5] Of special interest were its five chapters and twenty-one canons on Church and state.[6] From the standpoint of the late twentieth century, the material in these chapters and canons would be regarded as unproblematic. For example, chapter 10 declares the Church a "perfect society" that has its own public law (completed in the 1917 and 1983 *Codes of Canon Law*). Chapter 13 insists that God is the author of both ecclesiastical and political societies, that they coexist with their own respective spheres of law, that they ought to help each other, and that the state should respect the rights of the Church. Chapter 14 rejects the idea that political morality consists only of principles of utility and public opinion and that rights of religion depend upon political expedience. Chapter 15 enumerates rights of the Church in matters of education, seminaries, religious orders, and property. The canons, too, would be familiar to anyone who has read *Dignitatis humanae*. For example, the canons reject the propositions that "all rights among men are derived from the political State, and there is no authority but what is communicated by it" (can. 19); that "the supreme rule of conscience for public and social actions lies in the law of the political State, or in the public opinion of men" (can. 20); and that "it belongs to the Civil Power, by virtue of its supreme authority to judge and decree in matters of religion" (can. 21). Given the taut emotions besetting the relationship between the papacy and the European governments at that time (highlighted in 1870, when the pope lost his jurisdiction over the city of Rome and declared himself a prisoner in the Vatican), cooler judgment prevailed. There would be no conciliar decree or declaration on Church and state.[7]

From 1870 until the end of World War II, the problem of the Church's liberty *ad extra* was pursued in two ways. First, popes issued encyclicals and other directives on the Church's relation to civil governments. Leo XIII (1878–1903) wrote some one hundred ten encyclicals and other teaching letters, more than thirty of which dealt in one way or another with civil government and the Church's relationship to it. While some of the Leonine encyclicals would not outlast the particular occasion or problem they addressed, others were masterpieces of political theology that would transcend the era.[8] Second, through the diplomatic instrument of concordats,[9] the Church attempted to protect its liberty country by country. Most famous was the 1801 Concordat with Napoleon, which lasted until 1905. Several dozen other concordats were signed with European and South American regimes.

The most striking thing about this period is that, although the Church was equipped on the one hand with philosophical and theological doctrines on the relationship between Church and the states (in the abstract), and on the other with an ad hoc diplomatic policy realized via concordats, the Church lacked a middle-level policy that could bring together the speculative and diplomatic poles. During the nineteenth century, the Congregation for Extraordinary Ecclesiastical Affairs, first brought into being during the French Revolution, became part of the popes' "kitchen" cabinet. The title of this curial department conveys a sense of that era. Although it can be labeled the era of Catholic intransigence—against the revolutions, against confiscation of Church properties, against usurpation of the papal states, and indeed against modernity itself—a more apt characterization is the era of emergency. As political Christendom crumbled under the revolutions of the nineteenth century and then vanished altogether in the wars of the twentieth century, the situation was politically so volatile as to defy the development of a single policy on the part of the Church.

The Church's contemporary doctrine of religious liberty began in the 1940s, during the pontificate of Pope Pius XII (1939–1958). First, as a Vatican diplomat and secretary of state and then as pope during the Second World War and its aftermath, Pius XII demonstrated a keen interest in precisely the issues—theoretical and practical—necessary to develop an articulated papal position on Church and state. His Christmas addresses in 1942 and 1944 represented a significant breakthrough in the Roman estimation of the modern states. It was Pius XII who abandoned the older Roman policy of intransigence toward modern democratic governments and who began the process of making the necessary distinctions for shaping a new approach to Church-state relations. In this regard, Pius XII can be credited with two things. First, he did not speak as though the Church were still situated within political Christendom. Second, he took as normative the democratic regimes' self-understanding of the nature and scope of their authority: namely, as governments legally limited by constitutions and morally limited by a commitment to human rights.[10] Though Pius XII was critical of certain aspects of democratic government, his concerns were expressed in the manner of an internal, rather than a merely external, criticism. Contemporary teaching on Church and state unfolds in terms that are recognizably Pian.[11]

The Second Vatican Council

The Second Vatican Council addressed the issue of the Church's liberty, both *ad intra* and *ad extra*. With respect to the former, the most important sources for examination are the Constitution on the Church (*Lumen gentium*, 1964) and the Decree on the Office of Bishops (*Christus Dominus*, 1965). As for the latter, the main sources are the Constitution on the Church in the Modern World (*Gaudium et spes*, 1965) and the Declaration on Religious Liberty (*Dignitatis humanae*, 1965).

Dignitatis humanae is the text that will serve as the anchor of my exposition and analysis. The reason is easily explained. *Dignitatis humanae* attempts to supply what had been missing for two centuries, namely, a "middle-level" position that unifies principle and policy. Before I turn to *Dignitatis humanae*, it is necessary to describe the relevant details of the declaration during and after the council.

At the ninth public session of Vatican Council II, on December 7, 1965, Pope Paul VI promulgated the Declaration on Religious Liberty. There were more *non placet* votes registered for *Dignitatis humanae* than for any other document the council approved.[12] Since 1965, the far Left and the Right have been in heated agreement that this pamphlet-sized document augers a revolution. Archbishop Lefebvre, for example, refused to sign it and would eventually lead a schismatic movement based in part on his displeasure with *Dignitatis humanae*.[13] Even those who are not interested in radicalizing *Dignitatis humanae* have tended to make claims on its behalf that extend beyond what the document actually says.[14]

In order to properly interpret *Dignitatis humanae*, one should remember that it is a middle-level approach to the cluster of problems and issues summarized under the rubric "religious liberty." It is not a complete exercise in either the theory or the practice of Church-state relations. The relationship between Church and state (and more broadly between religion and society) is an enormous subject, thrown across a vast historical, social, philosophical, and theological canvas. In order to understand *Dignitatis humanae*, one must delineate the range of problems that were put on the council's table. Compared with the great conciliar constitutions (for example, *Lumen gentium* and *Gaudium et spes*), where the council broadly spoke its mind and supplied exceedingly rich contexts for taking stock of things, *Dignitatis humanae* is very short, terse, and anything but loquacious.[15]

Situating the Issues

At the council, the subject of religious liberty was considered and debated in light of three different models of how the Church might be situated vis-à-vis temporal authorities. The models were not merely abstract, for each had a historical track record.

The first model is that of political Christendom. Since the eighth century, the Catholic Church was wedded to Western society in the form of a single, though differentiated, *corpus mysticum*. Today, many speak of a theologico-political, or Church-state, "problem." For centuries, however, Church and state formed a single body, internally differentiated by two authorities, each of which was thought to share in Christ's *triplex munus* of priest, prophet, and king. The king participated in Christ's rule *pedes in terra* (feet on earth), while the episcopal authority imaged Christ's rule *caput in caelo* (head in heaven). As Ernst Kantorowicz noted in *The King's Two Bodies*, nearly a millennium of Church-state relations in the West was conducted within a model that is scarcely imaginable to the contemporary mind.[16] Today one rarely thinks of the state as a body, much less one shared with the Church. Although the organic model that governed the relationship between Church and state underwent many permutations, it nonetheless persisted in one form or another into the nineteenth century. At each step along the way, the language of self-governance changed, for both the Church and states, according to new notions of what it meant to be a juridical and moral person or *self*.[17] Despite the variety and permutations of the model, Leo XIII generally summarized it in *Immortale Dei* with the phrase *Fuit aliquando tempus*: "There was once a time when States were governed by the philosophy of the Gospel."[18]

This is not the forum to detail this complicated, fascinating, and often troubled history. Although this model was for the most part practically obsolete by the time of the Second Vatican Council, it was not entirely defunct. A scattering of countries still gave special recognition to Catholicism, either by way of constitutional law or concordat. Moreover, centuries of Church teaching were developed within the orbit of this model, including the papal encyclicals of the nineteenth century. Although recent popes never taught that harmonious relations between the Church and civil government require special assistance and recognition of the true religion by the state, such was the ideal. This ideal was rooted in two points of theology. First, the obligation to recognize and serve the truth of religion is not restricted to individuals. Societies, as well as individuals, bear an obligation to perform acts that satisfy the virtue of religion. Of course, precisely how societies are to do so without usurping the functions of the Church has been a complicated and controverted issue from the beginning of political Christendom in the West. Second, the kingship of

Christ is both spiritual and temporal. It would be a contradiction of fundamental Christology to believe that Christ's reign is only spiritual.

Undoubtedly certain bishops and theologians wanted this model to be the crucible of *Dignitatis humanae* and thus vindicate either the Left or the Right on matters of Church doctrine, the modern revolutions, and the general situation of the Church in modernity. Most bishops wanted a useful middle-level statement that would change the emphasis of the Church's teaching without contradicting fundamental theology. *Dignitatis humanae* adopted a carefully calculated silence on the establishment of religion, at least insofar as it was understood according to the older model.

The second model can be called the neutralist or separationist regime, according to which the Church enjoys a negative liberty vis-à-vis civil authority. What is most important is the ground of the negative liberty. It is one thing to say that a government constitutionally, by positive law, lacks authority over matters religious (for example, "Congress shall make no law respecting an establishment of religion"); it is quite another thing to assert that government on principled grounds must remain neutral on religion as such. Both are capable of generating a kind of negative liberty. The latter example, however, has more far-reaching implications. The neutralist regime can imply: (1) a radical privatization of religion—at its most extreme refusing to recognize the moral and juridical status of religious bodies; (2) a reduction of the moral and juridical status of the Church to that of other private associations; and (3) a denial that civil authority has any participation in the veridical order of truth.

Although the bishops were not experts in political philosophy, they were most likely not unfamiliar with the general lines of the neutralist regime. Furthermore, whereas the bishops remained mostly silent about political Christendom, they were careful to frame the civil right of religious liberty in such a way that it did not imply either a theoretical or practical endorsement of neutralism.

The third model has already been mentioned. This is where the status and liberty of the Church are conflated with the status and liberty of the state itself. In modern times, this model goes back to the Peace of Augsburg (1555), which effected a settlement of religious conflict in Germany on the basis of the formula *cuius regio, eius religio* ("whoever rules, his religion"). Far from being a flimsy legal device for a temporary modus vivendi in Germany, *cuius regio* established itself as a fundamental doctrine of state during the age of absolutism. In Catholic nations, *cuius regio* often vested itself in the titles and claims of ancient Christendom (for example, "the Most Christian Prince," "Monarch, by the Grace of God"), when princes were sworn to a quite different ideal of service to the Church. It was not always easy to distinguish where *cuius regio* meant princely service and protection of the Church according to the first model and where it amounted to a thinly disguised hijacking of the Church by the temporal authority. It was in the interest of the regalist party to obfuscate and to make the new doctrine look like the old one. For the bishops at the Second Vatican Council, this model was well known. Not only had it bedeviled Church-state relations in Europe for three centuries, but it had also reappeared in the communist states after World War II in the form of puppet churches. Interestingly, when the archbishop of Krakow died in 1962, the Polish government vetoed seven candidates before agreeing to Karol Wojtyla, who proved to be problematic for them after his election as pope in 1978. The communist state's exercise of the traditional right of the *placet* had nothing to do with political theology, but it showed clearly enough the perdurance of the *cuius regio* doctrine. Bishop Wojtyla of Krakow became a major player on the committee that drafted *Dignitatis humanae*.

Interpreting the Silence about Establishment

In *Dignitatis humanae*, article 1, the reader finds a clear statement of the scope of the declaration: "So while this religious freedom which men demand in fulfilling their obligations to worship God has to do with freedom from coercion in civil society, it leaves intact the traditional Catholic teaching on the moral duty of individuals and societies toward the true religion and the one Church of Christ."

It might prove surprising, if not frustrating, that *Dignitatis humanae* puts to one side theoretical treatment of the issues that directly touch, in American terms, upon establishment of religion. Instead, *Dignitatis humanae* treats the civil liberties required for the protection and fulfillment of the duty of man to worship God. Undoubtedly, the discussion of religious liberty will have implications for the establishment of religion. One implication is mentioned very briefly in *Dignitatis humanae*, article 6. In circumstances in which one religion is given "special civil recognition," the rights of other citizens and religious communities should be "recognized and respected."

A reader might reasonably say, after all these centuries of church and society constituting a kind of *corpus mysticum* and after all the various and sundry establishments of religion, it hardly seems possible that the "official" reckoning with this history would be reduced to the disclaimer in article 1, regarding what the council leaves untouched, and the rather terse sentence of article 6 on the need for the state to respect the rights of minorities in situations in which the Church is privileged in the constitution or by a concordat, or treaty, between the state and the Holy See. The correct response is that it is not possible because *Dignitatis humanae* does not undertake such a reckoning. For the Second Vatican Council, it was quite enough to tackle the problem of the religious civil liberties of individuals, communities, and the Church herself.

In addition to the fact that the drafters of *Dignitatis humanae* could not agree on how to formulate and resolve every problem, we can offer other reasons for their decision to emphasize religious liberty rather than the establishment or disestablishment of religion. First, it would have taken a Herculean effort to sort through fifteen hundred years of history for the purpose of identifying which governmental expressions of Catholicism (or for that matter, of religion) were good, merely acceptable, or unacceptable. Second, by the

1960s the most pressing problems facing the Church were how to induce secularist regimes to respect freedom of religion and how to use the Church's moral and spiritual resources to support constitutionally limited government in the wake of the world wars. Third, although it might come as a surprise to many American jurisprudents, the Catholic Church did not, and does not, believe that disestablishment is a principle superior to free exercise.

Finally, both Vatican II and John Paul II addressed the need for a theology of social liberty, especially in regard to the laity and sacralization of culture. *Gaudium et spes*,[19] article 43, invites the laity "to impress the divine law on the affairs of the earthly city" (*lex divina in civitatis terrenae vita inscribatur*). The Decree on Laity, *Apostolicam actuositatem*, similarly notes at article 7 that "the whole Church must work vigorously in order that men may become capable of rectifying the distortion of the temporal order and directing it to God through Christ." The *Catechism of the Catholic Church* asserts that "the social duty of Christians is to respect and awaken in each man the love of the true and the good. It requires them to make known the worship of the one true religion which subsists in the Catholic and apostolic Church.... Thus, the Church shows forth the kingship of Christ over all creation and in particular over human societies."[20]

In a certain respect, this theological reflection has just begun. One can see why, in 1965, it would have been precipitous to force *Dignitatis humanae* to attempt to resolve the issue of how religious liberty and confession of religious truth on the part of civil society might be synthesized in a distinctly contemporary mode—one in which democratic institutions prevail, the civil liberties of all are duly honored, and christianization or rechristianization has progressed to the point that the essence of the Gospel has worked its way into a fully public manifestation. *Dignitatis humanae* does not rule it out, but by the same token it does not bring it into view as a pressing problem. Just as *Dignitatis humanae* does not revisit all of the past problems, it refuses to project its teaching, by way of hypothesis, into the distant future.

Dignitatis humanae therefore declares: (1) that the Church ought to be free to be about its business, which includes the obligation of the laity to sacralize culture, (2) that everyone has the duty and therefore the right to freely fulfill their obligation to worship God, and (3) that this right ought to be given constitutional expression. I use the term "everyone" because *Dignitatis humanae*, article 6, insists that the duty to respect involves "individual citizens, social groups, civil authorities, the Church and other religious communities." I take this to mean that, whatever relationship might obtain between the Church and civil society and regardless of what the state does or does not do, everyone must respect liberty against external coercion in matters religious. That includes the imaginary scenario of a culture successfully evangelized. The Church declares itself to be a claimant and a supporter of this order of liberty with respect to the duties of the state and to the wider and deeper order of human society.

Thus, the council adopted a centrist position. It identified the principles proximate to the relevant subject (immunity of individuals and religious communities from external coercion), it drew a conclusion in the practical order (constitutional recognition of the principles), it took note of a few possible implications (what must obtain in states that give special recognition to Catholicism), and it remained discreetly silent about the rest, especially about governmental exemplifications of religious truth. This silence can be fairly interpreted as meaning that the Church does not rest its case for liberty on the confessing state. It would be a mistake to make *Dignitatis humanae* say anything more—or less. One might ask whether *Dignitatis humanae* is completely silent, however, on the posture of government toward truth. The answer is no.

Rejection of Liberal Neutrality

The first part of *Dignitatis humanae* (nos. 2–8), titled *Libertas religiosae ratio generalis*, treats religious liberty according to the general principle of human dignity. The dignitarian position is developed in terms of natural law.[21] In explicating the *ratio generalis*, the council had to distinguish its position from what I have called the liberal model. The liberal model can generate a negative liberty in the civil order in either the natural law or liberal paradigm. First, one could argue that the individual enjoys by natural right a self-expressive autonomy, untethered to any antecedent obligation. This kind of liberal dignitarian position exists in recent U.S. constitutional law, specifically in privacy and free-exercise case law.[22] *Dignitatis humanae*, article 2, however, asserts that "the right to religious freedom has its foundation not in the subjective attitude of the person, but in his very nature." This "nature" is not known exclusively from thin considerations, denuded from every theological and religious source. Second, one could also argue that government is incapable of making judgments on matters religious. In his Memorial and Remonstrance, for example, James Madison insisted that "Religion is wholly exempt from its cognizance."[23] *Dignitatis humanae*, articles 5–6, on the other hand, contends that government has an obligation to promote the free exercise of religion.

Dignitatis humanae, article 3, states that man has been made to participate in divine governance. The Eternal Law sweetly (*suaviter*) disposes man to fulfill his duty to know and to assent to the truth. Such reference to Wisdom 8:1 has a long history in Catholic theology. It was one of Saint Thomas's favorite biblical texts for describing divine governance.[24] In recent times, popes have cited the passage in order to admonish governments to heed the divine exemplar (*Mit brennender Sorge* and *Summi pontificatus*, for example).[25] Before the state imposes its laws and sanctions, men are already moved by God through the causality of their own nature to seek and adhere to religious truth. Religious obligation is a principle antecedent to human custom and positive law. Thus, *Dignitatis humanae* does not proffer a merely anthropocentric doctrine of conscience: "It is through his conscience that man sees and recognizes the demands of the divine."[26]

Therefore, the right of religious liberty is situated in something more than a mere faculty of liberty. Conscience is the mediation of a discourse between man and God. *Dignitatis humanae*, article 3, appeals to Saint Thomas's discussion of divine authority over the *actus interior*, the interior act of human judgment and conscience, and article 2 insists that "acts of this kind cannot be commanded or forbidden by any merely human authority." Coercion of conscience, then, violates human dignity *and* divine right (*DH* 3): "To deny man the free exercise of religion in society, when the just requirements of public order are observed, is to do an injustice to the human person and to the very order established by God for men."

Thus, *Dignitatis humanae* goes on to say that limits on religious liberty, as regards the *actus exterior*, have to be derived from that same order. The passage just cited uses the phrase "when the just requirements of public order are observed." As various drafts of *Dignitatis humanae* were debated, Bishop Karol Wojtyla of Krakow made a crucial intervention when he asked that *Dignitatis humanae*, article 7, make clear that when the state limits liberty, it do so *ordini morali objectivo conformes*—"in conformity with the objective moral order."[27] In Catholic parlance, this means in accordance with natural law. The qualification was necessary for two reasons. First, the qualification emphasizes that external limits on freedom are not drawn from principles completely alien to those that ground religious liberty itself. The common good and individual conscience are not located in separate orders of moral truth. Second, the qualification was necessary in order to make clear to the communist states that "public order" cannot be a pretext for overriding basic moral principles.[28]

Negative liberty is therefore developed by *Dignitatis humanae* in terms of the substantive obligation of individuals to pursue, assent to, and order their lives according to religious truth. Because the principle expresses an obligation, it cannot be reduced either to individual liberty or to governmental incompetence. When government recognizes the right of religious liberty, it is not respecting an empty liberty. Moreover, *Dignitatis humanae* contends that the absence of human authority over the interior act of conscience requires government to respect not only the individual's psychological dimension but also God's jurisdiction. Thus, natural law creates a norm for what constitutes an *ultra vires* act on the part of government.

Positively, government, "the purpose of which is the case of the common good in the temporal order, must recognize and look with favor on the religious life of citizens." However, "if [the government] presumes to control or restrict religious activity it must be said to have exceeded the limits of its power" (*DH* 3). Here, then, is the proposition. Government should actively promote, but not usurp, religious acts. While *Dignitatis humanae* does not try to provide a list of policies that would comport with religious liberty, *Dignitatis humanae*, articles 5–6, explicitly mentions facilitating the right of parents to have their children educated religiously.

Dignitatis humanae advocates a robust policy of "accommodation" not dissimilar to *Zorach v. Clauson*[29] and *Wisconsin v. Yoder*.[30] Yet, by way of comparison, these two decisions are not entirely apt because both are set within the context of the Supreme Court's neutralist/separationist doctrine.[31] Since *Everson v. Board of Education*,[32] the court has held that the establishment clause forbids government at any level from aiding and promoting religion—not just preferential aid to a particular denomination or religion, but aid to religion in general. In *Lemon v. Kurtzman*,[33] the prohibition on preferential aid was expanded to include the intention and motivation of legislators, who are constitutionally bound to have "secular" intentions.[34] The court interprets Madison to mean that government must not "cognize" matters religious—not just to refrain from imposing its jurisdiction *over* religion but to make no judgments according to dictates of religion.

Over the fifty-plus-year career of separationist jurisprudence, the free exercise clause has become like an appendix that cannot do any useful work; correlatively, when it works, it conflicts with the establishment clause.[35] The core problem is the separationist logic. Because free exercise of religion seems to favor rights of religion (in contrast to, say, free exercise of sport),[36] U.S. courts seem increasingly comfortable reducing specifically religious claims to those of free speech or free expression. By making one government duty reside in the establishment clause and another reside in protection of free speech, the court does not have to balance two facets of religion in public life. The price paid for this bifurcation of religious issues is that, rather than enjoying a substantive right to religious liberty, citizens enjoy an all-purpose right to free speech, which cannot be limited by restraint as to content, religious or otherwise.[37] In effect, religious liberty is rendered completely subordinate to a doctrine of disestablishment. Religious liberty can therefore materialize only by migrating to another sector of the First Amendment—usually freedom of speech.

This is not the place to consider the confusions and dead ends of U.S. First Amendment jurisprudence vis-à-vis religious liberty. What matters, though, is that *Dignitatis humanae* does not create such confusion. Of course, this is easier said than done because *Dignitatis humanae* prescinds, for the most part, from concrete matters of policy, where conflicts inevitably arise. Even so, it is important to note that *Dignitatis humanae* does not embody a separationist or neutralist logic.

The second point is that, on the issue of the competence of government in *Dignitatis humanae*, article 3, the second schema, the *Declaratio prior*, said that the "State is not qualified [*ineptam esse*] to make judgments of truth in religious matters." After vigorous debate, this sentence was abandoned in the penultimate draft—and for good reason. First, it might have been construed to mean that government lacks even the epistemic warrant to judge that religion is good, thus undercutting the argument of *Dignitatis humanae* itself; second, it could obscure the responsibilities of government on mixed matters, such as marriage and abortion; third, it almost certainly would have favored the neutralist and indifferentist doctrines that *Dignitatis humanae* otherwise took such great pains to avoid. While it is true that it does not provide a detailed map of the acceptable range of government's cognizance of religion, *Dignitatis humanae* does not remove government altogether from the veridical order—that is, the order of truth—in matters religious.[38]

Rejection of *Cuius Regio*

Dignitatis humanae is unusually loquacious about an important problem: the freedom of the Church. The most critical passage is found in article 13:

> Among those things which pertain to the good of the Church and indeed to the good of society here on earth, things which must everywhere and all times be safeguarded and defended from all harm, the most outstanding surely is that the Church enjoy that freedom of action which her responsibility for the salvation of men requires. This is a sacred liberty with which the only begotten Son of God endowed the Church, which he purchased with his blood. Indeed it belongs so intimately to the Church that to attack it is to oppose the will of God. The freedom of the Church is the fundamental principle governing relations between the Church and public authorities and the whole civil order.
>
> In human society and in the face of government the Church claims freedom for herself in her character as a spiritual authority, established by Christ the Lord, upon which there rests, by divine mandate, the duty of going out into the whole world and preaching the Gospel to every creature. The Church also claims freedom for herself in her character as society of men who have the right to live in society in accordance with the precepts of the Christian faith. . . .
>
> Ecclesiastical authorities have been insistent in claiming this independence in society. At the same time the Christian faithful, in common with the rest of men, have the civil right of freedom from interference in leading their lives according to their consciences. A harmony exists therefore between the freedom of the Church and the religious freedom which must be recognized as the right of all men and all communities and must be sanctioned by constitutional law.

Whereas *Dignitatis humanae* proceeds cautiously on other questions, the wording here at article 13 is decisive: "the most outstanding surely is that the Church enjoy that freedom of action which her responsibility for the salvation of men requires." Such freedom is called "sacred" (*libertas sacra est*) because it is endowed by Christ. Accordingly, the council speaks without qualification of a "fundamental principle" (*principium fundamentale*) in the relation between the Church and governments—one that cannot be unseated by considerations of "prudence," whether those considerations be introduced by the Church or by the state. In reaching this fundamental principle, it was crucial to distinguish it from the general right of religious liberty grounded in human dignity. The Church's "sacred liberty" stems from divine mandate directly rather than via secondary causality. This is the reason that *Dignitatis humanae*, article 13, speaks of a *concordia* but not a conflation of the two titles to freedom.

Unlike the question of whether the state should somehow manifest or exemplify the claims of the one true Church—a question that *Dignitatis humanae* declined to treat, even by way of historical survey—*Dignitatis humanae* does indeed treat the obverse of that question. It rules out the regalist doctrines that would make the Church an organ of the state. This is the problem that has haunted the modern history of Church-state relations (mostly, but not exclusively, in Europe). Wilhelm Emmanuel von Ketteler, bishop of Mainz, whose thoughts on this subject were influential during the pontificates of Pius IX and Leo XIII, took sober measure of the *cuius regio* ideology.[39] While giving due honor to the monarchies of old, Bishop von Ketteler contended that *cuius regio* was "nothing more than destructive idolatry."[40] Rather than looking to Rome for a model of independent spiritual authority, the nations wanted to revive the powers of the ancient Caesars. According to Seneca, Nero said, "Have I of all mortals found favor with Heaven and been chosen to serve on Earth as vicar of the gods? I am the arbiter of life and death for the nations."[41] Hence, von Ketteler's accusation that monarchy at that time amounted to little more than "pagan ultramontanism."[42]

This history is indisputably the background of *Dignitatis humanae*, article 13, though the totalitarian regimes of eastern Europe and Asia were likely in the forefront of the drafters' minds.[43] *Dignitatis humanae*, article 13, recites practically verbatim important sentences of Leo XIII's letter, *Officio sancissimo*, to the Church in Bavaria. Bavaria experienced what was called a "covert *Kulterkampf*."[44] Pope Leo wrote: "Of the rights of the Church that it is Our duty everywhere and always to maintain and defend against all injustice, the first is certainly that of enjoying the full freedom of action she may need in working for the salvation of souls. This is a divine liberty, having its author the only Son of God, Who, by shedding of blood, gave birth to the Church."[45] As one noted commentator pointed out, the phrase "freedom of the Church" occurs more than one hundred times in the Leonine corpus.[46]

The Church's formulation of precisely what it rejected in the *cuius regio* doctrine was considerably sharpened in the century preceding Vatican II. As noted earlier, Vatican I announced that the corporate unity of the Church does not consist of a federation of autonomous local units. During the 1860s Camillo Tarquini developed a canonical position that the Church is a *societas perfecta*, which has the ends and powers characteristic of a political community in its own right.[47] Leo XIII frequently reiterated Tarquini's claim. While the Church's authority cannot be reduced to the same proximate source as the authority of other human communities[48] and while its ultimate end transcends that of the state, its constitution nevertheless resembles that of a civil community. After the Second World War, Pius XII gave two important allocutions on the theme of the Church as a *societas perfecta*.[49] Although the idea of the Church as a juridical and moral person was not especially new, the emphasis placed upon the point represented a change of sensibilities since the era of political Christendom. In the modern world, the problem was not so much the establishment of Church by the state but rather its differentiation from the state.[50] What was most important was that the Church could be differentiated without reducing itself to the status of other private associations. In other words, religious liberty considered only in the light of the *ratio generalis* would misrepresent what the Church claimed for her own liberty.

Dignitatis humanae, article 13, therefore, should be read alongside the Vatican II decree on bishops, *Christus Dominus*, issued five weeks before *Dignitatis humanae*. *Christus Dominus*, article 20, states that, "Since the apostolic office of bishops was instituted by Christ the Lord and is directed to a spiritual and supernatural end, the sacred ecumenical council asserts that the competent ecclesiastical authority has the proper, special, and, as of right, exclusive power to appoint and install bishops."

The finishing touch was made in the 1983 *Codex iuris canonici*, which stated that "No rights or privileges of election, appointment, presentation or designation of bishops are conceded to civil authorities."[51]

Critics of *Dignitatis humanae* have complained that article 13, despite its Leonine credentials, derogates from the tradition of the Church. Although *Dignitatis humanae* clearly states the obligation of the state not to absorb the Church or to regard the Church merely as one private party among others, *Dignitatis humanae*, article 13, does not speak of the state's obligation (ideally) to confess the true religion. Archbishop Lefebvre, for one, protested that the line "Libertas Ecclesiae est principium fundamentale" was wrong because the issue was not merely the state's duty to the Church but its duty to "recognize the social royalty of Our Lord Jesus Christ."[52] A complete response to this objection entails a patient and thorough survey of where the conciliar documents take up the social ramifications of Christ as priest, prophet, and king. Here it suffices to reiterate a point made earlier, namely that *Dignitatis humanae*, article 1, put the issue of corporate obligations to confess the truth to one side. Instead, the bishops investigated the narrower issue of the civil liberty of human persons in matters religious and subsequently addressed the question of the liberty and mission of the Church.

Still others have objected that the Church has claimed the wrong principle, even for Herself. Michael Davies, for example, noted that "Pope Paul VI made it clear that he certainly interpreted *Dignitatis humanae* as meaning that freedom *alone* for the Church can be considered normal in principle."[53] Davies referred to Pope Paul VI's homily at the close of Vatican II on December 8, 1965. On this occasion, the message (*Aux governants*) was read by Achille Cardinal Lienart of Lille, France. Davies was perplexed by the sentence, "she asks of you only liberty, the liberty to believe and to preach her faith, the freedom to love her God and serve Him, the freedom to live and to bring to men her message of life."[54] Davies was perhaps misled by John Courtney Murray, who quoted the same sentence in support of his personal thesis that *Dignitatis humanae* renounces all special privileges and establishments for the Church and that her claim is freedom, nothing more.[55]

In this case Murray was wrong. In the first place, Murray, who usually counseled narrow and focused readings of the issues under review, here tried to make *Dignitatis humanae* (after the fact of its promulgation) resolve something that it expressly said it would not take up. In the second place, a doctrinal reading of "nothing more" cannot be supported by *Dignitatis humanae*, which not only asks the state to preserve liberty within the context of a "just... public order" but also asks the temporal authorities to appreciate that, according to the Church's own understanding, its liberty is grounded in a divine mandate. Recall the opening words of *Dignitatis humanae*, article 13: "Among those things which pertain to the good of the Church and indeed to the good of society here on earth,... the most outstanding surely is that the Church enjoy the freedom of action." Indeed, *Dignitatis humanae* insists that the Church's liberty derives first from Christ (hence, the *principium fundamentale*) and also (*etiam*) from her character as a society of men.

After the council, Murray voiced a different opinion: "This unique theological title, however, cannot be urged in political society and against government. The mandate of Christ to his Church is formally a truth of the transcendent order in which the authority of the Church is exercised and her life as a community is lived. Therefore it is not subject, or even accessible, to judgment by secular powers as regards its truth or falsity."[56] However, this was Murray's opinion, which in my view is contradicted by *Dignitatis humanae* and *Gaudium et spes*.

In the third place, the sentence that perplexed Davies was taken out of context. Here is the text of *Aux governants* read by Achille Cardinal Lienart:

We proclaim publicly: We do honor to your authority and your sovereignty, we respect your office, we recognize your just laws, we esteem those who make them and those who apply them. But we have a sacrosanct word to speak to you and it is this: Only God is great. God alone is the beginning and the end. God alone is the source of your authority and the foundation of your laws. Your task is to be in the world the promoters of order and peace among men. But never forget this: It is God, the living and true God, who is the Father of men. And it is Christ, his eternal Son, who came to make this known to us and to teach us that we are all brothers. He it is who is the great artisan of order and peace on earth, for He it is who guides human history and who alone can incline hearts to renounce those evil passions which beget war and misfortune. It is He who blesses the bread of the human race, who sanctifies its work and its suffering, who gives it those joys which you can never give it, and strengthens it in those sufferings which you cannot console. In your earthly and temporal city, God constructs mysteriously his spiritual and eternal city, his Church. And what does this Church ask of you after close to two thousand years of experiences of all kinds in her relations with you, the powers of the earth? What does the Church ask of you today? She tells you in one of the major documents of this council. She asks of you only liberty, the liberty to believe and to preach her faith, the freedom to love her God and serve Him, the freedom to live and to bring to men her message of life. Do not fear her. She is made after the image of her Master, whose mysterious action does not interfere with your prerogatives but heals everything human of its fatal weakness, transfigures it and fills it with hope, truth and beauty. Allow Christ to exercise his purifying action on society. Do not crucify Him anew. This would be a sacrilege for He is the Son of God. This would be suicide for He is the Son of man. And we, his humble ministers, allow us to spread everywhere without hindrance the Gospel of peace on which we have meditated during this council. Of it, your peoples will be the first beneficiaries, since the Church forms for you loyal citizens, friends of social peace and progress.[57]

As the text makes clear, Paul VI was not suggesting that the Church's liberty consists *only* of a negative freedom, which is to be discussed (*ad extra*) *only* in procedural terms. Paul VI does not ask the states to establish or even to privilege Catholicism; rather, he asks them to respect its sanctifying mission and power in society.[58]

Conclusion

First, the beginning of wisdom in reading *Dignitatis humanae* is to respect its silences. It should not be read as a treatise on the establishment of religion. As discussed, the silence of *Dignitatis humanae* on this matter evinces prudence that should not be dismissed as a mere pragmatic resignation in the face of disagreement. Moreover, establishment and disestablishment of religion mean different things, depending on the particular legal culture. As noted in connection with American jurisprudence, *Dignitatis humanae*'s position on religious liberty would probably count as favoring the establishment of religion. Second, we should pay attention to those issues that *Dignitatis humanae* does settle. *Dignitatis humanae*, articles 2–8, advances a principled argument for religious liberty, grounded not in subjective disposition or in empty liberty but in man's nature. Moreover, religious liberty is not subordinated, as it is in U.S. law, to a neutralist doctrine of disestablishment. How the notion of "the objective moral order" would permit the state, in particular cases, to limit the right is not described in any detail. Finally, *Dignitatis humanae*, article 13, certainly puts to rest any notion of establishment drawn from the *cuius regio* tradition, where the Church is established "in" the state.

In view of the precise points and limits of *Dignitatis humanae*, three general considerations can be concluded. First, *Dignitatis humanae* provides, at least in principle, a way to correct the concordat policy that so hampered the Church prior to World War II. As noted earlier, after 1789, the Church attempted to protect its liberties by cutting the best deal it could, country by country. *Dignitatis humanae* provides a framework that effectively integrates principle with policy and diplomacy, and it does so in language readily identifiable to states. To be sure, the principles of moral and constitutional liberties are not uncontested. Significant differences exist among states and international bodies about the interpretation and application of moral or human rights. The Church experiences continuing crises in Africa and Asia, where both individual and corporate religious liberty remain unprotected. The Chinese government, for instance, has reserved to itself the right to nominate bishops for the Patriotic Catholic Association since 1957, and has continued to do so into the pontificate of Pope Benedict XVI, which shows that the *cuius regio* doctrine is not completely dead.[59] In Sudan, there is terrible persecution of Catholics. Certain factions in India reject the idea that the Church is free to evangelize and incorporate converts. The main point is that *Dignitatis humanae* spells out clearly enough what the Church expects in whatever country it finds itself and not merely by way of a Chinese, a Sudanese, or an Indian policy. While all of this does not eliminate the need for diplomacy, it mitigates the ad hoc policies that so limited the Church in the era of concordats.

Second, *Dignitatis humanae* does not make a new case for the liberty of the Church. It does, however, recognize that the Church's claim for its own liberty must be complemented with a claim for the liberty of others. Such a policy is necessary for the Church's credibility and consistency. Provided that one avoids extreme interpretations, such as conflating the two distinct titles to liberty, *Dignitatis humanae* is rightly credited as a major development in the way the Church situates itself in the political world. The liberty of the Church does not require political hegemony. On balance, *Dignitatis humanae* much better serves the liberty and mission of the Church, which now comprises more than one billion Catholics, including adherents in missionary lands, where the Church's greatest external problem is the lack of constitutionally protected civil liberty.

Third, *Dignitatis humanae* represents a broader spirit of detachment from the problem of the state. Historically, the Catholic Church has been wedded to many different kinds of political societies. It has tried to achieve some measure of concord with ancient emperors (pagan and Christian), tribal chieftains, kings, leagues of cities, absolute monarchs, colonial governments, revolutionary governments, and, during the last century, constitutional democracies. This history is a kind of double-edged sword. On the one hand, whenever the concord was deep and long lived, the Church became dependent upon a political culture. The Church, naturally enough, mourned the demise of its own twin. On the other hand, the long and varied history gives the Church a certain psychological and spiritual advantage. Having seen so many different regimes come and go, the Church can cultivate a spirit of detachment.

Detachment has always been understood, of course, from a theological standpoint. The Church, after all, is *in* but not *of* the world. In every generation, the Church has asserted that she is a society not only different from but also independent of the state. In the post-1789 world, the Church was forced to learn (or relearn) how to distance its affairs from the state. Gradually, after much trial and error, the Roman Church saw how to interpret and adapt itself to this distance between Church and the state (namely, to a position that is not a twin of the Church but recognizes, respects, and protects civil liberties). In the documents of Vatican II and in the work of the present papal magisterium, the state is an instrumental good whose purpose is to protect the flourishing of societies other than the state itself. The twentieth century was a dreadful school in which everyone, including the Church, had to learn how to demystify the state. *Dignitatis humanae* takes a rather sober view of the powers of the state. Not only does it have nothing to say about the temporal powers that reflect *imago Dei*, but it also mentions nothing about the notion of *two swords*. Rather, the theological language is reserved chiefly for the Church, family, culture, and nations.[60] Although it must at this point remain a matter of speculation, the Church's position today is all the more timely because the nation-states of the post-Napoleonic world are undergoing a profound transformation. No one is quite sure what will remain of them in this era of globalization.

NOTES

1. Earlier versions of this chapter appeared in the *George Washington University Law Journal* (2000): 1035–58, and in Russell Hittinger, *The First Grace: Rediscovering the Natural Law in a Post-Christian World* (Wilmington, Del.: ISI Books, 2003), 215–41.

2. "By divine ordinance, the Roman church possesses a pre-eminence of ordinary power over every other church, and this jurisdictional power of the Roman pontiff is both episcopal and immediate" (*Pastor aeternus* [1870], no. 3). See also Robert A. Graham, *Vatican Diplomacy: A Study of Church and State on the International Plane* (Princeton, N.J.: Princeton University Press, 1959), 215.

3. Religions and churches fared differently in post–Napoleonic Europe. Jews, for example, were liberated from the political and legal vestiges of the older Christendom. While it is dangerous to generalize, one can say that Protestants were not so affected by the move to national churches, for this was their experience before the revolutions. Catholicism, however, was hit hard—not only in the material sense of having lost properties and monasteries and in the political sense of having ecclesiastical government interrupted or suppressed but also in the spiritual and theological sense, for the doctrines of state supremacy contradicted the Church's understanding of its own origin, nature, and mission.

4. Pius IX, *Quanta cura* (1864). Two propositions relate to broad cosmological questions (nos. 1, 2); 19 to authority of human reason and indifferentism in its moral mode (nos. 3, 4, 6–12, 14–18, 56–60); 6 to progress and culture (nos. 5, 12, 13, 32, 40, 80); 59 to specific church-state issues and political morality (nos. 15, 19, 20, 23–38, 39–55, 57–71, 73–80); and 5 to ecclesiology (nos. 21, 22, 35, 38, 72). By my count, only 7 of the propositions are *not* related to the issue of church and state.

5. *Allgemeine Zeitung* (Augsburg; Jan. 21, 1870). Leaked by Döllinger. See also Émile Ollivier, *L'église et l'état au Concile du Vatican*, 3d ed., vol. 2 (Paris: Garnier Frères, 1877), 46–48.

6. *Mansi* (Ioannes Dominicus), *Sacrorum conciliorum* (Nova et amplissima collectio), vol. 51, Arnhem, the Netherlands (Pays-Bas) and Leipzig (1926). *Primum schema constitutionis* De Ecclesia Christi, 539–54, chaps. X–XV, 543–51; canons I–XXI, 551–53.

7. The one untroubled relation was with the United States. In 1783 the apostolic nuncio in France, via Benjamin Franklin, asked the Second Continental Congress for permission to establish a vicar apostolate and to reorganize dioceses in the United States. In effect, he was asking Congress to exercise the ancient privilege of the *placet*. Congress wrote back: "That Dr. Franklin be desired to notify to the apostolic nuncio at Versailles that Congress will always be pleased to testify their respect to his sovereign

and State; but that the subject of his application to Dr. Franklin, being purely spiritual, is without the jurisdiction and powers of Congress, who have no authority to permit or refuse it, these powers being reserved to the several states individually." Graham, *Vatican Diplomacy*, 336.

8. See ibid., 228. See generally *Quod apostolici muneris* (1878); *Diuturnum* (1881); *Immortale Dei* (1885); *Officio sanctissimo* (1887); *Libertas* (1888); and *Praeclara gratulationis* (1894).

9. A concordat is a public treaty between the Church and the state that regulates relations in some area of mutual concern. Most likely, the first concordat was the Concordat of Worms (1122), which tried to settle the investiture controversy. For a reliable study of the concordats, see generally Graham, *Vatican Diplomacy*. The 1801 Concordat was the model for the nineteenth-century concordat policy. See William Roberts, "Napoleon, the Concordat of 1801, and Its Consequences," in *Controversial Concordats*, ed. Frank J. Coppa (Washington, D.C.: Catholic University of America Press, 1999), 34–80.

10. In the 1944 address the following lines were particularly important: "Moreover [and this is perhaps the most important point] beneath the sinister lightning of the war that encompasses them, in the blazing heat of the furnace that imprisons them, the peoples have, as it were, awakened from a long torpor. They have assumed, in relation to the state and those who govern, a new attitude—one that questions, criticizes, distrusts. Taught by bitter experience, they are more aggressive in opposing the concentration of dictatorial power that cannot be censured or touched, and call for a system of government more in keeping with the dignity and liberty of the citizens . . . to avoid for the future the repetition of such a catastrophe, we must vest efficient guarantees in the people itself. . . . If, then, we consider the extent and nature of the sacrifices demanded of all the citizens, especially in our day when the activity of the state is so vast and decisive, the democratic form of government appears to many as a postulate of nature imposed by reason itself." Pius XII, Christmas address, "True and False Democracy" (*Benignitas et humanitas*) (1944), *AAS* 37 (1945): 13. This address is cited at the outset of *Dignitatis humanae* 1.1.

11. Pius XII is cited no less than seven times in *Dignitatis humanae*.

12. The final tally: *placet* 2,308, *non placet* 70.

13. See generally Michael Davies, *The Second Vatican Council and Religious Liberty* (Long Prairie, Minn.: Neumann Press, 1992), who presents a sympathetic survey of objections on both the Left and the Right. See also Brian Harrison, *Religious Liberty and Contraception* (Melbourne, Australia: John XXIII Fellowship Co-op, 1988), who has created a more critical survey of the same range of opinions. The most complete account of the history and doctrine of *Dignitatis* is the six-volume study by Father Basile, O.S.B., *La liberté religieuse et la tradition catholique: Un cas de développement homogène dans le magistère authentique* (Abbaye Sainte-Madeleine du Barroux, 1998).

14. See generally Richard J. Regan, *Conflict and Consensus: Religious Freedom and the Second Vatican Council* (New York: Macmillan, 1967), 147, who presents an earlier work by a disciple of John Courtney Murray). See also John T. Noonan Jr., "Development in Moral Doctrine," *Theological Studies* 54 (1993): 662–77.

15. *Dignitatis humanae* is a *declaratio*, which differs from a *constitutio* and a *decretum*. Constitutions and decrees have binding force upon the whole Church. A declaration, on the other hand, is reserved for matters and persons who are not under the public law of the Church. Hence, the document on non-Christian religions (*Nostra aetate*, 1965) is also called a *declaratio*.

16. See generally Ernst H. Kantorowicz, *The King's Two Bodies: A Study in Mediaeval Political Theology* (Princeton, N.J.: Princeton University Press, 1957).

17. See generally David Nicholls, *Deity and Domination: Images of God and the State in the Nineteenth and Twentieth Centuries* (New York: Routledge, 1989). See also Frances A. Yates, *Astraea: The Imperial Theme in the Sixteenth Century* (Boston: Routledge & K. Paul, 1975), who examines the evolving doctrines of political theology in modernity.

18. See *Immortale Dei* (1885), no. 21. "There was once a time when States were governed by the philosophy of the Gospel. Then it was that the power and divine virtue of Christian wisdom had diffused itself throughout the laws, institutions, and morals of the people, permeating all ranks and relations of civil society. Then, too, the religion instituted by Jesus Christ, established firmly in befitting dignity, flourished everywhere, by the favor of princes and the legitimate protection of magistrates; and Church and State were happily united in concord and friendly interchange of good offices. The State, constituted in this wise, bore fruits important beyond all expectation."

19. Translation of conciliar documents from *Sacrosantum Oecumenicum Conclium Vaticanum II: Constitutiones, decreta, declarationes* (1993).

20. *Catechism of the Catholic Church*, no. 2105. In the material quoted, the *Catechism* notes *Dignitatis humanae* 1; *Immortale Dei*; and *Quas primas*. Undoubtedly, the three are cited together to emphasize their continuity.

21. The second part of *Dignitatis humanae* (nos. 9–15), under the heading *Libertas religiosa sub luce revelationis*, focuses specifically on the liberty of the Church. In no. 12 of his first encyclical, *Redemptoris hominis* (1979), John Paul II contended that the two parts be read together. The civil right is grounded in human dignity, not only as it is understood on the historical and philosophical plane but also in light of what the Church understands about herself:

> By Christ's institution the Church is its guardian and teacher, having been endowed with a unique assistance of the Holy Spirit in order to guard and teach it in its most exact integrity. In fulfilling this mission, we look towards Christ himself, the first evangelizer, and also towards his Apostles, martyrs and confessors. The *Declaration on Religious Freedom* shows us convincingly that, when Christ and, after him, his Apostles proclaimed the truth that comes not from men but from God ('My teaching is not mine, but his who sent me,' that is the Father's), they preserved, while acting with their full force of spirit, a deep esteem for man, for his intellect, his will, his conscience and his freedom. Thus the human person's dignity itself becomes part of the content of that proclamation, being included not necessarily in words but by an attitude towards it. This attitude seems to fit the special needs of our times. Since man's true freedom is not found in everything that the various systems and individuals see and propagate as freedom, the Church, because of her divine mission, becomes all the more the guardian of this freedom, which is the condition and basis for the human person's true dignity. (no. 34)

22. See *Planned Parenthood v. Casey*, 505 U.S. 833 (1992). ("At the heart of liberty is the right to define one's own concept of existence, of meaning, of the universe and of the mystery of human life. Beliefs about these matters could not define the attributes of personhood were they formed under compulsion of the State.")

23. James Madison, "Memorial and Remonstrance against Religious Assessments" (1785), reprinted in *Church and State in the Modern Age: A Documentary History*, ed. J. F. Maclear (New York: Oxford University Press, 1995), 60. The Memorial and Remonstrance, directed against a pending bill in the Virginia General Assembly, formed no part of the U.S. Constitution or the Bill of Rights (ibid., 59). It was only after the Second World War that the Supreme Court made Madison's remonstrance an

interpretive key to First Amendment jurisprudence. See *Everson v. Board of Education*, 330 U.S. 1, 12 (1947).

24. Of the many uses of Wis 8:1 by Thomas, see *Summa contra gentiles* III, 97; *Summa theologiae* I, q. 22, a. 2; and q. 103, a. 8; I–II, q. 110, a. 2; II–II, q. 23, a. 2, and q. 161, a. 1.

25. Here, *Dignitatis humanae*, no. 2, cites no. 7 of Pius XI's encyclical against the Nazis, *Mit brennender Sorge*: "Whoever follows that so-called pre-Christian Germanic conception of substituting a dark and impersonal destiny for the personal God, denies thereby the Wisdom and Providence of God who reacheth from end to end mightily, and ordereth all things sweetly."

26. It is the same position argued in *Gaudium et spes* 16, where conscience is said to be a *sacrarium* (a holy place): "For man has in his heart a law inscribed by God. His dignity lies in observing this law, and by it he will be judged. His conscience is man's most secret core, and his sanctuary. There he is alone with God whose voice echoes in his depths." This teaching is reiterated by John Paul II in *Veritatis splendor*: "Saint Bonaventure teaches that 'conscience is like God's herald and messenger; it does not command things on its own authority, but commands them as coming from God's authority, like a herald when he proclaims the edict of the king. This is why conscience has binding force.' Thus it can be said that conscience bears witness to man's own rectitude or iniquity to man himself but, together with this and indeed even beforehand, conscience is *the witness of God himself*, whose voice and judgment penetrate the depths of man's soul, calling him *forliter et suaviter* to obedience" (no. 58).

27. Still, critics complain that *Dignitatis humanae* adopts an emaciated liberal notion of public order. To set things absolutely clear, the *Catechism of the Catholic Church*, at no. 2109, states: "The right to religious liberty can of itself be neither unlimited nor limited only by a 'public order' conceived in a positivist or naturalist manner. The 'due limits' which are inherent in it must be determined for each social situation by political prudence, according to the requirements of the common good." To emphasize continuity with previous teachings, the *Catechism* cites Pius VI, *Quod aliquantum* (1791), and Pius IX, *Quanta cura* (1864).

28. The issue of public order, or what American jurisprudence would call "compelling state interest," has a long and troubled history in Catholic relations with modern states. The first article of the 1801 Concordat with Napoleon reads as follows: "The Catholic, Apostolic, and Roman religion shall be freely practi[c]ed in France; its worship shall be public, in conformity with police regulations which the Government shall judge to be necessary for public tranquility." *Church and State through the Centuries: A Collection of Historic Documents with Commentaries*, ed. and trans. Sidney Z. Ehler and John B. Morall (Westminster, Md.: Newman Press, 1954), 252. From the outset, the Vatican argued that article 1 was an all-purpose instrument for governmental regulation of the Church.

29. 343 U.S. 306 (1952).

30. 406 U.S. 205 (1972).

31. See ibid., 234–35n22; *Zorach*, 343 U.S., 314. The better comparison is to the Champaign program, which was ruled unconstitutional in *McCollum v. Board of Education*, 333 U.S. 203, 210–11 (1948).

32. 330 U.S. 1 (1947).

33. 403 U.S. 602 (1971).

34. See ibid., 612–13.

35. Justice Potter Stewart noted this problem in his concurring opinion III *Sherbert v. Verner*, 374 U.S. 398, 413–18 (1963) (Stewart, J., concurring). In *Sherbert*, a Sabbatarian

was denied unemployment benefits because she was unable to work on Saturdays for religious reasons (ibid., 399). The majority agreed that the free exercise clause required the state to accommodate her religious beliefs, but the problem of a conflict between the two clauses was apparent. See ibid., 409–410 (Stewart, J., concurring). The separationist logic enjoins government from favoring, aiding, promoting, or cognizing religion, while the free exercise clause commands government to accommodate religious belief, even in the instance of a law or policy that the state is otherwise entitled to make. See ibid., 414–15. Justice Stewart noted: "And the result is that there are many situations where legitimate claims under the Free Exercise Clause will run into head-on collision with the Court's insensitive and sterile construction of the establishment clause" (ibid., 414).

36. See, for example, *City of Boerne v. Flores*, 521 U.S. 507, 536–37 (1997) (Stevens, J. concurring). In response to Congress's bid to codify a broader interpretation of the free exercise clause, which requires government to show compelling state interest when its otherwise valid laws impair free exercise of religion, Justice Stevens said, "In my opinion, the Religious Freedom Restoration Act of 1993 (RFRA) is a 'law respecting an establishment of religion' that violates the First Amendment to the Constitution. . . . Whether the Church would actually prevail under the statute or not, the statute has provided the Church with a legal weapon that no atheist or agnostic can obtain. This governmental preference for religion, as opposed to irreligion, is forbidden by the First Amendment" (ibid.). The free exercise clause does suggest that religious liberty enjoys special constitutional favor and protection. U.S. Constitution Amendment I.

37. See, for example, *Rosenberger v. Rector*, 515 U.S. 819 (1995); *Capital Square Review Bd. v. Pinette*, 515 U.S. 753 (1995); *Lamb's Chapel v. Center*, 508 U.S. 384 (1993); *Widmar v. Vincent*, 454 U.S. 263 (1981); see also *Chandler v. James*, 180 F.3d 1254, 1265 (11th cir. 1999), which notes that "government violates the First Amendment when it denies access to a speaker solely to suppress the point of view he espouses; suppression of religious speech constitutes viewpoint discrimination, the most egregious form of content-based censorship." Significantly, the court in *Chandler* held that while the First Amendment protects free speech against content discrimination, the Constitution forbids religiously proselytizing speech by private parties in public schools (ibid.). Hence, the specifically and substantively "religious" aspect of speech is still intercepted by the separationist logic.

38. Father Basile's study has best covered the reason for and implications of dropping the phrase *ineptam esse*. See *La liberté religieuse et la tradition catholique*, particularly vol. I/B, 613ff, and 584, where he correctly concludes that the state's limit is "*une incompétence juridictionnelle en aval, non une incompétence gnoséologique en amont*" (a jurisdictional incompetence as to the source, not an epistemological incompetence downstream from the source). This is classic higher-law doctrine. For to say that there is an authority higher than the state implies a jurisdictional limit but not necessarily an epistemological deficit.

39. Wilhelm Emmanuel von Ketteler, "Freedom, Authority, and the Church," in *The Social Teachings of Wilhelm Emmanuel von Ketteler: Bishop of Mainz*, trans. Rupert J. Ederer (Washington, D.C.: University Press of America, 1981), 145.

40. Ibid.

41. Lucius Annaeus Seneca, *Moral Essays*, trans. John W. Basore (New York: Putnam's Sons, 1928), 357.

42. Von Ketteler, "Freedom, Authority, and the Church," 141.

43. The long background referred to is the *cuius regio* doctrine that the church is established in the state. Closer to the historical foreground is a variant of this position.

The French Separation Law (Dec. 9, 1905) unilaterally abrogated the 1801 Concordat. See "Separation of Church and State in France: Law of December 9, 1905," in Ehler and Morall, *Church and State through the Centuries*, 355–71. The most important and controversial portions of the law (nos. 18–24) transferred practical administration of the Church into the hands of associations of laymen. See ibid., nos. 18–24, 366–68. In his encyclical *Vehementer nos*, Pius X objected that the law "despoils the Church of the internal regulation of the churches in order to invest the State with this function" (no. 9). Despite the language of "Separation," the law tried to effect the same result as the older *cuius regio* regimes without a formal state "confession."

44. Graham, *Vatican Diplomacy*, 278. In Bavaria, for example, Maximilian taught that "The doctrine of the two powers is a monstrosity of priestly ambition. The church is in the state and not the state in the church" (ibid., 278).

45. *Officio sanctissimo* (1887), no. 13.

46. John Courtney Murray, "The Issue of Church and State at Vatican II," *Theological Studies* 27 (1966): 580–606, reprinted in *Religious Liberty: Catholic Struggles with Pluralism*, ed. Leon Hooper (Louisville, Ky.: Westminster/John Knox Press, 1993), 207.

47. See Graham, *Vatican Diplomacy*, 228–32, for a discussion of Cardinal Tarquini's influence upon canon law.

48. Complaining that the title to freedom is reduced to that of other associations, Leo XIII noted in *Immortale Dei*, no. 27, that "the Catholic religion is allowed a standing in civil society equal only, or inferior, to societies alien from it; no regard is paid to the laws of the Church, and she who, by the order and commission of Jesus Christ."

49. See Pius XII, "Allocution, Juridical Jurisdiction of the Church: Its Origin and Nature," in *The Canon Law Digest: Officially Published Documents Affecting the Code of Canon Law 1942–1953*, vol. 3, trans. T. Lincoln Bouscaren (1954), 587–93. See also Pius XII, "Allocution, Juridical Power of the Church Compared with That of the State," in *Canon Law Digest*, vol. 3, 593–99.

50. As late as the papal conclave of 1903, three states asserted the right to veto papal elections. Indeed, at that conclave, Franz Josef of Austria, via Cardinal Puzyna, bishop of Krakow, exercised the veto to prevent the election of Cardinal Rampolla.

51. *Code of Canon Law*, 1983, canon 377, no. 5. The exact words *societas perfecta* are used in neither the 1917 nor the 1983 codes. The concept is indisputably operative, however. In the 1983 code, canon 113, no. 1 asserts: "The Catholic Church and the Apostolic See have the status of a moral person by divine disposition." This means two things: (1) that the church is a bearer of rights and obligations beyond what might be ascribed by positive law, and (2) that the church is something that transcends the individuals who compose her. Canon 1254, no. 1, asserts: "The Catholic Church has an inherent right, independently of any secular power, to acquire, retain, administer and alienate temporal goods, in pursuit of its proper objective." Canon 1311 also states that "The Church has its own inherent right to constrain with penal sanctions Christ's faithful who commit offenses."

52. Davies, *Second Vatican Council and Religious Liberty*, 183.

53. Ibid., 184.

54. Murray, "Issue of Church and State at Vatican II," 212.

55. Ibid.

56. Ibid., 209. Murray contended (210) that the autonomy of the state is violated if the Church claims liberty on anything but secular grounds.

57. *Constitutiones, decreta, declarationes*, 1086.

58. Consider, too, Paul VI's homily at the last general session of the council, the day before his message *Aux gouvernants*: "The theocentric and theological concept of man and the universe, almost in defiance of the charge of anachronism and irrelevance, has been given a new prominence by the council, through claims which the world will at first judge to be foolish, but which, we hope, it will later come to recognize as being truly human, wise and salutary" (Paul VI, homily, Dec. 7, 1965).

59. Benedict XVI's "Letter to the Bishops, Priests, Consecrated Persons and Lay Faithful of the Catholic Church in the People's Republic of China" (May 27, 2007) suggests a new dialogue on this issue, though Benedict holds firm to Roman teaching in the conciliar documents *Christus Dominus* and *Dignitatis humanae*.

60. See, for example, John Paul II, "Freedom Cannot Be Suppressed," address to the UN General Assembly (Oct. 5, 1995), in *Pope Speaks* 41 (1996): 32, 36 (discussing the rights of nations as distinct from the state).

19

The Declaration on Christian Education, *Gravissimum Educationis*

Don J. Briel

In his overview of *Gravissimum educationis*, Bishop Johannes Pohlschneider argued that the declaration demonstrated both continuity and progress in relation to earlier Church teaching on the role of religious education within the Church and civil society. In a later review of the declaration, Ulrich Gunzer asserted that *"Gravissimum educationis* is an important step between the rather dark, apodictic-sounding encyclical on education by Pius XI in 1929 and the two communications by the Apostolic See in 1977 and 1982."[1] Despite the implicit critique of the earlier encyclical, Gunzer is certainly correct in arguing that the council's declaration drew upon Pius XI's 1929 encyclical, *Divini Illius Magistri.* The declaration presupposed, Gunzer maintained, a fundamental continuity with a long series of papal affirmations of the Church's commitment to the religious education of the young. He asserted that it was equally insistent in its condemnations (which extended throughout the nineteenth and twentieth centuries) of tendencies toward a state monopoly in education, the violation of parents' primary rights in their children's education, and the Church's central role not only in the moral and religious education of the young but also in their wider educational formation for life in the world and their preparation for the next. There is, nonetheless, a good deal that is new in *Gravissimum educationis,* much of which reflects a rather more optimistic anthropology and a positive evaluation of emerging technology that marks the council's reflections as a whole.

Bishop Pohlschneider suggested that progress beyond the vision of *Divini Illius Magistri* can be found in the "new attitude of openness to the world which is characteristic of Vatican II";[2] that openness is particularly evident in *Gaudium et spes.* In the specific case of *Gravissimum educationis,* the openness includes going beyond the limits of a focus merely on the Catholic school by turning the attention of the Church to the broader need for the Christian education of the increasing number of Catholic students in non-Catholic schools, especially through the formation of Catholic teachers for these schools, as well as a new emphasis on their religious instruction and pastoral care. In addition, *Gravissimum educationis* stressed the new realities of technology and communication, which, though not neglected by *Divini Illius Magistri*, are portrayed with a particularly positive emphasis as especially promising for the education of young people and for fulfilling the newly awakened human desire for participation in society at all levels. Finally, in light of the council's pervasive emphasis on human dignity, the declaration recognized the universal right to education, including the rights of unbelievers, and the Church's obligation to participate in confronting the challenges to this universal task of human formation.

However, the general and rather ambiguous notion of this new emphasis on the openness to the world continued to raise certain difficulties for the development of a coherent approach to education in the period immediately following the council. Moreover, it inevitably led to the new reflections from the Sacred Congregation for Catholic Education on the specific challenges and opportunities of Christian education in *The Catholic School* (1977), *Lay Catholics in Schools: Witnesses to Faith* (1982), and *The Religious Dimension of Education in a Catholic School* (1988). As Archbishop Beck of Liverpool pointed out in a reflection in *The Tablet* on November 6, 1965, the general trend of the council's discussions reflected a shift from the juridical and triumphant notions of the Church. This necessarily involved a move away from the earlier emphasis on the Church as a perfect society to what Archbishop Beck called "the more pastoral spirit as 'the People of God' on its march through history to the eschatological destiny, or as the Mystical Body of Christ with each of its members having a supernatural function."[3] Although this shift offered certain pastoral and theological advantages, it also entailed inevitable ambiguities, especially concerning the relations of the Church and the state with regard to the emerging demand for universal education and the promotion of opportunities for social participation. As Beck pointed out, there was "a tendency in the final statement to play down the rights of the Church, to stress parental responsibility and rights, and to emphasize, perhaps a little vaguely, the apostolic qualities of Catholic education offered by the Church as a voluntary association. This is a significant change of emphasis and many think that the council's statement should for this reason have dwelt more fully on the distinction between civil society and the state."[4]

A year earlier, Bishop James Malone had stressed the same point in a speech on the council floor, in which he insisted that a clear and explicit distinction needed to be made between "society itself and the state or government which is society's political arm or instrument."[5] Malone referred positively to Pius XI's "great encyclical on education, *Divini Illius Magistri*," which had provided a more comprehensive and nuanced account of the complexity of the relations among the family, the Church, and civil society in the responsibility to educate the young. Furthermore, he insisted on the danger (perhaps never effectively resolved within the declaration) of depending too heavily upon simply affirming the rights of parents and the Church in the area of education when confronted with increasingly coercive demands of the state for an educational monopoly. Rather, he insisted that "the school is not *simpliciter* the extension of the home or family; the teachers are not *simpliciter* delegates of the parents or even of the Church. Neither is the school *simpliciter* the agent much less the servant of the state. Each agent in education has a proper and legitimate interest in the education of its children, but each from its own point of view and within the limits of its own competence."[6]

Both Archbishop Beck and Bishop Malone sought to clarify the ways in which the state and the Church contributed to and articulated the particular conditions of the common good of civil society, especially in the area of education.

In *Divini Illius Magistri*, Pius XI had drawn upon the language of the three necessary societies, which are distinct but harmoniously combined by God. Two of these societies, the family and civil society, belong to the natural order, while the third, the Church, belongs to the supernatural order. He insisted that the family comes first, intended by God for the "generation and formation of offspring," but he acknowledged that the family is an imperfect society, incomplete in itself, whereas the civil society is a perfect society because it embodies all that is necessary for the temporal well-being of the community. In this sense, civil society has a legitimate preeminence over the family, which must participate in the larger civil society in order to achieve temporal perfection. The Church itself is a society "of the supernatural order and of universal extent," a perfect society because it has in itself all of the means required for its own end, which is "the eternal salvation of mankind."[7] The pope then proceeded to develop the necessary interrelations of the three societies and warned about the increasing tendencies on the part of civil society to repress the educational rights of families and of the Church and to establish a tyrannical control over all forms of education. Such a monopoly would exclude from the schools all religious and moral formation on the part of the Church and family and thereby repress the genuine religious and cultural pluralism inherent in modern cultures. This threat, identified with remarkable consistency by popes at least since Pius VII had warned about the increasing danger of state usurpations of education, took on a new urgency with the emergence of various totalitarian systems in the twentieth century. In 1937 in *Mit brennender Sorge*, Pius XI had spoken directly to Catholic parents in condemning the German Reich's violation of their parental rights by restricting their children's access to Catholic schools; he insisted that "we should never cease frankly to represent to the responsible authorities the iniquity of the pressure brought to bear on you and the duty of respecting the freedom of education."[8]

In *Nostis et nobiscum* Pius IX had similarly warned in 1849 that the enemies of religion and human society are seeking to corrupt the young by a perversion of their minds and hearts, and he insisted that the principal aim of these efforts was to detach schools from the authority and pastoral care of the Church. Of course, Pius IX did not hesitate to invoke the privileges and rights of the institutional Church when it was confronted by the hostility of new forces of statism, rationalism, racism, and atheism (many of which were cited as pressing threats to Catholic schools in early drafts of the schema *De scholis catholicis,* forerunner of *Gravissimum educationis,* but were later shifted to other conciliar texts or eliminated as insufficiently pastoral in tone). In the absence of a clear sense of the institutional reality of the Church and its relationships both to the family and to civil society, a certain fundamental ambiguity was perhaps inevitable. This ambiguity, hardly limited to the council's reflections on Christian education, reflected a deeper theological tension, which Joseph Ratzinger clarified when he emphasized the fact that "theology still oscillated between two extremes. There was the enthusiastic affirmation of the world on the one hand, based on the idea of the Incarnation (and carried to its most radical point by Teilhard de Chardin) and, on the other hand, a radical theology of the cross, not by any means lightly to be dismissed as Platonistic or even Manichaean."[9]

Ratzinger insisted that within this context emerged the recognition of certain problems to which the council could give no definite answers. He listed three specific examples: new directions in moral theology; Christian education; and the reform of canon law. Each would require considerable postconciliar reflection and debate in order to clarify its specific implications.

Gravissimum educationis begins with a sustained emphasis on the critical importance of education in the modern world, in which it is both easier and more urgent to educate both young people and adults. The council fathers noted an increasing desire on the part of men and women to participate in social and political life. The development of new technologies, modern scientific developments, and means of communication has enhanced the ability to forge new connections with others and increased the general interest in education.

The council noted that the right to an education, especially the primary rights of children and parents, has been increasingly recognized in a variety of public documents, including the United Nations' *Universal Declaration of Human Rights* (1948) and the *Declaration of the Rights of the Child* (1959). New efforts at universal education have begun despite the fact that much of the world lacks rudimentary education and many others are deprived of an education in which the claims of truth and love are interrelated. This stress on the interrelation of truth and love in a genuine human formation has a consistent and sustained expression within the declaration. Because the Church has the obligation to proclaim the mystery of salvation to all and to restore all things in Christ, no area of human life, even the secular, is alien to man's heavenly calling. It is in this wider context that the council identified the general aim of education: "For a true education aims at a formation of human persons which is directed towards their final end and at the same time towards the good of society of which they are members, and in whose functions, on becoming adults, they will take part."[10] In this sense, education will give human persons an ability "gradually to acquire a more perfect sense of responsibility in correctly improving their own lives by continual effort and in aiming at true freedom, overcoming obstacles with great courage and perseverance."[11]

This humanistic education will necessarily involve both new approaches to sex education (in which the interrelation of love and truth is too often conspicuously absent) and the acquisition of skills necessary for a productive social and economic life. But these goals must be pursued within the context of the right of the young "to be stimulated to weigh moral values with a correct conscience, to embrace them with personal commitment, and to know and love God more perfectly."[12] The responsibility for this right lies not only with parents and the Church; rather, all public authorities have the responsibility to see that young people are not deprived of this sacred right. Members of the Church have a particular and direct responsibility to ensure that this right is universally available and to confront the obstacles, financial, geographical, and cultural, that might impede the fulfillment of that right.

The Church's obligations to Christian education go beyond the universal task of forming mature human persons to include the specific obligation of the formation of the baptized and to gradually introduce them into the mystery of salvation. In doing so, young people need to become more aware of the gift of faith; to learn to worship the Father in spirit and in truth, especially in the liturgy; to be conformed in their personal lives to the new man created in justice and holiness of truth; to develop to a mature measure of the fullness of Christ and to strive for the growth of the mystical body; and to become aware of their calling and thus to contribute to the Christian formation of the world and to the good of the whole society.

Within this wider context of Christian formation, parents are to be understood as the primary and principal educators, for the family is the first school of the social virtues and provides the first experience of a wholesome human society and of the Church. Of course, this insight, already present in the educational philosophy of the Holy See throughout the last two centuries, found a new manifestation in the thought of Pope John Paul II, who insisted in *Familiaris consortio* that the family is a community of human life, a community of persons united in love, and is in this sense the foundation of all of civilization. He insisted that both the history of mankind and the history of salvation pass by the way of the family.

In order to fulfill its educational responsibility, the family needs the help of the whole community, including civil society, which is required to do all that is necessary for the temporal common good. There is then a principle of subsidiarity in the relations of families and civil society in which society must protect the rights and duties of parents and others who share in education and give them the necessary aid in order for their wishes to be fulfilled. However, in a special way, the Church too has a responsibility within this broader relation of obligations: the responsibility of announcing salvation to all, communicating the life of Christ to believers, and assisting all men and women to come to the fullness of life. As a mother, the Church must give her children an education by which their whole life is imbued with the spirit of Christ. This will promote the perfection of the human person, the good of earthly society, and the building of a world that is more human. Within this larger vision of education, one can speak of four specific aims of Catholic education: catechetical instruction; an education that nourishes life according to the spirit of Christ; an education that leads to intelligent and active participation in liturgical mystery; and an education that gives motivation for apostolic activity.

Catholic schools have a special role to play within this larger context of Christian education. It arises out of the "primary and inalienable right and duty of parents to educate their children." Public authorities have a fundamental obligation to support this right and to guarantee it in terms of public subsidies (*GE* 6). Any attempt to impose a monopoly of education is opposed to the native rights of the human person. Archbishop Beck had argued that Christian education could no longer be understood "in a narrow and negative sense as the specific privilege of a closed community."[13] Rather, within the larger civil society, the Church plays an indispensable moral and religious role on which the common good of that society as a whole ultimately depends. Clearly, the council sought to overcome the perceived alienation of the Church from the world and to insist on their ultimate complementarity within the mystery of salvation, in which all are called to work "for the restoration of all things in Christ."[14] Beyond this, the council insisted that all schools, secular as well as religious, must incorporate moral and religious instruction within their curriculum. In this sense, the Church has an obligation to serve the religious needs of Catholic students in non-Catholic schools. This can be accomplished through the profound witness of Catholic teachers and by the apostolic activity of fellow Catholic students. In addition, the Church must make available the ministry of priests and trained laypeople who can present to these students the doctrine of salvation. It is the particular duty of parents to ensure that their children receive this doctrine, and civil authorities are called upon to protect these rights within the context of a religious pluralism that increasingly defines modern cultures.

Catholic schools are called to create "the atmosphere of the school community, animated by the evangelical spirit of freedom and love. Its function is to help adolescents to develop their own personalities in such a way that they may at the same time grow according to the new creation which they have become through baptism" (*GE* 8).

It is in this sense that alumni of Catholic schools are to become a saving leaven within the broader human community and that Catholic schools continue to retain the utmost importance within the larger task of Christian education. This "privileged" position of Catholic schools, criticized by some council fathers (especially from parts of Latin America), must be seen, then, in the light of the special responsibility of Catholic school graduates to contribute to the universal task of Christian education.[15]

The council stressed the central role of Catholic teachers in the schools and mandated that suitable preparation in both secular and religious knowledge be made available for their full formation. These teachers, "intimately linked in charity to one another and to their students and endowed with an apostolic spirit," can not only by their formal instruction but also by the quality of their lives bear witness to Christ, the unique teacher. As such, teaching is a genuine and vital apostolate of the Church, one that is affirmed in a manner unique within the conciliar texts in the conclusion of *Gravissimum educationis*. The declaration recognized that significant new efforts for the formation of Catholic faculty were a pressing requirement.

In addition to existing elementary and secondary school programs, the council acknowledged a need for new professional and technical schools, new centers for adult education and for students with special needs, as well as new schools to prepare a new generation of teachers for religious and general education. In all of its educational apostolate, special attention should be given to the needs of the poor, not only those in economic poverty but also those who are deprived of the assistance and affection of a family or who are strangers to the gift of faith.

Within the context of higher education, the declaration affirms a need for individual subjects to be pursued "according to their own principles, method and liberty of scientific inquiry" so that a deeper understanding may be gained according to the example of the doctors of the Church, especially Saint Thomas Aquinas. This is necessary in order to attain a more extensive realization of the ultimate harmony of faith and science. For this reason, the Church must also have a living and critical presence within secular institutions. The council recognized that, in order to meet these broad goals, a new and sustained collaboration on the diocesan, national, and international levels would have to occur.

In 1966 Joseph Ratzinger had referred to *Gravissimum educationis* as unfortunately a rather weak document. A year later he was more specific about the declaration's particular limitations and strengths within the context of the council's larger work. He indicated that "One unfortunately has to say that the text wasn't treated by the council fathers with any specific affection," and from his point of view this is a further indication that the council members were tiring as they moved toward conclusion.[16] As a result, the declaration failed to develop all of the possibilities of education implied by the anthropology of the council. However, this should not be understood as a weakness; rather it implies a task left for future generations, who will still be guided by faith but will function in a situation different from that of the council. In order to address that task, the Church would have to confront the apparent conflict, unresolved in *Gravissimum educationis*, that was implicit in its oscillation between a modern view of the human person, the emerging, progressive hope of technological developments, and a biblical language that seemed somehow not fully compatible with the progressive optimism of the council's anthropology. This oscillation is often expressed within the council texts as a dilemma that involves the claims of faith and the claims of freedom. For Ratzinger, this is manifested in a primary way in the council's account of the relationship of the Christian and the Church to the technological world, for he saw an emerging position "which seeks to solve the problem by identifying to a high degree Christian hope with modern confidence in progress."[17] This led Ratzinger to suggest that, despite all disavowal, there remains in the council's anthropological statements "an almost naive progressivist optimism which seemed unaware of the ambivalence of all human progress."[18] This led him to raise the question—crucial to a coherent account of the Church's role in education—of the relation between this progressivist view and Christian hope, for he again insisted that the world is not redeemed by machinery but by love, a love seen without illusion. The task then would be for the Church to "establish critical norms by which to judge the technological."[19] But how might this critical hope be realized in a new understanding of the role of Christian education within the larger progressivist impulse of modern cultures?

Of course, it would be a mistake to think that the council's optimism about the emerging world of technology and social communication was simply misplaced. Ratzinger insisted that the council, in a historic opening to the world, does not "bemoan and deplore" the new situation but rather begins by "delimiting its [the Church's] own sphere of competency." Faith offers guidance about the origins and destiny of man's life, but it does not provide ready answers for all specific questions. This new humility before the complexity of the emerging technological culture was perhaps initially expressed by many in Catholic education in a rather naïve affirmation of the liberating power of new technologies and an emphasis on the autonomy of civil society's new and mature vision of human life.[20] However, the larger question of this new human situation would require much more careful analysis and interpretation in the future, for the triumph of technology produces "a new orientation toward human existence, based on the opportunity to make things functional in the service of man. But this alters the basic relation of man to reality. He now views reality essentially from a functional point of view. He no longer approaches the world from the viewpoint of contemplation and wonder, but as one who measures, weighs and acts."[21] This new functional account of the human person increasingly defined the basic philosophy of educational reforms of the next generation and had a considerable impact on the vision and educational philosophy of Catholic schools and universities.

Less than five months after the council, Ratzinger, then professor of dogmatics and the history of dogma at the Catholic theology faculty at Tübingen, addressed German Catholic lay leaders. He questioned the significance of the council's general understanding of the human person for education (April 23, 1966, at Bad Honnef). In the first part of his reflections, Ratzinger dealt with the anthropology of *Gaudium et spes* and its explicit significance for education and cultural formation. Having served on the preparatory commission for the pastoral constitution, Ratzinger referred to the foundational character of the anthropology developed in *Gaudium et spes* for the whole of the council. He argued that the other council documents (and in a special way the declaration on Christian education) elucidate, unfold, and concretize that anthropology in very important ways.

Unlike several of his other commentaries on the council from these years, Ratzinger's essay here does not address the differences of opinion among the participants at the council, but it does speak to the contemporary ambivalence of the human situation that the final text intends to articulate. Despite accurately perceiving and criticizing the self-delusion that often accompanies contemporary accounts of the historical character of humanity and the new humanism of our own age, the council also acknowledged in a radically new way the unique need and opportunity to develop global responsibility and solidarity as the necessary but not sufficient condition of attaining the abiding vocation of full humanity. The ambivalence of our times is reflected in the "danger and necessity" of speaking today of the human being as a project of history. These particular historical challenges form the context for understanding what the council has to say about education and cultural formation. Not every change that calls for a new embrace of global responsibility is humanizing, but the task of humanization will not be fulfilled without embracing the historical demands of our time for greater responsibility. Ratzinger insisted that new approaches to education must be viewed within this larger anthropological context.

Under the heading of responsibility and brotherhood, Ratzinger moved beyond Marxist and liberal market visions of progress and indicated that universal progress cannot dispense with older self-understandings of humanity, but neither will these older notions be realized today without a new, more human extension of technology. An adequate vision of the future would also require the renewal and deepening of Christology in order for us to understand more fully the demand and possibilities of this humanizing promise of the modern age. This would be one of the most significant challenges for the Church in responding to the emerging claims of a contemporary technological culture.

Ratzinger argued that certain implications for education were drawn directly from the pastoral constitution itself. In coining and using (and from Ratzinger's point of view, perhaps overusing) the word *responsibilitas*, the council underlines a central focus of its anthropology. The corresponding freedom and autonomy to embrace this responsiveness has theological, Christological, and properly anthropological justification, as well as a Trinitarian dimension, all of which encourage as never before the pluralization and specialization of education, along with the perennial and now ever more acute need for synthesis.

When Ratzinger treated specifically the issue of Catholic schools, he argued that such schools cannot be insisted upon merely for the sake of the Church's institutional self-affirmation but only insofar as they are genuinely schools in the common understanding of the term and also truly Catholic. He argued that the text of *Gravissimum educationis* says too little about universities and theological faculties. However, he pointed out that "the text does still stress that quality must come before quantity, something that sadly is not accepted by all."[22] Ratzinger went on to suggest that the declaration implies that the need to improve quality restricts somewhat the exclusive claims of any given university or theological faculty to an autonomous pretension to excellence. In order to achieve the larger renewal of a Catholic vision of the intellectual life, "The faculties' accomplishing their goal demands a limitation of the solitary claims of any given institution."[23] The need for an integrated and organic expression of the distinctive claims of Catholic higher education would be taken up later by Pope John Paul II in the apostolic constitution *Ex corde Ecclesiae*.

Gravissimum educationis insisted that the larger task of explicating, clarifying, and developing the basic principles of the declaration remained to be accomplished, and it urged the Sacred Congregation for Catholic Education, bishops' conferences, canonists, and the faithful to take up the challenge to draw out the fuller implications of the declaration's teachings for an application to the specific conditions of modern cultures. The Congregation for Catholic Education fulfilled *Gravissimum educationis*'s explicit charge to develop more fully the declaration's affirmations of Christian education and the specific role of Catholic schools in three documents: *The Catholic School* (1977); *Lay Catholics in Schools: Witnesses to Faith* (1982); and *The Religious Dimension of Education in a Catholic School* (1988). In each of these documents, the congregation (with perhaps a greater awareness of the specific dangers of an increasing secularization of modern culture) reaffirmed the substance of the council's declaration on the central importance of Christian education and articulated more clearly certain modern obstacles to the Catholic school's ability to realize its goal of "the development of man from within, freeing him from that conditioning which would prevent him from becoming a more fully integrated human being."[24]

There is also a clearer recognition in these three documents that the withdrawal of religious orders and priests from ministry in Catholic schools and the relatively inadequate formation of new lay faculty has presented a situation in which it is increasingly evident that many schools had now become only nominally Catholic. They often strongly affirm the need for a "clear realization of the identity of a Catholic school and the courage to follow all the consequences of its uniqueness"[25] and warn that the educational aims of Catholic schools demand "constant self criticism and return to basic principles."[26] There is also a strongly worded caution that Catholic schools do not provide "a quick answer to contemporary problems, but they give a direction which can begin to solve them."[27] This suggests that the tendency to pursue contemporary relevance risks the loss of a prophetic and specifically Catholic educational mission. The three documents increasingly express concern for the pastoral and theological formation of lay faculty and for a conscious and explicit emphasis on the distinctiveness of a Catholic philosophy of education, one that cannot be measured simply by efficiency.

In its 1982 statement on the role of lay faculty in Catholic schools the congregation reiterated Newman's distinction between professional instruction in which one transmits a body of knowledge and education that aims to form the human person as a whole. In this sense, the lay teacher shares in the witness of the faith and, in order to realize that vocation, must receive a formation in social virtues for the common good in order to contribute to the creation of a civilization of love. The congregation noted that the prospects for Catholic education have to be evaluated within a context of realism combined with hope. It pointed out the significant obstacles to the realization of an organic Catholic philosophy of education: "Identity crisis, loss of trust in social structures, the resulting insecurity and loss of any personal convictions, the contagion of a progressive secularization of society, loss of the proper concept of authority and lack of a proper use of freedom."[28]

The congregation affirmed Ratzinger's earlier recognition of the tension between the theology of the cross and the optimistic language of human progress in the council's texts. It warned Catholic teachers of the dangers of the general atmosphere of secularization and unbelief and cautioned against a mentality that is merely experimental and critical. Moreover, it insisted on the central importance of leading students to an awareness of the transcendent and disposing them to welcome revealed truth. Lay teachers were explicitly encouraged to recall their obligations to assist students in forming a sense of their vocations within the Church and their obligations to participate in its sacramental and liturgical life; teachers would achieve this task most effectively through the personal witness of their own lives. From the point of view of Catholic doctrine, lay teachers were reminded that "what is asked for is not that one impart one's own doctrine, or that of some other teacher, but the teaching of Jesus Christ Himself."[29] In order to achieve this goal, the professional and religious formation of lay teachers would be a permanent and ongoing responsibility of the Church and the Catholic school.

These documents impart a growing sense of the ambiguities and dangers of the modern situation, as well as a reaffirmation of the remarkable confidence expressed by the council in the ongoing maturation of modern cultures. By the time of the publication of the 1988 document, *The Religious Dimension of Education in a Catholic School*, the congregation was forced to acknowledge a remarkable social conformity among young people, for whom concepts such as truth, beauty, and goodness had become so vague that they "do not know where to turn to find help; even when they are able to hold on to certain values, they do not yet have the capacity to develop these values into a way of life; all too often they are more inclined simply to go their own way, accepting whatever is popular at the moment."[30] The congregation noted the presence among young people of both an increasingly one-dimensional universe in which practical utility is the only value and at the same time a desire to transcend that limit. This leads to a certain depression that is one of the hallmarks of our time and often leads them to an "almost irresistible urge to focus in on themselves."[31]

The 1988 document develops Ratzinger's earlier awareness of the tension between the optimism toward the new technological and scientific discoveries, which promise a liberation of human hope and aspiration, and the Christian recognition that the world is redeemed through love. This recognition will have both Christological and ecclesiological implications. The congregation acknowledged that "students learn many things about the human person by studying science" but insisted that "science has nothing to say about mystery."[32] Teachers need to introduce students to the saving mystery of the love of the Father, revealed in and through the life and death of the Son. "Here is where students discover the true value of the human person: loved by God, with a mission on earth and a destiny that is immortal."[33] The recognition of the saving mystery of Christ leads inevitably to an acknowledgement of a filial respect for the Church at work in the world and of the central role of the sacraments, which the Church provides for the sake of salvation.

The 1988 document stressed that the religious dimension of the Catholic school is fundamental and transformative and is not to be understood merely as an additional contextualizing element. Increasingly and resolutely biblical and doctrinal, the language insists that the Catholic school is a genuine and proper instrument of the Church, "a place of evangelization, of authentic apostolate and of pastoral action—not through complementary or parallel or extra-curricular activity, but of its very nature: its work of educating the Christian person."[34] Throughout these three postconciliar documents on Catholic education we find progressively strong warnings about the dangers of a merely functional understanding of the human person, reaffirmations of the liberating power of an authentic Christian understanding of freedom, and a recognition of the reductionist tendencies in certain contemporary accounts of material and technological progress.

In a variety of addresses, but especially in the two apostolic constitutions, *Sapientia christiana* and *Ex corde Ecclesiae*, Pope John Paul II sought to clarify the distinctive role of the Catholic university within the larger context of Christian education and the demands of modern cultures; he also hoped to overcome the limitation in *Gravissimum educationis* with regard to higher education and theological faculties that Ratzinger had noted in 1966. Especially in *Ex corde Ecclesiae*, John Paul II stressed the fact that there is ultimately only one culture, not many—"that of man, by man and for man"—and that we must explore and clarify the dimensions of this universal human culture in the ongoing dialogue between the Church and the multiplicity of modern cultures. The Church has a key role to play in this dialogue, for there is a tendency to relativize cultures in a new awareness of their historical contingency and particularity. The Catholic university assists the Church in this dialogue because in a unique way it consecrates itself without reserve to the cause of truth. This is made possible because its privileged task is to unite existentially two orders of reality often placed in opposition to one another: "the search for truth and the certain knowledge of already knowing the fount of truth."[35] This organic vision of Catholic higher education must be incarnated in the specific conditions and limits of particular universities, but the philosophy of education that it presupposes is universal and comprehensive. Pope John Paul II clearly recognized the danger, which Ratzinger had already identified, of the claims of a radical institutional autonomy that began to find a systematic expression in the years immediately following the council. He cited conciliar texts, especially those of *Gravissimum educationis* and *Gaudium et spes*, with a striking continuity of theme and emphasis.

Gravissimum educationis is perhaps rightly understood to have certain weaknesses in the sense that it did not apply to the realm of Christian education with exceptional clarity and probity the complex implications of the council's larger reflections on the relations of the Church to the modern world.

However, the complexity of the anthropological and ecclesial issues raised and debated as the council concluded necessarily required ongoing reflection and application, as the council fathers themselves had stressed. There was a clear recognition, as Newman had pointed out a century earlier, that great ideas are grown into and not learned by heart; moreover, the reflection on the emerging development of the council's theological anthropology, its new openness to a developing technological culture, and the recognition of the new importance of emerging understandings of human rights and the role of the state within civil society would require complex and sustained treatment and reflection. The opportunities and challenges for the Church in the area of education continue to press heavily, not only in the education of young people but perhaps equally critically in adult education and religious and catechetical instruction. In this context, *Gravissiumum educationis* has much to tell us about the situation of the Church and its role in Christian education. However, the application of its teaching, although ongoing, continues to develop as the Church articulates the relation of the theology of the cross and the progressivist claims of contemporary cultures with greater precision.

NOTES

1. Ulrich Gunzer, *"Gravissimum Educationis,"* in *Lexikon für Theologie und Kirche,* 3d ed., vol. 4 (Freiburg: Herder, 1995), col. 993.

2. Johannes Pohlschneider, "Declaration on Christian Education," in *Commentary on the Documents of Vatican II,* vol. 4, ed. Herbert Vorgrimler (New York: Herder and Herder, 1969), 13.

3. G. A. Beck, "Christian Education," *The Tablet* (Nov. 6, 1965), 1233.

4. Ibid.

5. James Malone, council speech, Nov. 18, 1964, in *Council Daybook,* ed. Floyd Anderson (Washington, D.C.: National Catholic Welfare Conference, 1965), 281.

6. Ibid.

7. Pius XI, *Divini Illius Magistri* (Dec. 31, 1929), 12–13.

8. Pius XI, *Mit brennender Sorge* (Mar. 14, 1937), 39n11.

9. Joseph Ratzinger, *Theological Highlights of Vatican II* (New York: Paulist Press, 1966), 100.

10. Second Vatican Council, *Gravissimum educationis,* no. 1.

11. Ibid.

12. Ibid.

13. Beck, "Christian Education," 1233.

14. Ibid.

15. In 1964 Bishop Aloysius Henriquy argued on the council floor that Catholic schools must be understood as a means, not an end, and that if "these confessional schools prove to be less effective in fulfilling the mission and obligation of evangelization, then we must abandon them and find more effective means." *Council Speeches of Vatican II, Third Session,* ed. William K. Leahy and Anthony T. Mossimini (Glen Rock, N.J.: Deus Books, 1965), 325.

16. Ratzinger, *Theological Highlights of Vatican II,* 179.

17. Ibid., 157.

18. Ibid., 158.

19. Ibid., 160.

20. Ibid., 162.

21. Ibid.

22. Joseph Ratzinger, "Das Menschenbild des Konzils in seiner Bedeutung für die Bilding," in *Kulturbeirat beim Zentralkomitee der deutschen Katholiken*, ed. Christliche Erziehung nach dem Konzil Berichte und Dokumentation (Cologne: J. P. Bechem, 1967), 63.

23. Ibid., 65.

24. Sacred Congregation for Catholic Education, *Catholic School* (1977), no. 29.

25. Ibid., no. 66.

26. Ibid., no. 67.

27. Ibid.

28. Sacred Congregation for Catholic Education, *Lay Catholics in Schools: Witnesses to Faith* (1982), no. 26.

29. Pope John Paul II, *Cathechesi tradendae* (Oct. 16, 1979), cited in ibid., no. 59.

30. Congregation for Catholic Education, *The Religious Dimension of Education in a Catholic School* (1988), no. 9.

31. Ibid., no. 12.

32. Ibid., no. 76.

33. Ibid., no. 33.

34. Ibid.

35. Pope John Paul II, *Ex corde Ecclesiae* (1990), I, no. 4.

20

The Declaration on the Relationship of the Church to Non-Christian Religions, *Nostra Aetate*

Arthur Kennedy

On October 28, 1965, the seventh anniversary of Pope John XXIII's election to the papacy, the *Declaration on the Relationship of the Church to Non-Christian Religions* (*Nostra aetate*) was one of five documents approved and promulgated by the fathers of Vatican II. In addition to this declaration, three decrees and one other declaration were accepted on the same day; these last four were more directly concerned with the direction and the renewal of the inner life of the Church.[1] *Nostra aetate* has its basis in the inner mystery of the Church, and it does so in the context articulated in *Lumen gentium* (nos. 1, 8, and esp. 16), which specifies the mission, purpose, and historicity of the life of the Church and its presence in the world. From the viewpoint of ecclesiology, the theological vision of *Nostra aetate* is analogical to the sacramental "sign of intimate union with God and of the unity of all mankind" (*LG* 1).

Two principles should guide the reading of *Nostra aetate*. The first is that the Catholic Church rejects nothing that is true and holy in non-Christian religions. She regards with sincere reverence those ways of conduct and life, those precepts and teachings that, though different from the ones she holds and sets forth, nonetheless often reflect a ray of the truth that enlightens all men.[2] The second principle is grounded in what the Church has been given in Christ's teaching and commands. The Church proclaims—and ever must proclaim—Christ as the way, the truth, and the life (Jn 14:6), in whom God has reconciled all things to himself. The theological motivation of the Church in its outreach and care for other religions is thus grounded in her awareness of the fullness of life and love in Christ alone.

The intention of the declaration is to call Catholics to be faithful mediators and to manifest in their lives what is "true or good or holy" as they concretely and historically present Christ and the Church to others. For Catholics, this call to constant conversion and fidelity is parallel to the conversion that is underlined as essential to authentic ecumenism in *Redintegratio unitatis* (cf. no. 6). It is through the converted life that Catholics engage in the search for the unity of the Church and as converted that they seek the unity of mankind under God and stand against all forms of discrimination; moreover, in relation to the Jewish people, Catholics reject "hatred, persecutions, displays of anti-Semitism, directed against Jews at any time and by anyone" (*Nostra aetate* 4).

Thus the declaration promotes the recognition of points of common concern with other religions so as to establish true and authentic dialogue and understanding and to appreciate the way in which a religious sense of life is operative in shaping cultures. As to what the Church seeks from other religions, Augustin Cardinal Bea, in his commentary on *Nostra aetate*, notes that it is to be "nothing more than the attitude that she herself adopts in the declaration with regard to them: namely an attitude of respect involving serious consideration of the content of her message, together with readiness to admit candidly the presence of anything good or holy.... Lastly she asks them for genuine respect for her fidelity to the mission which she is sincerely convinced she has received from Christ."[3]

Development of *Nostra Aetate* at the Council

During the council three different contexts were proposed for placing a theological reflection on the relationship of Jews to the Church. The first context was as part of the Decree on Ecumenism; the second was within the Constitution on the Church; and the third was as a self-standing decree. During the discussion about the second possibility the media learned of the discussions of Jewish relations with the Church that were taking place in the council. Subsequently, several Arab leaders interpreted this as a political act, a form of support of the state of Israel, and a statement against Muslims. Bishops from countries with large Muslim populations indicated in council discussions that the council's intention when misread as a provocation could endanger the Catholic faithful of their dioceses. They wanted the statement to be withdrawn.

Because of concerns about these practical implications, Cardinal Cicognani, the Vatican secretary of state, became involved in responding to Arab governments and political leaders in order to clarify that the council was not engaged in political matters but that it was concerned about the religious relationship of the Jews and the Church. For the most part the news reporters, because they lacked ecclesial differentiations, were not helpful in giving factual accounts of the Church's intentions. This problem became even more acute when the World Jewish Conference announced the appointment of Chaim

Wardi of the Israeli Ministry of Religious Affairs as a representative to the Holy See, for this fed Arab fears and reopened the concerns of the secretary of state; as a result, the discussion of the declaration was halted.[4]

Four different drafts of the document treated the theological relations of Jews and Catholics. The first identified what theological and pastoral issues should be engaged; the second dealt with anti-Semitism, as well as the need for a correct catechesis on the passion and the role of the Jews in the death of Jesus (this draft was intended to be chapter 4 of the Decree on Ecumenism). The third was developed after Pope Paul VI's visit to Israel and Jordan in early January 1964 and identified the Church's beginning in the patriarchal faith of Israel; it stated that, although God had acted definitively in the new covenant through Christ, the covenant with Israel continued. It also developed further discussion on corporate Jewish guilt and deicide.

It was this draft that captured the bishops' vision; they spoke with each other, often at length, on both the importance of the council's making a statement and what its foci should be. The prior drafts had in a sense prepared them, in consultation with theological *periti*, to engage the questions as their own. It also led to requests from a number of bishops to speak of Church relations with other world religions. In his Easter message of March 1964 Pope Paul VI referred to this broader sense and importance of conversation with other religions: "Every religion contains a ray of light that we must neither despise nor extinguish, even though it is not sufficient to give man the truth he needs, or to realize the miracle of the Christian light in which truth and life coalesce. But every religion raises us towards the Transcendent Being, the sole ground of all existence and all thought, of all responsible action and all authentic hope."[5]

The fourth draft presented a completely new context because of the broadening of theological issues into the reflections on divine creation and the universal hope of redemption, while maintaining the ecclesiology and Christological dimensions of what was being called the *Declaration on the Relationship of the Church to Non-Christian Religions*. The new context now drew on the synthesis and transpositions made possible by the Catholic understanding of the unity of truth in faith and reason that the bishops understood as a constant in tradition. In the opening to the declaration, this was brought to bear with regard to the Church's theological and philosophical tradition, as well as every created person's hunger for God.

At the same time it maintained the absolute uniqueness of Judaism to Christianity in being called into a covenantal relationship with God. Thus *Nostra aetate* begins not with a focus on the Jewish people, where one might have expected it to begin, but rather with the cogent remark of Saint Augustine, who, knowing his own pagan heart and its longing, realized after his conversion that his heart had been drawn into the heart of Christ, the truth of all peoples: "Our hearts are restless until they rest in Thee." Saint Augustine's vision, with its naming of the universal quest for the ultimate, eternal answer to the human longing for the overcoming of life's limits, for the release from suffering, and for the desire to be loved, provided a sense of tradition that the bishops knew well. Thus, we find that when the Church sought with such fervor, anguish, and hope to recognize its profound bond to God's creation of "Israel"—of the Jewish people as the first religious community of his presence and love—the Church reappropriated its most ancient awareness of God's infinite care and longing for all of his people.

The Church and the Jewish People

The task of developing and presenting the declaration to the council was assigned to Augustin Cardinal Bea. Immediately after the council concluded, he published a commentary on *Nostra aetate* that provided insights into its structure, themes, and expressions.[6] While the declaration begins with the Church's understanding of its relationship with other religions, he notes, the primary concerns during the council had been with the Jews. Thus the commentary, which covers the entirety of *Nostra aetate*, emphasizes the relationship with the Jews. He offers a clear account of the term the "Jewish people" as used in the declaration: "The term indicates . . . those descendents of Abraham whom God chose for himself and constituted as the people of Israel, with whom he concluded an alliance, slowly educating them and revealing himself and his salvific designs to them in the course of their history—and all this in preparation for the coming of Christ and the redemption of mankind."[7]

It is especially Saint Paul who both participated in and named the enormous complexity of the identity and differences, as well as the continuity and discontinuity, between synagogue and Church. Moreover, his Epistle to the Romans is the focus of the declaration's attention to the naming of the mystery, namely the relationship of Jewish and Christian self-awareness. *Nostra aetate*, article 4, follows with precision Saint Paul's testimony on the Jews as chosen people in covenant with God.

The Church had always treated Judaism as unique to its life and Jewish people as those chosen by God in history to make known the divine promise of redemption and to offer the hope of the Messiah. It knew this continuity through the fact that Judaism's prayers and psalms are the Church's prayers; its feasts presage the Church's sacramental life; its sacred writings are what the Church reads and what the Fathers, as well as medieval and modern scholars, engage in commentary. Jesus, Mary, and Joseph, the Apostles, and the first followers and believers are Jewish, and this bond forever grounds the continuity with the Jewish people; "as the council searches into the mystery of the Church, it remembers the bond which spiritually ties the people of the New Covenant to the offspring of Abraham" (*Nostra aetate* 4). This continuity links Christian life not only to the Jewish religion through Jesus but also to the faith of Abraham and the patriarchs, as well as to the prophets and the kings. The continuity with the Jewish people exists forever. Thus did Pope John XXIII, in his first meeting with the Jewish leaders after his election, greet them with the words: "I am Joseph, your brother."[8]

The discontinuity of the Jewish-Christians and the broader Jewish community, under the guidance of the Sanhedrin, arises in its own response to the person and teaching of Jesus. Those who accept him as the awaited one of Israel are scandalized by the refusal of the Jews who do not accept him; the latter speak of Jesus as "a blasphemer," a mere man who equates himself with God. Saint Paul had named the difficulty of accepting Jesus in his self-revelation: "For Jews demand signs and Greeks look for wisdom, but we proclaim Christ crucified, a stumbling block to Jews and foolishness to Gentiles" (1 Cor 1:23).

The death of Jesus encapsulates the discontinuity of Jews and Christians, even as Jesus presents his judgment on the Romans, the Jewish leaders, and the crowd as simultaneously a reconciliation: "Father, forgive them, for they know not what they do" (Lk 23:34). Peter expressed this same response after Pentecost, when he healed the paraplegic and responded to those who were astounded and standing in Solomon's Portico: "And now my friends, I know that you acted in ignorance as did also your rulers. In this way God fulfilled what he had foretold through all the prophets, that his Messiah would suffer" (Acts 3:17–18).

The historical persecutions of the Christians recorded in Acts (cf. 5:17–32; 6:8–15; 7:54–8:3) deepened the divisions, especially as they occurred in a number of places where the apostolic preaching of Christ spread, as might have been anticipated, in the synagogues of the local Jewish communities throughout the eastern Roman Empire. The tension deeply affected Saint Paul's sense of bonds, as is clear in his visit to Thessalonica about AD 51 (see 1 Thess 2:14). However, as his letter to the Romans evidences, the local interferences did not suffice to override the deeper foundation of the relationship as he formulated it in Romans 9–11; perhaps he may have recalled his own "breathing threats and murder against the disciples of the lord" (Acts 9:1). He is concerned about the Roman church's dismissal of the Jews and the danger that the gentile Christians are failing to understand the full mystery of Christ and the Church with its bond to the Jews and their place in God's eternal plan. Emotionally he appeals: "I am speaking the truth in Christ. . . . I have great sorrow and unceasing anguish in my heart. For I could with that I myself were accursed and cut off from Christ for the sake of my own people, my kindred according to the flesh. They are Israelites, and to them belong adoption, the glory, the covenants, the giving of the law, the worship, and promises; to them belong the patriarchs, and from them, according to the flesh, comes the Messiah, who is over all, God blessed forever" (Rom 9:1–5).

Gentiles are not to be boastful, for they are not the root of the olive tree but its branches, which have been grafted on to it, and so are dependent on its primordial spiritual gifts. With this biblical metaphor of the olive tree, with all of its resonances about their being treasures and support in earthly life, as one's children are "like olive plants . . . around your table" (Ps 128:3), the council brings into the focus of Catholics the scriptural teaching about the relationship with the Jews, both in its bond and within it the separation. "As regards the gospel, they are enemies for your sake; as regards election they are beloved for the sake of their ancestors; for the gifts and the calling of God are irrevocable" (Rom 11:28–29).

The testimonies of the scripture, with both the paradox and the balance that constitutes the mystery in and for the Church, move forward into the patristic period. Now the struggle becomes one of apologetics, as defenses of the gospel's teaching and truth. During the patristic period, moreover, the church experienced the conversions of some Gentile philosophers who, with their accounts of the role of intelligence and reason in faith, became defenders of Christianity to secular pagan society. In relationship to the Jewish community the apologetics are met with a parallel response from Jewish teachers and rabbis. The debates translate the controversies to the new sphere of society.[9]

One of the key controversies that had already arisen in Paul was the meaning of "Israel" for both Church and synagogue. This was a topic that was analyzed by Justin Martyr (165). Justin, a convert from secular pagan philosophy, considered the teaching of Christ as the true philosophy and employed the type of philosophical dialogue that he was accustomed to in his study of the meaning of "Israel." This he engages both apologetically and dialogically in his "Dialogue with Trypho," which is considered to have been held in Ephesus in AD 135. After 124 chapters of Justin's defense of Christianity, the following question appears in chapter 125: " 'I wish, sirs,' I said, 'to learn from you what is the force [δύναμις] of the name Israel.' "[10] This became a central contention between Christians and Jews. Justin, whose principle context is apologetic defense, stated that, after the crucifixion, a discontinuity arose between the old people of God and the new, and yet close relations can exist between them. In spite of their differences the Church and Jews can talk reasonably together. Having grasped the difficulty, Justin summarized the various tensions and debates over the Church in its relation to Israel and the synagogue, but in the wider plane of philosophical commitments to dialogue.

Saint Augustine in one sense continued in a similar pattern of apologetics, but he possesses a much sharper sense of the details of mysterious relations with the Jews. Famous are his commentaries on the psalms and other Old Testament texts. His work continues to identify the new order of Christian reality and to address, most particularly in *De civitate Dei*, the entire matter of religion, politics, and culture. This text composed of twenty-two books spends the first ten addressing the issues of religion in the Roman Empire and the fact that the mythic and pagan religions were not the source of Rome's strength. He explores the details of the polytheism of that world and the political and cultural institutions that arose through their influences. He draws most particularly on Marcus Terentius Varro, who was among other things a historian of Roman religions, and Marcus Tullius Cicero for his analytical study of what constitutes a true religion.

In book X he contrasts paganism with Christianity and indicates that the fall of the empire is really a small matter in history when seen *sub specie aeternitate*. The second half of his work then presents the positive interpretation of the life of the two cities of heaven and earth and the personal and public consequences of each within their constant tension.

Books XV–XVIII detail the historical beginning of the heavenly city in the scriptures' account of the people chosen in the line of Abraham. "The traces of the holy city" are found throughout the account of the mystery of Israel in its relationship to God and to the continuing fulfillments of promises and events that appear in earlier moments of the people's history.[11] The Jewish people belong to the city of God at its beginning, as the root of an olive tree, and the themes of continuity and discontinuity continue.[12] Saint Augustine also states that it is important for Christians to treat Jews with humility and love, in fact because the Jews have received God's promise and belong to him until the endtime: "Let us proclaim [the divine testimonies] with great love for the Jews. Let us not proudly glory against the broken branches; let us rather reflect by whose grace it is, and by much mercy, and on what root, we have been engrafted. Then, not savoring of pride, but with a deep sense of humility, not insulting with presumption, but rejoicing with trembling, let us say: 'Come ye and let us walk in the light of the Lord.' "[13]

As for historical relations between Catholics and Jews during the medieval period, recent studies have uncovered materials and data that indicate that they were not quite as antagonistic as have often been supposed.[14] Norman Roth states that "An unfortunate common myth, shared widely by Jews and Christians is that the Church persecuted Jews, or at least preached discrimination against them, throughout the Middle Ages.... It is in the first place incorrect to speak of 'the Church' as though it were a monolithic entity; rather, one must consider the words and deeds of individuals, popes, theologians, bishops, or legal texts or canons of councils, etc."[15]

Roth indicates all of the influences that were involved in individuals who either had friendly relationships with or were hostile toward Jews. Thus he notes that Visigothic Spain, shaped "by Byzantine legal codes, and polemical ideas, and operating in a virtual theocracy, subjected Jews to persecution and unsuccessful efforts to convert them forcibly. This was not typical of the mediaeval period in general."[16] Roth documents the care of Jews by some bishops and the antagonisms of others, and the testimonies of warm relations are most often provided in Jewish sources. In an encyclopedic article on Christian-Jewish relations, Roth details the charities and care that existed between both peoples: Christians aiding Jewish neighbors during Sabbath and holiday observances; Jews providing gifts and foods to Christians. He also comments on how Jewish religious customs changed or new customs were created: "An interesting example is the creation of the *bar mitzvah* (son of the commandment) ceremony, at which a boy who had reached the age of thirteen (legal adulthood in Jewish law) was called to the reading of Torah in the synagogue. This was the direct influence of the equivalent Christian confirmation ceremony (prior to this period, the "coming of age" of a Jewish boy was purely a legal matter, dependent technically on his reaching puberty, but generally assumed to be the age of thirteen)."[17]

In the modern period, it is important to take note of the Jewish-Christian dialogue that was related to the "Patmos Circle," wherein Catholics, Protestants, and Jewish scholars engaged each other in understanding what was both common and different in their mutual religious beliefs.[18] What they turned to as a basis of dialogue was the common human reality of speech and word. Because all of the participants shared a bond in the acknowledgment of and faith in a divine revealed word of God, their study benefited in numerous ways, not the least of which was that the very study of the divine Word contributed to their mutual respect and recognition of the importance of the way in which human language conveys and constitutes a fundamental community of human relations that are open to God's communication.

Of particular importance were the conversations, letters, and texts of Franz Rozenzweig and Eugen Rosenstock-Huessy, with their study of and dialogue on how the pursuit of common speech and thinking leads to the discovery of meaning and truth in a shared experience of the mystery of God and each other in a mutual presence. Rozenzweig especially recognized the importance of a fundamental collaboration of Church and synagogue in iden-tifying a more than human hope and fulfillment for the world. Speaking of this dialogue of interiority, Harold Stahmer remarks that in their conversations "the authority of each tradition was represented in and through the named individuals in an ontological reality."[19] Their sense of a common project was to be servants of the mystery of God's presence to transform both the world and the culture in which they lived. These colleagues had a clear sense that receiving the mystery of God's Word called them to respect the word of others and to speak truthfully to each other. The transposition of respect for a reli-gion as an abstract difference becomes more fully possible and more system-atically necessary in the bond of truth as it is grasped by those who are in communication with one another; they are conscious of being mutually rela-ted to the mystery of God and yet divided; this discontinuity reveals both the continuity and the realization of difference and separation.

In order to draw together the wide and troubled history of Jewish and Catholic relations in the preparation for the council and in the new context of speaking truthfully to each other, it is important to recall that one of the major reasons for Pope John XXIII's insistence on a statement about Jewish-Catholic relations was the horrors of the death camps and the *Sho'ah*.[20] Likewise, more immediate concerns arose with the request by French Jewish professor Jules Isaac for an audience with Pope John XXIII. He wrote with the support of the Archbishop de Provenchères of Aix-en-Provence, where Isaac lived. Among the documents Professor Isaac brought in support of his request was one that asked the Church to recall or reappropriate the teaching on the Jews and the death of Jesus in the Roman Catechism of Trent. On June 13, 1960, Isaac met Pope John XXIII. Because of many Catholics not following the Roman Cate-chism's teaching, Isaac claimed, a "language of contempt" for the Jews had developed in some parts of the Church. The Jewish scholar wondered whether there was any hope that the fuller tradition could be recovered and healing be established. He recalled that the pope's statement to him was that "You have the right to more than hope."[21] He was sent to visit with Cardinal Bea. As Isaac said later, "This German Jesuit . . . showed himself completely *au fait* with the problems facing us. . . . In him I found a providential aid."[22]

Other Non-Christian Religions

As the relationship of the Church with the Jews has a history within the entire tradition, so do the relationships with other religions. Principally these later relations were worked out through the philosophical understanding of religion, along with certain cultural, social, and political engagements that occurred at various times in the Church's history.

From the time of Saint Paul's speech to the philosophers' meeting in the Areopagus in Athens and his preaching to the Gentiles, the Church has been engaged with members of other religions besides Judaism (see Acts 17:16–34). From the days when Greek converts to Christ began to employ their philosophy to inform others that Christianity was true and that its goal was to form people in virtue, the apologists argued that true religion benefited the whole of society.[23]

In *De civitate Dei* Augustine details the various polytheistic religions and finds that natural religion that is fully spiritual is religion in an authentic form. He also affirms that philosophical reason lifts humans beyond the materialism of deities who lead worshippers into various forms of corruption, which are given a transcendental and cultural legitimacy in the behaviors of the gods as told in the religious myths. The polytheism of the ancient world is countered by a move to philosophical reason that inculcates wisdom as love of transcendent truth and goodness as seen in the natural theology of Plato and Aristotle.

As theology established its relationship with the philosophical traditions, there opened up a way of understanding other religions in their accounts of a transcendent eternal being and the different visions of human release from suffering and evil. Thus Augustine's grasp of the significant difference in understanding religion that was formed in Platonic and Neoplatonic idealism was expanded in the writings of Thomas Aquinas, who places the activity of natural religion in the broad scheme of virtues. He speaks of religion as a "potential part of justice" and states that potential parts of a virtue "have something in common with the principal virtue; and . . . in some respect they fall short of the perfection of that virtue."[24] Regarding religion, which seeks "to render to God what is due him," it "is annexed to justice since . . . it consists in offering service and ceremonial rights or worship to 'some superior nature which men call divine.' "[25]

In another account of religion in the epistemic mode (truth) rather than that of virtue (good), Aquinas affirms that, given the expanse of wisdom that is available to men, they have the potential for knowing some truths about God through natural reason; moreover, this is especially important in Christian relations with "Mohameddans and pagans": "We must, therefore, have recourse to the natural reason, to which all men are forced to give their assent. However it is true, in divine matters the natural reason has its failings."[26] This perennial insight has been operative in the Church for centuries and has continually received reappropriations of its truthfulness. Thus Vatican

I affirms that "The same holy mother church holds and teaches that God, the source and end of all things, can be known with certainty from the consideration of created things, by the natural power of human reason: ever since the creation of the world, his invisible nature has been clearly perceived in the things that have been made. It was, however, pleasing to his wisdom and goodness to reveal himself and the eternal laws of his will to the human race by another, and that a supernatural way."[27]

In addition to the philosophical foundation for conversation about the truths of religion and faith, the Church at times, especially in the Middle Ages, sent out missionary ambassadors to religious and political leaders. In 1245 Pope Innocent IV sent two Franciscans, John of Plano Carpini (Perugia) and Lawrence of Portugal, with two official letters to the Emperor of the Tartars for the purpose of bringing an understanding of Christian faith and for learning about the Mongol peoples. Behind this was the pope's intention to seek a peaceful resolution to the conflicts and attacks on the Christians on the eastern borders of Europe and Russia.[28] The letter from Genghis Kahn to the pope, however, was not reassuring. In fact, it demanded the surrender of the Christian West; otherwise, there would be a brutal war.[29] The documentation of John of Plano Carpini is of considerable interest in its careful account of the land, customs, character, religion, political rule, military might and preparations for war, the nations that had already been conquered, as well as the protection and courtesy they received on their journey as they passed from tribe to tribe. The record showed that they both preached Christ to people on their trip and observed carefully the natural virtues and vices of the people.[30]

Nostra aetate retrieves the importance of the philosophical bonds for conversation on natural truths about God, and it integrates this work with the historical and dialogical dimension of the Middle Ages. Now, however, the conversation is placed in the broader contexts and understandings of differing cultures.

Concluding Reflections

A short time after the conclusion of the fourth and final session of the council, on December 8, 1965, Pope Paul VI created a series of dicasteries in the Roman Curia to carry forward the council's work into the life of the Church. In the case of the Jewish and non-Christian religions he established two commissions. Likewise, the constant attention of Pope John Paul II in fostering relations with the Jews, including his visit to the synagogue in Rome and to the Western Wall in Jerusalem, exhibits the fruits of the reappropriation and proper balance that *Nostra aetate* gives to the age-old tension of the continuity and discontinuity of the two religions.

Moreover, we cannot overlook the instructions in the *Catechism of the Catholic Church*, for they remind us that the Church did not first speak about the cause of Jesus' death in *Nostra aetate*, article 4. As the catechism notes, both the scriptures and tradition testify, and in 1566 the *Roman Catechism* of the Council of Trent explained that the principal agency of Jesus' death is "our sins."[31] By acknowledging the historical role of Jewish leaders and a crowd that had been assembled in calling for Jesus' death, it affirms the guilt of sinners in all times:

> We must regard as guilty all those who continue to relapse into their sins. Since our sins made the Lord Christ suffer the torment of the cross, those who plunge themselves into disorders and crimes crucify the Son of God anew in their hearts (for he is in them) and hold him up to contempt. And it can be seen that our crime in this case is greater in us than in the Jews. As for them, according to the witness of the Apostle, "None of the rulers of this age understood this; for if they had, they would not have crucified the Lord of glory." We, however, profess to know him. And when we deny him by our deeds, we in some way seem to lay violent hands on him.

The present situation for dialogue with other religions has advanced dramatically with the inclusion of genuine theological reflection, along with earlier cultural and catechetical concerns. Yet, these dialogues have a parallel in Saint Thomas Aquinas's realization in his *Summa contra Gentiles* of the need to prepare preachers to be able to speak with Muslims through reason insofar as they do not share a common revelation.

In his homily on the feast of Epiphany, January 6, 2006, Pope Benedict XVI offered theological meditation that integrates the Jewish covenant and religions of "the nations" with the mystery of Christ through an understanding of the journey of the magi to Bethlehem:

> At a superficial glance, God's faithfulness to Israel and his manifestation to the peoples could seem divergent aspects; they are actually two sides of the same coin. In fact, according to the Scriptures, it is precisely by remaining faithful to his Covenant of love with the people of Israel that God also reveals his glory to other peoples. Grace and fidelity (cf. Ps 89[88]: 2), "mercy and truth" (cf. Ps 85[84]: 11), are the content of God's glory, they are his "name," destined to be known and sanctified by people of every language and nation.
>
>   However, this "content" is inseparable from the "method" that God chose to reveal himself, that is, absolute fidelity to the Covenant that reaches its culmination in Christ. The Lord Jesus, at the same time and inseparably, is "a light revealing to the Gentiles the glory of your people Israel" (Lk 2:32), as the elderly Simeon was to exclaim, inspired by God, taking the Child in his arms when his parents presented him at the temple. The light that enlightens the peoples—the light of the Epiphany—shines out from the glory of Israel—the glory of the Messiah born, in accordance with the Scriptures, in Bethlehem, "the city of David" (cf. Lk 2:4).

NOTES

1. These others addressed the issues of holiness, as well as pastoral, educational practices, and institutions in the Church's self-constitution. They are the Decree on Bishops (*Christus Dominus*); Decree on Priestly Formation (*Optatam totius*); Decree on Appropriate Renewal of Religious Life (*Perfectae caritatis*); and the Declaration on Christian Education (*Gravissimum educationis*).

2. For these two principles see Augustin Cardinal Bea's commentary on *Nostra aetate*, published as *The Church and the Jewish People* (New York: Harper and Row, 1966), 45–46.

3. Ibid., 48.

4. Cf. J. Oscar Beozzo, "The External Climate," in *History of Vatican II*, vol. 1, ed. Giuseppe Alberigo and Joseph Komonchak (Maryknoll, N.Y.: Orbis), 388–98; also John M. Osterreicher, "Introduction and Commentary" (on *Nostra aetate*), in *Commentary on the Documents of Vatican II*, vol. 3, ed. Herbert Vorgrimler (New York: Herder and Herder, 1969), 41–46.

5. Quoted in Osterreicher, "Introduction and Commentary."

6. Augustin Cardinal Bea, *The Church and the Jewish People* (London: Geoffrey Chapman, 1966).

7. Ibid., 10.

8. The pope's baptismal name was Guiseppe.

9. Cardinal Bea noted that not all of the leaders of the patristic age always held this balance, and he named Ambrose and Chrysostom as examples.

10. *The Ante-Nicene Fathers*, vol. 1, *The Apostolic Fathers, Justin Martyr, Irenaeus*, ed. James Alexander Roberts and James Donaldson (Grand Rapids: Eerdmans, 1989).

11. Book XVI, 1.

12. Cf. *Adversus Judaeos*, 1, 2; 9, 14; *Contra Faustum Manichaeum*, 11.

13. Augustine, "In Answer to the Jews," in *Treatises on Marriage and Other Subjects* (New York: Fathers of the Church, 1955), 414.

14. Cf. Edward A. Synan, *The Popes and the Jews in the Middle Ages* (New York: Macmillan, 1965); Shlomo Simonsohn, ed., *The Apostolic See and the Jews*, vols. 1–3 (Toronto: Pontifical Institute of Mediaeval Studies, 1988–1991).

15. Norman Roth, "Bishops and Jews in the Middle Ages," *Catholic Historical Review* 80 (1994): 1.

16. Ibid., 2.

17. Norman Roth, "Christian-Jewish Relations," in *Medieval Jewish Civilization: An Encyclopedia*, ed. Norman Roth (New York: Routledge, 2003), 154.

18. The Patmos Circle was operative from 1915 to 1923. Among the major contributors to the conversation were Martin Buber, Karl Barth, and Gabriel Marcel.

19. Harold Stahmer, *"Speak That I May See Thee!" The Religious Significance of Language* (New York: Macmillan, 1968), 161.

20. The German bishops' conference initiated the opening of the archives of dioceses all over Germany and had the materials published in more than sixty-five volumes contained in the collection, which was titled *Veröffentlichungen der Kommission für Zeitgeschichte, Reihe A und B, Forshungen* (Paderborn, Germany: Ferdinand Schoningh).

21. Vigniani, "Jules Isaac e il dialogo ebraico-cristiano a venti anni della morte," *Vita Monastica* 166–67 (1986): 112.

22. Jean Tolat, *Juifs, mes frères* (Paris: 1962), 10.

23. Justin Martyr, *First Apology*, chaps. 19–27.

24. Saint Thomas Aquinas, *Summa theologiae*, II–II, q. 80, a. 1.

25. Ibid. Aquinas is quoting Cicero.

26. *Summa contra gentiles*, I, 2, 3.

27. *De fide*, 2, 13–14, in *Decrees of the Ecumenical Councils*, vol. 2, ed. Norman Tanner, S.J. (Washington D.C.: Georgetown University Press, 1990).

28. *The Mongol Mission: Narratives and Letters of the Franciscan Missionaries in Mongolia and China in the Thirteenth and Fourteenth Centuries*, ed. Christopher Dawson; trans. a nun of Stanbrook Abbey (New York: Sheed and Ward, 1955), 3–72.

29. Ibid., 85–86.

30. A more detailed and dialogical engagement with the Mongols and all of the nations and tribes between Constantinople and the Mongols is told in the account of *The Journey of Friar William of Rubruck to the Eastern Parts of the World 1253–55* (London: Hakluyt Society, 1900), 89–220.

31. *Catechism of the Catholic Church*, no. 598.

21

Anamnesis, Epiclesis, Prolepsis: Categories for Reading the Second Vatican Council as "Renewal within Tradition"

Geoffrey Wainwright

A major ecclesiastical council—particularly one that claims ecumenical status—may be approached in two ways, both of them essential to its understanding, interpretation, and evaluation; moreover, because the two approaches interact, they must not be separated. A council may be broadly considered as an event located within a preparatory history, where it then occurs in its own way and finally has effects in the ecclesial body. Alternatively, it may be more narrowly examined for its own deliverances, which are authoritatively promulgated in textual form. As a Protestant (and specifically a Methodist) sympathetic to viewing the Second Vatican Council as an instance of "renewal within tradition," I concentrate on two conciliar documents—the decree on ecumenism (*Unitatis redintegratio*) and the constitution on the sacred liturgy (*Sacrosanctum concilium*). These I set in relation to the two convergent "movements" in the history of the twentieth century that aimed at the recovery of full unity among Christians of institutionally divided traditions and the renewal of their intentionally common worship: the ecumenical movement and the liturgical movement. In the deepest sense, these two movements found their sources in apostolic and patristic Christianity (that is, in the common ground before the major divisions of the sixteenth, the eleventh, and even the fifth centuries), and in the longest run they sought to advance the Church—and indeed thereby the world—toward the consummation of God's Kingdom.

The documents of Vatican II attribute both movements to the contemporary work of the Holy Spirit under God's providential conduct of ecclesial and human history for the sake of the Gospel of Christ and the attainment of the divine purpose. *Unitatis redintegratio* observes in its opening paragraph:

> In recent times the Lord of the Ages has begun to bestow more generously upon divided Christians [*in christianos inter se disiunctos*] sorrow over their divisions and a longing for unity. Everywhere large numbers have felt the impulse of this grace, and among our separated brethren also [*inter fratres quoque nostros seiunctos*] there increases from day to day a movement, fostered by the grace of the Holy Spirit, for the restoration of unity among all Christians. Taking part in this movement, which is called ecumenical, are those who invoke the Triune God and confess Jesus as Lord and Savior. They do this not merely as individuals but also as members of the corporate groups in which they have heard the Gospel, and which each regards as his Church and indeed, God's. And yet, almost everyone, though in different ways, longs for the one visible Church of God, a Church truly universal and sent forth to the whole world that the world may be converted to the Gospel and so be saved, to the glory of God. (*UR* 1)[1]

For its part, the constitution on the liturgy declared that "zeal for the promotion and restoration of the liturgy is rightly held to be a sign of the providential dispositions of God in our time, a movement of the Holy Spirit in his Church. It is today a distinguishing mark of the life of the Church, and, indeed, of the whole tenor of contemporary religious thought and action" (*SC* 43).

While having the Catholic Church principally in view, that very first document to be promulgated from the council saw liturgical renewal as serving causes that were widely shared in the ecumenical movement: "This sacred council has several aims in view: it desires to impart an ever increasing vigor to the Christian life of the faithful; to adapt better to the needs of our times those institutions that are subject to change; to foster whatever can promote union among all who believe in Christ; to strengthen whatever can help to call all people into the fold of the Church. Accordingly, the council sees particularly cogent reasons for undertaking the reform and promotion of the liturgy" (*SC* 1).

The Liturgical Movement

We may begin, as the council itself did, with the liturgy. In the broader liturgical movement of the twentieth century, several initiatives from within the Catholic Church were welcomed within other ecclesial communities that were also seeking a pastoral reinvigoration of worship after scriptural and patristic patterns. Pius X's encouragement of more frequent communion among Catholics at Mass was matched by a move among some Reformation churches to more frequent celebrations of the Lord's Supper after a lack of willing communicants—continued from medieval times—had for four centuries reduced their regular Sunday service to the verbal form of prayers, psalmody, and proclamation. Liturgical historians in all camps fixed on Justin Martyr's outline from mid-second-century Rome as an ideal pattern of community worship on the Lord's day:

> The reading of the Scriptures (Old and New Testaments)
> The exposition of the readings
> The prayers of intercession
> The bringing of the bread and wine to the presiding minister
> The Eucharistic prayer spoken by the presider and sealed by the people's amen
> The breaking of the bread
> The sharing of the elements over which thanks have been given.[2]

Liturgical theologians, drawing on patristic categories, made the Paschal mystery central to the worship of the Church,[3] naturally locating Christ's death and resurrection in the entire story of salvation—itself understood in Trinitarian terms.[4]

The conciliar constitution on the liturgy declared at the start that, after the Old Testament "prelude," Christ achieved his work of "redeeming mankind and giving perfect glory to God . . . principally by the paschal mystery of his blessed passion, resurrection from the dead, and glorious ascension, where 'dying, he destroyed our death, and rising, restored our life'" (*SC* 5, quoting the Easter Preface of the Roman Missal). The "Christological concentration" of the liturgy is encoded by the seventh chapter of *Sacrosanctum concilium* in terms of the multiform presence of Christ in the liturgical celebrations of the Church: In the Mass "not only in the person of his minister . . . but especially in the Eucharistic species"; "in the sacraments, so that when anybody baptizes it is really Christ himself who baptizes" (cf. Augustine, *Tract. in Joan.* VI.1, 7); "in his word, since it is he himself who speaks when the Holy Scriptures are read in the Church"; and "when the Church prays and sings," according to the promise of Matthew 18:20. The presence and work of Christ are already set in a fully Trinitarian framework by the immediately preceding chapter of the same constitution:

> Just as Christ was sent by the Father, so also he sent the apostles, filled with the Holy Spirit. This he did so that they might preach the Gospel to every creature [cf. Mark 16:15] and proclaim that the Son of God by his death and resurrection had freed us from the power of Satan [cf. Acts 26:18] and from death, and brought us into the Kingdom of his Father. But he also willed that the work of salvation which they preached should be set in train through the sacrifice and sacraments, around which the entire liturgical life revolves. Thus by Baptism men are grafted into the paschal mystery of Christ; they die with him, are buried with him, and rise with him [cf. Rom 6:4; Eph 2:6; Col 3:1; 2 Tim 2:11]. They receive the Spirit of adoption as sons "in which we cry, Abba, Father" (Rom 8:15) and thus become true worshipers such as the Father seeks [cf. Jn 4:23]. In like manner as often as they eat the Supper of the Lord they proclaim the death of the Lord until he comes [cf. 1 Cor 11:26]. . . . From that time [of the apostles] onward the Church

has never failed to come together to celebrate the paschal mystery, reading those things "which were in all the Scriptures concerning him" (Lk 24:27), celebrating the Eucharist in which "the victory and triumph of his death are again made present" [Council of Trent, sess. 23: *Decree on the Holy Eucharist*, 5], and at the same time "giving thanks to God for his inexpressible gift" (2 Cor 9:15) in Christ Jesus, "in praise of his glory" (Eph 1:12) through the power of the Holy Spirit. (*SC* 6)

The eighth chapter of *Sacrosanctum concilium* then opens up the eschatological perspective: "In the earthly liturgy we take part in a foretaste of that heavenly liturgy which is celebrated in the Holy City of Jerusalem toward which we journey as pilgrims.... With all the warriors of the heavenly army we sing a hymn of glory to the Lord; venerating the memory of the saints, we hope for some part and fellowship with them; we eagerly await the Savior, Our Lord Jesus Christ, until he our life shall appear and we too shall appear with him in glory [cf. Phil 3:20; Col 3:4]."

This whole picture of the place of the liturgy within the Trinitarian history of salvation is summarized by liturgiologists in the technical terms of "anamnesis," "epiclesis," and "prolepsis." In the first two sections of this chapter I keep returning to those categories of "remembrance" of the past, "invocation" in the present, and "anticipation" of the future; they will help prepare for a more systematic account of the notion and reality of "renewal within tradition," which I discuss in the third section.

The revisions of the liturgical books undertaken by order of the Second Vatican Council are imbued with the theme of the Paschal mystery, and the rites are "shaped" correspondingly.[5] This may be illustrated, first, from the structure of the Eucharist in its fullness as both word and sacrament,[6] and the ecumenical importance of a common "return to the sources" does not go unnoticed. As to the service of the word:

- "The treasures of the Bible are to be opened up more lavishly so that a richer fare may be provided for the faithful at the table of God's word. In this a more representative part of the sacred scriptures will be read in the course of a prescribed number of years" (*SC* 51; cf. 35 [i]). It was the Church of South India—which brought Anglicans, Methodists, Presbyterians, and Congregationalists together in an organic union (1947)—that pioneered the recovery of an Old Testament reading to join Epistle and Gospel. The postconciliar Order of Readings for Mass (1969) connected the testaments typologically in order to bring out all that was "written in the Law, the Prophets, and the Psalms" concerning Christ (cf. Lk 24:25–27, 32, 44–46).[7] Thus the liturgical reading of the Scriptures—both "the writings of the prophets" and "the records of the apostles," as in Justin's day—constitutes an anamnesis of the decisive events in the story of revelation and redemption.
- "By means of the homily the mysteries of the faith and the guiding principles of the Christian life are expounded from the sacred text during

the course of the liturgical year. The homily, therefore, is to be highly esteemed as part of the liturgy itself" (SC 52). There is an ecumenical importance in the conciliar declaration that "the ministry of preaching is to be fulfilled most faithfully and carefully . . . [for] the sermon . . . is the proclamation of God's wonderful works in the history of salvation, which is the mystery of Christ ever made present and active in us" (SC 35 [ii]). Protestants have always stressed the sermon and viewed it as an "epicletic" moment in which the Holy Spirit may bring redeeming and sanctifying grace into the present life of the gathered congregation.

- "The 'common prayer' or 'prayer of the faithful' is to be restored after the gospel and homily. . . . By this prayer in which the people are to take part, intercession will be made for holy Church, for the civil authorities, for those oppressed by various needs, for all mankind, and for the salvation of the entire world [cf. 1 Tim 2:1–6]" (SC 53). By praying comprehensively for the furtherance of all that makes for God's Kingdom and the removal of all that obstructs it, intercession plays a "proleptic" role in the movement of history towards its divinely willed end.

As to the service of the sacrament, one of the most remarkable features of liturgical reform and recovery across the ecumenical board in the years surrounding Vatican II has been the composition of anaphoras, or Eucharistic prayers—often modeled on that found in the ancient church order associated with *The Apostolic Tradition of Hippolytus* or following the Syro-Antiochene pattern, which dates back to at least the fourth century. Examples are, respectively, the second and fourth Eucharistic prayers of the *Ordo Missae* of 1969. Rehearsing doxologically the decisive history of salvation, such prayers reach their high point in the recital of the Last Supper, at which Christ announced his impending sacrifice; and they immediately make the commanded anamnesis of his redemptive work (summed up in an acclamation such as "Christ has died, Christ is risen, Christ will come again"). The Holy Spirit is invoked upon the offerings, the people, and their actions—for the sake of their communion and unity. The anaphora passes by way of a mention of the saints into a concluding prospect of the glory of God's final Kingdom, with the heavenly banquet now to be sacramentally anticipated.[8]

The other most striking achievement of Vatican II's liturgical teaching and the work it set in motion falls in the realm of Christian initiation, and again credit is due to the more comprehensive liturgical movement. Liturgical scholars had brought to the fore—from the evidence of third-, fourth-, and fifth-century texts—the processes by which candidates were prepared for baptism and received into the sacramental community. Against that background the council decreed that

> the catechumenate for adults, comprising several distinct steps, is to
> be restored and brought into use at the discretion of the local ordinary.
> By this means the time of the catechumenate, which is intended as a
> period of suitable instruction, may be sanctified by sacred rites to be
> celebrated at successive intervals of time. (SC 64)

> Both rites for the baptism of adults are to be revised, not only the
> simpler rite but also, taking into consideration the restored catechu-
> menate, the more solemn rite. A special Mass "For the conferring of
> Baptism" is to be inserted into the Roman Missal. (SC 66)

The *Rite for the Christian Initiation of Adults* (RCIA; 1972) is indebted to historical and pastoral scholarship of a wide ecumenical range. In turn, the
Catholic *RCIA* has been imitated and adapted at the local level among Protestants. Relatedly, others have also been inspired by postconciliar revisions in
the Catholic rites that followed the instruction to "make more use of the baptismal features which are proper to the Lenten liturgy," some of which were
"restored" from "earlier tradition" (SC 109). The initiatory process finds its
normal climax at Easter (RCIA, 7–8, 21–40), the most solemn annual celebration of the Paschal mystery (SC 102). Orders for the Easter vigil—which
allow all of the faithful to renew their participation in the baptismal covenant—
have been officially provided in the new service books of several denominations.
Thus the churches find similar ways of engaging in the tasks of evangelization
and reevangelization in face of the common challenges posed by cultural secularization, neopaganism, and relativism.[9]

One final theme from *Sacrosanctum concilium* is that of language. In articles 36, 54, and 63 the constitution on the liturgy gave guarded permission or
prudent encouragement to the use of the vernacular. This was quickly taken
up, especially in the linguistic areas of the West. However, one may wonder
whether the circumstances were favorable to such rapid work of translation as
was undertaken for the provision of new service books. The Catholic Church,
for its own part, had in recent centuries only limited experience of liturgical
worship in the vernacular and hence a rather weak "linguistic sense" in that
connection. In the culture at large, social and ideological secularization made
contemporary language a somewhat weak vehicle to carry the transcendent
dimensions of the faith. These factors also affected the otherwise welcome
enterprise of establishing ecumenically agreed versions of items commonly
used in the liturgies of the churches. Concerns over these matters were increasingly felt in Rome in the last decade of the twentieth century, and corrective steps taken in the first decade of the twentieth.[10]

The Ecumenical Movement

The modern ecumenical movement began in the late nineteenth and early
twentieth centuries chiefly among the Protestant churches (including Anglican and Methodist), with some guarded interest on the part of the Orthodox; its
three strands concerned themselves with Faith and Order, Life and Work, and
Mission and Evangelism. In 1928, by his encyclical *Mortalium animos* Pius XI
forbade Roman Catholics to participate in the nascent movement toward the
recovery of Christian unity—for fear of doctrinal and ecclesial indifferentism.
Between the 1930s and the 1950s a more positive attitude toward ecumenism

developed within Catholicism, thanks to a number of factors: the work of Catholic pioneers such as Paul Couturier (with his advocacy of prayer for unity "as and how Christ wills") and Yves Congar (with his book *Chrétiens désunis*, 1937); a growing convergence of scholarly work in the areas of Bible and patristics; some shared aims in the domain of liturgy; pastoral collabora- tion in the circumstances of the Second World War; common cultural chal- lenges in a rapidly changing postwar world.[11] By 1959—but still surprisingly— Pope John XXIII was able to call an "ecumenical" council (in the Roman sense), whose purview would include in one way or another "the promotion of Christian unity" (and would entail a secretariat established for the purpose); and, in the broader sense of the term, "ecumenical" observers would partici- pate in and around the work of the council in its four sessions between 1962 and 1965.

The underlying question in ecumenism is that of ecclesiology or the proper identification of the Church and its unity. Such has been the case throughout the history of Christianity. The matter can be put in terms of our triad: anamnesis, epiclesis, and prolepsis. The decisive, original foundation of the Church by Christ was as *one* Church ("my Church," Mt 16:18): That is the unrepeated event to be "remembered." The unity of his disciples and those who should come to faith through their word was a necessary object of Christ's *prayer* ("that they all may be one," Jn 17:21): The Holy Spirit is fittingly "invoked" to ensure that unity (cf. Jn 20:22f.; 1 Cor 12:3–13; Eph 2:18; 4:3–5). An outcome of the unity and unified witness of Christ's followers was to be the *conversion of the world* to belief in Christ's mission from the Father ("that the world may believe—and know—that thou hast sent me," Jn 17:21–23): The achievement of the divine Kingdom is thus "anticipated." In sad and sinful reality, however, the unity of Christ's followers has from apostolic times been threatened (by controversy) and even disrupted (by heresy and schism), as the New Testament epistles in particular demonstrate (for example, 1 Cor 1:10–13; 10:17–19; 15:1ff.; 2 Pet 2:1–2; 1 Jn 2:18–27; 4:1–6). The recurrent question has therefore been: Where are we to find the one Church, united in truth and love? How are we to identify it?

In the third century, Cyprian of Carthage pictured the Church as the ark of salvation, from which heretics and schismatics simply fell off, their religious rites then counting for nothing since their communities lacked the Holy Spirit. When persons putatively baptized by the Novatianists sought admission to the true Church, they were to receive baptism at Catholic hands (which was not *re*baptism). Stephen of Rome, however, held that penance sufficed for ad- mission to the Church in such cases; he was interpreted by the North African Catholics to hold that "whoever is baptized in the name of Christ, no matter where, immediately obtains the grace of Christ." However, one may also argue that he was presaging Saint Augustine's position that "whether the minister be Peter, Paul, or Judas, it is Christ who baptizes"—so that baptism administered among the Donatists was not to be "repeated"; it was (in later terminology) "valid," although it was not "efficacious" until persons so baptized were rec- onciled to the Catholic Church.[12]

Pope Boniface VIII, in the ecclesiastical and political circumstances of the early fourteenth century, declared it "absolutely necessary to the salvation of every human creature that he be subject to the Roman pontiff" (*Unam sanctam* [1302]). In its seventh session (March 1547), the Council of Trent anathematized anyone who denied that "true" baptism was given by heretics when the rite was administered with water in the name of the Trinity and "with the intention of doing what the Church does" (cf. canons 2 and 4 on baptism), but the ecclesial or salvific quality of such acts performed outside canonical bounds appeared questionable in light of the practice of "conditional baptism" toward those who subsequently sought admission to the Catholic Church. By the late nineteenth and early twentieth centuries, however, hints were emerging of an increasingly charitable interpretation of the "truth" of baptism administered in other communities: Other Christians can be called "fratres," albeit "dissidentes," and, following a long (if intermittent) custom, the Eastern churches—with their succession of bishops—were allowed to be designated precisely as "churches."[13]

Such, in minimal detail, is the historical background against which the Second Vatican Council must be examined for continuity and change in its ecclesiological teaching under the aspect of baptism and other rites performed in communities that make ecclesial claims for themselves without being included in the Catholic Church.

The most detailed conciliar text on this matter is the third chapter of the Decree on Ecumenism, *Unitatis redintegratio*:

> In this one and only Church of God from its very beginnings there arose certain rifts [cf. 1 Cor 11:18–19; Gal 1:6–9; 1 Jn 2:18–19], which the Apostle strongly censures as damnable [cf. 1 Cor 1:11ff.; 11:22]. But in subsequent centuries more serious dissensions appeared and large communities became separated from full communion with the Catholic Church—for which, often enough, men of both sides were to blame. However, one cannot charge with the sin of separation those who at present are born into these communities and in them are brought up in the faith of Christ, and the Catholic Church accepts them with respect and affection as brothers. For men who believe in Christ and have been properly baptized are put in some, though imperfect, communion with the Catholic Church. Without doubt, the differences that exist in varying degrees between them and the Catholic Church—whether in doctrine and sometimes in discipline, or concerning the structure of the Church—do indeed create many obstacles, sometimes serious ones, to full ecclesiastical communion. The ecumenical movement is striving to overcome these obstacles. But even in spite of them it remains true that all who have been justified by faith in baptism are incorporated into Christ [cf. Council of Florence, Session 8 (1439), the decree *Exultate Deo*]; they therefore have a right to be called Christians, and with good reason are accepted as brothers by the children of the Catholic Church [cf. Saint Augustine, *In Ps. 32, Enarr. II, 29* (PL 36: 299)].

Moreover, some, even very many, of the most significant elements and endowments which together go to build up and give life to the Church itself, can exist outside the visible boundaries [*visibilia saepta*; cf. *LG* 8: *compages visibilis*] of the Catholic Church.[14]

Further, such Christians are viewed not simply as individuals but as located in bodies that "carry out many sacred actions of the Christian religion": "In ways that vary according to the condition of each church or community, these most certainly can truly engender a life of grace, and, one must say, can aptly give access to the communion of salvation. It follows that the separated churches and communities as such, though we believe they suffer from the defects already mentioned, have been by no means deprived of significance and importance in the mystery of salvation. For the Spirit of Christ has not refrained from using them as means of salvation which derive their efficacy from the very fullness of grace and truth entrusted to the Catholic Church."[15]

The interesting move here, if move it be, is to an ecclesiology that allows, on a basis of *baptism* and the *faith* that it signifies, for *degrees of communion* with the Catholic Church.[16] The "sole Church of Christ," the dogmatic constitution *Lumen gentium* firmly declares, "subsists in the Catholic Church, which is governed by the successor of Peter and by the bishops in communion with him" (*LG* 8; cf. *UR* 2–3). Specifically, with regard to unity as well as unicity, "The unity of the one and only Church, which Christ bestowed on his Church from the beginning, subsists in the Catholic Church, we believe, as something she can never lose, and we hope that it will continue to increase until the end of time" (*UR* 4). Within the Catholic Church is the "fullness" of communion: "It is through the faithful preaching of the Gospel by the Apostles and their successors—the bishops with Peter's successor at their head—through their administering the sacraments, and through their governing in love, that Jesus Christ wishes his people to increase, under the action of the Holy Spirit; and he perfects its fellowship in unity: in the confession of one faith, in the common celebration of divine worship, and in the fraternal harmony of the family of God" (*UR* 2). The separated brethren, whether individually or communally, "are not blessed with that unity which Christ wished to bestow on all those to whom he has given new birth into one body, and whom he has quickened to newness of life—that unity which the Holy Scriptures and the ancient Tradition of the Church proclaim." Nevertheless, they enjoy a real, if "imperfect," communion with the Catholic Church. From the side of the separated brethren, one may wonder whether both the unity and the catholicity of the Catholic Church might not be increased by their fuller participation. I in fact suggest that as an ecumenical possibility—encouraged by what *Unitatis redintegratio* says at the very end of chapter 4, at least in the matter of catholicity.

As a systematic theological background to this "communion ecclesiology" stands the notion of the sacramentality of the Church as a whole in its location "between" Christ and the particular sacraments. The notion of "the Church as sacrament" merits, in fact, a little exploration for our present purposes as we seek to read the Second Vatican Council as "renewal within tradition"—and that with ecumenical intent. Saint Augustine, in conformity with the New Testament's linguistic use of *mysterium Dei*, declared that "the sacrament of God is none other than Christ."[17] Martin Luther had argued (polemically) that "the Sacred Scriptures have a single sacrament, which is Christ the Lord himself": "If I wanted to speak according to scriptural usage, I would have but one sacrament, and three sacramental signs."[18] By the mid-twentieth century a number of perfectly respectable Catholic theologians were finding at least analogical continuities in a line from Christ himself through the Church to the particular sacraments (and in reverse). In his book *Catholicisme* (1938), Henri de Lubac claimed that "if Jesus Christ is the sacrament of God, the Church is for us the sacrament of Christ."[19] This basic insight was expanded upon by Otto Semmelroth in *Die Kirche als Ursakrament* (1953); Edward Schillebeeckx, *Christus—Sacrament van de Godsontmoeting* (1958); and Karl Rahner, *Kirche und Sakramente* (1960).[20]

The sacramentality of the Church as a major ecclesiological category appears at the very beginning of the dogmatic constitution *Lumen gentium*:

> Christ is the light of the nations, and it is, accordingly, the heartfelt desire of this sacred council, being gathered together in the Holy Spirit, that, by proclaiming his Gospel to every creature (cf. Mark 16:15), it may bring to all men that light of Christ which shines out visibly from the Church. Since the Church, in Christ, is, as it were, a sacrament—a sign and instrument, that is, of communion with God and of unity among all humankind—she here purposes, for the benefit of the faithful and of the whole world, to set forth, as clearly as possible, and in the tradition laid down by earlier councils, her own nature and universal mission. (*LG* 1)

After that initial "lexical" note—"veluti sacramentum seu signum et instrumentum"—the council documents go on to use the sacramental designation of the Church rather readily: *Lumen gentium*, articles 9, 48, 59; *Gaudium et spes*, articles 42, 45; *Ad gentes*, articles 1, 5.[21]

Thus emboldened, we may further employ the notion of Church as sacrament to expound the conciliar ecclesiology, in particular according to our heuristic categories of anamnesis, epiclesis, and prolepsis and show its ecumenical fruitfulness by drawing on the long-standing dialogue—dating from immediately after the Second Vatican Council—between the Roman Catholic Church and the World Methodist Council. Concisely, "Christ the Lord founded one Church and one Church only" (*UR* 1): That is the decisive event, once accomplished and ever to be "remembered" (anamnesis) as the community gathers for worship—notably in "the wonderful sacrament of the Eucharist by which the unity of the Church is both signified and brought about" (*UR* 2; cf. *SC* 47). Again, "It is the Holy Spirit, dwelling in those who believe and pervading and ruling over the entire Church, who brings about that wonderful communion of the faithful and joins them together so intimately in Christ that he is the principle of the Church's unity" (*UR* 2; cf. *SC* 2, and 5 *ad finem*): That is what renders the "invocation" (epiclesis) of the Spirit ecclesiologically apt at every present moment. Third, "What has revealed the love among us is that the only begotten Son of God has been sent by the Father into the world, so that, being made man, he might by his redemption of the entire human race give new life to it and unify it. . . . The Church, then, God's only flock, like a standard lifted on high for the nations to see, ministers the Gospel of peace to all mankind, as it makes its pilgrim way in hope toward its goal, the fatherland above" (*UR* 2; cf. *SC* 2). That is the Church's life and witness in "anticipation" (prolepsis) of the final and universal Kingdom of God. In Trinitarian summary, urging the faithful to ecumenical activity that is "loyal to the truth we have received from the Apostles and the Fathers, and in harmony with the faith which the Catholic Church has always professed, and at the same time tending toward that fullness in which our Lord wants his Body to grow in the course of time," the council "places its hope entirely in the prayer of Christ for the Church, in the love of the Father for us, and in the power of the Holy Spirit" (*UR* 24).

Now comes our example from the dialogue between the World Methodist Council and the Roman Catholic Church. From its tentatively titled *Towards a Statement on the Church* (Nairobi, 1986), where the formulation of the goal is found for the first time in terms of "full communion in faith, mission, and sacramental life," the Methodist/Catholic dialogue proceeded in a strongly Trinitarian and increasingly sacramental mode to a fuller ecclesiology in *The Gift Given You in Christ: Catholics and Methodists Reflect Further on the Church* (Seoul, 2006).[22]

For our present purposes, particular interest resides in the Joint Commission's theological summary—in paragraph 137 of the Seoul report—of the potential benefits of reconciliation between Methodists and Catholics as "the mutual enhancement of each other's oneness, holiness, catholicity and apostolicity":

a. In an important sense, two uniting churches give to one another the gift of *unity*. In this case, two different aspects of unity would be valuably combined, one more structural and historical, the other more spiritual and eschatological. The Catholic Church believes that the unity Christ bestowed on his Church from the beginning "subsists in the Catholic Church" (*UR* 4; cf. *Ut unum sint*, 11), particularly because of the continuance in it of the Petrine ministry. In a sense, therefore, through this essential sign of visible unity, the Catholic Church can give the gift of unity to the Methodist Church. On the other hand, Methodists understand unity primarily as the spiritual unity of the body of Christ, which Christians must strive to make more visible in the world but which will remain imperfectly realized until the last day. This eschatological emphasis is important and reminds Catholics that unity is also a *vocation* that must inspire and challenge us each day towards an ever greater attainment of it.

b. The emphasis upon *holiness* which Methodists and Catholics already share means that we would give each other great solidarity and encouragement in our living of this mark of the Church and in our striving for an ever fuller realization of it. We would also have the joy of sharing the inspiring example of our saints.

c. Christian divisions prevent the Church from realizing "the fullness of *catholicity* proper to her" (*UR* 4; emphasis added). The firm commitment of Methodists and Catholics to ecumenism is indicative of our shared desire for ever greater catholicity, and that commitment and desire would be further strengthened by our unity. In accordance with its twofold meaning, the catholicity both of Catholics and also of Methodists would be enhanced by our unity: by an increased depth and balance of belief and by an increased vigor and scope of outreach.

d. Methodists can receive a vital sign of *apostolicity* from Catholics, namely, the apostolic succession of bishops. However, Catholics have much to gain from the commitment to apostolic mission, which is an explicit part of Methodist identity.

Within such a perspective of divine gift and human responsibility, of divine call and active human reception (and now I speak as an individual theologian rather than as cochairman of the commission), one may wonder whether the Catholic Church, as well as Methodism, might allow itself to be "completed," if not indeed "corrected." While "the Church is held, as a matter of faith, to be unfailingly holy," this holiness has to be addressed to all the faithful as a "call" (*LG* 39). Moreover, the Church as such, being "at once holy and in need of purification, follows constantly the path of penance and renewal [*sancta simul et semper purificanda, poenitentiam et renovationem continuo prosequitur*]" (ibid., 8; cf. *UR* 4: "ut ecclesia . . . de die in diem mundetur et renovetur"). Regarding catholicity, the conciliar decree on ecumenism declares that "the divisions among Christians prevent the Church from realizing in practice the fullness of catholicity proper to her in those of her sons and daughters who, though joined to her by baptism, are yet separated from full communion with her. Furthermore, the Church herself finds it more difficult to express in actual life her full catholicity in every respect" (*UR* 4: *Immo et pro ipsa ecclesia difficilius fit plenitudinem catholicitatis sub omni respectu in ipsa vitae realitate exprimere*). If the note of catholicity may receive less than full (dare one say?) "embodiment" in a Catholic Church, might one not say the same of unity?[23]

My intention in posing those questions is not to dismiss unity, any more than holiness or catholicity, into invisibility or postpone it into an indefinite future (such as the Congregation for the Doctrine of the Faith repeatedly warned against in *Mysterium Ecclesiae*, 1; and in *Dominus Iesus*, 17). Rather, I wish to suggest that a genuinely eschatological tension allows all of the "notes" of the Church to be confessed in a dynamic sense that fosters their perfect and tangible attainment, albeit within the limits of a pilgrim existence. In that way, other authentically Trinitarian churches and ecclesial communities—marked by the Gospel, the scriptures, baptism, the Lord's Supper, and active faith (cf. *UR* 20–23)—could be regarded as *part of* the "one holy catholic Church" while praying and working toward the fullness that would come to them—and to the

Roman Church—on the establishment of a more perfect communion with the apostolic Petrine See in structures that still demand elaboration. (I discuss the matter of a "universal ministry of unity" in the final section of this chapter.)

A Systematic Framework

In a nutshell, our categories of "anamnesis," "epiclesis," and "prolepsis"—in terms of which we have read the Second Vatican Council—correspond to the constancy of the character, action, and purpose of the Triune God revealed and played out in the history of salvation as this is so beautifully unfolded in, for instance, the second, third, and fourth chapters of *Lumen gentium*. That is the framework within which one may appropriately understand the notion and reality of "renewal within tradition." The time has now come to examine what light the documents of Vatican II shed on that exact notion and perhaps even to ask (in ecumenical friendship) how the council may have contributed to such a reality—to the benefit of relations between the Catholic Church and other communities with ecclesial claims.

What does Vatican II have to say about the principles, needs, and possibilities for renewal? A note is first needed about the word "new." In New Testament usage, the word "kainos" carries a far more significant sense than mere "novelty."[24] In connection with Christ and his work of redemption, the sacred texts speak of "the new covenant" (2 Cor 3:6; Heb 9:15), a "new commandment" (Jn 13:34), a "new man" (Eph 2:15; 4:24; Col 3:10) who walks in "newness of life" (Rom 6:4; cf. 7:6; 2 Cor 4:16), a "new creature" (2 Cor 5:15; Gal 6:15; cf. Titus 3:5), a "new name" (Rev 2:17; 3:12), a "new Jerusalem" (Rev 3:12; 21:2) where a "new song" is sung (Rev 5:9; 14:3), and indeed a "new heaven and a new earth" (Rev 21:1). All of this is an eschatological newness because Christ is "the last Adam" (1 Cor 15:45; cf. Rom 5:12–21), and therewith "the last days" have already dawned (Heb 1:2) and are upon us (Acts 2:17). At the institution of the Eucharist, Christ designates the cup of wine as "the new covenant in my blood" (1 Cor 11:25; cf. Mt 26:28; Mk 14:24; Lk 22:20); furthermore, borrowing from Hebrews 13:20 [*en haimati diathêkês aiôniou*], the Roman canon names it "the cup of my blood, the blood of the new and everlasting covenant [*novi et aeterni testamenti*]."

That is the semantic field—grounded in salvation history—in which the Second Vatican Council can speak of "renewal" in the Church, whether with reference to the liturgy or to unity. *Lumen gentium* saw the covenant with Israel as a preparation and prefiguration of "the new and perfect covenant which was to be ratified in Christ" (*LG* 9: *foederis illius novi et perfecti, in Christo feriendi*). *Dei verbum* declared that "the Christian economy, since it is the new and definitive covenant, will never pass away" (*DV* 4: *Oeconomia ergo christiana, utpote foedus novum et definitivum, nunquam praeteribit*). Such eschatological newness does not allow for repetition, but it does allow for renewal and may even, while the Church remains in its pilgrim phase, require it.[25] That is why the two principal documents of our investigation—*Sacrosanctum concilium* and

Unitatis redintegratio—can use the language of revision, restoration, and even reform[ation]. The location for all that is positive in these matters is the tradition of the Church, as comprehensively understood in *Dei verbum*:

> What was handed on by the apostles comprises everything that serves to make the People of God live their lives in holiness and increase their faith. In this way the Church, in her doctrine, life and worship, perpetuates and transmits to every generation all that she herself is, all that she believes.
>
> The Tradition that comes from the apostles makes progress (*proficit*) in the Church, with the help of the Holy Spirit. . . . The sayings of the Holy Fathers are a witness to the life-giving presence of this Tradition, showing how its riches are poured out in the practice and life of the Church, in her belief and her prayer. By means of the same Tradition the full canon of the sacred books is known to the Church and the Holy Scriptures themselves are more thoroughly understood and constantly actualized in the Church. Thus God, who spoke in the past, continues to converse with the spouse of his beloved Son. And the Holy Spirit, through whom the living voice of the Gospel rings out in the Church—and through her in the world—leads believers to the full truth, and makes the Word of Christ dwell in them in all its richness [cf. Col. 3:16]. (*DV* 8)

The conciliar constitution on the liturgy places its program under "the renewal of the covenant between the Lord and men in the Eucharist," from which "grace is poured forth upon us as from a fountain" (*SC* 10). On this principle, liturgical revision is possible and indeed necessary but only in accord with the divine institution and in organic continuity with sound tradition:

> In order that the Christian people may more certainly derive an abundance of graces from the sacred liturgy, holy Mother Church desires to undertake with great care a general restoration [*instauratio*] of the liturgy itself. For the liturgy is made up of unchangeable elements divinely instituted, and of elements subject to change. These latter not only may be changed but ought to be changed with the passage of time, if they have suffered from the intrusion of anything out of harmony with the inner nature of the liturgy or have become less suitable. In this restoration both texts and rites should be drawn up so as to express more clearly the holy things which they signify. The Christian people, as far as is possible, should be able to understand them with ease and take part in them fully, actively, and as a community. (*SC* 21)

> In order that sound tradition be retained, and yet the way remain open to legitimate progress [*ut sana traditio retineatur et tamen via legitimae progressioni aperiatur*], a careful investigation—theological, historical, and pastoral—should always be made into each part of the liturgy which is to be revised. Furthermore the general laws governing the

structure and meaning of the liturgy must be studied in conjunction with the experience derived from recent liturgical reforms and from the indults granted to various places. Finally, there should be no innovations [*innovationes*] unless the good of the Church genuinely and certainly requires them, and care must be taken that any new forms [*novae formae*] should in some way grow organically from forms already existing. (*SC* 23)

Article 50 of the constitution specifies the kinds of revision to be undertaken in the liturgy of the Mass:

The rite of the Mass is to be revised [*recognascatur*] in such a way that the intrinsic nature and purpose of its several parts, as well as the connection between them, may be more clearly manifested, and that devout and active participation by the faithful may be more easily achieved. For this purpose the rites are to be simplified, due care being taken to preserve their substance [*probe servata eorum substantia*]. Parts which with the passage of time came to be duplicated, or were added with little advantage, are to be omitted. Other parts which suffered loss through accidents of history are to be restored [*restituantur*], as may seem useful or necessary, in accordance with the shape they took in the days of the holy Fathers. (*SC* 50)

With regard to the liturgical calendar, "The liturgical year is to be so revised that the traditional customs and usages of the sacred seasons are preserved or restored to suit the conditions of modern times. Their specific character is to be retained so that they may duly nourish the piety of the faithful who celebrate the mysteries of Christian redemption and, above all, the paschal mystery" (*SC* 107).

Given the interplay between the "lex orandi" and the "lex credendi," matters of doctrine are, of course, involved in liturgical "renewal";[26] they come even more to the fore in the area of ecumenism since fundamental ecclesiology is there at stake. *Unitatis redintegratio* must also, therefore, be examined for what it says about the principles, possibilities, and needs of renewal within tradition. A likely guideline is provided by the concise formulation of Vincent of Lérins: "non nova, sed nove"—not new things, but in new ways. That would match what Pope John XXIII said in his address *Gaudet Mater Ecclesia* at the opening of the Second Vatican Council on October 11, 1962.[27] The authentic teaching of the Church, constantly transmitted by the Fathers and by ancient and modern theologians as far as the Council of Trent and the First Vatican Council, now needed to be presented to the world in contemporary forms of thought and speech: "The substance of the ancient doctrine—the deposit of faith—is one thing," said the pope, "and the language in which it is presented is another."[28]

The decree on ecumenism recognizes that there is "a task of renewal and reform" (*opus renovationis necnon reformationis*) to be accomplished in "faithfulness to Christ's will for the Church" (*UR* 4). Those terms are then repeatedly used in reference to the "movement toward unity" in its full ecumenical dimensions:

> Every renewal of the Church [*omnis renovatio ecclesiae*] essentially consists in an increase of fidelity to her own calling. Undoubtedly this explains the dynamism of the movement toward unity.
>
> Christ summons the Church, as she goes her pilgrim way, to that continual reformation of which she always has need, insofar as she is an institution of men here on earth [*ad hanc perennem reformationem qua ipsa, qua humanum terrenumque institutum, perpetuo indiget*]. Consequently, if, in various times and circumstances, there have been deficiencies in moral conduct or in Church discipline, or even in the way that Church teaching has been formulated—to be carefully distinguished from the deposit of faith itself—these should be set right at the opportune moment and in the proper way.
>
> Church renewal therefore has notable ecumenical importance. Already this renewal is taking place in various spheres of the Church's life: the biblical and liturgical movements, the preaching of the Word of God and catechetics, the apostolate of the laity, new forms of religious life and the spirituality of married life, and the Church's social teaching and activity. All these should be considered as promises and guarantees for the future progress of ecumenism. (*UR* 6)[29]

Authentic ecumenism is said to depend on "interior conversion," and this "newness of mind" (*novitas mentis*; cf. Eph 4:23) is ascribed to the Holy Spirit (*UR* 7), whose grace is required amid the conditions set by the humanity and the historicity of the Church. Thus, again, invocation (of the Holy Spirit) joins remembrance (of the faithfully transmitted past) in anticipation of the "full and perfect unity" that "God in his kindness wills" (*UR* 5).

I think I have shown, especially with attention to *Sacrosanctum concilium* and *Unitatis redintegratio*, that the documents of the Second Vatican Council allow for renewal within tradition—not least when set in relation to the broader ecumenical and liturgical movements with their concern for the recovery of full unity among Christians of institutionally divided traditions and the renewal of their intentionally common worship. How far has this happened? Having already recounted, in the first section of this chapter, some of the council's liturgical effects and located them within the wider liturgical movement among the churches, I here limit myself to the ecumenical movement toward the recovery of full ecclesial unity in the truth of the Gospel. I attend particularly to places where ecclesiological doctrine is affected and take into account the distinction between "the deposit of faith itself" and "the way in which Church teaching has been formulated."

Vatican II—and particularly the decree *Unitatis redintegratio*—marked the official entry of the Catholic Church into the ecumenical movement. Minimally, ecumenism requires only the assumption that Christianity exists in some sense beyond the institutional or canonical bounds of one's own community. Up to that point, the chief vehicle of the ecumenical movement had been the World Council of Churches. Its general secretary, the Dutch Reformed pastor W. A. Visser't Hooft, had said of the Second Vatican Council that it was "our business too": "Nostra res agitur."[30] According to the constitution of the World Council of Churches, the Roman Catholic Church could have entered into membership of that body without forfeiting its own ecclesiology or endorsing the ecclesial claims of other members in their own sense. The Catholic Church decided against membership, but a joint working group was set up with the World Council of Churches, which facilitated the appointment of Roman Catholic theologians to the Faith and Order Commission.[31] In his encyclical letter *Ut unum sint* (1995), Pope John Paul II declared "irrevocable" the Second Vatican Council's commitment to "the ecumenical venture"; he there paid repeated tribute to the work of Faith and Order, as well as to the work of several "bilateral dialogues" that had blossomed since Vatican II.[32]

In fact, a shift in the practice—and perhaps the understanding—of doctrinal dialogue was introduced by the Catholic Church's invitation of other "Christian world communions" to engage with itself in such dialogue one by one. Each has naturally concentrated on the particular matters that have historically been at issue between the Catholic Church and the respective bilateral partner. In one way or another, however, each dialogue has involved the dogmatic and structural shape of ecclesial unity—what is necessary and sufficient for the "unitatis redintegratio." I have already cited the dialogue between the World Methodist Council and the Roman Catholic Church as an example. We may now look at three more cases that, by their substance, methods, and prospects, are also important for the question of "renewal within tradition" in its ecumenical aspects.

For our purposes the most interesting feature in the dialogue between the Catholic Church and the Lutheran World Federation has been its treatment of the doctrine of justification, where anathemas were exchanged in the sixteenth century. It bears special significance on three counts: first, the original and deep-seated Lutheran conviction that this is "the point at which the Church stands or falls" (*articulus stantis vel cadentis ecclesiae*);[33] second, the theological procedures that were followed in constructing a "joint declaration on the doctrine of justification"; third, the fact that this *Joint Declaration on the Doctrine of Justification* received the authoritative affirmation of both parties at their highest ecclesial levels (in a signing at Augsburg on October 31, 1999). While "appropriating insights of recent biblical studies and drawing on modern investigations of the history of theology and dogma" (*Joint Declaration on the Doctrine of Justification*, 13), Lutherans and Catholics have found a "common way of listening to the Word of God in Scripture" (ibid., 8) and been convinced that "in their respective histories [the] churches have come to new insights" that require them to "examine the divisive questions and condemnations and see them in a new light" (ibid., 7): "This common listening, together with the theological conversations of recent years, has led to a shared understanding of justification. This encompasses a consensus in the basic truths" (ibid., 14)— such that "the corresponding doctrinal condemnations of the sixteenth century do not apply to today's partner" (ibid., 13) and "the remaining differences" of "language, theological elaboration, and emphasis" in the "explication" of the doctrine of justification are "compatible" with the consensus and therefore "no longer the occasion for doctrinal condemnations" (5; 14; 40).

The *Joint Declaration* begins substantively by displaying "The Biblical Message of Justification" (articles 8–12). Then "The Common Understanding of Justification" is set out in a concise, systematic—Trinitarian—statement (15–17). Most of the rest of the document is taken up "Explicating the Common Understanding of Justification": On each of seven historically controversial points, the parties begin with a common statement ("We confess together"), and then each respectively indicates what it wishes to assert and safeguard by its own characteristic language and emphases, while also reassuring the partner that it does not commit the errors of which it has been suspected or accused (cf. 19–39). The partners consider that the achieved consensus offers "a solid basis" for treating several other "questions of varying importance which need clarification," including "the relationship between the Word of God and church doctrine, as well as ecclesiology, ecclesial authority, church unity, ministry, the sacraments, and the relationship between justification and social ethics" (43). Such, according to the official common statement signed at Augsburg on October 31, 1999, is necessary "in order to reach full church communion, a unity in diversity, in which remaining differences would be 'reconciled' and no longer have divisive force." Meanwhile, "Lutherans and Catholics will continue their efforts ecumenically in their common witness to interpret the message of justification in language relevant for human beings today, and with reference both to individual and social concerns of our times" (ibid.).[34]

In this first example we have a case of a "renewal within tradition" that has proceeded anamnetically by listening—again and together—to the Word of God in scripture, which is the permanent source of the eschatologically new. In that light, ecumenical dialogue partners have proved themselves ready and able to reconsider their original points of difference and—without denying that certain positions needed, and still need, to be excluded—discover commonalities and complementarities that render continuing divisions groundless, at least on those matters. By such clarifications, one might even say, the traditionary process has been purified so that its substantive purpose—the conveyance of the Gospel through time and space—may be better served and the final Kingdom of God brought closer. Could it be that what has been happening with regard to the doctrine of justification has been occurring in other contexts—and without yet having received authoritative endorsement—in respect of other doctrines?

Our second example comes, in fact, from the international Anglican/Roman Catholic dialogue and its treatment of doctrine concerning "Mary the Mother of the Lord," particularly in the "agreed statement" of the International Commission, *Mary—Grace and Hope in Christ* (2005). About halfway through the document, when the historical recital picks up from the sixteenth century, we start to encounter heavy use of the term "re-reception" for both a notion and a reality:

One powerful impulse for Reformation in the early sixteenth century was a widespread reaction against devotional practices which approached Mary as a mediatrix alongside Christ, or sometimes even in his place.... Together with a radical re-reception of Scripture as the fundamental touchstone of Divine Revelation, there was a re-reception by the Reformers of the belief that Jesus Christ is the only mediator between God and humanity. This entailed a rejection of real and perceived abuses surrounding devotion to Mary. It led also to the loss of some positive aspects of devotion and the diminution of her place in the life of the Church.

In this context, the English Reformers continued to receive the doctrine of the ancient Church concerning Mary: it is summed up in their acceptance of her as the *Theotókos*, because this was seen to be both scriptural and in accord with ancient tradition. (nos. 44–45)

In the Roman Catholic Church, the continuing growth of Marian doctrine and devotion, while moderated by the reforming decrees of the Council of Trent (1543–1563), also suffered the distorting influence of Protestant-Catholic polemics. To be Roman Catholic came to be identified by an emphasis on devotion to Mary. The depth and popularity of Marian spirituality in the nineteenth and the first half of the twentieth centuries contributed to the definitions of the dogmas of the Immaculate Conception (1854) and the Assumption (1950). On the other hand, the pervasiveness of this spirituality began to give rise to criticism both within and beyond the Roman Catholic Church and initiated a process of re-reception. This re-reception was evident at the Second Vatican Council which, consonant with the contemporary biblical, patristic, and liturgical renewals, and with concern for ecumenical sensitivities, chose not to draft a separate document on Mary, but to integrate doctrine about her into the Constitution on the Church, *Lumen gentium* (1964)—more specifically, into its final section describing the eschatological pilgrimage of the Church (ch. VIII).... The fathers of the council consciously sought to resist exaggerations by returning to patristic emphases and placing Marian doctrine and devotion in its proper Christological and ecclesial context. (no. 47)

Meanwhile, the commission's report notes that "Mary has a new prominence in Anglican worship through the liturgical renewals of the twentieth century" (49), such that "in recent decades a re-reception of the place of Mary in corporate worship has been taking place across the Anglican communion" (50).

The notion of "re-reception" is interesting and merits closer systematic attention to what it implies in the way of affirmation, criticism, and development over the course of tradition. The writers of the Anglican-Roman Catholic statement agree that authentic doctrine (in this case concerning Mary) is—and must be—"consonant with" (58), "not contrary to" (59), and "in conformity with" (61) scripture; and they refer to Vatican II's constitution *Dei verbum* for "the central role of Scripture in the reception and transmission of Revelation." They conclude that "Revelation is received by the community of believers and transmitted in time and place through the Scriptures and through the preaching, liturgy, spirituality, life, and teaching of the Church, that draw upon the Scriptures" (61). Such a view clearly implies the need for a continuing means of determining fidelity to the permanent witness of scripture. The dialogue commission is aware that the "re-reception" proposed in the case of Mary would entail a "re-reception" also in the more comprehensive and indeed fundamental case of the magisterium, which is doctrinally responsible for securing the authenticity of all doctrines in relation to the definitive divine revelation: "Our hope is that the Roman Catholic Church and the Anglican Communion will recognize a common faith in the agreement concerning Mary which we offer here. Such a re-reception would mean the Marian teaching and devotion within our respective communities, including differences of emphasis, would be seen to be authentic expressions of Christian belief. Any such re-reception would have to take place within the context of a mutual re-reception of an effective teaching authority in the Church, such as that set out in *The Gift of Authority*" (63). With that, including the final mention of the commission's earlier report, we have arrived at our third example of a possible "renewal within tradition," which both the texts and the event of the Second Vatican Council might by their givenness justify (anamnesis), by their inspiration promote (epiclesis), and by their beginning effectiveness foreshadow (prolepsis).

In the encyclical that confirmed the Catholic Church's irrevocable commitment to the ecumenical cause (characterized in article 95 as "the full and visible communion of all those Communities in which, by virtue of God's faithfulness, his Spirit dwells"), Pope John Paul II sought to configure the claimed primacy of the Roman See more clearly and effectively as "a universal ministry of Christian unity." He cited the very phrase that the Fifth World Conference on Faith and Order at Santiago de Compostela in 1993 had used in calling for "a new study of the question" (cf. *Ut unum sint*, 89): "I am convinced that I have a particular responsibility in this regard, above all in acknowledging the ecumenical aspirations of the majority of the Christian Communities and in heeding the request made of me to find a way of exercising the primacy which, while in no way renouncing what is essential to its mission, is nonetheless open to a new situation" (95). Now within the Catholic Church itself, the Second Vatican Council—both in its texts and as an event—had treated the primacy at least in the manner of its exercise, if not also in its substance. The very fact of Pope John XXIII's convoking a council was significant, if papal maximalism might have rendered councils superfluous. The conciliar constitution on the Church attributes an exalted place to the college of bishops—as successors to the apostolic "college"—in expounding at length the hierarchical structure of the people of God (*Lumen gentium*, ch. 3). Yet the stated intention is not to deviate from the *Pastor aeternus* of Vatican I:

This sacred synod, following in the steps of the First Vatican Council, teaches and declares with it that Jesus Christ, the eternal pastor, set up the holy Church by entrusting the apostles with their mission as he himself had been sent by the Father (cf. John 20:21). He willed that their successors, the bishops namely, should be the shepherds in his Church to the end of the world. In order that the episcopate itself, however, might be one and undivided he put Peter at the head of the other apostles, and in him he set up a lasting and visible source and foundation of the unity both of faith and communion. This teaching concerning the institution, the permanence, the nature and import of the sacred primacy of the Roman Pontiff and his infallible teaching office, the sacred synod proposes anew to be firmly believed by all the faithful, and, proceeding undeviatingly with this same undertaking (*et in eodem percepto pergens*), it proposes to proclaim publicly and enunciate clearly the doctrine concerning bishops, successors of the apostles, who together with Peter's successor, the Vicar of Christ and the visible head of the whole Church, direct the house of the living God. (*LG* 18)

And again:

The college or body of bishops has for all that no authority unless united with (*nisi simul cum*) the Roman Pontiff, Peter's successor, as its head, whose primatial authority, let it be added, over all, whether pastors or faithful, remains in its integrity. For the Roman Pontiff, by reason of his office as Vicar of Christ, namely, and as pastor of the entire Church, has full, supreme and universal power over the whole Church, a power which he can always exercise unhindered. The order of bishops is the successor to the college of the apostles in their role as teachers and pastors, and in it the apostolic college is perpetuated. Together with (*una cum*) their head, the Supreme Pontiff, and never apart from him, they have supreme and full authority over the universal Church; but this power cannot be exercised without the agreement of the Roman Pontiff. (*LG* 22)

In connection, then, with our question of "renewal within tradition," how is Vatican II to be related to Vatican I in the matter of papal primacy? Immediately after the First Vatican Council, John Henry Newman took a diachronic view of the attainment of Catholic truth in this as in other doctrines: "Looking at early history, it would seem as if the Church moved on to the perfect truth by successive declarations, alternately in contrary directions, and thus perfecting, completing, supplying each other"; "If you look into history, you find popes continually completing the acts of their predecessors, and councils too—sometimes only half the truth is brought out at one time—I doubt not a coming pope, or a coming council, will so explain and guard what has been now passed by the late council, as to clear up all that troubles us now"; "Other definitions are necessary, and were intended, and will be added, if we are patient, to reduce the dogma to its proper proportions and place in the Catholic system."[35]

Following the Second Vatican Council, Walter Kasper and other Catholic theologians have considered that within the texts of Vatican II—as with earlier councils also—certain "juxtapositions" remain that allow and call for a subsequent theological synthesis.[36] In the "new situation" of which John Paul II spoke, might we pursue this task for the benefit of not only the Catholic Church but also the entire ecumenical cause? Doing so would constitute a continuation of the "patient and fraternal dialogue on this subject," to which the pope invited other "church leaders and their theologians." Given "the real but imperfect communion existing between us," we might thereby create "a dialogue in which, leaving useless controversies behind, we could listen to one another, keeping before us only the will of Christ for his Church and allowing ourselves to be deeply moved by his plea 'that they may all be one...so that the world may believe that you have sent me' (Jn 17:21)" (*Ut unum sint*, no. 96). The rhythm of anamnesis, epiclesis, and prolepsis is there clearly set forth: the primatial office—as intentionally a universal ministry of unity—is newly placed at the service of keeping the traditionary process in the Church faithful to its origin in the Gospel and its goal in the completion of God's Kingdom.[37]

Conclusion

From the texts of Vatican II it is clear that "renewal within tradition" was a coherent notion for the council and that the council intended to serve that purpose. It is not up to me, being only in "imperfect communion" with the Catholic Church, to estimate how far this aim has been internally received—its effects in Catholic thought and practice.[38] Ultimately, that is for the Lord of the Ages to judge. Meanwhile, an ecumenically engaged Protestant (Methodist) theologian has much reason for gratitude to the Second Vatican Council for its service to the twin causes of the recovery of full unity among Christians of institutionally divided traditions and the renewal of their intentionally common worship. I find myself thereby encouraged to continue along the road of an historically informed and empathetic retrieval of the past in its decisive and even divisive moments (anamnesis)—reliant upon the continuing guidance of the Spirit in the ecumenical movement that he is believed to have inspired (epiclesis)—toward a future that can be envisaged by a disciplined imagination in light of the revealed purpose of God (prolepsis).

NOTES

1. English versions are here taken—with an occasional minor adjustment—from *Vatican Council II*, vol. 1, *The Conciliar and Postconciliar Documents*, ed. Austin Flannery (Boston: St. Paul Editions, 1988).

2. Justin Martyr, *First Apology*, 67.

3. In the years before Vatican II, the Oratorian Louis Bouyer had already expounded the rites and offices of "the last three days of Holy Week" in the Tridentine liturgy in that way: *Le mystère pascal (Paschale sacramentum)* (Paris: Éditions du Cerf, 1945). In *Liturgical Piety* (Notre Dame, Ind.: University of Notre Dame Press, 1955), Bouyer extends the Paschal mystery to all of the features of the liturgy: the Mass, the sacraments, the calendar (not only Easter but also Advent, Christmas, and Epiphany), the commemoration of the saints, and the divine office. See also his *Eucharistie: Théologie et spiritualité de la prière eucharistique* (Tournai, Belgium: Desclée, 1966; in English, *Eucharist: Theology and Spirituality of the Eucharistic Prayer* [Notre Dame, Ind.: University of Notre Dame Press, 1968]). Father Bouyer was not blind to some faults and weaknesses in the liturgical movement, as the subtitle to the French translation of the second book mentioned shows: *La vie de la liturgie: Une critique constructive du mouvement liturgique* (Paris: Éditions du Cerf, 1960).

4. Importantly, Cipriano Vagaggini, *Il senso teologico della liturgia*, 4th rev. ed. (1957; Rome: Edizioni Paoline, 1965; in English, *Theological Dimensions of the Liturgy* [Collegeville, Minn.: Liturgical Press, 1976]).

5. See Irmgard Pahl, "The Paschal Mystery in Its Central Meaning for the Shape of Christian Liturgy," *Studia Liturgica* 26 (1996): 16–38. The "Christian mystery" or "Paschal mystery" headlines the liturgical sections of the postconciliar *Catechism of the Catholic Church* (1993).

6. "The two parts which in a sense go to make up the Mass, viz., the liturgy of the word and the Eucharistic liturgy, are so closely connected with each other that they form but one single act of worship" (*SC* 56). The point was emphasized in the council's teaching and decree concerning Sunday: "By a tradition handed down from the apostles, which took its origin from the very day of Christ's resurrection, the Church celebrates the paschal mystery every seventh day, which day is appropriately called the Lord's Day or Sunday. For on this day Christ's faithful are bound to come together in one place. They should listen to the word of God and take part in the Eucharist, thus calling to mind the passion, resurrection, and glory of the Lord Jesus, and giving thanks to God who 'has begotten them again through the resurrection of Christ from the dead, unto a living hope' (1 Pet 1:3)" (*SC* 106). The text here clearly echoes Justin Martyr concerning Sunday and its liturgy.

7. In many English-speaking Protestant churches a *Common Lectionary* (1983; rev. 1992), although based on the Roman, employs the typological principle quite broadly in the Sundays after Pentecost by matching readings from the Pentateuch with Matthew in his gospel year, the Davidic narratives with Mark, and the Prophets with Luke.

8. Service books in many Protestant churches now typically set forth what *The United Methodist Book of Worship* (1992) calls "Word and Table" as the "full" form of worship on the Lord's day. In its "Dublin Report" of 1976, the Joint Commission for Dialogue between the World Methodist Council and the Roman Catholic Church made a bold observation and claim: "In recent years ... there has been a notable recovery of Eucharistic faith and practice among Methodists, with a growing sense that the fullness of Christian worship includes both word and sacrament. Similarly among Roman Catholics there has been a renewal in the theology and practice of the ministry of the word. These developments have resulted in a remarkable convergence, so that at no other time has the worshipping life of Methodists and Roman Catholics had so much in common." See further Geoffrey Wainwright, "The Ecumenical Scope of Methodist Liturgical Revision," *Centro pro unione: Bulletin* 62 (2002): 16–26; also printed in *Liturgical Renewal as a Way to Christian Unity*, ed. James F. Puglisi (Collegeville,

Minn.: Liturgical Press, 2005), 35–59. Caution nevertheless remains in order; see my *"Ecclesia de Eucharistia vivit*: An Ecumenical Reading," *Ecumenical Trends* 33 (October 2004): 1–9.

9. The conciliar decree on the missionary activity of the Church—*Ad gentes*—emphasized the part played in evangelization by the liturgical catechumenate and the sacraments of initiation (*AG* 11, 14).

10. On the more recent twists and turns see Helen Hill Hitchcock, "A New Era of Liturgical Renewal: Foundations and Future," *Antiphon: A Journal for Liturgical Renewal* 10 (2006): 12–31. Given the major theme of the present book as "renewal within tradition," an anecdote may perhaps be permitted. On CNN television on June 15, 2006, during "In the Situation Room with Wolf Blitzer," it was announced by "our correspondent on faith and values" that the U.S. Catholic bishops had decided to replace the "traditional" [*sic*] response "and also with you" by "and with your spirit." So quickly had the memory of "et cum spiritu tuo" faded?

11. Such factors were recognized in *Unitatis redintegratio* as "ecumenically important" instances of the "renewal" that was already "taking place in various spheres of the Church's life" (*UR* 6).

12. See, briefly, Geoffrey Wainwright, *Christian Initiation* (London: Lutterworth Press, 1969), 58f., 98f. A more detailed discussion is found in Bernard Leeming, *Principles of Sacramental Theology* (Westminster, Md.: Newman Press, 1956), in particular 143–61, 497–520.

13. For examples of official Roman language from this period see Yves Congar, *Chrétiens désunis* (Paris: Éditions du Cerf, 1937), 381f.; or idem, *Dialogue between Christians: Catholic Contributions to Ecumenism* (Westminster, Md.: Newman Press, 1966), 200–202. Gustave Thils has shown that some post-Reformation Catholic theologians were unwilling to dismiss Protestants and their communities as simply "not-church"; see his *Histoire doctrinale du mouvement oecuménique* (Louvain, Belgium: Warny, 1955), 183–87; or, in more detail, his Louvain dissertation, *Les notes de l'Église dans l'apologétique catholique depuis la Réforme* (Gembloux, Belgium: Duculot, 1937).

14. "Elements or endowments" (*elementa seu bona*) have a more constitutive ring to them than the "traces of the Church" (*vestigia Ecclesiae*) that pioneering Catholic ecumenists detected in other communities. The nascent World Council of Churches had used the latter term with positive intent in its own ecclesiological searchings. In a more negative context, John Calvin had spoken thus of what had survived among the Papists from the dissolution of the Church (*"superesse ex dissipatione vestigia ecclesiae"*), "remains" (*reliquiae*) among the ruins (*Institutes*, IV.2.11–12). See Thils, *Histoire doctrinale*, 142–47, 187–97.

15. A note that refers to the Fourth Lateran Council, the Second Council of Lyons, and the Council of Florence indicates that the language of "church" here applies to "the East" (as *UR* 14–18 makes clear), while "the West" will have to make do with "separated churches and ecclesial communities"—without precise definition (*UR* 19–24).

16. In June 1959 a group of distinguished Catholic ecumenists composed a note in which "the value of baptism, however administered, as the distinguishing mark of Christians, and communion (*koinonia*) as the basis of the idea of the Church, are singled out as theological points that are crucial for any agreement." See *History of Vatican II*, vol. 1, ed. Giuseppe Alberigo (Maryknoll, N.Y.: Orbis, 1995), 24f., for this "Note du comité directeur de la 'conférence catholique pour les questions oecuméniques' sur la restauration de l'unité chrétienne à l'occasion du prochain concile."

17. Augustine, *Epistle* 187.34 (*PL* 33: 846).

18. Luther, *Disputatio de fide infusa et acquisita*, thesis 18, in *D. Martin Luthers Werke* (Weimar, Germany: Böhlau, 1888), vol. 6, p. 86; *De captivitate babylonica ecclesiae*, in ibid., p. 501. The principal scriptural text would be 1 Tim 3:16 (*mysterium/ sacramentum*; cf. also Mk 4:11; Rom 16:25; Eph 1:9f., 3:3–12, 6:19; Col 1:25–2:3, 4:3); the three "sacramental signs" for Luther at that stage were baptism, the Lord's Supper, and penance.

19. H. de Lubac, *Catholicisme*, 4th ed (Paris: Éditions du Cerf, 1947), 50 (abridged English trans., *Catholicism: A Study of Dogma in Relation to the Corporate Destiny of Mankind* [New York: Longmans, Green, 1950], 29).

20. For fuller references to these and other works see Geoffrey Wainwright, "Sacramental Theology and the World Church," *Proceedings of the Catholic Theological Society of America* 39 (1984): 69–83. No doubt the postwar theologians were encouraged by Pius XII's ecclesiological encyclical *Mystici Corporis* (1943).

21. The usage had already been introduced in the constitution on the liturgy, *SC* 5 ("From the side of Christ as he slept the sleep of death upon the cross came forth 'the wondrous sacrament of the whole Church'"—quoting from the liturgy of Holy Saturday in the preconciliar Roman Missal) and 26. Initial suspicions about the "novelty" of the concept are recounted by Joseph Ratzinger, who makes a strong theological case in favor of "Kirche als Sakrament"; see his *Theologische Prinzipienlehre: Bausteine zur Fundamentaltheologie* (Munich: Wewel, 1982), 45–57.

22. The Seoul report was officially published in the Pontifical Council for Promoting Christian Unity's Information Service, No. 123 (2006-iii/iv): 120–53. For the sustained Trinitarian ecclesiology in the Seoul report of 2006 see especially paragraphs 51–59, 65–96; for the sacramental consistency see especially paragraphs 45–50, 60–64, 102–104, 109, 131. Naturally there is much overlap of these dimensions and interweaving of these themes.

23. Protestants would want the contribution of their community to an eventual "reintegration of unity"—"the fullness of unity which Christ desires" (*UR* 4)—to be viewed as more "substantive" than the "accidental" enhancement that some pioneering Catholic ecumenists were willing to contemplate. See again Thils, *Histoire doctrinale*, 168, 174, 193f.

24. Admittedly, the novelty seekers of Athens wanted to "tell or hear *ti kainoteron*" (Acts 17:19–21); but the usual Greek word for "new" in the more trivial sense is "*neos.*"

25. The German Lutheran theologian Eberhard Jüngel neatly points out that the eschatologically new shows its newness precisely in its continuing power to renew: "Als das bleibend Neue wird das Eschaton an seiner *Wirkung* erkannt, die darin besteht, *neu zu machen*. . . . Als das *Erneuernde* ist es das bleibend Neue. . . . Als so verstandene Macht der Erneuerung ist das bleibend Neue ein Gottesprädikat" (147)—which Jüngel demonstrates in Trinitarian terms; see "Das Entstehen von Neuem" in E. Jüngel, *Wertlose Wahrheit: Zur Identität und Relevanz des christlichen Glaubens* (Munich: Kaiser, 1990), 132–50.

26. Vatican II itself had little to say directly about the *doctrine* of the sacraments *in genere* or the specific sacraments (but see *LG* 7, 11; and *UR* 22). It was only in the second half of the twentieth century that sacramental theologians began to engage with "the linguistic turn" in philosophy and "communication theory" in the human sciences ("performative language," "sign acts," and so on).

27. The text of the pope's opening address has a complex history; a critical edition (Latin and Italian) is provided by Giuseppe Alberigo and Alberto Melloni, "L'allocuzione *Gaudet Mater Ecclesia* di Giovanni XXIII (11 ottobre 1962)" in *Fede, tradizione, profezia:*

Studi su Giovanni XXIII e sul Vaticano II, Testi e ricerche di scienze religiose (Brescia, Italy: Paidea, 1984), 185–283.

28. Again, Eberhard Jüngel ("Das Entstehen vom Neuen," 133–37) notes that "new" theology is often called forth by changing cultural circumstances and opportunities; remembering the ultimate source of newness, such "paradigm shifts," to be fruitful, must remain within the greater paradigm of the divine revelation and redemption recorded in the Bible. That is no doubt the sense in which to take the "nouvelle théologie" of the years after World War II, which, though often controversial in its time, helped to lay the intellectual foundations for Vatican II.

29. Protestants may be specially interested in the fact that the phrase "renewal of the Church" is supported at its first occurrence by an appeal to the Fifth Lateran Council, sess. 12 (1517).

30. W. A. Visser 't Hooft, *Memoirs* (Philadelphia: Westminster Press, 1973), 335f.

31. The Benedictine Emmanuel Lanne and the Dominican Jean-Marie Tillard made significant contributions to Faith and Order's "Lima document" of 1982, *Baptism, Eucharist and Ministry*. This "convergence text" has special importance because it gained a nuanced but widely positive reception in official responses from the churches. The official response of the Roman Catholic Church came from the Secretariat for Promoting Christian Unity (after collaboration with the Congregation for the Doctrine of the Faith). It is found in *Churches Respond to BEM*, vol. 6, ed. Max Thurian (Geneva: World Council of Churches, 1988), 1–40. For commentary from the present writer see G. Wainwright, "The Roman Catholic Response to *Baptism, Eucharist and Ministry*: The Ecclesiological Dimension," in *A Promise of Presence: Studies in Honor of David N. Power, O.M.I.*, ed. M. Downey and R. Fragomeni (Washington, D.C.: Pastoral Press, 1992), 187–206.

32. See Geoffrey Wainwright, "*Ut unum sint* in Light of 'Faith and Order'—or 'Faith and Order' in Light of *Ut unum sint?*" in *The Papal Office and the Unity of the Church: An Ecumenical Dialogue on John Paul II's Encyclical "Ut unum sint" (That All May Be One)*, ed. Carl E. Braaten and Robert W. Jenson (Grand Rapids: Eerdmans, 2001), 76–97.

33. See Geoffrey Wainwright, "The Ecclesial Scope of Justification," in *Justification: What's at Stake in the Current Debates*, ed. M. Husbands and D. J. Treier (Downers Grove, Ill.: InterVarsity Press, 2004), 249–75.

34. The ecumenical scope of the *Joint Declaration on the Doctrine of Justification* has been extended and prolonged by a tripartite signing at Seoul, Korea, on July 23, 2006, through which the World Methodist Council became associated with the original declaration and had a statement that characterized Methodist soteriology in its "distinctive profile" affirmed by Lutherans and the Catholic Church.

35. These and other citations, taken from *The Letters and Diaries of John Henry Newman*, vol. 26 (Oxford, UK: Clarendon, 1974), are assembled in Wolfgang Klausnitzer, *Der Primat des Bischofs von Rom—Entwicklung, Dogma, ökumenische Zukunft* (Freiburg im Breisgau, Germany: Herder, 2004), 391f. (cf. 518f.).

36. Walter Kasper, "Die bleibende Herausforderung durch das II. Vatikanische Konzil: Zur Hermeneutik der Konzilsaussagen," in his *Theologie und Kirche* (Mainz: Grünewald, 1987), 290–99; cited by Klausnitzer, *Der Primat*, 431f., who also surveys other postconciliar theologians on this matter (427–50).

37. Ecumenical discussion around this topic stresses collegiality, synodality, and conciliarity as necessary dimensions of the exercise of primacy as a "universal ministry of unity." See, for instance, the summary statement of "advances in agreement" in the Second Anglican–Roman Catholic International Commission's *The Gift of Authority*

(1999), article 52; and, from a Methodist standpoint, Geoffrey Wainwright, "A Primatial Ministry of Unity in a Conciliar and Synodical Context," in *One in Christ* 38 (2003): 3–25. The time may now have come to progress from an "exchange of ideas" to an "exchange of gifts": See the Seoul report on the International Commission for Dialogue between the Roman Catholic Church and the World Methodist Council, "The Grace Given You in Christ: Catholics and Methodists Reflect Further on the Church" (2006).

38. I have, however, sympathetically interpreted Pope John Paul II's Eucharistic encyclical of 2003: "*Ecclesia de Eucharistia vivit*: An Ecumenical Reading," *Ecumenical Trends* 33 (Oct. 2004): 1–9; and I was able to contribute to the symposium organized by the Pontifical Council for Promoting Christian Unity to mark the fortieth anniversary of the conciliar decree on ecumenism in 2004: "*Unitatis redintegratio* in a Protestant perspective," *Pro Ecclesia* 15 (2006): 172–85. See also my article "A Remedy for Relativism: The Cosmic, Historical, and Eschatological Dimensions of the Liturgy according to the Theologian Joseph Ratzinger," *Nova et Vetera* (English) 5 (2007): 403–29.

22

The Challenges of Reform and Renewal within Catholic Tradition

Matthew L. Lamb

The introduction closed with the question of whether Vatican II would go down in history as a genuinely reforming council or fail at this task. Pope Benedict XVI has emphasized that the council will contribute to a genuine renewal of the Church and the world only when its teachings are understood and appropriated within the two millennial tradition of the Catholic faith. He spelled out the nature of a Catholic hermeneutics of reform within tradition by distinguishing between inevitable discontinuities of historical situations that are met by a profound continuity of the principles informing the truth of Catholic teaching down the ages. As he remarked in the address quoted at the beginning of this book, "It is precisely in this combination of continuity and discontinuity at different levels that the very nature of true reform consists." This is very different from the hermeneutics of discontinuity, which distorts the event of the council by privileging only what is new in its texts, as if the textual references to the continuity of deeper theological principles in past teachings are no more than compromises aimed at getting votes for the new.

   Such a mistaken emphasis upon the new as the "spirit" or "style" of the council also led not a few theologians to construct treatises on the church, liturgy, sacraments, ecumenism, and dialogue with world religions that focused almost exclusively on what was new in the teachings of Vatican II. Popes, especially Pope John Paul II and Pope Benedict XVI, and the synods of bishops always situated the teachings of Vatican II within a long magisterial tradition. Those who failed to understand the council within the whole living tradition of the Church at times criticized this as thwarting the spirit of Vatican II. Those whose works tend toward a hermeneutics of rupture charge that papal teachings seek "a restoration so that . . . it is difficult to find cohesion between magisterial documents and the spirit of the Second Vatican Council."[1]

However, it is not "restoration" but recognition by the popes that no ecumenical council can be properly understood except within the ongoing living tradition of the Church. No ecumenical council explicates the whole of the Catholic faith tradition. Councils are called to address specific questions and issues in the light of the truths revealed by Jesus Christ and consigned to the apostles and their successors to hand on faithfully until the Lord returns in glory. The council's authoritative documents reflect the way in which the basic principles of the Catholic faith are applied to the variety of historical circumstances at different times. To appreciate the continuity from the first ecumenical council of Nicea in 325 AD through the most recent council one must attend to the sacred mysteries revealed by the Triune God and expressed in the creeds and worship of the Catholic Church. Along with a lively faith and reverent worship, a profound study of the wealth of Catholic magisterial and theological teachings is incumbent upon Catholic theologians.

The challenge of providing an adequate understanding of Catholic teachings and tradition is that both faith and reason are needed. Fidelity to the Catholic magisterium requires an uncompromising dedication to intelligence and truth, to faith in Jesus Christ as "the way, the truth, and the life," and to the light of reason as the immaterial image of God "enlightening every human being coming into the world."[2] As Benedict XVI stated in his Regensburg lecture, "The courage to engage the whole breadth of reason, and not the denial of its grandeur—this is the program with which a theology grounded in Biblical faith enters into the debates of our time."[3] The light of faith elevates and heals the light of reason; it does not blind reason. One of the greatest challenges the Catholic theologian faces is the need to acquire a combination of linguistic skills, along with scholarly, philosophical, and theological habits of mind and heart, in order to appreciate and appropriate the truth and wisdom of the two millennial tradition of Catholic teaching.

It has become commonplace to criticize the council for not having stated this or that element or aspect of Catholic teaching. More perceptive writers have noted that the fault lies not with the council and its documents but with inadequate and misleading efforts to implement the renewal the council called for. These efforts were too often informed by theologies that failed to appreciate the fundamental continuity of Catholic tradition. After the council many Catholics in North America received doctoral training in programs that emphasized discontinuity. Departments of theology at Catholic universities in North America have many or even a majority of faculty members who did not get their doctoral degrees in Catholic programs. In Europe, some Catholic scholars internalized the liberal versus conservative framework of the media coverage of the council, which had a similar effect of promoting a hermeneutics of rupture rather than renewal and reform within tradition.

The chapters in this book have presented the documents of Vatican II within the fundamental continuity of Catholic tradition. Renewal and reform within this tradition are demanding projects for each generation of Catholics.

This volume is a very small contribution to this ongoing enterprise in the life of the Church. Centuries from now, if Vatican II is ranked with other reforming councils, it will be due to a fidelity in faith, worship, holiness, and scholarship as they relate to the Catholic Church's purpose of continuing the missions of the Word incarnate and the Holy Spirit—"as the Father has sent me even so I send you."[4] A common characteristic of all of the great reform councils in the Church has been the generations of saintly popes, bishops, priests, religious, laity, and scholars whose lives after the council embodied much fidelity and devotion. Media and management techniques are no substitute for fidelity to the great Catholic tradition and devoted scholarship to address the new situations confronting the Church with her God-gifted wisdom—ever ancient and ever new in its beauty, in the words of Saint Augustine. Vatican II called attention to this hallmark of the living tradition of the Church:

> Now what was handed on by the Apostles includes everything which contributes toward the holiness of life and increase in faith of the peoples of God; and so the Church, in her teaching, life and worship, perpetuates and hands on to all generations all that she herself is, all that she believes. This tradition that comes from the Apostles develops in the Church with the help of the Holy Spirit. For there is a growth in the understanding of the realities and the words that have been handed down. This happens through the contemplation and study made by believers, who treasure these things in their hearts (see Luke 2:19, 51) through a penetrating understanding of the spiritual realities which they experience, and through the preaching of those who have received through episcopal succession the sure gift of truth. For as the centuries succeed one another, the Church constantly moves forward toward the fullness of divine truth until the words of God reach their complete fulfillment in her. The words of the holy fathers witness to the presence of this living tradition, whose wealth is poured into the practice and life of the believing and praying Church.[5]

Will Vatican II be known in the future as a reform council? If it is not, the fault will lie neither in the event nor in the council's texts but in us— the generations of Catholics to whom the council repeated the invitation of the Lord Jesus Christ to faithful worship, holiness, and service. Thankfully, we are not alone in such a momentous invitation. "When we have entered the holy dwelling, whose dimensions are vaster than those of the universe, and have become members of the Mystical Body of Christ," Fr. Henri de Lubac wrote of the Church by quoting Paul Claudel:

> We have at our disposal for loving, understanding, and serving God not only our own powers but everything from the blessed Virgin in the summit of heaven down to the poor African leper who, bell in hand, whispers the responses of the Mass through a mouth half eaten away. The whole of creation, visible and invisible, all history, all the past, the present and the future, all the treasure of the saints, multiplied by

grace—all that is at our disposal.... All the saints and angels are with us. We can turn to the intelligence of Saint Thomas, the right arm of Saint Michael, the hearts of Joan of Arc and Catherine of Siena, and all the hidden resources that have only to be touched to be set in motion. Everything of the good, the great and the beautiful from one end of the earth to the other—everything that *begets* sanctity—it is as if all that were our work.... The Church transposes, and paints outside us on a vast scale, all that is in us almost without our knowing it. Our brief and blind impulses are wedded, taken up again, interpreted, developed, by vast stellar movements. Outside ourselves we can decipher at astronomic distances the text written on a microscopic scale in the furthest depths of the heart.[6]

It is in the light and warmth and wisdom of this New Law of Love, written in the hearts of all those baptized in the name of the Father, the Son, and the Holy Spirit, that the texts of Vatican II will assist in the vast tradition—the handing on—of the works of reform, renewal, and evangelization. At the beginning of this book Pope Benedict XVI quoted Saint Basil, who wrote of the trials and controversies attendant on the first Ecumenical Council of Nicea in 325 AD. We can conclude as he did: "If you think any point requires further elucidation, pray do not hesitate to pursue the investigation with all diligence.... The Lord will grant full explanation on matters that have yet to be made clear, according to the knowledge given to those who are worthy by the Holy Spirit. Amen."[7]

NOTES

1. See "Pope Subverts Vatican II, Historian Charges," *Catholic World News* (March 16, 2007); and the interview with G. Alberigo in *Corriere della sera* (March 15, 2007). Also see the extensive criticisms of distorted histories of Vatican II in Agostino Marchetto, *Il Concilio Ecumenico Vaticano II: Contrappunto per la sua storia* (Rome: Libreria Editrice Vaticana, 2006). English translation will be published.

2. John 1:9; 14:6.

3. Pope Benedict XVI, "Faith, Reason, and the University: Memories and Reflections," in James V. Schall, *The Regensburg Lecture* (South Bend, Ind.: St. Augustine Press, 2007), 147.

4. John 20:21.

5. Vatican II, *Dei verbum: Dogmatic Constitution on Divine Revelation*, no. 8.

6. Henri de Lubac, S.J., *The Splendor of the Church* (San Francisco: Ignatius Press, 1986), 239–40. He quotes Paul Claudel's *Interroge le Cantique des Cantiques*.

7. Saint Basil, *De Spiritu Sancto*, XXX, 77; *PG* 32, 213 A.

Index

Augustine (*continued*)
common good, 159
disorder, 17, 149, 166
interaction with cultures, 163
justice, 157, 158
missionary activity, 295
non-Christian religions, 402, 403, 405, 408n13
peace, 182n22
sacramental ecclesiology, 27
sacraments, 18, 109, 110, 142, 413, 417
autonomy
choice, 151, 152, 176, 247, 281, 355
of culture, 170, 180n12
human, 11, 150, 160, 168, 169, 171, 172, 177n2, 280, 367, 371, 391
of institutions, 391, 394
of society, 390
of the state, 381n56

baptism, 18, 32, 52, 52n1, 102, 213, 255, 257, 315, 316, 388, 415, 435n18
of adults, 416
conditional, 418
of faith, 40, 316
and grace, 232, 332
incorporation into Christ, 14, 40, 102, 273, 274, 293, 413, 418
and Lent, 416
and the liturgy of the word, 208
and membership in the Church, 276, 296, 316
necessity of, 30
and non-Catholics, 15, 332, 336n31, 340n110, 341n116, 418, 419, 422, 434n16
and unity, 332
validity of, 331, 332, 417–8
and worship, 104, 107
Barnabas, Epistle of, 110, 124n87
Barth, Karl, 408n18
Basil, St., ix, 442, 442n7
Baudoux, Maurice, 335n25
Baum, Gregory, 25, 35n2
Bea, Augustin, 83, 96n2, 97n19, 118, 124n77, 127n141, 128n160, 313, 316, 322, 331, 334n14, 335n16, 335n28, 335–6n31, 336n36, 340n109, 398, 400, 404, 408n6, 408n7, 408n9
Beane, Marjorie Noterman, 270n40
Beck, George A., 325, 384, 385, 388, 395n3, 395n13, 395n14
Benedict, St., 5, 134

Benedict XIV, Pope, 15, 115, 345
Benedict, XV, Pope, 289, 305n16
Benedict XVI, Pope, 3, 4, 5, 6, 7, 20n5, 20n6, 21n14, 39, 47, 69, 122n55, 131, 143n6, 145n41, 148, 154, 160, 163n3, 163n5, 163n6, 164n28, 188, 202, 308n89, 352, 356, 375, 382n59, 407, 439, 440, 442, 442n3. *See also* Ratzinger, Joseph
Beozzo, J. Oscar, 408n4
Bernard of Clairvaux, St., 6, 53n4, 98n21, 99n38, 99n40
Bevans, Stephen B., S.V.D., 306n29, 306n40, 307n57, 307n58, 307n64, 308n92, 309n99, 309n110, 309n116
biblical movement, 78, 96n10
bishops. *See* episcopate
Body of Christ. *See* Mystical Body
Boethius, 72n24
Boff, Leonardo, 35n7
Boniface VIII, Pope, 418
Bonaventure, 6, 255, 379n26
Bonet, E., 135
Bongaerts, L., 284n22
Bordeaux, Council of, 284n24, 337n54
Botte, Bernard, O.S.B., 125n109, 135n111, 225n66
Bouyer, Louis, 132, 133, 134, 136, 139, 143n15, 143n17, 143n19, 145n37, 145n50, 433n3
Brechter, Suso, 307n44, 307n63, 308n73
broadcasting, 355. *See also* communication, social
Brown, Raymond E., 99n34, 224n44
Buber, Martin, 307n63, 408n18
Bugnini, Annibale, 126n115, 126n116, 127n143
Burigana, Ricardo, 222n18
Burke, Thomas J. M., S.J., 356n2

Cajetan, 6
Calvin, John, 340n95, 434n14
canon law, 15, 132, 141, 180n16, 187–8, 189, 191, 192, 193, 198, 200, 203, 203n3, 203n5, 203n6, 203n8, 203n9, 203n10, 203n15, 203n16, 204n20, 204n21, 204n22, 204n23, 266, 269n26, 281, 312, 320, 333n7, 337n47, 360, 381n47, 381n51, 386. *See also* reform, of canon law
1917 code of, 14, 187, 194, 196, 203n7, 256–7, 260, 261, 262, 267n7, 269n24, 279, 280, 285n32, 285n33, 312, 333n5, 333n6, 334n7, 360

Capelle, Bernard, O.S.B., 113, 122n55, 126n112, 126n33

Capital Square Review Bd. v. Pinette (1995), 380n37

Cappadocians, 97n10. *See also* Basil, Gregory of Nyssa

Cappellari, Mauro, 36n28

Carbone, Vincenzo, 282n2

Cardijn, Joseph, 286n44

Carli, Luigi Maria, 203n1, 225n67, 328

Casado, Julian Herranz, 224n53

Casel, Odo, 122n46, 124n89, 139, 140, 146n53

catechetics. *See* education

catechism of Pius V, 138

Catechism of the Catholic Church, 72n22, 74n60, 130, 137, 138, 139, 143n7, 151, 162, 164n13, 306n27, 308n79, 366, 378n20, 379n27, 406, 409n31, 433n5

Catechism of the Council of Trent. See *Roman Catechism*

catechumenate, 28, 415, 416, 434n9. *See also* RCIA

Catherine of Siena, St., 442

Catholic Action, 14, 271, 275, 276, 279–80, 285n39, 285n41, 286n44

Catholic Worker Movement, 134

celibacy, 43, 193, 216, 221, 223n28, 239, 242

Celestine I, Pope, 33

Cereti, Giovanni, 338n66

Cerfaux, Lucien, 30, 96n9

Cessario, Romanus, 144n28

Chandler v. James (1999), 380n37

Chapp, Larry S., 179n10

charity, 8, 13, 16, 29, 43, 46, 50, 51, 105, 139, 182n23, 316, 356
  acts of, 255, 257, 260, 268n17, 275, 277, 279, 285n38, 296
  bond of perfection, 43, 44, 124n74
  in Christian life, 38, 40, 42, 44, 45, 46, 53n2, 198, 208, 211, 214, 216, 259, 264, 304, 318
  effects of, 39, 171, 174
  growth of, 43, 255
  as holiness, 41, 42, 43, 224n43
  as source of ministry, 41, 53n3, 257, 295, 322, 354
  source of, 39, 211, 212, 273
  spread of, 39, 226n81
  union in, 156, 211, 255, 325, 388

Charlier, Célestin, 99n41

chastity, 13, 177n4, 252, 255, 256, 258–9, 262, 269n31. *See also* evangelical counsels

children, 11, 17, 44, 158, 162, 167, 168, 175, 178n6, 179n8, 239, 355, 401. *See also* education, family, marriage, procreation; rights, of children
  of the Catholic Church, 418
  childlessness, 178n4
  education of, 17, 168, 195, 368, 382, 385, 386, 387, 388
  of God, 52n1, 59, 156, 164n10, 278, 299

Childs, Brevard, 95n3

China, Patriotic Catholic Association, 375

Christ
  divine nature, 29, 40, 57, 107, 292
  human nature, 29, 88, 99n40, 107
  hypostatic union, 27, 29, 88
  the last Adam, 423
  priesthood of, 101, 114, 208, 212, 214, 215, 224n49, 224n54, 274
  suffering of, 407
  Suffering Servant, 234
  Victim, 104, 105, 109, 248

Christian Family Movement, 286n44

Christmas, 407, 433n3

Christus Dominus, 12, 187–204, 315, 362, 372, 382n59, 408n1

chrismation. *See* confirmation

Church
  mission of, 6, 29–30, 150, 159–63, 221, 272, 275, 276, 279, 282, 290–1, 299, 302, 303, 304, 356, 372, 374, 375
  as mother, 105, 345, 346, 353, 387, 406, 424
  pilgrim, xiv, 18, 25, 30, 38, 43–6, 55, 63, 102, 103, 414, 421, 422, 423, 426, 429
  reality of, 82, 123n57, 306n30, 386
  as sacrament, 8, 18, 26–7, 29, 31, 35, 35n11, 38, 42–3, 112, 114, 163, 290, 291, 302, 353, 419, 420, 435n21
  as sign and instrument xiv, 26, 29, 38, 39, 52, 102, 172, 175, 233, 291, 302, 308n73, 329, 397, 420, 421
  as spouse of Christ, 41, 51, 52, 424
  threefold munera (prophetic/teaching; priestly, kingly) 12, 13, 189, 195, 197, 207, 208, 209, 210, 211, 212, 214, 215, 216, 217, 218, 221, 224n43, 224n49, 225n67, 234, 237, 238, 246, 247, 254, 273, 274, 363, 372

Leo XIII, Pope, 4, 20n4, 53n8, 78, 86, 108, 109, 122n47, 151, 181n18, 181n19, 253, 256, 260, 265, 267n7, 168n15, 268n21, 270n44, 312, 334n8, 341n115, 348, 361, 363, 371, 381n48

Leo XIII, *Rerum novarum*, 11, 151, 164n12, 169, 171, 180n14, 273, 285n35

Leo XIII, *Orientalium dignitas*, 15, 344, 347, 348

Leo XIII, *Praeclara gratulationis*, 15, 346, 377n8

Lercaro, Giacomo, 124n77, 135

Levering, Matthew, 141, 146n60

lex orandi, lex credendi, 425

liberty, 155, 180n13, 295, 300, 389

liberty religious, 16, 17, 48, 66, 161, 183n27, 299, 314, 359–82

Lienart, Achille, 372, 373

Lindbeck, George A. 25, 35n4

liturgical calendar, 93, 145, 425, 433n3

liturgical movement, 10

Liturgy, 32, 65, 66, 215, 243, 250n34, 320, 325, 387, 412, 413, 416, 417, 423, 424, 425, 430, 433n6, 435n21, 439. *See also* Eucharist; Mass; Paschal mystery; reform, liturgical; renewal, liturgical; worship, public
 action in, 10, 45
 earthly, 414
 heavenly, 414
 in history, 9, 205, 414
 and sacraments, 10, 129–46
 sign character of, 110, 115, 116, 117, 125n104, 127n138, 412
 summit of Church's activity, 10, 104
 theology of, 9, 101–28
 Tridentine, 137, 433n3
 unchangeable elements, 415

Liturgy of the Hours, 10, 101, 105, 110, 145n33, 239, 433n3

Lonergan, Bernard, 73n44

López-Gay, Jesus, S.J., 307n56

Lucal, John A., S.J., 183n24

Lumen gentium, xiv, 7–8, 10, 12, 13, 14, 25–36, 37–53, 64, 73n40, 109, 119, 147, 159, 163, 177n3, 189, 191, 193, 195, 199, 202, 206, 207, 213, 215, 216–8, 219, 223n38, 223n40, 224n54, 225n67, 226n71, 226n75, 226n83, 248n7, 251, 252, 254, 255, 257, 259, 267n2, 269n31, 273, 274, 275, 283n10, 283n11, 283n16, 290, 291, 297, 302n3, 305n18, 306n22, 314, 315,

316, 328, 336n34, 347n2, 353, 362, 397, 419, 420, 422, 423, 429, 430, 431, 435n26

Luther, Martin, 74n58, 321, 329, 336n38, 337n55, 420, 435n18

Lyons, Second Council of, 434n15

MacCulloch, Diarmaid, 305n10

MacIntyre, Alasdair, 21n7

Madison, James, 367, 369, 378n23

Maggiolini, Alessandro, 73n45

Magister, Sandro, 21n13

magisterium, 8, 9, 32, 34–5, 46, 56, 62, 66, 68, 78, 81, 82, 83, 92, 95, 130, 176n1, 179n7, 191, 201, 243, 250n34, 272, 273, 274, 275, 278, 281, 289, 301, 302, 304, 311, 318, 375, 430, 440
 doctrine on the role of, 191
 teaching of the ordinary and universal, 32, 34, 191

Malone, James, 384, 385, 395n5

Mansi, Iohannes Dominicus, 36n32, 376n6

Mar Ignatius Jacob III, Patriarch, 336n41

Marcel, Gabriel, 408n18

Marchetto, Agostino, 7, 21n11, 21n13, 70n2, 442n1

Marcion, 85, 100n45

Maritain, Jacques, 180n16

marriage, 11, 42, 43, 141, 157, 166–8, 175, 176, 177–8n4, 178n5, 178n6, 178n7, 179n8, 193, 242, 258, 259, 268n17, 319, 344, 369. *See also* children, family, procreation, sexuality; vocation, marriage as
 Church as spouse, 259, 424
 and homosexuality, 162

Marsili, Salvatore, O.S.B., 109, 118, 124n71, 124n73, 124n75, 125n97, 125n106, 126n113, 127n138, 128n157

Martimort, A.-G., 135

Martin, Francis, 72n28, 72n29, 74n54, 98n22

Martin of Rouen, J.M. 338n71

Marty, François, 206, 207, 220, 222n6

martyrdom, xiii, xiv, 43, 45, 93, 106, 152–3, 275, 347, 378

Mary, 8, 38, 40, 45, 46–51, 52, 239, 259, 267n8, 278, 349n11, 400, 430, 441
 in Anglicanism, 429
 Assumption of, 46, 48, 50, 323–4, 429
 doctrine on, 47, 49, 428, 429, 323, 324, 329, 428

CPSIA information can be obtained
at www.ICGtesting.com
Printed in the USA
BVHW040331010819
554824BV00005B/9/P

9 780195 332674